by the FCC—Standard (AM), Frequency Modulation (FM), Television, International, Auxiliary, Experimental, and others.

Parts IV and V deal with the hard facts of regulation—governmental requirements which must be met to get a license, responsibilities which must be assumed and conduct which must be avoided if one is to keep a license.

Part VI analyzes some of the current problems of broadcast regulation and suggests clarifying legislation and other remedial measures to make it more effective.

The book is an outgrowth of the author's experience and research over a period of twenty-five years. It not only presents and analyzes governmental policies and regulations, but provides a great amount of documented history explaining how the more important ones developed, both from the legislative and administrative points of view.

The reader will find the Appendices especially informative. The Communications Act of 1934, including the 1960 amendments, a detailed and documented chronology of the FCC plus biographical data and character studies of present commissioners and all former chairmen, CONELRAD regulations, Federal Trade Commission guides for advertising, recent policy statements of the FCC with respect to programming, the recently revised radio and TV codes of the National Association of Broadcasters—this and other material is reproduced for easy reference.

Walter B. Emery is a professor in the Television and Radio Department of Michigan State University. He has been a student of broadcasting and government for more than twenty-five years. He was the manager of an educational station and a program producer on commercial stations during the early days of radio—a period about which he writes in the first part of his book.

After completing a law degree at the University of Oklahoma in 1934, he went to Washington during the first Roosevelt administration and worked for a time on the legal staff of the then newly created FCC. This was followed by four years of teaching at the University of Wisconsin.

After holding professorships at the University of Oklahoma and Ohio State University, he returned to the FCC in 1943, where he served successively as attorney, examiner, Chief of the Renewals and Revocation Section, and Legal Assistant to former Chairman Paul A. Walker. In 1952, he left the government and for five years was employed as a general consultant by the Joint Council on Educational Television, after which he went to his present position in Michigan State University in 1957.

The author is a member of the Oklahoma Bar, and is licensed to practice before the FCC, the United States District Court, the U. S. Court of Appeals for the district, and the U. S. Supreme Court. He has been a frequent contributor over the past fifteen years to educational journals, writing on subjects mainly concerned with the broadcast media.

BROADCASTING AND GOVERNMENT:
Responsibilities and Regulations

BROADCASTING AND GOVERNMENT:

Responsibilities and Regulations

by

WALTER B. EMERY

Professor of Television and Radio, Michigan State University; Member of Oklahoma Bar, Federal Communications Commission Bar and licensed to practice before U. S. District Court, U. S. Court of Appeals for the District of Columbia and U. S. Supreme Court.

MICHIGAN STATE UNIVERSITY PRESS

Copyright © 1961

Michigan State University Press

Library of Congress catalog card number: 60-16416

Manufactured in the United States of America

★
★
★
★
★

To my wife, Olive Helen Emery,
without whose patience and
helpfulness this book would
not have been completed

Acknowledgments

This book is an outgrowth of more than twenty-five years of experience and study. I began doing research on it as early as 1945 when I was a member of the legal staff of the Federal Communications Commission. My first debt of gratitude, therefore, is to the FCC itself for entrusting me with important responsibilities for a period of almost ten years and making it possible for me to acquire first-hand knowledge concerning the problems of broadcast regulation, without which this book could not have been written.

I am particularly grateful to Paul A. Walker, former member and, for a time, Chairman of the FCC. He was appointed as an original Commissioner in 1934 and continued in the job until he retired in 1953. He brought me to the Commission in 1935, and at different periods, while he was there, I served as his legal assistant. I cannot overestimate the value of that association and the influence of his thinking which, to a considerable extent, is reflected in this book.

In my work at the FCC for brief periods in 1935 and 1936 and again from 1943 to 1952, I enjoyed the tremendous advantage of associating regularly with such men as Commissioner Rosel Hyde, who formerly was General Counsel, and who gave me my first job in what was then the Law Department of the Commission. My continued studies in the field of broadcasting and government and the writing I have done stem, in no small part, from the influence of these thoughtful and dedicated officials.

When I completed the preliminary manuscript of this volume, I submitted some parts of it to different staff members of the FCC and Federal Trade Commission. For their gracious and valuable assistance in reviewing the materials I must give acknowledgment. In so doing, however, I hasten to add that I, and not they, take full responsibility for the content of the book and for what errors of fact or interpretation it may contain. And particularly I want to stress that they cannot be held accountable for any of my criticisms of governmental policies or procedures, or recommendations for remedial action, since I did not solicit their advice or reactions to those parts of the book concerned with such matters.

A special word of thanks is due Gordon A. Sabine, formerly Dean of the College of Communication Arts and now Vice-President for Special Projects at Michigan State University. His genuine and intelligent interest in the subject of this book and the encouragement he gave me throughout its preparation have been invaluable. I also asknowledge my appreciation

to Kay Williams, Alison Cruise, and other members of his secretarial staff
who spent many hours typing most of the original manuscript.

I express my thanks to Frederick S. Siebert, now Dean of the College
of Communication Arts and a distinguished authority in the law of the
press, who has written the Foreword and made helpful suggestions, particularly regarding Chapter 22 dealing with legal restrictions on the use
of program materials. Also, the manuscript has benefitted greatly from the
constructive criticisms of my professorial colleagues, Leo Martin and Colby
Lewis at Michigan State University, and David Mackey, Professor of Communications, at Boston University. I am indebted to Robert Dye of Western
Michigan University for valuable assistance in the preparation of the
bibliography.

A work of this kind involves a tremendous amount of research and documentation. In this connection, I have appreciated, more than I can say, the
helpfulness of the Library staff at Michigan State University.

Contents

PART III. CHARACTER, CLASSIFICATION AND UTILIZATION OF RADIO FREQUENCIES

PART IV. PROBLEMS OF GETTING ON THE AIR

PART V. THE BROADCASTER AND ETHEREAL REALITIES

PART VI. A LOOK TO THE FUTURE

Foreword

What has been and what should be the function of government in the regulation of broadcasting?

These are the questions which this book attempts to answer. And they are important and difficult questions the answers to which will determine the course of radio and television broadcasting for the next generation.

Most of the legal questions relating to both radio and television broadcasting are relatively new. Very little precedent exists either from the point of view of the regulatory agencies or from that of the broadcasting media, and although some of the problems have been explored, no final answers have been given to some of the most important areas of controversy.

On the one hand, broadcasting is one of the media of mass communication and it is at least in part the inheritor of a long tradition in which the problems of the regulation of the printed media were worked out. For three centuries, the press fought to establish itself as an important element in the political and social structure, and this importance has been recognized by the inclusion of the guaranties of press freedom in the federal and state constitutions. Our society has accepted the principle that although the press may not be completely free of all governmental regulation, it should not be subject to any governmental regulation which impinges on the right of the publisher to express his sentiments, no matter how objectionable, on political and social issues.

To what extent is broadcasting the inheritor of this tradition? Theoretically and practically, broadcasting can perform many of the same essential functions as the press. In practice it has made great strides in this direction. On the other hand, radio and television broadcasting by the nature of their means of transmission must, as compared with the printed media, subject themselves to some degree of government regulation. To what degree has been a question for discussion and some action since the advent of radio, but many of the basic problems have not yet been solved. Because these questions are important, because they have not yet been completely solved, and because their solution is significant for our society, this is an important book.

The author, Walter Emery, is well qualified to discuss the problems of the relation of government to broadcasting. He has been director of a broadcasting station, teacher of broadcasting, attorney and examiner for the Federal Communications Commission, and student of legal and regulatory problems of broadcasting. In addition, he has been consultant to the Joint Council on Educational Television.

The history of the attempts to reconcile the historical tradition of freedom of expression as applied to broadcasting and the practical necessity for governmental regulation over the use of the air waves is a fascinating study which the author has presented in a concise and readable form. Part VI, A Look to the Future, brings together for the first time various proposals which have been made for changes in the content as well as the structure of governmental regulation of broadcasting.

Fred S. Siebert
Michigan State University

Introduction

It has been a little over a hundred years since Samuel Morse transmitted over a wire from Washington to Baltimore his historic message, "What hath God wrought?" More than eighty years have passed since Bell and Watson, in a little garret on Court Street in Boston, made the discovery that electricity could be made to transmit human speech. More than a half century ago Marconi thrilled the world by sending radio signals across the Atlantic Ocean.

Much of human progress in the past century may be attributed to the discoveries of these men and the tremendous developments in long distance communication which have followed their discoveries. Without the far-flung telegraph, telephone and broadcasting facilities of today, the intricate pattern of modern civilization and world community would be impossible.

A glimpse at the current dimensions of these communications media indicates the vital and indispensable part they have come to play in American life. For the calendar year 1958, Western Union operated more than four million miles of telegraph circuits, 21,200 telegraph offices and agencies, and some 56,000 direct teleprinter and "deskfax" connections to customers.[1] It has been estimated that the American people send more than 150 million telegrams each year.[2]

The telephone industry, comprising the Bell System and about 4,000 independent companies, operate nearly 70 million telephones, representing an industry investment of more than $24 billion, with annual gross revenues approaching $8 billion.[3] It has been reported that we Americans use the telephone more than one hundred billion times a year.[4]

In the international field, four cable and six radio companies furnish telegraph and telephone service between the United States and every important point on the globe. In 1958, the revenues of these carriers exceeded $100 million,[5] and during 1957, these companies transmitted more than 600 million words by telegraph and handled over a million and a half telephone calls.[6]

As of July 1, 1960, there were 3,483 standard broadcast stations (AM) on the air and an additional 98 under construction.[7] At the same time, there were 741 FM stations in operation and another 171 being built.[8] The box score for TV was 79 stations on the air and 74 more soon to be on the air.[9]

These figures impressively indicate that the communications industries have become big business in America. The broadcasting industry alone in 1958 reported revenues in excess of $1,553 million dollars.[10]

Educational broadcasting has now reached large dimensions. More than 160 noncommercial AM and FM stations are being operated by educational institutions.[11] About 50 educational TV stations are on the air, distributed among more than 25 states and serving areas with a total population of more than 45 million people.[12] According to the Joint Council on Educational Television, during the period from 1952 to 1958, considerably more than $50 million were spent by public and private interests to finance research in the educational uses of TV, to help build educational stations, and in other ways to promote educational telecasting.[13]

There are more than 200 million radio and television receivers in this country, almost two-thirds of the world's total supply. In fact, it is reported that we have far more receiving sets in the United States than bath tubs and running water. Four out of every five city homes and half the farm homes now have them. This far surpasses the number of homes with vacuum cleaners. Over ninety per cent of our people are within range of at least one TV station.[14]

As important and alluring as public broadcasting has come to be, quantitatively it is only a small part of the total picture. It is not generally realized, that for every station which transmits programs to the general public there are about eighty-five more stations providing other useful services. For example, there were, in 1959, more than 200,000 licensed stations contributing to the efficiency and safety of travel on land, water and in the air.[15]

Added to these are about 30,000 that serve public functions such as police and fire protection.[16] About 50,000 more are used by a wide variety of business and industrial enterprises.[17] There are numerous other services such as the Disaster Communications Service, Citizens Radio, Amateur Broadcasting with thousands of transmitters authorized by the FCC. In fact, at the close of the fiscal year 1960, the FCC had nearly 2.8 million broadcast authorizations on its books.[18]

These vast radio and broadcasting operations as well as the huge telegraph and telephone industries are so vital to the security and well-being of our people, it is unthinkable that they could be carried on effectively without some governmental regulation. Some have advocated in the past that management should be free to operate these facilities without public regulation. Few persons today, however, seriously entertain such a notion. If for no other reason, in the field of broadcasting the problem of technical interference accentuated by a crowded radio spectrum would be so great that such a system of unrestrained operation would not be feasible.

While there is common agreement that governmental control is necessary, there are honest and intelligent differences of opinion as to how much we should have. On the one extreme, there are some who believe in complete government ownership. In fact, many countries have this system, and private operation as we have it in America is the exception rather than the rule. On the other hand, there are those who urge that regulation should be limited to mere technical matters and that other restraints on free enterprise should be avoided.

There are varying shades of opinion between these two extremes. Speaking with respect to radio, a former chairman of the Federal Communications Commission stated that he believed in "having as few controls of radio as possible" and that government should exert a "minimum of interference with the lives and fortunes of its citizens."[19]

Speaking along the same line but expressing another shade of opinion, one of his predecessors at the FCC stated that what we need is "diversified and balanced control" and to achieve this balance "we must have effective government regulation."[20]

Whatever the individual differences of opinion may be, under the law, we are committed in this country to the basic principle that these communication mechanisms are "clothed with the public interest," and that the people through their government have a right to set the general standards for their operation, and that qualified persons may have the privilege of operating them providing they offer a worthwhile service.

The Federal Communications Commission has the statutory responsibility of regulating the many broadcasting stations which operate in this country as well as all telegraph and telephone facilities which provide interstate and foreign service. Other agencies of government including Congress, the White House, and Federal Trade Commission exercise functions which affect these operations.

The activities of these agencies and the multiplicity of policies and regulations which they have established and administer not only concern the enormous communication industries but they vitally affect the lives of all citizens. There is a real need, therefore, for an up-to-date book which covers the principal functions of these agencies and sets forth briefly the basic policies and rules which govern these industries and the services they provide the American people. This volume attempts to meet this need.

It cannot of course be a substitute for the *Federal Register* and reference services such as *Radio Regulation* by Pike and Fischer which report regularly the complete text of governmental orders, statements of policy and regulations. Nor can it take the place of expert legal and engineering counsel so often needed by the broadcaster and communications carrier to assure full and effective compliance with all governmental requirements. In fact, it is hoped that one of the purposes the book may achieve is to point up the necessity of expert counsel for those engaged in such a complex field of operation.

Avoiding the minutiae of regulation, its design is to bring together in one handy volume basic information essential to an understanding of how our unique regulatory system developed and how it operates and generally what qualification tests and rules of conduct must be complied with by those entrusted with the privilege of operating these communication media.

This book is mainly concerned with the FCC and its control of broadcasting. To understand fully, however, the factors that brought the FCC into being, some knowledge of the early developments of the telegraph and telephone industries is essential. Hence the chapter, "A Talking World," in Part I is included.

Since the FCC has the responsibility of regulating all telegraph and telephone service of an interstate and foreign character, what it does or does not do in these fields may be related to or may influence its actions with respect to broadcasting. It is appropriate, therefore, that some reference be made to its functions in these fields.

The work is divided into six major divisions. Part I discusses the primary technological, economic and social factors which led to the creation of the American system of broadcasting, combining private enterprise and limited governmental regulation. In addition to the developments in wire and wireless communication (including the fierce struggle for survival between the telegraph and telephone industries), there is a review of the mushroom growth of radio broadcasting following the First World War. Included in this review are some of the early microphone celebrities and types of programming which emerged, and the problems which plagued the young industry—technical interference and "chaos in the ether", wave piracy, hucksterism, censorship and monopoly—and the resulting public concern which precipitated legislative action and the establishment of the Federal Radio Commission in 1927 and its successor, the FCC, in 1934.

Part II defines the statutory powers and functions of the FCC and describes its organization and administrative machinery. Included is a discussion of conflicting points of view as to the extent of its powers and a historical review of legislative and administrative actions which have led to its present organizational structure and pattern of operation. There is a special chapter on the Federal Trade Commission and its controls over broadcast advertising. A glimpse is also taken at other agencies of government—Federal, state and local—which have influence or exercise controls over special areas and phases of broadcasting.

Part III is concerned with the broadcasting spectrum and the rules governing frequency allocation for the various classes of radio and television services—Standard Broadcast (AM), Frequency Modulation (FM), Television, International Broadcasting, and Auxiliary and Experimental Radio. Problems of classification, utilization and conservation of radio frequencies, with which the FCC is currently faced, are also discussed.

Parts IV and V deal with the hard facts of regulation—governmental requirements which must be met to get a license, responsibilities which must be assumed and conduct which must be avoided if one is to keep a license. As an outgrowth of the recent quiz scandals and payola practices, Congress, in 1960, enacted legislation imposing new restraints and responsibilities on radio and TV stations. All these, as well as other important license requirements, are fully covered.

Part VI analyzes some of the current problems of regulation and suggests clarifying legislation and other remedial measures, which, the author believes, would make regulation more effective.

Finally, it is believed that the reader will find the Appendix to be most useful. It contains those parts of the Communications Act, as amended which are related to broadcasting; a detailed and documented chronology of the FCC and its leadership from 1934 to 1960; recent FCC policy statements on program responsibilities of radio and television stations and the complete radio and television codes (as recently revised) of the National Association of Broadcasters; and FTC guides for broadcast advertisers plus other useful information.

In the preparation of this work, a high premium has been placed upon completeness and accuracy of documentation. Where Commission cases are referred to, citations in both the *FCC Reports* and Pike and Fischer's *Radio Regulation* (RR) are given if the publications were available at the times the cases were decided. The FCC suspended publication of its annual reports of decisions from 1950 to 1957 and Pike and Fischer did not begin their publication until 1945.

Where references are made to the *Federal Register* (Fed. Reg.), the Pike and Fischer citations are also given, if the matter referred to did not occur prior to 1945. Where specific FCC rules and regulations are recited, their section numbers are given and their locations in Pike and Fischer are also indicated. The complete text of cited regulations may also be found under the appropriate section numbers in Title 47, Telecommunications, *Code of Federal Regulations* (CFR).

Footnotes appear at the end of each chapter. Many of them contain not only the citations of documentary sources but clarifying, explanatory and supplementary materials that may be of interest and use to the reader.

NOTES

1. Federal Communications Commission, *Silver Anniversary Report,* for the Fiscal Year 1959, p. 7.
2. FCC News Release, No. 53599, December 31, 1957.
3. FCC *Silver Anniversary Report* for 1959, *op. cit.,* p. 6.
4. FCC News Release, *op. cit.*
5. FCC, *Silver Anniversary Report, op. cit.* p. 7.
6. FCC News Release, *op. cit.* p. 7.
7. FCC 26th Annual Report, p. 60.
8. *Ibid.*
9. *Ibid.,* p. 61.
10. *Ibid.,* p. 76.
11. *Ibid.,* p. 74.
12. JCET, *Educational Television Factsheet,* May and December 1959; also see *Four Years of Progress in Educational Television,* December, 1956, and subsequent status reports of JCET.
13. *Ibid.*
14. See FCC *Annual Report to Congress,* 1956, p. 1.

15. *Ibid.*, 1959, pp. 102, 103.

16. *Ibid.*, p. 103.

17. *Ibid.*, p. 102.

18. *Ibid.*, 1960, p. 6.

19. McConnaughey, George C., an address at the Meeting of the Committee of One Hundred of Miami Beach, Florida, January 8, 1957, FCC Release No. 40143.

20. Walker, Paul A., an address before the Third Annual Radio Conference sponsored by Stephens College, November 18, 1944.

PART I

Prologue to Regulation

CHAPTER 1

A Talking World

Do you not know that all the world is all now one single whispering gallery?—WOODROW WILSON

The vastness and efficiency of modern communication media contrast sharply with the limited and crude facilities in use during the early period of our nation's history. There were no telephones, no radios, and no ocean cables. There was some tinkering with telegraphy but its utility for communication had not yet been demonstrated. The postal service had been established, but stage coach travel was slow and it took days and days to get a message across the oceans, and communications to and from foreign countries required weeks and even months to reach their destinations.

The semaphore system had come into use and its enthusiasts envisioned its development on a nation-wide basis. Consideration was given to a plan by which intelligence could be relayed visually from city to city, using signalling stations placed a few miles apart.[1] But this system had obvious limitations. It could not be used at night or during cloudy weather. Considering its limited utility, it would be expensive to establish and maintain.

The pressing need for improved methods of communication in a rapidly expanding nation stimulated experimental studies. As early as 1837, Samuel Morse and Alfred Vail had demonstrated that intelligence could be transmitted over wires and recorded by means of electromagnetism.[2] The equipment which they first used had little to suggest the efficiency of modern telegraphic apparatus. After some improvements, however, Morse pleaded with Congress for an appropriation to build an experimental line between Washington and Baltimore. He aroused interest, but some Congressmen were skeptical. He was called a "crank" and ridiculed for visionary ideas. Some Congressmen thought it would be questionable politics to approve a subsidy to carry on a project which they associated with "mesmerism" and "animal magnetism."[3]

Despite the mockery, Morse was able to muster enough votes to get an appropriation. On March 3, 1843, Congress passed a bill giving him $30,000 to construct his telegraph line.[4] A year later the line was completed, and on May 24, 1844 it was formally opened with special ceremonies in the old Supreme Court room in the Capitol. Congressional leaders and other high government officials heaped praises and congratulations upon the proud and happy Morse.[5]

A New Era of Social and Economic Growth. The use of electromagnetic energy for long distance communication had definitely proved its worth. Henceforth it was destined to play an increasingly important part in the social and economic progress of the nation and the world.

By 1856, many telegraph companies had been organized and lines between many major cities had been established. This expansion continued at a rapid pace during the War between the States. In October, 1861, a line was completed to San Francisco providing service across the country.[6] President Lincoln, despite reverses at Bull Run, was not too busy to acknowledge receipt of several messages which came over the line during the first few days of its operation.[7]

The successful use of wire communication during the War gave impetus to its peace time development. The social and economic utility of this new facility was now generally recognized. Important negotiations and transactions, which formerly required weeks and even months to accomplish could now be completed in a few hours or days, and the parties were thus enabled to devote time and capital saved to new enterprises.

There followed a period of intense rivalry between telegraph companies. Cut-throat competition was the order of the day. Rates were drastically cut in some sections of the country. While a few small companies were able to survive this period of ordeal, many were unable to stand up against unrestrained competition and the economic power of giant monopoly.

While the war of wires was being waged, scientists were making new discoveries and developing new techniques. Technical improvements increased the carrier capacity of the wires. The development of apparatus for automatic transmission made it possible to send and record several thousand words per minute.

These developments and improvements were enormously helpful to news reporting. Following the construction of the Morse wire in the early days, telegraphic news reports carried by such papers as *The National Intelligencer* and the *Washington Madisonian* became popular features with the reading public. During the years that followed, with the improvement and extension of wire facilities, news agencies such as the Associated Press developed a thriving business. By the turn of the century, the newspapers of the country were sending news messages over Western Union facilities totaling hundreds of millions of words per year.

As Robert Thompson has pointed out in his excellent book, *Wiring a Continent,* the growth of the telegraph had a profound effect upon the life of the nation. He was referring to the early period of telegraph history, but what he had to say applies equally well to developments which came later. "Men from all walks of life and for a variety of reasons, employed the new means of communication."[8] Persons away from home could keep in close touch with their families. Urban life was made more secure by the use of telegraph for police and fire alarms. The farmer, merchant, banker, broker, the capitalist and the journalist constantly were broadening their base of operations as it became possible to transmit and receive intelligence quickly over hundreds and thousands of miles. In fact, the telegraph was a vital factor in the development of the American system of free enterprise.

Wires, Cables and World Community. Not all the developments by any means took place in this country. Scientists in Germany, Russia, France and other European countries did important experimental work in electrical communication and it achieved considerable growth in these countries during the forties and fifties. It had made a beginning during those early years in India, Australia, China, Japan, Turkey and some countries in Central and South America.[9]

It was only natural for men to begin thinking of connecting links among nations. Early in his career, Morse had predicted the spanning of the Atlantic and the ultimate development of a world-wide telegraphic network. After long and heroic efforts with many disheartening setbacks, the Atlantic Telegraph Company, under the courageous leadership of Cyrus Field, completed the construction of the first Atlantic cable.[10]

On August 5, 1858, a few days after the cable was laid, the New York *Evening Post* commented that "the hearts of the civilized world will beat in a single pulse, and from that time forth forevermore, the continental divisions of the earth will in a measure lose their conditions of time and distance . . ."

A few days later, the Queen of England sent a message over the cable to the President of the United States in which she prophesied that it would prove an additional link between Great Britain and the United States, "whose friendship is founded upon their common interest and reciprocal esteem."[11] President Buchanan replied, expressing the hope that the cable might "prove to be a bond of perpetual peace and friendship between the kindred nations, and an instrument destined by Divine Providence to diffuse religion, civilization, liberty and laws throughout the world.[12]

The first Atlantic cable functioned spasmodically for a time and then went completely dead. The approach of the War between the States prevented any immediate attempts to put down another one. Within one year after the War, however, two new cables were in successful operation providing a continuous flow of intelligence between the United States and Europe.[13] By 1870, a large part of the world was embraced by a network of telegraph wires. This expanding web of wires was having a vital effect upon international relations and the development of world community.

The Ring of the Magneto-Bell. While this vast telegraphic expansion was taking place, scientists were experimenting with the idea that human speech might be transmitted over wires. In 1876, Alexander Graham Bell, working in his laboratory in Boston, demonstrated that it could be done.[14] He had worked out an apparatus which included an electro-magnet, a U-shaped iron bar with a coil of wire wrapped around one limb and a

5

thin plate of iron attached to the other. A membrane diaphragm was stretched across the tube to serve as a mouthpiece. After some experimentation, he was able to produce undulations of electric current in the circuit, corresponding to the vibrations in the voice, thereby transmitting continuous and intelligible speech.

Bell took advantage of every opportunity to demonstrate how the new contrivance worked. He exhibited it at the great Centennial Exposition in Philadelphia in 1876 where thousands of people from all parts of the world had a chance to view its operations.[15] The novelty of it interested people but few at that time realized its possibilities. Most persons considered it something to play with and afford amusement. They thought little of its economic and social utility.

The telephone instruments which were first used in the seventies were crude and inefficient. A crank had to be turned vigorously. One talked into an odd appearing mouthpiece, and yelling often was necessary to overcome the howls and hisses of static so that one might be heard and understood at the other end of the line. The telephone was built in separate parts and the connections between the magneto bell, transmitter and battery were run around and tacked on the wall. It was troublesome, expensive and unsightly. The pictures of the original telephone as carried in the advertisements of that day present an amazing contrast to the dial telephone of today so compactly built that it can be put in an overcoat pocket.[16]

Improvements came quickly. The original telephone with separate, sprawling parts was soon replaced with one more compactly built. The new model had the magneto bell mounted on a base board, behind which were concealed in a box all connecting wires for the transmitter. The battery box was attached to the baseboard and served as a miniature desk on which one could write while conversing on the phone.[17]

Public interest in the use of the telephone increased so fast that by March, 1881, there was only one city in the country with more than 15,000 people that did not have a telephone exchange.[18] There were frequent comments in magazines regarding the increasing value of these telephones to community life. In cases of sickness, fire, theft or other emergencies, they saved life and property. Business men were finding them essential to the development of trade. They facilitated social contacts and group enterprise.

The Struggle for Supremacy. The growth of telephonic communication presented a real threat to the telegraph industry. The telephone offered a convenience and personal contact not provided by the telegraph. It was one thing to read a short, printed message from a friend 200 miles away but it was something else to hear that friend's voice over the telephone. To meet the competition of the expanding telephone service, Western Union began building telephone exchanges of its own throughout the country.[19]

The Bell company retaliated by bringing suit for infringement of its patent. The legal contest was settled out of court in 1879, Western Union admitting the validity of the Bell patents. The Bell company agreed to purchase the Western Union telephone system and to stay out of the telegraph business.[20]

This arrangement gave the Bell interests a clear field for the development of telephone service. They organized a new company in 1890 and under the leadership of Theodore N. Vail, moved forward rapidly. Vail had already formulated plans for a nation-wide system of inter-connected telephones, using long distance lines. Five years later, the American Telephone and Telegraph Company was established in New York for the purpose of providing long distance service.[21] On October 18, 1892, Bell sent the first message over a wire from New York to Chicago, and by the end of the century telephone toll service had become a flourishing business.

Technological developments had improved the quality of long distance communication. A report of the American Institute of Electrical Engineers published in 1904 gave a good summary of major improvements. The efficiency of long distance circuits had been vastly improved. A large part of the country was supplied with long distance lines built of sturdy copper wire. Improved equipment replaced the clumsy hand-operated magneto machines which required the subscriber to furnish his own current and keep his battery in working condition. The old system had been superseded by the single central station battery, a few cells of which were able to do the work of many and could be maintained more economically and efficiently. In most large cities, underground cables had replaced the appalling and unsightly maze of wires above the streets.[22]

In 1905, the Bell system as a whole had more than 4 million subscribers and handled on an average more than 7,000 calls per minute, 460,000 an hour and close to 11 million a day. The distance of the calls varied from a few feet to more than 1600 miles. The Bell company was handling nearly forty times as many messages as the telegraph companies. More than 30,000 towns and cities were connected by the wires of the system.[23]

This was not all. Beginning in the early nineties, numerous smaller companies not connected with the Bell system were established. By 1901, independent exchanges were being operated in 45 states and in the territories, with an investment of 100 million dollars and over a million telephones.[24]

Not all the development had occurred in the United States. In 1878, only two years after Bell had invented the telephone, public telephone exchanges were opened in London, Manchester and Liverpool. By 1891, Glasgow, Paris and Berlin were operating similar exchanges. The expansion continued, and in 1910 all the principal cities in the world had telephone service. It was estimated there were about ten million telephones in use, nearly two-thirds of which were in this country. The total number had almost reached the 15 million mark by 1915.[25]

Wireless Wizardry. But the telephonic achievements which evoked exclamatory utterances from journalists of that day could not compare with the wireless wonders which were already on the way. As previously mentioned, in 1901 Marconi thrilled the world with the transmission of electromagnetic signals across the Atlantic Ocean.[26] In March, 1903, the first transoceanic radiogram appeared in the London *Times*. A few years later, De Forest transmitted speech across his laboratory, using an audion amplifier which he had invented.[27] This made voice amplification possible and was the basis for the development of radio telephony.

By 1915, the American Telephone and Telegraph Company had inaugurated regular telephone service between New York and San Francisco. It was this same year, with the use of the Audion tube, that Bell engineers were able to span the Pacific and Atlantic oceans by means of radio telephony.[28]

World War I brought many improvements in radio communication. By 1925, transoceanic telephony using radio waves had been developed to the point that it was almost as reliable as that by wire and cable. During the next few years, tele-communications developed rapidly and literally revolutionized the pattern of living in many parts of the world.

On December 31, 1932, telegraph and cable companies then reporting to the Interstate Commerce Commission had capital assets amounting to more than 250 million dollars. Western Union and International Telephone and Telegraph Corporation transmitted over 125 million messages that year. The telephone industry had an investment of over 5 billion dollars with an annual income running more than a billion. In 1932, there were over 17 million telephones in use in the country. There were nearly ninety million miles of wire, more than enough to reach from the earth to the moon and back again more than 150 times.[29]

In 1934, the year the Federal Communications Commission was created, a vast network of wires extended to every major part of the globe with more than 32 million telephones in use. What a century before had been a multiplicity of provincial habitations, widely separated by time and space and scattered over the face of the earth, was now a talking world with the various parts literally linked together by wires and electromagnetic waves.

NOTES

1. Harlow, Alvin F., *Old Wires and New Waves* (New York, 1936), pp. 32, 33.

2. Bureau of the Census, *Telephones and Telegraphs* (Washington, D. C., 1902), pp. 112, 113.

3. Harlow, *op. cit.*, pp. 84, 85.

4. *Ibid.*, p. 86.

5. Morse, Edward Lind, *Samuel F. B. Morse, Letters and Journals*, Vol. 2 (Boston, 1914), pp. 221-229.

6. Harlow, *op. cit.*, p. 313.

7. *Ibid.*

8. Thompson, Robert, *Wiring a Continent* (Princeton, 1947), pp. 444, 445.

9. Shaffner, Tal. P., *The Telegraph Manual; a Complete History and Description of the Semaphoric, Electric and Magnetic Telegraphs of Europe, Asia, Africa and America, Ancient and Modern* (Pudney and Russell, 1859).

10. Walter, Kellogg Towers, *From Beacon Fire to Radio* (New York, 1924), pp. 117-124.

11. *Ibid.*, p. 125.

12. *Ibid.*

13. *Ibid.*, p. 136.

14. Bureau of the Census, *op. cit.*, p. 66.

15. *Ibid.*

16. Rhodes, Fredrich Leland, *Beginnings of Telephony* (New York, 1929); and Kingsbury, John E., *The Telephone and Telephone Exchanges* (Longmans Green, 1915).

17. *Ibid.*

18. Bureau of the Census, *op. cit.*, p. 66.

19. *Ibid.*

20. *Ibid.*

21. Casson, Herbert N., *The History of the Telephone* (New York, 1910), pp. 173, 174.

22. *Ibid.*

23. *Ibid.*

24. MacNeal, Harry B., *The Story of Independent Telephony* (The Independent Pioneer Telephone Association, Washington, D. C.).

25. Casson, *op. cit.*, pp. 245-273; also Bureau of Census, *op. cit.*, 1906, pp. 68-78.

26. *The Radio Industry, The Story of Its Development,* as told by leaders of the industry (Chicago, 1928), p. 29.

27. *Ibid.*, pp. 55, 56.

28. *Ibid.*, p. 130.

29. Federal Communications Commission, *Report, Special Telephone Investigation,* 1937.

CHAPTER 2

Eliminating the Static

The ether is a public medium and its use must be for public benefit. . . .
The dominant element for consideration in the radio field is, and always
will be, the great body of the listening public, millions in number, country-
wide in distribution.—HERBERT HOOVER

The technological development of radio and its effective use in telegraphic and telephonic communication paved the way for broadcasting.
From about 1910 to the end of the first World War, sporadic, experimental attempts were made to broadcast programs for general reception.
For example, in 1910, standing on the stage of the Metropolitan Opera
House in New York City, Enrico Caruso sang an aria into a paper cone
attached to a musician's tripod. Inside the cone was a vibrating diaphragm
attached to a telephone wire which ran to the laboratory of the young
scientist, Lee W. De Forest, located some distance away. The voice of the
world famous tenor was carried over this wire and then transmitted
through space by De Forest to wireless operators on various ships at sea.[1]

As early as 1909, a radio telephone transmitting station in San Jose,
California (later assigned call letters KQW) began broadcasting. In 1917,
station 9XM at the University of Wisconsin (subsequently identified as
WHA) began experimental broadcasts of musical programs.[2]

During this early period, amateur operators, or "hams" as they were
popularly called, scattered in various parts of the country, with transmitting and receiving equipment located in pantries, basements and attics,
were entertaining one another with small talk and recorded music and
were exchanging ideas on the wonders of wireless telephony. In 1916, one
of these amateur operators by the name of David Sarnoff (later to become
one of the great leaders in the broadcast industry) proposed that regular
musical and talking programs be presented by radio. He suggested the
manufacture of a "radio music box," complete with amplifying tubes and
a loudspeaker telephone. He expressed confidence that within a few years
millions of these sets could be sold to the general public.[3]

Early Microphone Celebrities. His confidence was fully justified. Following the first World War, there was a rapid development in the radio
art. With technological improvements which came out of the War, imagina-

tive business men such as Sarnoff applied their minds to the development of broadcasting as a means of public entertainment and enlightenment, at the same time foreseeing its vast commercial possibilities.

Great talent was brought before the microphones. For example, Fritz Kreisler caused a sensation when he performed over KDKA in Pittsburgh's Carnegie Hall on January 26, 1922.[4] Likewise, people were thrilled over the broadcast of grand opera by a station in Chicago.[5] John McCormack, noted Irish tenor, and Lucrezia Bori, Metropolitan opera star, gave their initial radio performances on the New York station WEAF in January, 1925. Many persons in the New York area heard them and the theatres complained of the competition.[6]

Lighter music was featured by some stations and attracted large audiences. There were the Kansas City Night Hawks who brought jazz music and night club atmosphere to millions of fans in the Midwest. WOS in St. Louis featured Harry M. Snodgrass, known popularly as "King of the Ivories," at that time serving a three year term for forgery in the Missouri State Prison. Vincent Lopez became a national celebrity as he and his traveling orchestra broadcast popular rhythm over WEAF and other stations. The harmony team of Jones and Hare, "The Happiness Boys," made their debut on WEAF in December, 1923 and "The National Barn Dance" was in full swing several months later on WLS in Chicago.[7]

During the early twenties, station WEAF was broadcasting the popular news analysis of H. V. Kaltenborn, then Associate Editor of the *Brooklyn Daily Eagle* and whose fame spread rapidly, soon making him a national figure. About the same time, Harold "Red" Grange, famous All-American half-back, was bringing dramatic accounts of sports events over the facilities of WOC in Davenport, Iowa. Station WJZ in New York broadcast a World Series game for the first time in October, 1921 and about two years later Graham McNamee presented a play-by-play report of the Series in his first network sports assignment.[8]

For the first time in history a speech in the halls of Congress was broadcast when President Harding read his message on December 6, 1923. Woodrow Wilson broke his silence of four years when on Armistice Day of the same year he addressed the American public through microphones installed in his home.[9]

Advertising Values Recognized. The value of radio as an advertising medium was being increasingly recognized. For example, during the early twenties, numerous commercial companies used the facilities of station WEAF in New York to advertise their products. There was The Eveready Hour sponsored by the National Carbon Company, which urged listeners to buy the dry-cell Eveready battery for their receiving sets. To attract listeners, the company featured celebrities such as John Drew, Julia Marlowe, George Gershwin, Weber and Fields, and Irvin S. Cobb.[10] More and more advertisers sponsored programs, featured high priced talent and enlarged the markets for their products or services.

Educational and Religious Uses.   The educational values of radio were not overlooked during those early years. For example, Judith Waller, one of the great pioneer women in commercial radio, became widely known for her contributions to public service broadcasting, including her early leadership in the University of Chicago Round Table. In May, 1923, WJZ in New York began the first University of the Air, featuring talks on economic problems of the day.[11]

Many colleges and universities had their own stations and were bringing to eager listeners professional lectures, inter-collegiate debates, musical and dramatic shows and market reports. By 1925, some institutions were offering formal instruction by radio and there was much talk among educators about extending its use for the teaching of a wide variety of subjects to the general public.

Religious programs were featured by many stations in those early days. On January 2, 1921, KDKA broadcast the first "Church of the Air." As early as 1922, the "Great Commoner," William Jennings Bryan, was transmitting via radio his message of salvation to vast numbers of churched and unchurched people. In 1925, Reverend Howard O. Hough established the "First Radio Parish Church in America," a non-sectarian organization, using the facilities of Station WCSH in Portland, Maine. Father James R. Cox of Pittsburgh became widely known for his presentation of the Catholic message from the Old St. Patrick's Church through the facilities of WJAS.[12]

The "Peddlers of the Air".   But all was not sweetness and light. There were the "peddlers of the air" who victimized listeners with their "get rich quick" schemes. Astrologers, fortune tellers, experts on dandruff and falling hair and other quacks found ready access to the microphones in many communities.

The mercenary medicine men presented a special problem. Hucksters such as Dr. John R. Brinkley made extravagant claims for their medicine and cures, swelling their bank accounts with cash which flowed in daily from unsuspecting and trusting listeners. Dr. Brinkley broadcast a program of hillbilly music and medical talks over his station KFKB in Milford, Kansas. In connection with this program he advertised his famous "goat-gland" operation as a sure and effective means of revitalizing elderly gentlemen. He openly defied the American Medical Association and through his broadcast braggadocia and buffoonery attracted literally thousands of older men from all parts of the United States to his clinic in Milford. There he performed "revitalizing" operations for a fee which averaged about $750.

For years he exploited a publicly owned radio channel to hawk his medical quackery. Finally, the Federal Radio Commission cancelled his license and put a stop to his predatory practice in Kansas.[13] Unable to operate on an assigned frequency in this country, he subsequently secured a high-powered transmitter in Mexico and beamed his medical gullery back into this country, using the call letters XER. He established new hospitals in Del Rio, Texas and Little Rock, Arkansas where he continued his "revitalizing" therapy. For ten years thereafter he carried on his "border raids" and come-on games until in 1941 a wholesale reallocation of frequencies and reductions in transmitting power of stations along the border, resulting from a treaty with Mexico and other North American countries, dealt a death blow to his 100,000-watt XER.[14]

Robert J. Landry in his book, *The Fascinating Radio Business,* has given an interesting account of the hawking activities of Brinkley and other radio hucksters during those early days:

Brinkley was definitely the most colorful of the motley assortment of self-promoters who came to radio in the early years. There were hysterical clergymen, enemies of Wall Street, enemies of chain stores, enemies of Catholics, Jews and Negroes, promoters of patented heavens. Tea-leaf Kitty from Jersey City went on the radio and offered to answer any three questions in a sealed envelope for one dollar. The meaning of the stars, the stock market, the future life could all be learned by enclosing cash. Falling hair or teeth could be arrested—just write. Fortunes in real estate could be made overnight—just write. Home cures for this, that or the other thing were available—just write.[15]

Frenzied Competition for Radio Audience. In the whole history of scientific discovery there perhaps has never been so rapid a development of knowledge for popular use as in the field of radio. In 1920 there were only about three radio stations providing regular program service to the public. By 1924, there were more than 500 on the air with programs available to most of the homes in the country. The sales of radio receivers and other apparatus at that time were averaging about a million dollars a day. It was estimated that over 200,000 persons were employed in the broadcasting industry.[16] In homes, offices, workshops and hotels, in cities, towns and rural areas, Americans were huddled around receivers with earphones clamped to their skulls listening in awe and wonderment to programs coming through the "ether" from stations far and near.

Broadcasters vied with one another for the listener's attention and interest. Advertisers were looking for the programs and talent that would attract the most listeners and provide the best market for services and goods. Some stations stepped up their power, jumped frequencies and changed hours of operation at will in a frenzied effort to enlarge their coverage areas and audiences and achieve competitive advantage.

While some broadcasters entered into agreements with respect to power, use of frequencies and hours of operation, there were many others who refused to do so. In deliberate, cut-throat fashion, some broadcaster's attempted to interfere with and drown out the signals of lower-powered stations. Francis Chase, Jr., in his informal history of broadcasting, *Sound and Fury,* has described the general situation at that time as one where

13

"chaos rode the air waves, pandemonium filled every loud-speaker and the twentieth century Tower of Babel was made in the image of the antenna towers of some thousand broadcasters who, like the Kilkenny cats, were about to eat each other up."[17]

The Growth of Networks. Network operation had reached a fairly advanced stage by 1925. Its development had come rapidly. On January 4, 1923, with a special circuit set up between WEAF in New York City and WNAC in Boston, a program originating at WEAF was transmitted simultaneously by the two stations. According to official reports, this was the first network broadcast.[18]

WEAF was then owned by the American Telephone and Telegraph Company. At that time the Bell company claimed exclusive rights under certain patents and patent-licensing agreements to sell radio time and operate "toll broadcasting stations." By the end of 1925, it had expanded its network to include 26 stations as far west as Kansas City. The company was selling time to advertisers over a basic network of 13 stations at $2600 per hour with a gross income of about $750,000 per year.[19]

The Radio Corporation of America also got an early start in network broadcasting. In the spring of 1923, RCA acquired control of WJZ in New York City and later that year constructed and started operating WRC in Washington. Its first network broadcast occurred in December, 1925, and included WJZ and the General Electric Company station WGY in Schenectady.[20]

Because of the restrictive policy of the AT&T in refusing to furnish wire service to broadcasting stations not licensed under that company's patents, RCA was hampered in the early development of its network. For a time, the radio company was compelled to use telegraph wires. Their transmission quality was much inferior to that of the telephone lines operated by the Bell system.[21] Also, since the telephone company claimed the exclusive right to sell time for broadcasting, RCA made no charge for the use of its facilities and was handicapped in developing the commercial aspects of its network.[22]

In 1926, the Telephone Company withdrew from the broadcasting field and transferred its radio properties to RCA, Westinghouse, and General Electric, and agreed to make its lines available to RCA for network purposes.[23]

That same year, RCA formed a corporation, the National Broadcasting Company, to take over its network business with the outstanding stock owned by RCA, General Electric, and Westinghouse. Subsequently, RCA purchased all the stock interests of GE and Westinghouse in NBC and the latter company became a wholly owned subsidiary of RCA.[24]

The Columbia Broadcasting System was organized in 1927. Its original network consisted of 16 stations. By this time, NBC had increased its outlets to 48. This made a total of 64 stations affiliated with the two chain systems, providing regular network service to every part of the country.[25]

14

The Listeners Become Critical.   With the continued growth of cities and metropolitan areas, expanding industries, and developments in transportation, life in America was taking on an increasingly complex pattern. It was far removed from the simple life of the early American Indians who found smoke rings and fire-arrows adequate to meet their needs for long distance communication. Telegraph, telephone and radio had facilitated this remarkable social and economic growth and had become an indispensable part of a highly developed civilization. Communication lines and channels had become the nerve fibers through which the organization of a great democratic nation of 120 million people was made to function.

More and more the average citizen realized this. He became increasingly conscious that his individual comfort and happiness as well as that of the community and nation were dependent upon the efficiency of these media. The security of his home, family, and job, the welfare of his local institutions—the church, the school and other community enterprises—all were tied up with communications service. In the language of the courts, these public utilities were "clothed with the public interest," and the citizen was voicing more concern with the way they were managed and operated.

He became more critical. The free and unrestrained transmissions of radio operators on ships at sea too often interfered with the music, speeches, baseball scores, weather reports and market information that he and thousands of others were trying to get from broadcast stations.

Many listeners complained of excessive and offensive advertising on radio programs. They deplored frequent interruptions by sponsors advertising hair nets, soaps, facial creams, etc.

Censorship, Monopoly and Demagoguery Deplored.   There was complaint against censorship. Political speakers didn't like the idea of having to submit manuscripts to station managers, who often deleted portions of the speeches. Men like the elder Robert La Follette and Norman Thomas insisted there should be no censorship of their radio speeches because of the prejudice or fears of station managers.

There were bitter attacks against the growth of monopoly in the radio industry. Frequent editorials in newspapers and magazines deplored the growing concentration of control in a few large companies. The Federal Trade Commission condemned what it termed an illegal monopoly in the manufacture and sale of radio apparatus.[26] In 1924, Station WHO in Des Moines, Iowa refused to carry the speech of Senator La Follette in behalf of his candidacy for President on the Progressive ticket. He asserted that "a monopoly had been formed to prevent him from going on the air."[27]

In a letter to the *New York Times* dated August 28, 1924, Congressman Emanuel Celler protested against what he termed an "absolute monopoly" in radio. He charged that the monopoly was "manifesting itself against candidates for public office who desire to use the radio for campaign purposes."[28]

There were general grumblings at the time about propagandists, religious zealots and unprincipled persons with axes to grind and a motley of demagogues and hucksters seeking to reach radio audiences with their peculiar brands of publicity. There were protests against radio programs not in good taste, and the excessive use of phonograph recordings was vehemently condemned.

With respect to radio, the decade from 1920 to 1930 can most certainly and appropriately be referred to as "the roaring twenties." A fast and furious growth in the industry, wave piracy, offensive advertising, monopoly and other disturbing conditions brought demands from the public that the government do something to correct the situation generally thought to be a "conglomerate mess."

Interference Becomes Intolerable. Herbert Hoover, then Secretary of Commerce, found much of his time taken up answering letters, telegrams and telephone calls from listeners complaining about technical interference. Typical of the complaints were those which came as a result of two church broadcasts in Washington. For three successive Sundays in 1922, two stations in the Capitol City broadcast services from these churches at the same time on the same wave length. The result was anything but heavenly. What poured from the receivers was a pain-provoking jumble of noise that was more conducive to neuroses than quiet religious worship. Large numbers of distressed listeners appealed to Secretary Hoover to straighten out the tangle. "Dante's Inferno can be no worse than the noises that come to us in Florida," wrote one distraught listener to the Secretary.

From every section of the country came similar appeals for relief from static and interference. For example, on May 15, 1922, the Radio Broadcasting Society of America asked Secretary Hoover to revoke the license of Station WJZ in New York, alleging that it wantonly interfered with the operation of fifteen other stations.[29]

Hoover was tremendously interested in the problems of broadcasting and was eager to improve a situation which some authorities thought was threatening to kill the art and industry. However, his authority to regulate radio was limited. By a 1910 Congressional Act, it was made unlawful for a ship carrying fifty or more persons to leave any port of the United States unless equipped with efficient radio communication facilities.[30] The Secretary of Commerce and Labor (as he was then called) was given the power to make regulations for the proper execution of this law.

The Titanic disaster of 1912 prompted Congress to strengthen the safety provisions of the 1910 law. A new act was passed implementing treaty obligations of the United States in connection with the use of radio by ships at sea, and specifying procedure to be followed in transmitting and answering distress calls. Other provisions of the 1912 Act required every radio station to secure a license from the Secretary of Commerce and

Labor, made compulsory the employment of a licensed operator, and specified bands of frequencies for different classes of stations.[31]

But still the law gave the Secretary no discretionary power. There were no general standards by which he could choose among applicants for stations. He had no authority to specify particular frequencies, power, hours of operation or the period of a license. There were certain regulations in the law designed to prevent or reduce interference between stations, but in large measure, broadcasters chose their own wave lengths and operated much as they pleased.

Hoover and his staff gave a great deal of thought to what might be done to correct the situation. Because of his interest in their problems, troubled broadcasters and listeners sought his help and advice. As an unofficial arbiter, he was able to settle many serious conflicts and disturbances in the radio field. He became convinced, however, that the serious impediments to effective broadcasting in this country could not be removed until the government was given actual and not nominal authority to regulate the radio industry. Accordingly, he called a conference of radio experts to discuss the possibilities of new and remedial legislation.

New Legislation Recommended. The meeting assembled in Washington, D. C. on February 27, 1922. After two months of study and investigation, the conference unanimously recommended the immediate extension of the regulatory powers of the government, and drafted technical provisions for submission to Congress.[32]

Wallace H. White, Jr., then Congressman from Maine, took the lead in drafting a bill along the lines suggested, and stated that the proposed legislation would provide for a "traffic cop of the air." In submitting the report of the Committee on the Merchant Marine and Fisheries which had held hearings on the bill, Congressman White said in part:

On December 27, 1922, there were in operation in the country 21,065 transmitting radio stations. Of these, 16,898 were amateur stations, 2,762 were ship stations, 569 were broadcasting stations, 39 were coast stations, 12 were transoceanic stations, and there were a few others not necessary to be enumerated . . . There are, however, in addition to them, receiving stations to the estimated number of 2,000,000.

He further pointed out that 279 government stations were using 122 of the total wave lengths then available, leaving only 29 for more than 17,000 private stations of all classes. He said:

There must be an ordered system of communication on the air into which all users of the ether must be fitted or there can be no intelligible transmission by this means. It is as difficult for two stations in the same locality to simultaneously transmit on the same wave length as it is for two trains to pass each other upon the same track. A schedule for transmission of messages in the air is as essential as a schedule for the movement of trains upon land. The primary purpose of the pending bill is to give the Secretary of Commerce such powers of regulation and control as are needed to relieve the present congestion in and to bring about a more orderly and efficient use of the ether.[33]

Despite the chaotic situation, the House and Senate could not agree on legislation, so Hoover called a second conference in 1923. Important commercial, scientific, and public organizations were represented. Since Congress had failed to act, the main purpose of the meeting was to work out administrative methods to reduce the ever-increasing interference to radio reception. The result was a recommendation for reallocation of frequencies which would place all broadcasting stations in a band from 550 to 1,350 kilocycles and assign other frequencies for amateur, government and marine use. The Department of Commerce adopted the recommendations and the interference problem was considerably alleviated.[34]

But Hoover was still concerned over the inadequacy of the law. There were thousands of radio stations of various types operating in the United States and along the coasts. He was expected to see that they were inspected but he had only a few men to do the work. He kept urging Congress to give the government more power to regulate broadcasting and additional money to employ adequate personnel.

Hoover Calls More Conferences. Congress continued to study the problem and Hoover continued to call conferences. At the Third National Radio Conference which assembled on October 6, 1924, he declared that "we must have traffic rules, or the whole ether will be blocked with chaos, and we must have safeguards that will keep the ether free for full development."[35]

In a statement to the press on December 31, 1924, he referred to both the appreciative and critical attitudes of the public regarding radio and its impact upon American life:

Listeners are becoming more and more appreciative of the real service of radio and increasingly critical, both as to the character of the matter furnished them and as to the efficiency with which it reaches them.

The whole broadcasting structure is built upon service to the listeners. They are beginning to realize their importance, to assert their interest and to voice their wishes. Broadcasting must be conducted to meet their demand, and this necessarily means higher character in what is transmitted and better quality in its reproduction to the ears of the listener.

The broadcasters as a whole are alive to the situation. There is a growing realization on their part of the public responsibilities they assume in conducting an agency so greatly affecting the cultural progress of our people.[36]

At the Fourth National Radio Conference in November, 1925, he reiterated the need for effective regulation. "We must face the actualities frankly," said this engineer who later was to become President. "We can no longer deal on the basis that there is room for everybody on the radio highways. There are more vehicles on the roads than can get by, and if they continue to jam in, all will be stopped."[37]

"We hear a great deal about freedom of the air, but there are two parties to freedom of the air, and to freedom of speech, for that matter. Certainly in radio I believe in freedom for the listener . . . Freedom cannot mean a license to every person or corporation who wishes to broadcast his name or his wares, and thus monopolize the listener's set."[38]

He further observed that "we do not get much freedom of speech if 150 people speak at the same time at the same place". With 578 independent stations in operation, he expected that there would be a wide latitude for the expression of opinions on social, political and religious questions. He did not feel, however, that any broadcaster could rightly complain that he had been deprived of free speech if he was compelled to prove that there was "something more than naked commercial selfishness in his purpose."[39]

He then stated a philosophy that was to become the basis for government regulation of broadcasting in this country from that day to this; that "the ether is a public medium, and its use must be for public benefit;" and that the main "consideration in the radio field is, and always will be, the great body of the listening public, millions in number, countrywide in distribution. There is no proper line of conflict between the broadcaster and the listener . . . Their interests are mutual, for without the one the other could not exist."[40]

The Radio Act of 1927. That 1925 conference recommended legislation giving the Federal government authority to issue licenses, assign wave lengths, and determine the power of broadcast stations. But the Conference cautioned against extending governmental authority "to mere matters of station management, not affecting service or creating interference."[41] Governmental censorship was strongly opposed.

Two important developments the following year made new legislation imperative. A Federal court held that a station owner could not be punished for disregarding a frequency assignment made by the Secretary of Commerce.[42] Shortly thereafter, the Attorney General sounded the death knell for Federal regulation under the then existing law when he ruled that the Act of 1912 gave the Secretary no authority to limit frequency, power or time used by any station.[43]

Congress had been holding hearings intermittently for several years but never had been able to agree on legislation. The chaotic condition of radio in 1926, however, intensified the determination of Congressional leaders to compromise differences and get a law passed. The public was fed up on the nightly chorus of heterodyne squeals caused by a multiplicity of broadcasters operating on the same channels. Congress was impelled to act.

Out of the 1926 Congressional hearings, in which leaders in government, education, religion, industry and labor urged Congress to remedy the intolerable situation, came a bill which the House and Senate finally agreed upon. It became law on February 23, 1927.[44]

This Radio Act of 1927, while imperfect in some respects, was an important step in the direction of effective radio regulation. It provided for a commission of five members with authority to grant, renew or revoke station licenses. It was provided that after one year, all authority was to be vested in the Secretary of Commerce except that he would have no authority to revoke a license and would be required to refer to the Commission all applications for licenses, renewals or modifications thereof, about which there might be any controversy.

It was definitely established by the Act that the radio spectrum belonged to the public and that a broadcaster acquired no ownership rights in a frequency when granted a license. Before he could be granted a license or a renewal of one, he was required to show that the public interest would be served. Thus the government was given authority to make a systematic assignment of frequencies and, within limitations, to set standards and make rules for the operation of radio stations.[45]

Actually, the authority provided in the law never became vested in the Secretary of Commerce. Congress from time to time extended the one year limitation and the Federal Radio Commission continued to function as originally provided until the passage of the Communications Act of 1934 when all authority to regulate radio was vested in the Federal Communications Commission.

The Federal Radio Commission established the regular broadcasting band from 550 to 1,500 kilocycles, and provided for a 10 kilocycle separation between stations. A general reallocation of frequencies brought about a more equitable distribution of radio facilities throughout the country and eliminated much of the station interference.

"Radio Became the Fifth Estate". With the help of this new "traffic cop of the air," general radio reception rapidly improved. Interference was reduced. Static continued to be some bother, but became less troublesome as the years passed. Head phones were soon replaced by attractive table sets and cabinet models. By 1930, national networks were doing a flourishing business. Plans were underway for the erection of an immense structure in the heart of New York City to cost $250,000,000. It was to cover three square blocks and rise 60 stories in the air. It was to be called Radio City, house the studios of the National Broadcasting Company and become the radio center of the world.

Will Rogers was thrilling millions of listeners with his down-to-earth philosophy and humor. Jack Pearl, popularly known as Baron Munchausen, had become top billing with his comedy on the Lucky Strike Hour. He was the forerunner of a galaxy of radio stars who captivated the American people with their talent—Ed Wynn, Eddie Cantor, George Jessel, Joe Penner, and a host of others. There were the entertainment teams—the Duncan Sisters, Amos 'n Andy, Bergen and McCarthy, Fibber McGee and Molly, to mention only a few. Paul Whiteman's orchestra and the New

York Philharmonic Symphony had become network features and were being heard regularly from coast to coast.

The superbly modulated and melodious voice of Milton J. Cross was reaching the eager and appreciative ears of music lovers throughout the country as he announced the broadcasts of the Metropolitan Opera. Walter Damrosch had achieved his ambition to broadcast musical education to the nation. The Columbia Broadcasting System was bringing to the classrooms of America "The School of the Air," offering a variety of subjects designed to supplement formal instruction. The inimitable Ted Husing was reporting important sports events to millions of excited fans. The CBS "Church of the Air" had become an established radio pulpit for every major religious faith. Father Charles E. Coughlin was causing a national furor, espousing the cause of his National Union for Social Justice over an independent network.

In 1932, Harold La Fount, then a member of the Federal Radio Commission, reported that there were 17 million radio receivers in homes throughout the country.[46] Popular stars such as Kate Smith were estimated to have audiences approaching the 5 million mark.[47] According to a survey covering 16 groups of stations and embracing 93 cities, almost 25 million dollars were spent for radio advertising during 1932, with about half the amount expended to promote the sale of food, beverages, drugs, toilet articles, automobiles, and tobacco.[48]

Ted Husing, in his delightful book, *Ten Years Before the Mike,* attempted in 1935 to recapture the psychology of broadcasting during that early period:

... Big names of the stage, screen and concert platforms began to appear in the broadcast schedules. With symphony orchestras broadcasting Beethoven and eminent clergymen starting "churches of the air," the most finical artists could no longer look on radio as a cheap toy. As a result, delight undreamed of by the masses, music, drama, comedy, romance, travel, enlightenment of every sort—in a word (consulting my Webster), culture, pressed down and running over—began to flow freely from early morning till late night alike into the hovels of Pittsburgh steel workers and the mansions of Southampton millionaires. Radio became the Fifth Estate.[49]

Inadequate Regulation of Telephone and Telegraph Service. Rules established by the Federal Radio Commission had helped to alleviate the chaos which had characterized radio in its formative years and had given impetus to the rapid and healthy development of the broadcasting industry. This Commission, however, had no authority to regulate telephone and telegraph companies now doing an enormous interstate business. In 1910, Congress had provided for the Federal regulation of these companies but the law was never adequate.[50] Regulatory authority had been assigned to the Interstate Commerce Commission, but that agency was largely concerned with railroad transportation, and communications received comparatively little attention.

Numerous state commissions had been established but their ability to regulate industries which had become national in scope was seriously limited. They were powerless to regulate communication services extending across state lines and into foreign countries.

Felix Frankfurter, then a professor of law at Harvard University, expressed the opinion in 1930 that throughout the United States the machinery of utility regulation had shown strain. He made note of the growing public feeling that not only had the purposes for which these state commissions had been designed—to serve the interests of the consumers—not been realized, but that actually the regulatory systems had been operating to defeat these purposes.[51]

In 1932, Dr. W. W. Splawn, Special Counsel for the House Committee on Interstate and Foreign Commerce, which had undertaken a special study of communications companies in the United States, wrote that the "American people are entitled to know if they are being over-charged for service" and stressed the need for more effective regulation. He expressed the feeling held by many at the time that a new Federal commission should be created to make an intensive study of telephone and telegraph companies with particular respect to their accounts, their methods of figuring depreciation, their operating expenses, their contracts for service, and their political activities.[52]

The telegraph and telephone industries more and more were making use of radio for point to point communication in both their domestic and foreign business. At the same time, the expansion of the broadcasting industry depended greatly upon the use of wire and cable facilities, particularly in the development of network operations.

As previously pointed out, prior to 1926, the Bell System had owned and operated broadcast stations. It had established its own network, manufactured and sold broadcast transmitting equipment, and furnished wire facilities to other broadcasters. It restricted the use of wire facilities to promote its own broadcasting activities and to protect its patent position.

After July, 1926, when the company sold its stations, it limited its radio activities to the furnishing of wire facilities to broadcasters. By reason of its patent position, its extensive wire networks, and its restrictive policies, it had attained a dominant position in the broadcasting field. Despite this monopoly, and the almost total dependence of broadcasters upon the Bell System for network operation, the telephone company, prior to 1934, had not committed itself to the principle that the furnishing of wire service to broadcasters was a part of its public service responsibility.[53]

There was increasing public awareness of the inter-dependency of the radio and telephone business as well as that of the telegraph companies. It became apparent that the efficiency, economy and growth of these media depended greatly upon how well their operations were coordinated. It followed, therefore, that effective regulation of any one of them required an understanding of the others and the working relationships of them all.

Accordingly, experts in the communications field such as Dr. Splawn felt there was imperative need for the establishment of a comprehensive national policy covering all these media, with a single Federal agency designed and equipped to administer the policy and make rules implementing it.

Roosevelt and the FCC. It was the perception of this need that prompted President Roosevelt to initiate a study of the over-all problem during the summer of 1933. Pursuant to his directive, the Secretary of Commerce appointed a governmental committee to consider the formulation of a national policy.[54] This committee found that regulation at the Federal level was divided among various governmental agencies. Radio was under the jurisdiction of the Federal Radio Commission; to a limited extent, as already mentioned, the Interstate Commerce Commission was authorized to regulate interstate telephone and telegraph carriers but did very little to exercise its powers; minor jurisdictions over wire services, at one time or another, had been vested in the Postmaster General and the President. The Committee was of the opinion that this division of authority was not conducive to effective regulation and recommended that a new Federal commission be created to which all existing authority would be transferred.[55]

David Sarnoff, President of the Radio Corporation of America, appeared before the House Committee on Interstate and Foreign Commerce on May 16, 1934 and testified in support of the principle of unified regulation of the communications industry. He said:

We have always believed in the necessity for effective regulation of communications by a single governmental agency, and we pledge our complete support to the President's views as expressed to Congress in his message of February 26, in which he urged the creation of a single agency to be vested with the authority now lying in the Federal Radio Commission, together with that authorized over communications now vested in the Interstate Commerce Commission.

To make this authority complete, I would suggest that the present authority of the Postmaster General over communications covered in the Post Roads Act, which includes the power to fix rates for governmental telegrams, be also transferred to the new Commission. Similarly, the power of the Executive Department, covering the granting and regulation of cable landing licenses, should likewise be transferred to the new Commission. Only in this manner can the United States develop a unified and progressive communications policy, both national and international.

Foreign nations give much thought to the control and effective planning of their international communication services. The creation of a single Federal regulatory body in this country will mark a most constructive step in the communications history of the United States. We therefore hope that the Communications Act of 1934 will become law and that under that law the Federal Communications Commission will be promptly established.[56]

Many other important leaders in industry, government and education supported Mr. Sarnoff's point of view. And after extensive hearings and debate, the Congress enacted the Communications Act of 1934, abolishing the Federal Radio Commission and creating the Federal Communications Commission with authority to regulate all interstate and foreign communication by means of wire or radio. The President signed the bill and it became law on June 19, 1934.[57]

Thus it was that the basic Federal law governing communications was established. It was an outgrowth of a long evolutionary process which had been going on for many decades. The law has now been in effect for more than twenty-five years. It has been amended from time to time, but its basic features remain very much the same today as they were in 1934 when the law was adopted.

The story of how the Communications Act of 1934 and the FCC came into being is the story of America's struggle to achieve maximum benefits from communications under a system of democratic, free enterprise. Both literally and figuratively, our people sought to eliminate static in the field of communications. They chose private ownership and management but insisted that there be government regulation for the protection of the public interest.

In the next part of this book, the more important features and provisions of this law as adopted in 1934, will be reviewed and the powers, functions and organizational structure of the FCC which it created will be described. The study, of course, will have more meaning and value if made in terms of the technical, social, economic and cultural developments discussed in this and the preceding chapter.

NOTES

1. Shurick, E. P. J., *The First Quarter Century of American Broadcasting* (Kansas City, 1946), pp. 28-29; also, Husing, Ted, *Ten Years Before the Mike* (New York, 1935), pp. 17-18.
2. Shurick, *Ibid.*, pp. 46-47.
3. Dunlap, Jr., Orin Elmer, *Dunlap's Radio and Television Almanac* (New York, 1951), p. 58.
4. Shurick, *op. cit.*, p. 66.
5. Landry, Robert, Jr., *This Fascinating Radio Business* (New York 1946), p. 161.
6. *New York Times,* January 2, 1925, pp. 1, 3.
7. Shurick, *op. cit.*, pp. 59-61, 71, and personal recollections of the author.
8. *Ibid.*, pp. 121, 129-30.
9. *Ibid.*, pp. 265-266.
10. Chester, Giraud and Garrison, R. Garnet, *Radio and Televison* (New

York, 1950), p. 25; also, see Goldsmith, Alfred N. and Lescarboura, Austin C., *This Thing Called Broadcasting* (New York, 1930).

11. Shurick, *op. cit.*, pp. 141-142, 303.

12. *Ibid.*, 312-314, 320.

13. *KFKB Broadcasting Association*, FRC, June 13, 1930, affirmed 60 App. D.C. 79, 47 F.(2d) 670 (1931).

14. Pike and Fischer, *Radio Regulation*, Vol. I, pp. 41:201-202; contains background report on original North American Regional Broadcast Agreement which became effective March 29, 1941 and Mexico's ratification of this agreement.

15. Landry, *op. cit.*, p. 48.

16. Third National Radio Conference, *Recommendations for Regulation of Radio* (Washington, D. C., 1924), p. 2.

17. Chase, Francis, Jr., *Sound and Fury* (New York, 1942), p. 21.

18. Federal Communications Commission, *Report on Chain Broadcasting*, Commission Order No. 37, Docket No. 5060 (Washington, D. C., May, 1941), p. 6.

19. *Ibid.*

20. *Ibid.*

21. *Ibid*, p. 7.

22. *Ibid*, pp. 7-8.

23. *Ibid.*

24. *Ibid.*

25. *Ibid.*, pp. 21-23.

26. *New York Times*, January 28, 1924, p. 1; also *Federal Trade Commission Report* No. 1686, December 1, 1923.

27. *New York Times*, October 17, 1925, p. 3.

28. *Ibid.*, September 5, 1924, p. 6.

29. *Ibid.*, July 23, 1922, Section I, p. 17.

30. 36 Stat. 629 (1910).

31. 37 Stat. 199 (1912).

32. First National Radio Conference, *Proceedings* (Washington, D.C. February 27, 1922).

33. *House Reports*, (Vol. 1, 67th Congress, 3rd and 4th Sessions, 1922, 1923, Report No. 1416), p. 2.

34. *Radio Service Bulletin*, Bureau of Navigation, Department of Commerce, (April 2, 1923), pp. 9-10.

35. Third National Radio Conference, *Recommendations for Regulation of Radio* (Washington, D.C., October 6-10, 1924), pp. 1-2.

36. *New York Times*, January 1, 1925, p. 22.

37. Fourth National Radio Conference, *Proceedings and Recommendations for Regulation of Radio* (Washington, D.C., November 9-11, 1925), p. 6.

38. *Ibid*, p. 7.

39. *Ibid.*

40. *Ibid.*

41. *Ibid.* p. 34.

42. *United States v. Zenith Radio Corporation*, 12 F. (2nd) 616 (1926).

43. 35 Op. Att. Gen. 126 (1926).

44. 44 Stat. 1162-1174.

45. For good analysis of its provisions see Cushman, Robert E., *The Independent Regulatory Commissions* (New York, 1941), pp. 302-310.

46. *New York Times*, May 25, 1932, p. 22.

47. Landry, *op. cit.*, p. 306.

48. *Advertising and Selling,* November 26, 1930, p. 40.

49. Husing, *op. cit.,* pp. 107-108.

50. 36 Stat. 539, June 18, 1910.

51. Frankfurter, Felix, *The Public and Its Government* (New Haven, 1930), p. 93.

52. *Preliminary Report on Communications Companies* (H.R. 1273, 73rd Congress, 2nd Session, April 18, 1934), p. XXXI.

53. Federal Communications Commission, *Proposed Report, Telephone Investigation, Pursuant to Public Resolution No. 8, 74th Congress,* p. 470. Chapter 13 of this report, pp. 454-470, contains a detailed and accurate account of the Bell system's involvement in broadcasting activities up until 1934.

54. Senate Committee Print, S. Doc. 144, *Study of Communications by an Interdepartmental Committee,* (73rd Congress, 2d Sess. 1934).

55. *Ibid.*

56. *Hearings before the Committee on Interstate and Foreign Commerce, House of Representatives* (H.R. 8301, 73rd Cong., April 10, 1934), pp. 292-293.

57. 48 Stat. 1064, June 19, 1934.

PART II

The Basis and Scope
of Governmental Controls

CHAPTER 3

The Statutory Powers and Functions
of the FCC

When one segment of society, whether it be government or industry or some other, is vested with unlimited authority over radio, then freedom is threatened and democracy suffers. It is diversification and balance of control that we want in American radio.—PAUL A. WALKER*

One of the distinctive features of the Communications Act of 1934 is that it envisages private ownership and operation of telegraph, telephone and broadcasting facilities. Prior to the passage of the Act, however, there had been some pressures on Congress from time to time to establish a system of government ownership patterned after systems adopted in other countries. In the early days, for example, Samuel Morse tried to persuade Congress to take over telegraph communication. He thought it would be better if the government would assume complete control of its use and development.[1] He was supported in this view in 1845 by the Postmaster General who stated that "the use of an instrument so powerful for good or evil cannot with safety to the people be left in the hands of private individuals . . ."[2]

Many years later, in 1913, Postmaster General Burleson, influenced by Congressional agitations, publicly declared:

A study of the constitutional purposes of the postal establishment leads to the conviction that the Post Office Department should have control over all means of the communication of intelligence. The first telegraph line in this country was maintained and operated as a part of the postal service, and it is to be regretted that Congress saw fit to relinquish this facility to private enterprise . . .[3]

He observed that in other countries the government owned and operated communications services and he advocated that the government in this country do the same.[4]

There was a resurgence of this type of advocacy at the time of America's

* Former chairman of the FCC.

entrance into the First World War. It again reached a high pitch during the depression years as revolutionaries and agitators, encouraged by the social anxiety of the period, attempted a demolition job on the free enterprise system.

But Congress, always influenced by the traditional conservatism of the American community, consistently resisted this panacean advocacy. Unwilling to run the risk of what Justice Holmes called "interstitial detriments"[5] that may result from radical and abrupt social change, Congress rejected the idea of government ownership of communications media in this country.

At the same time, as heretofore pointed out, telecommunications had become so vital to American life that the public demanded that they be more strictly regulated by the government. And it was this growing psychology in the early thirties that precipitated Congressional action, resulting in the Communications Act of 1934. A basic feature of the law, therefore, is its establishment of a national policy regarding these media which makes the public interest paramount and sets up adminstrative machinery to execute this policy. At the same time, it provides for private operation with legislative restrictions against governmental intrusion and control. Important sections of the law as they pertain to broadcasting are reproduced in Appendix I, including the Communications Act Amendments, 1960, adopted by the 86th Congress and approved by the President on September 13, 1960.

Scope and Limits of Federal Authority. As stated in Section I, the broad purpose of the Communications Act (hereinafter sometimes referred to as the Act) is "to make available, so far as possible, to *all* the people of the United States a *rapid, efficient, nation-wide,* and *world-wide* wire and radio communication *service* with adequate facilities at *reasonable* charges . . ." (emphasis supplied), and the Federal Communications Commission was created, with centralized authority to carry out this policy and enforce the provisions of the Act.[6]

As pointed out in the previous chapter, the Radio Act of 1927 was repealed and the powers and functions of the Federal Radio Commission were assigned to the new agency. The limited authority with respect to wire communications vested in the Interstate Commerce Commission and the Postmaster General were likewise transferred.[7]

In the establishment of the 1934 Act, Congress was careful not to encroach upon the authority of state governments. Section 2 makes it emphatic that no part of the Act applies to communications which are purely intrastate in character.[8] Its application is limited to interstate and foreign communication.[9] The FCC, therefore, cannot prescribe rules for communication services which are strictly local in character and do not cross state boundaries. For example, the rates charged and the service provided in connection with telephone calls and telegrams transmitted and received over wires that do not cross state boundaries are not regulated by the FCC. These are regulated by state public utility commissions. Congress recognized, however, that information available to these state agencies might be useful in dealing with interstate and foreign communication and provided in the Act that the FCC might "avail itself of such cooperation services, records, and facilities" as might be provided by any State commission.[10]

Under the "commerce clause" of the Constitution, Congress had the power to establish a federal agency to regulate interstate and foreign communications.[11] In the early administration of the Communications Act, however, the question was raised whether radio transmissions not crossing state lines constituted "interstate commerce" and were subject to federal jurisdiction. The courts answered this question in the affirmative. In 1933, the Supreme Court said that "no state lines divide the radio waves, and national regulation is not only appropriate but essential to the efficient use of radio facilities."[12]

Since any radio emission, regardless of its range, may affect or cause interference to other radio signals crossing state lines, it is subject to the regulatory authority of the FCC.[13] As Judge Freed in *U.S. v. Betteridge,* (N.D. Ohio, E. Div., 43 F. Supp. 53, 55) pointed out, because of the natural characteristics of electromagnetic waves "all transmissions of energy, communications or signals by radio, either use an interstate or foreign channel of transmission or so affect interstate or foreign channels as to require the regulation of their use" if the purposes of the Communications Act are to be carried out effectively.[14]

What this means is that the FCC has exclusive regulatory jurisdiction with respect to any type of radio transmission, and can require every station regardless of its power and range to have a license and to operate under rules established by the Commission. Attempts by state governmental agencies to exercise authority in this field are invalid and have been so held by the Federal courts.[15]

Monopoly Condoned and Condemned. When the Act was adopted, the telegraph and telephone industries had come to be recognized as "natural monopolies" in this country. History had shown the folly of free competition with wasteful duplication of facilities. Yet experience had also demonstrated that monopolies often resulted in abuse of power with infliction of unreasonably high and discriminatory rates upon the public. As protection against these predatory practices, Congress subjected both services and charges of interstate and foreign "carriers for hire" to FCC regulations.

Section 201 of the Act makes it the duty of these telegraph and telephone companies to furnish service on request and to connect with one another to establish through routes.[16] The section further declares that these public utilities must be fair and reasonable in their "charges, practices and classifications." Section 202 prohibits preferences in charges or services and 203 requires the publication of all rate schedules.[17]

The FCC was given authority to determine and prescribe reasonable charges and standards of service and to require carriers subject to the Act to file an inventory of all or any parts of their properties, classified by units and showing original costs and estimated costs of reproduction less depreciation. The Commission was also given "free access" to all properties of the carriers and their "accounts, records, and memoranda."[18]

While recognizing and sanctioning regulated monopoly in domestic wire communication services, Congress wanted to encourage competition between cable and radio in the foreign communication business. Wires and cables were first used for regular telegraph and telephone service between the United States and other countries. Subsequently, wireless transmission was developed, and, as heretofore pointed out, by 1934 radio telegraphy and telephony had become well established in the overseas service. Congress was concerned that no arrangements or agreements of any kind should be made which might unduly restrain competition between cable and radio as two separate and distinct means of international communication.[19] Accordingly, Section 314 of the Act provides that any such contrivances or deals involving unfair methods of competition are unlawful.[20]

Broadcasting: a Field of Free Competition. Unlike the telegraph and telephone industries, Congress recognized the field of broadcasting as one of free competition. Radio and television stations broadcasting programs intended to be received by the general public are not considered to be "common carriers for hire."[21] The Commission, therefore, was not given any authority to require stations to make their facilities available to every member of the public who might request them and has no power to determine or regulate the rates charged for the sale of broadcasting time.

To guard against the tendencies toward monopolistic control in broadcasting which had already developed in 1934, Congress declared in Section 313 of the Act that "all the laws of the United States" relating to unlawful restraints of trade are applicable to the manufacture and sale of radio apparatus and to broadcasting in general.[22] The section further provides that if any broadcaster is found guilty of the violation of any such laws the court hearing the case may revoke the license of the station. In the event the court assesses this extreme penalty, Section 311 prohibits the Commission from granting any further radio authorizations to the guilty party.[23]

Public Ownership of Broadcast Channels. The tangible facilities including wire and cables and other physical apparatus used by telephone and telegraph "carriers" and broadcasting stations are privately owned. While the use of these properties is regulated by the FCC, the actual title to the properties is vested in the carrier companies and the broadcast licensees. This is not true with respect to broadcast channels which they employ. Section 301 asserts with crystal clarity that one of the purposes of the Act is "to maintain the control of the United States over all the channels of interstate and foreign radio transmission."[24] It is provided that these channels can be used for limited periods of time only under licenses granted by federal authority and that no such license is to be construed as creating "any right beyond the terms, conditions, and periods of the license."[25]

The law states that "no station license shall be granted by the Commission until the applicant therefore shall have signed a waiver of any claim to the use of any particular frequency or of the ether as against the regulatory power of the United States because of the previous use of the same, whether by license or otherwise."[26]

General Powers of the FCC. Section 303 of the Act sets forth the general powers of the FCC with respect to broadcasting. The Commission is authorized to classify stations, prescribe the nature of their service, determine what power and type of technical facilities they shall use, the time they shall operate, where they shall be located and the areas they shall serve. It also may inspect equipment and installations and may designate and cause to be published the call letters of stations.[27]

One of the most important powers is that of allocating channels to the various classes of broadcasting service and the assignment of frequencies for station operation. In these functions, the Commission is under a statutory mandate to make "a fair, efficient, and equitable distribution of radio service" among the various states and communities.[28]

To prevent a recurrence of the bedlam in the ether which had bedeviled radio in earlier years, the framers of the 1934 Act gave the Commission specific authority to make regulations "necessary to prevent interference between stations."[29] But it was not enough simply to perform "traffic cop" functions. To carry out its powers and keep pace with a dynamic and fast growing industry, the Commission was required to "study new uses for radio, provide for experimental uses of frequencies and generally encourage the larger and more effective use of radio in the public interest.[30] It was also given authority to make such rules and regulations and prescribe such restrictions and conditions as might be necessary to carry out the provisions of the Act.[31]

Authority To Regulate Network Stations. At the time the Radio Act of 1927 was passed there was Congressional concern that networks might acquire monopolistic controls and unduly restrict competition in the industry. In the debates on the 1927 Act, Senator Dill expressed the feeling of anxiety prevalent in Congress and among independent broadcasters:

. . . the various radio organizations, including the Radio Corporation of America and the American Telephone and Telegraph Co., are going ahead and building up the chain stations as they desire without any restrictions because the Secretary of Commerce has no power to interfere with them. Unless this proposed legislation shall be enacted they will continue to do so and they will be able by chain-broadcasting methods practically to obliterate the independent small stations . . .[32]

While the commission would have the power under the general terms of the bill, the bill specifically sets out as one of the special powers of the Commission the right to make specific regulations for governing chain broadcasting . . ."[33]

This section of the bill, providing that the Radio Commission had the power to "make special regulations applicable to radio stations engaged in chain broadcasting", was passed and became Section 4 (h) of the Radio Act of 1927.[34] It was carried over verbatim and appears as Section 303 (i) of the 1934 law, giving the FCC the same power to make such regulations.[35] It was the exercise of this authority by the FCC which subsequently resulted in the adoption of the network regulations which now control the relations between the networks and their station affiliates and to which detailed reference is made in Chapter 18.

It should be noted here that only licensees of stations and not networks as such are covered by Section 303 (i). If these stations are affiliates, and their relationships with networks affect their ability to operate in the public interest, then the Commission is empowered by law to make special rules governing their operations. It goes without saying that the effect of exercising this power is an indirect control over the network organizations.

There has been growing sentiment in Congress during the past few years in favor of amending the law, giving the FCC direct regulatory authority over the networks. For example, a bill introduced in Congress in February, 1960 (HR 11340) by Congressman Oren Harris would bring TV and radio networks under FCC control, requiring "operating certificates" for networks with proscriptions against illegality in programs, failure to exercise control over matter broadcast, giving unfair advantages in matter broadcast to products and services in which networks have interests, and making contracts with affiliates not deemed to be in the public interest. However, there is strong opposition to such legislation from some segments of the broadcast industry, and whether Congress will provide for FCC regulation of the networks is highly problematical.

On May 4, 1960, the FCC expressed approval of bills pending in Congress which would give the Commission power to regulate networks. The Commission said it did not mean to suggest, however, "that the present responsibility of station licensees under the Act should in any way be diminished. Rather, the responsibilities which would be placed upon networks under these bills should complement, and not substitute for the existing responsibilities of broadcast stations." (FCC Mimeograph No. 88411).

Licensing Powers. Of all the powers possessed by the FCC none is more important than that which pertains to its licensing functions. Section 308(a) of the Act gives the Commission authority to grant construction permits and station licenses or modifications or renewals thereof. Paragraph(b) of the same section specifies that all such applications "shall set forth such facts as the Commission by regulation may prescribe as to citizenship, character, and financial, technical, and other qualifications of the applicant to operate the station," and other information pertaining to ownership of facilities, proposed frequency, power, hours of operation, and the purposes for which the station is to be used.[36]

At any time after the filing of an application, or during the period of a license, the Commission may require from the applicant or the licensee additional information to determine whether the application should be granted or denied or the license should be revoked.[37] Such information must be submitted in written form under oath or affirmation.[38]

No construction permit or station license, or any rights pertaining thereto may be transferred, assigned or disposed of in any manner without the prior approval of the Commission. Section 310(b) requires the filing of a written application for such transfer or assignment and the written consent of the Commission.[39]

If upon examination of any application, it appears that the applicant is not qualified or that a grant would not serve the public interest, the Commission has the power to deny the application. The applicant, however, must be given an opportunity for a public hearing before the decision is made final, as provided in Section 309(b).[40]

If the licensee fails to operate substantially as required by his license or fails to observe or violates any provision of the Act or regulation of the Commission, the agency may issue a cease and desist order with respect to the offense. In the case of willful or repeated violations of the law or regulations as described in Section 312, the more serious penalty of license revocation may be assessed. Before either a cease and desist order or license revocation can become final, however, the licensee must be given the opportunity for a hearing as prescribed in paragraphs (c), (d), and (e) of Section 312.[41]

As is discussed more fully in Chapter 21, Congress recently amended Section 503, granting the FCC authority to impose forfeitures for willful and repeated violations of the Act, certain sections of the Criminal Code, United States treaties, or FCC regulations.

Station Operators. The Commission has the responsibility of classifying and prescribing the qualifications of station operators and issues licenses in accordance therewith. Subject to the right of an operator to a formal hearing as provided in Section 303(2), the Commission is vested with power to suspend and revoke his license if convincing evidence shows him guilty of any of the following offenses:

1. Violation of any provision of the Act, treaty or other agreement binding on the United States or rules implementing the same.

2. Failure to carry out a lawful order of the master of a ship.

3. Willful damage to any radio installations.

4. Transmission of superfluous radio communications containing profane or obscene words; or willful transmissions of false or deceptive signals or communications.

5. Willful and malicious interference with any other radio communications.

6. Obtaining or attempting to obtain for himself or another an operator's license by fraudulent means.[42]

Program Controls. Section 326 of the Act specifically prohibits the Commission from censoring radio and television programs. It reads:

Nothing in this Act shall be understood or construed to give the Commission the power of censorship over the radio communications or signals transmitted by any radio station and no regulation or condition shall be promulgated or fixed by the Commission which shall interfere with the right of free speech by means of radio communication.[43]

There have been differences of opinion as to what this provision means. Some have contended that it precludes any concern on the part of the Commission with the program service of licensees, except in cases where there are violations of specific laws. A spokesman for this point of view is FCC Commissioner T.A.M. Craven. On November 19, 1958, the FCC adopted a public notice proposing to make certain revisions in Section IV of its renewal application form 303.[44] The changes proposed pertain to that part of the application form which elicits information regarding past program service of a station and that intended for the future. Commissioner Craven dissented to the proposed changes, contending that the Commission exceeds its authority when it requires applicants for broadcast facilities to file any program information except that which may be requested to determine whether a specific law would be or is being violated. He believes that the First Amendment to the Constitution and Section 326 of the Act forbid the Commission from exercising any authority over broadcast programming except where infractions against lottery laws and the like may be involved.[45]

Others have interpreted Section 326 differently. Relating it to other provisions of the Act, they believe that, while the Commission cannot tell a station what particular program or programs it can or cannot present, it does have the authority and the responsibility to review the over-all operation of a station when it comes up for renewal of its license to determine whether its operation has been in the public interest. This interpretation seems to be correct as confirmed by the legislative history of the Radio Act of 1927, the Communications Act of 1934, and the consistent administrative practice of the two commissions and court decisions.

Early Administrative Practice. The law directs the Commission to grant licenses and renewals of these licenses *only* if public interest, convenience and necessity will be served thereby. The original Federal Radio Commission which was established in 1927 assumed from the beginning that program service was an important factor in making this determination.

The renewal application forms used by it contained questions as to the amount of time devoted by the station to various types of programs.[46]

From 1927 to 1934, this original commission made reports to Congress regarding its practice of evaluating program service in connection with its consideration of renewal applications. By the time Congress was considering the replacement of the 1927 law with the Communications Act of 1934, there appeared to be little doubt that the government did have the authority and the responsibility to take program performance into account.

In Congressional hearings on one of the bills which culminated in the 1934 law, the National Association of Broadcasters presented a statement upholding this regulatory authority. It read in part as follows:

It is the manifest duty of the licensing authority in passing upon applications for licenses or the renewal thereof, to determine whether or not the applicant is rendering or can render an adequate public service. Such service necessarily includes broadcasting of a considerable proportion of programs devoted to education, religion, labor, agricultural and similar activities concerned with human betterment. In actual practice over a period of seven years, as the records of the Federal Radio Commission amply prove, this has been the principal test which the Commission has applied in dealing with broadcasting applications.[47]

In hearings upon the same bill, the Chairman of the Federal Radio Commission testified that "it is the duty of the Commission in passing on whether or not that station should be relicensed for another period, to say whether or not its past performance during the last license period has been in the public interest."[48] Fully informed of the procedure which had been followed by the Federal Radio Commission, Congress re-enacted the relevant provisions in the Communications Act of 1934.

When the 1934 Act was being considered by Congress there was a great deal of public agitation and pressure for a provision in the law which would require stations to set aside substantial portions of their broadcast time to be used by educational institutions and other non-profit organizations. In fact, the public feeling was so strong that 23 Senators voted for the Wagner-Hatfield Amendment which proposed to allocate 25 per cent of all radio broadcasting facilities to educational, religious, agricultural, labor, cooperative, and similar non-profit-making interests. While Congress did not adopt the amendment,[49] it did pass Section 307 (c) of the Act directing the FCC to make a study of the proposal and report to Congress its findings.[50]

The Commission did make a study, and in its report to Congress in 1935 it advised against the adoption of the legislative proposal. Its main reason for opposing it was that it already had adequate authority to achieve the ends that Congress had in mind. The Report in part said:

The Commission feels that present legislation has the flexibility essential to attain the desired ends without necessitating at this time any changes in the law.

In order for non-profit organizations to obtain the maximum service possible, cooperation in good faith by the broadcasters is required. Such cooperation should therefore, be under the direction of the Commission.[51]

FCC Program Powers Recognized by the Courts. From the very beginning, therefore, the FCC took the attitude that it did have the power to take into account program service as an important factor in its public interest determinations. Its view had been supported not only by legislative history and prior administrative practice, but by court decisions as well.

In the KFKB case referred to in the previous chapter, in which Dr. Brinkley's application for a renewal of license was denied, the Federal Radio Commission said:

The Commission is expressly precluded by the Radio Act of 1927 from exercising any power of censorship. At the same time, the Commission must, under the statutory standard, reach a decision that the nature of the program broadcast is in the public interest, convenience and necessity before it may grant an application. Upon the evidence adduced, the Commission feels constrained to hold that the practice of a physician's prescribing treatment for a patient whom he has never seen, and bases his diagnosis upon what symptoms may be recited by the patient in a letter addressed to him, is inimical to the public health, and safety, and for that reason is not in the public interest.

The testimony in this case shows conclusively that the operation of Station KFKB is conducted only in the personal interest of Dr. John R. Brinkley. While it is to be expected that a licensee of a radio broadcasting station will receive some remuneration for serving the public with radio programs, at the same time the interest of the listening public is paramount, and may not be subordinated to the interests of the station licensee. A license to operate a radio broadcasting station is a franchise from the public, and the licensee is a trustee for the public. Station KFKB has not been operated in the interest of the listening public and we, therefore, find that public interest, convenience and necessity will not be served by granting the application for renewal of its license.[52]

The United States Court of Appeals for the District of Columbia sustained the Commission's decision, holding that under Section 11 of the Radio Act of 1927 the Federal Radio Commission was "necessarily called upon to consider the character and quality of the service to be rendered and that in considering an application for renewal of a license an important consideration is the past conduct of the applicant."[53]

In its argument to the Court of Appeals, the Commission had contended that there had been no attempt on its part "to scrutinize broadcast matter prior to its release," and that administrative review of the station's past conduct was not censorship.[54] The Court agreed with this point of view.

38

In a 1932 case, the Court of Appeals again reaffirmed this postion. A Reverend Dr. Shuler owned KGEF in Los Angeles. The Commission denied his application for renewal of license on grounds that he attacked religious organizations, public officials, the courts, institutions and individuals; that these attacks often were not based upon facts; and that, in general, the programs of the station tended to be "sensational" in character rather than instructive or entertaining.[55] On appeal, the Court sustained the Commission's decision. In its opinion the Court said:

If it be considered that one in possession of a permit to broadcast in interstate commerce may, without let or hindrance from any source, use these facilities, reaching out, as they do, from one corner of the country to the other, to obstruct the administration of justice, offend the religious susceptibilities of thousands, inspire political distrust and civic discord, or offend youth and innocence by the use of words suggestive of sexual immorality, and be answerable for slander only at the instance of the one offended, then this great science, instead of a boon, will become a scourge, and the nation a theatre for the display of individual passions and the collision of personal interests. This is neither censorship nor previous restraint, nor is it a whittling away of the rights guaranteed by the First Amendment, or an impairment of their free exercise . . .[56]

Dr. Shuler appealed the case to the U. S. Supreme Court, but his petition for a writ of *certiorari* was denied.[57] This left no doubt, from a judicial point of view, that the Federal Radio Commission had the authority to evaluate past program performance in connection with its consideration of renewal applications.

Judicial Sanction of Network Regulations. The language prohibiting censorship, which appeared in Section 29 of the Radio Act of 1927, was reproduced verbatim in Section 326 of the Communications Act of 1934. It came up for consideration again by the Federal courts in connection with their review of the FCC's network regulations.

It is interesting to note that Commissioner Craven, in 1941, when he was serving his first term as a member of the FCC, dissented to the Commission's adoption of the network regulations on much the same grounds that he objects to requiring applicants and licensees to furnish information regarding program service. In a nineteen-page dissent, in which former Commissioner Norman Case joined, he said:

. . . The type of regulation specified by Congress for broadcasting clearly envisioned that the Communications Commission should not regulate the programs, the business practices or business policies of broadcast licensees.[58]

The network regulations were vigorously contested in the courts. Contentions similar to those made in the earlier cases were made that the Commission's powers were limited to technical matters, and that the right of free speech within the purview of the First Amendment and Section 326 of the Communications Act was abridged. The Supreme Court rejected these arguments and upheld the legal validity of the regulations. In answer to the contentions of the appellants, the Court said:

The Commission's licensing function cannot be discharged, therefore, merely by finding that there are no technological objections to the granting of a license. If the criterion of 'public interest' were limited to such matters, how could the Commission choose between two applicants for the same facilities, each of whom is financially and technically qualified to operate a station? Since the very inception of Federal regulation of radio, comparative considerations as to the service to be rendered have governed the application of the standard of 'public interest, convenience, or necessity.'[59]

The Court further said:

. . . we are asked to regard the Commission as a kind of traffic officer, policing the wave lengths to prevent stations from interfering with each other. But the Act does not restrict the Commission merely to supervision of the traffic. It puts upon the Commission the burden of determining the composition of that traffic.[60]

FCC Authority Limited by Public Interest Considerations. While possessing a wide range of discretion in the exercise of its powers, the Commission must always be guided by the "public interest, convenience, or necessity." If at any time, it fails to comply with this standard, the courts are available for redress.

For example, in choosing among applicants for limited radio facilities, the Commission may exercise administrative discretion, but the law requires that its judgments be based upon public interest considerations. Parties who are aggrieved by actions unsupported by substantial evidence or by "arbitrary" or "capricious" actions, not in accord with this statutory requirement may secure relief through appeal to the courts.

In this connection, the following discourse of the United States Supreme Court in a 1952 case is pertinent:

With the chaotic scramble for domestic air space that developed soon after the First World War, Congress recognized the need for a more orderly development of the air waves than had been achieved under prior legislation. Although the Radio Act of 1912 had forbidden the operation of radio apparatus without a license from the Secretary of Commerce and Labor, judicial decision left him powerless to prevent licensees from using unassigned frequencies, to restrict their transmitting hours and power, or to deny a license on the ground that a proposed station would necessarily interfere with existing stations. See *National Broadcasting Co. v. United States,* 319 U. S. 190, 212. Congress thereupon, in the Radio Act of 1927, created the Federal Radio Commission with wide licensing and regulatory powers over interstate and foreign commerce.

Congress did not purport to transfer its legislative power to the unbounded discretion of the regulatory body. In choosing among applicants, the Commission was to be guided by the 'public interest, convenience, or necessity', a criterion we held not to be too indefinite for fair enforcement. *New York Central Securities Corp. v. United States,* 287 U. S. 12. The statutory standard no doubt leaves wide discretion and calls for imaginative interpretation. Not a standard that lends itself to application with exactitude, it expresses a policy, born of years of unhappy trial and error, that is 'as concrete as the complicated factors for judgment in such a field of delegated authority'. *Federal Communications Comm'n v. Pottsville Broadcasting Co.,* 309 U. S. 134, 138.

Congress might have made administrative decision to license not reviewable. Although it is not suggested—or implied by the grant of power to review—that Congress could not have reserved to itself or to the Commission final designation of those who would be permitted to utilize the air waves, precious as they have become with technological advance, it has not done so. On the other hand, the scope of this Court's duty to review administrative determinations under the Federal Communications Act of 1934, 48 *Stat.* 1064, as amended, 47 U.S.C., Section 151 *et seq.,* has been carefully defined. Ours is not the duty of reviewing determinations of 'fact' in the narrow, colloquial scope of that concept. Congress has charged the courts with the responsibility of saying whether the Commission has fairly exercised its discretion within the vaguish, penumbral bounds expressed by the standard of 'public interest'. It is our responsibility to say whether the Commission has been guided by proper considerations in bringing the deposit of its experience, the disciplined feel of the expert, to bear on applications for licenses in the public interest.[61]

In the foregoing discussion, the principal features of the Communications Act and the general scope of the FCC's statutory authority have been analyzed. The next chapter describes the administrative and organizational structure developed by the FCC to exercise its powers and perform its functions.

NOTES

1. Morse, Edward Lind, *Samuel F. B. Morse, His letters and Journals* (New York, 1914), Vol. 2, pp. 228, 232, 240.

2. *Annual Report of the Postmaster General,* Document No. 2, December 1, 1845, p. 861.

3. *Report of the Postmaster General for the Fiscal Year Ended June 30, 1913,* Miscellaneous Reports, p. 15.

4. *Ibid.*

5. Holmes, Oliver Wendell, "Ideals and Doubts," 10 *Ill., L. R.* 2 (1915).

6. 48 Stat. 1064.

7. 48 Stat. 1101-1102.

8. 48 Stat. 1065.

9. *Ibid.*

10. 48 Stat. 1098.

11. *General Electric Company v. Federal Radio Commission,* 31 F. (2d) 630 (App. D.C. 1929).

12. *Federal Radio Commission v. Nelson Brothers,* 53 Sup. Ct. 627, 633-634.

13. *United States v. Gregg,* 5 F. Supp. 848 (S.D. Texas 1934); also see *C. J. Community Services, Inc., v. FCC,* 100 U. S. App. D.C. (379, 246 F. (2d) 660, 15 RR 2029 (1957).

14. *U.S. v. Betteridge,* 43 F. Supp. 53, 55 (N.D. Ohio, E. Div.).

15. See *City of New York v. Federal Radio Commission,* 59 App. D.C. 129, 36 F. (2d) 115 (1929); *Radio Station WOW v. Johnson,* 326 U.S. 120 (1944); *DuMont Laboratories v. Carroll,* 86 F. Supp. 813, 5 RR 2053 (E.D. Pa. 1949).

16. 48 Stat. 1070.

17. *Ibid.*

18. *Ibid.,* 1071.

19. 68 *Cong. Rec.* 2579; also see *MacKay Radio and Telephone Company v. Federal Communications Commission,* 97 F. (2d) 641, 645 (1938).

20. 48 Stat. 1087-1088.

21. 48 Stat. 1066; also see *Federal Communications Commission v. Sanders Bros.,* 309 U.S. 470 (1940).

22. 48 Stat. 1087.

23. 48 Stat. 1086.

24. 48 Stat. 1081.

25. *Ibid.*

26. *Ibid.*

27. 48 Stat. 1081.

28. 48 Stat. 1082-1083.

29. 49 Stat. 1475.

30. 48 Stat. 1082.

31. *Ibid.*

32. 50 Stat. 191.

33. 68 *Cong. Rec.* 2881. See also statements by Representative White, 68 *Cong. Rec.* 2579-2580, and by Senator Dill, 69 *Cong. Rec.* 12,352.

34. 68 *Cong. Rec.* 2881.

35. 44 Stat. 1164.

36. 48 Stat. 1082.

37. 48 Stat., 1084-1085.

38. *Ibid.*

39. *Ibid.*

40. 48 Stat. 1086.

41. 48 Stat. 1085.

42. 66 Stat. 716-717.

43. 48 Stat. 1082-1083.

44. 48 Stat. 1091.

45. *In the Matter of Amendment of Section IV (Statement of Program Service) of Broadcast Application Forms 301, 303, 314 and 315,* FCC Docket No. 12673, 1 RR 98:21.

46. *Hearing on Jurisdiction of Radio Commission,* House Committee on Merchant Marine and Fisheries (1928), p. 26.

47. Report by Federal Communications Commission, *Public Service Responsibility of Broadcast Licensees* (March 7, 1946), p. 10; also, *Hearings on Jurisdiction of Radio Commission,* House Committee on Merchant Marine and Fisheries (1928), p. 26.

48. *Hearings on H.R. 8301,* 73rd Cong., p. 117.

49. *Ibid.,* pp. 350-352.

50. 48 Stat. 1084.

51. Federal Communications Commission, *Report to Congress Pursuant to Section 307 (c) of the Communications Act of 1934,* January 22, 1935.

52. Transcript of Record, No. 5240, in *KFKB Broadcasting Association, Inc. v. Federal Radio Commission,* 60 App. D.C. 79, 47 F. (2d) 670 (1931); Statement of Facts and Grounds for Decision, p. 13.

53. *Ibid.,* p. 672.

54. *Ibid.*

55. Transcript of Record, No. 5561, in *Trinity Methodist Church South v. Federal Radio Commission,* 61 App. D.C. 311, 62 F. (2d) 850 (1932), p. 970.

56. *Ibid.*

57. *Ibid.,* 288 U.S. 599 January 16, 1933.

58. Federal Communications Commission, *Report on Chain Broadcasting,* Commission Order No. 37, Docket No. 5060 (May 1941), p. 117.

59. *National Broadcasting Company v. United States,* 319 U.S. 190, 216-17 (May 10, 1943).

60. *Ibid.,* p. 215.

61. *FCC v. RCA Communications, Inc.,* 346 U.S. 89-91 (June 8, 1953).

CHAPTER 4

How the FCC Is Organized and Conducts Its Business

In the last analysis, much depends on whether administration is heavy-handed and burdensomely bureaucratic or whether it is flexible and imaginative.—MARSHALL E. DIMOCK*

As prescribed in Section 4 of the Communications Act, the FCC is composed of seven commissioners chosen by the President with the advice and consent of the Senate, one of whom the President designates as Chairman.[1] As specified in the same section, the terms of the first commissioners ran for one, two, three, four, five, six and seven years, respectively, with all successive appointments made for seven years and until their successors are appointed and have qualified, except that they may not continue to serve beyond the expiration of the next session of Congress subsequent to the end of their fixed term. A person chosen to fill a vacancy is appointed only for the unexpired term of the Commissioner whom he succeeds.[2]

The Communications Act has very little to say about the qualifications of commissioners. It does require that they be citizens of the United States and no more than four of them may be members of the same political party. For the service they perform for the American people they draw annual salaries of $20,000 except for the Chairman who gets $20,500.[3]

Legislative Restrictions on Commissioners. As specified in the Act, while serving on the Commission, members are prohibited from having a financial interest in any of the following activities, enterprises or companies:
1. The manufacture or sale of radio apparatus or equipment for wire or radio communication.
2. Any kind of radio transmission of energy.
3. Any wire or radio communication.
4. Companies furnishing services or such apparatus to those engaged in wire or radio communication or to those manufacturing or selling such equipment.

* Professor and Head, Graduate Government Department, New York University.

5. Any company owning stock, bonds, or other securities of any such companies.[4]

The commissioners are further prohibited from participating in any hearing or proceeding in which they have a pecuniary interest and may not be employed by or hold any official relationship to any person subject to any of the provisions of the Communications Act. They may not own stocks, bonds, or other securities of any corporation over which the FCC has any jurisdiction. Nor may they be otherwise employed, or engage in any other business, vocation or profession while they are on the Commission.[5] Formerly, they could accept reasonable honorariums or compensation for the presentation or delivery of publications or papers. Recent legislation, however, prohibits this. (See 1960 Amendments to Act in Appendix I).

If a member terminates his service prior to the expiration of his appointed term, he must wait for a year before he may represent any person before the Commission in a professional capacity. This restriction does not apply, however, if he continues to serve out his appointed term.[6]

Transaction of Business. The seven commissioners function as a unit, and exercise general supervision over the work of the agency.[7] The Chairman, however, as provided in Section 5 (a) of the Act, serves as the chief executive officer of the Commission. It is his duty to preside at all meetings of the Commission, and to represent the agency in all legislative matters, (except that any other commissioner may present his own or minority views). He also represents the Commission in all matters requiring conferences or communications with other governmental officers, departments or agencies, and generally coordinates and organizes the work of the Commission.[8]

Four members of the Commission constitute a quorum for the transaction of business.[9] General sessions of the Commission are required to be held at least once a month at its principal offices in Washington, D. C. Special meetings, however, may be held elsewhere in the United States if economy and convenience will be served.[10] Biographical material pertaining to present FCC commissioners and past chairmen appears in Appendix 2. Also, a brief chronology of significant FCC events is set forth there.

The Commission has the legislative authority to take actions, make rules and regulations and issue orders, not contrary to law, as may be necessary to carry out its functions and may conduct proceedings in a manner "as will best conduce to the proper dispatch of business and to the ends of justice."[11]

Every vote and official action of the Commission must be recorded, and its proceedings (excluding its business meetings) shall be open to the public upon request of any interested party. One statutory exception to this is that the Commission may withhold publication of records or proceedings containing secret information affecting the national defense.[12]

Reports to Congress. A special matter of business required by law is the preparation and transmission of an annual report to Congress. This report must contain (1) information collected and considered by the Commission to have value in the settlement of questions relating to regulation of interstate and foreign transmissions by wire and radio; (2) information as to its work and accomplishments, and the adequacy of its staff and equipment. A former requirement for biographies of all persons employed during the year, their FCC positions and salaries, together with names of those who left the employ of the agency, was repealed in 1952.[13]

Personnel and Expenditures. Legislative authority for the selection of staff personnel appears in paragraphs (1) and (2) of Section 4(f) of the Act.[14] Subject to civil-service laws and the Classification Act of 1949, the Commission is authorized to appoint "officers, engineers, accountants, attorneys, inspectors, examiners, and other employees" as are necessary to carry out its functions.[15] It is provided that each commissioner may appoint a legal assistant, engineering assistant, administrative assistant, and a secretary to serve in his office, and may prescribe the duties of each.[16] In filling these particular jobs, he may disregard the civil-service laws but must comply with the requirements of the Classification Act of 1949.[17]

Paragraph (g) of Section 4 authorizes expenditures out of available appropriations as are necessary for the performance of Commission functions. All such expenditures, including necessary transportation expenses of commissioners or their employees, incurred while conducting any official business outside the city of Washington, are allowed and paid on the presentation of itemized vouchers approved by the Chairman or by such other members or officer as may be designated by the Commission.[18]

Original Organization of the FCC. The Communications Act, as adopted in 1934, provided that the Commission might divide itself into not more than three divisions, each to consist of at least three members. It was further provided that the Commission might direct that "any of its work, business or functions" might be assigned or referred to any division for action. In case of referral, the division was authorized to act on the assigned matter with all the jurisdiction and powers conferred by law upon the full Commission, and its action had the same force and effect as if taken by the Commission.[19]

As originally passed, the Act also authorized the agency to assign or refer any portion of its work to an individual commissioner or to a board composed of one or more employees. This authority, however, did not extend to investigations instituted on the Commission's own motion, or to those specifically required by the Act. Nor was it applicable to contested proceedings requiring the taking of testimony at public hearings, unless agreed to by the parties involved.[20]

Any action taken by an individual commissioner or a board with respect to an assigned matter had the same force and effect as if taken by the Commission. It was provided, however, that any party affected by any order, decision, or report of such commissioner or board might file a petition for rehearing by the Commission or a division. Any action by a division upon such a petition was subject to review by the Commission.[21]

Pursuant to these provisions, immediately after its creation the FCC established three divisions—Broadcast, Telephone, and Telegraph—each composed of two members with the Chairman of the Commission acting *ex officio* as a third member of each division.[22] The agency exercised authority over all matters not assigned to any division, and specifically retained jurisdiction over the allocation of frequency bands to the various classes of radio service and all matters involving two or more divisions. Pursuant to Section 405 of the Act, the full Commission was required to dispose of petitions requesting rehearing of cases decided by a division.[23]

This system of compartmentalized regulation did not prove satisfactory. There were jurisdictional disputes within the Commission. Differences in work load among the divisions required some commissioners to assume more responsibility than others. Because of the interrelationships of the telegraph, telephone and broadcast industries, a commissioner's competency in one area of regulation was limited by his lack of experience and knowledge in the others. As Harry Warner has pointed out, "the division system was not conducive to cooperation and mutual understanding, vested an unnecessary share of responsibility and power in each division and prevented a rounded development of each commissioner's knowledge and experience."[24]

FCC Divisions Abolished. Having become dissatisfied with the system, the Commission abolished the Telegraph, Telephone and Broadcast divisions on October 13, 1937 and assumed full responsibility for all their functions.[25] Henceforth, the Commission acted as a unit in regulatory matters relating to the three industries, with each commissioner having an equal voice in all policy determinations and other regulatory matters.

The organization at the staff level, as it was established at the time the Commission began operations in 1934, was not changed. It consisted of four departments with the heads thereof directly responsible to the full Commission. There was the Secretary and his assistants responsible for keeping records, maintaining dockets, and performing other functions essential to daily operations. The Legal Department headed by a General Counsel, was concerned with such matters as applications and complaints, carried on investigations, and handled litigation involving the Commission and the Courts.

The technical work was done by the Engineering Department with a Chief Engineer in charge. This included research on radio propagation, the installation, operation and maintenance of radio equipment, and such matters as the preparation and presentation of expert testimony at hearings conducted by the Commission. A special section of this department participated in international conferences concerned with the technical aspects of wire and radio communication and channel allocations. Still another section operated in the field, conducting examinations for radio operators, monitoring and inspecting station operations and assisting in field investigations.

The fourth department was the Accounting, Statistical and Tariff Department headed by a Chief Accountant. Its work was concerned with classification of services, depreciation and cost analysis, determination of rate schedules, and statistical studies relating to the communications industries.

Staff Organization Proves Inefficient. This departmental organization, with work arranged and divided on the basis of specialized knowledge and skills, was maintained for more than fifteen years. In the middle forties, however, faced with the prospect of a greatly increased work load after the War, the Commission began to think seriously in terms of a reorganization of its staff to achieve more economical and efficient operation. In August, 1945, Charles S. Hyneman, who had been serving as Director of the Foreign Broadcast Intelligence Service, a wartime service of the FCC, was assigned the task of helping work out a new organization.[26]

He was busy at the job for more than a year and a half. In his book, *Bureaucracy in a Democracy,* published in 1952, he described the organizational situation and problems at the FCC as he had found them while he was there. He pointed out that no man below the seven commissioners was in a position to coordinate and direct the work of the agency effectively. With respect to the manner in which the staff then disposed of cases, he wrote:

. . . Accountant, engineer, and lawyer negotiate in order to decide what questions shall be taken up next and how much work shall be done on the particular case. If agreement is reached (and it usually is) as to how men in the three divisions shall relate their work on a particular case, the individuals who actually do the work get their instructions from different superior officers and the original agreement is readily upset because someone forgets his part of the agreement or neglects to tell somebody else that a more pressing matter has arisen and he has reassigned his man to another task. The practical consequence of this situation is that the work which men in three different divisions do on a specific case is not well timed. Sometimes the case which should have gotten up before the commission last month, and which is scheduled to get there this month, does not actually get there until month after next. And it is not because men who analyze the cases lack competence or loaf on the job; it is because there is no one (short of the commissioners themselves) who has authority extending over all three divisions and is able to coordinate the work.[27]

After a detailed discussion of the operational demerits of this system, Mr. Hyneman stated that the commissioners had to choose between two sets of values:

They can organize the staff according to specialized knowledge or skill, suffer delays, and incur excessive costs in getting matters brought before them for attention, but have the assurance that the commissioners will get a full disclosure of the important considerations which they ought to take into account in making their decisions. Or the commissioners can organize the staff according to the industry (or area of affairs) to be regulated, have the assurance that there are men below them with ample authority to coordinate and direct all of the work on each and every problem that comes before the commissioners, and take a chance that these men will not, consciously or unconsciously, prejudice the decisions of the commissioners by failure to make available to them the information and points of view which they ought to consider. . . .[28]

The Hoover Commission, after a careful study of regulatory commissions, in 1949 made recommendations with respect to their internal organization. Its task force had recommended that agencies like the FCC, whose staffs were organized on a professional basis (e.g., with legal, engineering and accounting departments) reorganize on a functional basis in terms of the second alternative suggested by Mr. Hyneman.[29]

The Hoover Commission, in its report to Congress, favored vesting all administrative responsibility of the regulatory agency in its chairman, but had nothing to say about how the staff should be organized.[30]

Congress Becomes Concerned. Congress became increasingly concerned with the mounting backlog of work at the FCC and was especially unhappy about the slowness with which many cases were decided. After more than a decade of study including lengthy public hearings, the Senate Committee on Interstate and Foreign Commerce recommended that the Communications Act of 1934 be amended to provide, among other things, for a reorganization of the Commission along functional lines and to center administrative responsibility in the Chairman.

In its report to Congress on these amendments, submitted January 25, 1951, the Senate Committee said:

Section 5 of the bill is a revision of Section 5 of the law which deals with the organization of the Commission. The existing section of the law is an anachronism in that it provides for a permissive divisional organization of the Commission, which was adopted briefly shortly following enactment of the law in 1934 and then dropped. . . .

The most important subsection, and in the committee's opinion one of the most important of the entire bill here recommended, is subsection (b) which would reorganize the Commission into a functional organization. To make clear what the effect of this subsection would be, it should be explained that the Commission has been organized into three principal bureaus—Engineering, Accounting, and Legal. It also has, of course, other subsidiary sections and units but the bulk of its licensing work flows upward through these three bureaus. Regardless of the type of case involved, each of these three bureaus must independently, or occasionally in consultation, pass upon applications and other types of cases. Whether or not this system is responsible, the fact remains that the Commission's backlog of cases has continued to mount to alarming proportions. Hearing cases rarely get out in less than 2 years; some have been before the Commission as long as 4 to 7 years.

Citizens and taxpayers are entitled to greater consideration and better service from their Government than this.

Moreover, under this system, the three bureaus have become self-contained and independent little kingdoms, each jealously guarding its own field of operations and able to exercise almost dictatorial control over the expedition of a case. They can, and have, set at naught the best efforts of individual Commissioners to spur action.[31]

Communications Act Amended Requiring Establishment of Functional Organization. After consideration of reports from both Houses as well as the Conference Report,[32] Congress amended Section 5 of the Communications Act to provide for the changes recommended.[33] As amended, the section required the Commission, within six months, to "organize its staff into (1) integrated bureaus, to function on the basis of the Commission's principal workload operations, and (2) make such other divisional organizations as the Commission may deem necessary."[34] It was further required that each such integrated bureau should include "such legal, engineering, accounting, administrative, clerical, and other personnel" as the Commission might determine to be necessary.[35]

This amendment further directed the Commission to set up a new unit in the agency consisting of a "review staff" to assist in the preparation of summaries of evidence taken at adjudicatory hearings and by the compilation of facts material to exceptions and replies filed by interested parties after initial decisions and before oral argument, and "by preparing for the Commission or any member or members thereof, without recommendations and in accordance with specific directions from the Commission or such member or members, memoranda, opinions, decisions, and orders."[36]

Congress was concerned that this "review staff" be an independent group able to perform accurate and objective reporting functions, and with this end in mind provided (1) that it should be directly responsible to the Commission and not a part of any bureau or divisional organization thereof; (2) that none of its work should be supervised or directed by anyone other than a member of the review staff whom the Commission would designate as head of such staff; and (3) that no employee of the Commission not a member of the review staff should be allowed to perform any of the review functions.[37]

The original language of Section 5 of the Communications Act was further amended to provide for greater flexibility in the delegation of authority, and references to the Commission's authority to organize itself into "divisions" were deleted from the law.

Except for certain adjudicatory cases designated for hearing by the Commission and which must be conducted by it or an examiner as required by the Administrative Procedure Act,[38] the Commission was authorized to delegate functions as follows. It can, when necessary to the proper functioning of the Commission and prompt and orderly conduct of its business, "assign or refer any portion of its work, business, or functions to an individual commissioner or commissioners or to a board composed of one or more employees of the Commission."[39] Any such assignment may be amended, modified or rescinded at any time, and any person aggrieved by any action taken under such an assignment may file an application for review by the Commission.[40] The Commission, upon approval of such an application, may "affirm, modify, or set aside such order, decision, report or action," or order a rehearing thereon as provided in Section 405 of the Act.[41]

Actually, the functional organization required by the 1952 amendments, for the most part had already been established by the FCC before they were passed. The first step in the staff reorganization was taken in early 1950 and had been fully completed by March, 1952.[42]

Present FCC Organization. As it operates today, the FCC is divided into four bureaus and seven staff offices. The functions of these various units, as described in Part 0 of the Commission's Rules and Regulations, are briefly set forth below.

Broadcast Bureau. Among the more important functions of the Broadcast Bureau are (1) the processing of applications for broadcasting stations; (2) participation in hearings involving applications and rule making proceedings; (3) studying frequency allocations and drafting plans for their use in the broadcast services; (4) studying and establishing technical requirements for broadcasting equipment; (5) participation in government, industrial and international conferences concerning broadcast services and (6) the making of recommendations to the Commission concerning the promulgation of broadcasting rules and standards as well as recommendations relating to other functions mentioned.

The work load of the Broadcast Bureau is distributed among the Office of the Chief and seven divisions: namely, Broadcast Facilities, Renewal and Transfer, Complaints and Compliance, Rules and Standards, Economics, License and Hearing.[43]

A special *Office of Network Study* has been established in the Bureau to compile data relating to radio and television network operations to help the Commission develop and maintain an adequate regulatory program.[44]

Common Carrier Bureau. The work of the Common Carrier Bureau is handled by the Office of the Chief and four divisions: Telephone, Telegraph, International, and Domestic Radio Facilities. Its primary functions are concerned with the regulation of rates and services of telegraph and telephone companies and the licensing of their wire and radio operations. Its staff participates in international conferences and collaborates with representatives of state regulatory agencies and the National Association of Railroad and Utilities Commissioners in cooperative studies of matters which are of common concern to the FCC and state commissions.[45]

Safety and Special Radio Services Bureau. As previously mentioned, for every station broadcasting to the general public there are many others providing special radio services. It is the main function of the Safety and Special Radio Services Bureau to issue authorizations for these special operations. It also initiates any rulemaking proceedings with respect to them, studies frequency assignments and technical requirements for equipment, participates in international conferences and collaborates with other governmental agencies and industry groups interested in the problem of safety and special radio services, and plans and executes an enforcement program for such services, including educational campaigns conducted in collaboration with the Field Engineering and Monitoring Division.

In addition to the Office of the Chief, there are five Divisions in the Bureau: Aviation, Marine, Public Safety and Amateur, Industrial, and Land Transportation.[46]

Field Engineering and Monitoring Bureau. Another important phase of the Commission's work is handled by the Field Engineering and Monitoring Bureau. This unit consists of four divisions: namely, Engineering, Inspection and Examination, Monitoring and Field Operating Division and its associated field organization, consisting of district offices, their sub-offices, marine offices and monitoring stations located in major cities in various parts of the country. The locations of these various field offices and monitoring stations, including specific mailing addresses and personnel, are listed in Section 0.49 of the Commission's Rules and Regulations and are reproduced in Appendix III. This Bureau is responsible for all engineering activities in the field relating to broadcast stations including station inspections, monitoring, direction finding, signal measurement, and investigation.[47]

It also administers and enforces rules for commercial radio operators, and conducts examinations and issues licenses to these operators. It also processes data to determine whether proposed new or modified antenna structures will create hazards to air travel; and participates in international conferences relating to communications.[48]

Office of Hearing Examiners. All of these various bureaus are served by the Office of Hearing Examiners. In 1946, Congress passed the Administrative Procedure Act which, among other things, provides for the appointment of hearing examiners in the FCC and other federal administrative agencies. Under the provisions of this act, these examiners preside at and conduct adjudicatory proceedings assigned them by the agency and issue initial decisions. They are appointed subject to Civil Service laws, and cannot be removed from their offices except for good cause established by the Civil Service Commission after opportunity for hearing.[49]

Their functions are separated from those of other units in the Commission and, with limited exceptions, they are not permitted to consult with any person or party on any factual issue in a hearing unless upon notice and with opportunity for all parties to participate. They may not be supervised or directed by any FCC officer, employee, or agent engaged in the performance of investigative or prosecuting functions. In other words, they serve in a judicial role and are completely independent in the preparation of their opinions.

The Chief Hearing Examiner has administrative duties which include the assignment of examiners to preside at hearings and the time and place of hearings and the maintenance of hearing calendars. Upon advice of other examiners he recommends to the Commission changes in rules and regulations to simplify and expedite conduct of hearings; secures and prepares reports for the Civil Service Commission or other governmental agencies concerned with operations of the Office of Hearing Examiners; and serves as liaison for the Commission and the Examiners in securing advice or information from outside sources concerning the improvement of administrative procedures applicable to hearing cases.[50]

Other Offices in the Commission. The administrative affairs of the FCC are planned and directed by the *Office of Administration,* under the direction of the Executive Officer. The Executive Officer is responsible to the Chairman of the Commission and cooperates generally with the administrative staff of the agency in the development and improvement of administrative procedures. The Office is concerned with employment of personnel, budget, and the general housekeeping functions of the FCC. Also, under the general direction of the Defense Commissioner, and with the assistance of the various Bureaus and officers, it coordinates defense activities (other than CONELRAD and radio-frequency management activities of the Chief Engineer) of the Commission and keeps the Defense Commissioner informed as to significant developments in the area.[51]

The *General Counsel* represents the Commission in all litigation matters and, among other functions, advises the Commission with respect to proposed legislation concerning communications and assists in the preparation of Commission reports to Congress relating thereto; interprets general procedural rules of the agency as well as statutes, international agreements and regulations affecting its operation. He cooperates with other officers in rendering advice with respect to rulemaking matters and proceedings affecting more than one Bureau in the Commission.[52]

The *Office of Chief Engineer* has the following primary duties and responsibilities: (a) plans and directs broad programs looking toward the more effective use of communications in the public interest; (b) advises the Commission and the various Bureaus on matters of applied technical research; (c) advises and represents the Commission on the allocation of radio frequencies, including international agreements pertaining thereto; cooperates with the General Counsel in advising the Commission with respect to general frequency allocation proceedings not within the jurisdiction of any single Bureau.

This office also collaborates with the several Bureaus in the formulation of standards of engineering practice and the rules and regulations related thereto, and advises the Commission on such matters.[53]

As required by Section 5 of the Communications Act as amended in 1952 and already discussed above, a review staff has been set up in the Commission known as the *Office of Opinions and Review*. Section 0.141 of the Commission's Rules which describes the functions of the office reads substantially the same as the language in paragraph (c) of Section 5 of the Communications Act where the requirements for such an office are set forth.[54]

An important source of information for members of the public is the *Office of Reports and Information* which is responsible for releasing public announcements of the Commission. It prepares and makes available to the press, industry and general public informational materials and publications including annual reports relating to the Commission and its activities.[55]

The *Secretary* and his staff have the responsibility of signing all official correspondence and documents of the Commission; receive and record incoming and outgoing mail and maintain control correspondence files; keep minutes and records of Commission actions; maintain dockets of all hearing proceedings and have charge of library materials and facilities.[56]

Commission Delegations of Authority. As already pointed out, Section 5 of the Communications Act provides that the Commission may assign portions of its work to individual commissioners, or staff boards. In line with this authority, the Commission has delegated specific responsibilities to various Commissioners, committees and boards.

The responsibility for the general administration of internal affairs of the Commission is delegated to the Chairman of the Commission.[57] As provided in Section 0.213 of the Rules, in the absence of a quorum of the Commission, the Chairman or Acting Chairman may convene a board of Commissioners of those present and able to act. This Board may be empowered to transact business except that which has been delegated to individual commissioners or employees. This authority does not extend to the institution of investigations upon the Commission's own motion, or to rendering final decisions on such matters, or to investigations specifically required by the Communications Act, or to any hearing in adjudicatory matters as defined in the Administrative Procedure Act.[58]

The Telegraph Committee, composed of three commissioners, is authorized to act on all applications or requests of carriers engaged principally in record communication to construct, acquire, operate or extend telegraph lines, for temporary or emergency telegraph service, for supplementing existing telegraph facilities, or for discontinuance, reduction or impairment of telegraph service.[59] The *Telephone Committee,* composed of three commissioners, has similar authority with respect to carriers engaged in telephone communication.[60]

The Commission designates one of its members to serve as *Defense Commissioner* who takes responsibility for coordinating activities of the agency relating to national defense.[61] He is assisted by the *Division of Defense Coordination,* a unit of the Office of Administration, and by representatives of the various Bureaus and Staff offices discussed above.[62]

The Defense Commissioner has the responsibility of taking such action as will assure, in so far as possible, continuity of the Commission's essential functions and the protection of its personnel and property under war conditions.[63] In the event of enemy attack or other disaster disabling Commission functions in Washington, he assumes all the duties of the Commission until relieved by the *Emergency Relocation Board,* comprising such commissioners as are present and able to act, or, if none is available, members of the administrative staff in the order listed in Section 0.216 of the Rules.[64] A general discussion regarding operation of broadcast stations within the continental United States during enemy attack (CONELRAD) is set forth in Appendix IV.

A *Motions Commissioner* is named from time to time by the Commission to act upon such matters as petitions to intervene, specification of time and place of hearings to be conducted by a Hearing Examiner, petitions for dismissal of applications, etc.[65]

As provided in Section 0 of the Commission's Rules, the various Bureaus and Staff Offices are delegated authority to act upon numerous applications, requests, and other matters which are not in hearing status, relating to communication service in their particular areas.[66]

FCC Facilities and Work-load. To maintain the various offices described above and perform its functions, the Commission had only 1,281 employees in 1959 with total annual appropriations of less than 10 million dollars.[67] Personal services accounted for about 83 percent of this 1959 budget.[60]

As pointed out in the Introduction, the Commission has about 2.5 million radio authorizations outstanding, an increase of nearly 284,000 in 1959 over the number in 1958. During 1959, the Commission received nearly 600,000 applications of various kinds, an increase of almost 60,000 over the previous year. More than 1,500,000 pieces of mail were received or dispatched during the same period.[69]

During 1959, the FCC issued 134 initial decisions covering 176 applications. Of these, 99 concerned 140 broadcast applications. The many petitions and motions, oppositions and replies, protracted cases involving the taking of volumes and volumes of testimony, protests, court appeals—these and many other matters add greatly to the regulatory and adjudicatory burdens of the Commission.

The immensity of the communications industries and the comparatively small staff at the FCC responsible for their regulation, presents an increasingly serious problem. This problem is discussed more fully in Chapter 23.

1. 74 Stat. 407.
2. *Ibid.,* p. 408.
3. 70 Stat. 738, 739-40.
4. 48 Stat. 1066-67.
5. 66 Stat. 711.
6. *Ibid.*
7. *Ibid.*
8. 66 Stat. 712-713.
9. 48 Stat. 1068.
10. *Ibid.,* 1067 and 66 Stat. 714.
11. 48 Stat. 1068; also see 50 Stat. 191.
12. *Ibid.*
13. 50 Stat. 712; deletion referred to, 74 Stat. 245, 249.
14. 66 Stat. 711.
15. *Ibid.*
16. *Ibid.*
17. *Ibid.* The Classification Act of 1949 (separate from the Communications Act) requires that all jobs in the Federal Civil Service be classified and job descriptions approved by the Civil Service Commission.
18. 48 Stat. 1067; also, 66 Stat. 711-712.
19. 48 Stat. 1068-1070.
20. *Ibid.*
21. *Ibid.*
22. FCC Order No. 1, 1 FCC 3-4 (1934).
23. 48 Stat. 1095.
24. Warner, Harry P., *Radio and Television Law* (New York, 1953), p. 150.
25. Commission Order No. 20, 4 FCC 41.
26. Hyneman, Charles S., *Bureaucracy in a Democracy* (New York, 1950), p. xii.
27. *Ibid.,* p. 506.
28. *Ibid.,* p. 509.
29. Committee on Independent Regulatory Commissions; *A Report with Recommendations Prepared for the Commission on Organization of the Executive Branch of the Government,* (Appendix N); Government Printing Office, 1949.
30. *Ibid.*
31. Senate Report No. 44, 82nd Congress, 1st Session, submitted January 25, 1951; 97 *Cong. Rec.* 658.
32. House Report No. 2426, 82nd. Congress, 2nd. Session, submitted July 1, 1952; 98 *Cong. Rec.* 8807.
33. 66 Stat. 712-713.
34. *Ibid.*
35. *Ibid.*
36. *Ibid.*
37. *Ibid.*
38. 60 Stat. 244 (June 11, 1946).
39. 66 Stat. 713.
40. *Ibid.,* 713-714.
41. *Ibid.*

42. FCC, *Sixteenth Annual Report* (1950), pp. 15-18; also see *Nineteenth Annual Report* (1953), pp. 13-14.

43. FCC Rules and Regulations Concerning Radio, Section 0.12; 19 Fed. Reg. 4606 (1960).

44. *Ibid.*, Section 0.20.

45. *Ibid.*, Sections 0.21-0.28.

46. *Ibid.*, Sections 0.61-0.69.

47. *Ibid.*, Sections 0.41-0.49.

48. *Ibid.*

49. Administrative Procedure Act, Section 11, 60 Stat. 237.

50. FCC Rules, Sections 0.81-0.82.

51. *Ibid.*, Sections 0.91-0.92.

52. *Ibid.*, Sections 0.111-0.112.

53. *Ibid.*, Sections 0.121-0.126.

54. *Ibid.*, Section 0.141.

55. *Ibid.*, Section 0.151.

56. *Ibid.*, Sections 0.131-0.137.

57. *Ibid.*, Sections 0.3 and 0.211.

58. *Ibid.*, Sections 0.212-0.213.

59. *Ibid.*, Section 0.214.

60. *Ibid.*, Section 0.215.

61. *Ibid.*, Section 0.162.

62. *Ibid.*, Sections 0.163-0.164.

63. *Ibid.*, Section 0.162.

64. *Ibid.*, Section 0.216.

65. *Ibid.*, Sections 0.221-0.223.

66. *Ibid.*, Sections 0.224-0.341.

67. *FCC Annual Report to Congress,* 1959, p. 20.

68. *Ibid.*, p. 21.

69. *Ibid.*, p. 23-24.

CHAPTER 5

Other Governmental Agencies Concerned with Broadcasting

Any betrayal of public confidence by any station blackens the eye of all broadcasters. . . . Repairs are needed and you can make them. And if you need help from the government, it will be forthcoming. But don't lose faith in your own capacity, for if you do, you lose faith in freedom.—EARL W. KINTNER*

The Federal Trade Commission. While the FCC is the principal governmental agency with which the broadcaster must be concerned, there are many others at federal, state and local levels which exercise powers and perform functions which affect his operations. One of these is the Federal Trade Commission, whose basic function is to prevent "unfair methods of competition" and "unfair or deceptive acts or practices in commerce."[1] Since one of the primary concerns of this agency is with false and misleading advertising, its regulations and activities impinge directly upon the broadcaster who depends largely upon advertising for revenue to sustain his operations.

The Federal Trade Commission was created by the Federal Trade Commission Act passed by Congress in 1914.[2] This act provided that the Commission should have five members appointed by the President and subject to approval of the Senate. It provided that the original Commissioners were to be appointed for three, four, five, six and seven year terms, with successive appointments running for seven years. As is the case with the FCC, any person chosen to fill a vacancy is appointed only for the unexpired term of the Commissioner he succeeds. Not more than three Commissioners may be members of the same political party and no Commissioner may engage in any other business, vocation or employment.

The Chairman is designated by the President and is vested with the administrative management of the agency. Headquarters for the agency are located in Washington, D. C. The investigational work of the Commission is carried on by a *Bureau of Investigation* supported by nine field offices.

* Former Chairman, Federal Trade Commission.

These field offices are located in New York, Washington, Atlanta, Cleveland, Chicago, Kansas City, Seattle, San Francisco, and New Orleans.[3]

The trial work of the FTC is handled by a *Bureau of Litigation,* while voluntary compliance procedures are conducted by a *Bureau of Consultation.* Other important operating units include the *Bureau of Economics* which collects and analyzes economic information for the Commission; the office of the *Executive Director* with operational supervision over the various bureaus and exercising general administrative duties; a *General Counsel* who acts as principal legal officer and adviser, and, among other things, handles all matters arising out of compliance with the Commission's cease-and-desist orders and represents the Commission before the Federal district and appellate Courts.[4]

The statutory authority of the Commission is prescribed by the Federal Trade Commission Act of 1914, mentioned above, and as amended by the Wheeler-Lea Act of 1938 and the Oleomargarine Act of a later date. Originally, the Act prohibited only "unfair methods of competition." This made it necessary in every case of false or misleading advertising for the Commission to prove some injury to competition. The 1938 amendment, however, provided that any unfair or deceptive act or practice in commerce, regardless of its effect on competition, is unlawful.[5] This not only protects industry from unfair competition but protects all consumers from deceptive advertising.

Section 5 of the Federal Trade Commission Act makes unlawful any false radio or television advertising designed to induce listeners to purchase any commodities which move in interstate or foreign commerce.

What Is "False Advertising?". And what is "false advertisement" within the meaning of the Act? Sec. 15 states that it is an advertisement "which is misleading in a material respect." In determining whether any advertisement is misleading, "there shall be taken into account (among other things) not only representations made or suggested by statement, word, design, device, sound, or any combination thereof," but also the extent to which it fails to reveal material facts regarding consequences which may result from the use of the commodity under the conditions prescribed in the advertisement or under conditions considered to be customary or usual. The law further states that "no advertisement of a drug shall be deemed to be false if it is disseminated only to members of the medical profession, contains no false representations of a material fact, and includes, or is accompanied in each instance by truthful disclosure of, the formula showing quantitatively each ingredient of such drug."

The same section provides that, in the case of oleomargarine or margarine, an advertisement shall be deemed misleading in a material respect if . . . "representations are made or suggested by statement, word, grade designation, design, device, symbol, sound, or any combination thereof, that such oleomargarine or margarine is a dairy product . . ."

In the case of foods, drugs, devices or cosmetics, Section 12 of the Act declares false advertising to be unlawful whether or not these particular goods move in interstate or foreign commerce. The Act defines the term "food" to mean "(1) articles used for food or drink for man or other animals, (2) chewing gum, and (3) articles used for components of any such article."

The term "drug" includes "(1) articles recognized in the official United States Pharmacopoeia, official Homeopathic Pharmacopoeia of the United States, or official National Formulary, or any supplement to any of them; and (2) articles intended for use in the diagnosis, cure, mitigation, treatment, or prevention of disease in man or other animals; and (3) articles (other than food) intended to affect the structure or any function of the body of man or other animals; and (4) articles intended for use as a component of any article specified in clause (1), (2), or (3); but does not include devices or their components, parts, or accessories.

The Act defines "device" to include "instruments, apparatus, and contrivances, including their parts and accessories, intended (1) for use in the diagnosis, cure, mitigation, treatment, or prevention of disease in man or in other animals; or (2) to affect the structure or any function of the body of man or other animals."

The term "cosmetic" embraces "(1) articles to be rubbed, poured, sprinkled, or sprayed on, introduced into, or otherwise applied to the human body or any part thereof intended for cleansing, beautifying, promoting attractiveness, or altering the appearance, and (2) articles intended for use as a component of any such articles; except that such term shall not include soap."

Particular attention is called to the fact that Section 15 requires the FTC to consider not only direct falsehoods, but also failure to reveal material facts respecting consequences resulting from the use of the product. Under the authority of this section, the Commission requires the inclusion of warning statements in advertisements of potentially harmful products.[6]

Failure to Disclose Material Facts. Mention should also be made of cases involving advertisements which misrepresent the value of products for treatment purposes by failing to disclose material facts. For example, in a recent case, the FTC held that certain advertisements promoting the sale of medicinal preparations for use in treatment of conditions of the hair and scalp were misleading and unlawful. The manufacturer had falsely represented their therapeutic effect for the prevention of baldness and had falsely claimed that they would stimulate the growth of hair and prevent excessive hair fall. The Commission ordered the company to discontinue such advertisements on the grounds that they failed to reveal the fact that the vast majority of cases of excessive hair fall and baldness are known to dermatologists as male pattern baldness and that in cases of that type, the preparation in question would not stop excessive hair fall, prevent or overcome baldness or have any favorable influence on its underlying cause.[7]

Another type of advertising which has been subject to critical examination by the FTC is that which includes television demonstrations which are represented as proving the value of a product when in fact they do not. In a case decided June 11, 1959, the Commission, while it did not find the evidence sufficient to support the particular complaint involved, did enunciate clearly the principle that the use of such a demonstration, if untrue, constitutes an unfair trade practice within the meaning of Section 5 of the FTC Act, since it has "the tendency and capacity to mislead purchasers into believing they are buying a product which has been demonstrated or proven to have a certain quality or characteristic. The law is well settled that the public is entitled to buy what it thinks it is buying . . ."[8]

Administrative Procedure. Certain types of cases involving deceptive advertising are disposed of by administrative settlement or stipulation procedure established by the Commission. Where these processes are not successful in securing compliance with the law, formal complaints are issued against offenders and matters are set down for public hearing before examiners with counsel for the Commission assuming the general burden of proof. After all evidence is submitted and the record closed, the Examiner issues an initial opinion which may be reviewed by the Commission on its own initiative or at the request of the respondent in the proceeding.

If the allegations in the complaint are sustained by the evidence, the hearing examiner (or the Commission on appeal or review) then issues an order requiring the respondent to cease and desist from the false or misleading advertising. Subject to final review by the Federal Courts, the order becomes final. Failure to comply with the order subjects the offender to suit by the government in a U. S. District Court for recovery of a civil penalty of not more than $5,000 for each violation.[9]

In addition to the regular proceedings, the Commission may, in some cases, bring suit in a United States District Court and request the Court to enjoin the dissemination of advertisements of food, drugs, cosmetics, and devices intended for use in the diagnosis, prevention or treatment of disease, whenever it has reason to believe that such a proceeding would be in the public interest. If the court grants the request, the injunction remains in effect until the Commission has dismissed the complaint or it has been set aside by the Court on review, or until an order of the Commission to cease and desist has become final.[10]

Where it is proved that the use of a commodity is injurious to health or where there is intent to defraud or mislead, Section 14 of the Federal Trade Commission Act states that the offender is guilty of a misdemeanor and conviction subjects him to a fine of not more than $5,000 or imprisonment of not more than 6 months, or both. Succeeding convictions may result in a penalty of not more than $10,000 and not more than 1 year's incarceration, or both.[11]

Applicability of this criminal provision, however, is limited to the "manufacturer, packer, distributor or seller of the commodity to which the false advertisement relates," and specifically precludes publishers, broadcasting stations, or advertising agencies or media, providing they furnish the Commission on request the name and post office address of the party for whom the advertising was disseminated.[12]

The statute provides that the Commission shall certify this type of case to the Attorney General for institution of appropriate court proceedings.[13]

Complaints May Be Filed by Members of Public. Members of the public may file complaints with the Commission regarding deceptive and misleading advertising. No formality is required. A letter alleging deception with facts to support the charges is all that is required. Upon receipt of any such complaint, the Commission, through its Bureau of Investigation, considers the matter and determines whether to institute formal proceedings. It is the policy of the Commission not to disclose the identity of the complainant.[14]

If the Commission determines there is a valid basis for formal action, as provided by the law, it may proceed against the offender on one or all of three grounds: attacking the objectionable advertising as (1) an "unfair method of competition;" (2) as a "deceptive practice;" or (3) if food, drugs, cosmetics or devices are involved, as "misleading in a material respect."[15]

General Types of False Advertising. Several general types of deceptive advertising have been matters of serious concern to the Federal Trade Commission. One of these involves misrepresentations of one's business status or the advantages or connections which he may have, or claim to have, in the conduct of his business. Examples of this type are:

that certain distinguished authorities or personages are connected with his business;
that he has certain valuable contacts and arrangements with others;
that his business is for charity;
that he has Government endorsement;
that his business is an educational, religious or research institute or is nonprofit in character;
that he maintains scientific laboratories;
that the medical profession or the dental profession has endorsed his product;
that certain scientific tests have been made of his product;
and a host of other similar misrepresentations.[16]

A second type of advertising with which the FTC has been concerned is that which is deceptive concerning the comparative merits of products. For example, the audio portion of a TV commercial may well be within legal limits on the comparative merits of two products and at the same time the video portion may give the false and misleading impression of undesirability or unworthiness of the competitive product through slight-of-hand performances or other trick devices which may be skillfully employed.[17] There have been numerous cases in recent years involving this kind of deception in which the Commission has issued cease and desist orders.[18]

As mentioned above, false claims as to the efficacy of drugs and medicines constitute a third general type of advertising which has been declared unlawful. A fourth involves fictitious pricing or misrepresentation of comparative prices. Another is the bait-switch kind which advertises for sale at a low price a product described as desirable, and then when the customer offers to buy it on the terms suggested, he is switched to other merchandise either because the advertiser does not want to sell the article advertised or actually may not have it in stock, or for some other reason not in accord with fair business practice.[19]

Guides have recently been adopted by the Federal Trade Commission for the use of its staff in evaluation of pricing representations in advertising. While the guides do not purport to be all inclusive, the Commission has said "they are directed toward the elimination of existing major abuses and are being released to the public in the interest of obtaining voluntary, simultaneous and prompt cooperation by those whose practices are subject to the jurisdiction of the Federal Trade Commission." The complete text of these guides against deceptive pricing is reproduced in Appendix V.

FTC Monitoring Services. During the past decade the FTC has given increasing attention to false advertising on radio and television. It has a staff which regularly scans samples of commercial continuity of broadcasting stations. A sample form letter used by the FTC to elicit information along this line from broadcast licensees also appears in Appendix V.

In October, 1956, the new Radio and Television Advertising Unit was established by the Commission whose purpose is to monitor both aural and video presentations over broadcast media to discover any false advertising claims. A sizeable number of employees is assigned to the new unit and is actively engaged in the work in Washington and the various branch offices. Also, all professional members of the FTC staff have been requested by the Commission to report misleading radio and television advertising coming to their attention during off-duty hours, when that advertising appears to violate the FTC Act. This supplements the regular monitoring activities of the Commission.

The new monitoring unit employs equipment which records both aural and visual commercial continuity broadcast by stations. If an initial study suggests malpractice, an investigation of the matter is undertaken by a project attorney of the Commission. If he recommends prohibitive action against the advertiser and is supported by the Director of the Bureau of Litigation and by the Commission, the advertiser is then formally charged with having engaged in unfair methods of competition or unfair or deceptive acts, and is brought to trial before an examiner as previously described.

FTC Warns Against Illegal Huckstering. Recently, the Federal Trade Commission has stepped up its monitoring activities. Public reaction against rigged television shows and offensive advertising practices prompted the Commission to issue an official warning that it would scrutinize more carefully "advertising excesses that dance on the edges of the law." On November 1, 1959, the Commission announced that it had received many complaints from the public about TV advertising practices and was ready to "strike fast and hard" at "illegal huckstering by the irresponsible few."

The announcement further stated that the FTC would double its monitoring staff, make continuous rather than spot checks on all network commercials and speed investigations on non-network advertising throughout the country.

Network broadcasters were further warned that they would be required to supply all TV commercials for special scrutiny during the pre-Christmas period from November 15 through December 15, 1959. At the same time, the Commission reported that it already was investigating 53 cases involving objectionable commercials.

Chairman Earl W. Kintner pointed out that it was beyond the FTC's authority to police bad-taste ads but declared that the broadcasting industry had a responsibility to clamp down on advertising excesses.[20]

Stations Have Legal Right To Refuse False Ads. Broadcasting stations have the legal right to refuse to accept advertising which is false, misleading or otherwise harmful to the public interest. Most contracts for the sale of broadcasting time provide for this. A clause often incorporated in such contracts, and recommended by Standard Rate and Data Service, reads: "The right is reserved to reject or exclude copy which is unethical, misleading, extravagant, challenging, questionable in character, in bad taste, detrimental to public health or interest, or otherwise inappropriate or incompatible with the character of the publication or that does not meet with the approval of the Federal Trade Commission."

The Importance of Government Regulation Stressed. The importance of governmental regulation in the advertising field is indicated by the following remarks taken from a speech by Charles A. Sweeney, Legal Adviser for Radio and Television at the FTC, delivered in New York at the annual meeting of the Division of Food, Drug and Cosmetic Law, American Bar Association, July 12, 1957:

The increasingly important role of advertising as an essential of our continuously expanding economy not only justifies but demands such attention by the Federal government. The Commission is seriously mindful that the importance of advertising, especially in the field of foods and drugs because of the health aspect, has grown with our expanding economy and also in direct proportion to the lessening of direct, personal contact between producer and consumer. Few would deny today that advertising is indispensible to the maintenance and continued expansion of our American standard of living and our economic well-being.

It follows logically that the more important advertising becomes to the nation and its well-being, the greater the public interest in maintaining its integrity. That interest flows from the dependence of the buyer on this facility for knowledge essential to his intelligent selection of those goods which best suit his needs.

The seller has an equal interest in the integrity of advertising because of his desire to invest his advertising money with assurance that potential purchasers will have sufficient confidence in his claims to persuade them to select his products. This is an immediate and pressing interest. However, beyond that immediate interest, the seller must expect to rely increasingly upon the medium of advertising to acquaint the public with new products to be developed. For that reason any lessening of confidence in advertising not only will diminish the value of his advertising dollar but jeopardize or for practical purposes destroy this medium of contact upon which his business future so largely depends.

It is vital, for these reasons, that all of us recognize our common interest in utilizing the agencies and procedures provided by Congress to maintain the integrity and believability of advertising, of such importance to our economy and individual business well-being.

Food and Drug Administration. Not to be disregarded by the broadcaster are the functions and activities of the Food and Drug Administration. This agency, among other things, is charged with the responsibility of enforcing the Federal Food, Drug and Cosmetic Act.[21] It is empowered to prevent the misbranding and mislabeling of commodities. It is an operating division of the U.S. Department of Health, Education and Welfare with an Administrator who has wide discretion in promulgating standards of quality to be used in the marketing and sale of consumer goods.

There are the offices of the Administrator and his staff in Washington, D.C., with 16 district offices and 37 inspection stations distributed throughout the United States, equipped with testing laboratories and staffed with chemists and other technical personnel.[22] When violations of rules and regulations with respect to quality and labeling of commodities are discovered, the Administrator can resort to a number of corrective procedures as provided by law. He may attempt to secure compliance with rules and regulations by informal, administrative agreement in much the same manner as the Federal Trade Commission.[23] Or he may condemn adulterated or misbranded products offered for sale.[24] He also may recommend to the Department of Justice the seizure of such products, or the institution of injunction actions and criminal prosecutions.[25]

There is a working agreement between the Federal Trade Commission and the Food and Drug Administration by which it is acknowledged that the primary concern of the former agency is with advertising and that of the latter is with mislabeling.[26] The agreement provides for a close relationship between the agencies involving exchanges of information, and is designed to avoid jurisdictional conflicts and duplication of efforts and to strengthen enforcement procedures.

The President. As provided in Section 305 of the Communications Act, the President of the United States assigns all radio frequencies used by the Federal government. More than half of all available spectrum space is used by the various agencies of the Government including the expanding military establishment.

If he finds it necessary, the President is authorized by Section 606 of the Communications Act to exercise certain emergency powers in time of war. He may direct carriers to give communications preference or priority if they are essential to national defense and security. This section makes it unlawful for any person, during a war in which the United States may be engaged, to obstruct or retard interstate or foreign communication by radio or wire and the President is authorized to use the armed services to prevent any such obstruction or retardation of communications.[27]

Upon proclamation by the President that there exists war or a threat of war, or a state of public peril, disaster or other national emergency, or in order to preserve neutrality of the United States, he may suspend as he sees fit the rules and regulations applicable to any or all radio stations as prescribed by the FCC and may cause the closing of any such station. He may order the removal of its apparatus and equipment or he may authorize the use or control of any station or device, its apparatus and equipment by any department of the government under such rules as he may prescribe with just compensation to the owners.[28]

By an Executive Order issued December 10, 1951, the President delegated to the FCC, subject to certain limitations, the authority vested in him with respect to radio stations, except those owned and operated by any department or agency of the U.S. Government. With respect to government stations, subject to certain limitations, the authority vested in the President has been delegated to the head of each department or agency with which the stations are involved.[29]

The President has the advice and help of the Office of Civil and Defense Mobilization whose purpose is to "exercise strong leadership in our national mobilization effort, including both current defense activities and readiness for any future national emergency."[30]

The Director of OCDM, on behalf of the President, directs, controls, and coordinates all mobilization activities of the executive branch of the government. Pursuant to Executive Order 10461 of June 17, 1953, he assists and advises with the President respecting telecommunication functions in the executive branch including: (1) the coordination of the development of telecommunication policies, standards, plans and programs among the various government agencies to assure maximum security to the United States in time of national emergency with a minimum interference to non-government activities and (2) assigning radio frequencies to government agencies.[31] The Director coordinates his activities in this regard with the Federal Communications Commission. He is assisted by the Interdepartmental Radio Advisory Committee representing the various agencies of the government and by the Telecommunications Planning Committee, of which his Assistant Director for Telecommunications is Chairman.[32] The functions of the Assistant Director are not restricted to mobilization but are of continuing nature during normal as well as abnormal conditions.[33]

Mention has already been made of the President's power to appoint the members of the FCC and FTC and to designate their chairmen. While the law specifies that a limited number of commissioners may be members of the same political party, it goes without saying that the President has wide latitude in appointing those whom he thinks will reflect his own political and administrative ideas. Since the chairmen of these agencies hold their positions subject to the will of the President, their official conduct, needless to say, may be affected by attitudes and opinions which prevail at and radiate from the White House. A sense of loyalty and, in some cases, a realization that the same President may still be in office when time for reappointment comes around, can have a subtle, but none the less real influence upon the thinking and behavior of every Commissioner.

The Congress. Since their appointments and reappointments depend upon approval of the Senate, it is only natural that Commissioners should be concerned with what the Senators think of their actions. This is particularly true with respect to the Senate Interstate and Foreign Commerce Committee. Every presidential appointment and reappointment to one of these commissions is first passed upon by this Committee. Accordingly, opinions on communications matters expressed by individual Senators as well as the Committee as a whole are likely to receive careful consideration by commissioners.

Also, under the direction of its Chairman and with the assistance of staff experts, this Senate Committee makes continuing studies of problems in interstate and foreign commerce and has important responsibilities with respect to the initiation of legislation in this field. There is a close liaison between the Committee staff and that of the commissions and the exchange of information is most helpful in the development of legislation designed to improve regulatory processes.

The importance of other Congressional committees should be mentioned. The Committee on Interstate and Foreign Commerce in the House, like its counterpart in the Senate, is concerned with the operations of the FCC, FTC, and numerous other governmental bureaus. The appropriations committees of Congress also are able to influence the policies and activities of these commissions because of their power to approve or disapprove budget proposals submitted by these agencies.

Special Congressional committees have been appointed from time to time to investigate the operations of the FCC and other commissions and to study particular aspects of their operations and regulatory problems. The investigations and reports of these Congressional committees on occasions have seriously disrupted the normal operations of these commissions. This will be discussed more fully in Chapter 23.

The influence of individual Congressmen should not be overlooked. Because of inquiries, complaints and pressures from their constituents, they may be in frequent contact by telephone or correspondence with FCC and other government officials. In fact, a substantial portion of the correspondence of these agency officials is related to communications from individual Congressmen speaking in behalf of the people or of interests "back home." While it would be difficult to calculate their precise effects, it is safe to say that there have been times when these congressional communications have affected materially the consideration and ultimate outcome of matters pending before these bureaus.

The Courts. In the event that any parties over which the FCC, FTC and FDA have jurisdiction violate laws which these agencies administer, or fail to comply with lawful orders issued by them, the Federal District Courts are available to enforce compliance. For example, Section 401 of the Communications Act provides that these courts, upon application of the Attorney General of the United States at the request of the FCC may issue writs of mandamus commanding compliance with provisions of the law.[34] Similarly, these courts have authority to compel compliance with laws administered by the Federal Trade Commission and the Food and Drug Administration.[35]

Mention has already been made in Chapter 3 of Section 313 of the Communications Act which relates to the enforcement of the anti-trust laws. As pointed out, this section declares that all laws of the U.S. forbidding monopolies and restraints of trade are applicable to the manufacture and sale of radio apparatus and to interstate and foreign radio communications. The section further provides that whenever any civil or criminal proceeding is instituted in a Federal Court to enforce or review the orders of the Federal Trade Commission or other government agency with respect to these anti-trust laws, if the Court finds any radio licensee to be guilty, it may, in addition to the penalties imposed by the laws, revoke the license. Thereupon all rights under such license would cease subject of course to the licensee's right to appeal to a higher court.

Section 402 of the Communications Act provides that appeals may be taken from decisions and orders of the FCC to the United States Court of Appeals for the District of Columbia in any of the following cases:

(1) By any applicant for a construction permit or station license whose application is denied by the Commission.

(2) By any applicant for the renewal or modification of any such instrument of authorization whose application is denied by the Commission.

(3) By any party to an application for authority to transfer, assign, or

dispose of any such instrument of authorization, or any rights thereunder, whose application is denied by the Commission.

(4) By an applicant for authorization to locate and operate a broadcast studio or other place from which programs are transmitted or delivered to a radio station in a foreign country for the purpose of having them reach consistently the United States, whose application has been denied by the Commission or whose permit has been revoked by the Commission.

(5) By the holder of any construction permit or station license which has been modified or revoked by the Commission.

(6) By any other person who is aggrieved or whose interests are adversely affected by any order of the Commission granting or denying any application described above.

(7) By any person upon whom an order to cease and desist has been served under Section 312 of the Communications Act.[36]

It is provided in Section 402 that the decision of the District Court of Appeals on any of the above matters shall be final, subject, however, to review by the Supreme Court of the United States upon writ of *certiorari*.[37]

Section 402 sets forth detailed procedural requirements for appeals.[38] The appellate court may confirm or overturn the decision of the Commission. In the latter case, it remands the decision of the Commission to carry out the judgment of the Court.[39]

The laws governing the functions of the Federal Trade Commission and the Food and Drug Administration also provide for appeals to the U.S. Circuit Courts from decisions and orders of these agencies.[40]

The Department of Justice The Department of Justice is the agency generally responsible for the enforcement of Federal laws. Its affairs and activities are under the direction of the Attorney General, who supervises and directs the activities of U.S. district attorneys and marshals in the various judicial districts.

As provided in Section 401(c) of the Communications Act, it is the duty of any district attorney of the United States, upon application by the FCC to institute in the proper court and prosecute under the direction of the Attorney General all necessary proceedings for the enforcement of any provisions of the Act and for punishment of any violations thereof.[41] Similar assistance of the Attorney General and these district attorneys is available to the FTC and FDA, as provided in the laws governing these agencies.[42]

Special mention should be made of the anti-trust and criminal divisions of the Department of Justice. The former division is particularly concerned with the enforcement of Federal anti-trust laws by criminal actions and by civil suits in equity aimed to protect and restore competitive conditions to the American system of free enterprise. The Criminal Division has responsibility for and supervision over the enforcement of Federal criminal laws generally. Both are directed by Assistant Attorney Generals who are responsible to the Attorney General.

Prosecution of violations of Sections 313 and 314 of the Communications Act pertaining to anti-trust laws and preservation of competition in the broadcasting industry is the responsibility of the Anti-Trust Division. Violations of Section 1304 and 1464 of the U.S. Criminal Code, making it unlawful to broadcast lotteries and indecent and profane language, and violations of Section 14 of the Federal Trade Commission Act forbidding false advertising and Section 301 of the Food, Drug and Cosmetics Act prohibiting the mislabeling of foods, drugs and other commodities are prosecuted by the Criminal Division.

State and Local Agencies of Control. While the Federal Communications Commission has the primary responsibility for the regulation of broadcasting, the activity is affected to a considerable extent by governmental agencies and requirements at state and local levels. While by no means covering the many requirements and areas of activity of these agencies, the following are some of the more important ones which impinge upon broadcasting.

A large majority of radio and television stations are operated by corporations. In all states there exist general laws which prescribe procedure which must be followed in establishing corporations including those engaged in the broadcasting business. A certificate of incorporation must be approved by the Secretary of State or equivalent officer in the state government and the charter under which the station operates must authorize broadcasting activities.

While state statutes rarely expressly require corporations to adopt by-laws, they usually provide that they may do so and the implication is strong that they should. A failure to do so may in some cases actually lead to violation of state statutes in the transaction of corporate business.[43]

In drafting the charter and by-laws, the prospective broadcaster should consult with legal counsel familiar with corporation law in the state where the business is to be carried on.

State and Local Taxation. The Commerce Clause of the Federal Constitution prohibits states and localities from assessing any tax which directly or indirectly places an undue burden on or discriminates against interstate commerce. This rule, however, has not always operated to free interstate business such as broadcasting from all such levies. Some state courts have held that stations may be subject to a state tax if it is directed only at the local aspects of broadcasting.

While there is no uniform pattern for taxing radio and television stations at state and local levels, several types of levies have been made. One is the gross receipts tax. For example, the state of New Mexico imposed a 2 percent privilege tax on gross receipts derived from local business firms, but excluded gross receipts from network advertising originating in other states and those from national spot advertising on the grounds that they were interstate in character and therefore not subject to state assessment.[44]

Hawaii passed a law imposing a similar tax on the gross receipts of radio stations. Honolulu Station KPOA contested the validity of the tax in the courts, contending that all broadcasting is interstate in character, that Congress had preempted the subject matter of radio broadcasting to the exclusion of state and territorial legislation of every kind, including taxation, and that the assessments made against the station were invalid and unconstitutional.

The tax was upheld by the courts. It was held that Hawaii might levy a tax on gross receipts of a radio station located within the territory, where the station's broadcasts have commercial value only within the territory and income from broadcasts to the mainland by short-wave relay are excluded. Such a tax was held not to be a burden on interstate commerce. The fact that Congress had preempted the radio field and required broadcasters to secure licenses did not render them immune from taxation. It was reasoned by the courts that the character of radio communication does not prohibit a tax upon the state business any more than the interstate character of railroads, power companies, telephone, telegraph and express companies prevent taxes which do not aim to control interstate commerce.[45]

In an early case, *Fisher's Blend,* 297 U.S. 650, 56 S.Ct. 608, 80 L. ed. 956 (1936), a state occupation tax measured by gross receipts from two radio stations in the state of Washington was involved. In that case, the Court held that since the stations' income was derived from interstate commerce, the tax measured by gross receipts was a burden on interstate commerce. The Court indicated, however, that a gross receipts tax directed solely at a local aspect of broadcasting would not be invalidated.

The cases seem to show, therefore, that the courts must be satisfied that a tax measured by gross receipts is in some way related to activity within the state, either because the event taxed is a "local one," like the sale of advertising, or because the taxed income is intrastate commerce or is allocable to intrastate commerce.

The City of New York has worked out an apportionment formula by which interstate companies are taxed for the privilege of doing business there. The regulations there require that a radio station apportion to the City as "wholly taxable receipts" that "proportion of the gross receipts from the sale of sponsored time" which the number of radio families within the city bears to the total number of radio families covered by the station.[46]

Some municipalities have resorted to flat license taxes as a means of obtaining revenue from broadcasting stations. The courts have sustained this type of tax where it is shown that some proportion of the programs broadcast either originate in the local studios, are sponsored by local advertisers, or are primarily intended to reach a local audience. There have been exceptions though. An ordinance requiring all firms or persons operating a radio station to pay a license tax was struck down in *Whitehurst v. Grimes,* 21 F. (2d) 787 (E.D. Ky. 1927) as a direct tax on the business of radio broadcasting which the court said was interstate commerce and exclusively committed to the national government. *Tampa Times v. Burnett,* 45 F.Supp. 166 (S.D. Fla. 1942) was a similar case.

As of this writing, taxes are now being imposed on broadcast advertising by taxing authorities in five states: Arizona, Delaware, Indiana, New Mexico and West Virginia. An unsuccessful attempt was made in 1951 to impose a privilege tax on Oklahoma stations and a 5 percent tax on gross receipts of these stations. The privilege tax or license would have consisted of ten cents per watt, or $5,000 for a 50 kw station.[47]

In a recent ruling of the U.S. Supreme Court, it was held that the state might impose a tax on the net income of national business concerns, even though they may not have tangible assets in the taxing state, provided the levy is limited to that portion of the income derived from sales solely within the taxing state. (See 358 U.S. 450 Feb. 1959)

This decision would appear to make broadcast stations, station representatives, advertising agencies, program syndicators and networks liable for taxes in all states where they do business and derive income. According to *Broadcasting Magazine* for March 2, 1959, page 32, some 35 states now impose corporation taxes on companies located within their borders. Prior to the recent Supreme Court decision, companies had never paid income tax to a state in which they had no tangible property or assets.

The current practice with respect to taxation on broadcasting stations varies with the taxing authorities and courts in the different states and communities. With states and municipalities under increasing pressure to find new sources of revenue to meet the rising costs of government, it may be that stations will be called upon more and more to share in these costs.

Municipal Regulations. Some mention should be made of municipal regulations which impinge upon the broadcaster. These may include local ordinances to prevent interference to radio reception from various sources such as diathermy machines, industrial heating devices, and all types of electronic equipment capable of radiating electro-magnetic energy. Also, municipalities, by means of zoning and safety ordinances regulate the height and location of transmitting towers. These regulations are considered to be a valid exercise of state police power and designed to prohibit "nuisances" and other evils which affect the security and safety of the community.[48]

In a recent Pennsylvania case it was held that state and local authorities may not censor movies presented on television. In *Allen B. Dumont Laboratories v. Carroll,* 184 F. (2d) 153 (1951), the United States Court of Appeals for the Third District held that Congress had fully occupied the field of television regulation to the exclusion of any regulation by the states; that it had the constitutional right to do so, and that therefore a state could not censor motion picture films used in television broadcasts. The U.S. Supreme Court denied a writ of *certiorari* in the case, sustaining the decision of the lower court.[49]

Despite the decision in this case, some legal authorities feel that perhaps the Courts have not spoken the last word on this matter and there is speculation to the effect that in some cases, such as those involving unquestionable obscenity in films shown on television, judicial interpretation might take a different turn.[50]

NOTES

1. 52 Stat. 111 (1938).
2. 38 Stat. 717 (1914).
3. Federal Trade Commission, *Annual Report* (1958), p. III.
4. *Ibid.*
5. Wheeler-Lea Act, approved March 21, 1938, 52 Stat. 111, amending the Federal Trade Commission Act.
6. For excellent discussion of this matter, see "Remarks of Charles A. Sweeney," Legal Adviser for Radio and Television Bureau of Investigation, Federal Trade Commission, before The Nutrition Foundation, Inc. and Institute of Food Technology, Northern California Section, Berkeley, California, January 15, 1959. See also *Aronberg v. FTC,* 132 F(2d) 165 and *Gelb v. FTC,* 144 F(2d) 580.
7. See Sweeney, *Ibid.* Also, *In the Matter of Ward Laboratories, Inc. et al.,* FTC Docket No. 6346, decided March 4, 1959.
8. See *In the Matter of Hutchinson Chemical Corporation and Herman S. Hutchinson,* FTC Docket No. 7140.
9. 52 Stat. 114.
10. *Ibid.,* 115.
11. *Ibid.*
12. *Ibid.,* 116.
13. *Ibid.,* 116-117.
14. Federal Trade Commission, *Annual Report* (1957), p. 19.
15. *Ibid.,* pp. 6, 7.
16. Scott, Harold T., former Legal Adviser, Radio and Television Advertising, Federal Trade Commission; address to New Jersey Pharmaceutical Association, January 28, 1958.
17. *Ibid.,* p. 5.
18. See Federal Trade Commission, *Annual Reports* (1955, 56, 57 and 58).
19. *Ibid.*
20. See *New York Times,* November 2, 1959.
21. 52 Stat. 1041 (1938).
22. *U.S. Government Organization Manual* (1958-59), p. 348.
23. 52 Stat. 1043-45.
24. *Ibid.*
25. *Ibid.*
26. "The Regulation of Advertising", 56 Columbia L.R. 1036-1037 (November, 1956).
27. 48 Stat. 1104-5.
28. *Ibid.*
29. Executive Order on Emergency Control of Stations and Facilities, Executive Order No. 10312, signed December 10, 1951, 16 Fed. Reg. 12452.
30. *U.S. Government Organization Manual* (1958-59), p. 68.
31. *Ibid.,* p. 71.
32. *Ibid.*

33. *Ibid.*
34. 48 Stat. 1092.
35. 52 Stat. 114, and 1043-45.
36. 66 Stat. 718-19.
37. *Ibid.,* 720.
38. *Ibid.,* 719.
39. *Ibid.,* 720.
40. 52 Stat. 112-13 and 1055-56.
41. 48 Stat. 1093.
42. 52 Stat. 116-117 and 1046.
43. See Oleck, Howard L., *Non-Profit Corporations and Associations* (Englewood Cliffs, N.J., 1956), p. 173.
44. N.M. Stats., Section 76-1404 (1941).
45. *McGaw v. Tax Commissioners of Hawaii,* 40 Haw. 121, 9 RR 2055 (1953); affirmed *sub. nom.* McGaw v. Fase, 11 RR 2004 (9 Cir., October 30, 1954).
46. Article 214 of the New York City Regulations, *Radio Broadcasting Stations; Allocation of Receipts from Radio Broadcasting,* issued under the General Business and Financial Tax law.
47. See *Broadcasting* (November 11, 1957), p. 27.
48. For an excellent and comprehensive discussion of local ordinances affecting broadcasting see Rhyne, Charles S., *Municipal Regulations, Taxation and Use of Radio and Television,* Report No. 143 (1955), National Institute of Municipal Law Officers, Washington, D.C.
49. 340 U.S. 929.
50. See Rhyne, *op. cit.,* pp. 43-44.

PART III

Character, Classification
and Utilization of
Radio Frequencies

CHAPTER 6

The Nature, Measurement and Uses of Radio Waves

I must confess to a feeling of profound humility in the presence of a universe which transcends us at almost every point. I feel like a child who while playing by the seashore has found a few bright colored shells and a few pebbles while the whole vast ocean of truth stretches out almost untouched and unruffled before my eager fingers.—ISAAC NEWTON

As pointed out in Chapter 3, Section 303 of the Communications Act requires the FCC to classify broadcasting stations, assign bands of frequencies to the various classes of stations and prescribe the nature of their uses and services. Pursuant to this statutory mandate, the Commission has established detailed regulations providing for a systematic allocation of frequencies and classification of stations for different types of broadcasting service. Some knowledge of the nature of electromagnetic energy and the broadcast spectrum is necessary before these regulations can be fully understood and evaluated.

Broadcasting makes use of electromagnetic energy which exists in the form of waves. These waves travel at the speed of light (186,000 miles per second). To understand their properties and behavior, it is helpful to compare them with water and sound waves.[1] A pebble dropped in a pool causes an up and down movement of the water which is propagated on the surface in all directions with a certain velocity. Similarly, sound waves result from the movement or vibration of some physical material or body causing alternate condensations and rarefactions of air which we are able to "hear" because we possess auditory equipment which can detect varying conditions of the air.[2]

Electromagnetic waves are characterized by varying frequencies and lengths. The frequency is the number of cycles of vibration per second. The wave length is the distance the wave travels in one cycle. Or it may be described as the distance between the crests of the troughs of the wave.

The frequency is usually expressed in kilocycles (1000 cycles per second) and abbreviated *kc* or in megacycles (1 million cycles per second)

77

abbreviated *mc*. For example, a station operating on a frequency of 600,000 cycles per second is referred to as a 600 kc operation.

Radio communication is accomplished by transforming air vibrations into electromagnetic waves. This is done by a process called transduction. The sound waves set up by the voice or a musical instrument in a broadcasting studio strike a thin metal diaphragm in a microphone. An electrical current having the same vibrations is produced, and is carried by wire to amplifying tubes. These tubes increase the intensity of the current but do not change the frequency. This "audio-frequency" current, as it is called, is imposed on the carrier wave transmitted by the station. Electrical impulses oscillating back and forth between the antenna and the ground system of the station result in the emission of the carrier wave. This wave travels through space to a receiving set where the carrier current is modified so that sound currents corresponding with those at the broadcasting station are obtained, amplified and made intelligible to the human ear.[3]

The strength or field intensity of a wave at any receiving point depends upon numerous factors including the power and efficiency of the transmitting facilities, the distance from the transmitter to the receiver, the frequency, time of day, season, meteorological conditions, characteristics of the transmission path, etc.[4]

The field strength of a wave at any given point is measured in terms of volts or fractions thereof per meter. Unless in close proximity to the station, the electric field is always less than one volt per meter. Within a few miles the measure is in terms of millivolts per meter. As the wave travels farther and diminishes in intensity, it is measured in terms of microvolts per meter.[5]

The existence of other electric fields in an area of reception may produce interference problems. These "interference fields," as they are called, may result from a number of causes: atmospheric electricity or static, electrical devices such as diathermy machines and radio stations operating on the same or adjacent channels. In order for radio reception to be satisfactory, the field intensity of the desired wave must be strong enough and the receiving equipment good enough to overcome interference from the other electric fields existing in the area.[6]

Electromagnetic energy manifests itself in ways other than radio waves. It may take the form of electricity or be in the form of light, X-rays or cosmic rays, depending upon wave lengths and frequencies. When laid out in numerical order, these make up what is called the electromagnetic spectrum. Roughly, this is analogous to a piano key board with low frequency notes at one end and ascending in numerical order to the higher notes at the other. Similarly, it may be compared to a color sequence with the red end of the spectrum representing the lower frequencies and the blue end representing the higher ones.

At the lower part of the electromagnetic spectrum are the electrical waves which are comparatively long and have low frequencies. Above these, are the radio frequencies, starting at about 10,000 cycles per second with the wave being over 18 miles in length. At the upper end of this part, the waves have a frequency as high as 300,000 megacycles per second and measure only about one twenty-fifth of an inch in length. Above the radio spectrum in the area of visible light the waves become almost infinitesimal and have frequencies of millions of megacycles per second.[7]

The vast range of frequencies in the radio spectrum itself has been divided and classified by international agreement as follows:[8]

Very Low Frequency (VLF)	Below 30 kilocycles
Low Frequency (LF)	30 to 300 kc
Medium Frequency (MF)	300 to 3,000 kc
High Frequency (HF)	3,000 to 30,000 kc
Very High Frequency (VHF)	30,000 kc to 300 mc
Ultra High Frequency (UHF)	300 to 3,000 mc
Super High Frequency (SHF)	3,000 to 30,000 mc
Extremely High Frequency (EHF)	30,000 to 300,000 mc

Propagation Characteristics of Radio Frequencies. Just as the various parts of the electromagnetic spectrum as a whole differ in their form and behavior, so do the various frequency ranges within the radio spectrum itself exhibit different characteristics. For example, some radio waves travel in straight lines from the point of transmission to the point of reception. They are called direct waves. Others tend to follow the curvature of the earth and are called ground waves. Still others travel away from the earth and are reflected back. They are referred to as sky waves.

From about 35 to 250 miles above the earth, there are several layers of ionized atmosphere. These various strata make up what is called the ionosphere. They are formed as the ultra-violet rays from the sun reach the upper regions of air and electrify or ionize them. Their thickness and height vary from hour to hour with changes in the intensity flow of these rays from the sun. Radio waves traveling upward, striking the ionosphere, and reflecting back to earth, are called sky waves and constitute an important resource for radio transmission.

The four principal layers of the ionosphere are D, E, F_1 and F_2. During the daytime, the D layer lies about 37 miles above the earth. This is primarily a region of radio wave absorption, although some very long waves are reflected by it and provide some radio service. The E layer is about 70 miles above the earth. Still higher at about 140 miles is the F_1 region. Above this, at heights ranging from 185 to 250 miles is the heavily ionized F_2 strata.

These ionized layers reflect radio waves in much the same way that a mirror reflects light. A broadcast station transmits a wave which strikes the ionosphere, is reflected back to earth, and in a series of skips may travel a great distance before its energy is finally exhausted.

With respect to the utility of the different types of waves, in the lower frequencies (10 to 200 kc), ground waves predominate. These are capable of traveling long distances and their reception is comparatively stable and free from fading. To overcome atmospheric noises to which these frequencies are subject, however, greater power must be used, requiring high powered transmitting equipment and involving greater costs. Effective and profitable use of these frequencies is made to provide long distance point-to-point communication.

In the lower part of the next frequency range (200 to 2,000 kc), the ground waves continue to be important. Their attenuation, however, is more affected by the conductivity of the soil and irregularities of terrain over which they must travel and structures such as buildings, wire lines, etc., which lie in their pathway. These frequencies are useful for such services as aural broadcasting since they provide reasonably stable and moderately long distance transmission during both day and night. Like the frequencies in the 10 to 200 kc range, however, they must have substantial transmitting power to override atmospheric noises and be most effective.

Toward the top of the 200 to 2,000 kc range, relatively short distance ground-wave service is possible, especially over paths with poor conductivity. At these upper levels, skywaves become more important. While they are subject to the changes in the ionosphere, they are useful for long distance communication at night.

From 2 to 30 megacycles, skywaves become predominate. At night time when ionospheric conditions are favorable, long distance communication within this range can be achieved with relatively low transmitting power.

Frequencies above 30 mc are seldom reflected back to earth by the ionosphere. Useful propagation in this upper frequency range is achieved, however, with waves which travel directly from transmitting to receiving antennas and those which are reflected from the surface of the ground. Generally, the strength of the direct waves within line of sight is inversely proportional to the distance from the transmitter. Their effective use is for the most part limited to line-of-sight distance, and the height of the transmitting and receiving antennas are the principal factors which determine range of reception.[9]

Radio Service Classifications. In 1927, when the Federal Radio Commission was established, there was comparatively little knowledge regarding the propagation characteristics of the different bands of frequencies. The result was that many of the early assignments did not prove to be the most economical and efficient. As the years passed, however, the FRC and its successor the FCC, and the radio industry, through research and experimentation, acquired a better understanding of frequency behavior and, accordingly, the FCC has been able to parcel out the radio spectrum for more effective utilization.

The Commission has established three broad classifications of radio services: (1) Common Carrier, (2) Safety and Special Services, and (3) Broadcast. Common carrier services include wire and wireless facilities available to the general public for private messages, both domestic and international. In 1958, the long lines telephone system in the country had expanded to 32 billion circuit miles. Of this number, more than a third involved radio transmission including radio links, TV microwave relays, ship-to-shore telephony, etc.[10]

In 1959, there were more than 507,000 safety and special service stations authorized, employing more than 1.7 million transmitters, and providing a wide variety of services. As heretofore pointed out, radio is being used by ships, aircraft, trains, buses, trucks, and taxicabs. In industry it aids in the delivery of many products such as petroleum and electric power. Public agencies depend upon radio for police and fire protection, highway maintenance, and forestry conservation. It also plays an important role in defense, disaster and other emergency programs. The Commission has authorized its special use by amateurs and other individuals.[11]

As of the end of the fiscal year 1959, the Commission reported the chief categories under the broad classification of Safety and Special Services together with the number of authorizations and transmitters to be as follows:[12]

Class	Authorizations	Transmitters
Marine	84,947	93,649
Aviation	77,682	123,071
Land Transportation	59,894	442,471
Industrial	49,697	534,953
Public Safety	29,363	329,208
Amateur	195,776	195,776

The Broadcast Services, as classified by the Commission, include standard broadcasting (AM), frequency modulation (FM), non-commercial educational FM, television, and international. Added to these are the experimental, auxiliary and special broadcast services. As of August 10, 1960, 3,581 AM broadcast stations had been authorized and there were 8431 applications pending action of the Commission.[13] In the commercial FM category, there were 912 stations authorized with 142 applications not yet acted on.[14] On July 1, 1959 there were 165 educational FM stations on the air and two applications being processed by the Commission.[15]

As of August 10, 1960, 653 commercial TV stations had been authorized. Of this number, 533 stations (453 VHF and 80 UHF) were on the air and there were 115 applications pending. As of the same date, there were 47 educational TV stations on the air (35 VHF and 12 UHF).[16]

On July 23, 1958, the Commission authorized the first new international broadcast station since World War II. It is located at Belmont, California and its programs are beamed to Latin America. One other international broadcast station has been licensed by the FCC at Scituate, Massachusetts. All other international broadcast stations in this country are governmentally owned and operated by the United States Information Agency.[17]

Types of Radio Stations and Their Frequency Assignments. Part 2 of the FCC Rules and Regulations defines the exact nature and limits of each type of radio service and station.[18] Included in this part of the rules is a table of frequency allocations which has been adopted by the Commission, specifying the particular frequency bands to be used by each of these types of services and stations.[19]

Frequencies between 10 and 535 kilocycles are assigned largely to radio-telegraph stations and radio beacons used by ships and aircraft. The frequencies between 535 kc and 1605 kc are set aside for standard (AM) broadcast stations. Above this familiar AM band and extending to 25 megacycles are portions of the radio spectrum assigned to long distance radio telegraph and telephone communication, to ships at sea, planes in the air and international broadcasting.

In the region between 25 and 890 megacycles are the channel allocations for a variety of services including public safety, citizens radio, land transportation, industrial, etc. Also, FM and TV broadcasting occupy portions of this spectrum range. FM stations operate on channels between 88 and 108 megacycles. VHF television stations, receivable on standard sets, use specified frequencies within the 54 to 216 megacycle range. UHF TV stations are confined to the portion of the spectrum between 470 and 890 megacycles.

Beyond 890 megacycles, extending as high as 30,000 megacycles, space has been assigned to radio navigation, common carrier and mobile services and many other specialized radio services. Beyond the 30,000 mc point, frequencies are assigned mainly for experimental purposes and for developmental work in connection with new and improved services and equipment.

It is not possible to spell out an exact spectrum chart, because assignments of some of the radio services are widely scattered in different parts of the spectrum. For example, as of August 5, 1959, the amateur service carried on by more than 179,000 "hams" (as they are popularly called), used the following widely distributed frequencies: 1800-2000 kc, 3500-4000 kc, 7000-7300 kc, 14,000-14,350 kc, 21,000-21,450 kc, 28 to 29.7 mc, 50-54 mc, 144-148 mc, 220-225 mc, 420-450 mc, 1215-1300 mc, 2300-2450 mc, 3500-3700 mc, 5650-5925 mc, 10,000 to 1,500 mc, 21,000 to 22,000 mc, and numerous bands above 30,000 mc. Similar scattering of assignments is to be found in various parts of the radio spectrum between 5950 kc and 26,100 kc for international broadcasting stations.

The Commission has provided in its rules that the assignment and use of frequencies for different types of radio service must be in accordance with the table of frequency allocations mentioned above. In individual cases the Commission may authorize, on a temporary basis only, the use of a frequency or frequencies not in accordance with the table, if no harmful interference will be caused to an existing service, and provided exceptional circumstances justify such irregular utilization.[20]

Planning for More Effective Utilization of the Radio Spectrum. Increasing demands for spectrum space have presented serious allocation problems in recent years. The government, including the rapidly expanding military establishment, industry, education and a multiplicity of other social and business segments of our society have been clamoring for additional space in the radio spectrum to meet new communication needs. Existing broadcast services, to which reference has just been made, suffer because of overcrowding conditions in the limited areas of the spectrum to which they are assigned.

The problem of reappraising frequency allocations for government, military and civilian uses and working out plans for a more effective utilization of frequencies in these different areas, has become a critical and perplexing one. It has engaged the serious attention of the White House, Congress, the FCC, the broadcasting industry and numerous other governmental and business groups making use of radio.

On June 8 and 9, 1959, the Communications Subcommittee of the House Interstate and Foreign Commerce Committee, listened to a panel of experts discuss frequency allocation problems. Representatives of the Office of Civilian and Defense Mobilization, the Federal Aviation Agency, Department of Defense, the FCC, and the broadcasting and telecommunications industries, participated in the conference. The Chairman of the President's Special Advisory Committee on Communications, and several other distinguished experts also were involved.[21]

A number of suggestions were made at this conference to help meet the allocations problem. One group recommended that a Federal Spectrum Authority be established. Such an authority would have jurisdiction over the entire radio spectrum and would be empowered to make a division of frequencies and settle conflicts between government and non-government users. As described by a leading trade journal, it would be the "spectrum czar and bring to an end the amorphous dual jurisdiction exercised by the President and the FCC, established in 1934 in the Communications Act."[22]

Another group at the meeting urged the creation of a governing body or single administrator to exercise jurisdiction over the government portion of the spectrum. Still others suggested the establishment of a Presidential commission to study the matter of allocations. Certain members of the broadcasting industry called for a complete Congressional investigation of the spectrum before any move is made toward establishing new agencies of management and control.

On July 28, 1959, pursuant to studies growing out of the June conference, Congressman Oren Harris, Chairman of the House Interstate and Foreign Commerce Committee, introduced a bill in the House to establish in the executive branch of the government an independent agency to be known as the Frequency Allocation Board, composed of three members appointed by the President and approved by the Senate. The functions of the Board as stated in the bill would be as follows:

(1) to conduct on a continuing basis a thorough and comprehensive study and investigation of, and to develop long-range plans for, the utilization of the radio spectrum, including (but without being limited to) the allocation of radio frequencies in the radio spectrum between, and the utilization of such radio frequencies by, federal government users and non-federal government users, in order to ascertain the effectiveness of the utilization of the radio spectrum by, and the division of the radio spectrum among, federal government users and non-federal government users in the light of the needs of the national security and international relations of, and economic, social, educational and political activities in the United States, and the general welfare of its people;

(2) from time to time on its own initiative, or on application of the Federal Communications Commission or the Government Frequency Administrator, subject to section 206 and to international agreements to which the United States is a party, to allocate radio frequencies for federal government use and non-federal government use, as the Board deems appropriate, and to modify or cancel any such allocation;

(3) to advise the President in connection with matters concerning the foreign relations of the United States insofar as such matters relate to the utilization and division of the radio spectrum.

(4) The Board shall maintain tables of radio frequency allocations for federal government use and non-federal government use and shall make such tables available for public inspection.[23]

The bill would establish a Government Frequency Administrator to act for the President in the allocation of government frequencies among military and other federal government users.

The President's power over the radio spectrum in times of war and national emergency and the FCC's authority over frequency assignments for civilian uses would not be disturbed.

In its August 3, 1959 issue, *Broadcasting* magazine made the following editorial comment regarding the bill:

First tangible recognition of the need for complete overhauling of management of the critically important radio spectrum allocations as between government and non-government users is given in a bill (HR 8426) quietly introduced in the House last week. It would create a three-man Frequency Allocation Board —a sort of super-FCC but with power far broader than that vested in the FCC or perhaps in any other independent agency. Because of the bill's significance and scope, it must be assumed that its author, Chairman Oren Harris (D-Ark.) of the House Commerce Committee, does not expect passage at this session, now within weeks of adjournment. Rather, it looks to us like a trial balloon for study by interested groups during the Congressional recess.

There can be no doubt about the sincerity of Mr. Harris' intentions. He wants efficient management of the spectrum, to prevent hoarding of valuable frequencies by government but, at the same time, to protect the national security. Because broadcasters have a life-and-death stake in the sensitive allocation areas, particularly the vhf range in which tv and fm are assigned, extreme care and diligence must be exercised in appraising the new bill.

Is too much power given to three men? Should provision be made for appeal from board rulings? Should usual administrative procedures be followed in the functioning of the board or of the Government Frequency Administrator who would function under the President? Is the FCC unduly stripped of allocation functions?

These are just a few of the questions that crop up in a casual reading of the Harris Bill. It is for these reasons that all entities in broadcasting, who are responsible for direct service to the public, must give priority to analysis and interpretation of the Harris Bill.[24]

Whether the bill becomes law or not, it represents a constructive attempt to provide for a more effective use of radio frequencies of which there is a growing scarcity. Experts and authorities in the radio field are agreed that the present situation is chaotic and wasteful and there is little doubt that some action will be taken in the near future to correct it. The growing importance of radio services to the well-being of our national life makes conservation measures imperative.

NOTES

1. Filgate, John Thomas, *Theory of Radio Communication,* (Brooklyn, N.Y., 1929), p. 2.
2. Morecroft, John H., *Elements of Radio Communication* (New York, 2nd edition, 1934).
3. *Ibid.,* pp. 203-229.
4. *Ibid.,* pp. 97-102.
5. *Ibid.,* p. 98.
6. *Ibid.,* 111-112; Also see Warner, Harry, *Radio and Television Law* (New York, 1953), 225-227.
7. See Head, Sydney, *Broadcasting in America* (Boston, 1956), pp. 8-12 for an informative discussion on this subject.
8. International Telecommunications Union, Final Acts of the International

Telecommunication and Radio Conferences (Atlantic City, ITU, 1947), Radio Regulations, Chapter II, Article 2, Section II.

9. Much of the foregoing discussion of the propagation characteristics of different frequencies is based upon the excellent study of the Joint Technical Advisory Committee of the Institute of Radio Engineers, Radio-Television Manufacturers Association, *Radio Spectrum Conservation* (New York, 1952).

10. FCC, *24th Annual Report* (1958), p. 2.

11. FCC, *Silver Anniversary Report,* pp. 102-104.

12. *Ibid.*

13. *Broadcasting,* August 15, 1960, p. 102.

14. *Ibid.*

15. FCC, *Silver Anniversary Report,* p. 74.

16. *Broadcasting, op. cit.*

17. FCC, *24th Annual Report (1958)*, p. 118.

18. 23 Fed. Reg. 10437 (1958); also see 1 RR 52:21-153. Copies of these rules also may be secured at nominal cost from the Government Printing Office, Washington, D.C.

19. 23 Fed. Reg. 10440-63 (1958); also see 1 RR 52:45-58.

20. FCC Rules and Regulations, Section 2.103, 23 Fed. Reg. 10440 (1958); 1 RR 52:41.

21. *Broadcasting,* June 15, 1959, pp. 60-62.

22. *Ibid.,* p. 60.

23. 89th Congress (1st Session) H.R. 8426, July 28, 1959, referred to the Committee on Interstate and Foreign Commerce.

24. *Broadcasting,* August 3, 1959, p. 104.

CHAPTER 7

Standard Broadcast Stations (AM)

I believe we have a reasonably competitive system in AM. Some would say too much competition, but I think such persons would be reluctant to accept any alternatives there may be for the competitive system.—ROSEL H. HYDE*

As mentioned in the preceding chapter, standard broadcast or amplitude modulation (AM) stations, as they are called, operate on channels in the band of frequencies, 535-1605 kilocycles.[1] This space is only about one thirty-thousandth of the entire radio spectrum now in use. The many broadcast stations that operate in this small space are licensed to transmit programs primarily intended to reach the general public as distinguished from point-to-point communication.[2]

Within this "standard broadcast band" there are 107 channels, each channel having a 10 kc spread.[3] The frequency at the center of the channel is known as the carrier frequency and is the one on which the station operates. For example, if a station operates on an assigned frequency of 600 kc, its channel or band of frequencies is from 595 to 605 kc, and the channel is designated by the assigned carrier frequency. Beginning at 535 kc and continuing in successive steps of 10 to 1605 kc, there are 107 carrier frequencies assigned and used by standard broadcast stations.[4]

Types of AM Service Areas and Channels. These standard broadcast stations use both ground and sky waves. The area surrounding such a station, receiving a ground wave or signal strong enough to overcome ordinary interference and not subject to objectionable fading, is called the *Primary Service* area. As indicated in the previous chapter, primary coverage of a station depends upon numerous factors including the power of the station, the particular frequency, the character of the soil and topography over which the ground wave must travel, the extent of man-made noise in the area, certain atmospheric conditions, etc. For example, a station operating with 1 kw power in Texas on 550 kc frequency would provide primary service to a substantially larger area than a station operating on the same frequency in New Hampshire. The reason is that the low

* Member of the FCC.

flat sandy terrain of the Lone Star state is more conducive to electromagnetic wave transmission than is the hilly and rocky terrain of New England.

Roughly and empirically estimated, stations with different powers provide good, reliable ground wave service the following average distances:[5]

Power	Average Radius Miles
100 watts	30
250 watts	41
1 kw	63
5 kw	93
10 kw	115
50 kw	160

These values are averages only and cannot be used to calculate the precise coverage of any particular station. These coverage figures are no doubt too high for some stations, especially the low-powered stations.[6]

Beyond the primary service area lies the *intermittent* service area, served by the groundwave but subject to some interference and fading.

The *secondary service* area is that receiving skywaves which are not subject to objectionable interference but which do not always provide the best reception because of variations in intensity.[7] The range of these secondary service areas may vary from less than one hundred miles to a thousand miles or more. The service, however, in these extended areas, for the reason suggested, is not consistently dependable.

Ionospheric absorption of skywaves during daylight hours prevent their effective use for daylight broadcasting, and from sun-up to sun-set AM stations are dependent entirely upon groundwave propagation. After dark, however, as heretofore pointed out, the skywaves are reflected back to earth by the ionosphere and with reasonably good transmitting power and with no interference from other stations, they make possible at night a wider coverage area often reaching far beyond the groundwave contours. It should be pointed out that these skywaves at night, while providing extended service, may introduce complications which reduce the groundwave coverage.

In 1939, after extensive public hearings, the FCC adopted revised rules governing these AM stations.[8] Previously, the Commission had established three categories of channels for these stations: clear, regional and local. The revised rules retained these categories but in addition prescribed four general classes of stations.[9]

As defined in the FCC Rules, a *clear channel* is one on which stations operate with wide coverage. Their primary service areas and a substantial part of their secondary ones are protected from objectionable interference from other stations.[10]

A *regional channel* is one on which several stations may operate with no more than 5 kilowatts power and whose primary service area may be limited to a certain field intensity contour by interference from other stations operating on the same channel.[11]

The *local channel* is one assigned for the use of stations serving small areas whose power cannot exceed 250 watts and whose primary service areas may be restricted by the operation of other stations on the same channel.[12]

Classes of AM Stations and Frequency Assignments. As described in the FCC Rules, a *Class I station* is a dominant one operating on a clear channel with not less than 10 and not more than 50 kilowatts power, and designed to achieve relatively wide coverage. Its primary service area is free from all objectionable interference. Its secondary area is protected except that it may be subject to some interference from distant stations on the same channel or from those operating on adjacent channels.[13]

The Class I stations are subdivided into I-A and I-B groups. Those classified as I-A operate with no less than 50 kw power and no other stations are permitted to operate at night on the same frequencies.[14] During daytime, only Class II stations (described below) are permitted to share the frequencies. During daytime, these 1-A stations are protected to their 100 microvolts per meter (uv/m) groundwave contours from interference by stations on the same channels, and both day and night are protected to their 500 microvolts per meter (uv/m) groundwave contours from stations on adjacent channels.[15]

Of the 46 frequencies assigned as U.S. Clear Channels, 23 are occupied by 1-B stations.[16] The 1-B group operate with power not less than 10 or more than 50 kw and the channels they occupy[17] may also be assigned to other Class I or Class II stations operating unlimited time.[18] During night time hours, a I-B station is protected to its 500 uv/m 50 per cent skywave contour and during the day to its 100 uv/m groundwave contour from stations operating on the same channel. It is protected both day and night from stations on adjacent channels to its 500 uv/m groundwave contour.[19]

The Class II station is a secondary one on a clear channel with its primary service area limited by and subject to interference as may be received by Class I stations.[20] This type of operation is restricted to power not less than 250 watts nor more than 50 kilowatts.[21] When necessary, a Class II station must use a directional antenna or other means to avoid causing interference within the normally protected service areas of Class I or other Class II stations.[22]

These Class II stations normally provide primary service only, the extent of the coverage depending upon location, power and frequency of the station. It is recommended by the Commission that they be so located that the interference received from other stations will not limit their service areas to greater than the 2500 uv/m groundwave contour at night and 500 uv/m groundwave contour daytime.[23]

The following frequencies are assigned to Class II stations which do not deliver over 5 microvolts per meter groundwave or over 25 microvolts per meter 10 per cent time skywave at any point on the Canadian border, and for night-time operation are located not less than 650 miles from the nearest point on the border: 540, 690, 740, 860, 990, 1010 and 1580 kilocycles.[24]

In the continental United States, Class II stations operating daytime only with power not exceeding 1 kw and which do not deliver over 5 microvolts per meter groundwave at any point on the Mexican border, and those in Alaska, Hawaii, Puerto Rico, and the Virgin Islands which do not deliver over 5 microvolts per meter groundwave or over 25 microvolts per meter 10 per cent time skywave at any point on that border, use the frequencies 730, 800, 900, 1050, 1220 and 1570 kilocycles.[25]

The Class III stations operate on regional channels and are designed to provide service primarily to metropolitan districts and contiguous rural areas.[26] These stations are divided into A and B groups. The III-A stations operate with power not less than one or more than five kilowatts and are normally protected to their 2500 uv/m groundwave contours at night and their 500 uv/m groundwave contours daytime. Class III-B stations operate with power not less than 0.5 kw, or more than 1 kw nighttime and 5 kw daytime. Their service areas are normally protected to the 4000 uv/m contour at night and to the 500 uv/m contour during daytime.[27]

The Class III-A and III-B stations are assigned to the following frequencies designated as regional channels: 550, 560, 570, 580, 590, 600, 610, 620, 630, 790, 910, 920, 930, 950, 960, 970, 980, 1150, 1250, 1260, 1270, 1280, 1290, 1300, 1310, 1320, 1330, 1350, 1360, 1370, 1380, 1390, 1410, 1420, 1430, 1440, 1460, 1470, 1480, 1590 and 1600 kc.[28]

A Class IV station is one which operates on a local channel and is designated to render service primarily to a city or town and the suburban and rural areas contiguous to it.[29] The power of such a station may not be less than 100 watts nor more than 250 watts at night and 1 kw daytime.[30] The FCC Rules provide that it shall be protected to its 0.5 mv/m contour.[31] The following frequencies have been designated by the Commission as local channels and are assigned for use by Class IV stations: 1230, 1240, 1340, 1400, 1450 and 1490 kc.[32]

Previously, the Commission permitted the assignment of Class IV stations to regional channels under certain conditions. A revision of Section 3.29 of the Commission's Rules covering Radio Broadcast Services prohibited this, except that stations which had already been authorized at the time the rule was revised were not required to change their frequencies or power. Such stations, however, are afforded no protection against interference from Class III stations.[33]

Increase of Power for Local Stations Authorized. On May 28, 1958, the Commission adopted an order amending its rules to permit Class IV stations to increase their daytime power to 500 watts and, under certain conditions, to increase their power to 1 kw. It was set forth in the order, however, that increase in nighttime power for these stations would not be allowed, nor could directional antennas be used to reduce presently required separations between these Class IV stations.[34]

The Commission announced that applications for increase in power would be processed on a case-by-case basis except for two geographical locations. Stations requesting boosts in power cannot be located within an area 62 miles or less from the U.S.-Mexican border or in an area covering approximately the southern half of Florida, south of 28 degrees north latitude and 80-82 degrees west longitude in deference to agreements with other North American countries. Prior to the adoption of the May 28, 1958 order, the Community Broadcasters Association, Inc. had filed a petition with the Commission requesting a mandatory power increase for all Class IV stations or, in the alternative, blanket permission to increase power. The Commission denied this request, however, stating that it would decide each application on its merits.[35]

There are approximately 1,000 Class IV stations on the air and this amendment to the Rules will make possible considerable expansion in their service areas.

Of the 107 standard broadcast channels, 60 have been designated as clear channels and are assigned for use by Class I and Class II stations. Forty-six of these are used by the United States and the remainder are distributed among other nations of North America in accordance with the North American Regional Broadcast Agreement. Forty-one additional channels are designated as regional and are assigned for use by Class III-A and III-B stations. Six others are local channels on which Class IV stations operate.

The Clear Channel Controversy. Efforts of smaller stations to secure additional power and the almost wild scramble for spectrum space by many eager and enterprising have-nots in our society—all this is tied in with the long struggle to break up the clear channels and provide more frequencies for new stations in areas not now receiving adequate radio service.

In February, 1945, the Commission instituted a public hearing to explore the problems and consider proposals for improving the situation. For forty days the Commission listened to testimony on a number of issues. Evidence was received on such questions as (1) whether the number of clear channels should be increased or decreased; (2) what minimum and maximum power should be authorized for clear channel stations; (3) whether and to what extent power above 50 kw for such stations would affect the economic ability of other stations to operate in the public interest; (4) whether the present geographical distribution of clear channel stations and the areas they serve represent an optimum distribution of radio service throughout the country; (5) whether it is economically feasible to relocate clear channel stations so as to serve those areas which do not presently receive service; (6) what new rules, if any, should be promulgated to govern the power or hours of operation of Class II stations operating on clear channels; (7) what changes should be made with respect to geographical location, frequency, authorized power or hours of operation of any presently licensed clear channel station; (8) whether the clear channel stations render a program service particularly suited to rural needs; and (9) the extent to which service areas of clear channel stations overlap.[36]

Parties in that proceeding advocated numerous and diverse approaches to the problem of achieving more efficient use of the clear channels and of improving the deficiencies in the present service available to the public on these channels. Proposals for revising the clear channel allocations ranged all the way from exclusive nighttime use of selected clear channels by a single station operating at substantially higher powers than the present maximum of 50 kw, to the reclassification of selected clear channels as "local channels" on which it would be possible to assign over a hundred and fifty stations operating at maximum powers of 250 watts. Between these extremes a wide variety of proposals were submitted.[37]

As the Commission has pointed out, the record in the case "reflected two basically divergent views concerning the measures best calculated to improve the efficient use of the clear channel frequencies. Some parties urged that the chief goal should be to improve the capacity of the major clear channel stations (particularly the Class I-A stations) to provide a satisfactory signal to wide areas, and that this should be achieved by substantially increasing their power and by limiting (and, during the nighttime hours, excluding) co-channel stations. Other parties contended that the most desirable objective would be to increase the number of unlimited time stations on the clear channels and to reduce the degree of protection now afforded the latter throughout wide service areas."[38]

In June, 1946, the Commission announced the adoption of the policy of dismissing applications for station assignments or modifications of station assignments which were not permissible under the existing rules pending a resolution of the clear channel case.[39]

In May, 1947, a separate proceeding was initiated (FCC Docket 8333) to determine whether and the extent to which limitations should be imposed on daytime skywave radiation toward Class I-A and I-B stations operating on clear channels.[40]

In December, 1947, the two proceedings were consolidated and on January 19, 20, and 21, 1948, the Commission heard oral arguments on both matters.[41]

The proceedings, however, were again separated by the Commission in 1953, and in November, 1956, the Clear Channel Broadcasting Service filed a petition to reopen the record in the Clear Channel case, and again consolidate it with the daytime skywave case and afford opportunity to bring the records up to date. In response to this, the Daytime Broadcasters' Association promptly filed a petition requesting that the clear channel proceeding be dismissed, that the freeze on clear channel assignments be lifted, and that the Commission institute rule making on the Association's earlier request that daytime stations be authorized to operate additional hours.[42]

On September 17, 1957, as is more fully discussed later in this chapter, the FCC granted the request of the daytime broadcasters to consider the proposal to increase the hours for operation of their stations, but denied their request to dismiss the clear channel proceeding and remove the freeze on the processing of applications for Class II stations on the clear channel frequencies.[43]

On April 15, 1958, the Commission reopened the record in the clear channel case, stating that "it would be inappropriate, and inconsistent with sound and fair procedure, to attempt to arrive at final conclusions solely on the basis of the out-dated record before us."[44] At the same time, the Commission proposed to eliminate the exclusive nighttime use of Class I-A clear channels in New York, Chicago, Philadelphia, Pittsburgh, Rochester, Cleveland, Detroit, and St. Louis. The Commission also proposed to assign additional Class I stations to 12 western cities located in less well-served areas and to consider the possible assignment of Class II stations on those channels to other parts of the country that do not now have any primary groundwave service.[45]

In July, 1959, the Commission announced that it had instructed its staff to draw up a new proposal for rulemaking which, if adopted, would permit the assignment of some unlimited time Class II stations on Class I-A channels. These Class II stations, the Commission stated, would be not less than 10 kw in power, and their locations would be determined on the basis of need in areas without primary radio service.[46] Subsequently, the Commission did issue a proposal for rulemaking which would authorize new Class II stations on clear channels in the western part of the country where local broadcast facilities are limited.[47]

It is expected that this new proposal will be vigorously contested by the clear channel stations and other interested parties. It is not likely that a final decision in the matter will be made within the immediate future.

Should the Commission ultimately adopt the proposal, it has been reported by *Broadcasting Magazine* (July 27, 1959, p. 60) that estimates indicate that from 72 to 144 new Class II stations could be established in various sections of the country where there is comparatively little local radio service now available.

Field Intensity Requirements for AM Service Areas. As specified by the Commission, the field intensities of radio signals necessary to render primary service to different types of reception areas are as follows:

93

	Field Intensity Groundwave
Area	
City business or factory areas	10 to 50 mv/m
City residential areas	2 to 10 mv/m
Rural—all areas during winter or Northern areas during the summer	0.1 to 0.5 mv/m
Rural—southern areas during summer	0.25 to 1.0 mv/m

As Section 3.182(f) of the FCC Rules provides, all these values are based on an absence of objectionable fading, the usual noise level in the areas, and an absence of limiting interference from other broadcast stations. The values apply both day and night, but generally, fading or interference from other stations limits the primary service at night in all rural areas to higher values of field intensity than those recited.[48]

In determining the population of the primary service area, the following signal intensities are considered adequate to overcome man-made noise in towns of the population specified:

Population	*Field Intensity Groundwave*
Up to 2,500	0.5 mv/m
2,500 to 10,000	2.0 mv/m
10,000 and up	Values same as those listed in paragraph above for different types of cities.

The Commission has pointed out that these values are subject to wide variations in individual areas and especial attention must be given to interference from other stations. These specific values are not considered satisfactory in any case for service to the city in which the main studio of the station is located.[49]

Secondary service is delivered in the areas where the skywave for 50 per cent or more of the time has a field intensity of 500 uv/m or greater. To provide satisfactory secondary service in cities, it is considered necessary that the skywave signal approach the value of the groundwave required for primary service. But the secondary service is necessarily subject to some interference and extensive fading whereas the primary service area is not. Class I stations only are assigned on the basis of providing secondary service.[50]

The intermittent service is rendered by the groundwave and begins at the outer boundary of the primary service area and extends to the point where the signal has no further service value. This point may be where the signal has an intensity as low as only a few microvolts in some areas and as high as several millivolts in others, depending on noise level, interference from other stations, or objectionable fading at night. Only Class I stations are assigned so that their intermittent service areas are protected from interference from other stations.[51]

Time Classifications for Stations.   Each broadcasting station is authorized to operate in accordance with specified time classifications. These classifications are:

Unlimited time
Limited time
Daytime
Share-time
Specified hours

Unlimited Time stations operate without any restrictive time limits. Those authorized on a *limited time* basis are the Class II stations (secondary) which operate on clear channels only. They are permitted to operate during the day and until local sunset if located west of the dominant station on the clear channel. If located east thereof, they must close down when the sun sets at the dominant station. They may also operate during the night hours when the dominant station is off the air.[52]

Daytime stations operate during the hours between average monthly local sunrise and average local sunset. The opening and closing hours of operation for such stations are specified in their licenses. For example, a Class II daytime station operating on 1570 kc in the east central part of Illinois has the following sign-on and sign-off schedule:

January	7:15 A. M.	to 5:00 P. M.
February	6:45 A. M.	to 5:30 P. M.
March	6:00 A. M.	to 6:00 P. M.
April	5:15 A. M.	to 6:30 P. M.
May	4:45 A. M.	to 7:00 P. M.
June	4:30 A. M.	to 7:15 P. M.
July	4:30 A. M.	to 7:15 P. M.
August	5:00 A. M.	to 6:45 P. M.
September	5:30 A. M.	to 6:00 P. M.
October	6:00 A. M.	to 5:15 P. M.
November	6:30 A. M.	to 4:45 P. M.
December	7:00 A. M.	to 4:30 P. M.

Recently, the Commission amended its rules to permit daytime stations to sign off at 6:00 P.M. during months when local sunset is later than 6:00 P.M. (see Report No. 13-28, Pike and Fischer RR, July 27, 1960.)

As already indicated, the limitation and irregularity of these hours have been matters of grave concern to many daytime broadcasters. Reference has already been made to the petition filed by the Daytime Broadcasters Association, Inc. requesting that all daytime stations be authorized to operate from 5:00 A.M. or local sunrise (whichever would be earlier) to

95

7:00 P.M. or local sunset (whichever would be later) in lieu of the sunrise to sunset hours prescribed in the present rules.

In its petition, DBA asserted that there is a large unsatisfied need for local service during pre-sunrise and post-sunset hours. It was pointed out that in the United States over 900 communities, with a total population of more than 7,500,000, have available to them no locally licensed radio outlet other than daytime-only stations. It was argued by DBA that extended hours are necessary for daytime stations, notwithstanding the resulting interference to existing radio broadcast services, in order that the needs of these communities and surrounding areas for broadcast service may be more fully met.[53]

On September 19, 1958, the Commission denied this petition.[54] On October 20, 1958, DBA asked the Commission to reconsider its decision or, in the alternative, permit all daytime stations to operate from 6:00 A.M. or local sunrise (whichever is earlier) to 6:00 P.M. or local sunset (whichever is later). On January 7, 1959, the Commission refused to reconsider its decision regarding the "5 to 7" request and dismissed the DBA alternative request for "6 to 6" operation. At the same time, the Commission stated that it was not apprised of sufficient facts concerning the changes envisaged in the standard broadcast structure to render a decision upon the merits of the alternative request. Accordingly, the Commission instituted a formal inquiry to elicit further information.[55]

After receiving comments from interested parties and studying the record in the proceeding, on July 8, 1959, the Commission denied the "6 to 6" request. The reasons for the denial are succinctly set forth in paragraph 19 of the decision:

Upon careful review of the comments which have been filed, and a review of our decision in Docket No. 12274, we conclude that the losses of standard broadcast radio service, both groundwave and skywave in the various areas affected, which would result from an extension of the hours of operation of stations licensed for daytime operation must be determinative herein. We are unable to find an expression of any local need which is impossible of substantial fulfillment under existing rules for station licensing and which is so great or so pressing as to warrant widespread disruption of the existing radio service now enjoyed thereunder and relied upon daily by millions of citizens. Particularly, would it be undesirable and unwarranted to permit such disruption in those instances where the result as shown by the data would simply be the taking of regular service from rural farm areas and from small urban communities, which need radio vitally, and giving more stations—serving less area—to city and principal urban areas which are already relatively well supplied not only with standard broadcast radio programs but with other facilities for relaxation, intellectual stimulus, information and recreation. Moreover, this conclusion is strongly reinforced by a comparison of the 1,761,622 persons in 357 communities, now receiving only skywave service, who would gain in lieu thereof a local groundwave service, with the 25,631,000 persons in 1,727,000 square miles, now receiving skywave service, who would lose entirely the standard broadcast radio service now available to them.[56]

Share-time stations are restricted in their operation in accordance with a specified division of time with one or more stations using the same channel.[57]

Some stations are authorized to operate *specific* hours as stated in their licenses. (The minimum operating schedule for this type of station as well as all other standard broadcast stations is prescribed in Section 3.71 of the FCC Rules).[58]

NOTES

1. FCC Rules and Regulations, Part 3, Section 3.1, 1 RR 53:101.
2. *Ibid.*
3. *Ibid.,* Section 3.3, 1 RR 53:102.
4. *Ibid.*
5. *Fifth Annual Report of Federal Radio Commission* (1931), 30-31.
6. See Warner, Harry P., *Radio and Television Law* (New York, 1953), p. 233-34.
7. Section 3.11, 1 RR 53:103.
8. 4 Fed. Reg. 2714 (1939).
9. Section 3.22, 1 RR 53:131.
10. Section 3.21 (a), 1 RR 53:131.
11. *Ibid.,* Section 3.21(b).
12. *Ibid.,* Section 3.21(c). The FCC rules provide that there may also be assigned to these frequencies Class II stations operating unlimited time in Alaska, Hawaii, Virgin Islands and Puerto Rico. These stations are not permitted, however, to deliver over 5 microvolts per meter ground wave day or night or over 25 microvolts per meter 10 per cent time skywave at night at any point within the continental limits of the United States. See Section 3.25(a), FCC Rules, 1 RR 53:151.
13. *Ibid.,* Section 3.22(a), 1 RR 53:131.
14. Section 3.182(a) (1) (i), 1 RR 53:272. At this writing, these 1-A channels are: 640, 650, 660, 670, 700, 720, 750, 760, 780, 820, 830, 840, 870, 880, 890, 1020, 1040, 1100, 1120, 1160, 1180, 1200, and 1210 KC. See Section 3.25(a) of FCC Rules.
15. *Ibid.*
16. These 23 channels are: 680, 710, 810, 850, 940, 1000, 1030, 1060, 1070, 1080, 1090, 1110, 1130, 1140, 1170, 1500, 1510, 1520, 1530, 1540, 1550, and 1560 KC. See Sections 3.25(b) of the FCC Rules.
17. Section 3.182(a) (1) ii. 1 RR 53:272.
18. *Ibid.*
19. *Ibid.* A note under Section 3.25 (b) of the FCC Rules states that Class I and II stations are prohibited from delivering over 5 microvolts per meter groundwave or 25 microvolts per meter 10 per cent time skywave at any point of land in the Bahama Islands, and such stations operating at night shall be located not less than 650 miles from the nearest point of land in these islands.
20. Section 3.22(b), 1 RR 53:132.
21. *Ibid.*

22. *Ibid.*
23. Section 3.182(a) (2), 1 RR 53:272.
24. Section 3.25(c), 1 RR 53:151.
25. Section 3.25(d), 1 RR 53:151.
26. Section 3.22(c), 1 RR 53:132.
27. *Ibid.* Also, Section 3.182(a) (3) (i), 1 RR 53:273
28. Section 3.26, 1 RR 53:152.
29. Section 3.22(d), 1 RR 53:132.
30. *Ibid.*
31. Section 3.182(a) (4), 1 RR 53:273.
32. Section 3.27, 1 RR 53:153.
33. Section 3.29, 1 RR 53:155.
34. FCC Docket No. 12064, 17 RR 1541.
35. See *Broadcasting*, April 13, 1959, p. 54; also see Decision of the Commission denying petition for reconsideration and making its order final. 17 RR 1548a.
36. See *In the Matter of Clear Channel Broadcasting in the Standard Broadcast Band;* FCC Docket 6741, 1 RR 53:lix, p. 53:liii. The chronology of the Clear Channel case is recited succinctly here.
37. *Ibid.*, 23 Fed. Reg. 2612 (1958); 1 RR 53:xlix.
38. *Ibid.*
39. *Ibid.*
40. *Ibid.*
41. *Ibid.*
42. *Ibid.*, p. 53:1v.
43. *Ibid.*
44. *Ibid.*, p. 53:1.
45. *Ibid.*, pp. 53:1x5iii, 1xix, and 1xx.
46. *Broadcasting*, July 27, 1959, p. 60.
47. FCC Docket No. 6741, 24 Fed. Reg. 7739 (1959).
48. Section 3.182(f), 1 RR 53:274-275.
49. Section 3.182(g), 1 RR 53:275.
50. Section 3.182(i), 1 RR 53:275-276.
51. Section 3.182(j), 1 RR 276.
52. Sections 3.23(a) and 3.23(b), 1 RR 132.
53. In the Matter of Inquiry into the Advisability of Authorizing Standard Broadcast Stations to Operate with Facilities Licensed for Daytime Operation from 6:00 A.M. or Local Sunrise (whichever is earlier) to 6:00 P.M. or Local Sunset (whichever is later) FCC Docket No. 12729, 1 RR 53:xix at 53:xxiii and 53:xxiv.
54. *Ibid.*
55. *Ibid.*
56. 18 RR 1689, 1697.
57. Section 3.23(d), 1 RR 132.
58. See Chapter 17, p. 358, for statement of this minimum operating schedule.

CHAPTER 8

Frequency Modulation Broadcasting (FM)

First to make use of the 3-electrode tube for generating continuous electric waves which made radio broadcasting feasible, inventor of the long and widely used superheterodyne receiving circuit, and inventor of the new broadcasting by frequency modulation that so well avoids static as almost to defy the lightning. He is one of the leaders in accomplishing the miracle of radio communication, a reality so inconceivably novel that the imagination of no poet, no author of tales or fables, had ever anticipated.— Citation of the National Association of Manufacturers in selecting Edwin Armstrong as one of the National Modern Pioneers in 1940.

Prior to Pearl Harbor, great technological advances in the techniques of broadcasting had been made, but the remarkable developments which came out of the ensuing war surpassed any which had taken place before. Dazzling before a weary and war-ridden world were the brilliant prospects of a new electronics era destined to revolutionize life on this planet and to provide a valuable tool for exploration of outer space.

Advantages of FM. Frequency Modulation or FM, a new radio technique developed during the 1930's by Major Edwin F. Armstrong, had demonstrated its superior utility in military operations and was on the verge of a vast expansion in broadcasting.[1] Engineers had discovered and demonstrated that FM had several major advantages over Amplitude Modulation (AM) used in standard broadcasting.

First, it was discovered that FM was not affected nearly so much by static. Because atmospheric and electrical noises consist primarily of amplitude variations, they often got into the standard radio sets and ruined reception. FM, on the other hand, had an inherent advantage in avoiding these noises. Even though a storm might be raging, attended by frequent bursts of thunder and flashes of lightning, or though an electric train might be roaring past the door, radio reception would remain clear.

Another advantage was its ability to reproduce the entire tonal range from the deepest base to the highest overtones. Many music lovers found it more pleasurable to listen to symphony orchestras via FM because the varied tones produced by the different instruments in the studio came through with balance and clarity.

99

Also, FM made possible the operation of stations much closer together on the same channel without objectionable interference. This meant that many more towns and cities might have their own radio stations.[2]

Prior to the Second War, the FCC had held public hearings to explore the possibilities of FM broadcasting.[3] And on May 22, 1940, the Commission allocated 35 channels to the FM service in the 43-50 megacycle band. Five months later, there were fifteen stations in the country authorized to engage in FM broadcasting.[4] By the time of the World War II freeze on civilian construction which was imposed in 1941, the number had increased to about thirty.[5]

Post War Growth. It was not until after the War, however, that the enormous potential for FM broadcasting became generally recognized. Its superior advantages having been demonstrated in war maneuvers, there developed a wave of enthusiasm for its peace time use. Responding to this enthusiasm, the Commission conducted a series of allocation hearings, and on June 27, 1945, allocated the 88 to 108 mc band as the "permanent home" of FM. Of the 100 channels made available, the first twenty were assigned to non-commercial operation for educational groups and institutions.[6]

By July 1, only three days after the allocations were made, there were more than 400 applications for new FM stations on file with the FCC and the Commission had received hundreds of requests for information and application forms.[7]

But FM did not attain quickly the large measure of success envisioned by its enthusiasts. The expansion of standard broadcasting after the war and the flooding of the market with low-priced AM receiving sets and with comparatively few FM receivers available—all combined to make it difficult for FM stations. Many were compelled to leave the air for lack of audience and advertising revenue.

In 1949, just four years after the FM allocations were made, there were more than 700 commercial FM stations in operation. By 1956, this number had dropped to 530 and a large number of these were duplicating AM services.[8] Since that time there has been an increase and at this writing a new wave of enthusiasm for FM is sweeping the country.

As pointed out in the previous chapter, on June 30, 1958, 634 commercial FM stations had been authorized and 57 applications for new stations were pending. The following figures show the pattern of decline and growth of commercial FM from 1949 to 1958:[9]

Year	Grants	Deletions	Pending Applications	Licensed
1949	57	212	65	377
1950	35	169	17	493
1951	15	91	10	534

Year	Grants	Deletions	Pending Applications	Licensed
1952	24	36	9	582
1953	29	79	8	551
1954	27	54	5	529
1955	27	44	6	525
1956	31	37	10	519
1957	40	26	24	519
1958	98	24	57	526

Year	CP's on Air	Total on Air	CP's Not on Air	Total Authorized
1949	360	737	128	865
1950	198	691	41	732
1951	115	649	10	659
1952	47	629	19	648
1953	29	580	21	601
1954	24	553	16	569
1955	15	540	12	552
1956	11	530	16	546
1957	11	530	31	560
1958	22	548	86	634

One of the main reasons for the recent renewed interest in FM (figures on current status of FM recited on p. 81, Chapter 6) is the adoption of new rules by the Commission in 1955 authorizing FM stations to engage in certain types of specialized programming including news, music, weather reports, etc., for reception by business concerns and other subscribers who pay a fee for the service.[10] This will be considered more fully later in this chapter following a discussion of the basic classifications of FM service.

Classes and Service Requirements of FM Stations. Under present rules, commercial FM stations have been classified into A and B groups. The A group consists of those designed to render service primarily to a town or community other than a principal city and to the surrounding rural area. Such stations may not operate with more than 1 kilowatt effective radiated power and the power rating of their transmitters may not be less than 250 watts nor more than 1 kilowatt. They are normally protected to the 1 mv/m contour, but the Commission makes assignments in a manner to insure, insofar as possible, a maximum service to all listeners, whether urban or rural, giving consideration to the minimum signal capable of providing service.[11]

The following frequencies are designated as Class A channels and are assigned for use by Class A stations as described above:[12]

101

Frequency	Channel No.	Frequency	Channel No.
92.1	221	110.1	261
92.7	224	100.9	265
93.5	228	101.7	269
94.3	232	102.3	272
95.3	237	103.1	276
95.9	240	103.9	280
96.7	244	104.9	285
97.7	249	105.5	288
98.3	252	106.3	292
99.3	257	107.1	296

In Hawaii, the frequency band 98-108 mc is allocated for non-broadcast use and no channels from 251 through 300 in the band may be assigned for FM broadcast stations. Also, in Alaska, the frequency band 88-100 mc is allocated to government and other non-government services and channels 201 through 260 are not available for FM stations.[13]

The Class B FM stations are designed to provide service primarily to metropolitan districts or principal cities and the surrounding rural area, or to rural areas removed from large centers of population.[14]

The service area of a Class B station is not protected beyond the 1 mv/m contour, but assignments are made, insofar as possible, to insure a maximum service to all listeners within the coverage area. The standard power ratings of transmitters for FM stations must be 1 kw or more.[15]

Although some service is provided by tropospheric waves, the FCC considers the service area of an FM station to be only that served by the ground wave and to terminate at the point where this wave does not have sufficient intensity to be satisfactorily received. The field intensity considered necessary for service is as follows:[16]

Area	Median Field Intensity
City business or factory areas	1 mv/m
Rural areas	50 uv/m

A median field intensity of 3 to 5 mv/m must be placed over the principal city to be served, and for Class B stations, an intensity of 1 mv/m should be placed over the business district of cities of 10,000 or more population within the metropolitan district served. A field intensity of 5 mv/m should be provided at the place where the main studio is located, except, upon special showing of need, the FCC may authorize the location of the transmitter so that adequate service is not rendered to the studio locale. In no event, however, may this locale be beyond the 50 uv/m contour.[17]

Some particular area requirements with respect to Class B stations should be noted. Those located in Area I embracing a large portion of the Northeastern part of the United States (see Section 3.202 of FCC Rules, 1 Radio Reg. 53:391, for specific geographic limits), may not operate with an effective radiated power greater than 20 kilowatts and the antenna height is limited to 500 feet above average terrain. The same restrictions apply to stations in Area II (embracing the part of the United States not included in Area I) except that the use of greater power and antenna height is encouraged in those sections of Area II where it will not result in undue interference to other stations already authorized or in prospect at the time, and particularly, when it will provide service to rural areas that do not already have service.[18]

The following frequencies, except for Hawaii and Alaska, are designated as Class B channels and are assigned for use by Class B stations:[19]

Frequency	Channel No.	Frequency	Channel No.	Frequency	Channel No.
92.3	222	97.5	248	102.9	275
92.5	223	97.9	250	103.3	277
92.9	225	98.1	251	103.5	278
93.1	226	98.5	253	103.7	279
93.3	227	98.7	254	104.1	281
93.7	229	98.9	255	104.3	282
93.9	230	99.1	256	104.5	283
94.1	231	99.5	258	104.7	284
94.5	233	99.7	259	105.1	286
94.7	234	99.9	260	105.3	287
94.9	235	100.3	262	105.7	289
95.1	236	100.5	263	105.9	290
95.5	238	100.7	264	106.1	291
95.7	239	101.1	266	106.5	293
96.1	241	101.3	267	106.7	294
96.3	242	101.5	268	106.9	295
96.5	243	101.9	270	107.3	297
96.9	245	102.1	271	107.5	298
97.1	246	102.5	273	107.7	299
97.3	247	102.7	274	107.9	300

FCC Rules limiting FM assignments for Class A stations in Hawaii, discussed above, also apply to Class B stations. The assignment restrictions for Class A stations in Alaska are likewise applicable to B stations there.[21]

Subsidiary Communications Authorizations. As previously mentioned, commercial FM stations, in accordance with special FCC rules, may obtain Subsidiary Communications Authorizations (SAC) to provide specialized programs as an adjunct to their regular broadcasting service. A special FCC form (318) must be used in applying for this type of authorization and the nature and purposes of the SCA operation must be set forth in the application.[22] Section 3.293 of the Rules states that these services are restricted to programs "consisting of news, music, time, weather, and other similar program categories."[23]

Originally, the Commission authorized FM stations to conduct "functional" music operations on a "multiplex" basis at any time, or temporarily on a "simplex" basis providing they were transmitted outside regular broadcasting hours. When programs are "multiplexed", they cannot be heard on ordinary FM receivers since they are sent on subchannels simultaneously with regular programs on the main channel.

When the programs are "simplexed", they can be heard on standard FM receivers because they are transmitted on the same carrier frequency used for broadcasting. Special receivers sold or leased to commercial subscribers eliminate or amplify certain portions of the programs (usually the spoken words) by means of an inaudible supersonic (beep) signal.[24]

When simplex operation was authorized in 1955, the Commission emphasized that it was for a year only because of the unavailability of multiplex equipment and that, to protect the FM broadcast service, it would be necessary ultimately for all functional music operations to be conducted on a multiplex basis only.[25]

Authority to carry on simplex transmissions was extended for a year, but by July 1, 1957, multiplex equipment was available in sufficient quantities and since that time no further simplex operations have been authorized. The Commission, however, granted stations additional time to convert from simplex to multiplex equipment. As of July 30, 1958, 82 FM stations held SCA authorizations for multiplex operation.[26]

The Contest Over Simplex Operations. Station WFMF in Chicago contested the validity of the Commission's rules governing the SCA service insofar as they excluded such operation on a simplex basis. On appeal, the Commission contended that functional programming consisting of the presentation of a highly specialized program format with the deletion of advertising from the subscribers' receivers, and the exaction of a charge for these services, was "point-to-point" communication and not broadcasting within the meaning of Section 3(o) of the Communications Act.[27] The Court of Appeals, however, held otherwise. The court in part said:

. . . Broadcasting remains broadcasting even though a segment of those capable of receiving the broadcast signal are equipped to delete a portion of that signal . . . Petitioner, for example, has acquired a high degree of popularity with the Chicago free listening audience. Moreover, it receives substantial and growing revenues from advertisers specifically desiring to reach that audience. In this light, a finding that the programming of petitioner and broadcasters comparably situated is not directed to, and intended to be received by the public is clearly erroneous. Transmitted with the intent contemplated by Section 3(o), such programming therefore has the requisite attributes of broadcasting.[28]

Judge Danaher wrote a dissenting opinion. He stated that WFMF and the entire radio industry were on notice that the Commission would authorize only "multiplex" transmission by which there might be simultaneous sending of two or more signals within a single channel. "The Commission," he said, "made it abundantly clear that an FM broadcast band, already allocated to a particular area in the public interest, was not to be converted in large degree to commercial or industrial operations where the subscribers, and not the public, would control the receiving sets, decide when they should operate, at what volume, and what portions of what programs were to be deleted."[29]

He further declared that the Commission had decided as a matter of policy, "that FM bands were to be used for the purpose for which they had been allocated, and that functional music operations might be authorized on those FM bands only in a manner subsidiary to the main broadcasting service from which the licensee was to draw its financial sustenance. Its policy was evolved in the public interest, and was designed to achieve a far more effective use of the allocated FM frequencies, with greater opportunity to more licensees to achieve economically feasible FM broadcasting . . . The Commission simply decided that the specialized simplex service was not to be permitted to pre-empt the valuable spectrum space allocated to FM frequencies intended to be devoted to broadcasting. This was a public interest determination required to be made by law. Thus the Commission's rule-making was entirely within the Commission's competence."[30]

The Commission filed a petition for rehearing which was denied by the full court on January 16, 1959.[31] An appeal was taken by the Commission to the U.S. Supreme Court. But on October 12, 1959 the Supreme Court refused to review the case, thereby sustaining the lower court's ruling that the FCC's regulation requiring all SCA operations of FM stations to use multiplexing was illegal.[32]

On July 2, 1958, the Commission issued a *Notice of Inquiry* soliciting comments from the public on a number of questions relating to the feasibility of and the extent to which subsidiary FM communications should be authorized.[33] On March 11, 1959, the Commission enlarged the scope of the inquiry to afford interested parties an opportunity to submit further data and opinions directed specifically to the matter of stereophonic programming on a multiplex basis. Comments were requested with respect to the following questions:[34]

(a) Should stereophonic broadcasting by FM broadcast stations on a multiplex basis be permitted on a regular basis, and, if so, should such broadcasting take the form of a broadcast service to the general public, or should it be available only on a subscription basis under Subsidiary Communications Authorizations, or both?

(b) What quality and performance standards, if any, should be applied to a multiplex sub-channel used for stereophonic broadcasting?

(c) Should a specific sub-carrier frequency or frequencies be allocated for stereophonic broadcasting?

(d) Should the quality and performance standards applicable to the main channel be further relaxed, beyond the point already permitted for SCA operations, to accommodate stereophonic broadcasting and, if so, to what extent?

(e) What transmission standards regarding cross-talk between the main channel and stereophonic sub-channel should be adopted?

(f) Should FM broadcast stations engaging in stereophonic broadcasting be required to use a compatible system which allows listeners tuned only to the main channel to hear an aurally balanced program?

The March 11, 1959 *Notice* specified that statements should be filed on or before June 10, 1959. On June 3, 1959, however, the Commission extended the date to December 11, 1959. Subsequently, the date for filing comments was further extended to March 15, 1960.[35]

SCA Operating Requirements. As previously mentioned, the SCA applicant must set forth in his application the specific purposes for which he intends to use his authorization. Section 3.295 of the Commission's Rules provides that he is restricted to these purposes and that prior permission must be obtained to engage in any other activity.[36]

This section further provides:

(1) Supersonic tones or other similar devices may be employed with respect to material transmitted during SCA operation to promote or maintain its commercial marketability, with the station using appropriate actuating devices with the subscriber's receivers.[37]

(2) In arrangements with outside parties, the station must pass on all program material to be transmitted over its facilities, with the right to reject any which it deems inappropriate or undesirable. If the SCA operation is simplex in character, the licensee must be able at any time to substitute a program which it considers to be in the public interest.[38]

(3) The provisions of Section 3.290 requiring equal treatment for political candidates and Section 3.291 requiring the express authority of the originating station before programs may be rebroadcast are applicable when the FM station is engaged in SCA operations.[39]

(4) The requirements of Section 3.287 regarding station identification must be met on the main carrier when a station is engaged in SCA operations. The licensee may prevent their reception on subscribers' receivers through the use of supersonic tones capable of de-activating these specialized receivers.[40]

(5) The rules pertaining to announcements of recorded and sponsored programs as set forth in Sections 3.288 and 3.289 are applicable to the SCA operation when it is conducted on a simplex basis.[41] The station, however, may employ supersonic tones or other devices to prevent the reception of such announcements over subscribers' receivers.[42] The provision of 3.289 regarding sponsored programs are complied with if the SCA operator announces that the programs are being transmitted for a fee to commercial subscribers.

(6) Logs for the SCA operation are required to be kept in the following manner:[43]

(a) An entry must be made at the time of each station identification announcement (call letters and location).

(b) An entry must be recorded describing the material transmitted in each hour segment. If a speech is made by a political candidate, the name and political affiliations of such speaker must be entered.

(c) When the station is operated on a simplex basis and announcements of recorded and sponsored programs are required as specified above, entries must be made showing the times such announcements are made.

The requirements of Sections 3.281(b), (1)-(4) relating to the keeping of operating logs of FM stations are equally applicable during the periods of SCA transmission.[44] Similarly, the requirements of Section 3.265 regarding operators and Section 3.274 relating to remote control operation are applicable.[45]

Paragraph (j) of Section 3.295 specifies that each licensee must observe all technical rules and standards applicable to FM broadcast stations when conducting the SCA operation.[46] Specific technical standards applicable to SCA multiplex operations are set forth in Section 3.319 of the Commission's Rules.[47]

As previously indicated, SCA operations on a multiplex basis may be carried on without restrictions as to time. Simplex transmission, however, must be conducted outside the 36 minimum hours of regular broadcasting per week required of FM stations.[48]

Non-Commercial Educational FM. The Commission has established a special class of FM stations—Non-Commercial Educational FM broadcast stations. As previously indicated, the frequencies set aside for these stations include those between 88 and 92 megacycles. These twenty channels are assigned for educational use and commercial interests may not apply for them.

As pointed out in Chapter 3, when Congress was considering legislation to establish the FCC, there was a great deal of public support for a requirement that all broadcasting stations set aside substantial portions of broadcasting time for educational and cultural programs. This proposal was not adopted, but Congress did pass Section 307(c) of the Communications Act directing the Commission to make a study of it.[49]

Pursuant to this legislative mandate, the Commission conducted a hearing on the matter and invited educators and other interested parties to testify. Among the educational witnesses who testified in that 1935 proceeding was Dr. H. L. Ewbank of the University of Wisconsin. He urged the FCC to earmark a number of broadcasting channels to provide for non-commercial stations and that these be reserved for qualified educational agencies.[50]

This proposal was revived ten years later when the Commission conducted hearings on the allocation of frequencies above 25 megacycles to which reference was made earlier in this chapter. Educators representing such national organizations as the National Educational Association and the American Council on Education urged the Commission to reserve channels for educational FM broadcasting.[51] Accordingly, as pointed out above, on June 27, 1945, the Commission reserved 20 of the 100 FM channels (88 to 92 megacycles) for this purpose and in 1946 promulgated special rules governing the operation of stations on these channels.[52]

Progress Since 1944. In September, 1944, one institution of higher learning, the University of Illinois, was operating an FM station. At that time, construction permits had been granted to the Universities of Iowa, Kentucky and Southern California but the stations were not yet on the air. As of the same date, public school systems in Chicago, New York, San Francisco, and Cleveland were operating FM stations.[53]

With the assignment of special channels for education in 1945, the interest of educators was stimulated. The U.S. Office of Education was especially helpful in disseminating information regarding the availability of FM channels for education and urged schools to take advantage of the new opportunity.[54]

By December, 1945, more than 40 educational institutions had filed applications for new educational FM stations. Four years later, 58 such stations had been authorized.

Since that time, though the growth of educational FM has not been rapid, it has been steady as shown by the following figures:[55]

Year	Grants	Deletions	Pending Applications	Licensed
1949	18	7	9	31
1950	25	4	3	61
1951	19	6	2	82
1952	12	2	2	91
1953	13	1	3	106
1954	9	2	1	117
1955	7	3	1	121
1956	13	4	5	126
1957	17	5	2	135
1958	11	3	6	144

Year	CP's on Air	Total on Air	CP's Not on Air	Total Authorized
1949	3	34	24	58
1950	1	62	20	82
1951	1	83	12	95
1952	1	92	12	104
1953	0	106	10	116

Year	CP's on Air	Total on Air	CP's Not on Air	Total Authorized
1954	0	117	6	123
1955	3	124	3	127
1956	0	126	10	136
1957	0	135	13	148
1958	3	147	10	157

As of July, 1959, 179 educational FM stations had been authorized, of which number 165 were on the air. The number is steadily increasing. New impetus has been given to the growth of educational FM because of the FCC's recent proposal to authorize subsidiary communication operation by this type of station. (See FCC Public Notice-B, July 28, 1960).

Eligibility and Program Requirements. As provided in Section 3.501 of the Commission rules, the following channels are available for non-commercial educational FM broadcasting:[56]

Frequency (mc)	Channel No.	Frequency (mc)	Channel No.
88.1	201	90.1	211
88.3	202	90.3	212
88.5	203	90.5	213
88.7	204	90.7	214
88.9	205	90.9	215
89.1	206	91.1	216
89.3	207	91.3	217
89.5	208	91.5	218
89.7	209	91.7	219
89.9	210	91.9	220

Only non-profit educational organizations are eligible to apply for licenses to operate these educational FM stations. In determining eligibility of publicly supported educational organizations, the Commission takes into account whether they are accredited by their respective state departments of education. With respect to privately controlled educational organizations or institutions, their rating by regional and national accrediting associations is considered as a factor in determining eligibility. While the rules do not bar the holding of licenses by educational organizations without accreditation, they do place a heavier burden of proof on them to show that they are truly educational in character and have the resources and qualifications to operate an educational station in the public interest.[57]

The applicants for these educational FM stations must show that they will be used for the advancement of educational programs. The rules provide that the facilities may be used to "transmit programs directed to specific schools in a system or systems for use in connection with regular courses as well as routine and administrative material pertaining thereto and may be used to transmit educational, cultural, and entertainment programs to the public."[58]

At the time FM channels were reserved for education, there was considerable interest in the development of state-wide educational FM networks. Wisconsin did establish one which is still in operation today. Others were planned but did not materialize. In anticipation of network developments, the Commission provided in Section 3.502 of its Rules that in considering the assignment of a channel for noncommercial educational FM broadcasting, it would take into account the extent to which an application meets the requirements of any state-wide plan for such broadcasting, provided the plan affords fair treatment to public and private educational institutions at the various levels of learning and is otherwise fair and equitable.[59] This rule is still in effect but has had little applicability because plans for statewide educational FM networks have not developed on as wide a basis as was expected when the rule was adopted.

Each educational FM station is required to furnish a "non-profit and non-commercial broadcast service." No sponsored or commercial program may be transmitted and commercial announcements of any character are prohibited. These educational stations may transmit the programs of commercial stations. If they do, however, the rules say that all commercial announcements and references must be deleted.[60]

A public notice issued by the FCC on March 16, 1960, stating that all stations must identify on the air the suppliers of free records used in broadcasts, seemed to conflict with these rules governing noncommercial FM operations. This March 16 public notice was an interpretation by the FCC of Section 317 of the Communications Act which requires sponsorship identification of broadcast programs.[61] Under this interpretation, a failure of the educational FM station to identify the donors of records (those supplied the station without cost and not those sold), would have been a violation of Section 317 of the Act. At the same time, such identification would have contravened the Rules of the FCC against the use of commercial plugs on this type of station.

This conflict put educational FM broadcasters in the awkward position of not being able to use free records, and they were compelled to limit their broadcasts to recordings which they bought.

Recent legislation by Congress, however, has corrected this situation. As provided in Section 508 of the Communications Act, stations (both commercial and noncommercial) may use "free" records without being required to identify the donors.[62]

As previously pointed out, the number of educational FM stations has been growing steadily. A factor favorable to this development was the adoption of a rule by the FCC authorizing these stations to operate with power of 10 watts or less.[63] The equipment and cost requirements for these stations are comparatively low. Some manufacturers have package deals which make it possible to secure the basic equipment for such a station for as little as $3,000.00, not including studio facilities.

NOTES

1. See Armstrong, Edwin H., "A Method of Reducing Disturbances in Radio Signaling by a System of Frequency Modulation", 24 Proceedings of the Institute of Radio Engineers, No. 5, May, 1936, p. 689.
2. Walker, Paul A. and Emery, Walter B., "Post War Communications and Speech Education", *Quarterly Journal of Speech*, Vol. 30, No. 4, December, 1944, pp. 399-401. In this article, two former FCC officials discuss the advantages of FM transmission.
3. FCC Log. *A Chronology of Events in the History of the Federal Communications Commission from Its Creation on June 19, 1934, to July 2, 1956,* compiled by the FCC Office of Reports and Information, July, 1956, p. 21.
4. FCC News Release, Mimeograph No. 44578, October 31, 1940.
5. FCC News Release, Mimeograph No. 46405, January 15, 1941.
6. FCC Docket No. 6651. Also see *Broadcasting,* May 28, 1945, pp. 17, 24, 26, 28.
7. *FCC Annual Report,* 1945, pp. 19-20.
8. *Ibid.,* 1958, p. 131.
9. *Ibid.,* pp. 115, 131.
10. *Ibid.,* p. 115-116.
11. Section 3.203(a) 1 RR 53:392.
12. *Ibid.,* Section 3.203(b).
13. *Ibid.,* Section 3.203(c) and (d).
14. Section 3.204(a), 1 RR 53:393.
15. *Ibid.*
16. Section 3.311(c), 1 RR 53:494.
17. Sections 3.203 and 3.311(c), 1 RR 53:395, 494.
18. Section 3.204(2), 1 RR 395.
19. Section 3.204(2)(b), 1 RR 53:394.
20. *Ibid.,* Section 3.204(c).
21. *Ibid.,* Section 3.204(d).
22. Section 3.293, 1 RR 53:295.
23. *Ibid.*
24. *FCC Annual Report,* 1958, p. 116.
25. *Ibid.*
26. *Ibid.*
27. *Functional Music, Inc. v. Federal Communications Commission, Functional Music, Inc. v. United States et. al.,* U.S. Court of Appeals, District of Columbia Circuit, November 7, 1958, 274 F. (2d) 543; reported in 17 RR 2152.
28. 17 RR 2158.
29. 17 RR 2160.
30. *Ibid.*
31. *Broadcasting,* January 19, 1959, p. 9.
32. 361 U.S. 813, 80 S.C. Rep. 50, Oct. 12, 1959.
33. FCC Docket No. 12517, 1 RR 53:381.

34. 24 Fed. Reg. 1997 (1959); 1 RR 53:383-384.
35: 24 Fed. Reg. 10416 (1959); 1 RR 53:384.
36. 1 RR 53:489.
37. *Ibid.*, 53:490.
38. *Ibid.*
39. *Ibid.*, 53:486, 487.
40. *Ibid.*, 53:483.
41. *Ibid.*, 53:484-485.
42. *Ibid.*, 53:486.
43. *Ibid.*
44. *Ibid.*
45. *Ibid.*, 53:472, 475, 490.
46. *Ibid.*, 53:490.
47. *Ibid.*, 53:509.
48. See Sections 3.293 and 3.261, 1 RR 53:471, 489.
49. 48 Stat. 1084.
50. See transcript of record upon which was based the FCC's *Report To Congress Pursuant to Section 307(c) of the Communications Act of 1934,* January 22, 1935.
51. Testimony in FCC Docket No. 6651, 1944-45.
52. These rules were promulgated March 8, 1946, 11 Fed. Reg. 2839 (1946).
53. Emery and Walker, *op. cit.*, pp. 401-402.
54. *Ibid.*, p. 402.
55. *FCC Annual Report, 1958,* p. 131.
56. Section 3.501, 1 RR 53:521.
57. Section 3.503, 1 RR 53:522.
58. *Ibid.*
59. *Ibid.*, Section 3.502.
60. *Ibid.*, Section 3.503.
61. *In the Matter of Public Notice (FCC 60-239), March 16, 1960,* entitled "Sponsorship Identification of Broadcast Material," 25 Fed. Reg. 2406 (1960); 19 RR 1569.
62. For a full understanding of what is meant by "free" records, the full text of Section 508 should be consulted. See Appendix I.
63. 13 Fed. Reg. 4922, September 27, 1948.

CHAPTER 9

Television

So swiftly that America has barely awakened to its significance, television has reached from city to city across the nation. It has brought into millions of homes the magic of its immediacy and reality—transmissions of sight and sound combined, with an impact on practically all phases of life.
— DAVID SARNOFF*

As early as June, 1936, the FCC had promulgated rules governing visual broadcasting but because of the newness of the medium, did not establish any fixed standards for operations.[1] Considerable research and experimentation were carried on and by late March, 1939, there were 23 licensed TV stations authorized to engage in experimental broadcasting.[2] In the spring of 1939 and again in 1940, the rules governing television were revised.[3] The 1940 revised rules prescribed two classes of television stations:[4]

(1) "Experimental Research Stations" for the development of the television art in its technical aspects;
(2) "Experimental Program Stations" for the development and improvement of program service.

Subsequently, in March, 1941, a formal hearing was initiated by the Commission to consider the establishment of engineering standards, and to determine when television broadcasting should be placed upon a commercial basis.[5]

The outcome of this hearing was the adoption, on April 30, 1941, of rules and regulations and Standards of Good Engineering Practice governing commercial and experimental television stations.[6]

The Commission allocated 18 channels to television, the first nine being located in the 50 to 186 mc. band, and the second nine in the 186 to 294 mc. band.[7]

By January, 1942, there were a number of commercial and experimental television stations licensed to operate.[8] But the freeze on televison construction brought on by the War halted, for the time being, the development of television for civilian use.[9]

* Chairman of the Board, Radio Corporation of America.

After the cessation of hostilities, when it became evident that television would expand rapidly, the Commission began a long study looking toward amendment of its rules to provide for a systematic and efficient plan of allocating frequencies to meet the needs of the growing service. After public hearings, the Commission adopted a nation-wide allocation table and made 13 channels available for television broadcasting.[10] Subsequently, channel 1 was deleted from the television assignments and made available to fixed and mobile radio services. The Commission then proposed a distribution of the twelve VHF channels to a total of more than 340 cities in the United States.[11] However, in June and July, 1948, the Commission became concerned that the mileage separations it had proposed for TV stations were insufficient. Accordingly, it instituted further rule making proceedings and in September, 1948 declared a temporary freeze on all new television applications.[12]

These hearings continued intermittently until the latter part of 1951. In April, 1952, the Commission issued its final order in the proceedings, establishing a new fixed table of television assignments.[13]

During the hearings, there were some who urged the Commission not to adopt a nation-wide table of assignments and permit, as is the case in AM and FM broadcasting, the assignment of frequencies in terms of community needs and in accordance with established engineering standards. The Commission rejected this proposal, stating reasons as follows:

13. The Communications Act of 1934, among other things, establishes as a responsibility of the Commission the 'making available to all people of the United States, an efficient nationwide, radio service,' (Section 1) and the effectuation of the distribution of radio facilities in such a manner that the result is fair, efficient and equitable and otherwise in the public interest from the standpoint of the listening and viewing public of the United States (Section 303 and 307b). Our conclusion that these standards can best be achieved by the adoption of a Table of Assignments is based upon three compelling considerations: A Table of Assignments makes for the most efficient technical use of the relatively limited number of channels available for the television service. It protects the interests of the public residing in the smaller cities and rural areas more adequately than any other system for distribution of service and affords the most effective mechanism for providing for noncommercial educational television. It permits the elimination of certain procedural disadvantages in connection with the processing of applications which would otherwise unduly delay the overall availability of television to the people . . .[14]

The Commission assigned 70 UHF (Ultra High Frequency) channels between 470 and 890 megacycles in addition to the 12 VHF (Very High Frequency) channels between 54 and 216 megacycles which were already in use. At the same time, the new table of television assignments made available more than 2000 TV channels in almost 1300 communities throughout the United States, its territories and possessions.

Also, as a result of an impressive showing by educational organizations and interests in the TV allocation hearings, the Commission made channel assignments in 242 communities for noncommercial educational use, 80 of which were VHF and 162 UHF. As of the end of the fiscal year 1958, the FCC had increased the number to 257 (86 VHF and 171 UHF).[15] These channels are reserved for education and are not available for commercial use.

The Growth of Commercial Television. Since April, 1952, commercial television has shown an amazing growth. At the end of 1958, it was estimated that over 90 percent of the population was within service range of at least 1 TV station and that over 75 percent were within range of two or more stations. Nearly 50 million TV sets were in use with more than 80 percent of the homes having one or more such sets.[16]

As of April 25, 1960, *Broadcasting Magazine* reported 526 commercial television stations in operation.[17] Of this number, 449 were VHF and 77 UHF. Also, as of the same date, there were 119 applications for new stations on file and awaiting action of the Commission.[18]

While VHF television has advanced rapidly, UHF has had serious problems. As the Commission has said:[19]

. . . It is generally recognized, however, that the greatest difficulties are encountered in achieving successful operation of stations in the UHF band. Since there are only 12 channels in the VHF bands, it was contemplated in 1952 that extensive use of the 70 channels in the UHF band would be required to attain a nation-wide TV service. However, UHF stations have had great difficulty in getting established and in competing with VHF stations. The head start by the VHF system, the present disparity in performance between UHF and VHF transmitting and receiving equipment, and the small number of sets in use and being manufactured that are capable of receiving both UHF and VHF signals are the principal reasons for the difficulties experienced by UHF stations. Other factors, such as the preference of advertisers and other program sources for VHF and UHF outlets, have flowed from the principal reasons and aggravate the UHF difficulties.

The Television Allocations Study Organization (TASO), established in 1957 to study the technical aspects of both VHF and UHF, made its final report in March, 1959. Much of the report was unfavorable to UHF in its present state of development.

The Report concluded that (1) a UHF signal deteriorates more rapidly than a VHF signal as the distance from the transmitter increases; (2) a UHF receiving antenna is less efficient than a comparable VHF antenna; and (3) a UHF station costs more to operate than a comparable VHF outlet.

Factors favorable to UHF were found to be (1) the signal is almost impervious to man-made electrical noise and atmospheric interference;

(2) within limits of its signal range, UHF is on a par with VHF when it is operating over a level, smooth, treeless terrain.[20]

While the TASO study was a comprehensive one, as the report indicated, there is need for further research. It may well be, as more is learned regarding the propagation characteristics of UHF frequencies and as sending and receiving equipment is improved, the outlook for UHF television will become brighter.

In its 1961 budget proposal to Congress, the FCC earmarked two million dollars for a UHF research program. In the latter part of April, 1960, the House approved this proposal and it was expected that the Senate would go along. Subject to Congressional appropriation, the Commission announced that it would construct a superpower UHF transmitter on top the Manhattan area, that receivers would be placed throughout the city, and that a broad scale study over a two-year period would be made to determine the full capabilities of UHF in terms of both technical operation and programming.

The actual experiment, if authorized, will be done by a private research organization under contract with the FCC. It will be supervised, however, by the Commission. The National Bureau of Standards, the National Academy of Science, and possibly other educational and professional organizations are expected to cooperate in the study.

The possibility of using the experiment for in-school classroom instruction in the New York City area is being explored. Also, the networks will be invited to provide programs on a rotating basis so that side-by-side comparisons of UHF and VHF transmission and reception can be made.

Some members of the Commission and its staff and others knowledgeable in the field, have high hopes that this comprehensive study will provide answers to problems which now plague UHF and make possible its greater and more effective use for television service.[21]

The TV Table of Assignments and How It May Be Amended. Section 3.606 of the Rules contains a list of the cities throughout the United States with the particular TV channels assigned to each city. Those marked with an asterisk are reserved for education.[22]

Only channels which are listed in the Table of Assignments may be applied for. To make any changes in this table requires the filing of a formal petition with the Commission and a showing that the proposed changes will comply with the requirement for mileage separation of stations operating on the same or adjacent channels and that the public interest will be served.

As provided and graphically described in Section 3.609 of the Rules, the country is divided into three zones. For stations operating on the same channels, or co-channel stations as they are called, the minimum mileage separations in the various zones are as follows:[23]

Zone	Channels 2-13	Channels 14-83
I	170 miles	155 miles
II	190 miles	177 miles
III	220 miles	205 miles

For stations operating on adjacent channels, the minimum mileage separations for all zones are:[24]

Channels 2-13	Channels 14-83
60 miles	55 miles

Since the TV Table of Assignments was established many petitions to make channel changes have been filed with the FCC. Some have been granted while others have been denied, the action of the Commission depending upon the facts of each case and whether the public interest seemed to justify the proposed change. For information on all changes in the Television Table of Assignments approved by the FCC since the table was adopted in 1952, 1 RR 609-622 should be consulted.

In a statement to the Senate Committee on Interstate and Foreign Commerce on April 17, 1959, the Chairman of the FCC announced that the Commission was pursuing long range studies and negotiations to ascertain the practicability of making basic revisions in its present system of television allocations. At the same time, he announced that, because of the present scarcity of VHF channels in large markets and the pressing need for more television service, pending the completion of these long range studies the Commission would consider making exceptions, in appropriate cases, to the existing requirements for minimum separations.

Pursuant to this interim policy, the Commission has already formally proposed to assign new VHF channels to some areas and permit the establishment of stations, involving substandard or short-spaced separations on the same channels.[25]

Non-Commercial Educational Television. In the post-war television hearings, to which reference has been made above, educators made an impressive showing regarding the possibilities of using television for educational purposes. More than 70 witnesses appeared before the Commission and urged that TV channels be reserved for the exclusive use of education. More than 800 colleges, universities, state boards of education, school systems, and public service agencies submitted written statements urging the Commission to make the reservations. Distinguished professors pointed out how television could be used to extend the services of educational institutions in the sciences, arts, humanities, vocational education and other important areas of learning. As the Joint Council on Educational Television has pointed out, mayors, parent teacher groups, chambers of commerce, libraries, art associations, newspapers, civic groups, municipal

117

boards, clergymen, prominent members of Congress, men representing both of the major political parties, and others either testified or submitted written statements in behalf of these educational TV assignments.[26]

The Joint Council and a host of educational organizations including the American Council on Education, the National Education Association, the National Association of Land-Grant Colleges and Universities, the National Association of Broadcasters, the Council of Chief State School Officers joined in the crusade. The result of these joint efforts, as already pointed out, was the reservation of 242 channels (the number now is near the 260 mark) for the exclusive use of education with each state receiving one or more assignments.

The reservation of these channels parallels in a striking way the passage of the Morrill Act in 1859. This Act made available large areas of land in the public domain to help establish public colleges. From this has developed a nation-wide system of land-grant institutions that has become favorably recognized throughout the world. Similarly, the FCC's historic act of 1952 setting aside another part of the public domain, the broadcasting spectrum, for educational use has opened up a new and valuable frontier in American education.[27]

Following the FCC's action in 1952, numerous states held state-wide meetings to arouse interest in the activation of these reserved channels. Many committees were organized throughout the country to study the financial, programming and engineering problems of building educational stations.

Numerous governors and legislatures took definite steps to investigate the potentialities of educational television. Numerous foundations including the Fund for Adult Education, Ford Foundation, Twentieth Century Fund, Payne Fund, and others were early contributors to the educational TV movement.

On December 3, 1952, the Fund for Adult Education announced the formation of the National Citizens Committee on Educational Television with Milton S. Eisenhower and Marion B. Folsom as co-chairmen. Two days later, the Fund announced the formation of a National Educational Television and Radio Center. The purpose of this center, financed with an original grant of over a million dollars, was to aid in the exchange, circulation, and development of quality films and kinescopes to be used by educational television stations.[28]

In May, 1953, only one of the reserved TV channels had been activated. By the end of 1954, however, eight educational stations were on the air. Eight additional stations were in operation by the end of 1955 followed by five more in 1956, six in 1957, eight in 1958, and seven as of April, 1960.[29]

With almost 50 educational television stations on the air, a dozen more under construction and numerous others in the advanced planning stage— all this plus state-wide networks operating in Alabama, Florida, North

Carolina and Oklahoma and others being contemplated—there can be no doubt that educational TV has reached an advanced stage in its development and may now be considered firmly rooted in American life.

What the Joint Council on Educational Television said in 1954 is even more true today:[30]

The stresses and strains of this atomic age have imposed new problems on the citizen and the society in which he lives. His physical and psychological security is threatened in a tense and competitive world. Health, home, livelihood, retirement, social unrest, war—these and many other areas of individual concern make him eager to secure new and continuing knowledge. As our report shows, educational stations are now offering a wide variety of informational and instructional programs designed to help supply this knowledge speedily and effectively.

The American citizen also wants to make the most effective use of his leisure time and to benefit more fully from the cultural resources and influences so abundant in this country and other parts of the world. Accordingly, educational television stations are bringing into his home the reality and beauty of famous museums, art galleries, educational centers, parks and gardens, and historical sites. Also, they are making it possible for him to see and hear—on a regular basis—distinguished scholars in the fields of science, philosophy, literature, and so forth, and artists in the fields of painting, sculpture, music, dance, and drama.

It is clear that educational television has made and is making real progress. There are problems but these are gradually but surely being overcome. The facts clearly show that educational television is having a tremendous effect upon the educational and cultural life of the nation.

Eligibility and Operating Requirements for Educational TV Stations. Eligibility requirements for educational television stations are essentially the same as those for educational FM stations. Section 3.621 of the FCC Rules states that they may be licensed only to non-profit, educational organizations upon a showing that they will be used primarily to serve the educational needs of the community; for the advancement of educational programs; and to furnish a non-profit and non-commercial television broadcast service. In determining eligibility of public and private educational institutions to hold licenses, as is the case with educational FM stations, the factor of accreditation is also taken into account.[31]

While the rules that classify the services and prescribe the purposes for which educational FM and TV are substantially the same, there are a few differences which should be noted. Section 3.621 of the Rules pertaining to licensing requirements and character of service contains some language and provisions which do not appear in Section 3.503 covering the same subject regarding educational FM stations. For example, paragraph (a) of Section 3.621 is a bit more expansive than paragraph (a) of Section 3.503. It reads:

(a) Except as provided in paragraph (b) of this section, noncommercial educational broadcast stations will be licensed only to non-profit educational organizations upon a showing that the proposed station will be used primarily to serve the educational needs of the community; for the advancement of educational programs; and to furnish a non-profit and non-commercial television service.[32]

The language of paragraph (d) and (e) of Section 3.621 relating to educational TV stations does not appear at all in Section 3.503 of the noncommercial educational FM rules. These paragraphs read as follows:

(d) An educational station may not broadcast programs for which a consideration is received, except programs produced by or at the expense of or furnished by others than the licensee for which no other consideration than the furnishing of the program is received by the licensee. The payment of the charges by another station or network shall not be considered as being prohibited by this paragraph.

(e) To the extent applicable to programs broadcast by a noncommercial educational station produced by or at the expense of or furnished by others than the licensee of said station, the provisions of Section 3.654 relating to announcements regarding sponsored programs shall be applicable, except that no announcements (visual or aural) promoting the sale of a product or service shall be transmitted in connection with any program; provided, however, that where a sponsor's name or product appears on the visual image during the course of a simultaneous or rebroadcast program, either on the backdrop or in similar form, the portions of the program showing such information need not be deleted.[33]

These Rules require some interpretation. They prohibit educational TV stations from broadcasting any program for which pay is received. Exceptions to this permit the broadcast of recorded programs furnished by others or the use of programs, the costs of producing which are defrayed by others, provided the programs constitute the only consideration derived by the station. Also, the rules do not preclude a commercial network or station from paying line charges in connection with the furnishing of programs to educational TV stations.

In adopting the rules, it was the Commission's intention that educational TV stations should not sponsor the sale of goods, and commercial announcements are prohibited. In order that these stations might carry outstanding educational programs made available by commercial networks, the Commission did not require the deletion of visual images or pictorial material containing the name of the sponsor or his product. Aural commercials, however, in connection with such network programs, must be deleted by the educational TV station.

Business institutions may and do supply many fine educational programs to educational TV stations. Simple identification on the air of the institutions furnishing the programs does not contravene the rules against advertising on these stations, so long as the design is not to promote the business of the institution or the sale of its goods. However, the interpretation by the Commission of Section 317 of Communications Act (to which reference was made in the preceding chapter), which required stations, both commercial and non-commercial, when using free recordings to identify the commercial distributors, presented somewhat the same dilemma for education TV stations that it did for educational FM stations. As previously pointed out, however, recent legislation by Congress has eliminated the confusion.

NOTES

1. Fed. Reg. 536 (1936). For full story of Commission's concern with television and development of rules governing the service prior to the War see Warner, Harry P., *Radio and Television Law* (New York, 1953), pp. 620-667.
2. FCC Mimeograph No. 32563, February 27, 1939.
3. FCC Docket No. 5806, February 29, 1940, 5 Fed. Reg. 933 (1940).
4. FCC Mimeograph No. 39404, February 29, 1940, *Ibid.*
5. FCC Mimeograph No. 47053, January 28, 1941.
6. FFC Mimeograph No. 49832, May 2, 1941, 6 Fed. Reg. 2284.
7. *Ibid.*
8. FCC Mimeograph No. 57820, January 1, 1942.
9. FCC Memorandum Opinion, Mimeograph No. 59725, April 27, 1942.
10. FCC Docket No. 6780, November 21, 1945.
11. FCC Report and Order, Docket No. 8487, May 5, 1948.
12. FCC Log, *op. cit.*, p. 62; also Section 13 Fed. Reg. 5182 (1948).
13. FCC Sixth Report and Order, 17 Fed. Reg. 3905-4100, May 2, 1952.
14. *Ibid.*, P. 3906.
15. *FCC Annual Report*, 1958, p. 108.
16. *Ibid.*, p. 101.
17. *Broadcasting*, April 25, 1960, p. 104.
18. *Ibid.*
19. *FCC Annual Report*, 1958, p. 102.
20. *Broadcasting*, March 16, 1959, pp. 165-183.
21. See *Broadcasting*, April 25, 1960, p. 82, for report on and discussion of this research project. The project was authorized, and on October 5, 1960, the FCC announced that "the New York project for which Congress appropriated two million dollars is under the direction of the Commission's Chief Engineer and a special unit, aided by technical advice of the cooperating committees." (FCC Public Notice-B 94811, Oct. 5, 1960)
22. Section 3.606, 1 RR 53:602-622.
23. *Ibid.*, 53:627.
24. *Ibid.*, 53:628.
25. See *In the Matter of Amendment of Section 3.606, Table of Assignments, Television Broadcast Stations* (*Grand Rapids, Cadillac, Traverse City and Alpena, Michigan*), FCC Docket No. 13374, 25 Fed. Reg. 1055 (1960); 1 RR 53:589. Also see proposal relating to New Bedford, Massachusetts, Docket No. 13375, 25 Fed. Reg. 1056 (1960), 1 RR 53:595.

26. Joint Council on Educational Television, *Four Years of Progress in Educational Television,* (Washington, D.C. 1956), p. 20.

27. *Ibid.,* p. 1.

28. Based on information in files of JCET. Additional information about the functions of these organizations and the services they have provided may be obtained from the Joint Council on Educational Television, 1785 Massachusetts Avenue N.W., Washington D.C.

29. *Ibid.* See *JCET Educational Television Factsheet,* April 1960.

30. JCET, *Four Years of Progress in Educational Television, op. cit.,* pp. 18-19.

31. Section 3.621, 1 RR 53:633, 634.

32. *Ibid.*

33. *Ibid.*

CHAPTER 10

International Broadcasting

We here have an obligation to do everything within our power to strengthen the Voice of America. The voice that reaches out from our shores must be firm and clear. It must speak the truth in all the basic tongues of mankind. It must be heard throughout the world. The Voice of America must play its part in the fulfillment of the prophecy that "nation shall speak peace unto nation."—CHARLES R. DENNY*

International Broadcast Stations, as defined by FCC Rules, are those using frequencies between 5950 and 26,100 kilocycles, whose transmissions are intended to be received directly by the general public in foreign countries.[1]

Section 3.788 of the Rules provides that these stations "shall render only an international broadcast service which will reflect the culture of this country and promote international good will, understanding and cooperation. Any program solely intended for, and directed to an audience in the continental United States does not meet the requirements of this service."[2]

FCC Form 309 is used to apply for a construction permit to build one of these international broadcast stations.[3] This is followed by the submission of FCC Form 310 which requires a showing that construction has been satisfactorily completed and requests a license for operation.[4]

The Commission has stated that a license will be issued only after the applicant has made a satisfactory showing that

(1) there is a need for the service;

(2) that necessary program resources are available;

(3) that directive antennas and other technical facilities will be used to deliver maximum signals to the "target" area or areas for which the service is designed[5];

(4) that competent personnel will be used;

(5) that the applicant is technically and financially qualified and possesses adequate facilities to carry forward the service proposed; and finally,

(6) that the public interest will be served by the proposed international broadcast operation.[6]

* Former chairman of the FCC.

123

Such stations are licensed for unlimited time operation, except in certain cases where the hours may be specified.[7] They must operate with not less than 50 kw power and their signals must have a strength of at least 150 uv/m 50 per cent of the time in the distant target area.[8]

Assignment of Frequencies. Section 3.702 of the Rules says that frequencies in the bands allocated to the international broadcast service will be assigned to authorized stations for use at certain hours and for transmission to stated target areas.[9] Licensees may request the use of specific frequencies for particular hours of operation by filing informal requests in triplicate with the Commission not less than 15 days prior to the start of a new season.[10] These requests are honored to the extent that interference and propagation conditions permit.[11]

Not more than one frequency is authorized for use at any one time for any one program transmission except in instances where a program is intended for reception in more than one target area and the intended target areas cannot be served by a single frequency.[12]

In 1955, the World Wide Broadcasting Company, licensee of international broadcasting station WRUL, petitioned the Commission to reconsider its action in prohibiting the use of more than one frequency for transmitting programs to the same area. The station contended that other nations, particularly Russia, use multiple frequencies to transmit programs to the same area causing interference to certain frequencies used by United States international stations, making it necessary for the latter to use more than one to insure reception in a particular target area.

The Commission denied the petition on the grounds that such multiple frequency transmission to the same area is inconsistent with Article 43 of the Convention of the International Telecommunications Union which makes it incumbent upon the Commission to limit the number of frequencies and spectrum space to the essential minimum necessary to render satisfactory service. The Commission said, however, it would "take appropriate action" to protect the station from harmful interference caused by foreign stations operating in violation of international agreements.[13]

The Commission has pointed out that "all specific frequency authorizations will be made only on the express understanding that they are subject to immediate cancellation or change without hearing whenever the Commission determines that interference or propagation conditions so require and that each assignment of "frequency hours"[14] for a given season is unique unto itself and not subject to renewal, with the result that completely new assignments must be secured for the forthcoming season."[15]

The geographic areas to be served by an international broadcast station are described by the Commission in Section 3.792 of the Rules.[16] Licensees sending programs to more than one of these areas must specify one as *primary,* and state the reasons for the choice, with special reference to the nature and special suitability of the programming proposed.[17]

Commercial Programs Permitted. Stations operating in the foreign service are permitted to carry commercial or sponsored programs provided no more than the name of the sponsor and the name and general character of the commodity or service are advertised.

As provided in Section 3.788 of the Rules, several other restrictions relating to advertising apply: (1) a commodity advertised must be one regularly sold or is being promoted for sale on the open market in the foreign area to which the program is directed: (2) commercial continuity advertising an American utility or service to prospective visitors must be particularly directed to such persons in the foreign countries where they reside and to which the program is directed; and (3) where an international attraction such as a world fair, resort, etc., is being advertised, the oral continuity must be consistent with the purpose and intent of the provisions in this section.[18]

Operational Requirements. The FCC Rules contain specific requirements regarding equipment and operation of international broadcast stations. These requirements relate to power, frequency control, antenna design, auxiliary and alternate main transmitters, changes in equipment, keeping and preserving logs, etc. While the technical rules in many ways are substantially the same as those governing other broadcast stations, there are some differences made necessary because of the special character of the service. For example, antennas must be so designed and operated that the field intensity of the signal toward the specific country served will be 3.16 times the average effective signal from the station.[19] Also, not applicable to other types of stations, is the rule that station identification, program announcements, and oral continuity shall have international significance and be communicated in language particularly suitable for the foreign areas for which the service is primarily intended.[20]

Licenses for international broadcast stations are issued for one year only.[21] Unless otherwise directed by the Commission, each renewal application must be filed at least 90 days prior to the expiration date of the license.[22] FCC Form 311 is used in applying for the renewal.[23] As a part of the renewal application, a supplementary statement must be submitted showing the number of hours the station has operated on each assigned frequency, listing contract and private operations separately,[24] and reporting reception and interference and conclusions regarding propagation characteristics of assigned frequencies.[25]

Voice of America Broadcasting. There are only two private international broadcasting stations operating in this country under the rules discussed above. The Voice of America, however, an instrumentality of the United States Information Agency (USIA), operates a sizeable number of high powered short wave stations beaming programs to many parts of the world.

As provided in Section 305(a) of the Communications Act of 1934, radio stations belonging to and operated by any agency of the United States government, are not subject to the regulatory powers of the FCC as set forth in Sections 301 and 303 of the Act.[26] The only exception is that government stations (not including those on government ships beyond the continental limits of the United States) when transmitting any radio communication or signal relating to government business must conform to Commission regulations designed to prevent interference with other radio stations and the rights of others.[27]

Accordingly, the President, through delegated authority, assigns the frequencies to the USIA for the Voice of America transmissions. The program policies and pattern of operation of the Voice are determined by USIA. The director of the agency reports to the President through the National Security Council. Since one of the chief functions of the Voice is to report and interpret to foreign peoples policies and actions of the United States government and promote national security, its activities are closely coordinated with the White House, State Department, the Office of Civil and Defense Mobilization, the military establishment and other governmental organizations concerned with this country's position and participation in world affairs.[28]

Current Dimensions of the Voice. As of March, 1959, the Voice was operating 76 transmitters and providing programs in 37 languages to millions of people throughout the world. The Washington, D. C. facilities include 18 studios, equipment to make 40 disc or tape recordings simultaneously, ten tape-editing booths, a recording control, the Master Control, editorial offices and music and transcription libraries.

In April, 1959, the Voice announced plans for six new transmitters in Europe, West Africa, the Eastern Mediterranean and the Pacific to be added to the eight already established. This expansion program over a five year period, if funds are made available by Congress, will involve an expenditure of some 40 million dollars.

In early 1959, more than half of the Voice's 600 hours of broadcasting per week were being directed at the Soviet Union, the Eastern European satellites, Red China, North Korea and North Vietnam. These programs included newscasts of important happenings throughout the world, current reports on policies of the United States government and a variety of broadcasts concerning the life and culture of the American people.[29]

A few examples of regular Voice programs which attempt to project the image of America include a forum feature, *The Arts and Sciences in Mid-Century America;* a broadcast of jazz music called *Music USA;* and a dramatic show, *American Theatre of the Air.* These programs offer lectures and discussions by noted American experts in the natural and social sciences and humanities, leading artists in the popular music field, and distinguished actors performing under the auspices of the American National Theatre and Academy.[30]

More than 2,000 foreign stations regularly carry Voice "package programs." In March, 1959 more than 1,300 stations in South America were using its programs.[31]

The USIA provides a budget of about ten million dollars a year for Voice operations. In recent appearances before the House appropriations committee, officials of the agency have urged that funds be increased to expand its broadcasting activities to meet the competition of Communist Russia where the volume of foreign transmissions has been running more than four times as much per week as the volume in this country. Until recently more money was spent by Russia to jam reception of Voice programs than was spent to carry on all Voice operations.[32]

According to USIA Director George V. Allen, the Russians have reduced the amount of jamming of Voice broadcasts since Khrushchev's visit to this country in 1959. The reasons seem to be that jamming tends to cause interference to broadcasts by Russia and neighboring countries and is expensive in materials, manpower and money.

By 1962, the Voice expects to have 18 high-powered shortwave transmitters in operation on the East Coast. Their total value will be more than 25 million dollars. Long range plans call for the establishment of high powered, medium wave transmission in Liberia and the Mediterranean area, and increased power and facilities for short wave transmission at some of the Voice's present sites in England, Morocco, Greece, and the Philippines.[33]

Since its requests for funds are subject to approval by Congress, it goes without saying that the extent and nature of the broadcasting done by the Voice may be influenced considerably by attitudes of leaders on Capitol Hill as well as those in the Executive departments of the government. For example, in a recent attempt to compare the Voice's programs with those of Radio Moscow, the House Appropriations Committee asked for transcripts of one day's broadcasts by the stations. By random choice, the broadcasts of March 2, 1960 were selected. This was the day that Khrushchev landed at Kabul, Afghanistan. Radio Moscow reported that the Russian leader was "warmly greeted by thousands"; the Voice reported he "was enthusiastically greeted by a half million." *Newsweek* for May 2, 1960 noted that the House Committee forthwith reduced USIA's budget by $6.8 million.

NOTES

1. Section 3.701(a), FCC Rules and Regulations; 1 RR 53:731.
2. Section 3.788(a); I RR 53:749.
3. Section 3.711(a); I RR 53:737.
4. *Ibid.*
5. A target area, as defined by Section 3.701(m), 1 RR 53:731, is a geographic area in which the reception of particular programs is specifically intended and in which adequate broadcast coverage is contemplated.
6. Section 3.731; 1 RR 53:742. Also see *Report of Commission,* 13 RR 1501.
7. Section 3.761; 1 RR 53:745.

8. Sections 3.702(d) and 3.751; 1 RR 53:733, 742.

9. 1 RR 53:742.

10. *Ibid.* There are four seasons defined by the FCC Rules: Vernal Equinox, from February 1 to April 30; Summer, from May 1 to July 31; Autumnal Equinox, from August 1 to October 31; and Winter, from November 1 to January 31.

11. *Ibid.*

12. Section 3.702(f); 1 RR 53:734.

13. FCC Docket No. 10962; 13 RR 1510a.

14. The term "frequency hour", as defined by Section 3.701(b), 1 RR 53:731, means one frequency used for one hour.

15. Section 3.702(a); 1 RR 53:732.

16. 1 RR 53:753.

17. Section 3.702 (b); 1 RR 53:732.

18. Section 3.788; 1 RR 53:749.

19. Section 3.753; 1 RR 53:743.

20. Section 3.787(b); 1 RR 53:788.

21. Section 3.718; 1 RR 53:740.

22. Section 3.720; *Ibid.*

23. *Ibid.*

24. "Contract operations", as defined by Section 3.701(n), means any non-government operation of an international broadcast station pursuant to a contract with an agency of the United States Government and subject to Governmental control as to program content, target areas to be covered, and time of broadcast. "Private operation", as defined by paragraph (o) of the same section, is any operation not of a contract character. See 1 RR 53:731-732.

25. Section 3.791; 1 RR 53:751-752.

26. 48 Stat. 1083.

27. *Ibid.*

28. See *United States Government Organization Manual,* 1959-60, pp. 506-510; also see Annual Reports of USIA, 1954-59.

29. Based upon research and examination of documentary materials by the author made available by the Office of Research and Analysis, USIA, Washington, D. C.

30. *Ibid.*

31. *Ibid.*

32. *Ibid.*

33. See *Broadcasting,* April 25, pp. 86-87.

34. *Newsweek,* May 2, 1960, p. 13.

CHAPTER 11

Auxiliary and Other Special Types of Broadcasting

... these radio waves are made to perform all sorts of work. ...
Since they are public property, the deciding factor in determining how
many channels a certain type of service shall have, and who shall be en-
trusted with a channel within a type of service, must be the public interest.
—WAYNE COY*

FCC rules provide for the use of numerous auxiliary facilities which
contribute greatly to the economy, efficiency and quality of the regular
broadcast services already discussed. Without these adjunct operations,
the football game far removed from the station studio could not be brought
into our homes; an inaugural parade in Washington could not be transmitted to the television viewers throughout the nation; inhabitants in many
small, isolated communities in the West would have no local television
service; and much of the variety, immediacy and color that now character-
ize broadcasting in general would be missing.

Each of these important auxiliary services is subject to special regulations established by the FCC, and each has been assigned the use of particular bands of frequencies in the radio spectrum. Space will not permit a
detailed discussion of these regulations and channel allocations. It is
hoped, however, that the reader will find the following informational highlights helpful.

Remote Pickup Stations. All broadcast stations (standard, FM, Non-
commercial FM, TV and international broadcast) are eligible to apply for
and use remote pickup transmitters for a variety of purposes to support
their regular operations.[1] These pickup units are used to send programs
from remote points to the main transmitter for simultaneous or delayed
broadcasting and for the transmission of information and orders pertaining to such programs. They may be authorized to operate on a mobile
or fixed basis.[2]

Special temporary authority may be granted to operate, as remote
pickup stations, equipment already authorized for use by another class of

* Former chairman of the FCC.

129

station or equipment which, under the Communications Act of 1934, does not require a construction permit.[3]

These applications for temporary authority may be filed informally but should reach the Commission at least ten days previous to the date of operation. If received in less time, the Commission will accept the application if sufficient reasons for the delay are stated.[4]

These informal requests must set forth full particulars as to the purpose of the temporary remote pickup operation; give the name of the licensee whose equipment is to be used, the call letters, the type of equipment and the frequency or frequencies to be employed, time and date, location, transmitter power, and type of emission proposed.[5]

The frequencies used must be those especially assigned to the remote pickup broadcast service. Other frequencies under the jurisdiction of the FCC may be requested if effective transmission on the assigned ones is not possible and the programs to be broadcast relate to events of national interest and importance. In any case, it must be shown that the operation will not cause interference to any existing station. Under no circumstances, will frequencies in the so called Special Radio Emergency Service be authorized for these remote pickup operations.[6]

Special Rules for Miniature Low Power Auxiliary Stations. On July 30, 1958, the Commission adopted special rules for the operation of tiny transmitting devices, inconspicuously worn on the person, and used mainly for cueing and directing participants in rehearsals of programs as well as actual broadcasts. This small, portable equipment is a happy substitute for the clumsy telephonic apparatus and extension cords formerly used in the production of elaborate programs and has contributed further to the versatility of the broadcast media.

Only licensees of broadcast stations are eligible to use this auxiliary apparatus, and then only in connection with activities of a specified station or combination of stations. Their transmissions must be intended for reception at a point within the same studio, building, stadium or similarly limited indoor or outdoor area.

Only one application prepared in duplicate is required to be filed for one or more of these transmitting units, provided they are designed for operation in a common frequency band and are to be used with the same broadcast station or combination of such stations in a single city.

Adding further to the utility of this apparatus, the rules permit one licensee to use it in conjunction with broadcast stations of other licensees in the same area. If, however, it is to be used this way in other locations for a consecutive period of more than one day, the FCC Engineer in Charge of the radio district where the station is located and the FCC Engineer in the district where the operation is conducted must be notified in writing at least two days in advance of the operation.[7]

The power of these small pickups is limited to 1 watt and their operation is subject to the condition that no harmful interference will be caused to other stations of a fixed or mobile character.[8] Persons without operators' licenses may use them, but a licensed operator must be available to make immediate correction of any improper operation. If any adjustments or repairs are needed, they should be made by him or under his direction.[9]

Call letters are not assigned to these stations. An announcement, however, must be made over the transmitting unit at the beginning and end of each period of operation, identifying the type of operation, its location, and the call sign of the broadcast station with which it is being used.[10]

Studio Transmitter Link (STL) Stations. STL stations are fixed installations which serve the purpose of connecting studios of broadcast stations with their transmitters which, for some reason or another, it has been necessary or desirable to locate some distance away, often on a mountain top or other remote point to achieve efficient operation and satisfactory coverage.[11]

Only licensees of standard, FM and television broadcast stations (both commercial and noncommercial) are authorized to use these STL facilities and their use must be identified with and auxiliary to the main broadcasting operation.[12]

Inter-City Relay Stations. The FCC Rules provide for the establishment of inter-city FM and TV relay stations. Only FM and TV broadcasters may be authorized to use them.[13] In the case of FM relays, the FCC rules provide they will be authorized when suitable common carrier facilities are not available.[14] A verified statement must accompany the application giving reasons why common carrier facilities are not available or cannot be used if such is the case, and showing that the applicant, at the earliest time reasonably practicable, requested the appropriate company in the area to supply the transmission service. The letter of request as well as the company's reply must be submitted with the application.[15]

The same condition does not apply to television relays. On July 31, 1958, the Commission amended its rules to provide that television stations may have the option of operating their own private inter-city relay facilities or obtaining such facilities from common carriers. The Rules, however, specifically preclude the use of private relay stations as intermediate links in inter-city common carrier transmission. Under no conditions may they be directly connected with common carrier routes.[16]

In adopting this amendment, the Commission said that this new policy "will preserve the integrity of the nation-wide television program distribution system operated by the common carriers and at the same time will provide access to national network programs for television broadcast stations in small markets or with marginal operations."[27]

In further justification of the amendment, the Commission pointed out that "it will permit the establishment of modest local or regional networks of educational or commercial television stations, through the use of private inter-city relay systems. Stations operating in such local or regional networks may combine their efforts and resources to produce programs of local and regional interest which no one of the stations could afford to produce and lessen the dependence of TV stations on national network program sources."[18]

The Commission cautioned that the new rule was not intended to have broad application. It was designed to cover only those situations where television stations are located in relatively small communities at some distance from program service points on existing common carrier routes and where costs of connection would be disproportionately high when compared with prospects for profit from the linked operation of the stations.

"The situation which the present action seeks to remedy," said the Commission, "is one which is peculiar to the television industry, and such action is being taken in the interest of aiding the fullest possible development of television service in the United States."[19]

Operational Requirements for Auxiliary Stations. The FCC rules specify application procedure, and equipment and operation requirements for each type of auxiliary station. To summarize briefly, FCC Form 313 is used to request authorization for all three types of stations.[20] The form has a flexible format and also is used to apply for the license and any renewal thereof. The Rules specify frequency tolerances and power limitations for the different operations. Station and operator licenses must be conspicuously posted in the transmitter rooms of all stations. Requirements for keeping logs vary slightly, but hours of operation, frequency checks and pertinent remarks concerning operation are uniformly required to be recorded.[21]

Dimensions of Auxiliary Broadcasting. The Commission reported that at the end of the fiscal year 1959, almost 5,000 auxiliary stations had been authorized. More than 3,600 of these were remote pickup stations. More than 1,000 were of the auxiliary TV type, including low-power cueing devices, and more than 50 were studio-transmitter-links.[22]

In 1957, there were only about 2,600 auxiliaries in use. The higher figures in 1959 were due mainly to a rapid increase in the number of remote pickup facilities during the two year period.

Special Facilities for Television Broadcasting. As pointed out in Chapter 9, there are more than 500 regular TV stations on the air. Augmenting these, however, are more than 500 satellite, translator and booster stations, not to mention an estimated 700 community antenna systems serving widely scattered areas of the country.[24]

The development and use of these special types of broadcast media which project the signals and extend the coverage of regular TV stations, have made possible service in many communities and sections of the country which otherwise might not enjoy it.

Satellite Stations. In August, 1954, the Commission inaugurated a policy of considering applications for new UHF TV stations even though no local programming is proposed.[25] The purpose of this policy was to encourage the building of stations in smaller communities by eliminating the costs of studio equipment and local live performances. These stations, popularly known as "satellites," are licensed as regular TV operations and are required to comply with the technical rules and regulations already discussed. They are relieved, however, of the responsibility of originating local shows, though they may do so if they desire. Under present FCC policies, they may limit their broadcasts to the duplication of programs from other stations.

A number of television stations have been authorized to operate on this basis and are providing service to some small communities that otherwise might not receive it.

TV Translators. In May, 1956, the Commission adopted rules authorizing the establishment and operation of television broadcast translator stations.[26] These translator installations possess relatively inexpensive, low-powered equipment designed to receive "off-the-air" signals from other VHF and UHF television stations and convert them for retransmission on one of the upper 14 UHF channels (70 to 83) to areas where service is needed. They have no local studios and originate no local programs. Operating requirements have been relaxed to the barest minimum consistent with dependable service and protection of other stations from interference.

Section 4.732 of the FCC Rules provides that any qualified individual, organized group of individuals, broadcast licensee, or local, civic governmental body is eligible to secure a license for a TV translator station.[27] An appropriate showing must be made in the application that the applicant will be financially able to construct and operate the station for the period of the license.[28]

Upon appropriate proof of need, more than one translator may be licensed to the same applicant whether or not they serve substantially the same area.[29] A separate application, complete in all respects, must be submitted on FCC Form 313 for each station.[30] Only one channel will be assigned to each operation.[31]

The maximum operating power of these translators recently was increased from 10 to 100 watts[32] and experience reveals that they are capable of providing good reception out to an average distance of 15 to 20 miles.[33]

While the operating requirements are not severe, the Commission has established regulations to make sure that these translators do not interfere with other broadcast transmissions and do provide a reasonably high standard of service. Among the rules designed to accomplish these purposes are: (1) The antenna sites are required to be readily accessible and so located that they provide line-of-sight transmission to the entire service area.[34] For example, they should be situated well above trees to minimize the possibility of signal absorption by foliage; (2) only station equipment may be used which has been type-approved by the Commission;[35] (3)

installation of the stations must be under the direct supervision of a qualified electronics engineer, and any repairs or adjustments of operating apparatus must be made by or under the direction of a licensed first or second class radiotelephone operator;[36] (4) the choice of transmitting and receiving antennas is left to the discretion of the applicant, but the Commission has provided the following instruction:

. . . In general, the transmitting antenna should be designed to provide maximum signal over the area intended to be served and to minimize radiation over other areas, particularly those in which interference could be caused to the reception of other stations. The Commission reserves the right to require the use of a suitable directive transmitting antenna in order to permit the assignment of the same channel to two or more television broadcast translator stations located in the same general area. An application for construction permit for a new television broadcast translator station, or for changes in the facilities of an existing station, shall supply complete details of the proposed receiving and retransmitting antenna systems including an accurate plot of the field pattern of the transmitting antenna, if directive.[37]

Rapid Growth in Translator Broadcasting. The Commission reported that 245 translators had been authorized at the end of the fiscal year 1959, as compared to only 74 in 1957.[38] Close to a million dollars had been invested in translator facilities and over 180,000 all-channel TV receivers or UHF converters had been purchased in areas where these new transmitting facilities had been established.[39]

These translator stations are being operated by local governmental bodies, community groups, private concerns, and, in some places by licensees of regular TV stations who desire to extend their broadcast coverage.[40]

Repeater Stations. The Commission had had under consideration for more than four years a proposal to license on a regular basis booster or repeater stations, as they are called.[41] These devices differ from translators in that the received signal is retransmitted by the parent station. They are co-channel amplifiers and involve no frequency conversions as is the case with translator operations.

On May 3, 1960, in *C.J. Community Services, Inc. v. Federal Communications Commission,* the U.S. Court of Appeals for the District of Columbia held that the Commission has jurisdiction over these boosters, and that operation of them, causing interference to authorized stations, is a violation of the Act. The Court said, however, that the Commission had a statutory duty to provide for the issuance of appropriate licenses and suggested that it might "well get on with rule-making proceedings apparently contemplated in its Docket 11331 and its Docket 11611 in which is to be examined the feasibility" of boosters and other such devices. [See 100 U.S. App. D.C. 379; 246 F. (2d) 660; 15 RR 2033 (1957).]

In June, 1957, the Commission stated that it believed it was feasible to provide for the licensing of booster stations to be operated in the UHF television band with certain restrictions, but declined to license them in the VHF band.[42] It was proposed that UHF boosters be licensed only to operators of regularly assigned television stations, not to extend the normal range of these stations as do translators, but to help fill in and provide TV reception in "shadow" areas within the Grade A contours of stations where line-of-sight transmission is obstructed by terrain barriers.[43]

In a change of position, on December 30, 1958, the Commission announced that it would not make provision for licensing low power booster stations in either the VHF or UHF television broadcast bands. The Commission said it had concluded that UHF translator stations are adequate to meet the needs of small, remote communities at comparatively low costs; and that booster stations involve potential interference to existing television services.[44]

However, in a subsequent public notice, dated April 14, 1959, the Commission announced a further modification of its attitude on booster operations. It declared that it was recommending to Congress that the Communications Act be amended to legalize and permit the licensing of these repeater stations in the VHF band under certain conditions and, if that is done, to allow up to one year of time for existing boosters to comply with technical requirements to avoid interference to other stations.[45]

In the same notice the Commission stated that it had direct knowledge of over 300 booster stations which had been installed without FCC authorization, that experience indicated that VHF boosters might be operated with less interference than had previously been anticipated. Reversing its former position, therefore, the Commission said: "aware of the useful purpose served by these devices, and taking into account the investments made in those which have been installed, the Commission is now of the opinion that, if the Communications Act is appropriately amended, VHF repeaters could be licensed under conditions which will insure due protection to other users of the radio spectrum including aerial navigation services."[46]

The Commission further pointed out that Section 319 of the Act prohibits the Commission from licensing broadcast facilities constructed without a prior permit.[47] Accordingly, Congress will need to amend this section before the Commission can grant licenses to these repeater stations already installed.

Shortly after this announcement, in April, 1959, legislation was introduced in Congress designed to give the Commission the authority requested.[48] Pending Congressional action, the Commission announced that unlicensed boosters would have until September 30, 1959 to comply with regulations. Subsequently the Commission extended the time to June 29, 1960.[49]

On May 25, 1960, in Broadcast Action Report No. 3456, the Commission announced it had adopted rules, effective July 25, 1960, to provide for the use of boosters by UHF, TV broadcast stations. Their maximum effective radiated power is 5 kw and a signal in excess of 5 millivolts may not be placed at any point more than 68 miles from the parent TV station. The purpose of these boosters is to fill in "shadows" within a parent UHF station's Grade A service area and not to extend that area.

The FCC announced in late July, 1960, that it would begin processing applications for watt VHF boosters on September 6. These will enable parent VHF stations to extend their coverage to distant and remote communities. (See August, 1960, issue of *Broadcasting*, p. 84, for details. See 20 RR 153657 for full text of the Commission's Report and Order; also reported in 25 F.R. 7317)

Community Antenna TV Systems. In many communities over the country, community TV antenna systems are in use. These systems employ receiving antennas which pick up signals from regular TV stations and relay them by wire or cable to customers who pay a fee for the service. In some cases, the signals of distant TV stations are transmitted by microwave facilities supplied by common carriers and fed into the local cable distribution system.

Since CATV facilities, as they are popularly called, do not transmit over the air to the general public, they have not been required to secure authorizations from the Commission. The Commission has taken the position that it has no regulatory jurisdiction over their operations.[50]

It has been estimated that there are about 700 CATV systems in operation serving as many as a half million people.[51] Their widespread growth has aroused the concern of many broadcasters. Some have objected on the grounds that programs of regularly licensed stations are being unfairly and unlawfully pirated by the cable carriers. Some owners of small, local stations without network affiliations have protested having to compete with cable carriers that pick up network shows from distant stations and micro-wave them to the CATV units where they are distribtued to local customers.

In hearings before a Senate subcommittee on communications in July, 1959, a number of broadcasters from western states urged that CATV operators be required to secure licenses from the FCC; that they be required to secure permission of originating stations to distribute their programs; and that the FCC be required to take into account the impact of cable antenna and booster operations on local TV stations.[52]

At this writing, a case is pending in the United States District Court for the District of Idaho (Southern Division) in which station KUTV in Salt Lake City has requested the Court to enjoin Idaho Microwave, Inc., from picking up the programs of the Salt Lake City station and micro-waving them to a community antenna system in Twin Falls, Idaho for distribution to subscribers in that city.

In its formal complaint, the plaintiff station contends that it has a right in its electronic signals and programs and is entitled to be protected against their commercial use without the station's consent; that any such use by the defendant will be an unlawful interference with plaintiff's property, and will result in unfair competition and unjust enrichment of the defendant, and will appropriate the fruits of plaintiff's expenditure, skill and energies without any compensation therefor.[53]

The outcome of this case is being watched with interest by both broadcasters and owners of cable systems. Should the court grant the complaint, it will establish an important legal precedent that will militate generally against the use by cable operators of programs which they pick up off the air and distribute to paying customers without the broadcasters' consent.

Subscription Television. Another special broadcast service recently authorized by the Commission on a trial basis is subscription television. On February 10, 1955, the FCC adopted a Public Notice proposing to authorize this service and invited interested parties to file comments regarding the proposal.[54] The Notice listed numerous questions as to its legal validity and its possible effects on the public interest.

In the comments filed in response to the Notice, three systems for subscription TV were submitted for consideration and approval: (1) *Phonevision,* supported by Zenith Radio Corporation and Teco, Inc.; (2) *Subscriber-Vision* endorsed by Skiatron Electronics and Television Company and Skiatron Television, Inc., and (3) *Telemeter,* proposed by International Television Corporation.

During the week of September 15, 1957, the FCC was informed of two other methods: *Bi-Tran,* developed by Blonder-Tongue Laboratories, Inc., and *Teleglobe* by Teleglobe Pay-Television System, Inc.[55]

Briefly, the operating principles of these systems are as follows. Phonevision, Subscriber-Vision and Telemeter contemplate the encoding and scrambling of both images and sound transmitted via TV. Each requires the use of a decoding device attached to the receiver. Phonevision, and Subscriber-Vision would involve periodic billings, while Telemeter would require deposit of coins in a box associated with the decoder. All three systems provide, in different ways, for the dissemination to subscribers of information on how to activate the decoders and the procedure for recording charges and making payments.

Teleglobe involves the sending of the TV picture by conventional methods but the sound part of the transmission would be sent by wire and made available only to subscribing members of the public.

The Bi-tran system envisages simultaneous transmission of two programs on a single channel, one of which would be available without charge as at present, and the other subject to a fee and used for subscription TV operations.

The proponents of these various systems filed detailed comments urging the Commission to authorize the new service. The Joint Council on Educational Television filed a brief comment taking no definite position on the merits, but saying that educators should have the privilege of using subscription TV if the new service should be authorized.

The three major commercial networks vigorously objected. They were joined by the National Association of Radio and Television Broadcasters. The Joint Committee on Toll Television (said to represent a large percentage of the motion picture exhibitors in the country) and some television stations registered their disapproval.

Following the issuance of a public notice in May, 1957, announcing that it had concluded that it had the statutory authority to authorize toll TV,[56] the Commission adopted a Report on October 17, 1957 amending Section 3 of its rules to provide for subscripton TV.[57]

Questions as to Statutory Authority. While the Communications Act of 1934 does not specifically authorize the Commission to approve toll TV, the Commission, in justifying its action, relied upon certain general provisions of the Act. In the Report, reference is made to Section 301 which states that a basic purpose of the Act is "to provide for the use" of radio channels "under licenses granted by Federal authority."

The Commission also made reference to paragraphs (b), (e) and (g) of Section 303 of the Act which empower the Commission to prescribe the nature of the service to be rendered by each class of radio station; to regulate the kind of apparatus it uses, and to study new uses for radio, provide for experimental uses of frequencies, and generally encourage the larger and more effective use of radio in the public interest.

While acknowledging limitations on its power (such as the statutory bar against censorship) the Commission declared that there was nothing in the language of the Communications Act suggesting Congressional intent to prohibit the authorization of toll TV.

The Commission took note of arguments made against the legal validity of the system—that Section 1 of the law states the basic purpose of the Act to be that of providing communications facilities to *all* the people; that Section 3 (o) defines broadcasting as "the dissemination of radio communications intended to be received by the public" and that Congress, in passing the law, did not contemplate program service being made available only to such persons as were able and willing to pay a charge for it.

The Commission's response to these arguments was that Section 1 states the purpose of the Communications Act in broad terms but does not preclude the authorization of special services. For example, the Commission said, reference in the Act to "all the people of the United States" does not prevent the Commission from licensing stations for safety and other special purposes. Also, the Commission pointed out that it already licenses FM stations to provide musical programs to restaurants, department stores, etc.,—establishments that pay a fee for the service, and that the basic operating principles of subscription TV are essentially no different.

After considerable analysis of the legislative history of the Communications Act as it relates to toll TV, the Commission concluded that it did have the statutory power to authorize the service and that the only real question is whether the public interest will be served. In this connection, the Commission stated two fundamental issues:

(1) Will toll TV supplement the program choices, and with an increase in financial resources will it provide greater and better services to the people?

(2) Or will it seriously impair the capacity of the present system to provide advertiser-financed programming now free of direct charge to the public?

Arguments by Proponents. Proponents of toll TV have argued that under our present system of broadcasting, advertisers for the most part determine the type of programs that go out over the air; that their main concern is to reach the largest possible audience and that there is not the diversity and variety of programming that there might be; that with toll TV the listeners would determine the programs and that broadcasts of opera, Shakespearean drama, etc., while not attracting huge audiences, would attract enough viewers to make them economically worthwhile. They have argued that programs would be presented without commercials and that this would appeal to the general public.

Arguments by Opponents. Opponents of pay-as-you-see TV argue that the public will be asked to pay for what it now gets without charge and that the present broadcasting system will be destroyed. They argue that if toll TV can attract large audiences, enormous revenue will be derived which will tend to attract the best talent away from conventional TV; that with the loss of economic support from advertisers, the networks and stations will not be able to supply outstanding sustaining programs. They contend that toll TV can't offer anything the public doesn't already get. Why charge? Toll TV will be seeking the same big profits anyway, they say.

Trial Period. The Commission considered these various arguments and decided to authorize toll TV on a trial basis for three years, but to reserve judgment on whether it should be approved on a permanent basis. The Commission said:

While a trial may not be expected to give, in itself, a complete demonstration of the effects of a subsequently expanded subscription television service—should it be found desirable later to authorize it—it could, nevertheless, provide useful information concerning what subscription television can offer, how the public responds to what is offered, how the service would operate in practice, what, if any, abuses require curbing, whether it imposes a genuine threat to the free service (as distinguished from a challenge to that service to meet fresh competition of a new kind) what legislative and administrative safeguards would be desirable and effective, and a host of other important questions, such as the desirability of standardizing the equipment used, on which a largely argumentative record affords inadequate basis for final conclusions and decisions at this time.[58]

Conditions of Trial Operatons. In authorizing trial operations the FCC set forth a number of conditions:

(1) During the trial period any single toll TV system is limited to three markets.

(2) Authorizations were limited to cities having at least four commercial television stations. This was to make sure of continuing availability of free program service and at the same time allow maximum opportunities for competition between toll TV and the present system.

(3) Both VHF and UHF stations are eligible.

(4) Applications will be accepted from any holder of a construction permit or license for a television station or any person who files an application on FCC Form 301 requesting a construction permit and asking for a waiver of the rules as now preclude subscription TV.

(5) Systems must not cause interference to other stations and the reception must be good.

(6) Any franchise holder must provide the service to all stations in the community who want it.

(7) The station must be free to use more than one system if it wants to.

(8) The contracts between the franchise holder for TV operation and the station must be so worded as to permit any station contracting to present programs under one system to transmit them under any other system that meets the technical requirements of the Commission. Thus, more than one station will be free to participate in the trial operation of any individual system, more than one system will have an opportunity to be tried in the community, and any single station will have an opportunity if it desires and is authorized, to transmit subscription programs under more than one system.

(9) Licensees must be responsible for the choice of programs and must participate in determining the charges made to all subscribers.

(10) Programs must begin no later than six months after authorization unless more time is granted for good cause.

(11) Minimum hours of free programs must be broadcast.

(12) Periodical reports are required to be made to the Commission on the status of the trial operations.

(13) Technical regulations governing regular stations, such as the keeping of logs, were made applicable to toll TV operations.

Congressional Reaction. Following adoption of the report authorizing subscription TV under these conditions, the House Interstate and Foreign Commerce Committee, conducted six days of public hearings on the matter. Thereafter, on February 6, 1958, the Committee adopted the following resolution:

Resolved, that it is the sense of this Committee that the public interest would not be served by the granting of authorizations for subscription television operations as contemplated by the Federal Communications Commission in its First Report, adopted October 17, 1957, in Docket Number 11279, because

(1) It has not been established to the complete satisfaction of this Committee that authority to license such operations comes within the power of the Commission under the provisions of the Communications Act of 1934; and

(2) Such operations might lead at least to a partial blacking-out of the present system in particular communities, if not throughout the United States.[59]

Subsequently, numerous bills were introduced in both houses to prohibit or place restrictions on toll TV service and the Commission was informed that further Congressional hearings would be held on the subject.

In response, the Commission issued its Second Report on the matter, February 26, 1958, announcing that no applications for authorizations to conduct trial toll TV operations would be processed until thirty days following the *sine die* adjournment of the 85th Congress.[60]

More than a year having elapsed since this announcement, the Commission, on March 23, 1959, issued a Third Report in the proceeding stating that applications for trial subscription television operations would be accepted under conditions previously announced except that the trial of any particular television system would be limited to a *single* city and not to *three* as previously provided. Another new limiting factor added was that authorizations would be granted only on condition that the public would not be called upon to purchase any special receiving equipment.[61]

This action was followed two days later by the adoption of a resolution by the Senate Interstate and Foreign Commerce Committee (by a vote of 11 to 10) stating that it had no reservations to the approval of toll TV as contemplated in the Commission's Third Report.[62]

As yet, it is too early to determine what the outcome of the whole matter will be. It is clear, however, that Congressional opinion will be an important factor in toll TV's ultimate destiny.

The Zenith Radio Corporation announced in late March, 1960 that it had entered into an agreement with the RKO General Company to conduct a three year experiment in toll TV in Hartford, Connecticut under the conditions recently prescribed by the FCC. It announced that the two companies would request the Commission's approval for the ten million dollar experiment.[63]

Subsequently, Hartford Phonevision Company (subsidiary of RKO General, Inc.) filed an application with the FCC for authority to conduct trial subscription TV operations over its station WHCT (channel 18) in Hartford. On September 28, 1960, the FCC designated this application for a public hearing. In announcing this action, the Commission stressed that questions relating to a general toll TV service will have to await further hearings and the consideration of appropriate legislation. The only matter, therefore, immediately before the FCC in the present hearing is whether to authorize the limited trial operation proposed for a three-year period in Hartford.[64]

NOTES

1. FCC Rules and Regulations, Section 4.432; 1 RR 54:95.
2. Section 4.401; 1 RR 54:91.
3. Section 4.433; 1 RR 54:95.
4. *Ibid.,* p. 54:95.
5. *Ibid.*
6. *Ibid.*
7. Section 4.437(f); 1 RR 54:98.
8. Section 4.437(g); 1 RR 54:98.
9. Section 4.437(h); 1 RR 54:98.
10. Section 4.437(i); 1 RR 54:99.
11. Sections 4.501(a) and (b) and Section 4.601; 1 RR 54:111, 121; Also, see *FCC Annual Report,* 1958, p. 118.
12. *Ibid.*
13. Section 4.501(c) and 4.601(c); 1 RR 54:111, 121.
14. Section 4.531(c); 1 RR 54:113.
15. *Ibid.*
16. FCC Docket No. 11164, Fed. Reg. 6123 (1958). Also see FCC Report, 17 RR 1621.
17. 1 RR 1628.
18. *Ibid.*
19. *Ibid.,* p. 1629.
20. See FCC Form 313; 1 RR 98:237.
21. See Sections 4.451 through 4.581 and 4.651 through 4.682; 1 RR 54:99-118, and 129-132.
22. *FCC Silver Anniversary Report,* 1959, p. 71.
23. *FCC Annual Report,* 1956, p. 116.
24. *Ibid.,* 1958, pp. 105-108 and 1959, pp. 60-63; also see *Broadcasting* June 29, 1959, pp. 40-44 and July 6, 1959, pp. 64-69.
25. 19 Fed. Reg. 5144 (1954); 10 RR 1199.
26. 21 Fed. Reg. 3684 (1956); 13 RR 1563.
27. 1 RR 54:143.
28. *Ibid.*
29. *Ibid.*
30. See FCC Form 313, 1 RR 98:237.
31. Section 4.732(c); 1 RR 54:143.
32. FCC Docket No. 12567; 23 Fed. Reg. 9141 (1958); 17 RR 1736.
33. *FCC Annual Report,* 1958, p. 106.
34. Section 4.737; 1 RR 54:145-146.
35. Section 4.750; 1 RR 54:146.
36. *Ibid.,* p. 54:148.
37. *Ibid.*
38. *FCC Annual Report,* 1958, p. 106 and 1959, p. 71.
39. *Ibid.*
40. *Ibid.*

41. Docket 11331 (FCC 55-404).

42. *Ibid.* (FCC 57-700); 22 Fed. Reg. 4758 (1957). 1 RR 54:xiii.

43. *Ibid.*, 54:xviii.

44. 24 Fed. Reg. 220 (1959); 18 RR 1505; also see *Broadcasting,* January 5, 1959.

45. FCC Public Notice 72034, April 14, 1959; 14 RR 1514a.

46. *Ibid.*, p. 1514b.

47. *Ibid.*

48. S.C.R. 4 and H.C.R. 62, 86th Congress, First Session; also see *Broadcasting,* April 20, 1959, p. 76-77.

49. FCC Public Notice 72034, April 14, 1959; 18 RR 1514.

50. See FCC Report and Order, Docket No. 12443, 18 RR 1573, for comprehensive opinion of Commission that it has no authority to regulate CATV systems. The Commission contends they are not common carriers nor are they engaged in broadcasting as defined by the Communications Act and, therefore, concludes that there is no FCC jurisdiction. The opinion says that these systems are engaged in interstate commerce but that Congress will have to enact legislation before the Commission can regulate them.

51. *Broadcasting,* June 29, 1959.

52. *Ibid.*, July, 1959, pp. 64-69.

53. *KUTV, Inc., V. Idaho Microwave, Inc. and W. L. Reiher doing business as Cable Vision.* Complaint filed in U.S. District Court for the District of Idaho (S.D.). As of August, 1960, no decision had been handed down by the court.

54. Docket 11279 (FCC 55-165); 20 Fed. Reg. 988 (1955).

55. *Ibid.* (FCC 57-1153), 16 RR 1512.

56. *Ibid.*, p. 1513; Also see Commission's letter to Honorable Owen Harris, Chairman, Interstate and Foreign Commerce Committee, July 3, 1957; also see the Notice of May 23, 1957, 22 Fed. Reg. 3758 (1957); 15 RR 1689, and Memorandum of Law Concerning Authority of the Federal Communications Commission to Authorize Subscription Television Operations of the same date, 15 RR 1692.

57. Docket 11279 (FCC 57-1153; 22 Fed. Reg. 8313 (1957); 16 RR 1509.

58. *Ibid.*, 1522.

59. See Hearings before House Committee on Interstate and Foreign Commerce, 85th Congress, 2d Session, on Subscription Television, January 14, 15, 16, 17, 21, 22, and 23, 1958. The text of the Committee resolution is reported by the FCC in its Public Notice in Docket 11279 in 16 RR 1539-1540.

60. FCC Docket 11279; 23 Fed. Reg. 1574 (1958); 16 RR 1539.

61. *Ibid.*, 1540a; 24 Fed. Reg. 2534 (1959).

62. 1 RR 1540j.

63. See *Broadcasting,* April 4, 1960, pp. 35-37, for full report on plans for this experiment.

64. FCC Public Notice-B, No. 94442, September 28, 1960, 25 Fed. Reg. 9572 (1960).

CHAPTER 12

Experimental Radio and Broadcast Services

Except as otherwise provided in this Act, the Commission from time to time, as public convenience, interest, or necessity requires shall study new uses for radio, provide for experimental uses of frequencies, and generally encourage the larger and more effective use of radio in the public interest.
—Section 303 (g)of the Communications Act of 1934.

Section 303(g) of the Communications Act requires that the FCC "study new uses for radio, provide for experimental uses of frequencies, and generally encourage the larger and more effective use of radio in the public interest."[1] The Commission has implemented this provision by the establishment of various classes of experimental stations and the adoption of rules governing their operations.

Experimental Radio. Part 5 of the Commission's Rules and Regulations sets forth elaborately the licensing and operating requirements for experimental radio stations. The Commission has classified these stations into two groups: (1) those authorized to do research in the radio art not related to the development of an established or proposed new service, or to provide essential communications for research projects which could not be carried on without the use of such communications; and (2) those authorized to experiment with the development of data, or techniques for an existing or proposed radio service.[2]

These experimental radio operations are non-broadcast in character; that is, they may involve the experimental study of the propagation characteristics of certain frequencies, or the use of radio energy in connection with research projects in industry, or the development of improved transmitting or receiving equipment, etc.—projects in which broadcasting to the general public is not involved or is not an essential part.

Application and Licensing Procedure. Part 5 of the FCC Rules and Regulations, Sections 5.1 through 5.411, provide for the establishment of these stations, define their purposes, and prescribe the requirements for their operation.[3]

Applications to construct land (fixed and mobile) stations in this service, or to modify permits, must be filed on FCC Form 401. A separate application must be filed for each station. Where mobile units are to be used in connection with one operation, these several units may be requested in the one application.[4]

FCC Form 401 is also used to request licenses for operation after construction has been completed or to modify licenses already granted.[5]

The rules specify that FCC Form 405 must be used to apply for renewal of licenses. In this connection Section 5.55 (g) states that "a blanket application may be submitted for renewal of a group of station licenses in the same class in those cases where the renewal requested is in exact accordance with the terms of the previous authorizations. The individual stations covered by such applications shall be clearly identified thereon. Unless otherwise directed by the Commission, each application for renewal of license shall be filed at least 60 days prior to the expiration date of the license to be renewed."[6]

The rules provide for the filing of informal requests (usually in letter form) for special permission to operate these stations on a temporary basis in a manner different to that specified in the authorization, providing the requests in no way conflict with Commission rules. These requests must give the name and address of applicant; explain the purpose of the request and the need for special action; and inform the Commission regarding the class, type, location and date of the proposed operation. They must also specify equipment to be used, frequency desired, power output, type of radio emission and antenna height.[7]

In connection with all formal applications for construction permits for these experimental stations, a supplemental statement must be submitted with facts showing that the applicant is qualified to do the project proposed; that qualified personnel and adequate technical and financial resources are available; that an organized plan of experimentation has been worked out which promises to make a constructive contribution to the radio art, and that laboratory developments have reached the stage where actual transmission by radio is essential to further progress; and that harmful interference will not be caused to other stations.[8]

In addition, a statement must be submitted by the applicant confirming his understanding that all frequencies are assigned for experimental purposes only, and that the granting of authority to experiment as proposed shall not be construed as a finding by the Commission that the frequencies assigned are the best suited for the project, or that the applicant is qualified to operate any station other than experimental or that he may be so authorized. And finally, he must confirm his understanding that there will be no obligation on the part of the Commission to make provision for his type of operation on a regular basis.[9]

Operational Requirements. Sections 5.101 through 5.166 of FCC Rules contain the technical standards and operation requirements for these experimental radio stations. Requirements regarding frequency stability, types of emission that may be used, modulation, transmitter control and measurements, power and antenna heights, etc. are specifically set forth.[10]

The Commission expects adherence to these regulations, but in keeping with the exploratory and experimental character of these services, the Commission wisely allows some exceptions, "provided the applicant makes a satisfactory showing that the nature of the proposed program of experimentation precludes compliance therewith."[11]

These stations may make only such transmissions as are necessary to the conduct of the applicant's specified research project, and, unless permitted in the instrument of authorization, must not retransmit signals of any other station, or transmit programs intended for public reception.[12]

Unless specifically exempted, each station must announce its call letters at the end of each complete transmission. This is not required where the project calls for "continuous, frequent or extended use of the transmitting apparatus." In such case, the call letters should be announced at least every thirty minutes.[13]

Licensed operators are required. Their licenses together with that of the station must be conspicuously posted at the principal point of operational control. Records of operation must be maintained, and tower lights must be regularly checked as specified in the rules.[14]

Reports to the FCC on Experimental Program. The normal license period for experimental radio stations is for one year only[15], as against a period of three years for regular broadcast stations. Except in the case of stations providing essential communications for research projects, a report on the results of the experimental program authorized by the Commission must be submitted with and made a part of each application for renewal of license. The Commission may request other reports as it deems necessary during the period of a license, to evaluate the progress of the experimental program.[16]

Stations falling in the research group, as defined by the Commission and mentioned above, must include in their reports filed with renewal applications description of the experimentation conducted; detailed analysis of the results obtained; copies of publications covering the experimental work; a list of patents issued as a result of the research; and the number of hours the stations operated on each frequency assigned.[17]

Where a renewal of license is being requested for a radio facility essential to a research project not concerned with the radio art, the Commission requires a showing of need for continuing the authorization as part of the renewal application.[18]

With respect to stations classified as developmental, in addition to submitting the above data, they must provide comprehensive information as to the practicability of service operations, interference encountered, propagation characteristics and suitability of frequencies used, types of signals employed, and prospects for public support for the new service if established.[19]

Student Authorization for Radio Experimentation. On July 23, 1953, the Commission adopted special rules to encourage radio experimentation by students and instructors in educational institutions. These rules are reported at 23 Fed. Reg. 5775, and 1 RR 55:61-63. These authorizations may, in the discretion of the Commission, be granted to students of seventh grade or higher level.

As provided in Section 5.402 of the rules, an application may be filed in letter form, in duplicate, signed under oath and shall contain the following information:

(1) Name and address of applicant.

(2) A statement that the applicant is a citizen of the United States.

(3) Applicant's school and grade.

(4) A detailed description in narrative form of the project including the type and purpose of operation.

(5) Place of operation—street address, name of building, or other specific location.

(6) Date(s) of operation including the exact hours, when known, as well as the duration of each period of operation.

(7) Equipment to be used. If manufactured, list name of manufacturer and type number. For other equipment, describe in detail and furnish a circuit diagram.

(8) Frequency(ies) desired and range of frequencies which could be employed.

(9) The method by which the frequency of operation will be determined.

(10) Frequency tolerance.

(11) The means by which this tolerance will be maintained.

(12) DC plate power input to final radio frequency stage. If not known, indicate any known power rating of equipment and state whether this is power output of transmitter or radiated power, and whether average or peak.

(13) Type of emission, including a description of the modulation that will be applied, if modulated.

(14) Description of the antenna to be used, including height above ground.

Dimensions of Experimental Radio. In its 1958 annual report, the Commission pointed out several types of experiments being carried on in the experimental radio services.[20] For example, studies were being made to determine the height of the various reflecting layers in the ionosphere, which information is useful in making high frequency propagation forecasts.

Other licensees were investigating "scatter" phenomena, so called, which is developing as a new mode of long range communication, using VHF.

Experimental studies were being conducted, investigating propagation characteristics at the frequency of 8 kilocycles, which is just below the commonly accepted lower boundary of the radio spectrum. The antenna being used for the study was a section of high voltage power line several miles in length.

Other important experimentation in the development of new radio equipment is being carried on by colleges, universities, manufacturing concerns, and private laboratories, using radio frequencies assigned by the Commission in the experimental services.

"Another function of the experimental radio services," the Commission stated in 1958, "is to provide short-term authorizations for field-strength surveys and equipment demonstrations to prospective purchasers of new radio equipment. The demand for this type of operation has increased approximately 400 per cent in a little over 4 years and is still climbing. Experimental applications processed during the year totaled 2,854 as compared with 1,055 in 1952 and authorizations increased from 369 to 834."[21]

Because of the tremendous growth in experimental radio operations, there is the increasing problem of finding frequencies to meet the demand. More and more, researchers are compelled to share frequencies, and care must be exercised to see that regularly established services are not disrupted and that maximum utility from experimental frequencies is achieved.

Experimental Broadcast Services. In addition to stations in the experimental radio service, the Commission has provided in its rules for the establishment of experimental broadcast stations whose operations include the presentation of programs for public reception.

There are three types of these stations. One is the *Experimental Television Broadcast Station*. It is defined as one licensed for experimental transmission of "transient visual images of moving or fixed objects for simultaneous reception and reproduction by the general public." It of course also involves the transmission of synchronized sound and any license for such a station authorizes aural as well as visual transmissions.[22]

Its purpose is to carry on research and experimentation for the advancement of television broadcasting which may include tests of equipment, training of personnel, and experimental programs as are necessary.[23]

A second type of experimental broadcast station provided for in the Commission rules is that involving facsimile transmission.[24] FM stations may transmit still pictures, graphs, and printed or written matter to the general public on a simplex or multiplex basis. In the past a few authorizations have been granted for transmission of facsimile, but no stations are now engaged in this type of broadcasting.

The *Developmental Broadcast Station* is a third type. Its purpose is to carry on research and development primarily in radiotelephony for the advancement of broadcasting in general.[25] This kind of station may broadcast programs only when they are necessary to the experiments being conducted, but no regular program service may be carried on unless specifically authorized by the FCC.[26] Section 4.382 of the Rules states that if the license authorizes the carrying of programs, the developmental broadcast station may transmit the programs of a standard, or FM broadcast station or networks, provided, that during the broadcast a statement is made identifying the source of the programs and announcing that the program is being presented in connection with the experimental operation.[27]

Application and Licensing Procedure. FCC Form 309 is used in applying for permits to establish these three types of experimental broadcast facilities.[28] As is true with experimental radio stations already discussed, it must be shown in the application for each type of experimental broadcast station that the proposed operation complies with the general provisions of the Communications Act; that a definite program of technical research and experimentation has been worked out which indicates reasonable promise of substantial contribution to the development of the particular art; that the applicant has qualified personnel and is capable of proceeding immediately with such a program; and that the transmission of radio signals is essential to the proposed experimental research.[29]

Similar to the requirements in the experimental radio services, a supplemental statement must be filed with the application confirming the applicant's understanding that all operation upon the frequency requested is for experimental purposes only; that the frequency requested may not be the best suited for the particular project; and that it need not be allocated for any service that may be developed as a result of the experimentation; and that the frequency assignment is subject to change or cancellation without advance notice or hearing.[30]

After an application is granted, during the period of construction, the permittee (after notifying the Commission and the Engineer in Charge of the district in which the station is located) is free to conduct equipment tests.[31] Once these tests show compliance with conditions of the permit and technical requirements of the FCC, a license application may be filed on FCC Form 310 showing the station to be in satisfactory operating condition.[32] The station may then conduct service or program tests, provided, the Engineer in Charge of the district and the Commission are notified at least two days (not including Sundays, Saturdays and legal holidays) in advance of the beginning of such broadcasting.[33]

Each license specifies the maximum power that may be used by the station, and in no event may the actual operating power for an experimental broadcast station exceed more than 3 per cent of that authorized by the license.[34] A 5 per cent tolerance is allowed facsimile and developmental stations.[35] The license is issued subject to the condition that no objectionable interference will be caused other stations.[36]

More than one frequency may be assigned for these experimental broadcast operations provided the applicant has made an adequate showing of need, but the Commission does not authorize the exclusive use of any frequency by a single licensee.[37] Where interference will result from the simultaneous operation of experimental broadcast stations, licensees must try to arrange a satisfactory time division so that the interference will be avoided. If an agreement cannot be reached, then the Commission specifies the time division.[38]

The specific frequencies allocated to the various types of experimental broadcast stations are listed in the Commission's Table of Frequency Allocations which appears in Subpart B, Part 2 of the Rules and Regulations governing the operation of these stations.[39]

No person may own more than one experimental broadcast or facsimile station unless a showing is made that the character of the programs of research requires a licensing of two or more separate stations.[40] This limitation on ownership, however, does not appear in the rules relating to developmental and other types of experimental stations discussed in this chapter.

Licenses for these stations are granted for one year, and renewal applications (FCC Form 311) must be filed 60 days prior to the expiration of the licenses.[41] With respect to the experimental TV stations, a report must accompany the renewal application showing the following:

(1) Number of hours the station has operated.

(2) Full data on research and experimentation conducted including the type of transmitting and studio equipment used and their mode of operation.

(3) Data on expense of research and operation during the period covered.

(4) Power employed, field intensity measurements and visual and aural observations and the types of instruments and receivers utilized to determine the station service area and the efficiency of the respective types of transmissions.

(5) Estimated degree of public participation in reception and the results of observations as to the effectiveness of types of transmission.

(6) Conclusions, tentative and final.

(7) Program for further developments in television broadcasting.

(8) All developments and major changes in equipment.

(9) Any other pertinent developments.[42]

Less detailed reports are required to be submitted with applications for renewal of licenses of facsimile and developmental broadcast stations. A statement, however, must be filed showing the number of hours of operation, the research and experimentation conducted, developments and major changes in equipment, conclusions drawn from the study and a suggested program for further developments of the facsimile or developmental broadcast service.[43]

Equipment and Technical Operation. Licensees of these three types of broadcast stations may make changes in the equipment if (1) the operating frequency is not permitted to deviate more than the allowed tolerance; (2) the emissions are not outside the authorized band; (3) the power output complies with the license and the regulations governing the same; and (4) the transmitter as a whole or output power rating of the transmitter is not changed.[44] Section 4.351 (d) of the rules states that this last limitation does not apply to developmental broadcast stations licensed to operate in connection with the development and testing of commercial broadcast equipment.[45]

The Rules provide that experimental broadcast television and developmental stations transmitting below 450 megacycles must maintain their operating frequencies within plus or minus 0.01 per cent of those assigned.[46] Those transmitting above 450 megacycles must not deviate more than plus or minus 0.05 per cent.[47] If a lesser tolerance, however, is necessary to prevent interference the Commission will so specify.[48] For facsimile stations, the tolerance in every case is plus or minus 0.01, unless otherwise specified by the Commission.[49]

The necessary means must be provided and sufficient observations must be made to insure that these stations operate within the allowed frequency tolerance.[50] Each frequency measurement and the exact time it is made and the method employed must be entered in the station log.[51]

No regular schedule of operation must be maintained, but each type of station must actively conduct a program of research and experimentation substantially in accord with that proposed in the original application unless otherwise authorized by the Commission.[52]

Other operation requirements set forth in the rules include the maintenance of adequate records showing the operating hours of the station, programs transmitted, frequency checks, pertinent remarks concerning transmission, points of program origination and receiver location when relay or pickup stations are involved, and research and experimentation conducted.[53] Where antenna structures are required to be illuminated, inspections of the lighting must be made and recorded as specified in Part 17 of the Rules to which reference is made in Chapter 16.[54] All station records must be retained for a period of two years.[55]

No charge of any kind may be made by these experimental broadcast stations for the production or transmission of programs.[56] Call letters and station location must be announced at the beginning and end of each operation and at least once every hour during the broadcast period.[57]

Rebroadcasting of programs is not permitted without the prior written consent of the originating stations and, upon application, without securing the written authority of the Commission.[58]

One or more first or second class operators must be on duty at the place where the transmitting apparatus is located and in actual charge of its operation. He may be employed for other duties or for the operation of other broadcasting facilities so long as the operation of the transmitter at the experimental station is not unfavorably affected.[59]

Dimensions of Experimental Broadcasting. The Commission reported that there were 20 experimental TV stations in operation in 1959.[60] They were carrying on research in a number of fields.

This research ranged from the development of a hand-carried TV camera and transmitter to experimentation with directional antennas. One study related to repeater stations.[61] Preliminary studies indicated that a repeater, operating on the same channel as its parent station, might possibly improve UHF coverage in mountainous terrain. Among other researches, comparative studies were being made with respect to UHF and VHF transmissions.[62]

Applicants for the developmental type of operation usually are AM or FM licensees, and permission for short-term special operation may be granted to these licensees without their having to submit formal applications.

Thirty-six such authorizations were issued by the FCC in 1959, most of which went to broadcast licensees to experiment with stereophonic broadcasting.[63]

NOTES

1. 48 Stat. 1082.
2. FCC Rules and Regulations, Section 5.3 (c), (d) and (e); 1 RR 55:13.
3. 1 RR 55:12-411.
4. Section 5.55; 1 RR 55:12-17.
5. *Ibid.*
6. *Ibid.*
7. Section 5.56; 1 RR 55:18-19.
8. Section 5.57; 1 RR 59:19.
9. *Ibid.,* 53:19-20.
10. 1 RR 55:31-41.
11. Section 5.122; 1 RR 55:41.
12. Section 5.151(b) and (c); 1 RR 55:35.
13. Section 5.152; 1 RR 55:35.
14. Sections 5.155, 5.156, and 5.157, and 5.161; 1 RR 55:36-39.
15. Section 5.63; 1 RR 55:23.
16. Sections 5.204 and 5.255; 1 RR 55:51-52 and 54-55.
17. *Ibid.*
18. Section 5.204(d); 1 RR 55:22.
19. Section 5.255(d); 1 RR 55:54-55.
20. *FCC Annual Report,* 1958, pp. 171-172.
21. *Ibid.,* p. 172.
22. Section 4.101; 1 RR 54:31.
23. Section 4.012; 1 RR 54:31.
24. Section 4.201; 1 RR 54:51.
25. Section 4.301; 1 RR 54:71.
26. Section 4.382; 1 RR 54:75.
27. *Ibid.*
28. Section 1.322 (2); 1 RR 51:197.
29. Sections 4.131, 4.231, 4.331; 1 RR 54:33, 52, 72.
30. Sections 4.112 and 4.312; 1 RR 54:32, 71, 72.
31. Section 4.13; 1 RR 54:12.
32. *Ibid.,* and Section 1.325; 1 RR 51:198.
33. *Ibid.*
34. Section 4.132; 1 RR 54:33.
35. Section 4.232 and 4.332; 1 RR 54:52-53, and 72.

36. Sections 4.131(c); 1 RR 54:33.

37. Section 4.103, 4.131(b), 4.201, 4.231(b), 4.302, 4.331(b); 1 RR 54:31, 33, 51, 52, 71 and 72.

38. Sections 4.131(b), 4.231(b), 4.331(b); 1 RR 54:33, 52 and 72.

39. Section 2.103; 1 RR 52:41-58.

40. Sections 4.134 and 4.234; 1 RR 54:34 and 53.

41. Sections 1.328 and 4.15; RR 51:199 and 45:13-14.

42. Sections 4.113; 1 RR 54:32-33.

43. Sections 4.213 and 4.313; 1 RR 54:52 and 72.

44. Sections 4.151, 4.251 and 4.351; 1 RR 54:34, 53 and 73.

45. 1 RR 54:73.

46. Sections 4.161 and 4.361; 1 RR 54:34 and 73.

47. *Ibid.*

48. *Ibid.*

49. Section 4.261; 1 RR 54:53.

50. Sections 4.162, 4.262 and 4.362; 1 RR 54:34, 53 and 73.

51. *Ibid.*

52. Sections 4.163, 4.262, 4.363; 1 RR 54:34, 54 and 73.

53. See sections 4.164 through 4.184, 4.263 through 4.284 and 4.364 through 4.384; 1 RR 35-37, 54-56 and 74-76.

54. 1 RR 67:9-109.

55. Sections 4.181, 4.281 and 4.381; 1 RR 53:36, 55 and 75.

56. Sections 4.182, 4.282 and 4.382; 1 RR 53:36, 55 and 76.

57. Sections 4.183, 4.283 and 4.383; 1 RR 53:36, 55 and 76.

58. Sections 4.184, 4.284, 4.384; 1 RR 54:37, 56 and 76.

59. Sections 4.166, 4.266, 4.366; 1 RR 54:36, 54 and 74.

60. *FCC Annual Report,* 1959, pp. 70-71.

61. *Ibid.*

62. *Ibid.*

63. *Ibid.*

PART IV

Problems of Getting on the Air

CHAPTER 13

Qualifying for a License

The application for a construction permit shall set forth such facts as the Commission by regulation may prescribe as to the citizenship, character, and the financial, technical, and other ability of the applicant to construct and operate the station. . . .—Section 319 (a) of the Communications Act of 1934

Just anybody cannot get a license to operate a radio or television station. The Communications Act gives the FCC considerable discretion in determining the minimum qualifications for authority to operate stations, but in certain cases it specifically prohibits the Commission from granting licenses.

Statutory Ineligibility. The framers of the Communications Act were fearful that subversive elements might acquire control of the communications facilities to the detriment of national security. As early as 1932, the Secretary of the Navy had written to the Chairman of the Senate Interstate Commerce Committee stating that stations owned or controlled by foreign interests might be used "in espionage work and in the dissemination of subversive propaganda." He further declared:

It is not sufficient that the military forces have authority to assume control of radio stations in war. A certain amount of liaison between radio company executives and departmental officials responsible for government communications is required in peace time. Familiarity on the part of commercial executives of American radio companies with communication operating methods, plans, and developments of the military departments of the government is certainly to the best interests of the nation. Some of these matters are of a very secret nature. For the Navy Department to initiate and carry out this important contact with commercial companies, the divulging of confidential plans to directors is necessary. This is obviously impossible with even one foreigner on the board.

International companies must have agreements between their subsidiaries and the parent companies for a free exchange of information. Foreign personnel are transferred from one subsidiary to another so as to obtain intimate knowledge of the methods and equipment employed by other branches. It is impossible for a military service to work in close cooperation with or disclose its new developments to an organization which has foreign affiliations of this nature and employs foreign personnel.[1]

To make sure that the communications systems of the country would be absolutely free of foreign control, Congress adopted Section 310 (a) of the Communications Act prohibiting the granting of a license to any alien, foreign government, or any corporation organized under the laws of any foreign government. No corporation can hold a license if any officer or director is an alien or if more than 20% of the stock is owned or voted by aliens or foreign governments or corporations.

Paragraph 5 of this section gives the FCC discretionary power to refuse a license to any corporation directly or indirectly controlled by another corporation of which any officer or more than 25% of the stock is owned or voted by aliens, foreign governments or corporations or representatives thereof.

The FCC has consistently and strictly enforced the provisions of this section. Individuals applying for broadcasting facilities are required to prove their citizenship. Corporate applicants likewise must show that they are not subject to alien or foreign control.

In a 1938 case, the Commission denied an application for a construction permit when one of the individuals in a partnership was foreign born and claimed derivative United States citizenship through his stepfather but failed to present his certificate of derivative citizenship and did not prove that he had taken the oath to defend the constitution or had renounced his allegiance to his native country.[2]

In a 1939 case, the Commission held that the president and principal stockholder of an applicant corporation who was born abroad did not meet the legal requirements of Section 310 though he had come to this country when he was two years of age and claimed derivative citizenship through the naturalization of his father.[3]

The Commission was satisfied, however, with a "marginal" showing in another 1939 case, consisting of oral testimony by a stockholder in an applicant company as to the citizenship of an officer. The FCC gave credence to the testimony because the witness had been associated with the officer in a business way for many years and was well acquainted with his family.[4]

In 1955, the Commission held that a sufficient showing was made of compliance with paragraph 5 of Section 310(a) of the Act by a corporation with a large number of stockholders, where a sampling indicated that less than 25% of the stock was held by aliens or foreign governments or corporations, and no evidence was submitted to question the reliability of the sampling method used. The Commission recognized, however, that this method of proof might not be acceptable in all cases and under other circumstances.[5]

Monopolistic Practices. Section 313 of the Communications Act provides that if a court finds a party guilty of violating any of the anti-trust laws, it may, in addition to other penalties imposed, revoke any broadcasting license held by that party. In case of such court revocation, Section 311 of the Act directs the Commission to refuse any further permits or licenses to the offender.

In view of the mandatory features of Section 311, companies holding radio or television licenses and who are engaged in the manufacture, sale or trading of broadcasting equipment that enters or affects interstate or foreign commerce, must be particularly cautious to avoid any kind of arrangements or activities which might subject them to prosecution for monopolistic practices and unlawful restraints of trade.

Other Legal Disabilities. As will be discussed more fully later, persons desiring to operate broadcasting stations must first file written applications with the FCC asking for authority to construct the facilities and for licenses to operate them once construction is completed. In fact, except in cases of emergency involving danger to life or property or national security, Section 308(a) of the Communications Act specifically forbids the FCC from granting a construction permit, license or renewal of license without a written application having first been filed.

As set forth in Section 309(a) of the law, the Commission must be able to find that the public interest will be served before granting authority to build or operate a station. To aid the Commission in this function, the applicant is required to set forth in writing such facts as the Commission by regulation may prescribe as to his "citizenship, character, and financial, technical and other qualifications." In each case, the Commission must study these facts and be satisfied that the applicant is legally, financially, technically and otherwise qualified to operate a station in the public interest.

A corporation, partnership, association or other type of joint enterprise must establish itself as a legal entity and show its authority to engage in broadcasting activities before it can qualify for a construction permit or license. For example, two individuals, claiming to be a partnership, applied for a station, but the application was denied for the reasons that there was no written partnership agreement between the parties and they were not legally bound by any written instrument to contribute anything to the joint venture.[6]

In another case, involving a limited partnership,[7] the Commission held that the applicant was not legally qualified to receive a grant where it failed to show the statutory authority upon which it relied for its right to exist as a legal entity and presented for the record no partnership agreement or binding contract on the parties to contribute to the partnership funds.

Every profit and non-profit corporation is required to give evidence of its incorporation under state law and establish its legal identity and show

159

that broadcasting falls within the scope of its purposes and powers as set forth in its charter. The Federal Radio Commission, predecessor of the FCC, stated in 1932 that a "corporation has only such powers as are expressly granted in its charter or which are necessary for the carrying out of its express powers and the purposes of its incorporation."[8] This does not mean in every case that the instrument of authorization must specifically provide for broadcasting. The important test is whether it can reasonably be construed that the operation of a broadcasting station is appropriate or essential to the accomplishment of the general purpose set forth in the charter. Many educational institutions, for example, have qualified for licenses, even though the charter or the statutes which authorize their activities make no specific mention of broadcasting.

Financial Qualifications. As may be implied from Sections 308(a) and 319(a) of the Communications Act and prescribed in paragraph (3) of Section 3.24(b) of the Commission's Rules governing broadcast stations, there is a positive burden of proof on every applicant to show that he has the financial resources to build and operate the type of station proposed. In an early 1935 case, despite a showing by an applicant that he could secure money from friends to buy station equipment, his application was denied by the Commission on the grounds that he did not have enough finances to erect the station and maintain its operation and there was no proof that the station would be self-supporting.[9]

That same year, the Commission refused to grant a construction permit to an applicant because he proposed to build a station with money he had borrowed without security, the loan to be repaid in five years. On appeal, however, the Court of Appeals of the District of Columbia overruled the Commission and held that in the absence of a Commission rule or statutory prohibition against the use of borrowed funds, the applicant's plan for financing, with assured resources for five years, was adequate and that the Commission erred in disapproving it.[10]

In a more recent decision, an application of a California corporation for a television station was denied on the grounds that the applicant had only $32,500 available for construction and initial operation of the station. The estimated costs of construction ran almost $26,000, which did not include the cost of a monitor. With reference to the matter of financial inability the Commission said:

Where we consider the initial cost of operation for any reasonable period of time in the light of funds available to the applicant, together with our uncertainty with regard to the cost of composite equipment and the fact that no allowance has been made for the RCA monitor . . . that contingencies may arise which the applicant has not considered in its cost estimate . . . a substantial question as to the adequacy of the operating expense allocated for the purchase of film . . . we are unable to conclude that the applicant is financially qualified to construct, own and operate the proposed station.[11]

The Commission has established no hard and fast rules with respect to financial qualifications. Decisions have been based largely upon the facts of each case. Generally, the Commission has been fairly liberal in making grants where there is a reasonable proof that funds are on hand or will be available or can be secured to assure the construction and initial operation of the station. In making decisions on financial ability, the agency has taken into account such factors as costs of construction, estimated expense of operation for the first year, the size and type of market and possibilities of income, the previous income of the applicant, his present financial assets and liabilities, and ability of prospective donors or creditors, if any, to fulfil their pledges and commitments.

Technical Qualifications. The construction and operation of a broadcasting station requires special technical knowledge and skills. To qualify therefore for a permit or license, technical ability must be demonstrated. In an early 1936 case, the Commission stated a point of view which it more or less has followed through the years:

An indispensable element in passing upon any application for station licenses is the technical qualifications of the applicant. This does not mean that the applicant in every case must be personally qualified technically, but it does mean that if he is not personally qualified technically and does not propose to operate the station himself but through employees, then he should show that he has a competent staff to operate the proposed station for him, and their technical qualifications.[12]

In another 1936 case, a permit to build a station was denied on the grounds that technical ability of the applicant himself was insufficient and he declined to state the names of persons to whom he would entrust technical control.[13]

Where a Michigan company was seeking a special type of broadcasting station, the application was denied for the reason that no showing was made that there would be an adequate staff of engineers and technical facilities to effectuate the program of research and experimentation proposed. The company proposed to use the technical facilities of a university but this was held to be insufficient since the governing board of the institution had made no commitment in this regard and, in fact, had refused to assume any expense for such an operation.[14]

In a 1955 television case, the Commission stated that it did not expect an applicant to "achieve perfection in its first day of operation," and that the question with respect to technical qualifications is whether "staffing, studio and equipment plans are *adequate* to effectuate to a *reasonable* degree the programs it has promised." (Italics supplied).[15]

Character Qualifications. In addition to legal, financial and technical competencies, the Commission is given wide latitude in considering the general character qualifications of those seeking station licenses. This stems from the public interest features of the Communications Act and the fact that the Commission can require applicants to supply information regarding their character and behavior as it may relate to their ability to operate a station in the public interest. (See Sections 308(a) and 319(a) of the Communications Act). Since the use of a publicly owned channel is in the nature of a public trust, the Commission has attached great importance to elements of character such as honesty and reliability, moral, financial and social responsibility and respect for law and order.

In a 1937 case, the District Circuit Court of Appeals sustained the FCC in its denial of an application for a construction permit where, in addition to financial inability, the applicant failed to "make frank, candid, and honest disclosures of its organizational set-up, stock ownership, and connection with another licensee."[16] This same court took a similar position in a 1946 case where the Commission had questioned the honesty and candor of an applicant.[17]

In 1951, the application of a corporation for an FM station was denied, various misrepresentations of facts having been made and one of the three stockholders having demonstrated a lack of character qualifications because he had been "intemperate in his writings, sermons and broadcasts and was an expert in vituperation and vilification."[18] There again, on appeal, the Court confirmed the Commission's decision.

In some cases, where parties have failed to disclose material facts in applications regarding past conduct which is questionable, the Commission has resolved doubts in their favor, especially when the misconduct did not appear to have been willful and the parties have high professional standing and reputations for good character in the communities where they live. For example, the Commission decided that the failure of the principal stockholder in an applicant corporation to disclose his connection with a bankrupt corporation and to reveal that a number of his assets were in fact owned by his wife did not warrant a finding that there was intentional deception. There was an implication in the language of the Commission that the principal stockholder had not shown the highest degree of candor, but because of his generally good reputation and professional competency, the Commission gave him the benefit of the doubt.[19]

Public Responsibility and Respect for Law. In administrative practice, an applicant's sense of public responsibility and respect for law have always been considered by the FCC to be important character elements. Where serious deficiences in these respects have appeared, the agency has not hesitated to disqualify applicants.

In 1950, the U.S. Appellate Court for the District of Columbia agreed with the Commission in refusing a construction permit to a newspaper that had attempted to suppress competition by coercing advertisers to enter into exclusive contracts, and had refused to make space available to business concerns which also advertised over the local radio station, and also refused to print any reference to the station except unfavorable ones.

Whether this conduct actually violated the anti-trust laws the Court said was immaterial. It was enough that the behavior standards of the applicant in its business affairs and dealings with the public raised serious questions as to its ability to meet the requirements and responsibilities of a broadcast licensee.[20]

It has been held in another case that failure of a corporation to comply with state corporation laws reflects upon its character qualifications to become a licensee. The Commission declared that failure to comply with the state laws was a disqualifying factor plus the fact that two of the three incorporators had not looked at the application before it was filed and its preparation and submission to the Commission were carried on in "a confused and slipshod manner" and indicated a lack of ability and sense of responsibility essential for the operation of a radio station in the public interest.[21]

Certain individuals were disqualified from securing a license on the grounds that in the conduct of their private business, over a long period of time, they had violated and disregarded the regulatory laws of the states and the federal government. Even though their record did not involve any civil or criminal judgments against them, still the Commission and the Courts decided that they had not demonstrated sufficient sense of responsibility to qualify.[22]

In a later case, however, the fact that an applicant had been indicted on three occasions for alleged offenses but had been acquitted each time, was not considered by the Commission to reflect adversely on his character to operate a station.[23] Nor was arrest and conviction for giving a worthless check considered a reflection on the applicant's moral character when it was shown that through an oversight in the rush of business his bank account had been inadvertently overdrawn and when he had deposited funds immediately to take care of the check upon discovery of the error.[24]

In 1951, after a long study on the part of the FCC and its staff, the agency made a statement of uniform policy which it proposed to follow in cases where applicants have been involved in law violations. The Commission said:

In determining that an applicant is qualified to be a broadcast licensee the Commission must examine all pertinent conduct of the applicant. If an applicant is or has been involved in unlawful practices, an analysis of the substance of these practices must be made to determine their relevance and weight as regards the ability of the applicant to use the requested radio authorization in the public interest. Such a determination must be made on the facts of each case and no blanket policy may be enunciated. However, violation of a federal law, whether deliberate or inadvertent, raises sufficient question regarding character to merit further examination. Violation of federal laws does not necessarily make the applicant ineligible for a radio grant, since there may be extenuating or countervailing considerations. Innocent violations are not as serious as deliberate ones.

Another matter of importance is whether the infraction of law is an isolated instance or whether there have been recurring offenses which establish a definite pattern of misbehavior. Also there must be more concern with recent violations than with those which occurred in the remote past and have been followed by a long period of adherence to law and exemplary conduct. It is irrelevant to a determination of qualifications whether the finding of violation is in a civil or criminal case and the particular tribunal which makes the finding is not significant. And the Commission may consider and evaluate the conduct of an applicant insofar as it relates to matters entrusted to the Commission even though no suit alleging illegal conduct has been filed or has not been heard or finally adjudicated.[25]

In the Commission's Report, of which the above is a summary, certain basic considerations were set forth as guides to be followed in making a case to case determination of character qualifications where law violations are involved. These may be stated as follows:

(1) Was the violation willful or inadvertent?

(2) Was the infraction an isolated instance or have there been recurring offenses?

(3) Has the applicant been engaged in violations over a long period of time so as to show an antipathetic attitude toward the laws of the United States?

(4) Has the applicant recently engaged in illegal practices?

(5) Is the applicant presently engaged in such practices?

Involvement in Anti-Trust Litigation. While the Report had general applicability with respect to violation of all laws, the Commission's main concern was with violation of the anti-trust laws. The Report stressed the point that in setting up the Communications Act, Congress conceived as one of the Commission's major functions the preservation of competition in the radio field and the protection of the public interest. Accordingly, it was made clear that the Commission would view with much concern the proclivity of applicants to monopolize and drive out competition and would make it a major consideration in its determination of character qualifications to operate broadcast stations in the public interest.[26]

In *National Broadcasting Company v. United States,* 319 U.S. 190, 222, the Court gave judicial sanction to the Commission's point of view in this matter. In that case the Court had said that the Commission could exercise its judgment as to whether violations of the anti-trust laws disqualify an applicant from operating a station in the public interest and "might infer from the fact that the applicant had in the past tried to monopolize radio, or had engaged in unfair methods of competition, that the disposition so manifested would continue and that if it did it would make him an unfit licensee."[27]

During the period of time that the Commission had under study the adoption of its policy with respect to law violations, it withheld action on a number of applications for new broadcast facilities and for renewal of existing licenses filed by large companies with records of involvement in anti-trust litigation. One of these was Westinghouse Radio Stations, Incorporated. Westinghouse Electric, the parent company, had been named as a defendant in a number of anti-trust suits, but only once had it been found to have violated the laws against monopolies. The parent company also had been involved in several anti-trust proceedings resulting in consent decrees but in which there was no admission of guilt or court conviction.[28]

After a careful study of Westinghouse's record, the Commission concluded that there was insufficient evidence of character taint to warrant denial of license renewals. Accordingly, in April, 1952, the renewal applications were granted.[29] On April 1, 1953, the Commission granted the application of the company to increase the operating power of Station WOWO, action on which had been delayed until the disposition of the anti-monopoly questions. Subsequently, on June 29, 1955, the Commission issued its decision in a Portland, Oregon case involving four conflicting television applications for Channel 8 in that city, Westinghouse being one of the four applicants. While the company did not prevail in that comparative proceeding, the Commission again found no basis on which to impugn the character of the company because of alleged monopolistic practices, and the decision in the case favorable to another applicant turned on other grounds.

The Commission held that no adverse findings should be made against an applicant because of litigation in which it has been involved where the evidence consists chiefly of a recitation of the litigation without a showing of facts as they relate to the conduct of the applicant, and where no pattern of illegal conduct is proved. Facts of conduct and not mere allegations are important.

The Commission further said that *nolo contendere* decrees do not constitute proof of facts.[30] Nor do consent decrees reflect upon the conduct of the applicant where they are remote in time and no pattern of misbehavior can be established because of them.[31]

Paramount's Involvement in Anti-Trust Litigation. A more difficult case for the Commission to decide involved applications of Paramount Television Productions, Inc., and its subsidiary companies, seeking renewals of licenses and construction permits for numerous television stations. Along with those of Westinghouse, the applications of Paramount were kept in a pending status while the Commission was formulating its policy with respect to law violations mentioned above.

The Paramount companies had been involved in anti-trust litigation for more than 20 years. These cases included complaints alleging monopolistic practices and restraints of trade, both at federal and state levels.[32] On May

3, 1948, the United States Supreme Court handed down decisions in three cases involving anti-trust complaints against several companies owning or operating motion picture theatres and engaged in the production and distribution of films.[33] Paramount was one of the defendants in these cases. Proceedings in these cases were started in 1938 with a suit filed by the Government against Paramount Pictures, Inc., and several other motion picture companies, alleging violations of Section 4 of the Sherman Act.

The complaint charged that Paramount and other defendants, as distributors and exhibitors of motion picture films, had conspired to restrain and monopolize interstate trade in the exhibition of films in most of the larger cities of the country, and that they were guilty of a vertical combination of producing, distributing and exhibiting films contrary to the provisions of the Sherman Act.

Before the trial on these charges was held, negotiations for a settlement were undertaken, resulting in a consent decree entered on November 20, 1940. The consent decree contained no admission or adjudication of any issues of law or fact, other than the admission that the complaint stated a cause of action. The decree reserved to the government the right at the end of a three-year period to seek further relief. At the end of this period, the government, feeling that the decree had not proved effective, moved for trial against all the defendants.

After lengthy proceedings, the Federal District Court found the defendants substantially guilty of all the allegations of the complaint. On appeal to the Supreme Court, the judgment was affirmed with respect to charges of unreasonable restraints of trade. On certain questions relating to divorcement and arbitration, the District Court's findings were reversed and the matters sent back for redetermination.

In affirming the District Court's findings that the defendants had engaged in price-fixing conspiracies, the Supreme Court said:

The District Court found that two price-fixing conspiracies existed—a horizontal one between all the defendants, a vertical one between each distributor—defendant and its licensees. The latter was based on express agreements and was plainly established. The former was inferred from the pattern of price-fixing disclosed in the record. We think there was adequate foundation for it too. It is not necessary to find an express agreement in order to find a conspiracy. It is enough that a concert of action is contemplated and that the defendants conformed to the arrangement.[34]

In regard to the defendants' policies in granting clearances,[35] the Supreme Court upheld a finding that these arrangements were unreasonable and that many of them "had no relation to the competitive factors which alone could justify them."[36]

Furthermore, the lower court's findings were affirmed, that the defendants had been guilty of unfair competition in that they operated theatres, normally competitive, as units with profit-sharing agreements and had discriminated against independent exhibitors through various kinds of contract provisions. Other trade practices that were found to be unreasonable restraints of trade included formula deals, and block-booking. In regard to the latter practice the Supreme Court said:

. . . Block-booking prevents competitors from bidding for single features on their individual merits. The District Court (66 F. Supp. 349) held it illegal for that reason and for the reason that it 'adds to the monopoly of a single copyrighted picture that of another copyrighted picture which must be taken and exhibited in order to secure the first.' . . . The Court enjoined defendants from performing or entering into any license in which the right to exhibit one feature is conditioned upon the licensee's taking one or more other features. We approve that restriction.[37]

The District Court found that the defendants had a particular monopoly in the ownership of theatres, having interest in over 17% of the theatres in the United States from which they received 45% of the total domestic film rental. It found that in the 92 cities having populations over 100,000 at least 70% of all the first run theatres were affiliated with one or more of the defendants. The District Court enjoined the defendants from expanding their theatre holdings.[38]

The Supreme Court remanded the question of theatre ownership to the lower court. On remand of the case, Paramount entered into a consent decree under the terms of which it was split into two companies, not under common control, one to be concerned with pictures and the other with theatres. Under a plan of reorganization the old company was dissolved and its assets transferred to two new companies, namely Paramount Pictures Corporation and United Paramount Theatres, Inc.

The FCC was concerned that Paramount's monopolistic practices might carry over into the television field. It had received reports to the effect that Paramount and other motion picture industries had refused to make any of their films available for use by television stations. There also were restrictions imposed by some of these companies as to the appearances of actors under contract to the studio on television programs and to the use on television of stories or plays whose rights had been acquired by the studio.[39]

With respect to the weight to be attached to involvement in anti-trust litigation as regards character qualifications, attorneys for Paramount made a number of points which should be mentioned here. One point stressed was that anti-trust laws are highly complex and often-times difficult to understand; that a great deal of uncertainty as to the meaning of these laws prevails among businessmen, lawyers and the courts; that some practices now prohibited by the courts were formerly sanctioned by them. It was argued, therefore, because of the complexity and uncertainty of meaning of the anti-trust laws, that big business should not be charged with moral dereliction for violating them.[40]

It was further contended by legal counsel for Paramount that its involvement in the litigation described above had no real connection with the radio industry. "It does not reflect the character or qualifications of the defendant to serve the public interest." Nor was there any "claim in the Paramount case that the public was not adequately served by motion pictures, nor was there any claim of an exclusion of any picture from the public. On the contrary, it was conceded that the public in this case was not only given adequate, but the very best of theatre and amusement facilities." The counsel concluded, therefore, "public interest in radio, in the sense it is used in the Communications Act, is not even remotely involved in the Paramount case;" and further, "it cannot be fairly said that this type of activity in another field—activity of a kind which the government and the courts themselves were not certain about until recently—it cannot be said that such activity gives the slightest indication that businessmen would have a tendency toward monopoly in a different field."[41]

Despite these arguments, the Commission was unable to conclude that a grant of Paramount's pending applications for new broadcasting facilities and for renewal of its existing licenses would serve the public interest. Accordingly, they were designated for public hearing.

After a prolonged hearing in which Paramount's record and qualifications were thoroughly explored, the Commission granted the applications. The decision declared that with respect to Paramount and its subsidiaries who were existing licensees with records as broadcasters, it was impracticable to attempt to delve into and evaluate the entire history, remote as well as recent, of their activities in fields other than radio communications which might have involved anti-trust violations. The Commission further said that in general it would not consider any such activities which occurred more than three years before the filing of the applications.[42]

Subsequently, the Commission approved a merger of Paramount with the American Broadcasting Company. In the decision approving the merger, it was held that the policies of the motion picture concern with respect to its past use of film, talent or stories on television did not constitute a bar to a grant of license and transfer applications.[43]

In a case decided by the Commission in June, 1953, in which a question was raised as to whether recent conduct involving violation of the anti-trust laws was an absolute bar to getting a license, it was held that "a single violation or even a number of them, *ipso facto,* did not disqualify an applicant." Even though the applicant may have engaged in unlawful practices, in each case an analysis of the substance of these practices must still be made to determine their relevance and weight in terms of his ability to use the requested facilities in the public interest.[45] In support of this position the Commission quoted from its report setting forth policies to be followed in assessing qualifications of law violators, adopted in 1951 and referred to earlier in this chapter. The quotation is as follows:

Violations of Federal laws, whether deliberate or inadvertent, raise sufficient question regarding character to merit further examination. While this question as to character may be overcome by countervailing circumstances, nevertheless, in every case, the Commission must view with concern the unlawful conduct of any applicant who is seeking authority to operate radio facilities as a trustee for the public. This is not to say that a single violation of a federal law or even a number of them necessarily makes the offender ineligible for a radio grant. There may be facts which are in extenuation of the violation of law. Or, there may be other favorable facts and considerations that outweigh the record of unlawful conduct and qualify the applicant to operate a station in the public interest.[46]

No Hard and Fast Rules for Character Qualifications. No hard and fast rules can be drawn with respect to what constitutes adequate character qualifications to operate broadcasting stations in the public interest. The foregoing discussion with random reference to a few of the more important cases decided by the Commission simply suggests some types of behavior on the part of applicants, both individual and corporate, about which the FCC has raised questions. The Commission, by statute, is given wide latitude in determining character qualifications. Guiding principles have been established to which the public has a right to expect reasonable adherence by the FCC, but in the last analysis, each case must stand on its own merits, and be decided in terms of the particular facts involved. In any case, where the facts raise questions as to character and suggest inability to operate a station in the public interest, the burden of proof is always on the applicant to resolve any doubts and show that he does have the ability and can meet the requirements of law.

NOTES

1. Part of letter from the Secretary of Navy to the Chairman of the Senate Interstate Commerce Committee, March 22, 1932, Hearings on S. 2910, 73rd Congress, 2nd Session, p. 169.
2. *Sam Klaver,* 6 FCC 536 (1938).
3. *Mountain Top Trans Radio Corporation,* 7 FCC 180 (1939).
4. *Kentucky Broadcasting Corporation,* 6 FCC 776 (1939).
5. *Westinghouse Radio Stations, Inc.,* 10 RR 878 (1955).
6. *Carter and Wolfe,* 2 FCC 544 (1935).
7. *Chicago Broadcasting Association,* 3 FCC 277 (1936).
8. *Sun-Gazette Company* (FRC Docket No. 1300, March 18, 1932).
9. *Carl C. Struble,* 2 FCC 115.
10. *Heitmeyer v. FCC,* 68 App. D.C. 180; 95 F.(2d) 91 (1937).
11. *Orange Belt Telecasters,* 9 RR 1002a (1954).
12. *W. H. Kindig,* 3 FCC 313, 315, (1936).

13. *E. L. Clifford,* 2 FCC 573, (1935).

14. *Ann Arbor Broadcasting Co., Inc.,* 5 FCC 284, (1938).

15. *WKRG-TV, Inc.,* 10 RR 225 (1955), 268b.

16. *Greater Western Broadcasting Association v. FCC,* 68 U.S. App. D.C. 119, 94 F.(2d) 244.

17. *Calumet Broadcasting Corporation v. FCC,* 82 U.S. App. D.C. 59; 160 F.(2d) 285.

18. *Independent Broadcasting Co. v. FCC,* 89 U.S. App. D.C. 396; 193 F.(2d) 900; 7 RR 2066 (1951).

19. *Cherokee Broadcasting Company,* 13 RR 725 (1956).

20. *Mansfield Journal Co. v. FCC,* 86 U.S. App. D.C. 102; 180 F.(2d) 28, 5 RR 2074 e.

21. *Royal Broadcasting Corporation,* 6 RR 717 (1951).

22. *Bulova and Henshel (Mester),* 11 FCC 137, 3 RR 125 (1946), affirmed 70 F. Supp. 118, 332 U.S. 749 (1947).

23. *James A. Noe,* 4 RR 1441 (1949).

24. *Harold H. Thoms,* 7 FCC 108 (1939).

25. *In the Matter of Establishment of a Uniform Policy to be Followed in Licensing of Radio Broadcast Station Cases in Connection with Violations by an Applicant of Laws of the United States other than the Communications Act,* Docket No. 9572, 16 Fed. Reg. 3187 (1951); 1 RR 91:32 (1951).

26. *Ibid.*

27. 319 U.S. 190, at 222.

28. *Westinghouse Radio Stations, Inc.,* 10 RR 911 (1955).

29. *Ibid.*

30. A *nolo contendere* plea in a criminal prosecution is one which, without admitting guilt, subjects the defendant to conviction, but does not preclude him from denying the truth of the charges in a collateral proceeding.

31. *Westinghouse, op. cit.*

32. FCC Docket 7279, Vol. 3., Paramount Exhibit 4, San Francisco Hearing (TV).

33. *United States v. Paramount Pictures, Inc., et al.,* 334 U.S. 131; *United States vs. Griffith et al.,* 334 U.S. 100; *Schine Chain Theatres, Inc., et al. v. United States,* 334 U.S. 100.

34. *Ibid.,* p. 142.

35. A Clearance is the period of time elapsing between runs of the same feature in the same area.

36. *United States v. Paramount Pictures, Inc., et. al., op. cit.,* p. 146.

37. *Ibid.,* p. 157-58.

38. *Ibid.,* p. 167.

39. FCC Docket 9572, 16 Fed. Reg. 3187 (1951).

40. *Ibid.,* p. 92.

41. *Ibid.,* p. 9.

42. *Paramount Television Productions, Inc., et. al.* (Dockets 10031-10032); Fed. Reg. 8159 (1951).

43. *Paramount Pictures, Inc.,* 8 RR 135 (1952).

44. *ABC-Paramount Merger Case,* 8 RR 541 (1952).

45. *The Loraine Journal Co.,* 9 RR 406 (June 4, 1953).

46. *Ibid.,* p. 409.

CHAPTER 14

Competing with Other Applicants for Broadcast Facilities

The selection of an awardee from among several qualified applicants is basically a matter of judgment, often difficult and delicate, entrusted by the Congress to the administrative agency. The decisive factors in comparable selections may well vary; sometimes one applicant is superior to another in one respect, whereas in another case one applicant may be superior to its rivals in another feature. And . . . the Commission's view of what is best in the public interest may change from time to time. Commissions themselves change, underlying philosophies differ, and experience often dictates changes . . . All such matters are for the Congress and the executive and their agencies. . . . They are not for the judiciary.—JUDGE E. BARRETT PRETTYMAN, *230 F. (2d)204*

A single applicant for a broadcast station must show that he meets all the statutory requirements as set forth in the previous chapter. Furthermore, as set forth therein, he must show that he is financially, technically, legally and otherwise competent and possessed of good character before the Commission can grant him a license. His burden of proof, however, may become much heavier if he is competing with others for the same facilities. In such a case, he must show not only that he meets the minimum requirements of the statute, but that he is *better* qualified than the other applicants and that his plans and proposals for the establishment of a station will *better* serve the public interest.

As the U.S. Appellate Court for the District of Columbia has said, "a choice between two applicants involves more than the basic qualifications of each applicant. It involves a comparison of characteristics. Both A and B may be qualified, but if a choice must be made, the question is which is the better qualified. Both might be ready, able and willing to serve the public interest. But in choosing between them, the inquiry must reveal which would better serve that interest. . . . Comparative qualities and not mere positive characteristics must then be considered."[1]

In comparing qualities, the Commission has attempted to employ various criteria in determining which one, among multiple applicants, is best qualified to serve the public interest. At best, these criteria can be considered no more than guide posts, and the weight to be given any decisional factor in a comparative case is dependent upon the circumstances of that particular case.[2]

Local Ownership. In choosing among contenders for broadcasting facilities, the Commission has tended to prefer applicants owned and controlled by persons who reside and have their roots in the community where the station is to operate. This is based on the theory that they are likely to be more familiar with and responsive to local needs than non-residents and thus better qualified to operate a station in the "public interest." As will be pointed out later, however, in some cases applicants have overcome the disadvantage of non-residence by showing superior qualifications in other respects, including past broadcast experience and record of performance.

In an early 1935 case, involving two applications for the same radio channel, the Commission preferred an applicant company, of which a 51% stockholder had published a daily newspaper in the locality for many years and had been closely identified with local affairs, over an applicant that had no affiliation other than property investments in the community.[3]

Since that time, as revealed in a long line of cases, in comparing the qualifications of applicants, the factor of local ownership and residence has continued to hold a central position in the thinking of the Commission.[4]

Where local applicants have been able to show diversified ownership, representing various professions and business interests in the community, with participation and leadership in civic affairs, they have strengthened their positions in competitive proceedings. Furthermore, where they have proposed to integrate the ownership and management of stations and to recruit a competent staff from among citizens living in the local area, they have scored additional points of preference.

A typical expression of the Commission's attitude and judgment on these matters is found in the case, *Scripps-Howard Radio, Inc.,* 4 RR 525, decided in 1948. This involved two conflicting applications for a station in the same locality. As between the two, the Commission preferred the applicant corporation whose stockholders had diversified backgrounds, most of whom had resided in the local area for many years and had been active in the civic and philanthropic life of the community. The losing applicant was a newspaper organization controlled by a board of five directors, only one of whom lived in the city; two other officers of the corporation lived there but had no real voice in the establishment of policies and the management of the corporation.[5]

Broadcast Experience. The FCC has consistently viewed experience in broadcasting or related fields as an important aspect of qualifications in deciding cases involving competing applicants. For example, in *Utah Radio Educational Society,* 3 FCC 246 (1936), the Commission preferred an applicant whose principals were experienced in radio engineering as against an individual applicant without any radio experience. In a recent case, *Toledo Blade Co.,* 25 FCC 251, 15 RR 739 (1958), the Commission held that an applicant whose principals had had extensive experience in the operation of a local radio station over a long period of time was entitled to preference over applicants showing lesser experience. Other cases in point are *Scripps-Howard Radio, Inc.,* 11 RR 985 (1956); *Richmond Newspapers, Inc.,* 11 RR 1234 (1955); and *WHDH, Inc.,* 22 FCC 761, 13 RR 507 (1957).

Record of Past Performance. Since the early part of 1950, the Commission's decisions have reflected increasing emphasis upon the quality of past performance in the broadcast field as a determinative factor in comparative cases. For example, in *Petersburg Television Corporation,* 10 RR 567 (1954), it is stated that such factors as local residence, civic participation and integration of ownership and management are at most the basis for presumption of greater probability that programming commitments will be carried out or that the applicant will be sensitive to the area's needs, and are of minor importance where the applicants have a record of good past performance in the operation of broadcasting stations in the area.

In a 1954 case, the Commission concluded that an applicant which had compiled an outstanding operational record at its several broadcast stations over a period of years was entitled to a slight preference over an applicant with no record of past broadcast performance, but which had a higher degree of local ownership and integration.[6]

The Commission has taken the position that past broadcast records and broadcast experience are separate factors entitled to independent appraisal and weight and not to be considered as a single decisional factor in comparative cases. (See *Toledo Blade Co.,* cited above)

It is not necessary to discuss them here since they are dealt with in various chapters in Part V of the book, but there are many negative factors that can weigh against applicants in competitive proceedings. Violations of FCC rules and regulations, failure to report accurately or willful misrepresentation of facts to the Commission, unauthorized transfers of control of a station, abdication of licensee responsibility, failure to provide program service that meets the tests of public interest as prescribed by the FCC—these and many other types of derelictions (Discussed at length in later chapters), if part of a broadcaster's record, can work to his disadvantage if he is seeking additional radio or TV facilities in a competitive hearing.

Programming as an Element in Comparative Cases. In comparative proceedings, the program proposals of applicants are scrutinized carefully. In varying degrees, the Commission has given points of preference to applicants whose program proposals appear better designed to serve the particular needs and interests of the area in which the station will operate.

Often these points of preference become determinative in the outcome of a case.

The FCC decisions reveal both quantitative and qualitative comparisons of proposed plans for program service submitted by competing applicants. Depending upon the circumstances of the case, the Commission has awarded decisional preferences for superiority in over-all program design. In some instances, particular types of program service proposed such as local live programs planned especially to meet the needs of the area, including the discussion of vital issues of public interest in the community or religious and educational programs involving the local churches and schools, coverage of the local news—these and other specific features have tipped the scales in favor of some applicants.

It is only by a study of the particular facts in a case and the full text of the decision that one can understand fully the basis on which the Commission prefers one application over another. For example, since program rating in competitive cases is always a relative matter, the preferential weight to be given a proposal for full news coverage might depend upon the particular journalistic skills of the applicant as well as the community need for this type of service. Or a proposal to broadcast agricultural programs in an area largely urban in character would not have as much decisional significance as it would in one with a large rural population.

While the decisions of the Commission do not reveal any precise rating scales or standards of evaluation in connection with programming, excerpts from the conclusions in a few cases will suggest some guiding principles which have motivated the agency's thinking and judgment.

In *Tribune Co.,* 9 RR 719 (1954), the Commission expressed the view that local live programming is a factor of great importance in comparative consideration of broadcast applicants, but that a greater percentage is not itself determinative. Of more significance is the content and the promise for implementation of the proposal and the assurance of its effectuation.

Again, in *KTBS, Inc.,* 10 RR 811 (1955), the point was made that slight differences in emphasis and allocation of time are not important in appraisal of program proposals. Quantitative and statistical measurement is not enough. Furthermore, ordinarily proposals to carry network programs do not warrant points of preference but arrangements for broadcasting local live programs are considered more important in showing how the needs of the area will be served.

The primary question in program evaluation is whether the applicants have planned and propose a diversified, well-rounded service for the community, and mere differences in percentages of time to be devoted to various program types are not considered important.[7]

Numerical superiority, however, may achieve decisional significance if the statistical difference involves a kind of programming that clearly and effectively will serve community interests.[8]

The Commission has recognized that program proposals may be skillfully prepared but the important consideration is the basic competency of the applicant to provide a service which will meet the needs of the community from day to day.[9]

In a variety of comparative cases, the Commission has given preferential consideration to proposals to provide instructional broadcasts for in-school viewing,[10] to present programs dealing with "cultural arts,"[11] to provide time to local organizations for talks and discussions,[12] and to carry a "considerable number of regular agricultural programs,"[13]. Also, the Commission has made favorable mention of proposals to make time available for diversified, religious programs,[14] and to cover both national and local news and engage a special staff to prepare and present the newscasts.[15]

As reflected in various cases, applicants have scored points of preference for superior program plans based upon personally conducted surveys and discussions with leaders of civic, educational, religious and other community groups;[16] and for more comprehensive, detailed and well balanced program plans with specific limitations upon the amount of commercial programming to be carried by the station.[17] Also, commitments for larger and more competent staffs have elicited favorable comment from the Commission.[18]

Illustrative of the Commission's concern that applicants make careful studies of local needs and problems and plan programs accordingly, is a 1949 Michigan case.[19] This proceeding involved three applications for a station to operate on the frequency 1320 kc, with 1 kw power, unlimited time. Two of the applicants requested the facility in Lansing, Michigan. The third wanted it in Charlotte, Michigan, only twenty miles away. Since the applications were conflicting and mutually exclusive, the Commission designated them for a comparative hearing.

The successful applicant was station WILS in Lansing. In denying the Charlotte application, the Commission said:

The Charlotte Broadcasting Company has not demonstrated that the need of the Charlotte community for an outlet for local self-expression is more than merely theoretical. The applicant has not made a single contact with people in the Charlotte community who might cooperate with the proposed station in putting on musical, dramatic, educational or agricultural programs. . . . While the applicant's policy calls for sustaining time for civic and fraternal organizations there is no specific provision for programs by those organizations in the program schedule. Although the program schedule calls for 43.9 per cent of the operating time to be devoted to live programs, no arrangements have been made to secure talent for these programs with the single exception of a discussion with the President of the Ministerial Association with respect to religious programs. . . .

The preferential weight given to each of these program items has varied with the circumstances and comparative situation in each case. Not every aspect however of an applicant's program performance or his projected plans for the future gets favorable consideration. For example, in certain decisions, the Commission has declared its unwillingness to give any decisional weight to the fact that one network affiliation rather than another is anticipated,[20] or because one applicant intends to use network programs more during prime listening hours as against another who plans to present more wire and recorded broadcasts.[21] Nor will the Commission attach any importance to a failure to subscribe to a news film service where adequate arrangements otherwise have been made for local news film and leased wire service.[22]

In a number of cases, the agency has asserted unequivocally that it is not concerned one way or another whether religious programs are carried on a sustaining or commercial basis.[23] In *Southland Television Co.,* 10 RR 699 (1955), it attached no significance to the fact that one applicant emphasized film programs while other applicants stressed network programming.[24]

Limitations on Ownership of Stations. The Commission has established rules limiting the number of radio and television stations which may be owned or controlled by one party. Section 3.35 of the Rules covering standard (AM) broadcast stations provides that no license may be granted to any party who already owns, operates or controls another such station serving substantially the same primary service area, except on a showing that the public interest will be served. This is known as the duopoly rule and, in most cases, has served as a bar to the ownership or control of more than one station in the same community.

There have been exceptions to this rule, however. The Commission has said it would not grant duplicate facilities to the same party or interests unless it could be "overwhelmingly" shown that it would meet a community need which would otherwise not be met.[25] In a 1941 Hawaiian case,[26] the FCC did permit the Hawaiian Broadcasting System, which already was operating three of the only four stations in the Islands to acquire an additional one in the area. While expressing concern over the concentration of control which would result, the agency concluded that foreign language programs designed to promote Americanism and democratic principles which were proposed by the Hawaiian Company would serve an "overwhelming" need there and that a grant was justified.

In *Lubbock County Broadcasting Co.,* 4 RR 493 (1948), the Commission said that each case involving multiple ownership must be decided on its merits and that Section 3.35 of the Rules is not an absolute bar to a grant in every instance where there is overlap of service areas of two stations under common control.[27]

The prohibition against owning more than one station also applies even though the stations may be located in different communities, if, on the basis of the particular facts in the case, the Commission believes this multiple ownership would result in an undue concentration of control of broadcasting facilities contrary to the public interest.[28] Regardless of the facts, the rules preclude the single ownership of more than seven standard broadcast (AM) stations in the country.[29]

These same limitations with respect to multiple ownership apply to FM and television stations. Section 3.240 of the FCC Rules prohibits the ownership and control of more than seven FM stations.[30] Section 3.636 makes the same restriction applicable to television, except with the qualification that no more than five of the stations may be VHF, with the ownership and control of two additional UHF stations permitted.[31]

The Commission has not made these restrictive rules applicable to FM and television stations authorized for educational, non-commercial operation only. As previously pointed out, the special rules governing these stations provide that local and state school systems may use them for administrative and instructional purposes and no limit is placed on the number that a local or state educational organization may operate.

In competitive proceedings involving conflicting commercial applications, the matter of multiple ownership and possible concentration of control may become an important decisional factor. For example, in a 1947 case involving two applications for a new radio station in Grenada, Mississippi, the decision turned on this point. The Commission said:

> The chief distinction between the applicants, and the one which we believe is decisive, is the fact that (one) is the licensee of three other standard broadcast stations in Mississippi, while (the other) has no other broadcast interests. . . . It is our view that, unless there are countervailing considerations the public interest would be better served in choosing between two applicants by granting the application of the one which as compared with its competitor has fewer broadcast interests since such would tend towards a greater diversity of the ownership of broadcast stations.[32]

Recent competitive cases in which multiple ownership and diversification of control of mass media have been considered by the FCC as decisional factors are: *Triad Television Corporation,* 25 FCC 848, 16 RR 501 (1958); *Sucesion-Luis Pirallo-Castellaros,* 26 FCC 109, 16 RR 113 (1959).

A superior record of performance[33] or a closer identity with the community and a better program proposal in terms of local need[34]—these and other factors in comparative cases have been strong enough at times to overcome the multiple ownership and concentration of control factors. In the final analysis, the real test is: Which applicant is most likely to serve the interests and needs of the community taking into account all the pertinent facts?

It should be mentioned that the seven station ownership limitation of the FCC has been challenged in the courts. On May 21, 1956, the U.S. Supreme Court, however, affirmed the Commission's authority to impose such a restriction. The court held that the Commission was not barred from adopting rules that declare a present intent to limit the number of stations to prevent a concentration of control inimicable to the public interest and that the limitations were reconcilable with the Communications Act of 1934 as a whole. The Court did declare, however, that if any applicant could show adequate reasons in the public interest why the rules should be amended or waived in his case, he was entitled to a full hearing before the Commission, should he desire it.[35]

As Judge Miller indicated, in *McClatchy Broadcasting Co. v. FCC,* there is no fixed and inflexible standard by which all comparative cases can be decided. As he said, the Commission "has the duty, in choosing between competing applicants, to decide which would better serve the public interest. Where that interest lies is always a matter of judgment and must be determined on an *ad hoc* basis.[36]

As FCC Examiner Gifford Irion has pointed out, "dogmatic rules are not well adapted to administrative law, especially in comparative cases . . . There is no simple or easy method for deciding between applicants."

He has added, however, that

. . . there is good reason for saying that primary principles do not—or should not—change. If public interest requires selecting the party who will provide the best service and who gives the greatest assurance of so doing, then this must hold true in every case. The evidence by which he proves these things will, of course, vary from case to case, and that is why no single criterion should be invariably predominant. The task of counsel in a comparative proceeding is to form a theory of his client's case and to present the evidence so that one area of comparison leads logically into another. Ordinarily he will be unable to gain a preference on every point, but he certainly should have some rational theory explaining why the points on which he does prevail are those which should govern. If this standard of advocacy were maintained, not only during the hearing proper, but also on appeal to the full Commission, it may be fairly assumed that the decisions, both initial and final would likewise take on a desired quality of logic and consistency.[37]

NOTES

1. *Johnson Broadcasting Co. v. FCC,* 85 U.S. App. D.C. 40, 175 F.(2d) 351, 4 RR 2138 (1949).

2. *Hearst Radio Inc.,* 6 RR 994 (1951). For a detailed consideration of the various criteria used by the FCC in deciding competitive cases, see digest of cases in 2 RR M-2001 to M-2884.

3. *United States Broadcasting Corporation,* 2 FCC 208 (1935).

4. See *H. K. Glass,* 2 FCC 365 (1936); *Voice of Greenville,* 4 FCC 321 (1937); *Capital Broadcasting Co., Inc.,* 6 FCC 72 (1938); *Herbert L. Wilson,* 9 FCC 56 (1941); *Julio M. Conesa,* 11 FCC 200, 3 RR 158 (1946); *Town Talk Broadcasting Co.,* 11 FCC 919, 3 RR 769 (1947); *Norman Broadcasting Co.,* 13 FCC 1133; 5 RR 120 (1949); *Aladdin Radio and Television, Inc.,* 9

RR 1 (1953); *Mid-Continent Television, Inc.,* 9 RR 1271 (1953); *Southland Television Company,* 10 RR 699 (1955); *WKAT, Inc.,* 22 FCC 1254, 12 RR 1 (1957); *Hi-Lane Broadcasting Co.,* 13 RR 1017 (1957).

5. Other cases: *Southern Tier Radio Service,* 11 FCC 171, 3 RR 211 (1946); *Midwest Broadcasting Co.,* 11 FCC 817, 3 RR 764 (1947); *Wichita Broadcasting Co.,* 11 FCC 1010, 3 RR 865 (1947); *Kendrick Broadcasting Co.,* 9 RR 425 (1953); *City of Jacksonville,* 12 RR 113 (1956); *WHPH, Inc.,* 22 FCC 761, 13 RR 507 (1957); *Queen City Broadcasting Co.,* 23 FCC 113; 15 RR 645 (1957).

6. *McClatchy Broadcasting Company,* 9 RR 1190 (1954). Other cases along the same line: *Petersburg Television Corporation,* 10 RR 567 (1954); *Scripps-Howard Radio, Inc.,* 11 RR 985 (1956); *St. Louis Telecast, Inc.,* 22 FCC 625, 12 RR 1289 (1957).

7. *WOOD Broadcasting Corporation,* 10 RR 1119 (1956).

8. *WMBD, Inc.,* 11 RR 533 (1956).

9. *Television East Bay, Inc.,* 14 RR 1 (1956).

10. *WKRG-TV, Inc.,* 10 RR 225 (1955).

11. *Brush Moore Newspapers, Inc.,* 11 RR 641 (1956).

12. *Hi-Lane Broadcasting Company,* 13 RR 1017 (1956).

13. *Radio Station KFH Co.,* 11 RR 1 (1955).

14. *Richmond Newspapers, Inc.,* 11 RR 1234 (1955).

15. *Oregon Television, Inc.,* 9 RR 1401 (1954).

16. *Tuscaloosa Broadcasting Company,* 11 FCC 487 (1946).

17. *Bay State Beacon, Inc.,* 12 FCC 567 (1947), 3 RR 1455.

18. *Orlando Daily Newspapers, Inc.,* 11 FCC 760, 3 RR 624 (1946).

19. *Loving Broadcasting Company,* 5 RR 48 (1949).

20. *WSAV, Inc.,* 10 RR 402 (1955).

21. *WREC Broadcasting Service,* 10 RR 323 (1955).

22. *Superior Television, Inc.,* 11 RR 1173 (1956).

23. *WJR, The Goodwill Station, Inc.,* 9 RR 227 (1954); *Tampa Times Co.,* 10 RR 77 (1954); *KTBS Inc.,* 10 RR 811 (1955).

24. *Southland Television Co.,* 10 RR 699 (1955).

25. *Genesee Radio Corporation,* 5 FCC 183 (1938).

26. *The Hawaiian Broadcasting System,* 8 FCC 379 (1941).

27. *Lubbock County Broadcasting Co.,* 4 RR 493 (1948).

28. Section 3.35(b), FCC Rules and Regulations, 1 RR 53:160.

29. *Ibid.*

30. Section 3.240, 1 RR 53:417.

31. Section 3.636, 1 RR 53:641.

32. *Grenada Broadcasting Co.,* 12 FCC 1319 (1947); 3 RR 1159.

33. *Penn Thomas Watson,* 12 FCC 180.

34. *Norfolk Broadcasting Corporation,* 12 FCC 395, 3 RR 1699 (1947).

35. *United States et. al. v. Storer Broadcasting Company,* 351 U.S. 192, 13 RR 2161.

36. 239 F. 2d 15 (1956).

37. Irion, H. Gifford, "FCC Criteria for Evaluating Competing Applicants," *Minnesota Law Review,* Vol. 43, No. 3, p. 479, January, 1959. This is an excellent analysis of the criteria applied by the Commission and is based upon a detailed analysis of cases decided by the FCC. The problems of applying these criteria are clearly presented. Mr. Irion has served as an examiner with the FCC for a number of years and his opinions on this subject are an outgrowth of long study and experience.

CHAPTER 15

Getting Authority to Build a Station: Procedural Steps

*The determination of any particular proceeding requires a determination of the public interest, reached through procedure designed to give full protection to individual rights.—*GEORGE E. STERLING*

The detailed procedure for getting a license to operate a radio or television station is set forth in Part I of the FCC's Rules, entitled "Practice and Procedure." Part 3 of the Rules, "Radio Broadcast Services," explains the kind of showing an applicant must make before an authorization for a new standard broadcast station or an increase in existing facilities will be granted.

The purpose of this chapter is to provide a general understanding of the problems involved and the basic steps to be followed if a broadcast authorization is to be secured. The procedure is substantially the same whether the operation contemplated is standard (AM), frequency modulation (FM), television, or international broadcast.

As already stated, except under certain emergency conditions set forth in Section 308(a) of the Communications Act of 1934, the Commission is prohibited from granting construction permits, station licenses, or modifications thereof, or renewal of licenses, without *written* applications first having been filed.[1] As pointed out in Chapter 3, these applications must provide the Commission with certain types of information as specified in Section 308(b) of the Act.

Pursuant to this statutory mandate, FCC Application Form 301 has been designed. It has a flexible format and is required to be used to apply for authority to build a new AM, FM or television station or to make changes in existing broadcasting facilities.

With respect to standard broadcast stations, the requirements of Section 3.24 of the Commission's rules should be noted.[2] This section provides that an authorization for such a station will be issued *only* after a satisfactory showing has been made in regard to certain matters.

Showing Fair Distribution of Frequencies. First, the applicant must

* Former member of the FCC.

180

show that the frequency assignment requested "will tend to effect a fair, efficient, and equitable distribution of radio service among the several states and communities." This provision implements Section 307(b) of the Communications Act.

Following passage of the Radio Act of 1927, Congress became concerned that the Federal Radio Commission was concentrating grants of licenses in the Northern and Eastern parts of the country. Congressmen from the South and West protested this trend.[3] The result was the adoption of the Davis Amendment to help correct this situation.[4] Under this Amendment, the Federal Radio Commission was required to make an equal allocation of broadcasting facilities among five zones which had been established and to see that a fair distribution was made among the states in each zone according to population. The Radio Commission worked out a quota system based upon the population of each zone.[5]

With the demise of the 1927 Act, the Davis Amendment was embodied in Section 307(b) of the Communications Act of 1934. It was soon found, however, that allocation of facilities based largely on population did not lead to a "fair, efficient and equitable" distribution. The sparsely settled areas tended to suffer. Congress, therefore repealed the Davis Amendment in 1936. As amended, Section 307(b) now reads:

In considering applications for licenses, and modifications and renewals thereof, when and insofar as there is demand for the same, the Commission shall make such distribution of licenses, frequencies, hours of operation, and of power among the several States and communities as to provide a fair, efficient, and equitable distribution of radio service to each of the same.[6]

This is a very general and flexible provision which has been used by the Commission to justify preference of one applicant in a community which has no radio station over another in a second community which already has broadcasting facilities.[7] In other cases, the Commission has preferred one application over another because more people would be served by a proposed operation than by another.[8]

Showing That Objectionable Interference Will Not Result. A second showing required to be made in an application, as prescribed by Section 3.24 of the Rules, is that the proposed assignment and operation will not cause objectionable interference to other stations, or if such interference will be caused it must be shown that the need for the proposed service outweighs the need for the service which will be lost. Also, it must be shown that the proposed station will not suffer interference from other stations to an extent that it cannot provide a satisfactory service itself.

Objectionable interference has been defined as spurious or extraneous sound accompanying radio reception if it occurs as much as ten per cent of the time. This interference may result from a number of causes including atmospheric electricity or static, man-operated electrical devices, radio stations operating on the same channels or adjacent ones. Precise methods for determining objectionable interference with respect to standard broadcast stations are set forth by the Commission in Sections 3.182, 3.183, 3.184, 3.185 and 3.186 of the Technical Standards.[9] In selecting a suitable frequency and preparing the necessary technical showing, the services of a competent engineer are required.

Showing Financial, Legal, Technical and Character Qualifications. Paragraphs 3 and 4 of Section 3.24 call for a showing in the application that the applicant is financially and legally qualified and possesses good character and other qualifications. Paragraph 5 requires proof that the "technical equipment proposed, the location of the transmitter, and other technical phases of operation comply with the regulations governing same, and the requirements of good engineering practice." These paragraphs simply implement statutory provisions which have already been discussed in Chapter 13.

Showing That International Agreements Are Not Violated. Since radio waves do not stop at national boundaries, arrangement and agreements must be made with other countries to avoid objectionable interference and to achieve desirable international objectives. Accordingly, Paragraph 6 of Section 3.24 requires a showing in the application that the location and operation of a proposed station will not violate international agreements. Section 303(r) of the Communications Act gives the Commission the authority to make such a regulation. The United States has definite agreements with foreign countries designed to prevent interference among domestic and foreign stations. For example, we are signatories to what is known as the North American Regional Broadcasting Agreement. Canada and countries to the south of us are parties to the agreement. The Commission has scrupulously adhered to these agreements and has not permitted assignments or operations in this country which would interfere with those in other countries.[10]

Other Requirements. Paragraph (7) of Section 3.24 requires that an application for a standard broadcast station (AM) show that not more than one per cent of the population within the 25 millivolts per meter contour of the station shall reside in the one volt per meter area in the immediate vicinity of the transmitter. The rule does not apply where no more than 300 persons live within the small area. The rationale for this rule is that the signal of the station within a mile or so of the transmitter is so strong that it tends to override the signals of other stations and limits the inhabitants in this nearby area to the one local station. It is desirable, therefore, that the transmitter be located so that this limitation will affect as few people as possible.

Finally, the Commission says in Paragraph 8 of Section 3.24 that an application for an AM station must show that "the public interest, convenience, and necessity will be served through the operation under the proposed assignments."

FCC Application Form 301 Reviewed. FCC Application Form 301 has been designed with a flexible format and must be used by all applicants seeking authority to build new AM, FM or television stations or to make changes in existing ones. The form requires an applicant to submit various types of detailed information, including a description of the authority and facilities desired and facts showing ability to build and operate the station as proposed. Section 1 of the Form calls for items of information such as frequency and power requested, hours of operation, type of station desired and its location.

Section II requires proof of citizenship and a showing that the applicant is not subject to alien or foreign control. In addition, the legal authority under which the applicant is organized and is empowered to engage in broadcasting must be stated. Any license revocation, conviction for violation of anti-trust laws or crimes involving moral turpitude, unsatisfied judgments, or involvement in bankruptcy proceedings must also be reported. There are other questions as to officers and ownership of stock in applicant companies and some questions concerning intercorporate or contractual relationships, if any, directly or indirectly affecting the control of these companies.

Section II further calls for specific data concerning the present and past occupations, business and financial interests of applicants, their officers, directors and principal stockholders, and their connections, if any, with existing AM, FM or television stations or applications therefor which have been denied or are pending before the Commission.

Page 6 of Section II is designed especially for applicants seeking authority to build noncommercial, educational TV stations. Information as to the nature of the educational organization or institution, the laws under which it operates, and any accreditation which it may have must be supplied.

A detailed showing of financial ability must be made by all applicants in Section III. To complete this part of the form satisfactorily, a careful cost analysis of all station facilities must be made; specific items of expense must be indicated and sources and methods of financing the construction and initial operation of the station must be fully explained.

A statement regarding program service which the applicant proposes to provide is required in Section IV. The applicant must state the percentage of time that he expects to devote during a typical week of operation to various types of broadcasts, namely, entertainment, religious, agricultural, educational, news, discussion, talks, and miscellaneous programs. (See Appendix VIII re proposal to revise Section IV.)

Representations also must be made as to percentages of time to be devoted to network and local live programs plus wire service. Each applicant is also asked to state what its practice will be regarding the number and length of spot announcements. Included among other items of information requested under this section are the applicant's general plans for staffing the station, including the number of employees in each department, together with the names, residence and citizenship of key officials and departmental heads. The Commission now has under consideration proposed changes in the section of the application form (See Appendix VIII).

At the beginning of Section IV, there is a notice that the replies to questions therein constitute "a representation of programming policy upon which the Commission will rely in considering the application." Accordingly, applicants are cautioned to devote time and care and use their best judgment in preparing these replies. It is not expected by the Commission, however, that licensees "will or can adhere inflexibly in day-to-day operation" to the program representations made.

Technical Aspects of the Application. Section V of the form covers the technical aspects of the application. It must be prepared and signed by one having engineering knowledge. It calls for such information as frequency, hours of operation and power requested; location of station, transmitter and main studio; description of equipment including frequency and modulation monitors, antenna system, various coverage contours as proposed for day and night operation, and the methods employed to determine these contours; and maps clearly showing antenna location, general character of the city or metropolitan area to be served, buildings and other structures, and location of other transmitters and stations within a ten mile radius.

Considerably more technical data is required of applicants for television stations than from those seeking AM or FM facilities since both aural and visual equipment is involved. It must also be shown that the proposed location of the transmitter complies with the minimum separation requirements established by the Commission.

Section V-G calls for specific information regarding the proposed antenna and site which is submitted by the FCC for review by federal aviation authorities. Types of information requested include a list of landing areas within ten miles of the antenna site, exact distance to nearest airway within five miles, and the height of the proposed tower.

Commission Procedure for Processing Broadcast Applications. Three copies of the application and all exhibits must be prepared. Two additional copies (a total of five) of Section V-G and associated exhibits are required. The application must be personally subscribed and verified by the party in whose name it is filed or by one of the parties if there be more than one; or if a corporate applicant, by one of the officers of the company. Only the original need be signed and verified; the copies may be conformed.

If the applicant is physically disabled or absent from the continental United States, his attorney may execute and file the application. In his verification, however, he must set forth the grounds of his belief as to all matters not stated upon his knowledge and the reason why the applicant has not supplied the information or is unable to do so.

Except for Section V-G, information called for in Form 301 need not be refiled if it has already been submitted to the Commission in some other FCC form. This incorporation by reference is acceptable providing the form number, date of filing, and specific paragraph of the document containing the information are indicated, and the applicant states there has been "no change since the date of filing." In this connection, the Commission warns that any such incorporation makes the information referred to as well as the entire document containing it, whether confidential or otherwise, open for public inspection.

All applications for radio and television stations are required to be filed with the Secretary of the Commission.[11] They may be mailed or delivered personally to the Secretary's office in the New Post Office Building at 12th and Pennsylvania Streets, N.W., Washington, D.C. At the time of filing, the applicant must give notice in the principal area proposed to be served by the station, as recently required by legislation enacted by Congress (see Appendix I). Upon receipt in the Secretary's office, applications are dated and forwarded to the Broadcast Bureau for review.[12] If a preliminary review shows the application to be substantially incomplete or defective, it is returned to the applicant with a brief statement concerning its defects. Or if there are only minor omissions, it may be accepted for filing and a letter addressed to the applicant requestiong additional information.[13]

When the application appears to be in complete form, copies are distributed to appropriate staff members in the Broadcast Bureau. Section 1.354 of the Rules provides that the Commission will act on all applications for new stations or for major changes in the facilities of stations already authorized, such as frequency, power, hours of operation, station location, or substantial change in directional antenna system. The Chief of the Broadcast Bureau, however, is authorized to act on applications for minor changes such as those involving changes of equipment or relocation of studios or transmitter site not materially affecting the operation or service area of the station.[14]

Applications for new broadcasting stations or for major changes in facilities already authorized may not be granted by the Commission earlier than 30 days from the date that the Commission gives public notice that such applications have been accepted for filing.[15] Each is given a file number and is processed as nearly as possible in the order in which it is filed, except that the Broadcast Bureau is authorized to group together those which involve interference conflicts and where it appears that they must be designated for a consolidated public hearing.[16]

Section 1.356(d) of the Commission Rules provides that applications for noncommercial educational stations may be acted upon at any time after "Public Notice" is given of their acceptance by the Commission. Recent Congressional legislation, however, precludes such grants earlier than 30 days from the date of the notice of filing.[17]

After the FCC staff has made an engineering, legal and accounting study of an application, a memorandum is prepared and the Chief of the Broadcast Bureau places it on the agenda for Commission action. If there are questions concerning the qualifications of the applicant, or if the proposed operation of the new station would cause objectionable interference to an existing one, or the staff feels that there are other reasons why a grant of the application would be against the public interest, these matters are set forth in the memorandum for the consideration of the Commission.

Upon the basis of the information submitted by the staff, the Commission determines the action to be taken. If it appears that the public interest will be served, the application is granted and a construction permit is issued.[18] On the other hand, if the Commission is unable to make such a finding, the applicant and all interested parties are informed of any objections or questions. The applicant then may make a formal reply. If, upon consideration of this reply, the Commission is still in doubt, the application is then designated for a public hearing on the unresolved questions. The burden of meeting the specified issues and proving that a grant of the application will serve the public interest then falls upon the applicant.[19]

Pre-Grant Procedure. Section 309(c) of the Act formerly specified that grants of applications were subject to protest for a period of thirty days. During that time, any party in interest might formally register opposition and request a public hearing.[20] Congress, however, in the recent 1960 Amendments to the Communications Act, abolished the protest procedure and in lieu thereof has provided that any party in interest may file with the Commission a petition to deny any application (whether as originally filed or as amended) at any time prior to the day the Commission grants it. The petitioner must serve a copy of such a petition on the applicant. The applicant is afforded an opportunity to make a formal reply. If the application and the pleadings raise serious questions as to whether a grant of the application will serve the public interest, the Commission must designate the application for public hearing on specified issues, giving due notice to the applicant and other parties in interest. On the other hand, if the application and the petition raise no material questions, the Commission must make the grant, deny the petition, and issue a concise statement of reasons for denying the petition.[21] (For more detailed information regarding petitions, interventions, and other pre-grant procedure, see 1960 Amendments to Communications Act in Appendix I.)

Hearing Procedure. As provided in Section 1.140 of the Rules, when an application is set for hearing, the Secretary of the Commission mails an order to the applicant setting forth the reasons for the Commission's action and the issues to be heard.[22] If there are competing applications for the same channel, they will be designated for a consolidated hearing and all applicants will be notified by the Secretary of the issues on which their qualifications will be compared and the basis on which the winner will be selected.

The notice of hearing is published in the *Federal Register,* and, when possible, at least 60 days advance notice is provided.[23]

Any applicant has the right to withdraw or ask dismissal of an application without prejudice prior to its designation for hearing, but after that time such requests are considered only upon written petition served upon all parties involved in the proceeding and are granted by the Commission only for good cause shown.[24]

If an applicant desires to avail himself of the opportunity for a public hearing, he or his attorney must file with the Commission in triplicate a written appearance within twenty days from the mailing of the FCC hearing notice by the FCC Secretary, stating that the applicant will appear and present evidence on the issues specified. Unless a request is made to dismiss the application prior to the expiration of the 20 days or a petition is filed to accept an appearance at a later date, a failure to enter an appearance within the prescribed period will result in a dismissal of the application with prejudice for failure to prosecute.[25]

While hearings may be conducted by one or more Commissioners, in most cases, an examiner is designated to preside in accordance with Section 11 of the Administrative Procedure Act.[26] Under the law, the examiner is an independent officer, empowered to administer oaths, issue subpoenas, examine witnesses, rule on questions of evidence, take depositions, regulate the course of hearings, maintain decorum, hold conferences for the settlement or simplification of issues with the consent of parties, and perform other functions essential to the conduct of adjudicatory proceedings by Federal administrative agencies.[27]

After the taking of testimony, the examiner officially closes the record and, after certification, files it in the office of the Commission Secretary. Ten days are allowed for necessary corrections of the transcript.[28]

The applicant and other parties may file with the examiner proposed findings of fact and conclusions of law which become a part of the record in the case. These are required to be filed within 20 days after the record is closed, unless additional time is allowed.[29]

Upon the basis of the complete record, the examiner prepares an initial decision which must contain findings of fact and conclusions, as well as the reasons therefor, upon all material points in the case, and must contain a recommendation as to what disposition of the case should be made by the Commission. The initial decision is transmitted to the Secretary who makes it public immediately and files it in the docket of the case.[30]

Appeal and Review of Initial Decisions. As provided in Section 1.153 of the Rules, within 30 days of the public release of an initial decision, or such other time as the Commission may specify, any of the parties may appeal to the Commission by filing exceptions.[31] The Commission, on its own motion, may, within 20 days after the time for filing exceptions expires, order that an initial decision shall not become final pending review by the Commission.[32]

Either on its own initiative or upon appropriate request from a party, the agency may take one or more of several actions with respect to initial decisions which are subject to review. It may (1) hear oral argument on the exceptions; (2) require the filing of briefs; (3) before or after oral argument or the filing of exceptions or briefs, reopen the record and/or remand the proceedings to the presiding officer to take further testimony or evidence or make further findings or conclusions. The Commission may itself issue a supplemental initial decision or cause one to be issued by the presiding officer.[33]

Section 1.153 also provides that unless exceptions are filed within the required time, or unless the Commission takes one or more of the actions enumerated in the preceding paragraph, the initial decision becomes final and effective after 50 days from time of public release of the full text thereof.

Any exception to an initial decision must point out with particularity alleged errors and must contain specific references to the page or pages of the transcript, exhibit or order on which the exception is based.[34]

Within the time allowed for the filing of exceptions any party may file a statement in support of an initial decision, in whole or in part. Such a supporting statement, as well as any exception, may be accompanied by a separate brief or memorandum of law which is limited to 50 double-spaced typewritten pages. Ten days, or such other time as the Commission may specify, are allowed for the filing of reply briefs to which the same page limitation applies.[35]

If exceptions have been filed, any party may request oral argument not later than five days after the time for filing replies to the exceptions has expired.[36] If no request for oral argument is filed within the time allowed, parties are deemed to have waived their rights thereto. Those wishing to participate in an oral argument must file written notice of intention to appear and participate within five days from the date of the Commission's order. A failure to do so constitutes a waiver of the opportunity to participate.[37]

Following oral argument, the Commission issues a final decision in the case.[38] This decision contains findings of fact and conclusions upon all material issues, as well as the reasons therefor; rulings on all relevant and material exceptions filed, and an appropriate order granting or denying the application.[39]

Within 30 days from the day the full text of a final decision is released, or, if such a document is not issued, from the date of "Public Notice" announcing the action, petitions for reconsideration and rehearing may be filed with the Commission.[40] Only persons aggrieved or whose interests are adversely affected by the decision may file such petitions. Persons not parties to the proceeding must show clearly what their interests are and show good reason why they were unable to participate.[41]

Petitions for reconsideration or for rehearing, as provided in Section 1.191 of the Rules, may request numerous types of relief including (1) reconsideration; (2) reargument; (3) reopening of the proceeding; and (4) amendment of any finding of the Commission.[42] The rule provides, however, that only newly discovered evidence or that which should have been taken in the original proceeding will be admissible in a rehearing.[43] It also states that the filing of a petition under this section, without a special order of the Commission, does not excuse any person from complying with or obeying any decision, order, or requirement of the Commission, or operate in any manner to stay or postpone the enforcement thereof. But if good cause can be shown, the Commission may stay the effectiveness of its order pending a decision on the petition.[44]

Court Review of FCC Decisions. Any applicant for a construction permit, competitive or otherwise, whose application has been denied by the Commission, may appeal the decision to the United States Court of Appeals for the District of Columbia. As provided in Section 402 of the Communications Act, notice of appeal must be filed with the Court within 30 days following public notice of the decision, and must contain a concise statement of the nature of the proceedings, the reasons for the appeal and proof of service of a true copy of the notice and statement upon the Commission.[45]

Within five days of an appeal, the Commission must notify all interested parties and within thirty days must file with the Court a copy of the order complained of, a full statement in writing of the facts and grounds relied upon in support thereof, and the originals or certified copies of all papers and evidence presented to and considered by it in reaching its decision.[46]

The Court is required to hear and determine the appeal at the earliest convenient time. As provided in Section 10(e) of the Administrative Procedure Act, the Court may set aside the decision of the Commission if the findings and conclusions are "arbitrary, capricious or involve an abuse of discretion, or otherwise are contrary to law, or if not supported by substantial evidence."[47]

Section 402(h) of the Communications Act describes the procedure and disposition of a case in the event of court reversal. It reads:

In the event that the court shall render a decision and enter an order reversing the order of the Commission, it shall remand the case to the Commission to carry out the judgment of the court and it shall be the duty of the Commission, in the absence of the proceedings to review such judgment, to forthwith give effect thereto, and unless otherwise ordered by the court, to do so upon the basis of the proceedings already had and the record upon which said appeal was heard and determined.[48]

Paragraph (j) of the same Section provides that "the court's judgment shall be final, subject, however, to review by the Supreme Court of the

United States. Under Section 1254 of Title 28 of the United States Code, the appellant, the Commission or any interested party intervening in the appeal, or the circuit court itself, may petition the higher court to review the case.[49]

NOTES

1. 48 Stat. 1084.
2. FCC Rules and Regulations, Section 3.24, 1 RR 53:132a.
3. 69 *Cong. Rec.* 4489 (1928).
4. Act of March 28, 1928, 45 Stat. 373.
5. FRC General Order No. 40, *Second Annual Report of FRC* (1928), 11.
6. Act of June 5, 1936, 49 Stat. 1475.
7. See Warner, Harry P., *Radio and Television Law* (New York, 1953), p. 293, for discussion of this point.
8. *Ibid.*, pp. 294-297.
9. Section 3.182 *et al.*, 1 RR 53:271-53:313.
10. See various treaties with countries in this hemisphere, 1 RR 41:11-41:196.
11. Section 1.302; 1 RR 51:192.
12. Section 1.306; 1 RR 51:193.
13. *Ibid.*
14. 1 RR 51:228.
15. Section 309(b); Communications Act Amendments, 1960, approved September 13, 1960.
16. Section 1.154(c); 1 RR 51:228-229.
17. Section 309(b); Communications Act Amendments, 1960.
18. Section 1.361; 1 RR 51:362.
19. Section 1.362(a); 1 RR 51:251.
20. 70 Stat. 3.
21. Sections 309(d) and (e); Communications Act Amendments, 1960.
22. Section 1.140; 1 RR 51:141.
23. *Ibid.*
24. Section 1.312; 1 RR 51:196.
25. Section 1.140; 1 RR 51:163.
26. Section 1.143; 1 RR 51:142.
27. Section 1.144; 1 RR 51:165.
28. Section 1.147; 1 RR 51:146.
29. Section 1.149; 1 RR 51:166.
30. Section 1.151; 1 RR 51:167.
31. Section 1.153; 1 RR 51:168.
32. Section 1.153(b); 1 RR 51:168.
33. Section 1.153(c); 1 RR 51:168.
34. Section 1.154(a); 1 RR 51:169.
35. Section 1.154(c); 1 RR 51:169.
36. *Ibid.*
37. *Ibid.*
38. Section 1.157(a); 1 RR 51:171.
39. Section 1.157(b); 1 RR 51:171.
40. Section 1.191; 1 RR 51:173.
41. *Ibid.*

42. Section 1.91(d); 1 RR 51:174.
43. Section 1.191(e); 1 RR 51:174.
44. Section 1.191(g); 1 RR 51:174.
45. 66 Stat. 719.
46. *Ibid*; also Rule 37(a) and (b), Title VII, Federal Communications Commission, General Rules, U.S. Court of Appeals, D.C. Circuit; 1 RR 40:28.
47. Section 10(e); Administrative Procedure Act, 60 Stat. 237.
48. 1 RR 10:123.
49. *Ibid*.

CHAPTER 16

Building the Station and Getting a License

Upon the completion of any station for . . . which a permit has been granted, and upon it being made to appear to the Commission that all the terms, conditions, and obligations set forth in the application and permit have been fully met, and that no cause or circumstance arising . . . since the granting of the permit would . . . make the operation . . . against the public interest, the Commission shall issue a license . . . for the operation of said station.—Section 319(c) of the Communications Act of 1934

When an application is granted by the Commission, whether it be with or without a hearing, the applicant receives a construction permit to build the station. The construction of the station must proceed in exact accordance with the specifications and conditions set forth in the authorization. If any changes are to be made, the prior approval of the Commission must be secured by filing an application for modification of permit. The same form (301) is used for this purpose as is used for the original application.

At this point, a few words of caution are appropriate. Section 319 (a) of the Communications Act prohibits the Commission from granting a license for the operation of any station the construction of which is begun or is continued unless a permit for this construction has been granted.[1] The reason Congress adopted this provision in the law was to free the Commission from any pressure for a license which might be exerted because of expenditures made before a construction permit was granted.[2]

The Commission has interpreted this statutory prohibition to mean that an applicant is denied the right to operate a station constructed in whole or in part without a permit having been previously issued. This does not mean that premature construction precludes the Commission from issuing a permit, or that it is to be held against a competing applicant in a comparative proceeding, if the construction was not undertaken by that applicant for the purpose of influencing or "pressuring" the Commission into a favorable decision.[3]

Mention should be made of a recent amendment to Section 319(d) of the Act which provides that the FCC may waive the requirement for a permit for the construction of a station that is "engaged solely in rebroadcasting television signals if such station was constructed on or before the date of the enactment" of the amendment (74 Stat. 363). This was designed to make possible the validation of a large number of community antenna TV systems constructed without permits first having been received from the FCC.

In line with the statutory mandate in Section 319(b), the Commission requires that construction of a station must begin within 60 days from the date the permit is authorized, and must be completed within eight months from that time, unless, upon proper request, additional time is granted due to causes beyond the control of the permittee which have prevented completion within that period.[4]

During the eight months, studios must be built or arranged for; a tower and antenna must be erected; a transmitter, monitors, indicating instruments, and various other kinds of equipment, depending on the type of station, must be secured and installed. Required technical studies must be completed, such as field intensity measurements for stations employing directional antennas.

Technical Standards and Requirements. In the building of the station, how much and what types of equipment must be installed? What are the specifications as to performance? The answers to these questions are set forth in detail in Section 3 of the Commission's Rules.

The importance of these technical rules and standards cannot be overestimated. It is essential that the transmissions of a broadcasting station be efficient and reliable, free of objectionable interference and otherwise acceptable if a maximum utility from the channel on which the station operates is to be achieved and the public interest is to be fully served. This would not be possible without some regulations and uniform technical standards specifying types of equipment to be used and quality of performance required.

While the technical standards provide for some flexibility, the Commission has cautioned that "it is not expected that material deviation therefrom as to fundamental principles will be recognized unless full information is submitted as to the reasonableness of such departure and the need therefor."[5]

The Commission has further said that these standards will be changed from time to time as the radio art progresses and as new engineering knowledge is acquired.[6]

It is not possible within the limits of this chapter to cover all the detailed technical rules and standards. The purpose here is simply to present some of the high lights which must be taken into account by those who hold construction permits and have been authorized by the FCC to build stations. For detailed technical requirements regarding the various types of equipment and standards of performance of AM, FM, Television and International Broadcast stations, Part 3 of the Rules should be studied.

Transmitters. Transmitting equipment must be capable of satisfactory operation in terms of the authorized power of the particular type of station. The limits of modulation, as precisely prescribed in the Rules, and the degree of carrier shift and the amount of hum and extraneous noise are specifically limited. The design of transmitters must be such that they may readily be adjusted. Adequate provision must be made for changing power output to compensate for excessive variations in line voltage or other factors which affect the output. Automatic frequency control equipment must be installed, capable of maintaining operation on the assigned frequency or within specified limits thereof.[7]

The transmitter and associated equipment must be so constructed and adjusted that emissions are not radiated outside the authorized band which would cause interference to the communications of other stations.[8]

The utility and efficiency of the transmitter depend to a great extent upon its location. The Commission, therefore, has specified four primary objectives to be kept in mind in selecting a site for a transmitter. These are: (1) to serve adequately the center of population in which the studio is located and to give maximum coverage to adjacent areas; (2) to cause and experience minimum interference to and from other stations; (3) to present a minimum hazard to air navigation; (4) to insure maximum field intensities and adequate service to both business and residential sections.[9]

Transmitters must have suitable indicating instruments for determination of operating power and other equipment as is necessary for proper adjustment, operation and maintenance of the indicating instruments, the scale permitted, and the degree of accuracy which is required.[10]

Auxiliary and Alternate Main Transmitters. Upon a showing of need for an auxiliary transmitter, the Commission may issue a license for one under the following conditions which are set forth in the Rules. It may be installed either at the location of the main transmitter or at another location; it must be ready for operation if the regular transmitter fails or is being modified or repaired; it must have control equipment capable of maintaining operation on the assigned frequency as required by the Commission; and its maximum rated power may be less but in no case more than that authorized for station operation.[11]

The Commission may authorize the use of alternate main transmitters providing a technical need is shown. Such authorization may be justified where the station is on a twenty-four hour schedule and alternate use of transmitters is needed to maintain continuous and satisfactory operation, or when developmental work requires alternate operation. It is required that the two transmitters be located at the same place and have the same power rating, except where the operating power during the day is different from that at night when appropriate variations in power ratings of transmitters is permitted. Also, the external effects from both transmitters must be substantially the same as to frequency range and audio-harmonic generation.

Radiating Systems. Each broadcasting station is required to have an efficient radiating system which complies with the Standards of Good Engineering Practice. The antenna system must meet the minimum requirements for height or field intensity.

As the Commission has pointed out, to obtain maximum efficiency from antennas, good ground systems must be employed, involving the use of a sizeable number of evenly spaced buried radial wires. Also, if the location of the transmitter site in the center of a city necessitates placing the antenna on top of a building for best service, this building should not be surrounded by taller structures, especially if they are located in the direction which the antenna is particularly designed to serve. When higher than the antenna itself, they tend to cast radio shadows which may materially reduce the coverage of the station.

The Commission has cautioned against locating broadcasting stations in areas with high signal intensities caused by overhead electrical power and telephone lines, or where the wiring and plumbing are old and improperly installed. These conditions give rise to what is called "cross-modulation interference". Antennas are only permitted in down-town sections when the power of the station does not exceed 500 watts.

Important considerations to be taken into account in locating technical facilities outside of urban areas include the topography in the vicinity of the station, the ground conditions and the type of soil between the transmitting site and the principal area to be served, distance to airport and airways, and space dimensions for the antenna and ground system.

Modulation and Frequency Monitors. Each broadcast station must have in operation, either at the transmitter or at the place where the transmitter is controlled, both frequency and modulation monitors of the types approved by the Commission. Only monitoring equipment which meets the specifications set forth in the Rules may be used in the construction and operation of the station.[12]

This requirement does not apply to low power non-commercial educational FM stations. With respect to them, Section 3.552 (d) of the Rules reads:

(d) The licensee of such noncommercial educational FM broadcast station licensed for transmitter power output of 10 watts or less shall provide for the measurement of the station frequency by a means independent of the frequency control of the transmitter. The station frequency shall be measured (1) when the transmitter is initially installed, (2) at any time the frequency determining elements are changed, and (3) at any time the licensee may have reason to believe the frequency has shifted beyond the tolerance specified by the Commission's rules.

Safety Regulations. The construction and operation of technical facilities of all broadcast stations must comply with numerous safety regulations. For example, high voltage equipment including transformers, filters, rectifiers and motor generators must be protected to prevent injury to operating personnel. The antenna and associated parts must be constructed so as not to constitute a hazard to life or limb; metering equipment with a potential of more than 1,000 volts, must be protected by suitable devices and be so installed that it may be read easily and accurately without the operator having to risk contact with high powered circuits.[13]

Transmitter panels or units must be wired in accordance with standard switchboard practice. The monitors and the radio frequency lines to the transmitter must be totally shielded. This also applies to the crystal chamber, together with the conductor or conductors to the oscillator circuit.[14]

Installations must be constructed in suitable quarters providing for the comfort of operators. Studio equipment should be designed to comply with normal safety. There are no specific requirements with respect to design and acoustical treatment of studios except that noise level should be kept as low as reasonably possible.[15]

Construction, Marking and Lighting of Antenna Towers and Supporting Structures. Part 17 of the Commission Rules contains specific requirements with respect to the location, construction, marking and lighting of antenna towers and structures. These Rules were issued pursuant to provisions in the Communications Act which vest in the Commission the authority to issue licenses in terms of the public interest and to require the painting and/or illumination of broadcasting towers and supporting structures to avoid menace to air travel.[16]

Proposed antenna sites and structures involving no hazard to air navigation are considered and approved by the FCC itself. Under other conditions, however, applications for broadcasting towers are referred to the Airspace Subcommittee of the Air Coordinating Committee for special study.* See Appendix VI for detailed requirements regarding the construction, marking and illumination of towers.

Type Accepted Equipment. Transmitters, frequency and modulation monitors and other kinds of broadcast equipment, may be type-accepted by the Commission upon request of manufacturers, provided data is submitted showing that they meet technical requirements set forth in the Rules. Application for type approval may be in the form of a letter addressed to the Secretary of the Commission, specifying the particular Rules under which approval is requested and describing the equipment and stating the size and weight of each component. In most instances, the Commission advises the applicant to ship the equipment prepaid to the Chief,

---

* This Committee has now been abolished by Executive order, and the FCC has proposed to replace it with the Federal Aviation Agency (See FCC Docket 13384, 1 RR 67:vii).

Laboratory Division, P. O. Box 31, Laurel, Maryland together with operating instructions and circuit diagrams.

A separate request for type acceptance must be submitted for each different type of equipment. It must be filed in triplicate and signed by the applicant or his duly authorized agent who must certify that the facts asserted are true and correct. Additional certification by a qualified engineer who performed or supervised the equipment test is also required.

Lists of type-approved and type-accepted equipment are available for inspection at the Commission's offices in Washington, D.C. and at each of its field offices. These are published in three parts:

Part A, Television Broadcast Equipment
Part B, Aural Broadcast Equipment
Part C, Other than Broadcast Equipment

Files containing information about equipment submitted by the manufacturers and other persons pursuant to the Commission's Rules are not open to public inspection.[17]

If equipment for sale has been type-accepted by the Commission, persons authorized to build stations may purchase it and use it for construction without further approval of the Commission.

Getting the License. The equipment used and the construction of the station must comply with all the technical standards and requirements set forth above. Once this is accomplished, tests must be made and proofs of performance submitted to the Commission. An application for a license to cover the construction permit must then be filed. FCC Form 302 is used for this purpose. It is a comparatively short form calling for information as to the beginning and completion dates of construction; the actual building costs incurred and current financial position of the station. The most important part of the application must be prepared by an engineer describing equipment installed and reporting tests and measurements of performance.

Having filed the license application and given proof of good station performance, a request may then be made for Commission authority to begin program tests. The Rules require that this request be filed with the Commission at least 10 days in advance of the time desired for commencement of the tests. At the same time, the Engineer in Charge of the District in which the station is located must be notified.

The Commission reserves the right to change the date for the beginning of program tests or to suspend them if the public interest requires. They remain valid, however, unless suspended or revoked by the Commission, during the time the license application is under consideration. As soon as the Commission acts on the application, the program test authority is automatically terminated.

If all the terms of the construction permit have been met and the operation of the station is shown to be in accordance with the Rules and Standards, the Commission grants a license for regular operation as required by Section 319(c) of the Act. That section reads:

Upon the completion of any station for the construction of which a permit has been granted, and upon it being made to appear to the Commission that all the terms, conditions, and obligations set forth in the application and permit have been fully met, and that no cause or circumstance arising or first coming to the knowledge of the Commission since the granting of the permit would, in the judgment of the Commission, make the operation of such station against the public interest, the Commission shall issue a license to the lawful holder of said permit for the operation of the station. Said license shall conform generally to the terms of said permit . . .[18]

Section 307(d) of the Act provides that no license for a broadcasting station may be issued for more than three years and Commission Rules limit the normal license to this period.[19] In order to relieve the workload of the Commission staff, however, original licenses are issued to expire in accordance with staggered schedules and usually run less than three years. Expiration dates for original licenses are specified in the Rules depending upon the state in which stations are located.[20] Renewals are granted at three year intervals thereafter, except in the case of International Broadcast Stations where licenses run for one year only.[21]

By the 1960 Communications Act Amendments, referred to in Chapter 15, Section 307(d) was amended, giving the Commission authority to grant licenses for shorter periods than three years, if, in its judgment, public interest would be served.[22] Accordingly, the Commission has amended its rules, providing for license terms less than three years if the public interest justifies (see Section 3.34 of FCC Rules).

Each license granted by the Commission must contain a statement that (1) the licensee acquires no right in the use of the frequencies assigned beyond the term specified nor in other manner than that authorized; (2) that the rights granted under the license may not be assigned or otherwise transferred in violation of the Act; and (3) that the license is subject to Section 606 of the Act, giving the President emergency war-time powers.[23]

NOTES

1. 48 Stat. 1089.
2. See *WSAV, Inc.,* 10 RR 402, 430 J (1954), for discussion of the legislative history of Section 319(a) of the Act. Also see H.R. Rep. No. 417 to accompany H.R. 4557, P.L. 321, 83rd Congress, 1st Sess. (1953), 68 Stat. 35 (1954).
3. *Ibid.,* Also see *WJIV-TV, Inc. v. Federal Communications Commission,* U.S. Court of Appeals, D.C. (January 12, 1956), reported in 13 RR 2049.
4. For example, see Section 1.314; 1 RR 51:196.

5. FCC Technical Standards, Sections 3.181 (d) and 3.301 (b); 1 RR 53:271, 491.

6. Standard Broadcast Technical Standards, Sections 3.181 (e) and 3.301 (b); 1 RR 53: 271, 491.

7. See Section 3.40 of FCC Rules, 1 RR 53:166 for Standard Broadcasting and other appropriate sections covering transmitters in the FM and television service.

8. *Ibid.*

9. See Sections 3.188, 3.315; 1 RR 53:313, 501, 502 for detailed information regarding transmitter locations of AM and FM stations. These sections of the Rules should be consulted carefully. Regarding television, transmitter location must accord with the mileage separations prescribed by Sections 3.610 and 3.611, 1 RR 53:627, 628, and 629.

10. Sections 3.40, 3.317, 3.687; 1 RR 53:166, 505, 689.

11. Sections 3.63, 3.64, 3.321, 3.637, 3.638; 1 RR 53:206, 207, 208, 511, 642, and 643.

12. Sections 3.56, 3.60, 3.552, 3.553, 3.690, 3.691; 1 RR 53: 203, 552, 553, 695, 696.

13. Sections 3.56, 3.60, 3.552, 3.553, 3.690, 3.691; 1 RR 53:203, 552, 695, 696.

14. *Ibid.*

15. *Ibid.*

16. Section 303 (q), Communications Act of 1934, 48 Stat. 1083.

17. Sections 3.48-3.50, 3.331-3.332 and 3.694; 1 RR 53:175-180, 512-515.

18. 66 Stat. 718.

19. 66 Stat. 714.

20. Sections 3.34, 3.218, 3.518, 3.630; 1 RR 53:158, 405, 526, 638.

21. Section 3.718; 1 RR 53:740.

22. Section 3, Communications Act Amendments, 1960.

23. *Ibid.,* Section 4.

PART V

The Broadcaster and Ethereal Realities

CHAPTER 17

Technical Requirements for Operation of Broadcast Stations

One of the most essential duties incumbent upon the licensee of a broadcast station is that of insuring the continuous efficient operation of the transmitting equipment and failure of this equipment, due to causes reasonably within human control, whereby the public is deprived of service, denotes a state of carelessness and mismanagement which the Commission will not condone.—4 FCC 521 (1937)

The FCC has established detailed technical requirements for the operation of all broadcast stations (AM, FM, non-commercial, educational FM, Television and International). These are found in Part 3 of the Commission's Rules governing these various types of stations. For complete and detailed information regarding technical requirements, Part 3 should be consulted.

Authorized Power. These rules provide that the actual operating power of stations shall be maintained "as near as practicable" to that which is authorized in the license. A small degree of variation for each type of station is permitted but definite limits are prescribed. In cases of uncontrollable emergency, the power may be reduced below the stated limits for a period not to exceed ten days providing the Commission and the Engineer in Charge of the radio district are notified promptly when the emergency begins and ends and when normal licensed power is resumed.[1]

Assigned Frequency. The operation of a station must not deviate materially from its assigned frequency. Slight ranges of deviation are permitted, depending on the type of station. In standard (AM) broadcasting, the operation must be maintained within 20 cycles of the assigned frequency.[2] In FM, the allowable tolerance is 2,000 cycles above or below the assigned frequency,[3] except in the case of non-commercial, educational stations operating with 10 watts or less power, the tolerance is plus or minus 3,000 cycles.[4] In television, the carrier frequency of the visual transmitter must be maintained within 1000 cycles of the one authorized, whereas, the center frequency of the aural transmitter must be maintained 4.5 mc, plus or minus 1000 cycles, above the visual carrier frequency.[5]

Modulation Requirements. All stations are required to maintain modulation as high as possible consistent with good quality of transmission, and specific percentages of modulation are prescribed for the various kinds of stations. For detailed requirements regarding modulation, Commission Rules should be consulted.[6]

Repairing and Replacing Defective Equipment. In the event that operating equipment such as indicating instruments, monitors, etc. become defective, they must be repaired or replaced as soon as possible. In the case of defective monitors, they may be operated for a period of sixty days providing (1) log entries are made showing the time the monitor was removed and restored to service, and (2) the FCC Engineer in Charge of the radio district in which the station is located is immediately notified both after the instrument is found to be defective and after it is repaired or replaced and proper operation has been restored.[7] Informal request for additional time to complete repairs may be made of the Radio Engineer in Charge of the district in which the station is located.

While a modulation monitor is out of order, the degree of modulation of the station must be checked by suitable means as prescribed by the Rules to assure that modulation is maintained within tolerances prescribed. Where emergency conditions require operation without the use of the frequency monitor, the frequency of the station must be measured by an external source at appropriate specified intervals and the results recorded in the station log.[8]

In the event that indicating instruments fail or do not operate correctly, the Commission has prescribed the precise methods by which power shall be determined pending repair or replacement of the defective instruments.

Equipment Tests and Station Inspections. The licensees of AM and FM broadcasting stations are required to make equipment tests at least once a year, and one must be made during the four-month period preceding the date on which the renewal application is filed. The data required from these tests are set forth in the Rules and must be kept on file at the transmitter and retained for a period of two years and, upon request, be made available during that time to any duly authorized representative of the Federal Communications Commission.[9]

All licensees must make their stations available for inspection by representatives of the Commission at any reasonable hour. The Field Engineering and Monitoring Bureau with twenty-four field offices and eighteen monitoring stations distributed throughout the country is responsible for inspections in the field.[10] As previously mentioned, the locations of these offices and monitoring stations are listed in Appendix III.

Requirements Regarding Operating Schedules.

a. Standard Broadcast Stations (AM)

Except on Sundays, the licensees of all standard broadcast stations

(AM) must maintain a minimum operating schedule of two-thirds of the total hours they are authorized to broadcast between 6 A.M. and 6 P.M., local standard time, and two-thirds of the authorized time between 6 P.M. and midnight. An exception is made in cases of emergency due to causes over which the licensee has no control. Under such circumstances, the station may cease operation for a period not to exceed 10 days, but the Commission and the Engineer in Charge of the radio district in which the station is located must be notified in writing immediately.[11]

The station must operate or refrain from operating during the experimental period (from midnight to local sunrise) if directed by the Commission in order to facilitate frequency measurement or determine interference.[12]

If the license of a station specifies the hours of operation, this specific schedule must be adhered to except when emergencies, as mentioned above, permit cessation of operation for a limited time or when the station may be ordered by the Commission to operate or refrain therefrom during the experimental period.[13]

b. Share-Time Stations

As previously pointed out, some stations are authorized to share time on the same channel. If the licenses of such share-time stations do not specify hours of operation, the licensees must attempt to reach an agreement as to their respective time schedules. Three original copies of this written agreement must be filed by each licensee with each application for renewal of license. One copy is retained by the Commission, one sent to the Engineer in Charge of the radio district in which the station is located, and one returned to the licensee to be posted with the station license and considered as a part thereof.[14]

If the share-time license specifies a proportionate time division, the agreement must maintain this proportion. If none is specified, the licensees must agree upon a time division. Unless authorized by specific terms in the licenses, simultaneous operation of the share-time stations is not permitted.[15]

If the licenses do not specify hours of operation, the stations may agree to divide time during the experimental period. Such agreements do not have to be submitted to the Commission.[16]

The Commission will not permit a departure from the regular operating schedule set forth in the time-sharing agreement until it is superseded by another agreement signed by the licensees affected and filed in triplicate by each licensee with the Commission prior to the time of the proposed change. If time is of the essence, the schedule may be changed before the written agreement is filed, provided the Commission and the Engineer in Charge of the radio district are notified.[17]

If licensees authorized to share time cannot agree on a division, the

Commission must be notified at the time renewal applications are filed. Upon receipt of such applications the Commission then designates them for hearing. Pending the outcome of the proceeding, the stations must adhere to the time schedules previously agreed upon.[18]

The Rules covering the broadcast stations (FM and Television) have nothing to say about share-time arrangements. It can be assumed, however, that the same basic rules relating to AM stations are applicable to them as well.

c. Daytime, Limited and Specified Hour Stations

As has already been discussed, stations with licenses which specify operation from sunrise to sunset, commence and cease operations each day in accordance with times set forth in the license. Uniform sunrise and sunset times are specified by the Commission for all the days of each month. Section 3.23 of the Rules states the operating requirements for stations classified as "limited" or "specified hour" stations.[19]

d. FM and TV Stations

All FM broadcast stations are licensed for unlimited time operation. A minimum of 36 hours per week during the hours from 6 A.M. to midnight, consisting of not less than 5 hours in any one day, except Sunday, must be devoted to broadcasting.[20]

Non-commercial educational FM stations are not required to operate on a regular schedule and no minimum number of hours of operation is specified. The Commission has said, however, that the actual operation during a license period will be taken into account in connection with the consideration of renewal applications where it appears that the channels available are insufficient to meet the demand. These same rules apply to non-commercial educational television stations operating on reserved channels.[21]

Commercial television stations are licensed for unlimited time operation. The schedule for each station is prescribed by the Commission as follows: at least two hours daily in any five broadcast days per week and a total of at least twelve hours per week during the first eighteen months of operation; at least two hours daily in any five broadcast days per week and at least sixteen, twenty, and twenty-four hours per week for each successive six-month period of operation. Thereafter, at least two hours in each of the seven days and not less than a total of twenty-eight hours per week of broadcasting is required.[22]

Time devoted to test patterns, or to aural presentations accompanied by the incidental use of fixed visual images which have no substantial relationship to the subject matter of such aural presentations, may not be considered in computing periods of programs service.[23]

Requirements Regarding Operators. Section 318 of the Communications Act provides that no person shall operate the transmitting apparatus of any broadcast station without holding an operator's license issued by the FCC.[24] This statutory requirement has been implemented in the rules and regulations of the Commission.

Standard (AM) and FM Broadcast Stations. One or more radio operators holding valid radiotelephone first-class operator licenses must be in actual charge of the transmitting equipment of a standard or FM broadcasting station and must be on duty either at the transmitter location or remote control point. There is an exception to this rule.[25] Where a broadcast station is authorized for non-directional operation with power of 10 kilowatts or less, it may be operated by a person with a license other than first-class if the equipment is so designed that the stability of the frequency is maintained by the transmitter itself within the limits of tolerance specified; and when none of the activities necessary to be performed to maintain normal transmission may cause off-frequency or result in any unauthorized radiation.[26]

Except when under first-class supervision, lower grade operators are permitted to make only the following adjustments of transmitting equipment:[27]

1. Those necessary to commence or terminate transmitter emissions as a routine matter.
2. External ones required as a result of variations of primary power supply.
3. External ones necessary to insure modulation within the limits required.
4. Adjustments necessary to affect any change in operating power which may be required by the station's instrument of authorization.
5. Make adjustments necessary to effect operation on a CONELRAD authorization, providing the station's full-time first-class operator has previously instructed such person concerning transmitter adjustments necessary for CONELRAD operation.

If the transmitter apparatus is not operating in accordance with the station's authorization and none of the above adjustments is corrective, operators not holding first-class licenses and not under immediate first-class supervision are required to turn off the transmitter.[28]

As pointed out above, the licensee of a standard broadcast station must have one or more first-class operators in full time employment whose primary duties shall be to insure the proper functioning of the transmitting equipment. An operator may be employed, however, for other duties or for operation of other stations in accordance with the class of license he holds. Such duties, however, must not interfere with the proper operation of any broadcast transmitter for which he is responsible.[29]

In the event a licensee operates both a standard and FM station in the same community, a regular full-time first-class operator or operators at one station may be employed concurrently at the other, providing the performance of duties at the one does not interfere with his duties at the other.[30]

Non-Commercial Educational FM Stations. The operator requirements for non-commercial educational FM stations are largely the same as those for standard and FM stations. There are a few exceptions, as follows:

If the transmitter output is in excess of 10 watts but not greater than 1 kw, a second-class operator may perform the duties of a first-class one. If the power output is 10 watts or less, a second-class operator is adequate and he need not be in regular full-time employment at the station.[31]

Television and International Stations. One or more licensed first-class operators must be on duty at the place where the transmitting apparatus of each television and international broadcast station is located and in actual charge of its operations. This applies whether the operation is commercial or non-commercial. The operator may, at the discretion of the licensee, be employed for other duties or for the operation of another station or stations, providing these interfere in no way with his work at any television or international broadcast station for which he is responsible.[32]

Posting Licenses. All broadcast stations are required to post their licenses and any other instruments of authorization in a conspicuous place and in such manner that all terms are visible, at the place the licensee considers to be the principal control point of the transmitter. A photocopy of the license and other instruments of authorization must be posted at all other control points.[33]

The licenses of operators, regardless of classification, must also be posted at the regular place of duty. Originals (not copies) are required.

Keeping Logs. Section 303 (j) of the Communications Act gives the Commission authority to "make general rules and regulations requiring stations to keep such records of programs, transmissions of energy, communications, or signals as it may deem desirable." Pursuant to this authority, the Commission requires all broadcast stations to maintain program and operating logs. As provided in Sections 3.111, 3.281, 3.581, 3.663, and 3.781 of the Rules, the various types of broadcast stations are required to make the following entries in the program logs:[34]

(1) The time each station identification announcement (call letters and location) is made.

(2) A brief description of each program broadcast such as "music", "drama", "speech", etc., with the name or title thereof; the name of the sponsor, with the time of the beginning and ending of the complete program. If mechanical records are used, the entry must show the exact type, whether a record, transcription, mechanical reproduction, both visual and aural, and the time it is announced as such. If a speech is made by a political candidate, the name and political affiliation of the speaker must be entered.

(3) An entry showing that each sponsored program broadcast has been announced as sponsored, paid for, or furnished by the sponsor.

(4) An entry showing for each network program the name of the network originating the program.

Separate logs for technical operation must be maintained and include entries as follows:

(1) The time the station begins to supply power to the antenna, and the time it stops.

(2) The time the program begins and ends.

(3) An entry of each interruption to the carrier wave, its causes, and duration.

(4) An entry of the following each 30 minutes:
    a. Operating constants of last radio stage of aural transmission (take plate current and plate voltage).
    b. Transmission line readings.
    c. Frequency monitor readings.

If regular operation is carried on during the "experimental" period, the same requirements as to keeping program and operating logs apply. If the use of the entries specified above does not adequately describe the operation during this period, they may be modified or supplemented to provide a full description.

Where an antenna structure is required to be lighted, the licensee must observe the tower lights at least once every 24 hours or maintain automatic equipment with indicators designed to register any failure of the lighting. The failure of any code or rotating beacon or top tower light not corrected within 30 minutes, regardless of cause, must be recorded and reported immediately by telephone or telegraph to the nearest air ways communication station or office of the Civil Aeronautics Administration. Similar recording must be made and notification must be given upon resumption of the required illumination.

At intervals not exceeding three months, all automatic or mechanical control devices, indicators and alarm systems associated with the tower lighting must be inspected to insure proper functioning.

The station with an antenna structure requiring illumination must make the following entries in the logs:

(a) The time the tower lights are turned on and off each day if manually controlled.

(b) The time the daily check is made, if an automatic alarm system is not provided.

(c) Entries showing the failure of a tower light and the nature of the failure; date and time the failure was observed; date, time and nature of adjustments, repairs or replacements; and identification of air ways communication station (Civil Aeronautics Administration) which was notified of any light failure and the date and time of such notification.[85]

Retention of Logs. Logs for the various types of stations must be retained for a period of at least two years. Under certain conditions, the licensee may be required to keep them for a longer period. The Commission has stated that logs involving communications incident to disaster or which may be pertinent to an investigation by the Commission and about which the station has been notified, must be retained until the Commission specifically authorizes in writing their destruction. The same rule applies to retention of logs which may relate to any claim or complaint against the station until such matters have been disposed of or have been barred by the statute limiting the filing of suits.[36]

Keeping Logs in Orderly Manner. The rules require that logs be kept in an orderly manner and be sufficiently detailed that the "data required of the particular class of station are readily available". Key letters or abbreviations, if properly explained, may be used to facilitate the keeping of the station records.

Licensees are cautioned that each station log must be kept by a competent person or persons familiar with the facts, and who is required to sign the log both when starting and going off duty. No obliterations, erasures or destruction is permitted within the period of retention. Necessary corrections can be made only by the person originating the entry who may strike out the erroneous portion of the log, initial the correction and indicate the date it is made.

The rules also provide for the keeping of "rough logs". These may be transcribed into condensed form, but in such case the original log or memoranda and all portions thereof must be preserved and made a part of the complete log.[37]

Uniform Definitions and Program Logs. The Commission has adopted uniform definitions of basic program categories. Such classifications must be shown upon the face of the program log so that the licensee may submit descriptive data concerning its program service, as required by the FCC, in connection with applications for new facilities or license renewals. These uniform definitions and classifications are set forth in Appendix VII.[38] It should be pointed out, however, that the Commission has proposed to modify its present application forms, involving changes in these program categories and has announced that rule-making proceedings will be instituted soon pursuant to this purpose.[39] Until new rules are adopted, however, program classifications, as defined in Appendix VII, must be used.

1. FCC Rules, Sections 3.57, 3.267, 3.567, and 3.689; 1 RR 53:204, 473-474, 567-568 and 694-695.
2. Section 3.59, 1 RR 53:205.
3. Section 3.269, 1 RR 53:474.
4. Section 3.569, 1 RR 53:544.
5. Section 3.689, 1 RR 53:694-695.
6. See Sections 3.55, 3.268, 3.317(f)(1), and 3.687(b) 7; 1 RR 53:203, 474, 507 and 687.
7. Sections 3.56, 3.58, 3.252(b) and (c), 3.253 (b) and (c), 3.552 (b) and (c), 3.553 (b) and (c), 3.688 (f), 3.690 (f), 3.691 (f); 1 RR 53:203, 204, 452, 453, 532, 533, 694, 695, 696.
8. Sections 3.56, 3.252, 3.253, 3.553, 3.690; 1 RR 53:203, 204, 452, 453, 695.
9. Sections 3.47, 3.254; 1 RR 53:172, 173, 452, 453, 454.
10. Section 0.49, 1 RR 51:30-35.
11. Section 3.71, 1 RR 53:209.
12. *Ibid.*, Section 3.72.
13. *Ibid.*, Section 3.73.
14. *Ibid.*, Section 3.74.
15. *Ibid.*
16. *Ibid.*, Section 3.76.
17. Section 3.77; 1 RR 53:209-210.
18. *Ibid.*, Section 3.78.
19. Section 3.23, 1 RR 53:132.
20. Section 3.26, 1 RR 53:471.
21. Sections 3.561, 3.651 (b); 1 RR 53:541, 651.
22. Section 3.561(a), 1 RR 53:651.
23. *Ibid.*
24. 50 Stat. 56, c, 58.
25. Sections 3.93, 3.265; 1 RR 53:214, 472.
26. Section 3.565, 1 RR 53:541.
27. *Ibid.*, 53:541-542.
28. *Ibid.*
29. *Ibid.*
30. Section 3.265, 1 RR 53:472-473.
31. Section 3.565, 1 RR 53:542.
32. Sections 3.661, 3.764; 1 RR 53:660, 746.
33. Sections 3.92, 3.264, 3.564, 3.660, 3.661, 3.763, 3.764; 1 RR 53:213, 471, 415, 659, 746.
34. 1 RR 53:218, 481, 551, 660, 747.
35. Sections 17.37, 17.38; 1 RR 67:27, 28.
36. Sections 3.122, 3.282, 3.582, 3.664, 3.782; 1 RR 53:224, 482, 552, 661, 748.
37. Sections 3.114, 3.115, 3.284, 3.285, 3.584, 3.585, 3.664, 3.784, and 3.785; 1 RR 53:225, 483, 553, 661, 662, 748.
38. 1 RR 53:219-224.
39. See FCC Public Notice 91874 (July 29, 1960), 25 Fed. Reg. 7291 (1960); 20 RR 1901.

CHAPTER 18

FCC Rules Implementing Statutory Requirements Regarding Broadcast Programming

The Commission would be remiss in its duties if it failed, in the exercise of its licensing authority, to aid in implementing the statute, either by general rule or by individual decisions.—Chief Justice EARL WARREN, *354 U.S. 284*

While Section 326 of the Communications Act prohibits the FCC from exercising censorship over the programs presented by radio and television stations, there are a number of provisions in the law which impose requirements on broadcast licensees with respect to certain aspects of programming. Pursuant to these provisions, the Commission has adopted specific regulations which should be considered.

Station Identification. Section 303 of the Communications Act gives the FCC authority to designate call letters for all stations and to require their publication by the stations in such manner as will contribute to the efficiency of their operation and to the enforcement of the Act. Accordingly, Sections 3.117, 3.287, 3.587, 3.652 and 3.787 of the Commission's Rules require the different types of broadcast stations to make identification announcements, including call letters and location.[1]

Standard broadcast stations are required to make such announcements at the beginning and ending of each time of operation. Paragraph (a)(1) of Section 3.117 of the Rules, specifies announcements on the hour during station operation.[2] Paragraph (a)(2) of the same section states they must be made also either on the half hour or at the fifteen minute interval following the hour and at the fifteen minute interval preceding the next hour.[3]

There are exceptions to this requirement. The identification may be omitted on the hour if it would interrupt "a single consecutive speech, play, religious service, symphony, or operatic production of longer duration than 30 minutes."[4] In such cases it need only be made at the beginning of the program, at the first interruption of the "entertainment continuity" and at the conclusion of the program.[5]

In the case of variety shows, baseball games or similar programs longer than 30 minutes, the identification announcement must be made within five minutes of the hour and of the times specified in paragraph (2)(a) of Section 3.117.[6] In all other programs, it must be made within two minutes of the hour and of the times specified in paragraph (2)(a).[7]

The station identification requirements for *FM stations,* as stated in Section 3.287 of the Rules, are the same as those applying to standard stations. If one licensee, however, operates an FM and a standard broadcast station simultaneously, broadcasting the same programs over both facilities, the announcements may be made jointly for both stations during the period of simultaneous operation.[8]

The requirements for *non-commercial educational FM stations* are less exacting than those for other types of broadcast stations. Section 3.587 specifies that announcements be made (1) at the beginning and ending of each time of operation; and (2) within two minutes of each hour and of each half hour during operation. These latter announcements at the hour or half hour may be omitted, if making them would interrupt a single continuous program more than thirty minutes in length. In such cases, station identification need only be made at the beginning of the program, at the first interruption of the continuity, and at the conclusion of the program.[9]

Section 3.652 of the Rules provides that *television stations* must identify themselves at the beginning and ending of each operation and on the hour while broadcasting. The initial and closing identification must be presented both aurally and visually. Intervening ones on the hour may be by either one or the other means.[10]

There are special rules for *international broadcast stations.* Section 3.787 requires them to make announcements at the beginning and ending of each time of broadcasting and on the hour during operation.[11] The station identification, program announcements, and oral continuity must be made "with international significance", and designed for the foreign country or countries for which the service is primarily intended.[12] Single consecutive speeches, plays, etc. need not be interrupted with the station call letters, except at the first interruption of the "entertainment continuity" and at the conclusion of the program.[13]

Mechanical Reproductions. Until the latter part of 1956, FCC requirements were quite stringent with respect to identification of mechanical recordings. To make sure that the public was not deceived into believing that it was hearing live talent, all recorded programs had to be identified as such at the beginning and end of such programs and at certain specified intervals.

Following a public hearing, however, the Commission announced in October, 1956, that the rules then in effect imposed "a needless burden on broadcasters and detracted from the public's enjoyment of the programs."[14] Accordingly, the Commission amended the rules at that time requiring identification announcements only when the element of time is important and cutting down on the number and frequency required.[15]

As now in effect, the rules are uniform for standard, FM, non-commercial educational FM and television stations. They provide that no recorded program, "whether visual or aural, consisting of a speech, news, event, news commentator, forum, panel discussion, or special event in which the element of time is of special significance," may be broadcast without an appropriate announcement being made that it is recorded either at the beginning or end of the program.[16] The same rule applies to any other type of program in which the time element is important and presentation of which would create the impression that the event or program is in fact occurring simultaneously with the broadcast.[17]

Recorded programs of one minute or less need not be identified as such. Likewise, mechanical reproductions used for background music, sound effects, station program and sponsor identifications need not be announced as such.[18]

The waiver provision also applies to network programs transmitted in one time zone, recorded and rebroadcast later in another zone. However, the waiver applies only if the period of elapse between the beginning of the first and second transmissions does not exceed the time differential between the two locations.

The Rules provide that when a station broadcasts network programs at a later hour in accordance with the waiver, an appropriate announcement shall be made at least once each day between the hours of 10:00 A.M. and 10:00 P.M. stating that some or all of the network programs broadcast are delayed and presented by transcription.[20]

The exception is also applicable to network programs transcribed and rebroadcast one hour later because of the time differential resulting from the adoption of daylight saving time in some areas.[21]

Sponsored Programs. Section 19 of the Radio Act of 1927 provided that "all matter broadcast by any radio station for which service, money, or any other valuable consideration is directly or indirectly paid, or promised to or charged or accepted by, the station so broadcasting, from any person, shall, at the time the same is so broadcast, be announced as paid for or furnished, as the case may be, by such person."[22]

This language was lifted verbatim from the 1927 Act and became Section 317 of the Communications Act of 1934.[23] The Commission has implemented the provisions of this section with rules which are identical for Standard, FM, television and international broadcast stations.[24] Non-commercial educational FM and television stations are not permitted to sell time to sponsors, but Section 3.621(e) of the Rules specifically makes the statutory requirements of Section 317 of the Act applicable to non-commercial educational TV stations if they carry programs "produced by or at the expense of or furnished by others".[25] While the rules governing non-commercial educational FM stations do not so state, it is assumed that the statutory requirements of Section 317 of the Act are applicable to them as well.

In the case of any political program or any discussion of public controversial issues for which any films, records, transcriptions, talent, scripts, or other materials or services are furnished directly or indirectly as an inducement to the station to carry the program, an announcement to that effect must be made at the beginning and conclusion of the program, except if the program is no longer than five minutes, only one announcement need be made either at the beginning or end.[26]

The true identity of sponsors, donors or others covered by the provisions of Section 317 must be fully and fairly disclosed. Where the station knows that an agent is arranging for the program in behalf of a third party, the announcement must reveal the identity of this third party rather than the agent.[27]

Where programs advertise commercial products or services, a mere mention of the sponsor's corporate or trade name or his product is deemed sufficient, and only one such announcement need be made during the course of the program.[28]

Even if the program is one which does not advertise a product or service, if it is paid for in whole or in part by a corporation, committee, association or other unincorporated group, or uses materials or services provided by any such organization or group in the manner described above, the announcement must disclose the name of the group. Also, in each case, the station must require that a list of the chief executive officers or members of the executive committee or the board of directors of any such organization or group be made available for public inspection at the station carrying the program.[29]

FCC Action Against "Payola" Practices. On March 16, 1960, the Commission adopted a public notice entitled "Sponsorship Identification of Broadcast Material." The Commission indicated in this notice that on the basis of responses it had received to an inquiry of December 2, 1959, it appeared that stations had failed to comply with the requirements of Section 317 of the Communications Act and the Commission's Rules implementing it.

This action of the FCC was largely an outgrowth of "payola" practices in recent years which have evoked widespread public concern. In this notice, the Commission set forth several specific interpretations of Section 317 applicable to recordings broadcast by radio and television stations. These interpretations may be summarized as follows:

1. The receipt of any records by a station, intended by the supplier to be, or have the practical effect of being an inducement to play those particular records

or any other records on the air, and the broadcast of such records, requires an appropriate announcement pursuant to Section 317.

2. Appropriate announcements must accompany all broadcast material (playing of records, etc.) where a profit is to be derived from "record hops" or other non-broadcast activities, or where recorded or other broadcast exposure is being provided in exchange for donation of records, prizes, hall rental, etc. The parties deriving financial benefit from the "record hop" must be identified as well as any other parties furnishing consideration in exchange for any of the above types of broadcast exposure.

3. An appropriate announcement must be made where transportation and accommodation expenses or equipment operation and origination expenses incurred in "remote" pickups have been paid in whole or in part by persons or organizations as an inducement to broadcast program material containing, e.g., pictures or descriptions of a place, product, service, or event. The announcement must disclose the fact that consideration was provided, and by whom, as an inducement for the broadcast presentation.

4. "Trade out" announcements and "plugs" violate Section 317 unless it is disclosed that the particular matter broadcast is commercial and is supported by some form of consideration.

5. "Teaser" announcements and broadcast of similar subject matter without explicit identification of the sponsor are contrary to Section 317.

6. The playing of musical selections from current motion pictures under any kind of arrangement with a local theatre or distributor, or as a "bonus" for purchase of spot announcements, without sponsorship announcement is likewise unlawful.

7. Stations must use their utmost diligence to inform themselves of situations in which their employees or independent contractors have outside financial interests which are being promoted over these stations, and to require appropriate announcements to be made as required by Section 317.[30]

FCC's Interpretation of Statute Questioned. The National Association of Broadcasters, the Federal Communications Bar Association, the networks and other segments of the broadcast industry raised questions regarding these interpretations by the Commission and formally requested further proceedings.

In April 1960, the Commission issued a *Notice of Inquiry* stating that it would consider comments as to whether clarification of its interpretations was desirable, and gave interested parties opportunity to file such comments on or before May 2, 1960.[31]

In response to the April 1, 1960 Notice, voluminous comments were filed with the Commission. Many parties particularly objected to the Commission's interpretation of Section 317 which requires that all free records, when played over a station, be accompanied with announcements identifying the donors and stating that these records are furnished without cost.

In many of the comments, it was contended that the legislative history of Section 317 does not call for such a strict interpretation. It was argued

216

that early discussions in Congress regarding the purpose of the section as originally conceived, indicate that the section was mainly intended to prevent "disguised" advertising.[32]

Section 317 was carried over from the Radio Act of 1927. In explaining the origin and purpose of its provisions as they were stated in Section 19 of that original act, Congressman Celler, in 1926, said:

The author of the section sought to follow the law of the District of Columbia against newspapers printing disguised advertising. That law which was a rider to the Post Office Appropriation Bill, August 1912, Sixty-second Congress, second session, (Vol. 37, Stat. L. 553-554), is as follows:

All editorial or other reading matter published in any such newspaper, magazine, or periodical for the publication of which money or other valuable consideration is paid, accepted, or promised shall be plainly marked "advertisement." Any editor or publisher printing editorials or other reading matter for which compensation is paid, accepted, or promised without so marking the same, shall upon conviction in any court having jurisdiction be fined not less than $50 nor more than $500.[33]

The National Broadcasting Company argued that newspapers regularly receive gratuitous press releases and other "publicity hand-outs" from many different sources, the suppliers hoping that the information will be used to their benefit; that a portion or all of one of these press releases would not be a violation of the law. On the other hand, said NBC, if the newspaper is paid cash or other substantial consideration to run the reading material there would be a violation. It was asserted that this same principle ought to be applicable to broadcast stations.[34]

The Michigan Association of Broadcasters agreed with this point of view. In its comments to the FCC, the Association said:

We believe that this same rule of reason ought to apply to broadcast stations who receive, free of charge, records to be included in their libraries. Obviously, record companies and their distributors who make a practice of supplying these free materials to stations, have hopes that some of them will be used and that benefits therefrom will ensue. But where there is no understanding or agreement that any or all of the records will be used—no contractual obligation of any kind to play them on the station—it seems unreasonable to say that broadcast exposure without identification of the donors constitutes a violation of Section 317. As in the case of newspapers, however, if the record company or distributor *pays* the station to play the recordings a certain number of times, a broadcast announcement of this fact would be required to avoid violation of Section 317.[35]

Applicability of Section 317 to Discussion Programs. The legislative history of Section 317 does clearly show that Congress intended that the

217

source of programs involving discussion of political or controversial issues should be identified when broadcast. There can be no doubt that the *mere* supplying of such discussion programs is sufficient to constitute "valuable consideration" in the context of Section 317, and to require sponsor identification.

In a recent case, the Commission has made its position on this matter clear. In July, 1958, the Commission sent three Public Letters to three station licensees who had failed to reveal identity of an organization when those stations had televised kinescope summaries of Congressional hearings on a strike issue.[36] The organization had supplied the films free of charge and the stations received no material consideration except the films themselves. The Commission held that Section 317 of the Act and Section 3.654(a) of the Rules had been contravened. It was stressed that the person or group paying for or furnishing material in connection with the discussion of political matters or controversial issues of public importance should always be accurately and completely identified.

"We do not question the wisdom of this decision," said the Michigan Association of Broadcasters, "where points of view on controversial questions, especially those of a political nature, are being broadcast, the public is entitled to know who the sponsors are. Congress and the Commission have been concerned about this and, we think, rightly so. But the same reasons for this concern do not apply to pure entertainment including little or no discussion and where the consideration involved is the program itself. This is particularly true with respect to free musical recordings where there is no obligation on the part of stations to use any of the recordings."[37]

The Association further pointed out that many stations have built up large libraries of recorded music from which they draw regularly; that the current requirement that every record in these library collections (some of which contain hundreds of free records accumulated over the years) be accompanied with a commercial plug, is a serious burden on the broadcaster, degrades his program service, is offensive to the listeners, and works seriously against the public interest.

FCC Urged To Reconsider Its Interpretation. Along with other parties in the proceeding, the MBA urged the Commission to reconsider its interpretation of Section 317 as announced on March 16, 1960, and concluded its comments as follows:

. . . in view of the understanding of Section 317 which has prevailed among large segments of the broadcast industry for more than thirty years, and which appears to conflict with the recent views expressed by the Commission, we earnestly hope that the Commission will not take precipitous action in the matter. We suggest that the Commission suspend the effectiveness of its recent public notice, and institute rulemaking proceedings, looking toward a more careful and studied consideration of the whole problem. This approach will ensure that all interested parties will have an opportunity to provide information and express their views.

. . . .

Presently, there are many misgivings and much confusion in the broadcast industry as to the full import of Section 317 as interpreted at various times by the FCC. Rulemaking, as proposed, would alleviate most of these misgivings and provide clarification as to requirements and procedures. This would be of immeasurable benefit to the industry. More important, the public interest unquestionably would be served.[38]

There were professed differences of opinion among the FCC Commissioners as to the applicability of Section 317. Commissioners Hyde and Lee agreed with the Commission's Public Notice of March 16, 1960 in so far as it solicited comments, but, in a separate statement, expressed the view that the Commission's interpretive ruling may have gone beyond the intent and purpose of the Statute.[39] Accordingly, they favored suspending the effective date of the ruling until the Commission could have time to study the comments filed.

Subsequently, the Eighty-Sixth Congress, at its Second Session, amended Section 317 of the Communications Act, clarifying questions as to license responsibilities regarding announcements and disclosures of payments, received in connection with the broadcast of recordings and other program materials. This new legislation imposes severe penalties for violations of Section 317. The full text of the amendment is reproduced in Appendix I. In light of this new legislation, on September 20, 1960, the FCC withdrew its *Notice of Inquiry,* announcing that broadcast rules relating to sponsorship of broadcast material would remain in effect (Sections 3.119, 3.289, 3.654 and 3.789) until revised, except where superseded by Section 317 of the Act, as amended. [FCC Public Notice 60-1141, No. 93746, 25 Fed. Reg. 9177 (1960)].

Political Broadcasting. Section 315 of the Communications Act relating to the use of broadcasting facilities by candidates for public office, as originally adopted by Congress, was identical with Section 18 of the Radio Act of 1927.[40] While no station was obligated to carry political broadcasts, it was provided that if a station permitted any "legally qualified candidate" for public office to use its facilities, it must afford equal opportunities to all other such candidates. The section also specifically prohibited the station from censoring any material in broadcasts by political candidates.

In 1952, Congress amended Section 315 of the Communications Act by adding the provision that the charges made for broadcasts by political candidates could not exceed those made for "comparable use" of a station for other purposes.[41]

The FCC has adopted rules to carry out the provisions of Section 315 of the Act.[42] These rules are uniformly applicable to all types of broadcast stations. They incorporate the language of the statute making it optional with any station as to whether it will make its facilities available for political broadcasting, but where it does, requiring that all candidates be treated equally. Rates must be uniform and rebates are prohibited. A candidate may not be charged more than the rate a commercial advertiser would pay for comparable time to promote his business in the same area as that encompassed by the particular office for which the candidate is seeking election.

Discriminations or preferences as between candidates in "charges, practices, regulations, facilities, or services are strictly prohibited and no candidate may be subjected to any prejudice or disadvantage." No licensee can make any contract or other agreement which would have the effect of permitting one candidate to broadcast to the exclusion of others for the same office.

A complete record must be kept by the station of all requests for broadcast time by candidates for public office, together with an appropriate notation showing the disposition made by the licensee of such requests, and the charges made, if any, when broadcasting facilities are made available. These records must be retained for a period of two years and be open for public inspection.

Section 315 of the Act is applicable only to "legally qualified candidates." In the absence of statutory definition, it has been necessary for the Commission to define the term as it is used in the Rules. As described in Section 3.120 of the Rules relating to standard broadcasts stations, a "legally qualified candidate" is "any person who has publicly announced that he is a candidate for nomination by a convention of a political party or for nomination or election in a primary, special, or general election, municipal, county, state or national, and who meets the qualifications prescribed by the applicable laws to hold the office for which he is a candidate so that he may be voted for by its electorate directly or by means of delegates or electors, and who:

(1) has qualified for a place on the ballot or
(2) is eligible under the applicable law to be voted for by sticker, by writing in his name on the ballot, or other method, and
(3) has been duly nominated by a political party which is commonly known and regarded as such or
(4) makes a substantial showing that he is a bonafide candidate for nomination or office, as the case may be."

The rules with respect to treatment of political candidates on other types of stations (FM, non-commercial FM and TV) are identical to those discussed above. International broadcast stations are subject to Section 317 of the statute, but the Commission has not adopted specific rules applying it to them. It is assumed, however, should test cases arise, that the Commission would apply the same rules to international broadcasting that it does to domestic operations.

FCC's Interpretation of Section 315 Questioned. The Commission's interpretation of Section 315 recently was seriously questioned and criticized by numerous groups, including Congress, the networks, some stations and large segments of the press. Much of this criticism was an outgrowth of a case decided by the Commission on June 15, 1959, popularly known as the "Lar Daly Case".

The case grew out of the following facts. Primary elections for the office of Mayor of Chicago were scheduled for February 24, 1959. Richard J. Daley, Mayor of Chicago, was a candidate in the Democratic Primary; Timothy P. Sheehan was a candidate in the Republican Primary; and Lar Daly was a candidate in both. Prior to election time Lar Daly filed a complaint with the Commission alleging that certain Chicago television stations had, in the course of their newscasts, shown film clips of his opponents in connection with certain events and occasions; that he had requested equal broadcasting time over these stations but that his requests had been refused.

The film clips in question, each averaging less than a minute, involved interviews with one of the candidates as to why he chose to run for the office; moving pictures of the Democratic and Republican candidates filing petitions for the race; of Mayor Richard J. Daley in connection with the selection of the speaker for the Illinois House of Representatives and another involving the selection of the site for the Democratic National Convention; and the telecasts of the two candidates making speeches of acceptance. Also, there were two short telecasts of the Mayor, one issuing an official proclamation in connection with a drive for the March of Dimes, and the other greeting President Frondizi of Argentina, on his arrival at the Chicago Midway Airport.

After careful consideration, the Commission on February 19, 1959 advised the stations involved that under Section 315 of the Communications Act, Lar Daly was entitled to equal broadcasting opportunities.

The Columbia Broadcasting System contended that the film clips were shown as part of regularly scheduled news broadcasts and were handled by the station in routine fashion; that they were not designed to advance the cause of any candidate nor were they initiated directly or indirectly by a candidate; that they were under the exclusive control of the station and each film clip was included in the particular news program in the bona fide exercise by the station of its news judgment.[43]

CBS further alleged that where a station simply broadcasts the face or voice of a candidate as part of a regular news program, selects the event to be covered and controls every aspect of the broadcast, that it is not permitting the candidate "to use" its facilities in the sense Congress intended in Section 315. On the contrary, CBS said, in such situations the candidate is being used by the station. It was further argued that to impose a limitation on the exercise by a station of its bona fide news judgment would be a violation of free speech.[44] Numerous other arguments were advanced in support of its position.

The National Broadcasting Company and Westinghouse filed documents making many of the same points advanced by CBS.[45]

The Attorney General also opposed the Commission's interpretation and, as summarized by the Commission, his main contentions ran as follows: "that he does not support the holding that every time a candidate is shown on a regular news program, at the station's sole initiative, such showing constitutes a "use" by him since such holding might bar all direct news coverage of important campaign developments; that fair yet comprehensive news coverage can be assured not by applying Section 315 but by applying the "public interest" standard which requires fair presentation of public issues; that Section 315 does not state that any showing of a candidate on a radio or TV program entitles his opponents to "equal opportunities" to use the station's facilities; that instead it provides that "if any licensee shall permit any person . . . to use a broadcasting station it shall afford 'equal opportunities' to other candidates 'in the use of such broadcasting station'; and that this language is directed to 'use' by candidates of particular station facilities as part of their political campaign activities—not the station's reporting, as part of its news coverage, significant news events or campaign developments."[46]

In a 41 page decision adopted June 15, 1959, the Commission traced in detail the legislative history of Section 315 and dealt at great length with the arguments advanced by the petitioners.[47] Referring to the importance of the role of television in political campaigning, the Commission said:

. . . It is generally recognized that television can be a very valuable asset to a candidate and that the potential audience which a candidate may now reach is, because of television, far in excess of what it has been in the past. We believe that television has become an integral part of political campaigns and that with newspapers it is the most universal source of information for voters about the candidates. The candidate has several roles in which he may appear on television. The most obvious appearance is as a candidate campaigning for office. Of no less importance is the candidate's appearance as a public servant, as an incumbent office holder, or as a private citizen in a non-political role. It is, of course, in these latter roles that questions are raised about the applicability of Section 315 of the Act. While not always indispensable to political success, for some purposes television may enjoy a unique superiority in selling a candidate to the public in that it may create an impression of immediacy and intimate presence, it shows the candidate in action, and it affords a potential for reaching wide audiences.[48]

In the light of these facts, the Commission reaffirmed its position that *any* appearance by a political candidate on a newscast not initiated by him constitutes a "use" of the station's facilities by the candidate within the meaning of Section 315 of the Communications Act. This interpretation, the Commission said, is compelled by the legislative history of the section and by the possible benefits and advantages which accrue in favor of a candidate who is given exposure on television.

The Commission further held that the word "use" in Section 315 is synonymous with "appearance" and the word "appearance" is essentially the same as "exposure". And the Commission refused to view the problem of equalizing advantages through exposure of candidates on television and radio newscasts as one to be resolved through application of the overall "public interest" standard of fairness in presenting balanced programming.

The Commission did not agree with the petitioners that its interpretation involved any violation of freedom of speech or of the press. While news presentation is of great importance and vital to the public interest, a station does not have the same freedom of choice in presenting the news that a newspaper enjoys. This is because the station uses part of the radio spectrum which is public domain and its use is properly subject to Congressional control and limitations.

The following language appearing in paragraph 55 of the Commission's opinion is particularly noteworthy:

. . . we are of the opinion that there is no legal basis for exempting appearances by candidates on newscasts from Section 315, irrespective of whether the appearance was initiated by the candidate or not. We are further of the opinion that when a station uses film clips showing a candidate during the course of a newscast, that appearance of a candidate can reasonably be said to be a use, within the meaning and intent of Section 315. In short, the station has permitted a benefit or advantage to accrue to the candidate in the use of its facilities, thus placing itself under the statutory obligation to extend equal opportunities to opposing candidates in the use of its broadcasting station. In our opinion, only through this interpretation of Section 315 can Congress' unequivocal mandate that all candidates for the same office shall be treated equally be effectively carried out, taking into account the possible benefits or advantages which accrue in favor of a candidate thus given exposure on television. It may, of course, seem that such a holding is harsh or unduly rigid and that within the area of political broadcasts, it has a tendency to restrict radio and television licensees in their treatment of campaign affairs. *If* this be so, the short answer is that such a result follows not from any lack of sympathy on our part for the problems faced by licensees in complying with Section 315, which we are not at liberty to ignore. As the Court of Appeals observed in *Felix v. Westinghouse,* 186 F. 2d 1 (6 RR 2086), 'We must accordingly take the statute as the Congress intended it to be and leave it to that body to resolve the questions of public policy involved in the one construction or the other.'[49]

Congress, under great pressure from the broadcast industry and with the support of a substantial portion of the press, took action to resolve the questions. On September 14, 1959, Section 315 of the Communications Act was amended, specifically precluding its applicability to political candidates involved in "bona fide" newscasts.

As amended, the section now reads:

Sec. 315—(a) If any licensee shall permit any person who is a legally qualified candidate for any public office to use a broadcasting station, he shall afford equal opportunities to all other such candidates for that office in the use of such broadcasting station: provided, that such licensee shall have no power of censorship over the material broadcast under the provisions of this section. No obligation is hereby imposed upon any licensee to allow the use of its station by any such candidate. Appearance by a legally qualified candidate on any

(1) bona fide newscast

(2) bona fide news interview

(3) bona fide news documentary (if the appearance of the candidate is incidental to the presentation of the subject or subjects covered by the news documentary), or

(4) on-the-spot coverage of bona fide news events (including but not limited to political conventions and activities incidental thereto),

shall not be deemed to be use of a broadcasting station within the meaning of this subsection. Nothing in the foregoing sentence shall be construed as relieving broadcasters, in connection with the presentation of newscasts, news interviews, news documentaries, and on-the-spot coverage of news events, from the obligation imposed upon them under this Act to operate in the public interest and to afford reasonable opportunity for the discussion of conflicting views on issues of public importance.

(b) The charges made for the use of any broadcasting station for any of the purposes set forth in this section shall not exceed the charges made for comparable use of such station for other purposes.

(c) The Commission shall prescribe appropriate rules and regulations to carry out the provisions of this section.[50]

Section 2 of this amendatory act provides further that Congress will reexamine from time to time these new provisions to "ascertain whether they are effective and practicable and directs the FCC to make an annual report to the Congress setting forth (1) the information and data used by it in determining questions arising from or connected with such amendment, and (2) such recommendations as it deems necessary in the public interest."[51]

By legislation approved August 24, 1960, Congress suspended for the period of the 1960 presidential and vice-presidential campaigns the "equal opportunities" requirements of Section 315 with respect to nominees for the offices of President and Vice-President of the United States. The full text of this law appears in Appendix I.

Lotteries. Originally, Section 316 of the Communications Act prohibited the broadcasting of lottery programs or information regarding them.[52] As of September 1, 1948, this section was repealed by Congress and the substance of it incorporated in the U.S. Criminal Code. It now reads:

Broadcasting Lottery Information. Whoever broadcasts by means of any radio station for which a license is required by any law of the United States, or whoever, operating any such station, knowingly permits the broadcasting of any advertisement of or information concerning any lottery, gift enterprise, or similar scheme, offering prizes dependent in whole or in part upon lot or chance, or any list of the prizes drawn or awarded by means of any such lottery, gift enterprise, or scheme, whether said list contains any part or all of such prizes, shall be fined not more than $1,000 or imprisoned not more than one year or both.

Each day's broadcasting shall constitute a separate offense.[53]

In 1949, the Commission established rules defining and prohibiting the broadcast of lottery programs which it considered to come within the provisions of this section.[54] The rules, as originally contemplated, were uniformally applicable to all broadcasting stations, provided that an application for construction permit, license, or any other authorization for the operation of a station would not be granted where the applicant proposed to follow or continue to follow a policy or practice of broadcasting programs forbidden by the United States Criminal Code.

Programs outlawed by the Commission included those in connection with which a prize consisting of money or thing of value was awarded to any person whose selection depended in whole or in part upon lot or chance, if as a condition of winning or competing for such prize:

(1) Such winner or winners were required to furnish any money or thing of value or have in their possession any product sold, manufactured, furnished or distributed by a sponsor of a program broadcast on the station in question; or

(2) Had to answer correctly a question, the answer to which was given on a program broadcast over the station; or

(3) Had to answer the phone or write a letter in a prescribed manner or respond with a certain phrase if it had been broadcast over the station.

"Give-away" programs, so called, such as "Stop the Music", "What's My Name", and other similar features on the networks, which had attracted large national audiences, definitely fell within the ban of these rules. Two of the national networks challenged the validity of the rules in the Federal courts. They contended that the programs in question did not constitute lotteries as defined by Section 1304 of the Criminal Code, that mere participation of the home audience by simply listening to the programs did not constitute legal consideration, one of the essential elements of a lottery.

The case went to the U.S. Supreme Court on appeal. The high court, affirming the judgment of the U.S. District Court in the Southern District in New York, held that the Commission had the power to make rules to enforce Section 1304 which prohibits lotteries.[55] "Indeed," said Chief Justice Warren, speaking for the Court, "the Commission would be remiss in its duties if it failed, in the exercise of its licensing authority, to aid in implementing the statute, either by general rule or by individual decisions." But said he, "it would be stretching the statute to the breaking point to give it an interpretation that would make the give-away programs in question a crime."[56]

The Chief Justice concluded the decision as follows:

It is apparent that these so-called 'give-away' programs have long been a matter of concern to the Federal Communications Commission; that it believes these programs to be the old lottery evil under a new guise, and that they should be struck down as illegal devices appealing to cupidity and the gambling spirit. It unsuccessfully sought to have the Department of Justice take criminal action against them. Likewise, without success, it urged Congress to amend the law to specifically prohibit them. The Commission now seeks to accomplish the same result through agency regulations. In doing so, the Commission has over-stepped the boundaries of interpretation and hence has exceeded its rule making power. Regardless of the doubts held by the Commission and others as to the social value of the programs here under consideration, such administrative expansion of Section 1304 does not provide the remedy.[57]

This decision struck down those particular rules designed to ban "give-away" shows but left the Commission free to formulate rules prohibiting the broadcast of programs or information about them clearly involving all three essential elements of a lottery—prize, chance and substantial consideration. Accordingly, Section 3.122 of the Commission's Rules now in effect repeats the language of the Criminal Code and states in paragraph (b) that the determination whether a program falls within the statutory ban depends on the facts in each case but that in any event the Commission will consider a program in violation of the statute if there is connected with it a prize consisting of money or thing of value, given to a person chosen in whole or part upon lot or chance, and if the winner is required to furnish any money or thing of value or is required to possess any product sold, manufactured, furnished or distributed by a sponsor of a program broadcast on the station.[58]

Obscene and Indecent Language. Section 29 of the Radio Act of 1927 provided that "no person within the jurisdiction of the United States shall utter any obscene, indecent, or profane language by means of radio communication."[59] This same prohibition was included in Section 326 of the Communications Act of 1934.[60] In 1948, the language was deleted from Section 326, and with criminal sanctions added was transferred to the United States Criminal Code and reads as follows:

Section 1464. Broadcasting obscene language. Whoever utters any obscene, indecent, or profane language by means of radio communication shall be fined not more than $10,000 or imprisoned no more than two years or both.[61]

The FCC has never formulated rules to implement this section of the Code. There was one early case in which a Federal court attempted to give specific meaning to the statute as it was originally adopted and made a part of the Radio Act of 1927. In *Duncan v. United States,* 48 F.(2d) 128 (1931), the Court said that the test of whether language used in broadcasting is obscene or indecent is whether it would arouse lewd or lascivious thoughts in the minds of listeners. Such language as "grafting thief", "doggoned thieving", "lying . . . crook", "doggone his lousy picture", etc., was not held to constitute obscenity or indecency within the meaning of Section 29 of the 1927 Act since, the court said, these expressions had no tendency to excite libidinous thought on the part of the hearers. The Court held, however, that reference to an individual as "damned" and irreverent use of the expression "By God" constituted profanity and was a violation of the law.[62]

There have been no court cases construing the statutory language banning indecent, obscene or profane expressions as this language first appeared in Section 326 of the Communications Act or as it now appears in Section 1464 of the United States Criminal Code. Many programs presented over radio and television stations since 1934 have been the subject of complaints filed with the FCC by listeners, alleging that these programs were indecent, immoral, or profane. Traditionally, the FCC has associated these complaints with the official files of the stations and has reviewed them when the stations have come up for renewal of their licenses. In no case, however, has the Commission designated any renewal application for hearing or refused to renew a license on the basis of complaints that the station's programs have been of an indecent or profane character.

Since there is little court opinion by which the Commission may be guided and because the mores of communities and standards of decency differ so widely, there has been an understandable reluctance on the part of the FCC to take positive action in this area of regulation. There can be no doubt, however, that a program containing elements of vulgarity knowingly presented by a network or station and which would be shocking to the moral standards of a substantial number of listeners would give the Commission clear legal grounds on which to revoke or refuse to renew a license. At the same time, such an offense could involve the licensee in criminal proceedings that could lead to conviction under provisions of the Criminal Code.

As mentioned in Chapter 3, the Commission has authority to suspend the license of any operator who has transmitted "signals or communications containing profane or obscene words, language or meaning." Also, the language of Section 1464 is applicable to operators or other persons having access to broadcasting facilities as well as the licensees of stations, and any violation of the section would make them subject to criminal prosecution.

False Distress Signals and Rebroadcasting. Section 325 of the Communications Act prohibits the wilful utterance or transmission of any false or fraudulent signal of distress.[63] The same section provides that no broadcasting station may rebroadcast the program or any part thereof of another broadcasting station without the express authority of the originating station.[64]

This latter provision has been implemented by Commission rules. The Commission has defined the term "rebroadcast" as the "reception by radio of the program of a radio station, and the simultaneous or subsequent retransmission of such program by a broadcast station.[65]

The licensee of a station may rebroadcast a program of another station, providing it notifies the Commission, and certifies that authority for the rebroadcast has been received from the originating station.[66]

Network Regulations. As pointed out in Chapter 3, Section 303(i) of the Act gives the Commission power to make special regulations applicable to stations engaged in network broadcasting. The FCC has implemented this and other sections of the Act by the adoption of the network regulations. Prior to their adoption, the network contracts of NBC and CBS bound the affiliated stations for a period of five years. The networks themselves, however, were bound for only a period of one year.[67] The affiliated stations were prohibited from making their facilities available to any other national network during the five year period.[68]

The standard affiliation contracts originally gave the networks an option on all the time of the station for network commercial programs, subject to certain limitations. CBS contracts provided that a station might require not less than 28 days notice before the network could preempt time for programs and a station was not required to broadcast network commercial programs for more than 50 "converted hours" in any one week. A "converted hour" was understood to be the equivalent of one hour in the evening, two during the day, and two-thirds of an hour during Sunday afternoon. On the average, this meant that the network could preempt as many as 79 clock hours of the station's time during the week.[69]

Stations were given the right to reject a network program if it or the product advertised was objectionable, or if the station wanted to substitute a local sustaining program of public interest. NBC, however, required that the station prove that the substitution would be more in the public interest than the network program.[70]

While an affiliated station might substitute a local sustaining program for a network commercial under such conditions, it did not have the same freedom to substitute a local commercial program. If it did, it was compelled to pay to the network any increased revenue received from the substitution.[71]

Prior to the adoption of the chain broadcasting rules, there was no limitation on the number of networks which one company might own. NBC owned and operated the Blue and the Red networks with outlets in most of the major markets in the country. Nor were there restrictions on the number of stations which one network might own in the same community. NBC owned two stations in each of the following communities: New York, Chicago, Washington, and San Francisco as well as single stations in other larger cities.[72]

The affiliation contracts of NBC and CBS gave the chains full control over network station rates, and there were provisions in the NBC contracts designed to prevent outlets from securing revenues from the sale of time to advertisers for national spot business at rates lower than those set forth in the network rate card.[73]

On March 18, 1938, the FCC authorized an investigation "to determine what special regulations applicable to radio stations engaged in chain or other broadcasting are required in the public interest, convenience, or necessity."[74] A committee of three FCC commissioners was appointed to make the investigation.[75]

After long and careful study, including public hearings, the Committee issued a report on June 12, 1940.[76] This report contained a draft of proposed regulations which served as a basis for oral argument before the full Commission.

After full discussion was heard from interested parties, the Commission adopted specific network regulations on May 2, 1941.[77] These were restrictive in nature and their legality and propriety were vigorously challenged by the networks in the Federal courts. One of the principal contentions made against the regulations was that the Commission was "without jurisdiction to promulgate regulations which undertake to control indirectly the business arrangements of broadcasting licensees."[78] On May 10, 1943 the U.S. Supreme Court handed down its historic decision affirming the validity of the network rules.

Some amendments were made to these rules following their adoption in 1941.[79] Since April 12, 1944, with one exception, no further changes have been made. The regulations in effect today are as follows:

Exclusive Affiliation of Station. The Commission will not grant any application for a renewal of license or for increased or new broadcast facilities, if that station has any kind of "contract, arrangement, or understanding, express or implied, with a network organization under which the station is prevented or hindered from, or penalized for, broadcasting the programs of any other network organization."[80]

Territorial Exclusivity. The same rule applies if a station enters into any such arrangement which "prevents or hinders another station serving substantially the same area or a different area from broadcasting the network's programs not taken by the affiliate station." The Commission specifically says, however, that this does not preclude an arrangement by which the affiliate is granted the first call in its primary service area upon the programs of the network.[81]

Term of Affiliation. Network contracts are limited to two years but renewals may be made within six months prior to the commencement of a new contract period. Any kind of arrangement, express or implied, which provides for an affiliation with the network for longer than two years is strictly prohibited.[82]

Option Time. This rule originally provided that no license would be granted to a station which "options for network programs any broadcast time subject to call on less than 56 days' notice, or more time than a total of three hours within each of four segments of the broadcast day." These segments of the broadcast day are described by the Commission as follows: 8:00 a.m. to 1:00 p.m.; 1:00 p.m. to 6:00 p.m.; 6:00 p.m. to 11:00 p.m.; and 11:00 p.m. to 8:00 a.m. This meant that the affiliate might agree to give the network an option on as much as three hours of each segment of the broadcast day providing the network gave the station at least 56 days notice. Such an arrangement might not be exclusive as against other network organizations and might not prevent or hinder the station from optioning or selling *any* of its broadcast time to other network organizations. Any type of agreement preventing or hindering a station from the free scheduling of its programs or requiring that it get clearance from the network was prohibited.[83]

The Commission has amended the option regulation for TV stations (but not AM and FM stations), so that, as of Jan. 1, 1961, option hours within each segment of the broadcast day be reduced from 3 to 2½ hours [see 25 Fed. Reg. 9051 (1960)]. More flexibility was provided for the period of advance notice required before exercise of the option. Pertinent sections of this new rule, applicable to TV stations only, are:

Sec. 3.658(d). Option time. (1)(i) In no event may a station subject its time to call, under an option, for a network program to commence earlier than four weeks after notice of exercise of the option.

(ii) If a station has a written contract with one or more advertisers pursuant to which a non-network program series is being broadcast, the time so contracted shall not be callable under an option held by a network until the earlier of (a) the end of a 13-week waiting period or (b) the end of the program series so contracted.

(iii) If a station has entered into a written contract with an advertiser or advertisers for the broadcast of a non-network program scheduled to commence no later than four weeks after the network exercises its option for the same time segment, the network may not under its option require the station to substitute a network program until the earlier of (a) 13 weeks from the commencement of such non-network program or (b) the end of the program series so contracted.

(iv) If the station has contracted with more than one advertiser for the program series, the end of the program series for the purposes of this section shall be the latest of the several contract termination dates.

(2) No license shall be granted to a television broadcast station which options for network programs more than a total of 2½ hours within each of four segments of the broadcast day, as herein described. In determining the number of hours of option time, any network program which begins during the hours agreed upon by the network and station as option time and extends into non-option time, or which begins during non-option time, and extends into the hours agreed upon as option time, shall be considered as falling entirely outside option time. The broadcast day is divided into four segments, as follows: 8 a.m. to 1 p.m.; 1 p.m. to 6 p.m.; 6 p.m. to 11 p.m.; 11 p.m. to 8 a.m. (These segments are to be determined for each station in terms of local time at the location of the station but may remain constant throughout the year regardless of shifts from standard to daylight saving time or vice versa.) Time options may not be exclusive as against other network organizations and may not prevent or hinder the station from optioning or selling any or all of the time covered by the option, or other time, to other network organizations.

(3) As used in this section, an option is any contract, arrangement or understanding, express or implied, between a station and a network organization which prevents or hinders the station from scheduling programs before the network agrees to utilize the time during which such programs are scheduled, or which requires the station to clear time already scheduled when the network organization seeks to utilize the time. All time options permitted under this section must be specified clock hours, expressed in terms of any time system set forth in the contract agreed upon by the station and network organization. Shifts from daylight saving to standard time or vice versa may or may not shift the specified hours correspondingly as agreed by the station and network organization.

Right To Reject Programs. A station cannot enter into an arrangement or contract of any kind which prevents or hinders a rejection of network programs which the station reasonably believes to be unsatisfactory or unsuitable, or which, in its opinion, is contrary to the public interest, or which prevents it from substituting one of outstanding local or national importance.[84]

Network Ownership of Stations. Networks may not own or operate more than one station of each type (AM, FM, TV) where one of the stations would cover substantially the coverage area of the other, or where the existing facilities are so "few or of such unequal desirability (in terms of coverage, power, frequency, or other related matters) that competition would be substantially restrained."[85]

Dual Network Operation. It is further provided in the rules that the Commission will not grant a license to a station affiliated with a chain organization which maintains more than one network. This rule does not apply, however, if the networks are not operated simultaneously, or if there is no substantial overlap in the territory served by the group of stations comprising each such network.[86]

Control by Networks of Station Rates. Stations are prohibited from making any arrangements or agreements under which they are prevented or hindered by the networks from fixing or altering their rates for the sale of broadcast time other than that used by the networks.[87]

Recommended Revisions of Network Regulations. The Commission recently completed a long and comprehensive study of these network regulations. A network study group of the Commission has recommended revisions of these rules designed to give station licensees greater control over their programs. The new rules relating to option time are an outgrowth of these recommendations. Other proposals were made which may be the subject of future action by the Commission.[88]

Deceptive Contests. The Eighty-Sixth Congress, in 1959-60 conducted extensive public hearings with regard to the many quiz programs which had been carried by the networks and their affiliated stations. Many of these programs were found to be deceptive in character. The result was the passage of new legislation by Congress prohibiting them, as provided in Section 9 of the Communications Act Amendments, 1960, approved September 13, 1960, as follows:

Sec. 9. Title V of the Communications Act of 1934 (47 U. S. C., subchapter V), as amended by Section 7 (b) of this Act, is further amended by adding at the end thereof the following section: Prohibited Practices in Case of Contests of Intellectual Knowledge, Intellectual Skill or Chance

Sec. 509. (a) It shall be unlawful for any person, with intent to deceive the listening or viewing public—

(1) To supply to any contestant in a purportedly bona fide contest of intellectual knowledge or intellectual skill any special and secret assistance whereby the outcome of such contest will be in whole or in part prearranged or predetermined.

(2) By means of persuasion, bribery, intimidation, or otherwise, to induce or cause any contestant in a purportedly bona fide contest of intellectual knowledge or intellectual skill to refrain in any manner from using or displaying his knowledge or skill in such contest, whereby the outcome thereof will be in whole or in part prearranged or predetermined.

(3) To engage in any artifice or scheme for the purpose of prearranging or predetermining in whole or in part the outcome of a purportedly bona fide contest of intellectual knowledge, intellectual skill, or chance.

(4) To produce or participate in the production for broadcasting of, to broadcast or participate in the broadcasting of, to offer to a licensee for broadcasting, or to sponsor, any radio program, knowing or having reasonable ground for believing that, in connection with a purportedly bona fide contest of intellectual knowledge, intellectual skill, or chance constituting any part of such program, any person has done or is going to do any act or thing referred to in paragraphs (1), (2), (3), or (4) of this subsection.

(5) To conspire with any other person or persons to do anything prohibited by paragraphs (1), (2), (3), or (4) of this subsection, if one or more

of such persons do any act to effect the object of such conspiracy. (b) For the purpose of this section—

(1) The term 'contest' means any contest broadcast by a radio station in connection with which any money or any other thing of value is offered as a prize or prizes to be paid or presented by the program sponsor or by any other person or persons, as announced in the course of the broadcast.

(2) The term 'the listening or viewing public' means those members of the public who, with the aid of radio receiving sets, listen to or view programs broadcast by radio stations.

(c) Whoever violates subsection (a) shall be fined not more than $10,000 or imprisoned not more than one year or both.

NOTES

1. For AM stations, Section 3.117 of FCC Rules, 1 RR 53:226; FM stations, Section 3.287, 1 RR 53:483-484; TV stations, Section 3,652, 1 RR 53:652; International Broadcast Stations, Section 3.787, 1 RR 53:787-788.
2. 1 RR 53:226.
3. *Ibid.*
4. *Ibid.*
5. *Ibid.*
6. *Ibid.*
7. *Ibid.*
8. 1 RR 53:483.
9. *Ibid.*
10. 1 RR 53:652.
11. 1 RR 53:748-749.
12. 1 RR 53:749.
13. *Ibid.*
14. FCC Docket No. 11546, effective November 7, 1956, 21 Fed. Reg. 7768; 14 RR 1541, p. 1549.
15. *Ibid.*
16. Sections 3.118(a), 3.288 and 3.653; 1 RR 53:227, 484 and 653.
17. *Ibid.*
18. 1 RR 53:227, 484 and 653.
19. *Ibid.*
20. *Ibid.*
21. *Ibid.*
22. 44 Stat. 1170.
23. 48 Stat. 1089.
24. See Sections 3.119, 3.289, 3.654, 3.789; 1 RR 53:229, 485, 653 and 789.
25. 1 RR 53:634.
26. Sections 3.119(b), 3.289(b), 3.654(b), 3.789(b); 1 RR 53:228, 485, 654, and 750.
27. *Ibid.*
28. *Ibid.*
29. *Ibid.*
30. Sponsorship Identification of Broadcast Material, FCC Public Notice 85460, 25 Fed. Reg. 2406 (1960); 19 RR 1569-1577.

31. In the Matter of Public Notice (FCC 60-239) dated March 16, 1960, entitled "Sponsorship Identification of Broadcast Material," FCC Docket No. 13454, 25 Fed. Reg. 2926 (1960); 1 RR 53:xiii.

32. See Hearings on H. R. 5589 before the House Committee on the Merchant Marine and Fisheries, 69th Cong., 1st Sess. (1926); also, 67 *Cong. Rec.* 5488 (House, March 12, 1926).

33. 67 *Cong. Rec.* 5488 (House, March 12, 1926).

34. See NBC Comments on file with FCC, re Public Notice 85460.

35. See MBA Comments on file with FCC, re Notice of Inquiry, FCC Docket No. 13454.

36. 17 RR 553, 556a, 556d (1958).

37. Comments of Michigan Broadcasters Assoc., *op. cit.,* pp. 4-5.

38. *Ibid.,* pp. 8-9.

39. *Op. cit.,* FCC Docket No. 13454, 1 RR 53:xiv.

40. 44 Stat. 1089 and 48 Stat. 1088.

41. 66 Stat. 717.

42. Sections 3.120, 3.290, 3.657; 1 RR 53:229, 486, and 655.

43. See CBS pleadings filed in the *Matter of Petitions of Columbia Broadcasting Company for Reconsideration and Motions for Declaratory Rulings or Orders Relating to Applicability of Section 315 of the Communications Act of 1934, as amended, to Newscasts by Broadcast Licensees;* 18 RR 701. This opinion should be consulted for a comprehensive and detailed analysis of the legislative history of Section 315 and for a critical review of the various interpretations placed upon it.

44. *Ibid.*

45. *Ibid.*

46. *Ibid.,* p. 911.

47. *Ibid.,* pp. 701-744.

48. *Ibid.,* p. 713.

49. *Ibid.,* p. 736.

50. 73 Stat. 557. For discussions in Congress leading up to adoption of this amendment see Senate Report, Paragraph 10:1102; House Report, Paragraph 10:1103; Conference Report, Paragraph 10:1104. Also see 105 *Cong. Rec.* 13171-13195, July 28, 1959; 14863-14886, August 18, 1959; 16308-16313, September 2, 1959; and 16342-16347, September 3, 1959.

51. *Ibid.*

52. 48 Stat. 1088-1089.

53. 18 U.S.C., Section 1304.

54. Adopted August 18, 1949, FCC Docket No. 9113; effective date postponed by FCC order of September 21, 1949; 14 Fed. Reg. 5998 (1949).

55. *FCC v. A.B.C., Inc.,* 347 U.S. 284, 10 RR 2030.

56. *Ibid.,* pp. 289, 294.

57. *Ibid.,* pp. 296-297.

58. Section 3.122. 1 RR 53:232-233; adopted May 19, 1954, 19 Fed. Reg. 3054 (1954) effective June 26, 1954.

59. 44 Stat. 1172-1173.

60. 48 Stat. 1091.

61. 18 U.S.C., Section 1464.

62. *Duncan v. United States,* 48 F.(2d) 134.

63. 48 Stat. 1091.

64. *Ibid.*

65. Sections 3.121, 3.291, 3.655; 1 RR 53:230, 487 and 3.655.

66. *Ibid.*

67. *FCC Report on Chain Broadcasting,* Commission Order No. 37, FCC Docket No. 5060, May, 1941, p. 35.

68. *Ibid.*

69. *Ibid.,* pp. 36-37.

70. *Ibid.,* pp. 38-39.

71. *Ibid.,* pp. 39-40.

72. *Ibid.,* pp. 44-45.

73. *Ibid.,* pp. 43-44.

74. *Ibid.,* p. 1.

75. *Ibid.*

76. *Ibid.,* pp. 1-2.

77. *FCC Report on Chain Broadcasting, op. cit.* Also see 6 Fed. Reg. 2282, 2292, 5257 (1941).

78. 319 U.S. 209.

79. See 1 RR 53:241-243.

80. Sections 3.131 for AM broadcasting and 3.658(a) for television; 1 RR 53:241 and 657.

81. *Ibid.,* Section 3.132 and 3.658(b).

82. *Ibid.,* Section 3.133 and 3.658(c).

83. *Ibid.,* Sections 3.134 and 3.658(d).

84. *Ibid.,* pp. 53:242 and 658; Sections 3.135 and 3.658(e).

85. *Ibid.,* Section 3.136 and 3.658(f).

86. Sections 3.137 and 3.658(g); 1 RR 53:243 and 658.

87. *Ibid.,* Sections 3.138 and 3.658(h).

88. *Network Broadcasting, Report of the Study Staff to the Network Study Committee,* Federal Communications Commission, October 3, 1957. This is a monumental study with a wealth of information for the student concerned with the regulatory problems of broadcasting.

CHAPTER 19

Broadcasting Programs in the Public Interest

Democracy thrives more on participation at its base than upon instruction from the top.—CLIFFORD JUDKINS DURR*

As pointed out in Chapter 3, the law directs the FCC to grant licenses and renewals thereof *only* if public interest will be served. Any violations of the specific laws and regulations pertaining to programming discussed in the preceding chapter are of course contrary to the public interest, and could constitute grounds for revocation of a station license. But compliance with these statutory and regulatory requirements is not enough. The Commission has held (and the courts have agreed) that licensees have positive responsibilities to provide a program service that serves the needs of the community.

Early FCC Concern with Program Standards. In the late thirties, the Commission gave serious consideration to the establishment of rules governing program service for broadcasting stations.[1] A Committee of the Commission made a study of the problem and recommended that minimum standards be set as guides for licensees. In connection with this recommendation, the Committee stated:

It is very difficult to prescribe 'standards of public service' uniformly for all broadcasting stations because initiative and reasonable freedom of action are essential to the American system of broadcasting. The problem is also complicated by the fact that the requirements of broadcast service differ in the various sections of the nation, and within these sections each community presents its individual dissimilarities. Also, the economic factor is different for each class operating in different communities. While it is the primary duty of each station licensee to offer programs which will fully satisfy the public needs in the particular area served, it is obvious that some general principles might apply to the industry as a whole . . . However, it is needless to state that such standards should be minimum standards and they should be utilized solely as guides and subject to variation in accordance with changed conditions and even then should not be requirements of the Commission.[2]

* Former member of the FCC.

The Commission took no action on this proposal and no specific criteria for evaluation of program service were adopted at that time.

Some Congressmen had criticized the Commission for being lax in establishing and enforcing standards for broadcast programming; had charged that it had made little effort to require stations to operate in the public interest.[3]

In addition, during the early forties, the Commission increasingly received complaints from the public regarding program service. Many people were unhappy with the large number of broadcasts involving fortune telling, false and misleading advertising, suggestive programs bordering on obscenity, etc. The Commission received many letters complaining that stations were over-commercialized; that too little broadcast time was provided for local live talent and community organizations; that discussion of local issues was neglected and, in some cases, stations were unfair and biased in the presentation of news; and that there were too few programs of an educational, cultural and religious nature.

At long last, the FCC decided to do something positive about the situation. Accordingly, it retained Dr. Charles Siepmann, formerly with the British Broadcasting Corporation, to direct a study and come up with some proposed criteria which the Commission might establish for the evaluation of radio program service.

Adoption of the "Blue Book". The result of this study was the adoption and publication by the FCC in March, 1946 of the report, *Public Service Responsibility of Broadcast Licensees,* popularly known as the Blue Book. Essentially, what this report said was that the licensee of a broadcasting station has a primary responsibility for determining program service, but that the Commission has a statutory duty of which it may not divest itself. Accordingly, the Commission proposed in the Blue Book to give consideration to four program service factors in determining whether a station had operated in the public interest: (1) the carrying of sustaining programs to provide a "balanced" program structure; (2) the carrying of local live talent programs; (3) the carrying of programs dealing with important public issues, and (4) elimination of advertising excesses.

The Commission said that the sustaining program has five distinctive and useful functions. It helps:

1. To secure for the station or network a means by which in the overall structure of its program service it can achieve a *balanced* interpretation of public needs.

2. To provide programs which by their very nature may not be sponsored with propriety, such as some programs sponsored by religious, educational, governmental, or welfare groups.

3. To serve significant minority tastes and interests, such as providing programs of classical music or those of a literary nature.

4. To serve the needs and purposes of non-profit organizations such as educational institutions.

5. To provide a field for experiment in new types of programs, free of restrictions that obtain with reference to programs in which the advertiser's interest in selling goods predominates.

The Commission prescribed no particular percentages of time for the different program categories, but did stress that the licensee had the responsibility of attempting to achieve a "balanced program schedule" in terms of the particular needs of the community served by the station.[4]

Actually, this was no radical or drastic departure from previous FCC policy. It simply pulled together and codified some basic program factors which the Commission and its predecessor, the FRC, had evolved and applied in deciding individual cases for two decades. It did give notice to the broadcast industry, however, that in the future it would scrutinize applications more closely in terms of these specific criteria. Licensees were warned that they would be required to give an account of program performance in connection with applications for renewal of license.

New Renewal Application Form. In line with the principles stated in the Blue Book, the Commission designed a new renewal application form (303) in 1946 requiring applicants to state how much broadcast time they had devoted to the following program categories: entertainment, religious, agricultural, educational, news, discussion, talks, and miscellaneous programs.

This new form elicited information regarding the number of spot announcements carried by the station, the amount of time used for network shows and recordings, and that devoted to local live programs. The division of time as between commercial and noncommercial programs also was required to be reported.

These calculations were to be based upon an analysis of the program logs of the station for a seven-day period comprising a composite week announced by the FCC and of which days the licensees were to be given no advance notice.[5]

This application form not only required the licensee to report data reflecting past program performance but also to indicate what percentages of time for the various program classes were proposed for future operation.

Program Performance Questioned by FCC. Shortly after the Blue Book was released, the FCC withheld action on a number of applications for renewal of license where station operations did not measure up to the standards set forth. The Commission questioned whether these stations had operated in the public interest and designated their applications for public hearing.

In a 1947 case, the Commission questioned one station's performance on these grounds: (1) During the license period, it had carried a large number of commercial spot announcements, averaging more than 2,000 per week; (2) had failed to broadcast any programs dealing with controversial issues in the community; (3) had provided very little time for local live talent; and (4) had broadcast comparatively few educational programs.

In the hearing, the licensee promised to provide more time for school broadcasts, including lectures, recitals, musicals, sports, and drama. Moreover, the applicant pledged that it would devote at least 30% of its total broadcast time to local live programs, and would cut down on the quantity and frequency of commercial announcements.

In view of these promises, despite a poor record of past performance, the Commission granted the renewal application.[6]

A similar result was reached by the Commission in another 1947 case. Here again a renewal application was set down for a public hearing on essentially the same issues. The evidence adduced at the hearing showed over-commercialization, heavy use of recordings with comparatively little time devoted to broadcasts containing local live talent. But the station introduced evidence to show that it had adopted changes in program policy and had made definite commitments to provide a more varied and better "balanced" service to the community. The station received an official slap on the wrist by the FCC for inferior performance, but in view of promises to do better in the future, the Commission decided to give the station a second chance and renewed the license for another three-year period.[7]

A third Blue Book case decided in 1951 should be noted. It involved an application for renewal of a station license and a competing application for the same facility. The new applicant contended that the existing licensee had failed to keep its promises to the Commission; that station operation had fallen far below FCC program standards, and that the new applicant could provide a more worthwhile service in the public interest.

After a long and highly publicized hearing, the Commission denied the competing application and granted the renewal of license. In substance, the Commission decided that while the licensee's programming had been unbalanced in the past, improvements had now been made and a "well-rounded" service was proposed for the future. The Commission, therefore, was not disposed to prefer a new applicant and dispossess an existing licensee, when the latter recognized its substandard performance and had taken steps and made proposals under oath to improve its service.[8]

Blue Book Standards Have Not Been Officially Repudiated. The Blue Book standards have not been officially repudiated by the Commission, though present FCC rule-making proceedings will soon, no doubt, establish new policies and requirements. While no station license renewal has been refused for failure to comply with them, in a considerable number of cases in the past ten years, action on renewal applications has been held up temporarily where there appeared to be material deviation from these standards. In these cases, the practice of the Commission has been to study the over-all performance of the station during the preceding license period as reflected in the renewal application; and to review all serious complaints against the station received from the public over the three-year period. Where the over-all review indicates a failure to provide a "balanced" program service in terms of factors set forth in the Blue Book or otherwise raises questions as to whether the station has served the public interest, the Commission may write the licensee to this effect and ask for comment.

Where the responses of stations have acknowledged their deficiencies and indicated an intention to improve their service, in most cases, the Commission has been able to resolve questions without further delay, obviating the necessity for a public hearing.

In 1958-59, eight radio stations in Georgia operated on temporary licenses for more than a year. Renewals were held up by the FCC because the stations had carried little or no agricultural, educational and religious programming. The Commission had under advisement the question of whether to hold public hearings. On July 15, 1959, as a leading trade journal reported it, these stations, "which had been sitting on an FCC hot seat for more than a year were removed from their uncomfortable positions."[9] By a 4 to 2 vote (one Commissioner was absent and didn't vote) all these licenses were renewed. It is assumed that the licensees made satisfactory explanations of their past performance and gave adequate assurances to the Commission that their future programming would serve the public interest.

FCC Concern with Over-All Programming. The Commission has made it clear that its chief concern is with the over-all operation of stations measured in terms of the local needs, and not individual programs or particular formats or ways in which they are presented. Broadcasters are afforded a wide range of discretion and freedom in the choice of individual programs. While possessing no power of censorship, the Commission "does review over-all operations of broadcast licensees in connection with renewal of licenses, but it does not judge the licensee's fulfillment of its public interest obligations in the light of a particular program or series of programs broadcast during a limited period of time, and it seeks to avoid any possible invasion of the discretion vested in the licensee to determine the program material to be presented and to make other decisions involved in day-to-day operations. . . ."[10]

On May 20, 1960 the Commission announced the establishment, effective June 1, 1960, of a new Complaints and Compliance Division in its Broadcast Bureau to deal with complaints concerning radio and TV programming and to assist in the over-all evaluation of station operations at renewal time. Former Chairman Ford explained the reasons in an FCC Public Notice (Mimeograph No. B-88758, May 20, 1960) as follows:

We took this step because of our conviction that vigorous, timely, and systematic action in this area is essential to ensure that broadcasters fully discharge their obligation to operate in the public interest. I wish to emphasize that our decision in no way undercuts or limits the basic responsibility of licensees to take self-corrective measures, where these are required. But we believe that these self-corrective measures will be more effective—and enduring—if the Commission has adequate resources and machinery to discharge its own obligations under the Communications Act.

Our program contemplates stepping up very sharply our thoroughness and effectiveness in handling complaints. Currently, we receive 120-150 complaints weekly on broadcast matters, in addition to the matters recently brought to light, among others, by the Federal Trade Commission, by Congressional committees, and by the replies from stations and networks to our recent questionaire on Section 317 practices. To arrive at a sound judgment as to the merits of some of the practices complained of we must be able to send trained staff directly into the field to dig up the essential facts—objectively and thoroughly. While there is a place for and some utility in obtaining formal, written statements of explanation from licensees involved in individual cases, it is not an adequate substitute in many instances for direct, field investigation.

I don't want to convey the impression that the Commission has never sent investigators in the field before. However, where the complaints on their face are substantial, whether they involve an individual station or go to a general industry practice, we must have the wherewithal to look into all such substantial complaints by going to the source and drawing together all of the relevant facts—pro and con—needed to dispose of complaints on their merits. This is a prime obligation we owe to the public.

The second prong of our program involves checking into selected stations on a regular, continuing basis. We have some 1,700 stations coming up annually for renewal, and while we have some information on each of these stations when we make our renewal decisions, we do not have available an analysis in depth of the operations of each such station. We rely primarily on information, statistical and otherwise, submitted by the stations and on the presence or absence of any complaints filed against the stations or other information coming to the Commission's attention which bears on the operations of licensees.

Now, we propose to undertake an audit in detail of a limited number of selected stations so that we can have a much more penetrating and more rounded view of how effectively stations discharge their stewardship in the public interest. We intend, among other items, to check on program logs, Section 317 compliance, political broadcast records, and other pertinent station controls, records, and procedures related to the Commission's non-technical rules and regulations and other statutory and treaty requirements; to examine the extent, nature, and disposition of complaints coming directly to the stations; to ascertain whether representations made in connection with license applications are reasonably complied with, as, for example, participation by broadcast licensees in actual station management and operation.

For these station audits, we will use, as one of our tools, sample monitoring of station programs which will be compared with the logs of the stations, and the representations of the stations to the Commission, as well as a general check on station compliance with Commission rules and regulations.

If abuses are uncovered, remedial action will be required. In those cases where licensees are found to have abused their trusteeship flagrantly, provision has been made for formal hearing proceedings. Moreover, hearings in the field will be required in some cases, to provide a proper forum to determine whether the service provided by stations has been in the public interest.

The decision reached by the Commission that systematic investigation of complaints and regular station audits, including program monitoring, are required in the public interest has come only after a full consideration of all the facts. We are persuaded that without impairing the basic responsibility of licensees, the program as outlined is essential to strengthening the Commission's processes. The program undoubtedly will have a very significant impact on the industry. It should stimulate licensees to establish and maintain policies and practices more closely related to the public interest; and may well serve to raise the general level of broadcasting service.

The Commission urged that Congress provide the necessary funds ($300,000) to effectuate the proposed program in its first year.

According to former Chairman Ford:

We would have a staff of 25 persons (exclusive of secretarial and clerical assistants) who may be in the field at least half of the time. Obviously, the first year will be experimental. We cannot tell at the moment with precision the specific number of complaints we will designate for full-field investigation, or the number of stations we will audit. There are some 5,000 broadcast stations operating in 2,000 communities throughout the nation. We would do well with the proposed staff if we could reach as many as 100 communities for full audit. The stress, however, will not be placed on mechanically covering a prescribed number. Rather we intend to develop means of effectively screening various types of situations and to focus our resources where they will do the most good.

On July 29, 1960, the Commission released a report with respect to its powers over programming and what it considers to be the responsibilities of broadcast licensees. The Commission said that rules will be made "at the earliest practicable date" looking in the direction of establishing general standards and requirements to guide stations in their operations. The Commission stressed the obligation of the licensee "to make a positive, diligent and continuing effort to determine the tastes, needs and desires of the public in his community and to provide programming to meet those needs and interests." Because it represents an important policy statement of the Commission, the full text of the report is reproduced in Appendix VIII. It should be studied carefully by all broadcasters and students of broadcasting.

Particular Types of Programs in Official Disfavor. As heretofore pointed out in Chapter 3, the old Federal Radio Commission denied a renewal application where it was shown that the owner prescribed medical treatments for listeners, basing his diagnosis simply upon symptoms recited in letters addressed to the station.[11] In another case, the FRC denied an application for renewal of license where the owner used the facilities to attack religious organizations, public officials, courts, etc., without due regard to the facts.[12]

The FCC, successor to the FRC, has never denied an application for renewal of license of a broadcast station solely on program grounds, but in many decisions it has expressed disapproval of certain types of programs as contrary to the public interest. The more objectionable ones to which the Commission has taken exception are:

Broadcasts prescribing medical treatments[13]
Broadcasts of horse racing information[14]
Advertising birth control preparations[15]
Astrology and fortune telling programs[16]
Fraudulent advertising[17]
Liquor advertising[18]
Lottery broadcasts[19]
Obscene and vulgar programs[20]
Unwarranted attacks on persons and organizations and defamatory statements[21]
Racial and religious attacks[22]

The Federal Radio Commission enunciated the principle that broadcast stations could not be used exclusively to serve the special interests of certain individuals or groups.[23] Stations were not to be mere adjuncts of particular business enterprises;[24] nor should they become mouthpieces for certain social, economic, political, or religious philosophies to the exclusion of others.[25]

The FCC adopted and has maintained a similar policy and has insisted that broadcasting stations not be used simply as tools of special interests or for the dissemination of propaganda.

Educational and Religious Programs Favored. From the very beginning, the FCC has looked with favor upon the broadcasting of educational and religious programs, and has many times made pronouncements that such programming serves the public interest. There have been many times during the past twenty-five years, that the Commission has withheld action on renewal applications and placed stations on temporary licenses because they had devoted little or no time to these types of programs. And it was only after securing assurance from these stations that some such programs would be carried, that the Commission renewed their licenses on a regular basis.

The Commission and individual Commissioners have stressed in various statements and decisions that a well balanced program structure designed to meet community needs should include some broadcasts by educational institutions and religious organizations. For example, in *WKRG-TV, Inc.,* 10 RR 268(1954), the Commission said that instructional broadcasts for in-school viewing are a type of programming to be encouraged and is illus-

243

trative of the kind of policy which "gears proposed programs to major local needs."

In *Mid-Continent Broadcasting Co. (WTIX)*, FCC Public Notice No. 23360 (September 7, 1955), 12 RR 1286, the Commission had raised a question as to whether the station's license should be renewed. After deliberation, the Commission resolved the doubt in the station's favor and did renew the license without a public hearing. Former Commissioner Doerfer dissented, however, saying that the station had failed to carry any religious, educational or discussion programs and had not met the minimum program standards required by the Commission.

In terms of the consistent policy of the FCC since its creation in 1934, it is risky business for any station to come up for renewal of its license without being able to show some broadcast time devoted to education and religion.

Station Advocacy Prohibited by Mayflower Decision. Prior to 1949, the FCC held to the policy that a station licensee could not be an advocate on controversial questions and did not have the privilege of editorializing as do the newspapers. In the famous *Mayflower* decision of 1940, the Commission said:

. . . under the American system of broadcasting it is clear that responsibility for the conduct of a broadcast station must rest initially with the broadcaster. It is equally clear that with the limitations in frequencies inherent in the nature of radio, the public interest can never be served by a dedication of any broadcast facility to the support of partisan ends. Radio can serve as an instrument of democracy only when devoted to the communication of information and the exchange of ideas fairly and objectively presented. A truly free radio cannot be used to advocate the causes of the licensee. It cannot be used to support the candidacies of his friends. It cannot be devoted to the support of principles he happens to regard most favorably. In brief, the broadcaster cannot be an advocate.

Freedom of speech on the radio must be broad enough to provide full and equal opportunity for the presentation to the public of all sides of public issues. Indeed, as one licensed to operate in a public domain the licensee has assumed the obligation of presenting all sides of important public questions, fairly, objectively and without bias. The public interest—not the private—is paramount. These requirements are inherent in the conception of public interest set up by the Communications Act as the criterion of regulation. And while the day to day decisions applying these requirements are the licensee's responsibility, the ultimate duty to review generally the course of conduct of the station over a period of time and to take appropriate action thereon is vested in the Commission.[26]

The Scott Case. In 1946, this philosophy of the Commission was tested by Robert Harold Scott who requested that the licenses of three California stations be revoked because they had refused to give or sell him time to broadcast his atheistic views. He contended that the existence of a Deity was a controversial matter and that he was entitled to time to dispute with religious groups who aired their views. The stations replied that this was not a controversial question, that there were comparatively few atheists and that the matter was not of sufficient public interest to justify discussion. The Commission dismissed the complaint but stated:

We recognize that in passing upon requests for time, a station licensee is constantly confronted with most difficult problems. Since the demands for time may far exceed the amount available for broadcasting a licensee must inevitably make a selection among those seeking it for the expression of their views. He may not even be able to grant time to all religious groups who might desire the use of his facilities, much less to all who might want to oppose religion. Admittedly, a very real opportunity exists for him to be arbitrary and unreasonable, to indulge his own preference, prejudices, or whims; to pursue his own private interest or to favor those who espouse his views, and discriminate against those of opposing views. The indulgence of that opportunity could not conceivably be characterized as an exercise of the broadcaster's right of freedom of speech. Nor could it fairly be said to afford the listening audience that opportunity to hear a diversity and balance of views, which is an inseparable corollary of freedom of expression. In making a selection with fairness, the licensee must, of course, consider the extent of the interest of the people in his service area in a particular subject to be discussed, as well as the qualifications of the person selected to discuss it. Every idea does not rise to the dignity of a 'public controversy,' and every organization regardless of membership or the seriousness of its purposes, is not *per se* entitled to time on the air. But an organization or idea may be projected into the realm of controversy by virtue of being attacked. The holders of a belief should not be denied the right to answer attacks upon them or their belief solely because they are few in number.

The fact that a licensee's duty to make time available for the presentation of opposing views on current controversial issues of public importance may not extend to all possible differences of opinion within the ambit of human contemplation cannot serve as the basis for any rigid policy that time shall be denied for the presentation of views which may have a high degree of unpopularity. The criterion of the public interest in the field of broadcasting clearly precludes a policy of making radio wholly unavailable as a medium for the expression of any view which falls within the scope of the constitutional guarantee of freedom of speech.[27]

The Commission Reconsiders the Mayflower Decision.   The decision of the Commission in the *Mayflower* case holding that a licensee could not be an advocate met with disfavor from some segments of the broadcast industry. The National Association of Broadcasters, for example, asked that the Commission reconsider its decision. The result was that the Commission held public hearings in March and April of 1948 to determine whether its policy should be changed.

Testimony was presented by 49 witnesses representing the broadcasting industry and various interested organizations and members of the public. On June 1, 1949, the Commission issued a report announcing that stations might editorialize providing they offered opportunities for opposing points of view. The Commission said:

... the Commission believes that under the American system of broadcasting the individual licensees of radio stations have the responsibility for determining the specific program material to be broadcast over their stations. This choice, however, must be exercised in a manner consistent with the basic policy of the Congress that radio be maintained as a medium for free speech for the general public as a whole rather than as an outlet for the purely personal or private interests of the licensee. This requires that licensees devote a reasonable percentage of their broadcasting time to the discussion of public issues of interest in the community served by their stations and that such programs be designed so that the public has a reasonable opportunity to hear different opposing positions on the public issues of interest and importance in the community. The particular format best suited for the presentation of such programs in a manner consistent with the public interest must be determined by the licensee in the light of the facts of each individual situation. Such presentation may include the identified expression of the licensee's personal viewpoint as part of the more general presentation of views or comments on various issues, but the opportunity to present such views as they may have on matters of controversy may not be utilized to achieve a partisan or one-sided presentation of issues. Licensee editorialization is but one aspect of freedom of expression by means of radio. Only insofar as it is exercised in conformity with the paramount right of the public to hear a reasonably balanced presentation of all responsible viewpoints on particular issues can such editorialization be considered to be consistent with the licensee's duty to operate in the public interest. For the licensee is a trustee impressed with the duty of preserving for the public generally radio as a medium of free expression and fair presentation.[28]

Reactions Against FCC's Current Policy on Editorialization. The policy of the Commission expressed in the editorialization opinion is still in effect. One aspect of the Commission's policy, however, has been most unpopular with some segments of the broadcast industry. It is that which requires broadcast licensees to make an affirmative effort to secure the expression of points of view opposed to those in the editorials carried by the stations. The Commission has said that it does not believe "that the licensee's obligations to serve the public interest can be met merely through the adoption of a general policy of not refusing to broadcast opposing views where a demand is made of the station for broadcast time."

The Commission has further stated "that broadcast licensees have an affirmative duty generally to encourage and implement the broadcast of all sides of controversial public issues over their facilities, over and beyond their obligation to make available on demand opportunities for the expression of opposing views. It is clear that any approximation of fairness in the presentation of any controversy will be difficult if not impossible of achievement unless the licensee plays a conscious and positive role in bringing about balanced presentation of the opposing viewpoints."[29]

Radio and Television Codes. The broadcasting industry has made efforts to provide effective self-regulation with respect to programming. The National Association of Radio and Television Broadcasters has adopted codes for radio and television stations. While these specific codes have not been officially approved or disapproved by the FCC, various Commissioners from time to time have informally made favorable reference to these Codes and have urged broadcasters to take action, individually and cooperatively, to improve the quality of their programs to avoid governmental controls. These NARTB codes, as recently revised, are included in Appendix IX for convenient reference. Also included is a sample code of station WJR in Detroit.

In Conclusion. In conclusion, it may be said that programs specifically prohibited by statute such as lotteries and broadcasts of an indecent and obscene character are contrary to the public interest and must be avoided. But more than this, the FCC holds that the licensee has a positive responsibility to provide a program service designed to meet the varied needs of the particular community in which the station is located.

The primary responsibility for determining what this program service will be vests in the licensee. The FCC has no powers of censorship and would violate the law if it attempted to restrain a station from carrying any program or series of programs, or to impose its judgment on the day-to-day operation of the station. At the same time, it is clear that the law requires the FCC to make a decision as to whether a station has operated in the public interest when that station comes up for renewal of its license. This decision is based upon the showing made in the renewal application and any substantial complaints or commendations with respect to the station's service received from the public during the license period.

The Commission has not established any hard and fast formula applicable to every station and community. It has stressed the importance of providing a balanced program service—balanced in the sense that a reasonable effort is made to serve the religious, educational, cultural and economic needs of the community and to afford reasonable access to the microphone or camera for the expression of different points of view on important public issues.

If the renewal application and the complaints filed against the station during the license period indicate that the station's over-all performance has fallen below these standards, and that the licensee has made little effort to ascertain community needs and interests and attempt to serve them, then questions may be raised requiring further study before action is taken on the application. The practice of the Commission in such cases has been to place the stations on temporary licenses, and through informal correspondence and investigation, elicit additional information and ascertain more fully the plans of licensees for future operations.

In most instances, these informal inquiries have resulted in a resolution of any questions raised regarding station operation and the FCC has granted the license renewals without further procedure. There have been a few cases, however, as previously pointed out, where the Commission has not been satisfied with station responses to these initial inquiries and has required licensees to go through formal public hearings in the communities where the stations are located. In these hearings a detailed and critical study of station performance is made in terms of specifically stated issues, the qualifications of the licensee are re-examined, and a written record of all evidence in the proceeding is assembled and used as a basis for making a final decision in the case. If the new policies of the Commission are carried out, more careful scrutiny of program service, involving more public hearings, can be expected.

As already discussed in Chapter 15, recent legislation affords interested parties the opportunity of filing petitions with the FCC requesting that applications for broadcast authorizations (including renewals) be denied. At the time of filing, the applicant must give public notice in the community where the station operates. Petitions for denial may be filed within 30 days of the date the application is accepted for filing by the FCC. If the petition raises substantial questions as to whether the station has been operating in the public interest, the FCC must designate the renewal application for a public hearing. The Commission may, if it so chooses, hold the hearing in the community where the station is located and the petitioner, as well as other interested parties, may have opportunity to participate and present evidence as to whether the station has operated in the public interest and whether the station's license should be renewed. (See Appendix I for details regarding this new legislation and its provisions.)

NOTES

1. Committee Report on Proposed Rules Governing Standard Broadcast Stations and Standards of Good Engineering Practice, FCC Docket No. 5072-A, April 1, 1939, p. 30.

2. *Ibid.*

3. See 84th *Cong. Rec.* 1164-66, February 6, 1939.

4. *Public Service Responsibility of Broadcast Licensees,* Report of FCC, March 7, 1946.

5. See Appendix VII for definitions of program categories and for reproduction of Section IV of Renewal Application Form 303. The commission has under consideration modification of this Section of the form.

6. *Walmac Co.,* 12 FCC 91, 3 RR 1371 (1947); also see *Community Broadcasting Co.,* 12 FCC 85, 3 RR 1360 (1947).

7. *Eugene J. Roth,* 12 FCC 102, 3 RR 1377 (1947).

8. *Hearst Radio Inc.,* 6 RR 994 (1951).

9. *Broadcasting Magazine*, May 25, 1959, p. 64; also, July 20, 1959, p. 78.

10. *Captain James E. Hamilton*, 16 RR 170 (1957). Other cases in point: *Brush-Moore Newspapers, Inc.*, 11 RR 641 (1956); *Appalachian Broadcasting Co.*, 11 RR 1327 (1956); *Travelers Broadcasting Service Corporation*, 12 RR 689 (1956); *WKAT, Inc.*, 22 FCC 117, 12 RR 1 (1957).

11. See Chapter 3, Footnote 51, p. 43.

12. See Chapter 3, Footnote 55, p. 43.

13. See *Bremer Broadcasting Co.*, 2 FCC 200; other cases listed in 2 RR-M-2366e.

14. *Standard Cahill Co., Inc.*, 1 FCC 227 (1935); *Joliet Broadcasting Company*, 4 RR 1225 (1948); *American Broadcasting Company, Inc.*, 7 RR 1129 (1952). The Commission has taken the position that the *amount* of time devoted to horse racing programs and the *amount* of information presented for the benefit of betters are important in determining whether such programs are against the public interest.

15. *Knickerbocker Broadcasting Co., Inc.*, 2 FCC 76 (1935).

16. *Nellie H. and W. C. Morris*, 2 FCC 269; *Farmers and Bankers Life Insurance Corporation*, 2 FCC 455; and *Radio Broadcasting Corporation*, 4 FCC 125.

17. See *Scroggin and Company Bank*, 1 FCC 194; *Bremer Broadcasting Co.*, 2 FCC 79; *WREG Broadcasting Service*, 10 RR 1323 (1955). A cooperative arrangement has been arrived at whereby the Federal Trade Commission advises the FCC of questionable advertising broadcast over radio and television stations and the FCC communicates such information to the stations involved. See 14 RR 1262.

18. The Commission has stated that no federal law prohibits the broadcasting of advertisements for alcoholic beverages and the Commission's authority with respect to the matter is limited to the consideration of applications for renewal of license. . . . In states and localities where sale or advertising of alcoholic beverages is prohibited by law, such sale or advertising by radio would of course be contrary to the public interest. Where there are no laws prohibiting such sale or advertising, the problems raised are the same as those raised by any other program which may have limited appeal to the radio audience. In some circumstances the broadcasting of liquor advertisements may raise serious social, economic and political issues in the community, thereby imposing an obligation upon the station to make available time, if desired, to individuals or groups desiring to promote temperance and abstinence. *Broadcast Programs Advertising Alcoholic Beverages*, 5 RR 593 (1949).

19. See *KXL Broadcasters*, 4 FCC 186 (1937); also see *Metropolitan Broadcasting Corporation*, 5 FCC 501 (1938).

20. *Bellingham Publishing Co.*, 6 FCC 31, 32 (1938); also see Warner, Harry, *Radio and Television Law*, pp. 334-339.

21. *Ibid.*, pp. 384-385.

22. *KFKB Broadcasting Association, Inc. v. F.R.C.*, 60 App. D.C. 79, 47 F(2d) 670, 672 (1931).

23. *Ibid.*

24. *Third Annual Report of F.R.C.* (1929), p. 34.

25. *Ibid.*

26. *The Mayflower Broadcasting Corporation*, 8 FCC 333 (1940).

27. *Re Scott*, FCC Mimeo. 96050, July 16, 1946.

28. *In the Matter of Editorializing by Broadcast Licensees*, Docket No. 8516, 13 FCC 1246, 14 Fed. Reg. 3055, 1 RR Section 91:21 (1949).

29. *Ibid.*, p. 6.

CHAPTER 20

Changes in Ownership and Control
of Stations

In passing on application for transfer of control of a broadcast licensee corporation, the Commission's primary consideration from the standpoint of public interest is not the relationship between the contract price and the items to be transferred, but rather the qualifications of the proposed transferee and its ability to provide the public with an improved broadcast service.—7 FCC 315 (1939)

As Section 310(b) of the Communications Act provides, no license for a broadcast station may be assigned or the control of a station transferred without the prior written consent of the Commission. This section originally read:

The station license required hereby, the frequencies authorized to be used by the licensee, and the rights therein granted shall not be transferred, assigned, or in any manner either voluntarily or involuntarily disposed of, or indirectly by transfer of control of any corporation holding such license, to any person, unless the commission shall, after securing full information, decide that said transfer is in the public interest, and shall give its consent in writing.[1]

Also, as originally adopted, Section 319(b) of the Act provided that no construction permit or any rights pertaining thereto could be transferred without the consent of the Commission.

In 1952, both sections were amended. The provision relating to transfer of construction permits was deleted from 319(b) and merged with Section 310(b). The latter section now reads:

No construction permit or station license, or any rights thereunder, shall be transferred, assigned, or disposed of in any manner, voluntarily or involuntarily, directly or indirectly, or by transfer of control of any corporation holding such permit or license, to any person except upon application to the Commission and upon finding by the Commission that the public interest, convenience, and necessity will be served thereby. Any such application shall be disposed of as if the proposed tranferee or assignee were making application under Section 308 for the permit or license in question; but in acting thereon the Commission may not consider whether the public interest, convenience and necessity might be served by the transfer, assignment, or disposal of the permit or license to a person other than the proposed transferee or assignee.[2]

When FCC Approval Must Be Secured. In 1948, in accordance with statutory provisions in effect at the time, the Commission released a public statement pointing out that the assignment of a license or transfer of control of a station may not be effected until after the Commission has given written consent.[3] Any kind of agreement, written or oral, or any sales of stock in a corporate licensee or changes in a partnership arrangement which shifts the major control of the station must first be approved by the Commission.

With respect to sales of stock in a licensee corporation, the Commission has stated that a transfer of control takes place requiring prior approval when:

(1) An individual stockholder gains or losses affirmative or negative control. (Affirmative control consists of control of more than 50% of voting stock; negative control consists of control of exactly 50% of voting stock.)

(2) Any family group or any individual in a family group gains or loses affirmative or negative control.

(3) Any group in privity gains or loses affirmative or negative control.

In its instructions to licensees the Commission gives the following examples of transfers of control or assignments requiring *prior* written consent:

(1) A, who owns 51% of the licensee's or permittee's stock, sells 1% or more thereof to B.

(2) X corporation, wholly owned by Y family reduces outstanding stock by purchase of treasury stock which results in family member A's individual holdings being increased to 50% or more.

(3) A and B, man and wife, each own 50% of the licensee's or permittee's stock. A sells any of his stock to B.

(4) A is a partner in the licensee company. A sells any part of his interest to newcomer B or existing partner C.

(5) X partnership incorporates.

(6) Minority stockholders form a voting trust to vote their 50% or more combined stockholdings.

(7) A, B, C, D, and E each own 20% of the stock of X corporation. A, B, and C sell their stock to F, G, and H at different times. A transfer is effected at such time as C sells 10% or more of his stock. In other words, a transfer of control occurs at such time as 50% or more of the stock passes out of the hands of the stockholders who held stock at the time the original authorization for the licensee or permittee corporation was issued.[4]

Agreements such as management contracts may involve transfers of control requiring *prior* consent of the Commission. For example, in one case the facts showed that the National Broadcasting Company had been employed as an exclusive agent of Westinghouse Electric and Manufacturing Company to supply all broadcast programs for Westinghouse stations. The Commission held that, by entering into this agreement in 1932, rights and privileges granted under the license to all intents and purposes had been transferred without the written consent of the Commission in violation of Section 310(b).[5]

The Commission had designated the renewal applications of the stations for hearing. Westinghouse petitioned for reconsideration and grant without a hearing on the grounds that the old agreement with NBC had been terminated and a new one had been made by which Westinghouse would supply its own programs for local broadcasting. With the abrogation of the 1932 contract and the pledge that henceforth the licensee would exercise control over the stations, the Commission granted the petition and renewed the licenses.[6]

Application Forms. The application forms used for requesting approval of assignments and transfers are prescribed in Section 1.329 of the Commission's Rules of Practice and Procedure. They are *FCC Form 314 (Assignment of License)* and *FCC Form 315 (Transfer of Control).*

Since the Commission is under a statutory duty to pass on the qualifications of any assignee or transferee, the considerations are substantially the same as those involved in original applications. Section 1 of these forms elicits information regarding the frequency, power, and hours of operation of the station involved. A full statement of reasons for requesting the assignment or transfer must be given by both the seller and purchaser.

Other items of information which must be submitted include original and replacement costs and present values of the station properties, a current balance sheet, and the price or consideration involved in the transaction. Copies of the contract of sale and all instruments affecting the assignment or transfer must be attached to the application.

The assignee or transferee must give information as to his legal and financial qualifications. He must submit specific and detailed data regarding funds or property furnished by parties other than the applicant and the conditions under which such financial help is provided.

A statement regarding proposed program service must be given in Section IV similar to that required in an application for a construction permit (FCC Form 301) referred to in Chapter 15.

A short form (FCC Form 316) may be used in those cases where the control shifts from one legal entity to another but where the ownership remains substantially the same. As stated in Section 1.329(b) of the Rules, this short form may be used in the following situations:

(1) Assignment from an individual or individuals (including partnerships) to a corporation owned and controlled by such individuals or partnerships without any substantial change in their relative interests;

(2) Assignment from a corporation to its individual stockholders without effecting any substantial change in the disposition of their interests;

(3) Assignment or transfer by which certain stockholders retire and the interest transferred is not a controlling one;

(4) Corporate reorganization which involves no substantial change in the beneficial ownership of the corporation;

(5) Assignment or transfer from a corporation to a wholly owned subsidiary thereof or vice versa, or where there is an assignment from a corporation to a corporation owned or controlled by the assignor stockholders without substantial change in their interest; or

(6) Assignment of less than a controlling interest in a partnership.

Section 1.329 of Commission Rules states that transfer and assignment applications "should be filed with the Commission at least 45 days prior to the contemplated effective date of the assignment or transfer of control."

Section 1.330 provides that in case of death or legal disability of an individual permittee or licensee, a member of a partnership or a person controlling a corporate licensee, the Commission must be notified promptly in writing. Within 30 days, an application on short Form 316 must be filed with the Commission requesting consent to an involuntary assignment to a person or entity legally qualified to succeed to the station properties under the laws of the place having jurisdiction over the estate involved.

Financial, Contractual and Ownership Reports. So that the Commission may keep itself fully informed at all times regarding the financial status, ownership and control of stations, certain reports are required. Section 1.341 of the Rules specifies that the licensee of each commercially operated standard, FM, television, or international broadcast station shall file with the Commission on or before April 1 of each year, on FCC Form 324, broadcast revenue and expense statements for the preceding calendar year together with a statement as to investment in tangible broadcast property as of December 31 of such year.[7]

As provided in Section 1.342, these stations must also file copies of the following contracts, instruments, and documents together with amendments, supplements, and cancellations, within 30 days of their execution:[8]

(a) Contracts relating to any kind of network service, including transcription agreements or contracts for the supplying of film for television stations which specify option time, but not contracts granting the right to broadcast music such as ASCAP, BMI, or SESAC agreements;

(b) Contracts relating to present or future ownership or control, including but not limited to the following:

    (1) Articles of partnership, association, and incorporation, and changes in such instruments;

(2) Bylaws, and any instruments effecting changes in such bylaws;

(3) Any agreement, or document providing for the assignment of a license or permit or affecting, directly or indirectly, the ownership or voting rights of the common, preferred, voting or non-voting stock such as agreements for stock transfer, for issuance of new stock, or the acquisition of stock owned by the licensee or permittee. Pledges, trust agreements, options to purchase stock and other executory agreements are required to be filed.

(4) Proxies with respect to stock running for a period more than a year; and those regardless of time, given without full and detailed instructions binding the nominee to act in a specified manner. For those given without such instructions, a statement must be filed showing the number of such proxies, by whom given and received, and the percentage of outstanding stock represented by each proxy. There is an exception when there are more than 50 stockholders. In such cases complete information need be filed only regarding proxies given by those who are officers or directors, or who have 1% or more of the corporation's voting stock. In cases where the licensee or permittee has more than 50 stockholders and those giving proxies are neither officers or directors nor hold 1% or more of the stock, the only information required is the name of any person voting 1% or more of the stock by proxy, the number of shares he voted in this way, and the total number of shares voted at the particular stockholders' meeting in which the proxies were involved.

(5) Mortgage or loan agreements containing provisions restricting the licensee's or permittee's freedom of operation, such as those affecting voting rights, specifying or limiting the amount of dividends payable, the purchase of new equipment, the maintenance of current assets, etc; or

(6) Any agreement reflecting a change in the officers, directors or stockholders of a corporation, other than the licensee or permittee, having an interest, direct or indirect, in the licensee or permittee.

(c) Contracts relating to the sale of broadcast time to "time brokers" for resale.

(d) Contracts relating to Subsidiary Communications Authorization Operation, except contracts granting licensees or permittees engaged in SCA the right to broadcast copyright music.

(e) Time sales contracts with the same sponsor for 4 or more hours per day, except where the length of events (such as athletic contests, musical programs, and special events) broadcast pursuant to the contract is not under control of the station.

(f) Management consultant agreements with independent contractors; contracts relating to the utilization in a management capacity of any person other than an officer, director, or regular employee of the station; management contracts with any persons, whether or not officers, directors, or regular employees which provide for both a percentage of profits and a sharing in losses.

Agreements which need not be filed with the FCC are those with persons regularly employed as station managers or salesmen; contracts with program personnel, with chief engineers or other technical employees, with attorneys, accountants, or consulting radio engineers, performers, station representatives, labor unions, or similar agreements.

As specified in Section 1.343 of the Rules, each licensee of a standard, FM or television station, whether operating or intending to operate on a commercial or non-commercial basis, must file an Ownership Report (FCC Form 323) at the time the application for renewal of station license is required to be filed. Licensees owning more than one standard, FM, or television broadcast station need file only one ownership report at three year intervals. These reports must provide the following information as of a date not more than 30 days prior to the time they are filed with the Commission:[9]

(a) In the case of an individual, the name of such individual;

(b) Regarding a partnership, the names of the partners and the interest of each;

(c) As to a corporation, association, trust, estate, or receivership:

    (1) The name, residence, citizenship, and stockholdings of officers, directors, stockholders, trustees, executors, administrators, receivers, and members of any association.

    (2) Full information as to family relationship or business association between two or more officials and/or stockholders, trustees, executors, administrators, receivers, and members of any association;

    (3) Capitalization with a description of the classes and voting power of stock authorized by the corporate charter or other appropriate legal instrument and the number of shares of each class issued and outstanding; and

    (4) Full information on FCC Form 323 with respect to the interest and identity of any person having any direct, indirect, fiduciary, or beneficiary interest in the licensee or any of its stock. For example, where A is the beneficial owner or votes stock held by B, the same information should be furnished for A as is required for B. Or where X corporation controls the licensee, or holds 25% or more of the number of outstanding shares of either voting or non-voting stock of the licensee, the same information should be furnished with respect to X corporation as is required in the case of the licensee, together with full data as to the identity and citizenship of the person authorized to vote licensee's stock.

The same information should be supplied as to Y corporation if it controls X or holds 25% or more of the number of outstanding shares of voting or non-voting stock of X and as to Z corporation if it controls Y corporation or holds 25% or more of the number of outstanding shares of either voting or non-voting stock of Y and so on back to natural persons.

All licensees must include in the Ownership Report a list of all contracts still in effect required to be filed under Section 1.342 of the Rules as mentioned above, and must report any interest they may have in any other broadcast station.

A permittee of a station must file an Ownership Report within 30 days of the date of grant by the Commission of an application for an original construction permit containing the items of information mentioned. A supplemental Ownership Report must be filed within 30 days after any change occurs in the information required by the Ownership Report (Form 323) including:[10]

(1) Any change in capitalization or organization;
(2) Any change in officers and directors;
(3) Any transaction affecting the ownership; direct or indirect, or voting rights of licensee's or permittee's stock;
(4) Any change in the officers, directors, or stockholders of a corporation other than the licensee or permittee such as X, Y, or Z corporation described above.

Some exceptions should be noted. With respect to the ownership reports required to be reported as explained above, corporations or associations having more than 50 stockholders or members need only file the information regarding those stockholders or members who are officers or directors, and regarding others who have one percent or more of either the voting or non-voting stock of the corporation or voting rights in the association.[11]

Competing Applications in Assignment and Transfer Cases Not Permitted. As Section 310(b) of the Act now reads, if a request is made for approval of a station transfer or assignment, the Commission is not permitted to entertain and consider competing applications as is true where authority to build a station is being applied for. This, however, has not always been the case.

Several years prior to 1952, the Commission adopted a procedure requiring that all transfer and assignment applications be advertised in a local newspaper, twice weekly for at least three weeks after the filing of the application stating "the terms and conditions of the proposed assignment or transfer and the name of the proposed assignee or transferee." It was further provided that "any other person desiring to purchase the facilities upon the same terms and conditions" might file an application to this effect with the Federal Communications Commission within sixty days.

The Commission withheld action during the sixty days. If no competing applications were filed during that time, the pending one was granted if the Commission decided it was in the public interest. If a competing application was filed, the Commission might still grant the original one without a hearing if the buyer chosen by the licensee appeared to be the best qualified to operate the station and the public interest would be served. If, however, this determination could not be made, then the Commission designated the original and any competing applications for a consolidated hearing "to determine among other things which of the applicants is best qualified to operate the station in the public interest."[12]

If the Commission preferred the competing applicant, he and the licensee were given thirty days to submit a contract for the transfer of assignment on the same terms as stated in the original application or upon such other terms agreed upon and approved by the Commission.[13]

In 1952, Congress annulled this procedure. Section 310 (b) was amended, prohibiting competing applications in transfer and assignment cases, but still requiring that the Commission pass on the qualifications of those seeking to buy stations and to determine whether such sales would serve the public interest.

In support of the amendment, the Senate Interstate and Foreign Commerce Committee in its report to Congress, in part said:

One of the purposes of the proposed new language in this subsection is to annul the so-called Avco procedure adopted several years ago by the Commission to prevent a licensee from selling his property to a proper person of the choice but requiring an opportunity for others to make bids for any radio station proposed to be sold. The committee believes that there is no provision of present law which authorized the Commission to employ such a procedure and it deems such procedure an unwise invasion by a government agency into private business practice.

The committee regards it significant that the Commission dropped the so-called Avco procedure several months ago as unsatisfactory and a cause of undue delay in passing upon transfers of licenses. It should be emphasized that the Commission's authority to see to it that stations are operated in the public interest and to determine whether the proposed transferee possesses the qualifications of an original licensee or permittee is not impaired or affected in any degree by this subsection. In fact, the latter requirement is expressly stated. . . .[14]

The Business of Buying and Selling Stations. The buying and selling of stations has increased considerably during the past few years. More than 800 AM, FM and TV stations, or about 20% of the total number of stations on the air, changed hands during the fiscal year 1958.[15] This was almost a 50% increase over the number that was transferred in 1955.

The prices paid for broadcast stations in 1958 were substantially higher than those paid in prior years.[16] According to a recent survey conducted under the auspices of the Communications Research Center at Michigan State University, the Commission approved 461 transfers of control and assignments of license (excluding the *pro forma* ones and those not involving substantial consideration) during the calendar year 1958. The total financial consideration involved in these transactions amounted to more than $104,000,000.

The average prices paid for the different types of station during that year were as follows:

AM stations $ 116,810.00
FM stations   19,300.00
TV stations   2,144,900.00

During this period, the FCC approved one package deal involving the sale of three stations (AM, FM, and TV) in Philadelphia at a price of about $20,000,000.[17] In Providence, Rhode Island, a similar package deal involved consideration of more than $6,500,000.[18] In the latter case, the television station involved had been in operation for about six years and its original construction cost amounted to about a million dollars.[19] For more detailed information regarding sales of stations, in 1958, see Appendix X.

"Trafficking" in Licenses.   The Congress and the FCC have expressed concern from time to time over what has been called "trafficking" in licenses—the business of buying and selling stations, realizing large profits which have little relationship to the actual value of the tangible broadcast properties but are derived from what some critics are pleased to call the "exploitation" of radio and television channels in choice markets.

As early as August, 1937, Congressman Wigglesworth of Massachusetts introduced a resolution in the House looking toward an investigation of the FCC. In this resolution, reference was made to the alleged evils of monopoly in broadcasting, "trafficking in licenses, capitalization of Federal licenses at the expense of the public."[20]

Again he made reference to this problem in a speech to the House five years later in which he declared "that time after time I have stood in the well of this House and inveighed against the practice of the Commission giving its approval to the transfer of stations or the control of those stations for considerations far in excess of the value of the physical assets so transferred—a practice, in other words, involving the sale of government licenses, with all the possible dangers to the public that we have seen involved in the capitalization of licenses in other fields."[21]

On April 20, 1949, Senator Johnson of Colorado, then Chairman of the Senate Interstate and Foreign Commerce Committee, stated that it was not the intent of the Communications Act that permits and licenses should be "peddled" to second parties. "In Washington," said he, "liquor licenses are transferred for substantial sums, but broadcast licenses ought not to be sold over the bargain counter like beans in the corner grocery."[22]

The Avco Case.   In 1945, The Aviation Corporation engaged primarily in the manufacturing of aircraft and airplane parts applied to the Commission for approval of the purchase of 73% of the stock of The Crosley Corporation, licensee of Station WLW in Cincinnati, Ohio. The FCC granted the application despite the fact that part of the purchase price attributable to the station facilities was not segregated from the total amount paid for the other properties of the Crosley Corporation. The price for the "entire package" was $16,060,000.00, but there was no testimony in the hearing on the application assessing any value to the broadcast properties.

With respect to the price paid for these, the majority of the Commission stated they had no jurisdiction to pass on the matter. While they suspected that the price was in excess of the fair value of the station properties and that a portion of the total consideration was being paid for the radio frequency, they said they were unable to deal with this problem since Congress had furnished no administrative standards. Until Congress, therefore, provided remedial legislation, the majority of the Commission held to the view that consideration of the price to be paid for a station should be limited to three questions:

(1) Does the price suggest trafficking in licenses? Is there evidence that the station is being acquired merely for the purpose of resale at a large profit rather than to provide a public service?

(2) Is the applicant financially qualified to pay the price?

(3) Is the price so high that the purchases would over-commercialize the operation at the expense of public service programming?

There was a dissenting opinion in the case in which two Commissioners stated that the Commission had the legal authority to pass on the purchase price of a station. They admitted that there was no set formula by which the Commission could determine whether a part of the sale price represented an exploitation of a publicly owned frequency, but they contended that the judgment should be made in terms of the circumstances of each case.[23]

One year later, in a case proposing transfer of control of broadcast facilities to a network, involving consideration of more than $3,000,000, the Commission again held that it did not have the legal power to disapprove a sale and transfer of a station simply on the grounds of price and cited its decision in the Avco case.[24] The FCC approved the deal, but again there was a dissenting opinion by the same two Commissioners who had dissented in the Avco case the year before.

In 1955, the Commission approved the assignment of a TV construction permit and the assignment of a license of a station already in operation to a single applicant at specified prices. Commissioners Webster and Bartley dissented and voted for a public hearing on the applications. In his dissent, Commissioner Webster said:

While the Communications Act provides for the assignment of a construction permit or the transfer of a corporation holding such a permit, it is silent as to whether any monetary consideration can properly be involved. Accordingly, without legal restriction in this connection, it must be assumed that certain payments are proper. However, the Commission, since its inception, has steadfastly taken the position that trafficking in frequencies is not in the public interest. But unfortunately, it has never seemed to be able to arrive at a policy under which it could determine what constitutes trafficking in frequencies, and, as a result, it has vacillated from one extreme to another.

In 1952, the Commission denied an application (BMP-5803) to extend the construction permit for Station WERL, East Rainelle, West Virginia and dismissed as moot an application (BAP-170) to assign the permit for that station on the ground that, although only a couple of thousand dollars was involved, an extension of the permit and the assignment thereof would be tantamount to a sale of the frequency. Since that time the Commission has approved assignments and transfers of bare permits where the payment of many thousands of dollars has been involved.

I do not take the position that the Commission should or could promulgate a hard and fixed rule under which it would determine what payments can legitimately be made where the assignment or transfer of a bare permit is concerned. But I think the Commission should now pause long enough in its consideration of construction permit assignments and transfers to enable it to determine whether it proposes to abandon the Commission's long-standing policy against trafficking in frequencies, and, if not, to set up some general guide for determining what constitutes trafficking of that nature. For I contend that the Commission can set up a general policy in this connection which would at least permit us to achieve a certain degree of consistency.[25]

Since this decision, Commissioner Bartley has dissented in a number of other cases where the Commission has approved sales of stations at prices much in excess of the actual value of the broadcast properties and where the sellers have had the licenses only a short period of time.[26]

Is the Transfer in the Public Interest? There are differences of opinion among authorities as to the extent to which the Commission may consider the sale price of a station in connection with transfer and assignment applications. The majority of the Commission has held the position that they have no legal authority to make a determination as to the propriety or validity of any particular price. A minority has held a contrary view.

Whichever view is correct, the basic question in all transfer cases is whether the proposed change of ownership will serve the public interest. The Commission obviously has the authority to consider this question. Price standing alone is not particularly significant. If, however, it appears that a prospective purchaser, because of the high price to be paid for the station, will "over-commercialize" his operation and neglect public service programming, or because of limited resources may have difficulty meeting installment payments and financing the operation of the station, then the Commission may properly raise the question whether the public interest will be served by approval of the transfer.

Originally, there was a great deal of concern in Congress that the ownership of stations might gravitate into the hands of a few wealthy entrepreneurs. There was a fear that those with the "bulging pocketbooks" would buy up the choice broadcasting facilities and monopoly would result.

This fear to some extent still persists, but with the multiple ownership rules now limiting the number of stations that may be owned by any one individual or group, there is less justification for the fear.

In any case, the real test is whether a transfer will serve the public interest. The question is not so much how much the purchaser pays for the station but how much service will he be able to give the community.

A bill introduced in the 86th Congress (HR 11340) proposed to amend Section 310(b) of the Communications Act prohibiting the transfer of any broadcast license held for less than three years unless, after public hearing, it is affirmatively established that, because of an unforeseen change in circumstances affecting the licensee, approval of the proposed transfer would serve the public interest.

While the Commission had reservations about the necessity of holding hearings in every transfer case, it did support the principle of the bill. On May 4, 1960, the Commission, in formal comments, said in part:

We believe that the subsection will have a salutary effect, not only in checking the practice of quick transfers by licensees tempted to traffic in licenses, but also in discouraging the entry of persons with such propensities into the broadcast field. Consequently, we believe that in the long run the policy so established will greatly simplify the problems we have encountered in transfer applications. Although we anticipate that transfer applications falling within the purview of subsection (d) may not be as numerous as in the past because of the rigid policy, and although we do expect that the required field hearings will result in some increase in the Commission's workload, we endorse the principle of the amendment.

The 86th Congress adjourned, however, without passing the bill. On December 7, 1960, the FCC issued a notice proposing to require hearings (in most cases) involving applications for assignment of licenses and transfers of control of broadcast stations within three years of their acquisition.

NOTES

1. 48 Stat. 1086.
2. 66 Stat. 716.
3. Procedure on Transfer and Assignment of Licenses, 4 RR 342.
4. FCC Form 323 with instructions; Section 98, Table of Forms, 1 RR 308.
5. *Re Westinghouse Electric and Manufacturing Company,* 8 FCC 195, 196 (1940). For other cases on management contracts see network proceedings before FCC, Docket No. 5060 (1938).
6. *Ibid.*
7. 1 RR 51:206-207.

8. *Ibid.*, 51:207-208.

9. *Ibid.*, 51:206-207.

10. *Ibid.*, 51:210.

11. *Ibid.*, 51:211.

12. See Warner, *op. cit.*, Footnotes 1, 2, 3, and 4, pp. 574-576.

13. *Ibid.*

14. *Senate Report No.* 44, 82nd Cong., 1st Sess., submitted January 25, 1951, 1 RR 10:280.

15. *FCC Annual Report*, 1958, p. 132.

16. *Ibid.*, p. 121.

17. *Ibid.*

18. Survey of Transfers of Broadcast Stations for Calendar Year 1958, Communications Research Center, Michigan State University.

19. *Ibid.*

20. 81 *Cong. Rec.*, p. 9406.

21. 88 *Cong. Rec.*, p. 551.

22. 95 *Cong. Rec.*, p. 4783.

23. *Powel Crosley, Jr. (Avco Case)*, 11 FCC 1 (1946). See *Re Jackman*, 5 FCC 496 (1938), and *Bulova and Henshel (Mester)* 11 FCC 137, 3 RR 125 (1946), aff'd 70 F. Supp. 118, 332 U.S. 749 (1947). Also see other cases dealing with "trafficking" in licenses digested in 2 RR M-2855-2858b.

24. *Edward J. Noble.* 11 FCC 569, 3 RR 449 (1946).

25. *E .D. Rivers, Sr.*, 12 RR 281 (1955).

26. *Telrad, Inc.*, 13 RR 1124 (1956); *Universal Broadcasting Company, Inc.*, 14 RR 569 (1956).

CHAPTER 21

Broadcaster Beware!

Licensees and their principals are expected to display a high degree of public responsibility and obedience to the law as they are in a very real sense, guardians of a public trust.—FCC, 12 RR 1225

Broadcast licenses are not granted in perpetuity. As heretofore pointed out, licensees acquire no property rights in radio or television channels. The use of these channels may be withdrawn from those who fail to comply with the law and the regulations or otherwise do not operate their stations in the public interest.

Grounds for Revoking Licenses and Issuing Cease and Desist Orders. As provided in Section 312(a) of the Communications Act, as recently amended, the Commission has the authority to revoke broadcast licenses or construction permits to construct stations for any of the following reasons:[1]

(1) for false statements knowingly made either in the application or in any statement of fact which may be required pursuant to Section 308;

(2) because of conditions coming to the attention of the Commission which would warrant it in refusing to grant a license or permit on an original application;

(3) for willful or repeated failure to operate substantially as set forth in the license;

(4) for willful or repeated violation of, or willful or repeated failure to observe any provision of this Act or any rule or regulation of the Commission authorized by the Act or by a treaty ratified by the United States;

(5) for violation of or failure to observe any final cease and desist order issued by the Commission under this section; or

(6) for violation of Section 1304, 1343, or 1464 of Title 18 of the United States Code.

Section 312(b) provides that "where any person (1) has failed to operate substantially as set forth in a license, (2) has violated or failed to observe any rule or regulation of the Commission authorized by this Act or by a treaty ratified by the United States, the Commission may order such person to cease and desist from such action."

However, as pointed out in Chapter 3, before a cease and desist order may be issued or a broadcast authorization (permit or license) may be revoked, the Commission must first give the permittee or licensee an opportunity to show cause why the contemplated action should not be taken. He must be supplied with a statement of the matters with which the Commission is concerned and a time and place for a public hearing must be specified. The respondent station must be given at least thirty days from the time he receives the notice to prepare for the hearing.[2]

If, after a hearing, or a waiver thereof, the Commission concludes that the station should discontinue the practice in question, or if it is decided that the offense is sufficiently serious that the permit or license should be withdrawn, an appropriate restraining or revocation order is issued. This order must recite when it is to become effective and must contain a statement of findings and the reasons therefore.[3]

In every case, where a hearing is conducted pursuant to Section 312 of the Act, the Commission must proceed with the introduction of evidence and assume the burden of proof.[4]

The provisions of Section 9(b) of the Administrative Procedure Act are made applicable to the institution of proceedings relating to revocation of licenses and the issuance of cease and desist orders. The pertinent part of Section 9(b) reads as follows:

. . . Except in cases of willfulness or those in which public health, interest, or safety requires otherwise, no withdrawal, suspension, revocation, or annulment of any license shall be lawful unless, prior to the institution or agency proceedings therefore, facts or conduct which may warrant such action shall have been called to the attention of the licensee by the agency in writing and the licensee shall have been accorded opportunity to demonstrate or achieve compliance with all lawful requirements. In any case in which the licensee, has, in accordance with agency rules, made timely and sufficient application for a renewal or a new license, no license with reference to any activity or a continuing nature shall expire until such application shall have been finally determined by the agency.[5]

For good cause, the Commission may institute revocation proceedings at any time against permittees and licensees and there have been numerous cases where the Commission has done so. More often, however, where misconduct is involved, the Commission has administered legal sanctions against the offending stations by refusing to grant renewal of licenses.

Misrepresentations of Facts to the Commission. One of the surest ways to jeopardize or lose a broadcast permit or license is to misrepresent or conceal essential facts from the Commission. This is illustrated by the following cases.

In 1937, the Commission refused to grant a construction permit when it was discovered that the applicant did not make frank, candid and honest disclosures as to its organizational setup, stock ownership and its connection with another station. On appeal, this action of the Commission was sustained by the U.S. Court of Appeals for the District of Columbia.[6]

In a 1940 case, the Commission revoked a station license where the applicant had made untrue statements in his original applications and had given false testimony at the hearing on these applications. The action was taken, despite the contention of the licensee that the community would be left without any local radio service.[7]

Two years later, however, the Commission refused to revoke a license where it was shown that the licensee over a period of time had misrepresented the facts regarding ownership, control and financing of the station. The countervailing facts, as recited by the Commission, were that the station had had erroneous advice from its legal counsel; had not appeared to act in bad faith; and deletion of the station license would leave the community without any local radio service and would be detrimental to the war effort.[8]

In 1947, the Commission refused to grant renewal of a station license because the licensee had concealed from the Commission various transfers of stock; had denied the existence of an oral agreement it had made to re-issue certain stock to a party who would vote it and who would serve as a director of the corporation. Also, in its original application for a construction permit, the licensee had filed a balance sheet showing over $25,000 in the bank whereas the actual amount was less than $400.

The Commission held that whatever might have been the motive, the willful concealment and misrepresentation of facts by the licensee could not be excused. The Commission further held that under the facts of the case, a showing that the station was rendering a satisfactory service was not enough to warrant a renewal of the license.[9]

In 1953, the Commission granted a renewal of license and set aside an order of revocation of a construction permit for another station where a partnership agreement and new methods of financing had not been reported promptly. The Commission concluded that the dereliction was due to ignorance and negligence and not to a deliberate desire to commit wrong. Also, the Commission noted that new owners were in charge of the two stations, were respected in the local communities, and that there was need for broadcast service in the areas involved.[10]

The Commission has emphasized that the Communications Act of 1934, as amended, "contemplates that applicants for a permit or license shall establish those qualifications which would support a finding that a grant to them would serve the public interest. This of necessity presupposes a candid, honest and complete disclosure as to all facts underlying the application and deemed by the Commission to be essential. It is also expected and required that applicants satisfactorily establish that they comprehend the responsibilities imposed upon licensees of radio broadcast stations. . . ."[11]

In *Federal Communications Commission v. WOKO, Inc.,* 329 U.S.

223, the U.S. Supreme Court expressed its point of view on the matter of concealment and misrepresentation of facts to the FCC. In that case the Commission found that station WOKO in Albany, New York had rendered an acceptable service to the community; that for a twelve year period one man and his family received all dividends paid by the licensee company though he and his family owned only 24% of the stock. The facts further showed that he was a network vice-president and had obtained the stock on assurance that he would help secure a network affiliation for the station and provide other benefits.

In reports to the FRC and later to the FCC, this family ownership was concealed and it was represented that the stock was held by others. The station's general manager appeared on behalf of the licensee at various hearings and testified falsely regarding the identity of the corporation stockholders and the shares held by each.

Upon discovery of these misrepresentations, the FCC refused to renew the station license. On appeal, the U.S. Court of Appeals for the District of Columbia reversed the Commission. The Supreme Court, however, reviewed the lower court's opinion and sustained the Commission.[12]

The licensee contended that no finding had been made that the facts concealed were material to the Commission's decision-making responsibilities. The Supreme Court answered that this was beside the point, and declared that "the fact of concealment may be more significant than the facts concealed. The willingness to deceive a regulatory body may be disclosed by immaterial and useless deceptions as well as by material and persuasive ones. We do not think it is an answer to say that the deception was unnecessary and served no purpose."[13]

Another contention made by the licensee was that a majority of its stockholders had no part or knowledge of the concealment or deception. The Court replied that "this may be a very proper consideration for the Commission in determining just and appropriate action. But as a matter of law, the fact that there are innocent stockholders can not immunize the corporation from the consequences of such deception. If officers of the corporation by such mismanagement waste its assets, presumably the state law affords adequate remedies against the wrongdoers. But in this as in other matters, stockholders entrust their interests to their chosen officers and often suffer for their dereliction. Consequences of such acts cannot be escaped by a corporation merely because not all of its stockholders participated."[14]

The final language of the opinion, reflecting the Supreme Court's attitude toward misrepresentation or concealment of facts and the scope of the Commission's authority in this regard, should be noted:

Lastly, and more importantly, the Court of Appeals suggested that in order to justify refusal to renew, the Commission should have made findings with respect to the quality of the station's service in the past and its equipment for good service in the future. Evidence of the station's adequate service was introduced at the hearing. The Commission on the other hand insists that in administering the Act it must rely upon the reports of licensees. It points out that this concealment was not caused by slight inadvertence nor was it an isolated instance, but that the station carried on the course of deception for approximately twelve years. It says that in deciding whether the proposed operations would serve public interest, convenience or necessity, consideration must be given to the character, background and training of all parties having an interest in the proposed licensee, and that it cannot be required to exercise the discretion vested in it to entrust the responsibilities of a licensee to an applicant guilty of a systematic course of deception.

We cannot say that the Commission is required as a matter of law to grant a license on a deliberately false application even if the falsity were not of this duration and character, nor can we say that refusal to renew the license is arbitrary and capricious under such circumstances. It may very well be that this station has established such a standard of public service that the Commission would be justified in considering that its deception was not a matter that affected its qualifications to serve the public. But it is the Commission, not the courts, which must be satisfied that the public interest will be served by renewing the license. And the fact that we might not have made the same determination on the same facts does not warrant a substitution of judicial for administrative discretion since Congress has confided the problem to the latter. We agree that this is a hard case, but we cannot agree that it should be allowed to make bad law.[15]

Unlawful Assignment of Control. As explained in Chapter 20, Section 310(b) makes it unlawful to transfer the control of a station without the consent of the Commission. In some instances licenses have been lost because of this violation.

In *United States Broadcasting Corporation*, 2 FCC 208 (1935), applications for license renewal and for full time operation were denied where it appeared the station had carried on a mediocre program service, was in financial difficulties and where there had been a transfer of control without the consent of the Commission.[16]

In another case, the Commission revoked a license where there had been two unauthorized transfers of control, at least one of which was willful; where incomplete and erroneous ownership reports had been filed, some stock transfers had not been reported, and the officers, directors and stockholders had been negligent and indifferent to their responsibilities to the public and the Commission.[17]

There have been many instances involving violations of Section 310(b) where the Commission has granted renewal of licenses. In such cases, the Commission has resolved doubts in favor of the licensees because of countervailing factors. For example, in *Farmers Broadcasting Service, Inc.,* 8 RR 415 (1953), 50 percent of the stock in the licensee company was issued to new stockholders without the Commission's consent and there was failure to report intention to sell additional stock. The Commission decided however that there was no active concealment of facts and that the errors committed were not deliberate but due to ignorance of corporate procedure.[18] Considering all the circumstances, the Commission approved a renewal of the station's license.

In a 1953 case, applications for transfer of control and renewal of license were granted despite the fact there had been misrepresentations to the Commission and an unauthorized transfer of control. Any doubts were resolved in favor of the licensee for the reason that the offenses had been committed some years in the past and the perpetrators of the illegal acts no longer were connected with the management of the station and a useful and needed broadcast service was being provided the public.[19]

The Commission decided in 1956 that a prior unauthorized shift of control was not a bar to license renewal where the change was more technical than actual; that the same persons, a family group, continued to own the corporation in which one now had a majority interest, and where the same management and operating policies were still in effect.[20]

Illegal Delegation of Control over Radio Programs. Any kind of arrangement by which the licensee delegates or abdicates its responsibility for programming violates section 310(b) of the Act and may result in a loss of license. For example, in a 1948 case, the Commission held that a contract by which a city, licensee of a station, transferred to a private commercial organization substantial control over about 85% of the broadcast time, with the right of the latter to seek injunctive relief in case of breach or threatened breach by the city, was an abdication of the licensee's duties in violation of the law. The city was required to rid itself of the contract and regain control of the station.[21]

In 1949, the Commission announced the reservations of broadcast time by sellers of stations to be illegal. The Commission declared that "under the Act a station licensee is fully responsible for the operation and control of his station and he cannot properly divest himself by contract or otherwise of such responsibility. The obligation to operate in the public interest is the licensee's alone. It is not in the public interest and is inconsistent with the nature of the rights conferred by a license for owners of radio stations as part of the consideration for the transfer of such stations to reserve a right to the use of radio time on the station being sold, to attempt to obtain a right of reverter of license, or to obtain other rights which under the Act can be exercised only by licensees."[22]

The Commission has implemented this policy with the following specific regulations:

Special rules relating to contracts providing for reservation of time upon sale of a station.—(a) No license, renewal of license, assignment of license, or transfer of control of a corporate licensee shall be granted or authorized to a standard broadcast station which has a contract, arrangement or understanding, express or implied, pursuant to which, as consideration or partial consideration for the assignment of license or transfer of control, the assignor of a station license or the transferor of stock, where transfer of a corporate licensee is involved, or the nominee of such assignor or transferor retains any right of reversion of the license or any right to the reassignment of the license in the future, or reserves the right to use the facilities of the station for any period whatsoever.

(b) In the case of assignment of license or transfer of control of a corporate licensee approved by the Commission before the effective date of this section February 15, 1949, involving a contract, arrangement or understanding of the type covered by paragraph (a) of this section and the existence and terms of which were fully disclosed to the Commission at the time of execution, the Commission will give consideration to the issuance of a license despite the existence of such contract, arrangement or understanding, if the parties thereto modify such contract within 6 months from the effective date of this section. Such modifications will be considered on the facts of each case but no such modifications will be approved unless the modified contract contains at least the following provisions:

(1) A maximum limitation of the time subject to reservation so that no more than 12 hours per week shall be subject to reservation, of which no more than 4 hours shall be on any given day.

(2) A clause providing that the licensee reserves the right to reject or refuse programs which he reasonably believes to be unsatisfactory or unsuitable or for which, in his opinion, a program of outstanding local or national importance should be substituted, but provision may be made for the substitution of other radio time for programs so rejected or for the payment at the station card rate for the time made unavailable.

(3) A prohibition against the resale or reassignment of any of the broadcast time reserved by such modified contract.

(4) An express negation of any right with respect to reversion or reassignment of license.

(5) An express provision setting forth a definite expiration date of the contract, arrangement or understanding. Such expiration date shall not extend beyond February 15, 1964 and shall in no event extend beyond the expiration date originally provided for in any such contract, agreement or understanding, in the event that such expiration date is a date prior to February 15, 1964.

(6) An express provision giving to the licensee the right to terminate the contract, arrangement or understanding for substantial cause, including, but not limited to, the assignment of license or the transfer of control of a corporate licensee, consistent disagreement over programs between the parties, or the acquisition of a network affiliation by the licensee, upon the payment of a lump sum or periodic payments, and providing that the amount initially fixed shall thereafter decrease as the amount of time reserved is decreased by performance of the contract. Any such payment should not be so unduly large as to constitute in practice an effective deterrent to the licensee exercising the right of termination. In determining whether

the amount is unduly large, the Commission will consider the amount by which consideration in return for the transfer of the station was decreased by reason of the reservation of time or the present value of the radio time still reserved and unused as of the date of the exercise of the right of termination.[23]

In a 1950 case, the Commission stated that the licensee is responsible for the selection of programs and must maintain a continuous and positive control over programming. Retention of a negative or veto control with the delegation of responsibility to a time broker is not sufficient.[24]

Violations of the Communications Act. Violations of law in general as they relate to character qualifications of broadcast licensees have already been discussed in Chapter 13. Licensees of course are expected to observe strictly all provisions of the Communications Act itself. Failure to do so can lead to serious consequences.

There are penal provisions which should be mentioned. Section 501 of the Act provides that "any person who willfully and knowingly does or causes or suffers to be done" anything prohibited or declared to be unlawful, or likewise fails to do anything required, shall, upon conviction, be fined not more than $10,000 or be imprisoned for a term not more than one year, or both. In case of second offenses, the term of imprisonment may be extended to two years.[25]

As pointed out in Chapter 3, it is the responsibility of U.S. District Attorneys to carry out under the direction of the Attorney General all necessary proceedings for the enforcement of this and other provisions of the Communications Act.[26]

While the Commission itself has no authority to enforce criminal sanctions, as previously pointed out, it does have the power to revoke licenses or may refuse to renew them where violations of the Act are involved.

Violations of FCC Rules and Regulations. In the business and programming affairs and technical operation of the station, management must be alert at all times to make sure that FCC rules and regulations are strictly observed. Section 502 of the Communications Act specifies penalties for willful violation of these rules. It reads:

Any person who willfully and knowingly violates any rule, regulation, restriction, or condition made or imposed by the Commission under authority of this Act, or any rule, regulation, restriction, or condition made or imposed by any international radio or wire communications treaty or convention, or regulations annexed thereto, to which the United States is or may hereafter become a party, shall, in addition to any other penalties provided by law, be punished, upon conviction thereof, by a fine of not more than $500 for each and every day during which such offense occurs.[27]

Here again we are dealing with criminal provisions of the statute, responsibility for the enforcement of which vests in the Attorney General. The Commission, however, has the authority to revoke or refuse to renew licenses for violations of its rules the same as it may for violation of any of the provisions of the Communications Act.

In an early 1932 case, the U.S. Court of Appeals of the District of Columbia sustained a decision of the Federal Radio Commission, denying license renewal because the station involved had violated regulations by using excessive power, by permitting the station to be operated by a person not having a license and had not met the requirements as to announcement of station call letters and identification of phonograph records.[28]

In 1935, the FCC denied a renewal application where it appeared, among other things, that the station's transmitter was not being properly modulated and spare parts were such that they could not be used for replacement.[29]

In other situations, stations have lost their licenses for failing to maintain operating schedules as required by the Commission, for defective equipment and repeated violations of technical rules, for failure to log the names of political speakers, and for not requiring station personnel to sign station logs, etc.[30]

The Commission has taken into account extenuating circumstances and has set aside revocation orders or granted renewal of licenses despite infractions of rules. For example, in a 1949 case, the Commission revoked the license of a station because of almost 150 technical irregularities. The order of revocation, however, subsequently was set aside, because the licensee was operating from a new site and a special inspection had shown that the violations had been corrected.[31]

Likewise, in a Puerto Rican case, a revocation order was set aside where there had been numerous engineering violations. Extenuating circumstances included attempts at improvements in technical operation. Also, the station had been in operation only a short time and the Commission thought there was a good prospect that it would continue to improve its service. Moreover, there was no evidence that the misconduct in question was willful or deliberate.[32]

Forfeitures. By a recent amendment of Section 503 of the Act, the Commission is empowered to impose forfeitures (1) for willful and repeated failure of a station to operate substantially as authorized; (2) for failure to observe any rule or regulation of the Commission or to comply with any final cease or desist order; (3) for violation of Section 317(c) or Section 509(a)(4) of the Act or Section 1304, 1343, or 1464 of Title 18 of the United States Code. No forfeiture liability, however, may attach until the licensee has received written notice and has had an opportunity to show in writing why he should not be held liable. (See Section 7,

Communications Act Amendments, 1960, Appendix I, for details regarding maximum penalties and administrative procedure.)

Network Regulations. The network regulations have already been discussed in Chapter 18. A historic case involving violation of these regulations was *Don Lee Broadcasting System,* 14 FCC 993, 5 RR 1179 (1950). In that case, the Commission found that the network in question had forced its affiliates to "accept arrangements under which they could not freely accept programs from another network organization;" had pressured them "to agree to accept regularly network programs on less than 56 days' notice," and "to treat as network option time far more than the 3 hours in each of the segments of the broadcast day permitted by the rules." The record in the case further showed that the affiliates were compelled to surrender, contrary to the regulations, their rights to reject network programs which they reasonably believed to be contrary to the public interest and their right to substitute programs of outstanding local importance for network programs. As the Commission said, "in order to force the affiliates to comply with the network demands, the affiliates were subjected to unremitting and insistent pressure from the network in the form of written and oral communications, 'follow up' activities on the part of network officials, and, on occasion, implied threats to cancel station network affiliation. In at least one instance, moreover, the network refused to grant an affiliation with a new station if it were managed by a manager of another of its affiliates who had, in the past, proved 'uncooperative' with respect to the network's demands to relinquish local option time, and to shift programs, and had shown reluctance to accept the network's judgment as to what constituted good programming for the local station."[33]

Despite these violations of the network rules as shown by the record, the Commission concluded:

We find ourselves in a difficult situation in deciding this case. This is not due to any deficiency in the record for we are convinced that the attitude which responsible Don Lee officers displayed in this record with respect to the Commission's chain broadcasting regulations—an attitude which can at best be characterized as one of indifference—warrants critical examination of the qualifications of the applicant to be a broadcast licensee. We are, however, faced with the important practical difficulties in this case which arise from the fact that the only sanction we have to apply is denial of license—an action which will put the licensee out of business. Except (in an aggravated case), the Commission is reluctant to impose a sentence on a licensee which not only terminates his existing operations but would preclude him from holding any other radio licenses. Had we the authority to order a suspension, assess a penalty or impose some other sanction less than a 'death sentence' we should have no hesitancy whatsoever in doing so in this case. In view of the foregoing, we are disposed to afford Don Lee a final chance to demonstrate its ability to comply with the Commission's rules and regulations in the light of the enunciation of their scope and import in this decision. In reaching this conclusion, the Commission has given careful consideration to the affidavit filed by Lewis Allen Weiss on January 6, 1949, in which he undertook to personally guarantee that, in the future, Don Lee would not, in any manner, violate the Commission's chain broadcasting regulations.[34]

Had the Commission been empowered to assess penalties (as it is now) at the time this case was decided, it no doubt would have assessed one against the network involved. Now having sanctions less than the "death sentence", the Commission may be able to deal more effectively with willful and repeated violations of network regulations should they occur.

In deciding this Don Lee case, the Commission stated what it considered to be the basic purpose and policy underlying the chain broadcasting regulations of which all broadcasters should be aware and careful to observe:

. . . These regulations were promulgated to insure that the licensees of radio stations who become affiliated with the various networks did not, formally or informally, surrender control of the day-to-day operation of their stations to the networks. Licensee responsibility is an integral part of the statutory scheme for regulating the radio industry under which persons or groups are granted limited renewable franchises to utilize the radio spectrum for broadcasting in the public interest. In granting licenses the Commission considers the operational plans and policies proposed by the licensee; the licensee's ability to carry out his proposals; his ties with the community in which the station is located; and all other facets of the licensee's character and qualifications to own and operate the station and serve the community in which it is located. Pursuant to this careful evaluation the Commission seeks to choose those applicants who propose an operation best calculated to serve the public interest and best qualified to carry out the proposed plans. The Communications Act makes the individual licensee responsible for the operation of his station and requires that he maintain control of that operation in order to carry out the proposals made to the Commission. Unless the licensee retains complete control of his station, the Commission has no one whom it can hold responsible for the operation of the station and the Commission's statutory duty to insure that broadcast licensees operate their stations in the public interest would be effectively frustrated.

The network regulations are designed to insure that control of the individual stations is not forfeited to a network organization and with which such stations are affiliated. The networks, as such, are not licensed by the Commission and are under no statutory obligation to serve the public interest. The chain broadcasting regulations, therefore, are designed to govern the conduct of the individual stations rather than the networks. Thus they provide that no license shall be issued to a station which violates any of the regulations. Where, however, a station has been induced to violate one or more of the regulations because of pressure or coercion from a network, it is the network which is primarily responsible for the violations of the regulations. For an individual station does not deal with a network as an equal, particularly when it is a small station. Consequently, when a network, which has induced its affiliated stations to violate the regulations, is also the licensee of various radio stations, serious questions are raised as to the qualifications of that network to continue as a licensee of such broadcasting stations even though since its operation of its own stations does not come within the scope of the chain broadcasting rules, the network's activities do not involve any violations of the rules with respect to its own stations.

The chain broadcasting regulations have clear application not only to prohibited relationships between network and stations which are expressed in formal written agreements, but to prohibited relationships which may be established through tacit understandings or courses of conduct which have the same effect as formal written agreements. The regulations enjoin stations from 'having any contract, arrangement, or understanding, express or implied' which establish the specified prohibited relationships. A tacit understanding imposed by a network upon it affiliates under which the stations affiliated with the network are expected to operate and do in fact generally operate contrary to the provisions of the chain broadcasting regulations is as much a violation of those rules as if the forbidden course of conduct were the result of a formally written contract spelling out the forbidden practices.[35]

Defamation. The common law and state statutes recognize the right of every man to be protected from false and defamatory references. In legal parlance, a defamatory imputation is one which tends to lower a man's reputation among responsible and respectable people, or causes him to be shunned or avoided, or to become the object of contempt, hatred or ridicule. Such a derogatory reference broadcast from a radio or television station may subject the station to an action for damages in a state court.

Traditionally, two types of defamation have been recognized by the courts—slander and libel. Slander involves spoken words, whereas libel consists of written or printed words or pictures. More liability attaches to the latter because of its permanence of form and greater damaging effects.

When are defamatory remarks on radio and television slanderous and when are they libelous? This has been a troublesome and controversial matter. It has been held that a defamatory radio or television broadcast read from a script was libelous in character.[36] In 1956, a New York court sustained a complaint which alleged a libelous statement on television not based upon a prepared script.[37]

In this New York case, the specific question was raised whether a telecast not read from a prepared script constituted libel or slander. The Court said in part:

This precise question has not been passed upon by our appellate courts, nor apparently in any other jurisdiction. *Hartmann v. Winchell* (supra) held that the 'utterance of defamatory remarks, *read from a script* into a radio microphone and broadcast constitutes libel' (296 N.Y. at P. 298; italics supplied). It expressly did not reach the question 'whether broadcasting defamatory matter which has not been reduced to writing should be held to be libelous because of the potentially harmful and widespread effects of such defamation' (p. 300).[38]

The New York Court concluded that the defamatory remarks, though not read from a script and though extemporaneous in character, nevertheless constituted libel because of the likelihood of "aggravated injury" inherent in the medium of broadcasting.[39] The *North Carolina Law Review* for April, 1958 reviewed the development of the law on whether televised defamation is libel or slander and concluded that the New York Court was correct.[40]

The weight of opinion in recent years seems to be that all broadcast defamation should be classified as libel on the grounds that the potential for harm should be the important factor and not permanence of form.[41] Some writers, however, have taken the opposing view.[42]

In any case, whether the defamation be classified as slander or libel, all broadcasters must use due care to see that false and derogatory statements do not go out over the air. In a number of early radio cases, the doctrine of absolute liability for defamation as applied to newspapers was followed by the courts.[43] In a 1939 case, however, a Pennsylvania court refused to follow this doctrine. The facts of this case were that NBC had leased its facilities to an advertising agency which in turn had engaged Al Jolson as the featured entertainer on a sponsored program presented over the network. The script of the particular program in question was prepared in advance and was submitted to the network and approved. While the program was in progress, Jolson deviated from the script and made an extemporaneous remark to the effect that the Plaintiff operated a "rotten hotel." The Plaintiff brought an action for defamation and was awarded $15,000 by a jury in the lower court.

On appeal, the judgment was reversed, the higher court holding that "a broadcasting station that leases its time and facilities to another whose agents carry on the program is not liable for an interjected defamatory remark where it appears that it exercised due care in the selection of the lessee, and having inspected and edited the script, had no reason to believe an extemporaneous defamatory remark would be made.[44]

With respect to defamation by radio and television, the laws in the various states vary and courts are not uniform in their construction of the statutes. All licensees, however, should be familiar with the laws as applied in the states where their stations operate. Management should be particularly careful to see that no statements go out over the air which, for example, falsely accuse persons of crimes, impute immoral conduct, suggest the existence of an infectious or loathsome disease, or do harm to a person in his profession or business, etc. Generally, whether broadcast licensees are liable for such statements depends upon whether the statements are true or false, the degree of care exercised by the licensee in connection with any questionable broadcast, and whether the utterances are made by station employees or by outside persons having no official connection with the station.

Political Broadcasting. In Chapter 18, mention was made of Section 315 of the Communications Act relating to the use of broadcast facilities by political candidates. The language in the section which prohibits the station from censoring any material used in such broadcasts has been troublesome. In 1951, the FCC held that the broadcaster has no authority to censor a broadcast by a political candidate, whether on the ground that it contains defamatory matter or for any other reason. The Commission warned that all licensees would thereafter be expected to comply fully with this provision of the law.[45]

Since that time a number of suits have been filed in state courts against broadcast stations charging defamation in political broadcasts and asking damages for alleged injuries. These cases have held that the stations are immune from such damage suits since they are prohibited from censoring the broadcasts of the political candidates.[46] There has been language in some of these cases, however, which indicates that the courts might have allowed damage claims had the facts been different. For example, in a 1955 case decided by the Connecticut Supreme Court of Errors, it was held that the defendant radio station was not liable for damages. The Court said the station was immune under the circumstances but implied the decision might have been otherwise had it been shown that the defendant company "maliciously permitted its facilities to be used, or that it knew that the facts stated were false and yet allowed the broadcast, or otherwise acted in bad faith."[47]

In a 1958 North Dakota case, the Supreme Court in that state pointed out that Section 315 of the Communications Act states "in clear and specific language that where candidates for political office are permitted to use the facilities of a station such 'shall have no power of censorship.' "[48] The Court further said that "since power of censorship of political broadcasts is prohibited it must follow as a corollary that the mandate prohibiting censorship includes the privilege of immunity from liability for defamatory statements made by the speakers.[49] The Court further reasoned that it "could not believe that it was the intent of Congress to compel a station to broadcast libelous statements and at the same time subject it to the risk of defending actions for damages.[50]

There was language in the case, however, which suggested possible exceptions. The Court quoted from an Illinois case in which the U.S. Supreme Court had referred to "narrowly limited classes of speech, the prevention of which have never thought to raise any constitutional problem. These include the lewd and obscene, the profane, and libelous and the insulting or 'fighting' words—those which by their very utterance inflict injury or tend to incite to an immediate breach of the peace. It has been well observed that such utterances are no essential part of any exposition of ideas, and are of such slight social value as a step to truth that any benefit that may be derived from them is clearly outweighed by the social interest in order and morality."[51]

This case was appealed to the U.S. Supreme Court and the decision of the North Dakota Court was affirmed. The Supreme Court held that a broadcasting station may not censor defamatory statements contained in speeches broadcast by legally qualified candidates for public office, and the licensee of the station is immune from any liability for such statements.[52] This decision of the high court laid to rest any question regarding the matter and now provides an unequivocal mandate which all stations must follow.

NOTES

1. 66 Stat. 716-717. See Section 6 of Communications Act Amendments, 1960, for recent changes in 312(a).
2. *Ibid.*
3. *Ibid.*
4. *Ibid.*
5. 60 Stat. 237 at 242.
6. *Great Western Broadcasting Association v. FCC,* 68 App. D.C. 119, 94 F.(2d) 244 (1937).
7. *Revocation of Station License of Station WSAL,* 8 FCC 34 (1940).
8. *Panama City Broadcasting Company,* 9 FCC 208 (1942). See also *Ocala Broadcasting Company, Inc.,* 9 FCC 223 (1942).
9. *Broadcasting Service Organization, Inc.,* 11 FCC 1057, 3 RR 979 (1947).
10. *Big State Broadcasting Corporation,* 8 RR 161 (1953).
11. *Balboa Radio Corporation,* 6 RR 649 (1953).
12. 329 U.S. 223.
13. *Ibid.,* p. 227.
14. *Ibid.*
15. *Ibid.,* pp. 228-229.
16. 2 FCC 208 (1935).
17. *Station KWIK,* 6 RR 567 (1950); also see *Station WXLT,* 6 RR 378 (1950); *Station KXXL,* 5 RR 1206 (1950).
18. Also see *Joseph C. Calloway,* 5 FCC 345 (1938); *J. L. Robinson,* 5 FCC 623 (1938); *John R. Frazier,* 5 FCC 649 (1938); *East Texas Broadcasting Co.,* 8 FCC 479 (1941); *ABC-Paramount Merger Case,* 8 RR 541 (1953).
19. *St. Joseph Valley Broadcasting Corp.,* 8 RR 766 (1953).
20. *News Publishing Co.,* 13 RR 1061 (1956).
21. *WOAX, Inc.,* 12 FCC 960; 4 RR 344 (1948).
22. *In the Matter of Promulgation of Special Rules Relating to Contracts Providing for Reservation of Time upon Sale of Station,* Docket No. 8774, 14 Fed. Reg. 179 (1949).
23. 1 RR 53:243-244.
24. *Master Broadcasting Corp.,* 6 RR 621 (1950).
25. 48 Stat. 1100.
26. *Ibid.,* 1043.

27. 48 Stat. 1100-1101.

28. *Brohy v. FRC,* 61 App. D.C. 204, 59 F.(2d) 879 (1932).

29. *United States Broadcasting Corporation,* 2 FCC 208 (1935).

30. See *Greater Kampeska Radio Corp.,* 5 FCC 514 (1938); affirmed 71 App. D.C. 117, 108 F. (2d) 5 (1939); *Charles C. Carlson,* 12 FCC 902; 3 RR 1887 (1948); *Radio Station WPBP,* 4 RR 1087 (1948).

31. *Radio Station WINZ,* 5 RR 715 (1949).

32. *Inter-Amercian Radio Corporation* 7 RR 676 (1951).

33. *Don Lee Broadcasting System,* 14 FCC 993, 5 RR 1179 (1950).

34. *Ibid.,* pp. 1010-1011.

35. *Ibid.*

36. *Hartman v. Winchell,* 296 NY 296, 73 N.E. (2d) 30; Also *Gearhart v. WSAZ, Inc.,* U.S. District Court, E.D. Ky., March 9, 1957, 150 F. Supp. 98.

37. *Shor v. Billingsley, et al,* New York Supreme Court, New York County, November 28, 1956, 158 NY 5 (2d) 476, 14 RR 2053.

38. *Ibid.,* 14 RR 2054.

39. *Ibid.,* 2054-2056.

40. 36 *N.C.L. Rev.* 355 (April, 1958); also see the *University of Kansas City Law Review,* 26 *U.K.C.L. Rev.* 69 (December, 1957).

41. 37 *B.U.L. Rev.* 378 (1957); 32 *Tulane L. Rev.* 136 (December 1957); 71 *Harv. L. Rev.* 384 (December 1957); 43 *Corn. L. Q.* 320.

42. See 31 *St. John's Law Review* 314 (May, 1957).

43. *Sorenson v. Wood,* 123 Neb. 348, 243 N.W. 82 (1932), appeal dismissed *sub. nom; KFAB Broadcasting Co. v. Sorenson,* 290 U.S. 599 (1933); *Coffee v. Midland Broadcasting Co.,* 8 F. Supp. 889 (W.D. Mo., 1934); *Knickerbocker Broadcasting Co.,* 179 Misc. 787, 38 N.Y.S. (2d) 985 (1942).

44. *Summit Hotel Co. v. National Broadcasting Co.,* 336 Pa. 182 (1939).

45. *WDSU Broadcasting Corporation,* 7 RR 766 (1951).

46. *Farmers Educational and Cooperative Union of America,* North Dakota Supreme Court, April 3, 1958, 17 RR 2001; also, *Lamb v. Sutton, et. al.,* U.S. District Court, M.D. Tenn., July 29, 1958, Civil Actions No. 1925, 1936, 17 RR 2099.

47. *Charles Parker Company v. Silver City Crystal Co.,* Conn. Supreme Court of Errors, August 1, 1955, 12 RR 2057 at 2062. In *Dansell v. Voice of New Hampshire, Inc.,* New Hampshire Supreme Court, Merrimack County, April 29, 1954, Equity No. 123, 10 RR 2045, the Court actually held that Section 315 of the Communications Act did not prohibit the censorship of libelous material in a political broadcast or protect the station against liability for libel or slander. The Court said only the censorship of words as to their political and partisan trend is prohibited by Section 315.

48. *Farmers Educational and Cooperative Union of America,* North Dakota Division v. WDAY, Inc., N.D. Sup. Ct., 17 RR 2007.

49. *Ibid.,* p. 2008.

50. *Ibid.,* p. 2007.

51. *Beaubarnais v. Illinois,* 343 U.S. 250, 96 L. Ed. 919, 72 S. Ct. 725.

52. 18 RR 2135 (June 29, 1959).

CHAPTER 22

Copyright and Other Legal Restrictions on Broadcast Use of Program Materials

*The notion of property starts, I suppose, from confirmed possession of a tangible object and consists in the right to exclude others from interference with the more or less free doing with it as one wills. But in copyright, property has reached a more abstract expression. . . . The grant of this extraordinary right is that the person to whom it is given has invented some new collocation of visible or audible points—of lines, colors, sounds or words. The restraint is directed against reproducing this collocation, although but for the invention and the statute any one would be free to combine the contents of the dictionary, the elements of the spectrum, or the notes of the gamut in any way that he had the wit to devise. . . .—*JUS-TICE HOLMES

The creative works of others may not be used by radio and television stations except with the permission of the owners and under the conditions which they prescribe. Even though these works have not been copyrighted, they are protected prior to duplication for sale by common law as interpreted and applied in the several states.

Once these original materials are placed on the market for general sale, statutory copyright must be relied on for protection against their unauthorized use.

Dramatic and Dramatico-Musical Materials. Section 1(d) of the U.S. Copyright Code confers the following exclusive rights regarding the performance of dramatic works:

To perform or represent the copyrighted work publicly if it be a drama or, if it be a dramatic work and not reproduced in copies for sale, to vend any manuscript or any record whatsoever thereof; to make or to procure the making of any transcription or record thereof by or from which, in whole or in part, it may in any manner or by any method be exhibited, performed, represented, produced, or reproduced; and to exhibit, perform, represent, produce, or reproduce it in an manner or by any method whatsoever;[1]

The courts have definitely established that these performance rights apply to operas, operettas, musical comedies, or other dramatic-musical works as well as ordinary dramas and stage plays. Any radio or television adaptions of these various dramatic forms are subject to the same exclusive rights.

It has also been clearly established that motion picture and kinescopic photoplays fall within this category and the exhibition of them on television without license would infringe Section 1(d) quoted above.

There is some question as to whether the provisions of this section are applicable to the exhibition of what may be termed non-dramatic motion pictures and kinescopes. However, some authorities believe that the courts will lean in that direction and hold the unauthorized exhibition of such materials as illegal.[2]

It is the "public performance" of the above types of material which is prohibited without the permission of the owners. The courts have held that radio and television broadcasts are "public performances" within the meaning of the statute.[3] All broadcast stations, therefore, whether they be commercial or noncommercial, must secure clearances from the copyright owners before putting such materials on the air.

Music Materials. In the case of dramatic works as described above, unauthorized "public performance" is enough to infringe the Copyright Code. In the case of musical compositions and mechanical recordings, not dramatic in character, there is the added requirement that they be publicly performed "for profit." All commercial stations operating for profit must secure clearances for such musical compositions and recordings. It has been held that the unlicensed broadcast of a copyrighted musical composition by means of a phonograph recording on a sustaining program of a non-profit radio station, which devoted a third of its time to advertising programs and used the revenue to defray operating costs, was a "performance for profit" within the meaning of the Copyright Act, entitling the copyright owner to an injunction and damages.

The facts of this case were that Debs Memorial Fund, Inc. owned and operated Station WEVD in Brooklyn, New York, and was organized as a business corporation under Article 2 of the Stock Corporation Law of New York. The Fund had by-laws providing for non-profit sharing operation, with all profits and surplus being used for the enlargement of the station's facilities and for improving the educational and cultural activities thereof. The Court stated that the basic purpose of the Fund was philanthropic and educational.

The Court held that "it can make no difference that the ultimate purposes of the corporate defendant were charitable or educational. Both in the advertising and sustaining programs, Debs was engaged in an enterprise which resulted in profit to the advertisers and to an increment to its own treasury whereby it might repay its indebtedness and avoid an annual deficit." The reasoning of the Court seemed to be that by providing a musical program such as the one in question, the station increased its number of listeners and made it more desirable as a station for paid advertising.[4]

The question arises whether the same rule applies to educational radio and television stations which operate on a strictly non-profit and non-commercial basis. The answer appears to be no. There is an important difference between these stations and the Debs one in that they are prohibited from carrying any advertising at all. Also, the FCC rules definitely preclude any type of commercial or profit-making operation on the part of educational stations using reserved channels. Therefore, it appears that they are not required to get permission to use copyrighted music or recordings thereof from the owners.

The American Society of Composers, Authors, and Publishers. Radio and television stations generally draw upon the resources of the American Society of Composers, Authors, and Publishers for recorded music. This society has a large repertoire of copyrighted music which is available for use by stations under contractual arrangements and on payment of an annual license fee.

The following definition of "users of music" appears in the current Articles of Association of the Society:

'User' means any person, firm or corporation who or which
1. owns or operates an establishment or enterprise where copyrighted musical compositions are performed publicly for profit, or
2. is otherwise directly engaged in giving public performance of copyrighted musical compositions for profit.

In 1946, ASCAP attempted to enlarge its licensing activities to include educational institutions. Several schools in the East reluctantly entered into contracts with the Society paying annual fees for the use of music in the Society's repertoire. But some educational organizations strenuously objected and refused to accede to a demand for payment of a license fee.[5] Negotiations resulted in ASCAP arrangements favorable to the educators.

The term "user" as presently defined by the society includes all commercial broadcast stations, but would not appear to include non-commercial stations operated by non-profit institutions. The standard practice for educational stations is to secure ASCAP licenses for nominal fees with freedom to use all the music in the ASCAP repertoire so long as no public performance for profit is involved.

What has just been said must be qualified. The ASCAP contracts state that members are assigned the public performance rights "of the separate numbers, songs, fragments or arrangements, melodies or selections forming part or parts of musical plays and dramatico-musical compositions, but that the owner reserves and excepts from the assignment the right of performance of musical plays and dramatico-musical compositions in their entirety, or any part of such plays or dramatico-musical compositions on the legitimate stage."[6]

What this means is that the ASCAP license gives the broadcast station the right to use the separate songs and parts of musical plays, operas, operettas, oratorios, and the like, but not the right to use these dramatico-musical compositions in their entirety or any parts of them if they are picked up and transmitted from the "legitimate stage."

The rights for the performance of these dramatico-musical works in their entirety or parts thereof on the legitimate stage are spoken of as "grand rights." They are not assigned to ASCAP but are retained by the copyright proprietor, and no public presentation of the works in their totality or parts on the legitimate stage, either on a profit or non-profit basis, can be made without his consent. Securing such consent in each individual case is a matter of negotiation between station management and the coypright owner.

It should be mentioned that music may not be integrated on the sound track of motion picture film or kinescope and used by broadcast stations without the consent of the coypright holder.

Broadcast Music, Inc. BMI, the competing organization of ASCAP, charges license fees in terms of station rate cards. An important difference between the BMI and ASCAP contracts is that with the former the broadcaster obtains both "grand" and "small" rights in all musical compositions in the BMI repertoire for both radio and television.

Since educational broadcast stations do not sell time and have no rate cards, they are able to negotiate contracts with BMI for performance rights without charge except for the payment of a nominal annual fee the same as assessed by ASCAP.

Performing and Recording Rights to Literary Works. On July 17, 1952, Congress amended Title 17 of the U.S. Copyright Code to extend to authors the performing and recording rights in non-dramatic literary works, the law becoming effective January 1, 1953. The amendment gives to such authors exclusive rights as follows:

(c) To deliver, authorize the delivery of, read, or present the copyrighted work in public for profit if it be a lecture, sermon, address or similar production, or other nondramatic literary work; to make, procure the making of any transcription or record thereof by or from which, in whole or in part, it may in any manner or by any method be exhibited, delivered, presented, produced, or reproduced; and to play or perform it in public for profit, and to exhibit, represent, produce, or reproduce it in any manner or by any method whatsoever. . . .[7]

Under the law prior to this amendment, the writers of poems, short stories, magazine articles or novels were imperfectly protected against the unauthorized performance of their works. It was pointed out to Congress that if poems, short stories, magazine articles or novels were published in book form first, the copyright statute gave no performance protection. Congress responded with proposed legislation designed to remedy this situation.

The legislation as originally introduced would have granted copyright protection even if a performance were "non-profit" in character.[8] The effects of such legislation would have barred a teacher from reading excerpts from a copyrighted book in the classroom, a minister from reading such materials in the pulpit, or a speaker from doing the same at a civic meeting. When these effects were pointed out, the bill was changed to limit the copyright protection to *performances for profit* only.[9] As the law reads, therefore, it is not a violation of the copyright law for a broadcasting station operating noncommercially to use copyrighted material, whether in the form of poems, short stories, magazine articles or similar publications. This rule applies to live shows produced by a non-commercial educational station or to the use of transcriptions of this material.

While there is some difference of opinion among authorities, this amendment appears to provide that no person may make a transcription or recording of a copyrighted work without payment of royalties. This applies whether or not the purpose of making the recording is "non-profit" or not. Recordings can be made *only* when the permission of the copyright owner has been obtained. Accordingly, neither a commercial or noncommercial station may make a transcription of a literary work without prior clearance from the author, nor may it copy a record or a transcription which it has received without securing appropriate clearances.

Kinds of Materials Which May be Copyrighted. The following types of materials may be copyrighted and all commercial radio and TV stations should make sure they have been cleared before using them in broadcasts.[10]

(a) Books, including composite and cyclopedic works, directories, gazetteers, and other compilations.

(b) Periodicals, including newspapers.

(c) Lectures, sermons, addresses prepared for oral delivery.

(d) Dramatic or dramatico-musical compositions.

(e) Musical compositions, including words and music.

(f) Maps and charts.

(g) Works of art; models or designs for works of art.

(h) Reproductions of works of art.

(i) Drawings or plastic works of a scientific or technical character.

(j) Photographs.

(k) Prints and pictorial illustrations including prints or labels used for articles of merchandise.

(l) Motion picture photoplays.

(m) Motion pictures other than photoplays.

(n) Scripts.

With the exceptions previously pointed out, educational stations operating strictly on a non-profit basis may use copyrighted materials without securing clearance.

The Doctrine of Fair Use. The limited use of published copyrighted materials for purposes of review and criticism is permissable. Where brief references or quotations from such works are used on educational broadcasts, no problem is involved. Whether there is fair use depends on the nature and purpose of the quotations, the quantity quoted and the extent to which the material might prejudice the use or sale of the original work. Obviously the presentation of a full-length copyrighted play or dramaticomusical in a telecourse on dramatic literature or music appreciation would not be fair use. However, a few short quotations or characterizations used for illustrative purposes would constitute fair use.

No clearly defined rules with respect to fair use can be stated. In *Shapiro, Bernstein and Company, Inc. v. Collier and Son,* the Court stated some general principles that are helpful: "The extent and relative value of the extracts; the purpose and whether the quoted portions might be used as a substitute for the original work; the effect upon the distribution and objects of the orginal work."[11]

Protection of Program Ideas. The Courts have held that radio and television ideas which have been reduced to tangible and concrete form and possessing the attributes of novelty and originality are considered protectable interests. Both common law and statutory copyright law afford protection. Should an unauthorized use of a concrete original idea be attempted, the offender may be liable for legal damages and may be enjoined in a court of equity from further use of the program idea or format.[12]

In order for the creator of the program to avail himself of judicial protection he should, at once, reduce to writing the concrete facts regarding the basic ideas and format of the program. This statement should contain the name of the creator of the program, the date of its origination, descriptive facts regarding its format indicating its originality and novelty. The statement should include assertions by the creator that the program idea is the result of independent and creative effort on his part, that he claims a property interest therein and that it is not to be used without his permission. The statement should be dated and retained in his files for future reference and use.

If the program idea or any scripts, films, or kinescopes pertaining thereto are permitted to be used by others, it should be made perfectly clear in writing that no property rights therein are being given up; and that, under no circumstances, can any use be made without the written consent of the proprietor. Nothing should be done which may be construed as making the program idea available for general use.

Unfair Competition. In an early case, *International News Service v. Associated Press,* 248 U.S. 215 (1918), the Supreme Court extended the doctrine of unfair competition to cover misappropriation of another's goods—"to misappropriation of what equitably belongs to a competitor."

The facts of this case were that the Plaintiff and Defendant were rival news gathering agencies. The International News Service copied news items from the bulletin boards and early editions of the Associated Press and telegraphed these items to its subscribers on the West Coast.

The Court held that while Associated Press could assert no property right in news as against the general public, as against a competitor, there was a kind of quasi-property right. The Court said that AP had acquired these rights in its news:

. . . as the result of organization and the expenditure of labor, skill, and money and which is salable by complainant for money, and that defendant in appropriating it and selling it as his own is endeavoring to reap where it has not sown . . . Stripped of all disguises, the process amounts to an unauthorized interference with the normal operation of complainant's legitimate business precisely at the point where the profit is to be reaped, in order to divert a material portion of the profit from those who have earned it to those who have not; with special advantage to defendant in the competition because of the fact that it is not burdened with any part of the expense of gathering the news. The transaction speaks for itself, and a court of equity ought not to hesitate long in characterizing it as unfair competition in business.[13]

The doctrine of this case has been extended to enjoin a broadcasting station from pirating news from a newspaper. The Associated Press brought an injunction against KVOS, a radio station in Bellingham, Washington, claiming that the station was engaged in unfair competition when it broadcast the news contained in member papers before the papers could be distributed to their subscribers. The U. S. Circuit Court of Appeals for the Ninth Circuit sustained the injunction.[14] Also, stations have invoked this doctrine against competing stations who have appropriated to their use without permission the content of sports programs.[15]

While the law of unfair competition has and may be invoked by broadcast stations, Harry Warner has observed that "the public policy which abhors monopolies aided by the pragmatic experience of the courts precludes the wholesale substitution of common law and statutory copyright by the law of unfair competition. It is submitted that the law of unfair competition should be invoked to protect intellectual property when the latter is outside the protective scope of common law and statutory copyright. Thus unfair competition complements statutory copyright; it cannot and should not be employed where the copyright law provides a remedy."[16]

Right of Privacy. The right of privacy may be defined as the right of every person to "be left alone", to demand that his private affairs shall not be exhibited to the public without his consent. It assures him private existence and protection from public gaze.[17]

This right of privacy has been given wide legal recognition by courts. In New York it has been sanctioned by statute in relation to advertising. The New York law reads:

Section 50, Article 3 of the Civil Rights Law.—Right of Privacy.—a person, firm, or corporation that uses for advertising purposes, or for the purpose of trade, the name, portrait, or picture of any living person without having first obtained the written consent of such person, or if a minor, of his or her parent or guardian, is guilty of a misdemeanor.

Broadcasting stations are under obligation to respect an individual's right of privacy. Under certain conditions, however, an individual may lose this right—for example, by becoming a public figure, or becoming a part of a news event, or by being involved in court proceedings or other official matters of public interest.

Dr. Frederick S. Siebert has provided a succinct statement on this subject with respect to television which is helpful and informative:[18]

Television stations, both commercial and noncommercial, are facing an entirely new set of problems in the area of privacy because of the visual presentation.

All types of stations undoubtedly have the right to broadcast pictorial material about news events and persons in the news. This right, however, does not guarantee to the station the privilege of access with cameras and recording equipment to all types of news events. News events occurring in public places may be reported both by camera and recorder. Public places include streets, parks, and other sites to which every member of the public has access without payment or restriction.

Most news occurrences, however, take place in what might be called semiprivate places, such as government buildings, sports arenas, or controlled-admission halls. Television stations may report events occurring in such sites only with the permission of the authority controlling admission to the site.

The right of the individual to protest televising his person depends on whether or not he is currently newsworthy and on whether or not the cameraman has legal access to the site. For example, an educational station may not televise the picture of a person without his consent unless he is in the news. The station, however, if given permission to televise a football game, does not have to get permission from each individual player or from each member of the audience who might appear on the screen.

The Right of Privacy and the Courts. The doctrine of right of privacy is a relatively new legal concept. As already mentioned, courts generally recognize the principle, but there are often differences of opinion among judges as to when the individual's privacy ends and the public's right to know begins. For example, there is considerable controversy as to what extent radio and television shall have access to trials. Some courts take the position that the mass media have no constitutional right to require trial participants to submit to photography or sound recordings. They hold it is an invasion of the right of privacy. Also, they object on the grounds that it is an interference with court procedure that may prevent the defendant from getting a fair trial.[19] While the American Bar Association has had the matter under study, its Special Committee on Canons of Ethics has recently recommended only minor changes in the language of Canon 35 "without in any way qualifying its adamantine prohibition against photographing, broadcasting, or televising of courtroom proceedings other than ceremonial proceedings such as the formal portions of naturalization proceedings."[20]

On the other hand, some courts are moving in the direction of loosening the restrictions against electronic journalism. Their position is that the defendant gives up his right of privacy when he becomes involved in a public trial and, in recognition of the public's right to be informed, broadcast media should have access to the courtroom.[21]

As Dr. Siebert has pointed out, the two basic questions a radio or television station must consider in connection with individual privacy, are (1) whether the person subjected to broadcast exposure is a part of a situation or event which is clearly newsworthy, and (2) whether the photographer or recorder has legal access to the site. Also, since broadcast media have a special obligation to serve community needs, the question must always be considered, whether the public's right to know does not take precedence over the individual's desire to be free of public gaze.

NOTES

1. 61 Stat. 652 (1947).

2. See Warner, Harry P., *Radio and Television Law* (New York, 1953), p. 315, for discussion of this point; also see 66 Stat. 753 (1952), which may be invoked to protect motion pictures other than photoplays.

3. *Select Theaters Corporation v. Ronzoni Marcaroni Co.*, 59 U.S.P.Q. 288 (DC NY 1943); *Associated Music Publishers v. Debs Memorial Radio Fund*, 46F Supp. 829 (DC NY 1942), affirmed, 141 F(2d) 852 (2d cir. 1944) *cert.* denied 323 U.S. 766.

4. *Ibid.*

5. See Warner, *op. cit.*, pp. 403-404.

6. ASCAP agreement with members executed in 1941 and expiring in 1965. See Warner, *op. cit.*, for full discussion of these ASCAP contracts.

7. 66 Stat. 752.

8. HR 3589, 82nd Congress, 1st Session, introduced April 6, 1951.

9. HR 1160, 82nd Congress, 1st Session (1951), accompanied HR 3589.

10. See Warner, *op. cit.*, Chapter III, "The Subject Matter of Copyright Protection", pp. 40-91, for detailed and authoritative discussion re materials which must be cleared before used on radio or television stations.

11. *New York Tribune, Inc. v. Otis and Company*, 39 F Supp. 67 (DC NY 1941).

12. *Stanley v. Columbia Broadcasting System*, 35 Cal. (2d) 653, 221 P. (2d)

73 (1950); *Cole v. Phillips H. Lord, Inc.,* 262 App. Div. 116, 28 NYS (2d) 404, (1941); 16 *University of Chicago Law Review* 323 (1949).

13. 39 Sup. Ct. Reporter, 72-73.

14. *Associated Press v. KVOS,* Fed. Supp. 279 (1934); also see 80 F (2) 575 (1935).

15. *Pittsburgh Athletic Co. v. KQV Broadcasting Co.,* 24 F Supp. 490 (WD Pa. 1938); Also, *Mutual Broadcasting System, Inc. v. Muzak Corp.,* 177 Misc. 489, 30 NYS (2d) 419 (Sup. Ct. 1941); and *Southwestern Broadcasting Co. et al. v. Oil Center Broadcasting Co.,* 210 SW (2d) 230 (Texas Civ. App. 1947).

16. Warner, *op. cit.,* p. 931.

17. 4 *Harvard Law Review* 193, 195; *Melvin v. Reid* 112 Cal. App. 285, 297 Pac. 91 (1931).

18. Siebert, Frederick S., "Clearance, Rights and Legal Problems of Educational Radio and Television Stations". National Association of Educational Broadcasters (1955).

19. See *Atlanta Newspapers, Inc., et al. v. Grimes et al.,* Georgia Superior Court, April 14, 1959; also see 43 A. B. A. J. 419 (May, 1957); *Tribune Review Publishing Co. v. Thomas,* 153 F. Supp. 486 (W. D. Pa., 1957); and 330 P. (2d) 734 (Okla. Crim. App. 1958).

20. 16 FCC B. J. No. 1, 66.

21. See "The Right to Report by Television," by Fred S. Siebert, 34 *Journalism Quarterly* 333 (Summer, 1957); also in same issue, "Equality of Access for Radio in Covering Washington News," by Theodore F. Koop of CBS, p. 338; and "Electronic Journalism in the Colorado Courts," by Hugh B. Terry of KLZ. Denver, p. 341.

PART VI

A Look to the Future

CHAPTER 23

Overcoming Barriers to Effective Broadcast Regulation

. . . The mountain of work of the Commission never shows any signs of letting up. We are on a tyrannical treadmill of en banc *meetings, executive sessions, oral arguments and hearings—interspersed with trips up to Capitol Hill. And apparently there are more trips to the Hill to be added to our treadmill.—*WAYNE COY*

For the year ending June 30, 1959, the FCC received and processed more than 12,000 broadcast applications for new AM, FM and TV stations, and for authority to modify existing operation. It received more than 250,000 additional applications for authority to operate amateur, aviation, industrial, land transportation, marine and public safety stations.[1]

The Commission handled about 25,000 complaints of station interference in 1959 and conducted more than 15,000 investigations involving a sizeable number of field inspections.[2]

Besides the variety and multiplicity of services provided in the broadcasting field, the Commission processed the same year more than 5,000 applications from telephone and telegraph companies for extension and enlargement of their commercial facilities.[3]

This service was provided free of charge to a broadcasting industry whose worth runs into the billions and which had a gross income of more than a billion dollars in 1959; to a telephone industry worth about twenty billion dollars with gross annual revenues of almost seven billion, and a telegraph industry with a land line investment of two hundred and fifty million and annual income exceeding two hundred and forty million. To this must be added the cable and radio companies under the jurisdiction of the FCC which provide international telephone and telegraph service with yearly income running more than one hundred million dollars.[4]

To regulate these vast industries, all of which have the free use of publicly-owned radio channels and special franchises for telecommunications, the FCC received from Congress in 1959, less than ten million dollars, and had only about 1200 employees to do the work.[5] It readily be-

* Former chairman of the FCC; now deceased.

comes apparent that one of the main reasons the Commission hasn't done a better job of regulating these huge industries is that its resources are pathetically inadequate.

It simply is impossible for the Commission to handle this enormous volume of business in the most efficient manner with the limited facilities available. Not only the general public, but the broadcasting industry itself suffers from this situation. For example, in the past, there often have been protracted delays in the processing of applications for new stations or modifications of existing facilities. The decisions in important cases have been held up for months (and even years) because of lack of personnel. Petitions from industry for changes in rules often must be kept in a pending status for inordinate periods of time because there isn't the manpower available to evaluate them and act on them. Often broadcasters who have spent large amounts of money in competitive proceedings must remain in suspense for months waiting for an overworked staff to digest the records and get the cases ready for Commission action.

Special Competency of FCC Commissioners Required. Additional money and a larger staff are, of course, only part of the answer to the problem of securing efficient broadcast regulation. The more important consideration is the securing of personnel, both at the Commission and staff levels, *competent* to deal with the increasingly complex regulatory problems at the FCC.

Generally speaking, since the creation of the FCC in 1934, the members of the Commission have been high-caliber men. (See biographical material relating to present and past commissioners in Appendix II.) Their qualifications have compared favorably with those of members of the numerous other independent commissions and boards of the Federal government. But there have been times when appointments to the FCC, as well as other agencies of government, have been motivated more by political and partisan considerations than by genuine concern for high and special qualifications needed to perform the duties of public office.

While political considerations have played some part in the appointment of Federal judges, traditionally there has been a concern that persons appointed to these judicial offices should have special qualifications for their jobs. They must have unquestioned integrity, a high sense of public responsibility, and the special training, experience and skills needed to perform in a judicial role. Where attempts have been made to appoint persons not measuring up to these standards, bar associations and other professional groups interested in the proper administration of justice have vigorously protested. Generally, public opinion in this country demands a high degree of competency of those who must pass judgment on the behavior and rights of citizens and who must settle multifarious and complicated questions of law in our democratic society.

No less should be demanded of persons who serve on commissions such as the FCC. In fact, in some respects, they ought to have even higher qualifications. An FCC commissioner must act in a three-fold capacity. He must serve in a legislative role in the formulation of rules and regulations to implement laws passed by Congress. He must see that these rules are administered properly. And he must serve as judge in many cases coming within the jurisdiction of the FCC. He is required to wear three hats and he must be able to change these hats when the duties of his office require.

Communications media have become increasingly important in American life. This fact becomes so very real when we contemplate what the situation would be if we suddenly were deprived of all telephone, telegraph, and radio communication. The FCC has tremendous legislative, administrative and judicial powers with respect to a large part of these facilities. And since the jurisdiction of courts is very much limited, this means that the decisions of the Commission are to a large extent final. Their decisions crucially affect the position and operational pattern of these media as they function to meet the needs of the nation.

The men, therefore, who serve on the FCC should have the highest qualifications. They should have superior intellects with demonstrated ability to do creative, constructive and objective thinking. Their educational and professional backgrounds should be such that they have developed a deep and profound understanding and appreciation of the critically important role that mass media play in a free, democratic society. And above all, they should have unquestioned personal integrity, a high sense of social responsibility, and a capacity for independent thought and action.

Factors Militating Against High Level Appointments. While the qualification tests suggested are high, there have been and still are members of the Commission who measure up to these tests. There are at least three factors, however, that have often militated against the recruitment of high level officials at the FCC. These are: (1) comparatively low salaries not commensurate with the heavy responsibilities of office; (2) short tenure and lack of financial and professional security; and (3) pressures from outside the agency which make it difficult for Commissioners to exercise and maintain independence of judgment and action.

Except for the Chairman (who gets an annual salary of $20,500), members of the FCC draw annual salaries of $20,000.[6] They are required to devote full time to their jobs and may not be employed otherwise. These salaries, in this writer's opinion, should be raised considerably. They are low when compared with the income of many executives in the communications industries regulated by the FCC. While non-pecuniary incentives should be important to those who work for the government, it is not realistic to expect to attract consistently high caliber men to public office when the salaries paid are far below those paid in industry for jobs with comparable responsibilities. This is especially true when it is considered that a commissioner is appointed for a limited term only.

The regular term of an FCC commissioner is now only seven years.

Quite often it is less than this when the commissioner is appointed to fill an unexpired term. It would be well to give consideration to lengthening this period to ten or possibly twelve years. This longer tenure, in addition to providing more financial security, would give a commissioner more time to become familiar with the complex regulatory problems of the agency and to make his maximum contribution to its operations. It would also be more conducive to his exercise of independent judgment since he would not be subject as often to the political hazards and ordeal that usually accompany reappointment.

Still more important, commissioners, like judges, should be free of pressures from Congress, the White House, and the industries they regulate. Many competent men are hesitant to accept positions on regulatory commissions for fear they may not be able "to call the shots as they see them." As is the case with Federal judges, they should be fully insulated and protected from outside pressures and intimidations and free to perform their tasks with the knowledge that they will not have to suffer reprisals of any sort because of any official decisions made or actions taken.

To guard against commission "packing" tendencies, Congress and professional groups particularly concerned with FCC operations should scrutinize most carefully each appointment and reappointment to the agency at the time it is made. No person should be approved for membership on the Commission, who has committed himself to take direction from any party leadership or who might be inclined to become a "rubber stamp" for the party in power or become the spokesman for any special interest group.

Congress and the FCC. A larger staff and higher standards for the selection of Commissioners will go far in improving the quality of broadcast regulation. There is another problem, however, that must be solved if the FCC is ever to achieve maximum efficiency. It has to do with the attitude and relationship of Congress toward the agency. It is a situation so serious that it deserves special consideration.

It has now been almost four years since the Congressional Subcommittee on Legislative Oversight began its investigative activities in Washington. As of February, 1959, the Subcommittee had spent more than $300,000, held more than 80 days of public hearings, listened to more than 130 witnesses recite 11,000 pages of testimony, all pertaining largely to charges made against the FCC.[7]

There can be no doubt that the Subcommittee was helpful in drawing attention to some of the serious regulatory problems of that agency and revealed some misfunction and malpractice that needed correction. (The Subcommittee has made specific recommendations for legislative action which are discussed in the next chapter). Ironically, however, the very Congress that has brought to light the unhappy conditions at the FCC has had a great deal to do with creating them. The long-standing antipathy which Congress has manifested with respect to the agency has made it difficult for the FCC to achieve the high level of performance of which it is capable.

The Investigation-Ridden FCC. Probably no other agency of the Federal government has been the object of as much vilification and prolonged investigation by Congress as has the FCC. In fact, its recent bath of fire brought on by the spectacular exploits of the House Subcommittee on Legislative Oversight was but a continuation of an ordeal to which the bedraggled agency has been subject more or less constantly since Sam Rayburn breathed the breath of life into it in 1934.

It may surprise many to know that the FCC has been under Congressional investigation or the threat of one virtually every year since it was established. The same may be said of its predecessor, the Federal Radio Commission, created in 1927 but which succumbed after six years of pelting from angry and hostile law-makers in Washington.

The Radio Act of 1927 established the Federal Radio Commission with authority to assign radio frequencies, grant, renew and revoke licenses and, within limitations, to set standards and make rules for the operation of radio stations. But Congress was never happy with this original "traffic cop of the air." Almost from the very beginning, it seemed to be viewed by its progenitors on Capitol Hill as a delinquent creature, not to be trusted, and requiring frequent discipline.

Shortly after it was created, a resolution was introduced in the House to investigate the agency.[8] Subsequently, a similar resolution was introduced in the Senate, to authorize an investigation of its personnel, records, documents, and decisions, "with particular reference to the conduct and deportment of the several members of the Commission while engaged in exercising judicial or quasi-judicial functions under the Radio Act of 1927. . . ."[9]

A few days later, Senator Huey P. Long requested the Senate to make a formal inquiry of the FRC with respect to its handling of a radio case involving conflicting interests in Shreveport and New Orleans, based upon allegations that the decision had been "changed and rechanged, reversed and re-reversed by reason of pressure exerted from the White House."[10]

Early Attacks of the FCC. But the move of the "kingfish" from the Louisiana back-country to bring the FRC to public trial didn't materialize. Before there was time to get the inquisition under way, the agency had drawn its last breath, and its functions had been swallowed up by the newly created FCC, empowered by Congress to regulate all interstate and foreign communication by means of wire or radio, including the vast telephone and telegraph industries.

This new agency had the initial blessing of New Dealers in Washington. However, Roosevelt's signature on the Communications Act of 1934 was hardly dry before the FCC was under severe attack from irate Congressmen. They took it to the proverbial woodshed frequently, and during the first seven years of its life introduced eleven different resolutions in the House and Senate to subject it to formal investigation.[11]

There was an incredible ambivalence exhibited by Congress in its attacks against the FCC during that early period. A good example of this was the behavior of Congress before and after the Commission adopted the network regulations in May, 1941. For fifteen years prior to their adoption, in virtually every session of Congress, the evils of monopoly in the broadcasting industry were oratorically deplored and the FCC was frequently chided for not riding herd on network practices. Accordingly, as previously discussed, in 1938, the FCC instituted a general investigation of the broadcasting industry, its particular target being the operations of the radio networks.

Interestingly enough, while the Commission was carrying on this rigorous proceeding and was promulgating these regulations, no fewer than six resolutions were introduced in the Congress to investigate the distraught agency.[12] These various investigatory moves were aided and abetted by a growing number of unsuccessful and disgruntled (and in some cases embittered) applicants for radio stations. But much of this probing spirit in Congress resulted from complaints of powerful (and at times vindictive) leadership in the broadcasting industry, unhappy with governmental controls, and infuriated by the possibility of stricter regulations.

The rules, as finally adopted by the FCC, were relatively mild in light of the strong position taken by Congress against radio monopoly and its insistence for more than a decade that network operations be regulated. Despite this, the regulations evoked a flood of critical comment from Capitol Hill castigating the Commission for assuming arbitrary powers over the program and business affairs of networks and stations. Almost immediately, a resolution was introduced in the Senate to investigate the FCC to determine whether the regulations were arbitrary and capricious, abridged the rights of free speech, and violated the First Amendment.[13]

Shortly thereafter, the Supreme Court issued the famous Felix Frankfurter opinion (to which reference has already been made) upholding the legality of the regulations. But it afforded the FCC with no relief from the Congressional flail. On the contrary, it intensified the hostility of the dissident Congressmen who were now determined to drive the "bureaucratic rascals" from Washington.

The Cox Investigation. The inquisitional scene shifted from the Senate to the House where the stage had been set for a full dress and spectacular probe of the FCC. The stage manager for this sensational drama was the tempestuous Congressman Eugene Cox from Georgia. In early January, 1943, he introduced House Resolution No. 21 to set up a select committee to scrutinize the organization, personnel and activities of the FCC.[14] Within three weeks, the House had approved the resolution and Congressman Cox was appointed to direct the show.[15]

The fierce and sensational manner in which he and Eugene Garey, the

Committee's first general counsel, carried on the investigation attracted national attention. As for the FCC, it was a demoralizing and bitter experience. Members of the Commission and its staff, not yet recovered from a decade of almost uninterrupted ordeal in their relations with Congress, were now pulled away from their normal regulatory duties and were required to prepare loads of informational data for the Select Committee and were interrogated under oath regarding FCC policies and procedures.

The author remembers most vividly the intensity with which the House Committee pressed their charges against the Commission. The morale of the employees dropped to an abysmally low point. He recalls the weary and frustrated feelings of a staff which had long cringed under the Congressional whip-lash for failure to control network practices, and now was flayed by the same Congress for attempting to regulate those practices, and was accused of exceeding its powers and meddling in the business affairs of stations and networks.

While the Commission writhed under this torturous treatment, FCC sympathizers at the White House and other political powers in Washington interceded backstage. Counter forces were set in action in the House and the Senate. The charge was made that Congressman Cox had accepted a $2500 interest in a new radio station in his home state after having used his Congressional position to influence the Commission to grant the application.[16]

Embarrassed by this accusation (no formal charges were ever made against him), he resigned as Chairman of the Committee in a diatribe which he emitted to his colleagues and to packed galleries in the House Chamber, September 30, 1943.[17]

He was succeeded as Chairman by Congressman Lea of California.[18] General Counsel Garey carried on for another five months and concluded that he had had enough. Senator Warren Magnuson (then a member of the lower House and on the Committee) had complained publicly that the FCC had been investigated for 13 months, that 1800 pages of testimony had been taken, with half of it consisting of words from counsel and Committee members, and all before the Commission was permitted to present its case.[19] In a huff, Mr. Garey withdrew from the Committee.[20] His parting shot was that the investigation was being converted into a "sheer whitewashing affair, wholly responsive to political pressures and dominated by political expediency."[21]

He was succeeded by John J. Sirica, who tried to pump new life into the investigation. By this time, however, the counter forces in Congress had taken full command. Unable to develop the kind of report which he thought the facts required, he resigned on November 28, 1944, stating that he did not want anyone to be able to say that he was a party to a "whitewash."[22]

The final report of the Select Committee was submitted to the House on January 2, 1945.[23] It contained no startling disclosures of FCC misconduct. In fact, it was the opinion of some experts who had followed the proceedings closely that the report pretty much absolved the Commission from the charges made against it.

The "Blue Book" Controversy. The year that followed was one of the few in the history of the FCC that the *Congressional Record* shows no formal moves to investigate the agency. The respite, however, was short lived, and the Commission had hardly had time to draw a deep breath before it was under severe attack from Congressional Hill. And here again Congress demonstrated its remarkable facility for chameleon-type behavior.

One of the complaints of some Congressmen for many years had been that the Commission had been lax in establishing and enforcing standards for broadcast programming; that despite many complaints, the Commission had made little effort to require stations to operate in the public interest.

At long last, the FCC decided to do something about it. Paul A. Porter, brilliant and imaginative, and with an impressive record as a public official, received the Presidential nod for chairmanship of the Commission. During his tenure which lasted a little over a year, he brought in Dr. Charles Siepmann, formerly with the British Broadcasting Corporation, to direct a study and come up with some proposed criteria which the Commission might establish for the evaluation of radio program service.

The result of this study was the adoption and publication by the FCC in March, 1946 of the report, *Public Service Responsibility of Broadcast Licensees,* popularly known as the Blue Book and which was discussed in Chapter 19.

Congressional reaction to this FCC publication was immediate. Despite his previous castigation of the Commission for failure to set general standards, and even before he had time to read the Blue Book carefully, Congressman Wigglesworth of Massachusetts made derogatory reference to it in a House speech, saying that some people construed it as "indicating an interest on the part of the FCC to assume unlawful control over what the people shall or shall not hear over the air."[24] He further declared that "there is imperative need for improvement in standards of administration by the Commission and for remedial legislation. Both are essential to impartial and efficient regulation and to equality of opportunity and freedom of speech over the radio . . ."[25]

Not to be outdone, fiery Senator Tobey of New Hampshire dropped a companion resolution in the Senatorial hopper to determine how much the FCC had censored and controlled programs of broadcasting stations, and the extent it had restricted or might restrict freedom of speech as guaranteed by the Constitution of the United States. A short time later, Congressman Wolverton of New Jersey gave the House notice that he was introducing a resolution to authorize an inquiry and complete study of the FCC.[26]

It was shortly after this that the writer was appointed Chief of the Renewals and Revocation Section of the Commission. It was his job, with the help of a small staff, to process all renewal applications of broadcast stations and recommend appropriate action to the Commission in terms of the program criteria set forth in the Blue Book.

He served in the position for about four years but felt handicapped because of conflicting attitudes in the Commission and on Capitol Hill. While the courts had said the FCC had the responsibility to exercise authority in the program field, some Congressmen persisted in saying publicly that the Commission was guilty of censorship when it did and that it had misconstrued the original intent of Congress.

Needless to say, this cleavage militated against any real, effective application of the program criteria which the Commission had enunciated, and engendered a kind of frustration and impuissance which, except for a few cases, made the approval of renewal applications pretty much of an automatic process.

Only two cases have been cited where Congressional intrusions and ambivalence have made it difficult for the FCC to formulate positive policies and take effective action on matters relating to the public interest. Others could be mentioned. Suffice to say, all too often have the energies and resources of the Commission been diverted from important regulatory tasks by investigating rigmarole which makes the headlines but which, in too many instances, has failed to serve useful and constructive purposes.

What makes the situation worse is the awareness of the Commission that in the establishment of basic policies, whatever road it may take, the rigmarole is likely to result and Commission character is likely to be impugned. This accounts in part for the Commission's tendency to delay action on important matters such as the clear channel case (still undecided after fifteen years) and toll TV which has been the subject of so much heated controversy in Congress for more than five years.

It is not meant by the writer to suggest that Congress should not be concerned about the conduct of administrative agencies. Unquestionably, one of the important functions of Congress is to investigate and expose inefficiency and irresponsibility in public administration. The investigative process, however, carried on more or less continuously over a long period of time can have a most damaging effect on a federal agency. This has been the case with the FCC. At no time in its twenty-six years of life has it in fact been independent in its operations. While some Congressional inquiries have been constructive in character and have been enormously helpful to the FCC, there have been too many of a destructive nature, designed to serve special interests in and outside Congress. Their punitive and often inquisitional character over a long period of time has created in the public mind an image of depravity with respect to the FCC that severely handicaps the agency in the exercise of its functions. It is the opinion of the writer that until Congress changes its own ways and corrects this situation, the FCC will never begin to approach its full capacity for achievement and public service.

The White House and the FCC. This is also true with respect to the White House and its staff. As previously pointed out, members of the FCC are appointed by the President who designates the Chairman. It is only natural, therefore, that Commissioners should feel some sense of loyalty to the executive leadership at 1600 Pennsylvania Avenue. Members of the Commission also know full well that if their conduct is not pleasing to the President, he is not likely to reappoint them. This has a subtle but none the less real influence on the thinking and actions of Commissioners —an influence which does not exist with respect to Federal judges who have life tenure and owe no allegiance to any individual or group.

Extending the terms of office of FCC members as suggested above would be helpful. The real solution, however, must come from a deep and profound concern at the White House for responsible and efficient administration. While there have been many meritorious appointments to the FCC and other independent commissions in Washington, there have been some in both Republican and Democratic administrations which were motivated largely by political expediency. In these cases, not enough consideration was given to the special competencies required to perform the difficult tasks of a government agency whose functions vitally affect the lives of all the Amercian people.

No person should be appointed to the FCC simply because he has been helpful to the party, or simply because he has been associated with and has the support of some special interest group, or because he is a friend of the President or a Congressman or other leaders in the party. While it is not meant to suggest that such things constitute disqualifying factors, quite obviously they should not be major considerations in appointing men to administer the highly important and complicated affairs at the FCC.

Once competent men are appointed who meet the high qualification tests suggested, they should be completely independent in the performance of their duties and free to make decisions without pressures or reprisals of any sort from the White House or any other political source. In this respect, they should have the same protection as that enjoyed by the courts.

The Total Citizenship Has a Responsibility. The FCC itself, Congress and the White House must bear their appropriate share of the responsibility for the failure of broadcast regulation to reach the highest level of efficiency in this country. To point the finger of criticism at these agencies alone, however, would be most unfair and would oversimplify the problem. The total citizenship has a responsibility.

Recent studies of the Special Subcommittee on Legislative Oversight of the House Committee on Interstate and Foreign Commerce clearly reveal a shocking disregard by many citizens for moral and ethical values which traditionally have been basic to American culture. In the feverish, competitive struggle of special interest groups to gain control and capital-ize on scarce natural resources such as radio and television channels, all too often contestants have succumbed to the temptation to ignore the ground rules and resort to *ex parte* pressures to win the victory.

Another manifestation of the growing indifference to ethical standards among our citizenship were the recent exposures of the deceptive tactics employed in certain quiz shows carried by the networks. While the networks and sponsors of these shows deserve criticism for the colossal hoax perpetrated on the American people, it must not be overlooked that it never could have happened without the participation of individual citizens, willing to bemean themselves to secure quickly the big dazzling cash rewards.

Irresponsibility and misconduct in government mirror to some extent the general lack of concern for and a breakdown in the moral code. As citizens, we can hardly expect our governmental officials who serve us in Washington to exhibit a higher standard of moral and ethical conduct than we ourselves exhibit. If the citizen representing himself or some group rushes to Washington and contrives a situation where he can make *ex parte* representations to a Commissioner, or enlists the aid of a Congressman or a member of the White House staff to secure a favorable decision from the FCC, he is just as guilty of misconduct as a Special Assistant to the President or a Congressman would be if he made a call to the FCC for the purpose of influencing the outcome of a case.

The problem, therefore, of overcoming barriers to effective broadcast regulation is the responsibility of all the people and not just those who represent us in the nation's Capital. In fact, the very preservation of all democratic government depends to a large extent upon the moral choices made by individual citizens.

A recent Report to the President of Michigan State University from its Committee on the Future of the University highlighted this point and stressed the importance of university training along this line:

If educated persons are to be effective citizens in the world, they must be prepared to make difficult moral choices as individuals and as members of social groups. A democracy cannot survive unless its members recognize their responsibilities for the ethical as well as the technical implications of the public and private decisions being made. The university is not an institution for indoctrination, but the university experience should equip the student to examine his ethical position and to analyze and define the value systems necessary to the maintenance of a free society.[28]

Not only universities, but education at all levels should recognize here one of its most challenging opportunities to meet one of the most critical needs of our time.

1. *FCC Annual Report,* 1959, pp. 75, 105.

2. *Ibid.,* p. 143.

3. *Ibid.,* p. 128.

4. *Ibid.,* pp. 125-127.

5. *Ibid.,* p. 20. Congress has allowed some additional funds for 1960, but the total amount is still grossly inadequate.

6. Section 4(d), Communications Act of 1934, as amended in 1956, 70 Stat. 736.

7. *Broadcasting,* February 23, 1959, p. 62.

8. H. Res. 80, 75 *Cong. Rec.* 1057, December 21, 1931.

9. 78 *Cong. Rec.* 965, May 28, 1934.

10. *Ibid.,* p. 10558.

11. See House Res. 394, 80 *Cong. Rec.* 456, January 15, 1936; Senate Res. 245, 80 *Cong. Rec.* 3427, March 9, 1936; House Res. 442, 80 *Cong. Rec.* 3468, March 9, 1936; House Res. 313, 81 *Cong. Rec.* 8880, August 14, 1937; House Res. 321, 81 *Cong. Rec.* 9295, August 16, 1937; House Res. 342, 81 *Cong. Rec.* 9683, August 21, 1937; Senate Res. 149, 81 *Cong. Rec.* 6786-6787, July 6, 1937; House Res. 365, 82 *Cong. Rec.* 720, December 2, 1937; House Res. 70 and 72, 84 *Cong. Rec.* 805, January 25, 1939; Senate Res. 251, 86 *Cong. Rec.* 3731, April 1, 1940; House Res. 51, 87 *Cong. Rec.* 79, January 8, 1941.

12. In addition to resolutions listed in previous footnote, see Senate Res. 251, 86 *Cong. Rec.* 3731, April 1, 1940; House Res. 51, 87 *Cong. Rec.* 79, January 8, 1941.

13. See Senate Res. 133, 87 *Cong. Rec.* 3950-51, May 13, 1941.

14. See House Res. 21 introduced by Congressman Cox, 89 *Cong. Rec.* 26, January 6, 1943; unanimously approved by the House Rules Committee.

15. See 89 *Cong. Rec.* 235.

16. See resignation speech of Congressman Cox made on the House floor making reference to this charge, September 30, 1943, 89 *Cong. Rec.* 7937.

17. *Ibid.*

18. 89 *Cong. Rec.* 8035, October 4, 1943.

19. 90 *Cong. Rec.* 2123, February 29, 1944.

20. *Broadcasting,* February 28, 1944, p. 9.

21. *Ibid.*

22. *Ibid.,* December 4, 1944, p. 16.

23. *Ibid.,* January 28, 1945, p. 13.

24. 92 *Cong. Rec.* 2219, March 13, 1946.

25. *Ibid.,* p. 9803-9804, July 24, 1946.

26. 93 *Cong. Rec.* 2899, March 31, 1947.

27. Senate Res. 307, 92 *Cong. Rec.* 9803-9804, July 24, 1946.

28. *A Report to the President of Michigan State University from the Committee on the Future of the University,* East Lansing, Michigan, 1959.

CHAPTER 24

Proposals for Legislative Action

Congress has a big responsibility in this field; and the inquiry it has begun can be one of the most important it has ever undertaken—but only if it is followed through.—New York Times

In the first session of the 86th Congress which adjourned in September, 1959, more than 250 bills relating to broadcasting were introduced.[1] As an outgrowth of the long and highly publicized hearings of the House Legislative Oversight Subcommittee, more than 20 bills were introduced to provide for more effective regulation of the broadcasting industry.[2]

Out of all this, the only measure approved by both houses during that first session was S 2424, amending Section 315 of the Communications Act.[3] As pointed out in Chapter 21, that section formerly provided that if a station granted broadcasting time to one political candidate it was required to grant equal time to other candidates. The recent amendment, as previously mentioned, specifically exempts stations from this requirement if a candidate appears only as a part of a bonafide newscast, news interview or similar type of program.

One of the most constructive things which came out of the studies of the Legislative Oversight Subcommittee, and which received comparatively little publicity, was a comprehensive and thoughtfully prepared report making recommendations to Congress for legislative action.[4] While there are parts of this document with which one may take issue, in the opinion of the writer, it is by far the best report made by any special Congressional committee that has ever investigated the Commission. It recognizes that both Congress and the FCC must share the responsibility for the FCC's failure at times to function most efficiently in the public interest. The proposals of the Subcommittee deserve careful and critical consideration.

Wider Latitude for Staff Consultation Suggested. One proposal of the Subcommittee urges Congress to amend Section 5 (c) of the Communications Act to provide wider latitude for consultation by the Commission with members of its staff in the preparation of decisions. In support of this proposal, the Subcommittee in part said:

This so-called 'separation of functions' required by the Communications Act precludes both commissioners and hearing examiners from the use of Commission personnel for advice and consultation when problems arise. Yet, the Commission is expected to perform the function of providing the final decision in each case, based on a massive body of evidence, summaries of evidence provided by the 'review staff,' with whom they are equally unable to consult, and upon whatever further information in the way of proposed findings and conclusions, exceptions, and supporting reasons they receive from the pleadings of the interested parties.

As a result of this situation, the Commission is provided with a staff of experts, with whom it cannot consult without reopening the record, allowing the interested parties to be present, giving opportunity for reply, and needlessly adding to the size and volume of testimony which, in all probabilty, in the more difficult cases, already extends to thousands of pages. The judicial imputation of expertise to Commission decisions under these circumstance is in effect a legal fiction.[5]

This analysis of the situation deserves careful consideration. As the law now stands, the Commission is precluded from consulting with its General Counsel, Chief Engineer, Chief Accountants and their staffs to secure information and advice in preparation of decisions.[6] This restriction seriously handicaps the Commission in disposing of the large volume of cases that must be decided. Both quantity and quality of output have been affected.

There would seem to be no valid reason why members of the Commission should not be free to call upon appropriate members of the staff for help and advice, so long as those staff members have not been engaged, directly or indirectly, in the prosecution or investigation of the case. It undoubtedly would help avoid protracted delays which have been a source of concern to the Commission and the public.

Commissioners Should Write Their Opinions. Another related suggestion is that one Commissioner be made responsible for the writing of the opinion in each adjudicatory case, with the rotation principle followed to distribute equally the work load among the Commissioners.

This proposal should be given careful consideration. In all Federal court cases, one judge prepares and delivers the opinion of the court. This practice might very well be followed in those cases where Commissioners are acting in a judicial capacity.

The involvement of an individual Commissioner in the actual writing and signing of an opinion, permitting him to draw freely upon staff resources for information and advice, would definitely place responsibility at the Commission level. This might do much to restore public confidence in the agency, which, to some extent, has suffered because of a widespread belief that the staff and not the Commission itself plays the major role in deciding cases. Such personal involvement would stimulate the critical faculties of the Commissioner, give him a better knowledge of the facts and a deeper understanding of the issues in the case. This no doubt would contribute to the quality and soundness of opinions and make for greater consistency in Commission decisions.

An objection to this proposal which has been made is that the Commissioners are now overloaded with work and would not have the time to write opinions. This problem, which of course is a real one, might be met if Congress would amend the present law, increasing the number of FCC members, and providing the Commission with wider latitude to consult with staff personnel.

Compulsory Hearings for Station Grants. At the present time, hearings are held in all cases involving competing applications for broadcast facilities. A single application may be granted without a hearing if the Commission finds it to be in the public interest. However, until the recent adoption of the Communications Act Amendments (already discussed in previous chapters), the law provided that "interested parties" might file formal protests against these non-hearing grants.[7] Whether valid or not, the Commission was compelled by law to consider such protests and to hold up decisions in cases until these protests were disposed of. Furthermore, a decision of the Commission on a protest was subject to appeal in the courts and this could further delay final action in the case.

All this added to the work-load of the Commission and at times was responsible for inordinate delays in decisions. This became a source of concern to the Commission as well as to applicants who had to spend extra money in litigation and wait long periods of time before getting a final "go" signal to begin construction of a station.

In view of this situation and the fact that the "gold rush" days of 1952 are over and there is no longer an avalanche of requests for new stations, the legislative Subcommittee suggested that it might be better simply to designate for hearing all applications for licenses, including requests for transfers.[8] The argument advanced was that this would avoid "the unpleasant 'after effects' of Commission decisions which so often never became final until they have progressed to the Courts."[9]

The Subcommittee further stated that in the future "instead of new applications for frequencies, there will be an increasing amount of 'horse trading' among channel owners, and it is through the back door of transfer that the major part of future television license change seems to lie."[10] It was recommended, therefore, that hearings in all such instances should be scheduled, with the Commission required, in the public interest, to examine the qualifications of the assignee alongside those of the present owner. In particular, when multiple owners seek to buy additional facilities, hearings should be held in order to develop full information."[11]

Subsequent to the Subcommittee's report, Congress, as previously mentioned, eliminated the protest procedure referred to above. Now, "interested parties" may, within thirty days, file petitions with the Commission asking that any application be denied. If the reasons advanced appear to be valid, the Commission is required to designate the application for public hearing. If not, the Commission, if it finds the public interest will be served, can make a grant without further delay.

In the light of this new development, to require the holding of public hearing on non-competitive applications to the extent suggested by the Subcommittee, would impose an unnecessary administrative burden on the Commission. With full opportunity now afforded "interested parties" to register formal objections to the grant of an application, and with the Commission obliged by law to consider these objections before taking action, new legislation providing for compulsory hearings, as proposed, does not appear to be necessary.

A Temporary Study Committee on Procedure Needed. An overall study of administrative procedures of the FCC and other independent agencies of the federal level is needed. Careful consideration should be given to the elimination of prolonged, involved and expensive procedures in whatever area of Commission activity they may exist. To the end that improvements may be effectuated, it would be helpful if a temporary study committee (possibly financed by an appropriate foundation) could be set up to make a comprehensive and critical review of the present situation. The Commission of course should be represented on such a committee. Other members might include leaders in the broadcast industry and education, and legal and engineering experts concerned with regulatory procedures at the FCC as well as representatives of Congress who are knowledgeable in the field.

The members of the committee should be chosen carefully because of their specialized knowledge and their ability to think constructively and contribute to the solution of these procedural problems.

Position of Hearing Examiner Should Be Appraised. This same committee could concern itself with another related proposal of the House Subcommittee which calls for a reexamination of the position of the Hearing Examiner in the Commission. The Subcommittee raises questions regarding the operation of the present examiner system as established under the Administrative Procedure Act in 1952, particularly the method of recruiting hearing officers which requires approval of their qualifications by the Civil Service Commission. The Committee suggests considering the establishment of an independent "Office of Federal Administrative Practice" to perform this function. In this connection, the Report of the Subcommittee states:

It would seem that the recruitment and selection of the desired caliber of hearing examiner requires that such tasks be performed by an agency having a major and continuing interest in the field of administrative proceedings. In this way a full understanding of the problems involved in such proceedings and of the capacities required for hearing examiners would be brought to bear in the consideration of what men should be retained as examiners.[12]

306

The Report further recites that "it has been frequently observed that proceedings before such hearing examiners are of too great length, as is often the opinion of the hearing examiner himself," and suggests that the Congress might be helpful "in the direction of eliminating irrelevant and immaterial matters, which currently take up undue time in administrative proceedings."[13]

Whatever the merits of these suggestions may be, they quite appropriately could be studied along with the procedural problems connected with the granting of licenses discussed above.

Ex Parte Representations in Adjudicatory Cases Should be Clearly Prohibited by Law. Another proposal urged by the Subcommittee is that additional legislation should be enacted prohibiting the making of any *ex parte* or extra record representation to any commissioner or any employee of the Commission regarding any proceeding of record, either of a rule-making or adjudicatory character. The Subcommittee would make this applicable to all persons including members of Congress and the executive branch of the government. Any oral or written communications regarding such cases would be required to be made a part of the official record. A failure to comply with these requirements would result in severe civil and criminal penalties. These rules against *ex parte* representations are applicable to Federal courts and certainly they ought to be applicable to administrative agencies in so far as rule-making and adjudicatory proceedings are concerned.

Differences Between Commissions and Courts Should Be Recognized. A word of caution is appropriate here. The important differences between regulatory commissions such as the FCC and courts should be clearly understood. The FCC is far more than a court. It is a public service agency, not only obliged to decide cases, but to conduct experimentation and research and under the continuing obligation to promote "the larger and more effective use of radio in the public interest."[14] The doors of the Commission, therefore, should always be open to members of the public seeking information about the problems of broadcasting, and Commissioners and members of their staff should be free to discuss these problems with outside persons so long as they do not relate to matters in hearing status.

FCC Must Keep Itself Informed. Also, there is another important point to remember. If wise policies and regulations are to be adopted, the Commission and its staff must keep fully informed regarding developments in the communications field. It would not be desirable, therefore, to isolate and insulate them from the public to the same extent as judges who deal only with adjudicatory matters. They should be free to move with intelligent discretion outside Commission walls and talk freely with those who are in a position to provide information that will be helpful in meeting the complex regulatory problems relating to broadcasting and other communication services.

The competent FCC official will make a clear distinction between his legislative and judicial functions. In this sense he has a more difficult job than the judge who serves solely as an adjudicator, and whose official purview is always limited to the written record. The competent Commissioner knows when to talk and when not to talk. He has the obligation of silence and limited vision in adjudicatory cases, but he also has the obligation of communication and wide observation in other areas of his responsibility.

Any legislation, therefore, prohibiting extra-record representations should make this distinction in functions perfectly clear. Should there be the least statutory ambiguity in this respect, the effect would be to restrain and restrict the FCC official in imporant areas of responsibility outside the judicial realm where he ought to be mobile, inquisitive and communicative.

Service Fees for Broadcasters. Finally, the Congressional Subcommittee has recommended that the terms of Commissioners be lengthened and that thought be given to the idea of assessing fees against broadcasters for special services and privileges they receive from the government. The desirability of giving FCC commissioners longer terms has already been mentioned in a favorable light and need not be discussed further here. The proposal for the establishment of service fees has frequently been before Congress and the Commission in various forms over a long period of time and warrants special consideration. Some history should be cited.

As early as 1929, the old Federal Radio Commission received a Congressional slap on the wrist for not working out a system of service fees to be charged applicants for broadcasting facilities. In response, the Chairman of the FRC transmitted to the Senate such a proposal.[15] Congressional interest, however, flagged and the proposal was kept in cold storage for three years.

In 1932, Senator Dill recommended an amendment to the Radio Act which would impose nominal charges upon applicants for broadcast facilities and defray most of the operational costs of the FRC.[16] In support of this amendment he had said in a special report to the Senate that he thought the proposed fees were entirely just, "because without governmental regulation the interference between radio stations would amount to chaos so far as radio reception is concerned." He further explained that the radio stations charged for the use of their facilities and could "well afford to help pay the cost of regulation."[17]

Nothing happened legislatively, but after the FCC was established, there was a resurgence of this type of advocacy in Congress. With the expansion of radio and with mounting profits in the industry, the halls of Congress reverberated more frequently with oratory alleging excessive profiteering and exploitation of publicly owned radio channels and urging that commercial interests be required to pay something for these valuable franchises and to help defray the costs of governmental regulation.[18]

FCC Rebuked by Congress. Rebuked for not bringing to Congress a proposal, the FCC began a comprehensive study of the matter.[19] While this was going on, the House in 1941 approved a bill which would have imposed taxes ranging from 5 to 15 percent on net annual sales of radio time above $100,000.[20]

But the Senate Finance Committee under powerful pressure from the broadcasting industry, refused to go along with the House bill or the FCC proposal and again no legislation was passed.[21]

The following year, Congressman Wigglesworth rebuked the FCC for not recommending a tax plan in lieu of that which had been repudiated by the Committee the year before. He referred to the $30,000,000 net profits then accruing to the broadcast industry on an investment of only $40,-000,000. "It seems to me entirely illogical and unreasonable," he complained, "to allow the industry to continue to obtain any such return from licenses for which they pay nothing under present conditions in this country."[22]

As the broadcasting industry expanded after the War, Congressional grumbling against free use and commercial exploitation of publicly owned radio channels continued. In March, 1950, again responding to the persistent needling of Congress and at the specific request of the Senate Committee on Expenditures in the Executive Departments, the FCC submitted a report classifying its activities for which service fees might be assessed. These included processing all broadcast applications; all authorizations for telephone and telegraph services under FCC jurisdiction; equipment tests, station inspections, and miscellaneous filings such as petitions, motions, etc.[23]

Two years later, in a House debate on whether to cut the FCC's annual budget by $2,000,000, Congressman O'Konski from Wisconsin stated that he knew something about the FCC because he happened to be in the radio industry. "There is no reason under the sun," said he, "why the Federal Communications Commission should cost the taxpayers of this country one cent. . . . For as profitable a business as the radio and television business, it is incredible that they get their licenses for free."

"I know of one television station," he continued, "that was built at a total construction cost of $150,000, and a few weeks after they passed the requirements they sold that station for a million and a quarter dollars. They paid not one red penny for that license. . . . Let us give the Federal Communications Commission the money they need to let this industry expand and grow. But at the same time let us make the radio and television industry foot the bill."[24]

Less than seven months before, Congress had passed the Independent Offices Appropriation Act of 1952 authorizing the head of each governmental agency to prescribe by regulation such fees and charges as he determined to be fair and equitable "taking into consideration direct and indirect costs to the government, value to the recipient, public policy or interest served, and other pertinent facts."[25]

Persistent Congressional Pressure Brings FCC Action. With this enabling legislation applicable to administrative agencies in general, plus the persistent urging by Congressmen for twenty years that broadcasters and other communication companies operating across state lines should bear the cost of their regulation, the FCC at last felt there was a clear directive from Capitol Hill to take positive action. Accordingly, the Commission issued a notice of proposed rule-making, published in the Federal Register on February 3, 1954.[26]

This notice proposed to divide all applications for broadcast authorizations into two main categories. In one, a fee of $325 was to be charged for each broadcast application involving major analysis and action. In the other, a fee of $50.00 was proposed for applications requiring less time and effort to process, such as those involving minor changes in broadcasting equipment.

A schedule of smaller charges was proposed for handling applications for various types of radio stations used by ships, airplanes, land transportation, amateurs, etc. Fees also were included for applications from manufacturers asking for type approval of various kinds of broadcasting equipment and for inspections of radio stations on ships at sea.

In addition, a schedule of charges was set forth for applications from telephone and telegraph companies regulated by the FCC, involving acquisition, construction or extension of facilities, ranging from 30 to 350 dollars.

Congress Strikes a Fatal Blow. And now what was the reaction of Congress? Were there speeches commending the Commission for finally doing what it so often had been scolded for not doing? No such eloquence emanated from Capitol Hill. On the contrary, a week before the deadline for filing comments in the proceeding, the Senate Interstate and Foreign Commerce Committee, which exercises legislative jurisdiction over the FCC, unanimously passed a resolution and transmitted it to the Chairman of the Commission, saying that it had concluded, after inquiry, that any departure from the existing structure of licensing should be resolved specifically by the Congress itself and that the FCC should suspend the proceeding.[27]

This struck the fatal blow. Despite the enabling legislation passed only three years before and the intermittent agitations of Congress for service fees for almost three decades, the Commission simply could not buck the unanimous opposition of this powerful Senate committee. The case was dismissed and the piles of official papers accumulated by the FCC in the proceeding were consigned to the docket graveyard.[28]

It might serve the public interest, if the hearings on this matter could be revived and a system of small service and license fees adopted. A tax is not being suggested, only a system of small charges commensurate with the services rendered broadcasters is proposed. It takes only a little calculating to see that such a system would go far in making regulation self-sustaining and would provide additional funds to make it more effective.

The broadcasting industry might well support such a proposal, since the additional revenue which it would bring in could help speed up administrative processes at the Commission and avoid some of the inordinate delays in decisions from which the broadcasters have suffered in recent years.

In the light of history, however, it is clearly the responsibility of Congress and not the FCC to take the initiative in the matter.

FCC's Authority Over Broadcast Programming Should Be Clarified. Additional legislation of a fundamental nature is needed which was not mentioned in the Report of the House Subcommittee on Legislative Oversight. Of paramount importance is the need for statutory clarification as to the Commission's authority relating to programs carried by broadcast stations.

While the Courts have held that under the present law the Commission does have legislative authority to consider program service in the exercise of its licensing functions, there is some vagueness and ambiguity in the wording of the statute that has been troublesome. Section 326 of the Communications Act says the Commission cannot censor programs. Well, what is censorship? The courts have clearly held that the term, when interpreted in connection with the provisions of the Act, prohibits critical review by the FCC of particular programs carried by stations except where violation of specific laws such as the indecency or lottery statutes may be involved. They have not, however, precluded FCC review of the over-all performance of a station when it comes up for renewal of its license.

Despite this, there has been a tremendous amount of speaking and writing in and out of Congress for the past twenty-five years to the effect that Congress never really intended to give the Commission the power. As previously pointed out, one of the present Commissioners has stated recently that the FCC exceeds its authority when it requires applicants for broadcast facilities to file any program information except where infractions against lottery laws and the like are involved.[29] On the other hand, another Commissioner, as late as August 28, 1959, has stated that the Commission has a positive duty to review the over-all programming of a station when it comes up for renewal of its license.[30] Congress ought to eliminate the confusion by legislation to the extent constitutionally possible. There ought not to be a continuing debate over what the Commission's authority is.

In Conclusion. In conclusion, it can be said that the future of broadcast regulation will depend a great deal upon Congressional action. The recent Congressional probe was helpful in drawing attention to some of the serious regulatory problems of the FCC that need correction. Despite the sensational hearings on FCC operations, and the introduction of numerous bills in Congress to correct alleged evils, not a single piece of legislation

311

growing out of the probe was adopted during the 1st Session of the 86th Congress.

However, some important legislation designed to improve broadcast regulation and licensee responsibility was adopted during the 2nd session. Congress is to be commended for this. But the long and drawn out investigations conducted by Congress during the past four years have revealed many other critical problems that call for constructive legislation. It is hoped that Congress, upon the basis of extensive studies made and voluminous hearing records accumulated, will respond with the needed legislation. (See recent Landis report cited in bibliography)

The *New York Times* said on March 11, 1958, in referring to the investigation of the FCC, then attracting national attention, "Congress has a big responsibility in the field; and the inquiry it has begun can be one of the most important it has ever undertaken—but only if it is followed through."[31]

NOTES

1. *Broadcasting,* September 14, 1959, p. 64.
2. *Ibid.*
3. See *Cong. Rec.* 16308-16313, September 2, 1959 and 16342-16347, September 3, 1959.
4. *Regulation of Broadcasting, Half Century of Government Regulation of Broadcasting and the Need for Further Legislative Action;* a study for the Committee on Interstate and Foreign Commerce, House of Representatives, 85th Congress, Second Session on H. Res. 99, United States Government Printing Office, Washington, 1958.
5. *Ibid.,* pp. 157-158.
6. *Ibid.*
7. *Ibid.*
8. *Ibid.,* p. 166.
9. *Ibid.*
10. *Ibid.*
11. *Ibid.*
12. *Ibid.,* p. 169.
13. *Ibid.,* p. 170.
14. Section 303(g) Communications Act of 1934, 48 Stat. 1082.
15. See 70 *Cong. Rec.* 5058, March 2, 1929 and 72 *Cong. Rec.* 342, December 10, 1929. Also see Senate Document No. 47, 71st Congress, 2nd Session, 1929, for the full text of the FRC Chairman's letter.
16. 76 *Cong. Rec.* 542, December 16, 1932.
17. Senate Report No. 564, pp. 11, 12; 72nd Congress, 1st Session.
18. See speech on floor of House by Congressman Lawrence J. Connery, April 11, 1938, 83 *Cong. Rec.* 5284; also see discussion of Congressman Richard B. Wigglesworth, February 6, 1939, 84 *Cong. Rec.* 1164-1166.
19. *Broadcasting,* October 27, 1941, p. 9.
20. See remarks of Congressman Wigglesworth, 88 *Cong. Rec.* 551, January 22, 1942.
21. *Ibid.,* pp. 551-552.

22. *Ibid.*
23. 96 *Cong. Rec.* A1914, A1915, March 8, 1950.
24. 98 *Cong. Rec.* 2538, 2539, March 19, 1952.
25. 59 Stat. 597.
26. 19 Fed. Reg. 622-624.
27. 100 *Cong. Rec.* 3782, March 24, 1954.
28. *FCC Annual Report,* 1954, p. 16.
29. However, Commissioner Craven did vote to approve the Report and Statement of the Commission adopted July 27, 1960, which reads in part:

In the fulfillment of his obligation the broadcaster should consider the tastes, needs and desires of the public he is licensed to serve in developing his programming and should exercise conscientious efforts not only to ascertain them but also to carry them out as well as he reasonably can. He should reasonably attempt to meet all such needs and interests on an equitable basis. Particular areas of interest and types of appropriate service may, of course, differ from community to community, and from time to time. However, the Commission does expect its broadcast licensees to take the necessary steps to inform themselves of the real needs and interests of the areas they serve and to provide programming which in fact constitutes a diligent effort, in good faith, to provide for those needs and interests.

30. "The Role of the FCC in Programming," address of Commissioner Fredrick W. Ford before the West Virginia Broadcasters Association, White Sulphur Springs, West Virginia, August 28, 1959, FCC Mimeograph No. 77193.
31. *New York Times,* March 11, 1958, p. 28.

Communications Act of 1934, as Amended*

AN ACT

To provide for the regulation of interstate and foreign communication by wire or radio, and for other purposes.

Be it enacted by the Senate and House of Representatives of the United States of America in Congress assembled,

TITLE I—GENERAL PROVISIONS

PURPOSES OF ACT; CREATION OF FEDERAL COMMUNICATIONS COMMISSION

SECTION 1. For the purpose of regulating interstate and foreign commerce in communication by wire and radio so as to make available, so far as possible, to all the people of the United States a rapid, efficient, Nation-wide, and world-wide wire and radio communication service with adequate facilities at reasonable charges, for the purpose of the national defense, for the purpose of promoting safety of life and property through the use of wire and radio communication, and for the purpose of securing a more effective execution of this policy by centralizing authority heretofore granted by law to several agencies and by granting additional authority with respect to interstate and foreign commerce in wire and radio communication, there is hereby created a commission to be known as the "Federal Communications Commission", which shall be constituted as hereinafter provided, and which shall execute and enforce the provisions of this Act.

APPLICATION OF ACT

SEC. 2. (a) The provisions of this Act shall apply to all interstate and foreign communication by wire or radio and all interstate and foreign transmission of energy by radio, which originates and/or is received within the United States, and to all persons engaged within the United States in such communication or such transmission of energy by radio, and to the licensing and regulating of all radio stations as hereinafter provided; but it shall not apply to persons engaged in wire or radio communication or transmission in the Philippine Islands or the Canal Zone, or to wire or radio communication or transmission wholly within the Philippine Islands or the Canal Zone.

(b) Subject to the provisions of section 301, nothing in this Act shall be construed to apply or to give the Commission jurisdiction with respect to (1)

---

* Only parts of the Act relating to broadcasting have been included. The full text of the Act can be secured at nominal cost from the U. S. Government Printing Office, Washington, D. C. Also it is reproduced in Statutes at Large and Pike and Fisher IRR 10:11-157.

charges, classifications, practices, services, facilities, or regulations for or in connection with intrastate communication service by wire or radio of any carrier, or (2) any carrier engaged in interstate or foreign communication solely through physical connection with the facilities of another carrier not directly or indirectly controlling or controlled by, or under direct or indirect common control with such carrier, or (3) any carrier engaged in interstate or foreign communication solely through connection by radio, or by wire and radio, with facilities, located in an adjoining State or in Canada or Mexico (where they adjoin the State in which the carrier is doing business), or another carrier not directly or indirectly controlling or controlled by, or under direct or indirect common control with such carrier, or (4) any carrier to which clause (2) or clause (3) would be applicable except for furnishing interstate mobile radio land vehicles in Canada or Mexico; except that sections 201 through 205 of this Act, both inclusive, shall, except as otherwise provided therein, apply to carriers described in clause (2), (3) and (4).

DEFINITIONS

SEC. 3. For the purposes of this Act, unless the context otherwise requires—

(a) "Wire communication" or "communication by wire" means the transmission of writing, signs, signals, pictures, and sounds of all kinds by aid of wire, cable, or other like connection between the points of origin and reception of such transmission, including all instrumentalities, facilities, apparatus, and services (among other things, the receipt, forwarding, and delivery of communications) incidental to such transmission.

(b) "Radio communication" or "communication by radio" means the transmission by radio of writing, signs, signals, pictures, and sounds of all kinds including all instrumentalities, facilities, apparatus, and services (among other things, the receipt, forwarding, and delivery of communications) incidental to such transmission.

(c) "Licensee" means the holder of a radio station license granted or continued in force under authority of this Act.

(d) "Transmission of energy by radio" or "radio transmission of energy" includes both such transmission and all instrumentalities, facilities, and services incidental to such transmission.

(e) "Interstate communication" or "interstate transmission" means communication or transmission (1) from any State, Territory, or possession of the United States (other than the Philippine Islands and the Canal Zone), or the District of Columbia, to any other State, Territory, or possession of the United States (other than the Philippine Islands and the Canal Zone), or the District of Columbia, (2) from or to the United States to or from the Philippine Islands or the Canal Zone, insofar as such communication or transmission takes place within the United States, or (3) between points within the United States but through a foreign country; but shall not, with respect to the provisions of Title II of this Act, include wire communication between points within the same State, Territory, or possession of the United States, or the District of Columbia, through any place outside thereof, if such communication is regulated by a State commission.

(f) "Foreign communication" or "foreign transmission" means communication or transmission from or to any place in the United States to or from a foreign country, or between a station in the United States and a mobile station located outside the United States.

(g) "United States" means the several States and Territories, the District of

Columbia, and the possessions of the United States, but does not include the Philippine Islands or the Canal Zone.

(h) "Common carrier" or "carrier" means any person engaged as a common carrier for hire, in interstate or foreign communication by wire or radio or in interstate or foreign radio transmission of energy, except where reference is made to common carriers not subject to this Act; but a person engaged in radio broadcasting shall not, insofar as such person is so engaged, be deemed a common carrier.

(i) "Person" includes an individual, partnership, association, joint-stock company, trust, or corporation.

(j) "Corporation" includes any corporation, joint-stock company, or association.

(k) "Radio station" or "station" means a station equipped to engage in radio communication or radio transmission of energy.

(l) "Mobile station" means a radio-communication station capable of being moved and which ordinarily does move.

(m) "Land station" means a station, other than a mobile station, used for radio communication with mobile stations.

(n) "Mobile service" means the radio-communication service carried on between mobile stations and land stations, and by mobile stations communicating among themselves.

(o) "Broadcasting" means the dissemination of radio communications intended to be received by the public, directly or by the intermediary of relay stations.

(p) "Chain broadcasting" means simultaneous broadcasting of an identical program by two or more connected stations.

(q) "Amateur station" means a radio station operated by a duly authorized person interested in radio technique solely with a personal aim and without pecuniary interest.

(r) "Telephone exchange service" means service within a telephone exchange, or within a connected system of telephone exchanges within the same exchange area operated to furnish to subscribers intercommunicating service of the character ordinarily furnished by a single exchange, and which is covered by the exchange service charge.

(s) "Telephone toll service" means telephone service between stations in different exchange areas for which there is made a separate charge not included in contracts with subscribers for exchange service.

(t) "State commission" means the commission, board, or official (by whatever name designated) which under the laws of any State has regulatory jurisdiction with respect to intrastate operations of carriers.

(u) "Connecting carrier" means a carrier described in clause (2) of section 2 (b).

(v) "State" includes the District of Columbia and the Territories and possessions.

(w) (1) "Ship" or "vessel" includes every description of watercraft or other artificial contrivance, except aircraft, used or capable of being used as a means of transportation on water, whether or not it is actually afloat.

(2) A ship shall be considered a passenger ship if it carries or is licensed or certified to carry more than twelve passengers.

(3) A cargo ship means any ship not a passenger ship.

(4) A passenger is any person carried on board a ship or vessel except (1) the officers and crew actually employed to man and operate the ship, (2) persons employed to carry on the business of the ship, and (3) persons on board a ship

317

when they are carried, either because of the obligation laid upon the master to carry shipwrecked, distressed, or other persons in like or similar situations or similar situations or by reason of any circumstances over which neither the master, the owner, nor the charterer (if any) has control.

(x) "Auto-alarm" on a foreign ship means an automatic alarm receiver which has been approved by the country to which the ship belongs, provided the United States and the country to which the ship belongs are both parties to the same treaty, convention, or agreement prescribing the requirements for such apparatus. "Auto-alarm" on a ship of the United States subject to the provisions of Part II of Title III of this Act means an automatic alarm receiver complying with law and approved by the Commission. Nothing in this Act or in any other provision of law shall be construed to require the recognition of an auto-alarm as complying with Part II of Title III of this Act, on a foreign ship subject to such part, whose country or origin is not a party to a treaty, convention, or agreement with the United States in regard to such apparatus.

(y) (1) For the purpose of Part II of Title III, a "qualified operator" or "operator" on a foreign ship means a person holding a certificate as such complying with the provisions of the General Radio Regulations annexed to the International Telecommunication Convention in force, or complying with an agreement or treaty between the United States and the country to which the ship belongs.

(2) For the purpose of Parts II and III of Title III, a "qualified operator" or "operator" on a ship of the United States means a person holding a radio operator's license of the proper class, as prescribed and issued by the Commission.

(z) "Harbor" or "port" means any place to which ships may resort for shelter or to load or unload passengers or goods, or to obtain fuel, water, or supplies. This term shall apply to such places whether proclaimed public or not and whether natural or artificial.

(aa) "Safety convention" means the International Convention for the Safety of Life at Sea in force and the regulations referred to therein.

(bb) "Station license," "radio station license," or "licensee" means that instrument of authorization required by this Act or the rules and regulations of the Commission made pursuant to this Act, for the use or operation of apparatus for transmission of energy, or communications, or signals by radio, by whatever name the instrument may be designated by the Commission.

(cc) "Broadcast station," "broadcasting station," or "radio broadcast station" means a radio station equipped to engage in broadcasting as herein defined.

(dd) "Construction permit" or "permit for construction" means that instrument of authorization required by this Act or the rules and regulations of the Commission made pursuant to this Act for the construction of a station or the installation of apparatus, for the transmission of energy, or communications, or signals by radio, by whatever name the instrument may be designated by the Commission.

(ee) "Existing installation," as used in section 355 of this act, means an installation installed on a ship prior to November 19, 1952, in the case of a United States ship subject to the radio provisions of the Safety Convention, or one installed on a ship prior to a date one year after the effective date of this subsection in the case of other ships subject to Part II of Title III of this Act.

(ff) "New installation," as used in sections 355 and 356 of this Act, means an installation which replaces an existing installation or, in the case of a United States ship subject to the radio provisions of the Safety Convention, one installed on a ship subsequent to November 19, 1952, and, in the case of other ships subject to Part II of Title III of this Act, one which is installed subsequent to a date one year after the effective date of this subsection.

SEC. 4. (a) The Federal Communications Commission (in this Act referred to as the "Commission") shall be composed of seven commissioners appointed by the President, by and with the advice and consent of the Senate, one of whom the President shall designate as chairman.

(b) Each member of the Commission shall be a citizen of the United States. No member of the Commission or person in its employ shall be financially interested in the manufacture or sale of radio apparatus or of apparatus for wire or radio communication; in communication by wire or radio or in radio transmission of energy; in any company furnishing services or such apparatus to any company engaged in communication by wire or radio or to any company manufacturing or selling apparatus used for communication by wire or radio; or in any company owning stocks, bonds, or other securities of any such company; nor be in the employ of or hold any official relation to any person subject to any of the provisions of this Act, nor own stocks, bonds, or other securities of any corporation subject to any of the provisions of this Act. Such commissioners shall not engage in any other business, vocation, or employment. Any such commissioner serving as such after one year from the date of enactment of the Communications Act Amendments, 1952, shall not for a period of one year following the termination of his services as a commissioner represent any person before the Commission in a professional capacity, except that this restriction shall not apply to any commissioner who has served the full term for which he was appointed. Not more than four commissioners shall be members of the same political party.

(c) The commissioners first appointed under this Act shall continue in office for the terms of one, two, three, four, five, six, and seven years, respectively, from the date of the taking effect of this Act, the term of each to be designated by the President, but their successors shall be appointed for terms of seven years and until their successors are appointed and have qualified, except that they shall not continue to serve beyond the expiration of the next session of Congress subsequent to the expiration of said fixed term of office; except that any person chosen to fill a vacancy shall be appointed only for the unexpired term of the commissioner whom he succeeds. No vacancy in the Commission shall impair the right of the remaining commissioners to exercise all the powers of the Commission.

(d) Each commissioner shall receive an annual salary of $10,000, payable in monthly installments.*

(e) The principal office of the Commission shall be in the District of Columbia, where its general sessions shall be held; but whenever the convenience of the public or of the parties may be promoted or delay or expense prevented thereby, the Commission may hold special sessions in any part of the United States.

(f) (1) The Commission shall have authority, subject to the provisions of the civil-service laws and the Classification Act of 1949, as amended, to appoint such officers, engineers, accountants, attorneys, inspectors, examiners, and other employees as are necessary in the exercise of its functions.

(2) Without regard to the civil-service laws, but subject to the Classification

* This subsection (d) has been superseded by 5 U.S.C. Sections 2204 (4), 2205 (a) (45), 75 Stat. 737. The annual salary for the Chairman of the FCC now is $20,500 and for other members $20,000.

Act of 1949, each commissioner may appoint a legal assistant, an engineering assistant, and a secretary, each of whom shall perform such duties as such commissioner shall direct. In addition, the chairman of the Commission may appoint, without regard to the civil-service laws, but subject to the Classification Act of 1949, an administrative assistant who shall perform such duties as the chairman shall direct.

(3) The Commission shall fix a reasonable rate of extra compensation for overtime services of engineers in charge and radio engineers of the Field Engineering and Monitoring Bureau of the Federal Communications Commission, who may be required to remain on duty between the hours of 5 o'clock postmeridian and 8 o'clock antemeridian or on Sundays or holidays to perform services in connection with the inspection of ship radio equipment and apparatus for the purposes of Part II of Title III of this Act or the Great Lakes Agreement, on the basis of one-half day's additional pay for each two hours or fraction thereof of at least one hour that the overtime extends beyond 5 o'clock postmeridian (but not to exceed two and one-half days' pay for the full period from 5 o'clock postmeridian to 8 o'clock antemeridian) and two additional days' pay for Sunday or holiday duty. The said extra compensation for overtime services shall be paid by the master, owner, or agent of such vessel to the local United States collector of customs or his representative, who shall deposit such collection into the Treasury of the United States to an appropriately designated receipt account: Provided, That the amounts of such collections received by the said collector of customs or his representatives shall be covered into the Treasury as miscellaneous receipts; and the payments of such extra compensation to the several employees entitled thereto shall be made from the annual appropriations for salaries and expenses of the Commission: Provided further, That to the extent that the annual appropriations which are hereby authorized to be made from the general fund of the Treasury are insufficient, there are hereby authorized to be appropriated from the general fund of the Treasury such additional amounts as may be necessary to the extent that the amounts of such receipts are in excess of the amounts appropriated: Provided further, That such extra compensation shall be paid if such field employees have been ordered to report for duty and have so reported whether the actual inspection of the radio equipment or apparatus takes place or not: And provided further, That in those ports where customary working hours are other than those hereinabove mentioned, the engineers in charge are vested with authority to regulate the hours of such employees so as to agree with prevailing working hours in said ports where inspections are to be made, but nothing contained in this proviso shall be construed in any manner to alter the length of a working day for the engineers in charge and radio engineers or the overtime pay herein fixed.

(g) The Commission may make such expenditures (including expenditures for rent and personal services at the seat of government and elsewhere, for office supplies, law books, periodicals, and books of reference, for printing and binding) for land for use as sites for radio monitoring stations and related facilities, including living quarters where necessary in remote areas, for the construction of such stations and facilities, and for the improvement, furnishing, equipping and repairing of such stations and facilities, and of laboratories and other related facilities (including construction of minor subsidiary buildings and structures not exceeding $25,000 in any one instance) used in connection with technical research activities, as may be necessary for the execution of the functions vested in the Commission and as from time to time may be appropriated for by Congress. All expenditures of the Commission, including all necessary expenses for transportation incurred by the commissioners or by their employees, under their orders, in making any investigation or upon any official business in any other places than in the city of Washington, shall be allowed and paid on the presentation of itemized vouchers therefor approved by the chairman of the Commission or by such other member or officer thereof as may be designated by the Commission for that purpose.

(h) Four members of the Commission shall constitute a quorum thereof. The Commission shall have an official seal which shall be judicially noticed.

(i) The Commission may perform any and all acts, make such rules and regulations, and issue such orders, not inconsistent with this Act, as may be necessary in the execution of its functions.

(j) The Commission may conduct its proceedings in such manner as will best conduce to the proper dispatch of business and to the ends of justice. No commissioner shall participate in any hearing or proceeding in which he has a pecuniary interest. Any party may appear before the Commission and be heard in person or by attorney. Every vote and official act of the Commission shall be entered of record, and its proceedings shall be public upon the request of any party interested. The Commission is authorized to withhold publication of records or proceedings containing secret information affecting the national defense.

(k) The Commission shall make an annual report to Congress, copies of which shall be distributed as are other reports transmitted to Congress. Such report shall contain: (1) Such information and data collected by the Commission as may be considered of value in the determination of questions connected with the regulation of interstate and foreign wire and radio communication and radio transmission of energy; (2) Such information and data concerning the functioning of the Commission as will be of value to Congress in appraising the amount and character of the work and accomplishments of the Commission and the adequacy of its staff and equipment; provided, that the first and second annual reports following the date of enactment of the Communications Act Amendments, 1952, shall set forth in detail the number and caption of pending applications requesting approval of transfer of control or assignment of a broadcasting station license, or construction permits for new broadcasting stations, or for increases in power, or for changes of frequency of existing broadcasting stations at the beginning and end of the period covered by such reports; (3) (Repealed)* (4) An itemized statement of all funds expended during the preceding year by the Commission, of the sources of such funds, and of the authority in this Act or elsewhere under which such expenditures were made; and (5) Specific recommendations to Congress as to additional legislation which the Commission deems necessary or desirable, including all legislative proposals submitted for approval to the Director of the Bureau of the Budget.

(1) All reports of investigations made by the Commission shall be entered of record, and a copy thereof shall be furnished to the party who may have complained, and to any common carrier or licensee that may have been complained of.

(m) The Commission shall provide for the publication of its reports and decisions in such form and manner as may be best adapted for public information and use, and such authorized publications shall be competent evidence of the reports and decisions of the Commission therein contained in all courts of the

* Deleted by Pub. L. No. 554 (82d Cong.), July 16, 1952, 74 Stat. 245, 249. Required Commission report as to new employees and persons leaving the Commission's employ.

United States and of the several States without any further proof or authentication thereof.

(n) Rates of compensation of persons appointed under this section shall be subject to the reduction applicable to officers and employees of the Federal Government generally.

(o) For the purpose of obtaining maximum effectiveness from the use of radio and wire communications in connection with safety of life and property, the Commission shall investigate and study all phases of the problem and the best methods of obtaining the cooperation and coordination of these systems.

ORGANIZATION AND FUNCTIONING OF THE COMMISSION

SEC. 5. (a) The member of the Commission designated by the President as chairman shall be the chief executive officer of the Commission. It shall be his duty to preside at all meetings and sessions of the Commission, to represent the Commission in all matters relating to legislation and legislative reports, except that any commissioner may present his own or minority views or supplemental reports, to represent the Commission in all matters requiring conferences or communications with other governmental officers, departments or agencies, and generally to coordinate and organize the work of the Commission in such manner as to promote prompt and efficient disposition of all matters within the jurisdiction of the Commission. In the case of a vacancy in the office of the chairman of the Commission, or the absence or inability of the chairman to serve, the Commission may temporarily designate one of its members to act as chairman until the cause or circumstance requiring such designation shall have been eliminated or corrected.

(b) Within six months after the enactment of the Communications Act Amendments, 1952, and from time to time thereafter as the Commission may find necessary, the Commission shall organize its staff into (1) integrated bureaus, to function on the basis of the Commission's principal workload operations, and (2) such other divisional organizations as the Commission may deem necessary. Each such integrated bureau shall include such legal, engineering, accounting, administrative, clerical, and other personnel as the Commission may determine to be necessary to perform its functions.

(c) The Commission shall establish a special staff of employees, hereinafter in this Act referred to as the "review staff," which shall consist of such legal, engineering, accounting, and other personnel as the Commission deems necessary. The review staff shall be directly responsible to the Commission and shall not be made a part of any bureau or divisional organization of the Commission. Its work shall not be supervised or directed by any employee of the Commission other than a member of the review staff whom the Commission may designate as the head of such staff. The review staff shall perform no duties or functions other than to assist the Commission, in cases of adjudication (as defined in the Administrative Procedure Act) which have been designated for hearing, by preparing a summary of the evidence presented at any such hearing, by preparing, after an initial decision but prior to oral argument, a compilation of the facts material to the exceptions and replies thereto filed by the parties, and by preparing for the Commission or any member or members thereof, without recommendations and in accordance with specific directions from the Commission or such member or members, memoranda, opinions, decisions, and orders. The Commission shall not permit any employee who is not a member of the review staff to perform the duties and functions which are to be performed by the review staff; but this shall not be construed to limit the duties and functions

322

which any assistant or secretary appointed pursuant to section 4(f) (2) may perform for the commissioner by whom he was appointed.

(d) (1) Except as provided in section 409, the Commission may, when necessary to the proper functioning of the Commission and the prompt and orderly conduct of its business, by order assign or refer any portion of its work, business, or functions to an individual commissioner or commissioners or to a board composed of one or more employees of the Commission, to be designated by such order for action thereon, and may at any time amend, modify, or rescind any such order of assignment or reference. Any order, decision, or report made, or other action taken, pursuant to any such order of assignment or reference shall, unless reviewed pursuant to paragraph (2), have the same force and effect, and shall be made, evidenced, and enforced in the same manner, as orders, decisions, reports, or other action of the Commission.

(2) Any person aggrieved by any such order, decision, or report may file an application for review by the Commission, within such time and in such form as the Commission shall prescribe, and every such application shall be passed upon by the Commission. If the Commission grants the application, it may affirm, modify, or set aside such order, decision, report, or action, or may order a rehearing upon such order, decision, report, or action under section 405.

(3) The secretary and seal of the Commission shall be the secretary and seal of each individual commissioner or board.

(e) Meetings of the Commission shall be held at regular intervals, not less frequently than once each calendar month, at which times the functioning of the Commission and the handling of its work load shall be reviewed and such orders shall be entered and other action taken as may be necessary or appropriate to expedite the prompt and orderly conduct of the business of the Commission with the objective of rendering a final decision (1) within three months from the date of filing in all original application, renewal, and transfer cases in which it will not be necessary to hold a hearing, and (2) within six months from the final date of the hearing in all hearing cases; and the Commission shall promptly report to the Congress each such case which has been pending before it more than such three- or six-month period, respectively, stating the reasons therefor.

TITLE III—PROVISIONS RELATING TO RADIO

PART I—GENERAL PROVISIONS

LICENSE FOR RADIO COMMUNICATION OR TRANSMISSION OF ENERGY

SECTION 301. It is the purpose of this Act, among other things, to maintain the control of the United States over all the channels of interstate and foreign radio transmission; and to provide for the use of such channels, but not the ownership thereof, by persons for limited periods of time, under licenses granted by Federal authority, and no such license shall be construed to create any right, beyond the terms, conditions, and periods of the license. No person shall use or operate any apparatus for the transmission of energy or communications or signals by radio (a) from one place in any Territory or possession of the United States or in the District of Columbia to another place in the same Territory, possession, or District; or (b) from any State, Territory, or possession of the United States, or from the District of Columbia to any other State, Territory, or possession of the United States; or (c) from any place in any State, Territory, or possession of the United States, or in the District of Columbia, to any place in any foreign country or to any vessel; or (d) within any State when the effects of such use extend beyond the borders of said State, or when interference is caused by such use or operation with the trasnmission of such energy, communications, or signals from within said State to any place beyond its borders, or from any place beyond its borders to any place within said State, or with the transmission or reception of such energy, communications, or signals from and/or to places beyond the borders of said State; or (e) upon any vessel or aircraft of the United States; or (f) upon any other mobile stations within the jurisdiction of the United States, except under and in accordance with this Act and with a license in that behalf granted under the provisions of this Act.

ZONES

SEC. 302. [Repealed by Pub. L. No. 652 (74th Cong.), June 5, 1936, 49 Stat. 1475.]

GENERAL POWERS OF COMMISSION

SEC. 303. Except as otherwise provided in this Act, the Commission from time to time, as public convenience, interest, or necessity requires, shall—

(a) Classify radio stations;

(b) Prescribe the nature of the service to be rendered by each class of licensed stations and each station within any class;

(c) Assign bands of frequencies to the various classes of stations, and assign frequencies for each individual station and determine the power which each station shall use and the time during which it may operate;

(d) Determine the location of classes of stations or individual stations;

(e) Regulate the kind of apparatus to be used with respect to its external effects and the purity and sharpness of the emissions from each station and from the apparatus therein;

(f) Make such regulations not inconsistent with law as it may deem necessary to prevent interference between stations and to carry out the provisions of this Act: *Provided, however,* That changes in the frequencies, authorized power, or in the times of operation of any station, shall not be made without the consent of the station licensee unless, after a public hearing, the Commission shall determine that such changes will promote public convenience or interest or will serve public necessity, or the provisions of this Act will be more fully complied with;

(g) Study new uses for radio, provide for experimental uses of frequencies, and generally encourage the larger and more effective use of radio in the public interest;

(h) Have authority to establish areas or zones to be served by any station;

(i) Have authority to make special regulations applicable to radio stations engaged in chain broadcasting;

(j) Have authority to make general rules and regulations requiring stations to keep such records of programs, transmissions of energy, communications, or signals as it may deem desirable;

(k) Have authority to exclude from the requirements of any regulations in whole or in part any radio station upon railroad rolling stock, or to modify such regulations in its discretion;

(l) Have authority to prescribe the qualifications of station operators, to classify them according to the duties to be performed, to fix the forms of such licenses, and to issue them to such citizens of the United States as the Commission finds qualified; except that in issuing licenses for the operation of radio sta-

324

tions on aircraft the Commission may, if it finds that the public interest will be served thereby, waive the requirement of citizenship in the case of persons holding United States pilot certificates or in the case of persons holding foreign aircraft pilot certificates which are valid in the United States on the basis of reciprocal agreements entered into with foreign governments;

(m) (1) Have authority to suspend the license of any operator upon proof sufficient to satisfy the Commission that the licensee—

(A) Has violated any provision of any Act, treaty, or convention binding on the United States, which the Commission is authorized to administer, or any regulation made by the Commission under any such Act, treaty, or convention; or

(B) Has failed to carry out a lawful order of the master or person lawfully in charge of the ship or aircraft on which he is employed; or

(C) Has willfully damaged or permitted radio apparatus or installations to be damaged; or

(D) Has transmitted superfluous radio communications or signals or communications containing profane or obscene words, language, or meaning, or has knowingly transmitted—

(1) False or deceptive signals or communications, or

(2) A call signal or letter which has not been assigned by proper authority to the station he is operating; or

(E) Has willfully or maliciously interfered with any other radio communications or signals; or

(F) Has obtained or attempted to obtain, or has assisted another to obtain or attempt to obtain, an operator's license by fraudulent means.

(2) No order of suspension of any operator's license shall take effect until fifteen days' notice in writing thereof, stating the cause for the proposed suspension, has been given to the operator licensee who may make written application to the Commission at any time within said fifteen days for a hearing upon such order. The notice to the operator licensee shall not be effective until actually received by him, and from that time he shall have fifteen days in which to mail the said application. In the event that physical conditions prevent mailing of the application at the expiration of the fifteen-day period, the application shall then be mailed as soon as possible thereafter, accompanied by a satisfactory explanation of the delay. Upon receipt by the Commission of such application for hearing, said order of suspension shall be held in abeyance until the conclusion of the hearing which shall be conducted under such rules as the Commission may prescribe. Upon the conclusion of said hearing the Commission may affirm, modify, or revoke said order of suspension.

(n) Have authority to inspect all radio installations associated with stations required to be licensed by any Act or which are subject to the provisions of any Act, treaty, or convention binding on the United States, to ascertain whether in construction, installation, and operation they conform to the requirements of the rules and regulations of the Commission, the provisions of any Act, the terms of any treaty or convention binding on the United States, and the conditions of the license or other instrument of authorization under which they are constructed, installed, or operated.

(o) Have authority to designate call letters of all stations;

(p) Have authority to cause to be published such call letters and such other announcements and data as in the judgment of the Commission may be required for the efficient operation of radio stations subject to the jurisdiction of the United States and for the proper enforcement of this Act;

(q) Have authority to require the painting and/or illumination of radio towers if and when in its judgment such towers constitute, or there is a reasonable possibility that they may constitute, a menace to air navigation.

(r) Make such rules and regulations and prescribe such restrictions and conditions, not inconsistent with law, as may be necessary to carry out the provisions of this Act, or any international radio or wire communications, treaty or convention, or regulations annexed thereto, including any treaty or convention insofar as it relates to the use of radio, to which the United States is or may hereafter become a party.

WAIVER BY LICENSEE

SEC. 304. No station license shall be granted by the Commission until the applicant therefor shall have signed a waiver of any claim to the use of any particular frequency or of the ether as against the regulatory power of the United States because of the previous use of the same, whether by license or otherwise.

GOVERNMENT-OWNED STATIONS

SEC. 305. (a) Radio stations belonging to and operated by the United States shall not be subject to the provisions of sections 301 and 303 of this Act. All such Government stations shall use such frequencies as shall be assigned to each or to each class by the President. All such stations, except stations on board naval and other Government vessels while at sea or beyond the limits of the continental United States, when transmitting any radio communication or signal other than a communication or signal relating to Government business, shall conform to such rules and regulations designed to prevent interference with other radio stations and the rights of others as the Commission may prescribe.

(b) Radio stations on board vessels of the United States Shipping Board Bureau or the United States Shipping Board Merchant Fleet Corporation or the Inland and Coastwise Waterways Service shall be subject to the provisions of this title.

(c) All stations owned and operated by the United States, except mobile stations of the Army of the United States, and all other stations on land and sea, shall have special call letters designated by the Commission.

FOREIGN SHIPS

SEC. 306. Section 301 of this Act shall not apply to any person sending radio communications or signals on a foreign ship while the same is within the jurisdiction of the United States, but such communications or signals shall be transmitted only in accordance with such regulations designed to prevent interference as may be promulgated under the authority of this Act.

ALLOCATION OF FACILITIES; TERM OF LICENSES

SEC. 307. (a) The Commission, if public convenience, interest, or necessity will be served thereby, subject to the limitations of this Act, shall grant to any applicant therefor a station license provided for by this Act.

(b) In considering applications for licenses, and modifications and renewals thereof, when and insofar as there is demand for the same, the Commission shall make such distribution of licenses, frequencies, hours of operation, and of power among the several states and communities as to provide a fair, efficient, and equitable distribution of radio service to each of the same.

(c) The Commission shall study the proposal that Congress by statute allocate fixed percentages of radio broadcasting facilities to particular types or kinds of non-profit radio programs or to persons identified with particular types or kinds of non-profit activities, and shall report to Congress, not later than February 1, 1935, its recommendations together with the reasons for the same.

(d) No license granted for the operation of a broadcasting station shall be for a longer term than three years and no license so granted for any other class of station shall be for a longer term than five years, and any license granted may be revoked as hereinafter provided. Upon the expiration of any license, upon application therefor, a renewal of such license may be granted from time to time for a term of not to exceed three years in the case of broadcasting licenses and not to exceed five years in the case of other licenses, if the Commission finds that public interest, convenience and necessity would be served thereby. In order to expedite action on applications for renewal of broadcasting station licenses and in order to avoid needless expense to applicants for such renewals, the Commission shall not require any such applicant to file any information which previously has been furnished to the Commission or which is not directly material to the considerations that affect the granting or denial of such application, but the Commission may require any new or additional facts it deems necessary to make its findings. Pending any hearing and final decision on such application and the disposition of any petition for rehearing pursuant to Section 405, the Commission shall continue such license in effect. Consistently with the foregoing provisions of this subsection, the Commission may by rule prescribe the period or periods for which licenses shall be granted and renewed for particular classes of stations, but the Commission may not adopt or follow any rule which would preclude it, in any case involving a station of a particular class, from granting or renewing a license for a shorter period than that prescribed for stations of such class if, in its judgment, public interest, convenience, or necessity would be served by such action.

(e) No renewal of an existing station license shall be granted more than thirty days prior to the expiration of the original license.

APPLICATIONS FOR LICENSES; CONDITIONS IN LICENSE FOR FOREIGN COMMUNICATION

SEC. 308. (a) The Commission may grant construction permits and station licenses, or modifications or renewals thereof, only upon written application therefore received by it: provided, that (1) in cases of emergency found by the Commission involving danger to life or property or due to damage to equipment, or (2) during a national emergency proclaimed by the President or declared by the Congress and during the continuance of any war in which the United States is engaged and when such action is necessary for the national defense or security or otherwise in furtherance of the war effort, or (3) in cases of emergency where the Commission finds, in the non-broadcast services, that it would not be feasible to secure renewal applications from existing licensees or otherwise to follow normal licensing procedure, the Commission may grant construction permits and station licenses, or modifications or renewals thereof, during the emergency so found by the Commission or during the continuance of any such national emergency or war, in such manner and upon such terms and conditions as the Commission shall by regulation prescribe, and without the filing of a formal application, but no authorization so granted shall continue in effect beyond the period of the emergency or war requiring it: providing further that the Commission may issue by cable, telegraph, or radio a permit for the operation of a station on a vessel of the United States at sea, effective in lieu of a license until said vessel shall return to a port of the continental United States.

(b) All applications for station licenses, or modifications or renewals thereof, shall set forth such facts as the Commission by regulation may prescribe as to the citizenship, character, and financial, technical, and other qualifications of the applicant to operate the station; the ownership and location of the proposed station and of the stations, if any, with which it is proposed to communicate; the frequencies and the power desired to be used; the hours of the day or other periods of time during which it is proposed to operate the station; the purposes for which the station is to be used; and such other information as it may require. The Commission, at any time after the filing of such original application and during the term of any such license, may require from an applicant or licensee further written statements of fact to enable it to determine whether such original application should be granted or denied or such license revoked. Such application and/or such statement of fact shall be signed by the applicant and/or licensee under oath or affirmation.

(c) The Commission in granting any license for a station intended or used for commercial communication between the United States or any Territory or possession, continental or insular, subject to the jurisdiction of the United States, and any foreign country, may impose any terms, conditions, or restrictions authorized to be imposed with respect to submarine-cable licenses by section 2 of an Act entitled "An Act relating to the landing and the operation of submarine cables in the United States", approved May 24, 1921.

ACTION UPON APPLICATIONS; FORM OF AND CONDITIONS ATTACHED TO LICENSES

SEC. 309. (a) Subject to the provisions of this section, the Commission shall determine, in the case of each application filed with it which Section 308 applies, whether the public interest, convenience, and necessity will be served by the granting of such application, and, if the Commission, upon examination of such application and upon consideration of such other matters as the Commission may officially notice, shall find that public interest, convenience and necessity would be served by the granting thereof, it shall grant such application.

(b) Except as provided in subsection (c) of this section, no such application—

(1) for an instrument of authorization in the case of a station in the broadcasting or common carrier services, or

(2) for an instrument of authorization in the case of a station in any of the following categories:

(A) fixed point-to-point microwave stations (exclusive of control and relay stations used as integral parts of mobile radio systems),

(B) industrial radio positioning stations for which frequencies are assigned on an exclusive basis,

(C) aeronautical en route stations,

(D) aeronautical advisory stations,

(E) airdrome control stations,

(F) aeronautical fixed stations, and

(G) such other stations or classes of stations, not in the broadcasting or common carrier services, as the Commission shall by rule prescribe, shall be granted by the Commission earlier than thirty days following issuance of public notice by the Commission of the acceptance for filing of such application or of any substantial amendment thereof.

(c) Subsection (b) of this section shall not apply—

(1) to any minor amendment of an application to which such subsection is applicable, or

(2) to any application for—

(A) a minor change in the facilities of an authorized station,

(B) consent to an involuntary assignment or transfer under Section 310(b) or to an assignment or transfer thereunder which does not involve a substantial change in ownership or control,

(C) a license under Section 319(c) or, pending application for or grant of such license, any special or temporary authorization to permit interim operation to facilitate completion of authorized construction or to provide substantially the same service as would be authorized by such license,

(D) extension of time to complete construction of authorized facilities,

(E) an authorization of facilities for remote pickups, studio links and similar facilities for use in the operation of a broadcast station,

(F) authorizations pursuant to Section 325(b) where the programs to be transmitted are special events not of a continuing nature,

(G) a special temporary authorization for non-broadcast operation not to exceed thirty days where no application for regular operation is contemplated to be filed or pending the filing of an application for such regular operation, or

(H) an authorization under any of the proviso clauses of Section 308(a).

(d) (1) Any party in interest may file with the Commission a petition to deny any application (whether as originally filed or as amended) to which subsection (b) of this section applies at any time prior to the day of Commission grant thereof without hearing or the day of formal designation thereof for hearing; except that with respect to any classification of applications, the Commission from time to time by rule may specify a shorter perior (no less than thirty days following the issuance of public notice by the Commission of the acceptance of for filing of such application or of any substantial amendment thereof), which shorter period shall be reasonably related to the time when the applications would normally be reached for processing. The petition shall contain specific allegations of fact sufficient to show that the petitioner is a party in interest and that a grant of the application would be prima facie inconsistent with subsection (a). Such allegations of fact shall, except for those of which official notice may be taken, be supported by affidavit of a person or persons with personal knowledge thereof. The applicant shall be given the opportunity to file reply in which allegations of fact or denials thereof shall similarly be supported by affidavit.

(2) If the Commission finds on the basis of the application, the pleadings filed, or other matters which it may officially notice that there are no substantial and material questions of fact and that a grant of the application would be consistent with subsection (a), it shall make the grant, deny the petition, and issue a concise statement of the reasons for denying the petition which statement shall dispose of all substantial issues raised by the petition. If a substantial and material question of fact is presented or if the Commission for any reason is unable to find that grant of the application would be consistent with subsection (a), it shall proceed as provided in subsection (e).

(e) If, in the case of any application to which subsection (a) of this section applies, a substantial and material question of fact is presented or the Commission for any reason is unable to make the finding specified in such subsection, it shall formally designate the application for hearing on the ground or reasons then obtaining and shall forthwith notify the applicant and all other known parties in interest of such action and the grounds and reasons therefor, specifying with particularity the matters and things in issue but not including issues or requirements phrased generally. When the Commission has so designated an application for hearing the parties in interest, if any, who are not notified by the Commission of such action may acquire the status of a party to the proceeding thereon by filing a petition for intervention showing the basis for their interest at any time not less than ten days prior to the date of hearing. Any hearing subsequently held upon such application shall be a full hearing in which the applicant and all other parties in interest shall be permitted to participate. The burden of proceeding with the introduction of evidence and the burden of proof shall be upon the applicant, except that with respect to any issue presented by a petition to deny or a petition to enlarge the issues, such burdens shall be as determined by the Commission.

(f) When an application subject to subsection (b) has been filed, the Commission, notwithstanding the requirements of such subsection, may, if the grant of such application is otherwise authorized by law and if it finds that there are extraordinary circumstances requiring emergency operations in the public interest and that delay in the institution of such emergency operations would seriously prejudice the public interest, grant a temporary authorization, accompanied by a statement of its reasons therefor, to permit such emergency operations for a period not exceeding ninety days, and upon making like findings may extend such temporary authorization for one additional period not to exceed ninety days. When any such grant of a temporary authorization is made, the Commission shall give expeditious treatment to any timely filed petition to deny such application and to any petition for rehearing of such grant filed under Section 405.

(g) The Commission is authorized to adopt reasonable classifications of applications and amendments in order to effectuate the purposes of this section.

(h) Such station licenses as the Commission may grant shall be in such general form as it may prescribe, but each license shall contain, in addition to other provisions, a statement of the following conditions to which such license shall be subject:

(1) The station license shall not vest in the licensee any right to operate the station nor any right in the use of the frequencies designated in the license beyond the term thereof nor in any other manner than authorized therein.

(2) Neither the license nor the right granted thereunder shall be assigned or otherwise transferred in violation of this Act.

(3) Every license issued under this Act shall be subject in terms to the right of use or control conferred by section 606 of this Act.

LIMITATION ON HOLDING AND TRANSFER OF LICENSES

SEC. 310. (a) The station license required hereby shall not be granted to or held by—

(1) Any alien or the representative of any alien;

(2) Any foreign government or the representative thereof;

(3) Any corporation organized under the laws of any foreign government;

(4) Any corporation of which any officer or director is an alien or of which more than on-fifth of the capital stock is owned of record or voted by aliens or their representatives or by a foreign government or representative thereof, or by any corporation organized under the laws of a foreign country;

(5) Any corporation directly or indirectly controlled by any other corporation of which any officer or more than one-fourth of the directors are aliens, or of which more than one-fourth of the capital stock is owned of record or

voted, after June 1, 1935, by aliens, their representatives, or by a foreign government or representative thereof, or by any corporation organized under the laws of a foreign country, if the Commission finds that the public interest will be served by the refusal or the revocation of such license.

Nothing in this subsection shall prevent the licensing of radio apparatus on board any vessel, aircraft, or other mobile station of the United States when the installation and use of such apparatus is required by Act of Congress or any treaty to which the United States is a party. Notwithstanding paragraph (1) of this subsection, a license for a radio station on an aircraft may be granted to and held by a person who is an alien or a representative of an alien if such person holds a United States pilot certificate or a foreign aircraft pilot certificate which is valid in the United States on the basis of reciprocal agreements entered into with foreign governments.

(b) No construction permit or station license, or any rights thereunder, shall be transferred, assigned, or disposed of in any manner, voluntarily or involuntarily, directly or indirectly, or by transfer of control of any corporation holding such permit or license, to any person except upon application to the Commission and upon finding by the Commission that the public interest, convenience and necessity will be served thereby. Any such application shall be disposed of as if the proposed transferee or assignee were making application under Section 308 for the permit or license in question; but in acting theron the Commission may not consider whether the public interest, convenience and necessity might be served by the transfer, assignment, or disposal of the permit or license to a person other than the proposed transferee or assignee.

SPECIAL REQUIREMENTS WITH RESPECT TO CERTAIN APPLICATIONS
IN THE BROADCASTING SERVICE

SEC. 311. (a) When there is filed with the Commission any application to which Section 309(b) (1) applies, for an instrument of authorization for a station in the broadcasting service, the applicant—

(1) shall give notice of such filing in the principal area which is served or is to be served by the station; and

(2) if the application is formally designated for hearing in accordance with Section 309, shall give notice of such hearings in such area at least ten days before commencement of such hearing.

The Commission shall by rule prescribe the form and content of the notices to be given in compliance with this subsection, and the manner and frequency with which such notices shall be given.

(b) Hearings referred to in subsection (a) may be held at such places as the Commission shall determine to be appropriate, and in making such determination in any case the Commission shall consider whether the public interest, convenience or necessity will be served by conducting the hearing at a place in, or in the vicinity of, the principal area to be served by the station involved.

(c) (1) if there are pending before the Commission two or more applications for a permit for construction of a broadcasting station, only one of which can be granted, it shall be unlawful, without approval of the Commission, for the applicants or any of them to effectuate an agreement whereby one or more of such applicants withdraws his or their application or applications.

(2) The request for Commission approval in any such case shall be made in writing jointly by all the parties to the agreement. Such request shall contain or be accompanied by full information with respect to the agreement, set forth in such detail, form and manner as the Commission shall by rule require.

(3) The Commission shall approve the agreement only if it determines that

331

the agreement is consistent with the public interest, convenience or necessity. If the agreement does not contemplate a merger, but contemplates the making of any direct or indirect payment to any party thereto in consideration of his withdrawal of his application, the Commission may determine the agreement to be consistent with the public interest, convenience or necessity only if the amount or value of such payment, as determined by the Commission, is not in excess of the aggregate amount determined by the Commission to have been legitimately and prudently expended and to be expended by such applicant in connection with preparing, filing, and advocating the granting of his application.

(4) For the purposes of this subsection an application shall be deemed to be "pending" before the Commission from the time such application is filed with the Commission until an order of the Commission granting or denying it is no longer subject to rehearing by the Commission or to review by any court.

ADMINISTRATIVE SANCTIONS

SEC. 312. (a) The Commission may revoke any station license or construction permit—

(1) for false statements knowingly made either in the application of or in any statement of fact which may be required pursuant to Section 308;

(2) because of conditions coming to the attention of the Commission which would warrant it in refusing to grant a license or permit on an original application;

(3) for willful or repeated failure to operate substantially as set forth in the license;

(4) for willful or repeated violation of, or willful or repeated failure to observe, any provision of this Act or any rule or regulation of the Commission authorized by this Act or by a treaty ratified by the United States; and

(5) for violation of or failure to observe any final cease and desist order issued by the Commission under this section; or

(6) for violation of Section 1304, 1343, or 1464 of Title 18 of the United States Code.

(b) Where any person

(1) has failed to operate substantially as set forth in a license.

(2) has violated or failed to observe any of the provisions of this Act, or Section 1304, 1343 or 1464 of Title 18 of the United States Code, or

(3) has violated or failed to observe any rule or regulation of the Commission authorized by this Act or by a treaty ratified by the United States, the Commission may order such person to cease and desist from such action.

(c) Before revoking a license or permit pursuant to subsection (a), or issuing a cease and desist order pursuant to subsection (b), the Commission shall serve upon the licensee, permittee or person involved an order to show cause why an order of revocation or a cease and desist order should not be issued. Any such order to show cause shall contain a statement of the matters with respect to which the Commission is inquiring and shall call upon said licensee, permittee or person to appear before the Commission at a time and place stated in the order, but in no event less than thirty days after the receipt of such order, and give evidence upon the matter specified therein; except that where safety or life or property is involved, the Commission may provide in the order for a shorter period. If after hearing, or a waiver thereof, the Commission determines that an order of revocation or a cease and desist order should issue, it shall issue such order which shall include a statement of the findings of the Commission and the grounds and reasons therefor, and specify

332

the effective date of the order, and shall cause the same to be served on said licensee, permittee, or person.

(d) In any case where a hearing is conducted pursuant to the provisions of this section, both the burden of proceeding with the introduction of evidence and the burden of proof shall be upon the Commission.

(e) The provisions of Section 9(b) of the Administrative Procedure Act which apply with respect to the institution of any proceeding for the revocation of a license or permit shall apply also with respect to the institution, under this section, of any proceeding for the issuance of a cease and desist order.

APPLICATION OF ANTITRUST LAWS; REFUSAL OF LICENSES AND PERMITS IN CERTAIN CASES

SEC. 313. (a) All laws of the United States relating to unlawful restraints and monopolies and to combinations, contracts, or agreements in restraint of trade are hereby declared to be applicable to the manufacture and sale of and to trade in radio apparatus and devices entering into or affecting interstate or foreign commerce and to interstate or foreign radio communications. Whenever in any suit, action, or proceeding, civil or criminal, brought under the provisions of any of said laws or in any proceedings brought to enforce or to review findings and orders of the Federal Trade Commission or other governmental agency in respect of any matters as to which said Commission or other governmental agency is by law authorized to act, any licensee shall be found guilty of the violation of the provisions of such laws or any of them, the court, in addition to the penalties imposed by said laws, may adjudge, order, and/or decree that the license of such licensee shall, as of the date the decree or judgment becomes finally effective or as of such other date as the said decree shall fix, be revoked and that all rights under such license shall thereupon cease: *Provided, however,* That such licensee shall have the same right of appeal or review as is provided by law in respect of other decrees and judgments of said court.

(b) The Commission is hereby directed to refuse a station license and/or the permit hereinafter required for the construction of a station to any person (or to any person directly or indirectly controlled by such person) whose license has been revoked by a court under this section.

PRESERVATION OF COMPETITION IN COMMERCE

SEC. 314. After the effective date of this Act no person engaged directly, or indirectly through any person directly or indirectly controlling or controlled by, or under direct or indirect common control with, such person, or through an agent, or otherwise, in the business of transmitting and/or receiving for hire energy, communications, or signals by radio in accordance with the terms of the license issued under this Act, shall by purchase, lease, construction, or otherwise, directly or indirectly, acquire, own, control, or operate any cable or wire telegraph or telephone line or system between any place in any State, Territory, or possession of the United States or in the District of Columbia, and any place in any foreign country, or shall acquire, own, or control any part of the stock or other capital share or any interest in the physical property and/or other assets of any such cable, wire, telegraph, or telephone line or system, if in either case the purpose is and/or the effect thereof may be to substantially lessen competition or to restrain commerce between any place in any State, Territory, or possession of the United States, or in the District of Columbia, and any place in any foreign country, or unlawfully to create monopoly in any line of commerce; nor shall any person engaged directly, or indirectly through any person directly or indirectly controlling or controlled by, or under direct or indirect common control with, such person, or through an agent, or otherwise, in the business of transmitting and/or receiving for hire messages by any cable, wire, telegraph, or telephone line or system (a) between any place in any State, Territory, or possession of the United States, or in the District of Columbia, and any place in any other State, Territory, or possession of the United States; or (b) between any place in any State, Territory, or possession of the United States, or the District of Columbia, and any place in any foreign country, by purchase, lease, construction, or otherwise, directly or indirectly acquire, own, control, or operate any station or the apparatus therein, or any system for transmitting and/or receiving radio communications or signals between any place in any State, Territory, or possession of the United States, or in the District of Columbia, and any place in any foreign country, or shall acquire, own, or control any part of the stock or other capital share or any interest in the physical property and/or other assets of any such radio station, apparatus, or system, if in either case the purpose is and/or the effect thereof may be to substantially lessen competition or to restrain commerce between any place in any State, Territory, or possession of the United States, or in the District of Columbia, and any place in any foreign country, or unlawfully to create monopoly in any line of commerce.

FACILITIES FOR CANDIDATES FOR PUBLIC OFFICE

SEC. 315. (a) If any licensee shall permit any person who is a legally qualified candidate for any public office to use a broadcasting station, he shall afford equal opportunities to all other such candidates for that office in the use of such broadcasting station: *provided,* that such licensee shall have no power of censorship over the material broadcast under the provisions of this section. No obligation is hereby imposed upon any licensee to allow the use of its station by any such candidate. Appearance by a legally qualified candidate on any—

(1) bona fide newscast

(2) bona fide news interview,

(3) bona fide news documentary (if the appearance of the condidate is incidental to the presentation of the subject or subjects covered by the news documentary), or

(4) on-the-spot coverage of bona fide news events (including but not limited to political conventions and activities incidental thereto),

Shall not be deemed to be use of a broadcasting station within the meaning of this subsection. Nothing in the foregoing sentence shall be construed as relieving broadcasters, in connection with the presentation of newscasts, news interviews, news documentaries, and on-the-spot coverage of news events, from the obligation imposed upon them under this Act to operate in the public interest and to afford reasonable opportunity for the discussion of conflicting views on issues of public importance.*

* By Pub. L. No. 86-274, approved September 14, 1959, 73 Stat. 557, Congress amended subsection (a). Section 2 of this amendatory act reads as follows:

Sec. 2. (a) The Congress declares its intention to reexamine from time to time the amendments to Section 315(a) of the Communications Act of 1934 made by the first Section of this Act, to ascertain whether such amendment has proved to be effective and practicable.

(b) To assist the Congress in making its reexaminations of such amendment, the Federal Communications Commission shall include in each annual report it makes to Congress a statement setting forth (1) the information and data used by it in determining questions arising from or connected with such amendment, and (2) such recommendations as it deems necessary in the public interest.

(b) The charges made for the use of any broadcasting station for any of the purposes set forth in this section shall not exceed the charges made for comparable use of such station for other purposes.

(c) The Commission shall prescribe appropriate rules and regulations to carry out the provisions of this section.*

MODIFICATION BY COMMISSION OF CONSTRUCTION PERMITS OR LICENSES

SEC. 316. (a) Any station license or construction permit may be modified by the Commission either for a limited time or for the duration of the term thereof, if in the judgment of the Commission such action will promote the public interest, convenience and necessity, or the provisions of this Act or of any treaty ratified by the United States will be more fully complied with. No such order of modification shall become final until the holder of the license or permit shall have been notified in writing of the proposed action and the grounds and reasons therefor, and shall have been given reasonable opportunity, in no event less than thirty days, to show cause by public hearing, if requested, why such order of modification should not issue; provided, that where safety of life or property is involved, the Commission may by order provide for a shorter period of notice.

(b) In any case where a hearing is conducted pursuant to the provisions of this section, both the burden of proceeding with the introduction of evidence and the burden of proof shall be upon the Commission.**

ANNOUNCEMENT WITH RESPECT TO CERTAIN MATTER BROADCAST

SEC. 317. All matter broadcast by any radio station for which service, money, or any other valuable consideration is directly or indirectly paid, or promised

* Pub. L. 86-677 (S. J. Res. 207, approved August 24, 1960) provides:
Resolved by the Senate and House of Representatives of the United States of America in Congress assembled, that that part of Section 315(a) of the Communications Act of 1934, as amended, which requires any licensee of a broadcast station who permits any person who is a legally qualified candidate for any public office to use a broadcasting station to afford equal opportunities to all other such candidates for that office in the use of such broadcasting station, is suspended for the period of the 1960 presidential and vice-presidential campaigns with respect to nominees for the offices of President and Vice-President of the United States. Nothing in the foregoing shall be construed as relieving broadcasters from the obligation imposed upon them under this Act to operate in the public interest.

(2) The Federal Communications Commission shall make a report to the Congress, not later than March 1, 1961, with respect to the effect of the provisions of this joint resolution and any recommendations the Commission may have for amendments to the Communications Act of 1934 as a result of experience under the provisions of this joint resolution.

** Former Section 316 was repealed September 1, 1948, Pub. L. No. 772 (80th Cong.), 62 Stat. 862. The substance of it was incorporated in 18 U. S. C. 1304, which reads:

Sec. 1304. Broadcasting Lottery Information. Whoever broadcasts by means of any radio station for which a license is required by any law of the United States, or whoever, operating such a station, knowingly permits the broadcasting of, any advertisement of or information concerning any lottery, gift enterprise, or similar scheme, offering prizes dependent in whole or in part upon lot or chance, or any list of the prizes drawn or awarded by means of any such lottery, gift enterprise, or scheme, whether said list contains any part or all of such prizes, shall be fined not more than $1,000 or imprisoned not more than one year, or both. Each day's broadcasting shall constitute a separate offense.

to or charged or accepted by, the station so broadcasting, from any person, shall, at the time the same is so broadcast, be announced as paid for or furnished, as the case may be, by such person: provided, that "service or other valuable consideration" shall not include any service or property furnished without charge or at a nominal charge for use on, or in connection with, a broadcast unless it is so furnished in consideration for an identification in a broadcast of any person, product, service, trademark or brand name beyond an identification which is reasonably related to the use of such service or property on the broadcast.

(2) Nothing in this section shall preclude the Commission from requiring that an appropriate announcement shall be made at the time of the broadcast in the case of any political program or any program involving the discussion of any controversial issue for which any films, records, transcriptions, talent, scripts, or other material or service of any kind have been furnished, without charge or at a nominal charge, directly or indirectly, as an inducement to the broadcast of such program.

(b) In any case where a report has been made to a radio station, as required by Section 508 of this Act, of circumstances which would have required an announcement under this section had the consideration been received by such radio station, an appropriate announcement shall be made by such radio station.

(c) The licensee of each radio station shall exercise reasonable diligence to obtain from its employees, and from other persons with whom it deals directly in connection with any program or program matter for broadcast, information to enable such licensee to make the announcement required by this Section.

(d) The Commission may waive the requirement of an announcement as provided in this Section in any case or class of cases with respect to which it determines that the public interest, convenience, or necessity does not require the broadcasting of such announcement.

(e) The Commission shall prescribe rules and regulations to carry out the provisions of this section.

OPERATION OF TRANSMITTING APPARATUS

SEC. 318. The actual operation of all transmitting apparatus in any radio station for which a station license is required by this Act shall be carried on only by a person holding an operator's license issued hereunder. No person shall operate any such apparatus in such station except under and in accordance with an operator's license issued to him by the Commission: provided, however, that the Commission if it shall find that the public interest, convenience or necessity will be served thereby may waive or modify the foregoing provisions of this section for the operation of any station except (1) stations for which licensed operators are required by international agreement, (2) stations for which licensed operators are required for safety purposes, (3) stations engaged in broadcasting (other than those engaged solely in the functions of rebroadcasting the signals of television broadcast stations), and (4) stations operated as common carriers on frequencies below thirty thousand kilocycles: provided further, that the Commission shall have power to make special regulations governing the granting of licenses for the use of automatic radio devices and for the operation of such devices.

CONSTRUCTION PERMITS

SEC. 319 (a) No license shall be issued under the authority of this Act for the operation of any station the construction of which is begun or is continued after this Act takes effect, unless a permit for its construction has been granted by the Commission. The application for a construction permit shall set forth such facts as the Commission by regulation may prescribe as to the citizenship, character, and the financial, technical, and other ability of the applicant to construct and operate the station, the ownership and location of the proposed station and of the station or stations with which it is proposed to communicate, the frequencies desired to be used, the hours of the day or other periods of time during which it is proposed to operate the station, the purpose for which the station is to be used, the type of transmitting apparatus to be used, the power to be used, the date upon which the station is expected to be completed and in operation, and such other information as the Commission may require. Such application shall be signed by the applicant under oath or affirmation.

(b) Such permit for construction shall show specifically the earliest and latest dates between which the actual operation of such station is expected to begin, and shall provide that said permit will be automatically forfeited if the station is not ready for operation within the time specified or within such further time as the Commission may allow, unless prevented by causes not under the control of the grantee.

(c) Upon the completion of any station for the construction or continued construction of which a permit has been granted, and upon it being made to appear to the Commission that all the terms, conditions, and obligations set forth in the application and permit have been fully met, and that no cause or circumstance arising or first coming to the knowledge of the Commission since the granting of the permit would, in the judgment of the Commission, make the operation of such station against the public interest, the Commission shall issue a license to the lawful holder of said permit for the operation of said station. Said license shall conform generally to the terms of said permit. The provisions of Section 309(a), (b), (c), (d), (e), (f), and (g), shall not apply with respect to any station license the issuance of which is provided for and governed by the provisions of this subsection.

(d) A permit for construction shall not be required for Government stations, amateur stations, or mobile stations. With respect to stations or classes of stations other than Government stations, amateur stations, mobile stations, and broadcasting stations, the Commission may waive the requirement of a permit for construction if it finds that the public interest, convenience or necessity would be served thereby; provided, however, that such waiver shall apply only to stations whose construction is begun subsequent to the effective date of the waiver. If the Commission finds that the public interest, convenience and necessity would be served thereby, it may waive the requirement of a permit for construction of a station that is engaged solely in rebroadcasting television signals if such station was constructed on or before the date of enactment of this Act.

DESIGNATION OF STATIONS LIABLE TO INTERFERE WITH DISTRESS SIGNALS

SEC. 320. The Commission is authorized to designate from time to time radio stations the communications or signals of which, in its opinion, are liable to interfere with the transmission or reception of distress signals of ships. Such stations are required to keep a licensed radio operator listening in on the frequencies designated for signals of distress and radio communications relating thereto during the entire period the transmitter of such station is in operation.

DISTRESS SIGNALS AND COMMUNICATIONS

SEC. 321 (a) The transmitting set in a radio station on shipboard may be adjusted in such a manner as to produce a maximum radiation, irrespective of the amount of interference which may thus be caused, when such station is sending radio communication or signals of distress and radio communications relating thereto.

(b) All radio stations, including Government stations and stations on board foreign vessels when within the territorial waters of the United States, shall give absolute priority to radio communications or signals relating to ships in distress; shall cease all sending on frequencies which will interfere with hearing a radio communication or signal of distress, and, except when engaged in answering or aiding the ship in distress, shall refrain from sending any radio communications or signals until there is assurance that no interference will be caused with the radio communications or signals relating thereto, and shall assist the vessel in distress, so far as possible, by complying with its instructions.

INTERCOMMUNICATION IN MOBILE SERVICE

SEC. 322. Every land station open to general public service between the coast and vessels or aircraft at sea shall, within the scope of its normal operations, be bound to exchange radio communications or signals with any ship or aircraft station at sea; and each station on shipboard or aircraft at sea shall, within the scope of its normal operations, be bound to exchange radio communications or signals with any other station on shipboard or aircraft at sea or with any land station open to general public service between the coast and vessels or aircraft at sea; provided, that such exchange of radio communication shall be without distinction as to radio systems or instruments adopted by each station.

INTERFERENCE BETWEEN GOVERNMENT AND COMMERCIAL STATIONS

SEC. 323. (a) At all places where Government and private or commercial radio stations on land operate in such close proximity that interference with the work of Government stations cannot be avoided when they are operating simultaneously, such private or commercial stations as do interfere with the transmission or reception of radio communications or signals by the Government stations concerned shall not use their transmitters during the first fifteen minutes of each hour, local standard time.

(b) The Government stations for which the above-mentioned division of time is established shall transmit radio communications or signals only during the first fifteen minutes of each hour, local standard time, except in case of signals or radio communications relating to vessels in distress and vessel requests for information as to course, location, or compass direction.

USE OF MINIMUM POWER

SEC. 324. In all circumstances, except in case of radio communications or signals relating to vessels in distress, all radio stations, including those owned and operated by the United States, shall use the minimum amount of power necessary to carry out the communication desired.

FALSE DISTRESS SIGNALS; REBROADCASTING; STUDIOS OF FOREIGN STATIONS

SEC. 325. (a) No person within the jurisdiction of the United States shall knowingly utter or transmit, or cause to be uttered or transmitted, any false or fraudulent signal of distress, or communication relating thereto, nor shall any

338

broadcasting station rebroadcast the program or any part thereof of another broadcasting station without the express authority of the originating station.

(b) No person shall be permitted to locate, use, or maintain a radio broadcast studio or other place or apparatus from which or whereby sound waves are converted into electrical energy, or mechanical or physical reproduction of sound waves produced, and caused to be transmitted or delivered to a radio station in a foreign country for the purpose of being broadcast from any radio station there having a power output of sufficient intensity and/or being so located geographically that its emissions may be received consistently in the United States, without first obtaining a permit from the Commission upon proper application therefor.

(c) Such application shall contain such information as the Commission may by regulation prescribe, and the granting or refusal thereof shall be subject to the requirements of section 309 hereof with respect to applications for station licenses or renewal or modification thereof, and the license or permission so granted shall be revocable for false statements in the application so required or when the Commission, after hearings, shall find its continuation no longer in the public interest.

CENSORSHIP; INDECENT LANGUAGE

SEC. 326. Nothing in this Act shall be understood or construed to give the Commission the power of censorship over the radio communications or signals transmitted by any radio station, and no regulation or condition shall be promulgated or fixed by the Commission which shall interfere with the right of free speech by means of radio communication.*

USE OF NAVAL STATIONS FOR COMMERCIAL MESSAGES

SEC. 327. The Secretary of the Navy is hereby authorized, unless restrained by international agreement, under the terms and conditions and at rates prescribed by him, which rates shall be just and reasonable, and which, upon complaint, shall be subject to review and revision by the Commission, to use all radio stations and apparatus, wherever located, owned by the United States and under the control of the Navy Department, (a) for the reception and transmission of press messages offered by any newspaper published in the United States, its Territories or possessions, or published by citizens of the United States in foreign countries, or by any press association of the United States, and (b) for the reception and transmission of private commercial messages between ships, between ship and shore, between localities in Alaska and between Alaska and the continental United States: *Provided,* That the rates fixed for the reception and transmission of all such messages, other than press messages between the Pacific coast of the United States, Hawaii, Alaska, Guam, American Samoa, the Philippine Islands, and the Orient, and between the United States and the Virgin Islands, shall not be less than the rates charged by privately owned and operated stations for like messages and service: *Provided further,* That the right to use such stations for any of the purposes named in this section shall

* The prohibition against indecent programming was deleted by Pub. L. No. 772 (80th Cong.), 62 Stat. 862, September 1, 1948 and the substance was incorporated in 18 U. S. C. 1464, which reads:
Sec. 1464.—Broadcasting Obscene Language. Whoever utters any obscene, indecent, or profane language by means of radio communication shall be fined not more than $10,000 or imprisoned not more than two years, or both.

terminate and cease as between any countries or localities or between any locality and privately operated ships whenever privately owned and operated stations are capable of meeting the normal communication requirements between such countries or localities or between any locality and privately operated ships, and the Commission shall have notified the Secretary of the Navy thereof.

SPECIAL PROVISION AS TO PHILIPPINE ISLANDS AND CANAL ZONE

SEC. 328. This title shall not apply to the Philippine Islands or to the Canal Zone. In international radio matters the Philippine Islands and the Canal Zone shall be represented by the Secretary of State.

ADMINISTRATION OF RADIO LAWS IN TERRITORIES AND POSSESSIONS

SEC. 329. The Commission is authorized to designate any officer or employee of any other department of the Government on duty in any Territory or possession of the United States other than the Philippine Islands and the Canal Zone, to render therein such services in connection with the administration of the radio laws of the United States as the Commission may prescribe: *Provided,* That such designation shall be approved by the head of the department in which such person is employed.

TITLE IV—PROCEDURAL AND ADMINISTRATIVE PROVISIONS

JURISDICTION TO ENFORCE ACT AND ORDERS OF COMMISSION

SECTION 401. (a) The district courts of the United States shall have jurisdiction, upon application of the Attorney General of the United States at the request of the Commission, alleging a failure to comply with or a violation of any of the provisions of this Act by any person, to issue a writ or writs of mandamus commanding such person to comply with the provisions of this Act.

(b) If any person fails or neglects to obey any order of the Commission other than for the payment of money, while the same is in effect, the Commission or any party injured thereby, or the United States, by its Attorney General, may apply to the appropriate district court of the United States for the enforcement of such order. If, after hearing, that court determines that the order was regularly made and duly served, and that the person is in disobedience of the same, the court shall enforce obedience to such order by a writ of injunction or other proper process, mandatory or otherwise, to restrain such person or the officers, agents, or representatives of such person, from further disobedience of such order, or to enjoin upon it or them obedience to the same.

(c) Upon the request of the Commission it shall be the duty of any district attorney of the United States to whom the Commission may apply to institute in the proper court and to prosecute under the direction of the Attorney General of the United States all necessary proceedings for the enforcement of the provisions of this Act and for the punishment of all violations thereof, and the costs and expenses of such prosecutions shall be paid out of the appropriations for the expenses of the courts of the United States.

(d) The provisions of the Expediting Act, approved February 11, 1903, as amended, and of section 238 (1) of the Judicial Code, as amended, shall be held to apply to any suit in equity arising under Title II of this Act, wherein the United States is complainant.

SEC. 402. (a) Any proceeding to enjoin, set aside, annul, or suspend any order of the Commission under this Act (except those appealable under subsection (b) of this section) shall be brought as provided by and in the manner prescribed in Public Law 901, Eighty-first Congress, approved December 29, 1950.

(b) Appeals may be taken from decisions and orders of the Commission to the United States Court of Appeals for the District of Columbia in any of the following cases:

(1) By any applicant for a construction permit or station license whose application is denied by the Commission.

(2) By any applicant for the renewal or modification of any such instrument of authorization whose application is denied by the Commission.

(3) By any party to an application for authority to transfer, assign, or dispose of any such instrument of authorization, or any rights thereunder, whose application is denied by the Commission.

(4) By any applicant for the permit required by Section 325 of this Act whose application has been denied by the Commission, or by any permittee under said section whose permit has been revoked by the Commission.

(5) By the holder of any construction permit or station license which has been modified or revoked by the Commission.

(6) By any other person who is aggrieved or whose interests are adversely affected by any order of the Commission granting or denying any application described in paragraphs (1), (2), (3) and (4) hereof.

(7) By any person upon whom an order to cease and desist has been served under Section 312 of this Act.

(8) By any radio operator whose license has been suspended by the Commission.

(c) Such appeal shall be taken by filing a notice of appeal with the court within thirty days from the date upon which public notice is given of the decision or order complained of. Such notice of appeal shall contain a concise statement of the nature of the proceedings as to which the appeal is taken; a concise statement of the reasons on which the appellant intends to rely, separately stated and numbered; and proof of service of a true copy of said notice and statement upon the Commission. Upon filing of such notice, the court shall have jurisdiction of the proceedings and of the questions determined therein and shall have power, by order, directed to the Commission or any other party to the appeal, to grant temporary relief as it may deem just and proper. Orders granting temporary relief may be either affirmative or negative in their scope and applications so as to permit either the maintenance of the status quo in the matter in which the appeal is taken or the restoration of a position or status terminated or adversely affected by the order appealed from and shall, unless otherwise ordered by the court, be effective pending hearing and determination of said appeal and compliance by the Commission with the final judgment of the court rendered in said appeal.

(d) Within thirty days after the filing of an appeal, the Commission shall file with the court the record upon which the order complained of was entered, as provided in Section 2112 of Title 28, United States Code.

(e) Within thirty days after the filing of any such appeal, any interested person may intervene and participate in the proceedings had upon said appeal by filing with the court a notice of intention to intervene and a verified state-

341

ment showing the nature of the interest of such party, together with proof of service of true copies of said notice and statement, both upon appellant and upon the Commission. Any person who would be aggrieved or whose interest would be adversely affected by a reversal or modification of the order of the Commission complained of shall be considered an interested party.

(f) The record and briefs upon which any such appeal shall be heard and determined by the court shall contain such information and material, and shall be prepared within such time and in such manner as the court may by rule prescribe.

(g) At the earliest convenient time the court shall hear and determine the appeal upon the record before it in the manner prescribed by Section 10(e) of the Administrative Procedure Act.

(h) In the event that the court shall render a decision and enter an order reversing the order of the Commission, it shall remand the case to the Commission to carry out the judgment of the court and it shall be the duty of the Commission, in the absence of the proceedings to review such judgment, to forthwith give effect thereto, and unless otherwise ordered by the court, to do so upon the basis of the proceedings already had and the record upon which said appeal was heard and determined.

(i) The court may, in its discretion, enter judgment for costs in favor of or against an appellant, or other interested parties intervening in said appeal, but not against the Commission, depending upon the nature of the issues involved upon said appeal and the outcome thereof.

(j) The court's judgment shall be final, subject, however, to review by the Supreme Court of the United States upon writ of certiorari on petition therefor under Section 1254 of Title 28 of the United States Code, by the appellant, by the Commission, or by any interested party intervening in the appeal, or by certification by the court pursuant to the provisions of that section.

INQUIRY BY COMMISSION ON ITS OWN MOTION

SEC. 403. The Commission shall have full authority and power at any time to institute an inquiry, on its own motion, in any case and as to any matter or thing concerning which complaint is authorized to be made, to or before the Commission by any provision of this Act, or concerning which any question may arise under any of the provisions of this Act, or relating to the enforcement of any of the provisions of this Act. The Commission shall have the same powers and authority to proceed with any inquiry instituted on its own motion as though it had been appealed to by complaint or petition under any of the provisions of this Act, including the power to make and enforce any order or orders in the case, or relating to the matter or thing concerning which the inquiry is had, excepting orders for the payment of money.

REPORTS OF INVESTIGATIONS

SEC. 404. Whenever an investigation shall be made by the Commission it shall be its duty to make a report in writing in respect thereto, which shall state the conclusions of the Commission, together with its decision, order, or requirement in the premises; and in case damages are awarded such report shall include the findings of fact on which the award is made.

SEC. 405. After a decision, order, or requirement has been made by the Commission in any proceeding, any party thereto, or any other person aggrieved or whose interests are adversely affected thereby, may petition for rehearing; and it shall be lawful for the Commission, in its discretion, to grant such a rehearing if sufficient reason therefor be made to appear. Petitions for rehearing must be filed within thirty days from the date upon which public notice is given of any decision, order, or requirement complained of. No such application shall excuse any person from complying with or obeying any decision, order, or requirement of the Commission, or, operate in any manner to stay or postpone the enforcement thereof, without the special order of the Commission. The filing of a petition for rehearing shall not be condition precedent to judicial review of any such decision, order, or requirement, except where the party seeking such review (1) was not a party to the proceedings resulting in such decision, order, or requirement, or (2) relies on questions of fact or law upon which the Commission has been afforded no opportunity to pass. Rehearings shall be governed by such general rules as the Commission may establish, except that no evidence other than newly discovered evidence, evidence which has become available only since the original taking of evidence, or evidence which the Commission believes should have been taken in the original proceeding shall be taken on any rehearing. The time within which a petition for review must be filed in a proceeding to which Section 402(a) applies, or within which an appeal must be taken under Section 402(b), shall be computed from the date upon which public notice is given of orders disposing of all petitions for rehearing filed in any case, but any decision, order, or requirements made after such rehearing reversing, changing, or modifying the original order shall be subject to the same provisions with respect to rehearing as an original order.

GENERAL PROVISIONS RELATING TO PROCEEDINGS—WITNESSES AND DEPOSITIONS

SEC. 409. (a) In every case of adjudication (as defined in the Administrative Procedure Act) which has been designated for a hearing by the Commission, the hearing shall be conducted by the Commission or by one or more examiners provided for in Section 11 of the Administrative Procedure Act, designated by the Commission.

(b) The officer or officers conducting a hearing to which subsection (a) applies shall prepare and file an initial decision, except where the hearing officer becomes unavailable to the Commission or where the Commission finds upon the record that due and timely execution of its functions imperatively and unavoidably require that the record be certified to the Commission for initial or final decision. In all such cases the Commission shall permit the filing of exceptions to such initial decision by any party to the proceeding and shall, upon request, hear oral argument on such exceptions before the entry of any final decision, order, or requirement. All decisions, including the initial decision, shall become a part of the record and shall include a statement of (1) findings and conclusions, as well as the basis therefor, upon all material issues of fact, law, or discretion, presented on the record; and (2) the appropriate decision, order, or requirement.

(c) (1) In any case of adjudication (as defined in the Administrative Procedure Act) which has been designated for a hearing by the Commission, no examiner conducting or participating in the conduct of such hearing shall, except to the extent required for the disposition of ex parte matters as authorized by law, consult any person (except another examiner participating in the conduct of such hearing) on any fact or question of law in issue, unless upon notice and opportunity for all parties to participate. In the performance of his duties, no such examiner shall be responsible to or subject to the supervision or direction of any person engaged in the performance of investigative, prosecutory, or other functions for the Commission or any other agency of the Government. No examiner conducting or participating in the conduct of any such hearing shall advise or consult with the Commission or any member or employee of the Commission (except another examiner participating in the conduct of such hearing) with respect to the initial decision in the case or with respect to exceptions taken to the findings, rulings, or recommendations made in such case.

(2) In any case of adjudication (as defined in the Administrative Procedure Act) which has been designated for a hearing by the Commission, no person who has participated in the presentation or preparation for presentation of such case before an examiner or examiners or the Commission, and no member of the Office of the Chief Accountant shall (except to the extent required for the disposition of ex parte matters as authorized by law) directly or indirectly make any additional presentation respecting such case, unless upon notice and opportunity for all parties to participate.

(3) No person or persons engaged in the performance of investigative or prosecuting functions for the Commission, or in any litigation before any court in any case arising under this Act, shall advise, consult, or participate in any case of adjudication (as defined in the Administrative Procedure Act) which has been designated for a hearing by the Commission, except as a witness or counsel in public proceedings.

(d) To the extent that the foregoing provisions of this section are in conflict with provisions of the Administrative Procedure Act, such provisions of this section shall be held to supersede and modify the provisions of that Act.

(e) For the purposes of this Act the Commission shall have the power to require by subpena the attendance and testimony of witnesses and the production of all books, papers, schedules of charges, contracts, agreements, and documents relating to any matter under investigation. Witnesses summoned before the Commission shall be paid the same fees and mileage that are paid witnesses in the courts of the United States.

(f) Such attendance of witnesses, and the production of such documentary evidence, may be required from any place in the United States, at any designated place of hearing. And in case of disobedience to a subpena the Commission, or any party to a proceeding before the Commission, may invoke the aid of any court of the United States in requiring the attendance and testimony of witnesses and the production of books, papers, and documents under the provisions of this section.

(g) Any of the district courts of the United States within the jurisdiction of which such inquiry is carried on may, in case of contumacy or refusal to obey a subpena issued to any common carrier or licensee or other person, issue an order requiring such common carrier, licensee, or other person to appear before the Commission (and produce books and papers if so ordered) and give evidence touching the matter in question; and any failure to obey such order of the court may be punished by such court as a contempt thereof.

(h) The testimony of any witness may be taken, at the instance of a party, in any proceeding or investigation pending before the Commission, by deposition, at any time after a cause or proceeding is at issue on petition and answer. The

Commission may also order testimony to be taken by deposition in any proceeding or investigation pending before it, at any stage of such proceeding or investigation. Such depositions may be taken before any judge of any court of the United States, or any United States commissioner, or any clerk of a district court, or any chancellor, justice, or judge of a supreme or superior court, mayor, or chief magistrate of a city, judge of a county court, or court of common pleas of any of the United States, or any notary public, not being of counsel or attorney to either of the parties, nor interested in the event of the proceeding or investigation. Reasonable notice must first be given in writing by the party or his attorney proposing to take such deposition to the opposite party or his attorney of record, as either may be nearest, which notice shall state the name of the witness and the time and place of the taking of his deposition. Any person may be compelled to appear and depose, and to produce documentary evidence, in the same manner as witnesses may be compelled to appear and testify and produce documentary evidence before the Commission, as hereinbefore provided.

(i) Every person deposing as herein provided shall be cautioned and sworn (or affirm, if he so request) to testify the whole truth, and shall be carefully examined. His testimony shall be reduced to writing by the magistrate taking the deposition, or under his direction, and shall, after it has been reduced to writing, be subscribed by the deponent.

(j) If a witness whose testimony may be desired to be taken by deposition be in a foreign country, the deposition may be taken before an officer or person designated by the Commission, or agreed upon by the parties by stipulation in writing to be filed with the Commission. All depositions must be promptly filed with the Commission.

(k) Witnesses whose depositions are taken as authorized in this Act, and the magistrate or other officer taking the same, shall severally be entitled to the same fees as are paid for like services in the courts of the United States.

(l) No person shall be excused from attending and testifying or from producing books, papers, schedules of charges, contracts, agreements, and documents before the Commission, or in obedience to the subpena of the Commission, whether such subpena be signed or issued by one or more commissioners, or in any cause or proceeding, criminal or otherwise, based upon or growing out of any alleged violation of this Act, or of any amendments thereto, on the ground or for the reason that the testimony or evidence, documentary or otherwise, required of him may tend to incriminate him or subject him to a penalty or forfeiture; but no individual shall be prosecuted or subjected to any penalty or forfeiture for or on account of any transaction, matter, or thing concerning which he is compelled, after having claimed his privilege against self-incrimination, to testify or produce evidence, documentary or otherwise, except that any individual so testifying shall not be exempt from prosecution and punishment for perjury committed in so testifying.

(m) Any person who shall neglect or refuse to attend and testify, or to answer any lawful inquiry, or to produce books, papers, schedules of charges, contracts, agreements, and documents, if in his power to do so, in obedience to the subpena or lawful requirement of the Commission, shall be guilty of a misdemeanor and upon conviction thereof by a court of competent jurisdiction shall be punished by a fine of not less than $100 nor more than $5,000, or by imprisonment for not more than one year, or by both such fine and imprisonment.

TITLE V—PENAL PROVISIONS—FORFEITURES

GENERAL PENALTY

SECTION 501. Any person who willfully and knowingly does or causes or suffers to be done any act, matter, or thing, in this Act prohibited or declared to be unlawful, or who willfully and knowingly omits or fails to do any act, matter, or thing in this Act required to be done, or willfully and knowingly causes or suffers such omission or failure, shall, upon conviction thereof, be punished for such offense, for which no penalty (other than a forfeiture) is provided in this Act, by a fine of not more than $10,000 or by imprisonment for a term not exceeding one year, or both; except that any person having been once convicted of an offense punishable under this Section, who is subsequently convicted of violating any provision of this Act punishable under this Section, shall be punished by a fine of not more than $10,000 or by imprisonment for a term not exceeding two years or both.

VIOLATIONS OF RULES, REGULATIONS, AND SO FORTH

SEC. 502. Any person who willfully and knowingly violates any rule, regulation, restriction, or condition made or imposed by the Commission under authority of this Act, or any rule, regulation, restriction, or condition made or imposed by any international radio or wire communications treaty or convention, or regulations annexed thereto, to which the United States is or may hereafter become a party, shall, in addition to any other penalties provided by law, be punished, upon conviction thereof, by a fine of not more than $500 for each and every day during which such offense occurs.

FORFEITURES

Sec. 503. (a) Any person who shall deliver messages for interstate or foreign transmission to any carrier, or for whom as sender or receiver, any such carrier shall transmit any interstate or foreign wire or radio communication, who shall knowingly by employee, agent, officer, or otherwise directly or indirectly, by or through any means or device whatsoever, receive or accept from such carrier any sum of money or any other valuable consideration as a rebate or offset against the regular charges for tramission of such messages as fixed by the schedules of charges provided for in the Act, shall in addition to any other penalty provided by this Act forfeit to the United States a sum of money three times the amount of money so received or accepted and three times the value of any other consideration so received and accepted, to be ascertained by the trial court; and in the trial of said action all such rebates or other considerations so received or accepted for a period of six years prior to the commencement of the action may be included therein, and the amount recovered shall be three times the total amount of money, or three times the total value of such consideration, so received or accepted, or both, as the case may be.

(b) (1) Any licensee or permittee of a broadcast station who—

(A) Willfully or repeatedly fails to operate such station substantially as set forth in his license or permit,

(B) willfully or repeatedly fails to observe any of the provisions of this Act or of any rule or regulation of the Commission prescribed under authority of this Act or under authority of any treaty ratified by the United States,

(C) fails to observe any final cease and desist order issued by the Commission,

(D) violates Section 317 (c) or Section 509 (a) (4) of this act, or

(E) violates Section 1304, 1343, or 1464 of Title 18 of the United States Code, shall forfeit to the United States a sum not to exceed $1,000. Each day during which such violation occurs shall constitute a separate offense. Such forfeiture shall be in addition to any other penalty provided by this Act.

(2) No forfeiture liability under paragraph (1) of this subsection (b) shall attach unless a written notice of apparent liability shall have been issued by the Commission and such notice has been received by the licensee or permittee or the Commission shall have sent such notice by registered or certified mail to the last known address of the licensee or permittee. A licensee or permittee so notified shall be granted an opportunity to show in writing, within such reasonable period as the Commission shall by regulations prescribe why he should not be held liable. A notice issued under this paragraph shall not be valid unless it sets forth the date, facts, and nature of the act or omission with which the licensee or permittee is charged and specifically identifies the particular provision or provisions of the law, rule, or regulation or the license, permit, or cease and desist order involved.

(3) No forfeiture liability under paragraph (1) of this subsection (b) shall attach for any violation occurring more than one year prior to the date of issuance of the notice of apparent liability and in no event shall the forfeiture imposed for the acts or omissions set forth in any notice of apparent liability exceed $10,000.

PROVISIONS RELATING TO FORFEITURES

Sec. 504. (a) The forfeitures provided for in this Act shall be payable into the Treasury of the United States, and shall be recoverable in a civil suit in the name of the United States brought in the district where the person or carrier has its principal operating office or in any district through which the line or system of the carrier runs; provided, that any suit for the recovery of a forfeiture imposed pursuant to the provisions of this Act shall be a trial de novo; provided further, that in the case of forfeiture by a ship, said forfeiture may also be recoverable by way of libel in any district in which such ship shall arrive or depart. Such forfeitures shall be in addition to any other general or specific penalties herein provided. It shall be the duty of the various district attorneys, under the direction of the Attorney General of the United States, to prosecute for the recovery of forfeitures under the Act. The costs and expenses of such prosecutions shall be paid from the appropriation for the expenses of the courts of the United States.

(b) The forfeitures imposed by Parts II and III of Title III and Sections 503(b) and 507 of this Act shall be subject to remission or mitigation by the Commission, upon application therefor, under such regulations and methods of ascertaining the facts as may seem to it advisable, and, if suit has been instituted, the Attorney General, upon request of the Commission, shall direct the discontinuance of any prosecution to recover such forfeitures; provided, however, that no forfeiture shall be remitted or mitigated after determination by a court of competent jurisdiction.

(c) In any case where the Commission issues a notice of apparent liability looking toward the imposition of a forfeiture under this Act, that fact shall not be used, in other proceedings before the Commission, to the prejudice of the persons to whom such notice was issued, unless (i) the forfeiture has been paid, or (ii) a court of competent jurisdiction has ordered payment of such forfeiture, and such order has become final.

Sec. 505. The trial of any offense under this Act shall be in the district in which it is committed; or if the offense is committed upon the high seas, or out of the jurisdiction of any particular state or district, the trial shall be in the district where the offender may be found or into which he shall be first brought. Whenever the offense is begun in one jurisdiction and completed in another it may be dealt with, inquired of, tried, determined, and punished in either jurisdiction in the same manner as if the offense had been actually and wholly committed therein.

COERCIVE PRACTICES AFFECTING
BROADCASTING

Sec. 506. (a) It shall be unlawful, by the use or express or implied threat of the use of force, violence, intimidation, or duress, or by the use or express or implied threat of use of other means to coerce, compel, or constrain or attempt to coerce, compel, or constrain a licensee—

(1) to employ or agree to employ, in connection with the conduct of the broadcasting business of such licensee, any person or persons in excess of the number of employees needed by such licensee to perform actual services; or

(2) to pay or give or agree to pay or give any money or other thing of value in lieu of giving, or on account of failure to give, employment to any person or persons, in connection with the conduct of the broadcasting of such licensee, in excess of the number of employees needed by such licensee to perform actual services; or

(3) to pay or agree to pay more than once for services performed in connection with the conduct of the broadcasting business of such licensee; or

(4) to pay or give or agree to pay or give any money or other thing of value for services, in connection with the conduct of the broadcasting business of such licensee, which are not to be performed; or

(5) to refrain, or agree to refrain, from broadcasting or from permitting the broadcasting of a non-commercial educational or cultural program in connection with which the participants receive no money or other thing of value for their services, other than their actual expenses, and such licensee neither pays nor gives any money or other thing of value for the privilege of broadcasting such program nor receives any money or other thing of value on account of the broadcasting of such program; or

(6) to refrain, or agree to refrain, from broadcasting or permitting the broadcasting of any radio communication originating outside of the United States.

(b) It shall be unlawful, by the use or express or implied threat of the use of force, violence, intimidation or duress, or by the use of express or implied threat of the use of other means to coerce, compel, or constrain or attempt to coerce, compel, or constrain a licensee or any other person—

(1) to pay or agree to pay any exaction for the privilege of, or on account of, producing, preparing, manufacturing, selling, buying, renting, operating, using, or maintaining recordings, transcriptions, or mechanical, chemical, or electrical reproductions, or other articles, equipment, machines, or materials,

used or intended to be used in broadcasting or in the production, preparation, performance, or presentation of a program or programs for broadcasting; or

(2) to accede to or impose any restriction upon such production, preparation, manufacture, sale, purchase, rental, operation, use, or maintenance, if such restriction is for the purpose of preventing or limiting the use of such articles, equipment, machines, or materials in broadcasting or in the production, preparation, performance, or presentation of a program or programs for broadcasting; or

(3) to pay, or agree to pay any exaction on account of the broadcasting, by means of recordings or transcriptions, of a program previously broadcast, payment having been made, or agreed to be made, for the services actually rendered in the performance of such program.

(c) The provisions of subsection (a) or (b) of this section shall not be held to make unlawful the enforcement or attempted enforcement, by means lawfully employed, of any contract right heretofore or hereafter existing or of any legal obligation heretofore or hereafter incurred or assumed.

(d) Whoever willfully violates any provision of subsection (a) or (b) of this section shall, upon conviction thereof, be punished by imprisonment for not more than one year or by a fine of not more than $1,000, or both.

(e) As used in this section the term "licensee" includes the owner or owners, and the person or persons having control or management, of the radio station in respect of which a station license was granted.

DISCLOSURE OF CERTAIN PAYMENTS

Sec. 508. (a) Subject to subsection (d), any employee of a radio station who accepts or agrees to accept from any person (other than such station), or any person (other than such station), who pays or agrees to pay such employee, any money, service, or other valuable consideration for the broadcast of any matter over such station shall, in advance of such broadcast, disclose the fact of such acceptance or agreement to such station.

(b) Subject to subsection (d), any person who, in connection with the production or preparation of any program or program matter which is intended for broadcasting over any radio station, accepts or agrees to accept, or pays or agrees to pay, any money, service or other valuable consideration for the inclusion of any matter as a part of such program or program matter, shall, in advance of such broadcast, disclose the fact of such acceptance or payment or agreement to the payee's employer, or to the person for whom such program or program matter is being produced, or to the licensee of such station over which such program is broadcast.

(c) Subject to subsection (c), any person who supplies to any other person any program or program matter which is intended for broadcasting over any radio station shall, in advance of such broadcast, disclose to such other person any information of which he has knowledge, or which has been disclosed to him, as to any money, service or other valuable consideration which any person has paid or accepted, or has agreed to pay or accept, for the inclusion of any matter as a part of such program or program matter.

(d) The provisions of this section requiring the disclosure of information shall not apply in any case where, because of a waiver made by the Commission under Section 317(d), an announcement is not required to be made under Section 317.

(e) The inclusion in the program of the announcement required by **Section** 317 shall constitute the disclosure required by this section.

(f) The term "service or other valuable consideration" as used in this section shall not include any service or property furnished without charge or at a nominal charge for use on, or in connection with, a broadcast, or for use on a program which is intended for broadcasting over any radio station, unless it is so furnished in consideration for an identification in such broadcast or in such program of any person, product, service, trademark, or brand name beyond an identification which is reasonably related to the use of such service or property in such broadcast or such program.

(g) Any person who violates any provision of this section shall, for each such violation, be fined not more than $10,000 or imprisoned not more than one year, or both.

PROHIBITED PRACTICES IN CASE OF CONTESTS OF
INTELLECTUAL KNOWLEDGE, INTELLECTUAL SKILL, OR CHANCE

Sec. 509 (a) It shall be unlawful for any person, with intent to deceive the listening or viewing public—

(1) to supply to any contestant in a purportedly bona fide contest of intellectual knowledge or intellectual skill any special and secret assistance whereby the outcome of such contest will be in whole or in part prearranged or predetermined;

(2) by means of persuasion, bribery, intimidation, or otherwise, to induce or cause any contestant in a purportedly bona fide contest of intellectual knowledge or intellectual skill to refrain in any manner from using or displaying knowledge or skill in such contest, whereby the outcome thereof will be in whole or in part prearranged or predetermined;

(3) to engage in any artifice or scheme for the purpose of prearranging or predetermining in whole or in part the outcome of a purportedly bona fide contest of intellectual knowledge, intellectual skill, or chance;

(4) to produce or participate in the production for broadcasting of, to broadcast or participate in the broadcasting of, to offer to a licensee for broadcasting, or to sponsor, any radio program, knowing or having reasonable ground for believing that, in connection with a purportedly bona fide contest of intellectual knowledge, intellectual skill, or chance constituting any part of such program, any person has done or is going to do any act or thing referred to in paragraph (1), (2) or (3) of this subsection;

(5) to conspire with any other person or persons to do any act or thing prohibited by paragraph (1), (2), (3), or (4) of this subsection, if one or more of such persons do any act to effect the object of such conspiracy.

(b) For the purpose of this section—

(1) the term "contest" means any contest broadcast by a radio station in connection with which any money or any other thing of value is offered as a prize or prizes to be paid or presented by the program sponsor or by any other person or persons, as announced in the course of the broadcast;

(2) the term "the listening or viewing public" means those members of the public who, with the aid of radio receiving sets, listen to or view programs broadcast by radio stations.

(c) Whoever violates subsection (a) shall be fined not more than $10,000 or imprisoned not more than one year, or both.

UNAUTHORIZED PUBLICATION OF COMMUNICATIONS

Sec. 605. No person receiving or assisting in receiving, or transmitting, or assisting in transmitting, any interstate or foreign communication by wire or radio shall divulge or publish the existence, contents, substance, purport, effect, or meaning thereof, except through authorized channels of transmission or reception, to any person other than the addressee, his agent, or attorney, or to a person employed or authorized to forward such communication to its destination, or to proper accounting or distributing officers of the various communicating centers over which the communication may be passed, or to the master of a ship under whom he is serving, or in response to a subpoena issued by a court of competent jurisdiction, or on demand of other lawful authority; and no person not being authorized by the sender shall intercept any communication and divulge or publish the existence, contents, substance, purport, effect, or meaning of such intercepted communication to any person; and no person not being entitled thereto shall receive or assist in receiving any interstate or foreign communication by wire or radio and use the same or any information therein contained for his own benefit or for the benefit of another not entitled thereto; and no person having received such intercepted communication or having become acquainted with the contents, substance, purport, effect, or meaning of the same or any part thereof, knowing that such information was so obtained, shall divulge or publish the existence, contents, substance, purport, effect, or meaning of the same or any part thereof, or use the same or any information therein contained for his own benefit or for the benefit of another not entitled thereto—provided, that this section shall not apply to the receiving, divulging, publishing, or utilizing the contents of any radio communication broadcast, or transmitted by amateurs or others for the use of the general public, or relating to ships in distress.

WAR EMERGENCY—POWERS OF PRESIDENT

Sec. 606. (a) During the continuance of a war in which the United States is engaged, the President is authorized, if he finds it necessary for the national defense and security, to direct that such communications as in his judgment may be essential to the national defense and security shall have preference or priority with any carrier subject to this Act. He may give these directions at and for such times as he may determine, and may modify, change, suspend, or annul them and for any such purpose he is hereby authorized to issue orders directly, or through such person or persons as he designates for the purpose, or through the Commission. Any carrier complying with any such order or direction for preference or priority herein authorized shall be exempt from any and all provisions in existing law imposing civil or criminal penalties, obligations, or liabilities upon carriers by reason of giving preference or priority in compliance with such order or direction.

(b) It shall be unlawful for any person during any war in which the United States is engaged to knowingly or willfully, by physical force or intimidation by threats of physical force, obstruct or retard or aid in obstructing or retarding interstate or foreign communication by radio or wire. The President is hereby authorized, whenever in his judgment the public interest requires, to employ the armed forces of the United States to prevent any such obstruction or retardation of communication: provided, that nothing in this section shall be construed to repeal, modify, or affect either Section 6 or Section 20 of an Act entitled "An Act to Supplement Existing Laws Against Unlawful Restraints and Monopolies, and for Other Purposes."

(c) upon proclamation by the President that there exists war or a threat of war, or a state of public peril or disaster or other national emergency or in order to preserve the neutrality of the United States, the President, if he deems it necessary in the interest of national security or defense, may suspend or amend, for such time as he may see fit, the rules and regulations applicable to any or all stations or devices capable of emitting electromagnetic radiations within the jurisdiction of the United States as prescribed by the Commission, and may cause the closing of any station for radio communication, or any device capable of emitting electromagnetic radiations between 10 kilocycles and 100,000 megacycles, which is suitable for use as a navigational aid beyond 5 miles, and the removal therefrom of its apparatus and equipment, or he may authorize the use or control of any such station or device and/or its apparatus and equipment, by any department of the Government under such regulations as he may prescribe upon just compensation to the owners. The authority granted to the President, under this subsection, to cause the closing of any station or device and the removal therefrom of its apparatus and equipment, or to authorize the use or control of any station or device and/or its apparatus and equipment, may be exercised in the Canal Zone.

(d) Upon proclamation by the President that there exists a state or threat of war involving the United States, the President, if he deems it necessary in the interest of the national security and defense, may, during a period ending not later than six months after the termination of such state or threat of war and not later than such earlier date as the Congress by concurrent resolution may designate, (1) suspend or amend the rules and regulations applicable to any or all facilities or stations for wire communication within the jurisdiction of the United States as prescribed by the Commission, (2) cause the closing of any facility or station and its apparatus and equipment by any department of the Government under such regulations as he may prescribe, upon just compensation to the owners.

(e) The President shall ascertain the just compensation for such use or control and certify the amount ascertained to Congress for appropriation and payment to the person entitled thereto. If the amount so certified is unsatisfactory to the person entitled thereto, such person shall be paid only 75 per centum of the amount and shall be entitled to sue the United States to recover such further sum as added to such payment of 75 per centum will make such amount as will be just compensation for the use and control. Such suit shall be brought in the manner provided by paragraph 20 of Section 24, or by Section 145, of the Judicial Code, as amended.

(f) Nothing in subsections (c) or (d) shall be construed to amend, repeal, impair, or affect existing laws or powers of the states in relation to taxation or the lawful police regulations of the several states, except wherein such laws, powers, or regulations may affect the transmission of government communications, or the issue of stocks and bonds by any communication system or systems.

(g) Nothing in subsection (c) or (d) shall be construed to authorize the President to make any amendment to the rules and regulations of the Commission which the Commission would not be authorized by law to make; and nothing in subsection (d) shall be construed to authorize the President to take any action the force and effect of which shall continue beyond the date after which taking of such action would not have been authorized.

(h) Any person who willfully does or causes or suffers to be done any act prohibited pursuant to the exercise of the President's authority under this section, or who willfully fails to do any act which he is required to do pursuant to the exercise of the President's authority under this section, or who willfully causes or suffers such failure, shall, upon conviction thereof, be punished for such offense by a fine of not more than $5,000, except that any person who commits such an offense with intent to injure the United States or with intent to secure an advantage to any foreign nation, shall, upon conviction thereof, be punished by a fine of not more than $20,000 or by imprisonment for not more than 20 years, or both.

FCC Chronology and Leadership from 1934 to 1960

On March, 1958, Dr. Bernard Schwartz, who had formerly served as Legal Counsel for the House Subcommittee on Legislative Oversight investigating the FCC and other federal agencies, was quoted as having said to a Harvard Law School audience that these agencies had become "political dumping grounds for lame duck Congressmen" and that the caliber of appointments had been extremely low during the last 20 years.[1] Since he was primarily concerned with the activities of the FCC during his short-lived tenure with the Committee, we may assume that he had this agency mainly in mind when he made the derogatory remark.

With respect to the FCC, it cannot be properly said that the agency has been a "dumping ground" for lame duck Congressmen. In fact, of the 33 persons who have served on the Commission, only two served in Congress prior to their appointments. Nor is it correct to say that the caliber of appointments generally has been extremely low during the last twenty years. On the contrary, with some exceptions, those appointed to the FCC have been well qualified for their jobs.

THE FIRST DEMOCRATIC MEMBERS

The first FCC Chairman was Democrat *Eugene Octave Sykes*. He was from Mississippi, and prior to coming to Washington had served for eight years as a member of the Supreme Court of that state. He was appointed as an original member of the Federal Radio Commission in 1927 and continued in that office until the creation of the FCC in 1934 when Roosevelt made him Chairman of the new agency.[2]

Other original Democratic members who served under Mr. Sykes were Commissioner *Irvin Stewart* from Texas, attorney and educator, with a distinguished record as a professor at the University of Texas and American Univeristy, plus four years experience as Chief of the Electrical Communication Treaty Division in the Department of State and participation in several important international radio conferences, and who, because of his vast knowledge in the communications field and his writing skill, had been called upon by Congress to play a major role in drafting the Communications Act; *Paul A. Walker*, distinguished attorney who had achieved a national reputation as an able public utility regulator in his home state of Oklahoma, and aging attorney *Hampson Gary* who had had a long career in government and who resigned as Commissioner after less than six months of service.[3]

---

[1] *New York Times*, March 29, 1959, p. 36.

[2] *Who's Who in America*, 1940-41, p. 2518.

[3] Biographical material regarding these early Commissioners is taken from *Who's Who in America*, and press releases of the FCC.

The first Republican members were *Thaddeus Harold Brown* from Ohio, an attorney who had served as a member of the Ohio Civil Service Commission, had been Secretary of State in Ohio for four years and who, just prior to his FCC appointment, had been Vice-Chairman of the Federal Radio Commission; *Norman Stanley Case,* an attorney and former governor of Rhode Island and personal friend of Roosevelt when the latter was Governor of New York; and *George Henry Payne* from New York, author and journalist, and at one time Republican candidate for Governor in New York.

Mr. Sykes served as Chairman of the FCC only eight months. He continued as a Commissioner but stepped down as Chairman on March 9, 1935 and was succeeded by *Anning S. Prall,* a Democrat from New York State, who had served terms in Congress and previously was Commissioner of Taxes and Assessments in New York City and, at one time, had been President of the Board of Education there.

On July 23, 1937 Chairman Prall died and was succeeded by *Frank Ramsey McNinch* of North Carolina. Mr. McNinch had had a distinguished record as a governmental administrator and long experience in the field of utility regulation. With a professional background which included service as a member of the North Carolina House of Representatives and as Mayor of Charlotte, he accepted appointment to the Federal Power Commission in 1930. President Roosevelt designated him as Chairman of the FPC in 1933. He was Roosevelt's representative to the World Power Conference held at the Hague in July, 1935. He left the Chairmanship of the FPC at the suggestion of the President and took over the leadership of the FCC on October 1, 1937.

He remained at the FCC helm for a little less than two years when he resigned on August 31, 1939 to become Special Assistant to the Attorney General.

With the exception of Mr. Garey who resigned after a few months of service and Mr. Stewart whose short term expired June 30, 1937, all original members were still on the Commission when McNinch switched to the Justice Department.[4]

EARLY PROBLEMS AND ACCOMPLISHMENTS

The first five years were difficult and turbulent ones for these commissioners. The Commission had to be organized, the vast broadcasting and tele-communications industries had to be brought under regulatory controls, and the basic operational pattern of the Commission had to be established.

During the first year of its life, the Commission conducted hearings pursuant to Section 307(c) of the Communications Act and, as mentioned in Chapter 3, made a report to Congress with recommendations against requiring fixed percentages of broadcast facilities for educational purposes.

The Commission issued orders requiring licensees to file information regarding the ownership of broadcasting stations. Telephone and telegraph companies under the jurisdiction of the Commission were ordered to report current services, rates, contracts, and stock ownership. Under the leadership of Paul A. Walker, then Chairman of the Telephone Division, the Commission carried on an investigation of the American Telephone and Telegraph Company for three years which brought about substantial reductions in long distance telephone rates.[5]

[4] Biographical material regarding these early Commissioners is taken from *Who's Who in America* and press releases of the FCC.

[5] FCC Report, *Investigation of the Telephone Industry in the United States,* June 14, 1939, p. 602.

New rules and engineering standards for AM broadcast stations were approved.[6] Important hearings on radio frequency allocations were completed during this early period. Negotiations with other North American countries regarding the cooperative use of the radio spectrum and the avoidance of objectionable interference across national boundaries were completed. The result was the signing of the North American Regional Broadcasting Agreement in Havana on December 13, 1937.[7]

This was the period in which Mae West programs evoked wide-spread protests, and when Orson Wells caused "terror and fright" among millions of listeners with his "War of the Worlds" program. The Commission was pressed by the public to scrutinize more closely the programming of stations when they came up for renewal of their licenses.[8]

AN ANGRY CONGRESS

The problems of the Commission during these early days were aggravated by a hostile Congress. This antipathy was a carry over from the days of the Federal Radio Commission. That original "traffic cop of the air," as it was called, was never popular with Congress. As pointed out in Chapter 23, the FCC seemed to be even less popular. During the first four years of its life, it was the object of frequent charges and attacks from angry Congressmen. Growing dissatisfaction with the FCC's operations prompted the introduction of numerous resolutions in Congress to investigate the FCC.

THE CONTROVERSIAL MR. FLY

This was the unhappy situation which *James Lawrence Fly* faced when he took over the administrative reins of the FCC from Mr. McNinch on September 1, 1939. He was particularly well trained for the rough five years ahead. His educational and professional background included graduation from the U. S. Naval Academy, an LL.B. degree from Harvard and the practice of law in New York and Massachusetts. From 1929 to 1934, he was Special Assistant to the Attorney General and served as government counsel in actions involving restraint of trade under the Federal anti-trust laws. From 1934 to 1937, he headed up the legal department of the Tennessee Valley Authority and was its General Counsel for two years prior to his appointment as Chairman of the FCC on September 1, 1939.[9]

Less than three months after Mr. Fly took office, the Commission began public hearings on an order to investigate the radio networks. Despite vigorous and venomous protests from the broadcast industry, Mr. Fly was determined to see the investigation through to the bitter end. While the proceeding was under way, he was the subject of scathing attacks from industry spokesmen who were infuriated by his testy manner and the possibilities of stricter regulations.

He also received much tongue-lashing from Capitol Hill, and from 1939 to 1943, while he was in command at the FCC, no fewer than five resolutions were introduced in Congress to investigate the distraught agency. These various

[6] Rules and Regulations of the FCC, published in mimeograph form, FCC mimeograph No. 30764, Nov. 28, 1938. Also see *Fifth Annual Report of FCC* (1939).

[7] The full text of the agreement as approved by the signatories on December 13, 1939 appears in 1 RR 41:11-43.

[8] See Warner, Harry. *Radio and Television Law* (Washington, 1948), pp. 337-39.

[9] *Who's Who in America,* 1938-1939, p. 916.

investigatory moves were aided and abetted by a growing number of unsuccessful and disgruntled (and in some cases embittered) applicants for radio stations.

After prolonged hearings, in May, 1941, the Commission adopted its historic *Report on Chain Broadcasting,* establishing the network regulations.[10]

By this time, Commissioner Brown no longer was with the Commission, having encountered political difficulties on Capitol Hill and failing to secure confirmation of his reappointment by the Senate. Frederick I. Thompson, a Democrat and Newspaper publisher from Alabama, had been appointed and began service with the FCC on April 13, 1939. Ray C. Wakefield, an attorney and Republican from California and formerly Chairman of the public service commission of that state, took the oath of office on March 22, 1941. These new members joined Chairman Fly and Commissioners Walker and Payne in adoption of the majority report approving the network regulations.

As previously pointed out, T. A. M. Craven, who began his first term as Commissioner on August 25, 1937, vigorously dissented from the majority report and was joined in the dissent by Commissioner Case.

Chairman Fly was on the receiving end of much of the criticism which these network regulations evoked from Congress and the broadcast industry. Already bruised and battered by three years of the ordeal, he appeared before the Senate Interstate and Foreign Commerce Committee and adamantly denied the charges made against the Commission.[11]

Shortly thereafter, the Supreme Court issued the famous Felix Frankfurter opinion (*National Broadcasting Co. vs. U. S.,* 319 U.S. 190, May 10, 1943), upholding the legality of the regulations. But powerful political and economic forces had now combined to force the resignation of Mr. Fly. But he by no means was about to resign. He was determined to weather the storm, "come hell or high water."

He had the sympathetic support of Clifford J. Durr who had come on the Commission in November, 1941, about the time the network investigation began. Mr. Durr was a Democrat from Alabama. He was a brilliant lawyer, having graduated from the law school at the University of Alabama and later completed a degree in jurisprudence at Oxford University under a Rhodes scholarship. From 1933 to 1941, he had held a number of important legal positions in the Federal government. He was General Counsel and Director of the Defense Plant Corporation at the time of his appointment to the FCC.[12] He was a liberal in the true sense of the word and intensely devoted to the public interest.

Despite the prolonged pounding inflicted on him by the Cox Committee (discussed in Chapter 23), Mr. Fly did not give up his FCC job until December 1944. He resigned just a few weeks before the Committee released its report absolving the Commission of most of the major charges made against it.

WAR-TIME ACTIVITIES

While much of Mr. Fly's time and energy as Chairman was taken up with matters pertaining to the investigation, he and the other commissioners carried heavy administrative duties during the War. The Board of War Communications,

[10] FCC, *Report on Chain Broadcasting,* Commission Order No. 37, Docket No. 5060, May, 1941.
[11] Hearings before the Senate Committee on Interstate Commerce on S. Res. 113, 77th Congress, First Session, June 2 to 20, 1941, pp. 10106.
[12] *Broadcasting,* March 17, 1958, p. 54.

cooperating with the Office of Civilian Defense and other governmental agencies and the military establishment, made important contributions to the war effort.

Also, it was during this period that the Commission held hearings on the proposed merger of the Postal Telegraph and Western Union companies. After consideration of a long and involved record in the proceeding, the Commission approved the consolidation and thereby made possible a stabilization of the telegraph industry.[13]

Because of the continued growth of newspaper ownership of radio stations during the late thirties, the Commission under the leadership of Mr. Fly instituted a full scale investigation to determine whether a monopoly in mass media was developing. There was pressure from some sources for the establishment of rules which would impose limitations on newspaper ownership of stations.

After long public hearings in which the press strongly opposed any rules which would discriminate against newspapers, the Commission issued a report which it submitted to Congress.[14] No rules were established. The Commission simply said that in the future, each case involving newspaper ownership and raising questions of monopoly, would be decided on its merits. This policy enunciated under Mr. Fly's leadership has continued, more or less, to be the policy of the Commission ever since.[15]

POST-WAR LEADERSHIP

Following Mr. Fly's resignation on November 11, 1944, *Ewell Kirk Jett* was appointed interim Chairman. Prior to his appointment as a Commissioner, he had served as Chief Engineer. He had had a distinguished career as a radio engineer in the Navy, the Federal Radio Commission and the FCC, covering a span of 35 years. He had been a bulwark of strength down through the years in helping meet the many difficult engineering problems with which the Commission had been faced.[16]

But he was eager to retire from government service and had no desire to take over the full duties of Chairman. Accordingly, his interim appointment was terminated in about six weeks and he was succeeded by *Paul A. Porter* who had received the Presidential nod for the position.

Who's Who in America for 1944 gives the highlights of Mr. Porter's previous career as follows: He was educated at Kentucky Wesleyan College and University of Kentucky Law College. Later, he worked for several years as a newspaper reporter and editor. From 1934 to 1937, he was Special Counsel in the Department of Agriculture; and from 1937 to 1942 was Washington Counsel for the Columbia Broadcasting System. Subsequently, he was Deputy Administrator in charge of the rent division of the Office of Price Administration and at the time of his appointment to the FCC was Assistant Director of the Office of Economic Stabilization.[17]

Although Mr. Porter was with the Commission only a little over a year,

[13] 10 FCC 148-198, September 27, 1943.

[14] The hearings were conducted for a total of 25 days between July 23, 1941 and February 12, 1942. The record consisted of 3400 pages and 400 exhibits. 54 witnesses were called. See "The Newspaper Radio Decision" 7 *FCC Bar Journal* (1944), 11, 13.

[15] See Warner, *op. cit.*, pp. 205 to 212, for good discussion of the newspaper ownership hearings, the decision of the FCC and the problems involved.

[16] *Who's Who in America*, 1940-41, p. 1390.

[17] *Ibid.*, 1946-47, p. 1889.

some very significant developments occurred while he was there regarding frequency allocations for FM and TV broadcasting. With the War coming to a close, the Commission, under the previous leadership of Mr. Fly, had initiated public hearings relating to the allocation of frequencies above 25 megacycles. Mr. Porter and the Commission followed through with a number of important reports based upon these hearings.

On June 27, 1945, the Commission allocated the 88 to 108 megacycle band as the "permanent home" for FM broadcasting, reserving the first twenty channels in the band for noncommercial, educational broadcasting.[18]

After further hearings, on September 12 and 20, 1945, the Commission published rules and regulations and standards of good engineering practice governing the commercial FM broadcast service.[19]

It was also in connection with this proceeding, that the Commission allocated the 44 to 88 and 174 to 216 megacycle bands to television. Following hearings which began on October 4, 1945, the Commission, on November 21, 1945, made available thirteen VHF channels for commercial television with UHF channels provided for experimentation and future development.[20]

THE "BLUE BOOK" CONTROVERSY

Mr. Porter also gave leadership in the preparation and publication of the industry-shaking "Blue Book." Before he came on the scene, for years, certain Congressmen had been complaining that the Commission had been lax in establishing and enforcing standards for radio programs; that despite many complaints, little effort had been made to require stations to serve the "public interest."[21]

Commissioner Durr, who had already been on the Commission more than three years, felt strongly that something positive should be done about it. He was quite articulate and vocal in the expression of his views and had much to do with establishing a climate of receptivity in the Commission for definite action. Typical of his thinking was a speech he made during the War in which he said:

In thinking of radio, we are too much inclined to think in terms of what radio can bring to the people—a one-way pipeline of news, ideas, and entertainment—and too little in terms of its value as an outlet through which the people may express themselves. Democracy thrives more on participation at its base than upon instruction from the top . . . Round-table discussion of local problems by local people, and town meetings in which local people participate, may be as exciting and as important as similar types of programs on national and international affairs participated in by authorities of national or international reputation. Moreover, while programs by the local music society, the college department of music, the policemen's band, or the local little theater may not reach the technical perfection of similar performances by a national symphony orchestra or Hollywood professionals, they bring to the community a sense of participation and an awareness of cultural values that can never be piped in from studios in New York or Hollywood.

The world is now in the midst of a major crisis, greater than any that has hereto-

[18] Report of FCC on Allocations from 44 to 108 megacycles. Docket No. 6651, June 27, 1945.

[19] See Report of FCC, No. 84371, August 24, 1945.

[20] Report of the Commission Re. Promulgation of Rules and Regulations and Standards of Good Engineering Practice for Commercial Television Broadcast Stations (Docket No. 6780., Nov. 21, 1945).

[21] See speech of Congressman Wigglesworth on House Floor; 84 *Cong. Rec.* 1164-1166, Feb. 6, 1939.

fore occurred in its history. Following the war, when tremendous economic, political, and cultural adjustments will have to be made, the pattern of the future will depend upon our ability to make these adjustments in the right way. In this country, we are dedicated to the principles of democracy. If the pattern of the future is to be a democratic pattern, it cannot be imposed from the top; it must be based upon the desires, beliefs, and feelings of the people themselves. Democracy can function only in an atmosphere of full information and frank discussion. In determining the course of the future, radio can plan its part for good or evil, depending upon whether it is the voice of the few or an outlet for full information and free expression, as uncurbed by commercial as by political restraints.[22]

Mr. Durr believed that some minimum program standards should be set up by the Commission to be applied when stations come up for renewal of their licenses. Mr. Porter agreed, and during his one year tenure as FCC Chairman, Dr. Charles Seipmann, formerly with the British Broadcasting Corporation, was brought in to direct a study and come up with some criteria which the Commission might establish for the evaluation of radio program service.

The result of this study was the adoption and publication by the FCC in March, 1946 of the report, *Public Service Responsibility of Broadcast Licensees,* fully discussed in previous Chapters.

Only a few weeks before this report was released, Paul Porter resigned to accept the position of OPA Administrator. He was replaced by a brilliant young man then only thirty-two years of age, *Charles Ruthven Denny, Jr.,* who had been appointed Commissioner shortly after Mr. Porter received the Chairmanship.

Mr. Denny had a brilliant record as a student at Amherst and at Harvard Law School. He was admitted to the District of Columbia Bar in 1936, practiced law in the District for two years, and then joined the Department of Justice as an attorney. He was appointed Special Assistant to the Attorney General in 1941 and came to the FCC as Assistant General Counsel the following year.[23]

Not yet thirty years of age, he quickly acquired a masterful knowledge of regulatory problems at the FCC and demonstrated unusual administrative and organizational ability. He was made General Counsel in October, 1942 and during the next two years spent much of his time representing the Commission in the hearings conducted by the Congressional Select Committee to which reference has already been made.[24]

His stellar performance in these hearings was credited as having been an important factor in the issuance of the report by that committee which acquitted the Commission of most of the charges made against it. There can be no doubt that the favorable impression he made on Congress as well as his efficient handling of legal matters within the Commission, accounted for his appointment to the Commission on March 30, 1945.[25] With the departure of Mr. Porter, it was only logical that Mr. Denny should succeed him.

He was appointed Acting Chairman on February 26, 1946.[26] He continued in an acting capacity until December 4 of the same year when the President gave him full status as Chairman.[27]

[22] Durr, Clifford Judkins, "Freedom of Speech for Whom," FCC Mimeograph No. 79855.

[23] *Who's Who in America,* 1946-47, p. 599.

[24] See *FCC Log. A Chronology of Events in the History of the Federal Communications Commission from its Creation on June 19, 1934, to July 2, 1956;* compiled by the FCC Office of Reports and Information.

[25] *Ibid.,* p. 45.

[26] *Ibid.,* p. 49.

[27] *Ibid.,* p. 52.

Only a few weeks after he was appointed Acting Chairman, the Blue Book was issued. Industry and Congressional reaction was immediate. It was charged that the document had been adopted without rule-making proceedings and was therefore illegal; that it constituted censorship and violated Section 326 of the Communications Act and the First Amendment to the Constitution.[28]

Judge Thurman Arnold, former member of the United States Circuit Court of Appeals for the District of Columbia, took an opposite point of view. Speaking for the American Civil Liberties Union over the CBS network on June 1, 1946, he commended the FCC for its action. Said he, in part:

The Commission announced that hereafter in issuing and in renewing the licenses of broadcasting stations it would give particular attention to the program service that the station had been giving the public . . . The Commission followed the simple principle that this valuable public grant should be given to those who gave more public service in preference to those who gave less. The absence of such a standard in the past has been responsible for the abuses of our forums of the air. It is difficult to see how any rational man can quarrel with this sort of protection of the public interest, as a condition of a public grant.[29]

The Commission, under Mr. Denny's leadership, set up machinery to apply the criteria set forth in the Blue Book. Licensees were put on notice that their program service would be measured in terms of these criteria when their stations came up for renewal of their licenses.

Shortly thereafter, a number of hearings on renewal applications were held. Some stations received slaps on the wrist for over-commercialization or for not providing what the Commission called a "balanced program service." In no case, however, was a single renewal application denied for failure to adhere to Blue Book standards.[30]

Nevertheless, the very fact that the Commission had announced its intention to apply these program standards and, in a few instances, had required stations to go through expensive public hearings before their licenses were renewed, gave force and sanction to the standards which most licensees felt it would be risky to ignore.

A number of other significant actions were taken by the Commission while Mr. Denny was Chairman. Measures were adopted to streamline and speed up the processing of applications.[31] New rules for educational FM stations were adopted.[32] The international tele-communications conference began in Atlantic City on May 16, 1947 and continued until October 3 of the same year with Chairman Denny presiding.[33]

A COMMERCIAL BROADCASTER BECOMES CHAIRMAN

A treaty having been signed by all the participants, Mr. Denny resigned in October, 1947 as Chairman of the FCC to accept a position as General Counsel of the National Broadcasting Company.[34]

[28] Senate Resolution 307 introduced by the late Senator Tobey to investigate FCC control over radio programming was an outgrowth of these charges. See *Cong. Rec.*, 9803, 9804, July 24, 1946.

[29] Speech of Thurman Arnold over CBS Network, June 1, 1946, incorporated in *Congressional Record* by Congressman Hugh B. Mitchell. 92 *Cong. Rec.* A 3120-21, June 3, 1946.

[30] See *Walmac Co.*, 12 FCC 91, 3 RR 1371 (1947); *Eugene J. Roth*, 12 FCC 102, 3 RR 1377 (1947); *Hearst Radio, Inc.*, 6 RR 994 (1951).

[31] *FCC Log, op. cit.*, pp. 50-51.

[32] *Ibid.*, p. 56.

[33] *Ibid.*, p. 58.

[34] *Ibid.*

Commissioner Paul A. Walker, was appointed Acting Chairman less than one month later and held the position until December 26, 1947, when President Truman gave the Chairmanship to *Wayne Coy*.[35]

Like some of his predecessors, Mr. Coy had an impressive background. He graduated from Franklin (Indiana) College in 1926. He began his newspaper career at the age of 16 as a reporter, and later served as city editor of the *Franklin Star* and became editor and publisher of the *Delphi Citizen*.

In 1933, he was made a secretary to Governor McNutt of Indiana, directed the Governor's Commission on Unemployment Relief, and organized and administered Indiana's first Welfare Department. In 1935, he was appointed Indiana State Administrator and Regional Administrator for the Works Progress Administration. Two years later he went to the Philippines as administrative assistant to Mr. McNutt, then United States High Commissioner to those islands. Subsequently, Mr. Coy was made Assistant Administrator of the Federal Security Agency, followed by an assignment in 1941 as Special Assistant to the President and White House Liaison officer with the Office of Emergency Management.

In 1942, he was appointed Assistant Director of the Budget, a position which he held until February, 1944 when he left government service to become assistant to the publishers of the *Washington Post* and director of the paper's radio stations WINX-AM and WINX-FM.

Mr. Coy had been active on a number of committees of the National Association of Broadcasters. In 1946 and 1947, he headed an industry committee which cooperated with the Federal Communications Commission on the simplification of broadcast application forms. He had long been interested in frequency modulation broadcasting and had served as an officer and director of FM Broadcasters, Inc.[36]

Mr. Coy served as Chairman for four years. During this time, the Commission grappled with many difficult regulatory problems. On September 20, 1948, the Commission initiated public hearings on possible expansion of television broadcasting to include the UHF bands, the addition of color, and other improvements.[37] Shortly thereafter, all TV applications were "frozen" pending study of the general TV situation.[38] Long and exhaustive hearings were held intermittently, and after the issuance of five reports covering different phases of the TV proceeding, the Commission began the preparation of its final report and order looking toward lifting the television "freeze," adding 70 UHF channels, adopting a nation-wide allocation table with assignment of both VHF and UHF channels to communities throughout the country, and reserving 242 channels for education.[39]

Mr. Durr did not seek reappointment when his term expired on June 30, 1948 and had no opportunity to participate in these television hearings. His intelligent and constructive efforts, however, in behalf of educational broadcasting continued to have effect. The understanding and enthusiasm which he generated in the Commission with respect to educational FM carried over into the television proceedings and no doubt was an important factor in the Commission's decision to reserve television channels for education.

In this connection, the late Commissioner *Frieda B. Hennock,* who replaced

[35] *Ibid.,* p. 59.
[36] FCC Biographical Sketch of Chairman Wayne Coy, Mimeograph No. 14931, December 29, 1947.
[37] *FCC Log, op. cit.,* p. 62.
[38] *Ibid.*
[39] *Ibid.,* p. 75-76.

Mr. Durr,[40] should be mentioned. She was a Democrat from New York where she had practiced law and had been active in politics before coming to the Commission. She soon exhibited an active interest in reserving TV channels for education. Her animated and zealous advocacy during the hearings attracted nation-wide attention, and many have credited her with playing a major role in the Commission's decision to make the reservations.

In connection, with the channel allocations and the establishment of a nation-wide plan for television, there were many thorny technical problems. The knowledge and advice of Commissioners Edwin M. Webster and George A. Sterling, both career men who had served the Commission in an engineering capacity for many years, were most helpful in working out these problems.

One of the controversial questions that the Commission had to consider in the television proceeding was whether to establish a fixed table of assignments for the country at large with definite mileage separations for stations on the same or adjacent channels, or to provide that assignments would be made in terms of local demand and needs. The majority report resolved the question in favor of the fixed table. Robert Jones, a Republican from Ohio and a former Congressman, who became a Commissioner on September 5, 1947, dissented vigorously. The majority contended that the adoption of the fixed table of assignments would make for administrative simplicity and would provide for a more equitable and effective distribution of television facilities. Commissioner Jones disagreed. In concluding his dissenting opinion he said:

. . . Efficient distribution of channels and the provision of the maximum number of television stations have been sacrificed to achieve a misleading appearance of simplicity of administration. The public interest, convenience and necessity have been abandoned to the theoretical convenience of the Commission. The small communities are to be subjected to rules drawn upon considerations applicable primarily or wholly to large cities. The apparent simplicity of administration is an illusion that will disappear as soon as the number and complexity of conflicting applications under the standards emerge. The Commission thinks it has eliminated Section 307(b)* contests between cities (it has not eliminated them all); but by creating a scarcity of frequencies it has created a bigger problem in each city where there will surely be more applicants than there are channels. The administrative burden created by competitive applicants for the limited number of frequencies by this artificial scarcity or channel assignments will far outweigh the administrative burden they are trying to eliminate.[41]

Other important accomplishments of the Commission under the Coy administration should be noted. Of special importance was the adoption of the famous report authorizing broadcasters to editorialize subject to their affording broadcast time for the expression of opposing views.[42] The Commission underwent a reorganization; administrative and prosecutory functions were separated; hearing examiners were appointed in line with the Administrative Procedure Act, requiring that they act in a judicial capacity and decide cases independently. New bureaus were established to take care of expanding broadcast

[40] *Ibid.,* p. 62.

* Section 307(b) of the Communications Act provides that "in considering applications for licenses, and modifications and renewals thereof, when and insofar as there is demand for the same, the Commission shall make such distribution of licenses, frequencies, hours of operation, and of power among the several states and communities as to provide a fair, efficient, and equitable distribution of radio service to each of the same.

[41] *FCC Sixth Report and Order;* 17 Fed. Reg. 3905, 4100, May 2, 1952.

[42] *In the Matter of Editorializing by Broadcasting Licensees,* FCC Docket No. 8516; 13 FCC 1246; 14 Fed. Reg. 30 55; 1 RR 91:21 (1949).

services and many new rules and regulations were adopted to cover these services.[43]

The Wayne Coy administration came to a close when he resigned on February 21, 1952 to go into the television business. He was succeeded by *Paul A. Walker* whose tenure as Chairman lasted for eighteen months, and whose professional career is hereinafter presented in detail as a special case study in public administration.

REPUBLICAN LEADERSHIP FOR THE FIRST TIME

With the election of a Republican administration, *Rosel Hyde,* who had been a member of the Commission since April, 1946, was designated by President Eisenhower to succeed Commissioner Walker as the Chairman for the specified term of one year.[44] Upon expiration of the one year, the President having failed to take action, the Commission continued Mr. Hyde's position by electing him Acting Chairman.[45] He continued in this acting capacity until the President appointed *George C. McConnaughey* on October 4, 1954.[46]

During Mr. Hyde's administration, there were a number of important and significant developments. TV processing lines were established to speed up action on pending applications. A code of ethics for FCC employees was adopted. A $65,000,000 increase in interstate telephone rates became effective. The license term for TV stations was extended from one to three years. The multiple ownership rules were amended limiting control by one group or interest to 7 AM, 7 FM and 7 TV stations, with ownership of VHF stations limited to 5. Domestic telegraph rates were increased, yielding additional annual income to Western Union of $10,000,000.[47]

Mr. McConnaughey, a resident of Ohio, had been Chairman of the Renegotiation Board prior to his appointment as head of the FCC. His formal education included a Ph. B. degree from Denison University, and LL. B., Western Reserve University. He was admitted to the Ohio Bar in 1924. After practicing law for two years, he was employed by the city of Cleveland in a legal capacity from 1926 to 1928. From 1939 to 1945, he was chairman of the Ohio Public Utilities Commission and for three years during this period, served as chairman of the Ohio War Transportation Committee. He was president of the National Association of Railroad and Utilities Commissioners in 1944-45.[48]

Mr. McConnaughey's administration as Chairman of the FCC lasted about two years and nine months. Some developments during that period should be noted. FM broadcasters were authorized to engage in supplemental "funtional music" operations. A study of network operations was initiated. Rule making proceedings to consider the problems of UHF were instituted. The Commission called a public conference to consider the technical problems of UHF, out of which developed an industry committee known as TASO. This organization made allocations studies for more than two years and reported important data to the Commission in 1959.[49]

At no previous period in the history of the Commission was there more intense rivalry for the acquisition of broadcasting facilities. Applicants for

[43] *FCC Log, op. cit.,* 65-82.
[44] *Ibid.,* p. 88.
[45] *Ibid.,* p. 94.
[46] *Ibid.,* p. 97.
[47] *Ibid.,* pp. 82-97.
[48] *Who's Who in America,* 1958-59, p. 1830.
[49] *FCC Log, op. cit.,* pp. 97-112.

television stations spent hundreds of thousands of dollars in competitive proceedings. With some channels being sought valued at as high as ten million dollars each, enormous pressures of an extrajudicial character were brought to bear on Congress, the White House and the FCC to influence decisions in highly controversial cases.

Mr. McConnaughey's term expired on June 30, 1957 and he left the Commission to practice law. Prior to his departure, Congress, through its special House Committee on Legislative Oversight, was preparing to make serious charges against the Commission with particular respect to its handling and disposition of several important TV cases. It was this foreboding situation which *John Charles Doerfer* faced when he moved into the Chairman's office in July, 1957 and which plagued him and the Commission almost constantly during the three year period that he headed the agency. The following article is a detailed case study of his character, qualifications and administration as FCC Chairman.

JOHN CHARLES DOERFER'S DEMISE AS FCC CHAIRMAN *

On June 19 of this year, the Federal Communications Commission will be twenty-six years old. To put it mildly, its life has been hectic.

This agency that regulates all broadcasting and a vast portion of the telephone and telegraph industries in the country, since its birth in 1934, has been viewed more or less continuously by its progenitors on Capitol Hill as a delinquent child—congenitally weak and depraved, and requiring frequent discipline.

It has been under formal investigation by Congress or the threat of one every year since it was created. In fact, its recent bath of fire brought on by the spectacular exploits of the House Subcommittee on Legislative Oversight was but a continuation of the ordeal to which the bedraggled Commission has been subject most of its life.

Its general popularity rating has never been high. The broadcast industry has often complained bitterly because of FCC regulations, particularly when they relate to programming. Other groups have denounced the Commission for not imposing stricter program controls. It has been called almost everything in the book—incompetent, irresponsible, morally corrupt, bureaucratic, left wingish and even subversive.

The eleven men who have served as Chairman of the FCC have been clobbered unmercifully. One died in office. Three succumbed shortly after leaving the job. Of those still alive, two have related that they suffered serious health impairment as a result of the experience.

With the possible exception of James Lawrence Fly who ruled the FCC roost during the early forties, no chairman had a rougher time than John Charles Doerfer who resigned on March 10, 1960. He held the position for almost three years (the average term for FCC chairmen has been less than two years), and the hot seat kept him jumping most of the time.

He was appointed a member of the Commission in 1953 and was designated Chairman in July, 1957, replacing George McConnaughey who left the job to practice law. Even before President Eisenhower gave him the nod for the top post, the House Subcommittee on Legislative Oversight already had Doerfer and several other FCC Commissioners targeted for investigational fire. Dr. Bernard Schwartz, the "rule or ruin" professor (as he was later called by

* This article is by the author and appeared in the March 1960 issue of the *Telefilm Magazine*. It is reprinted with a few editorial changes by permission of *Telefilm*.

Congressman Harris), then Chief Counsel for the Subcommittee, had his staff searching the FCC files for evidence of villainy. And with the use of concealed tape recorders in their interviews at the FCC, they were conducting try-outs for the leading characters to be featured in the sensational drama to follow.

A few months later, the big show opened in the House Office Building on Capitol Hill. In a confidential memo prepared for the Subcommittee, Dr. Schwartz had accused the FCC Chairman and several other members of the Commission of official misconduct, undue fraternization with the broadcast industry, and fraud against the government. The memo had been leaked to the press without Doerfer having received any prior official notice of the charges. He was incensed, and appeared before the Subcommittee in public hearings to answer the charges.

Normally a mild man, he was in an angry mood as he faced a battery of news-hungry reporters and clicking cameras and began his testimony that afternoon on February 3, 1959. While he didn't question the right of a Congressional committee to investigate the Commission, he was deeply aggrieved and provoked by what he considered to be the irresponsible and sleuth-like tactics of Professor Schwartz and his staff. "It is my right," he declared, "as a public official and as a citizen to object strongly to the process of smearing reputations by distortions and innuendo."

With vocal acidity he referred to the "confidential" memo of Dr. Schwartz which had charged that he and other members of the Commission had failed to act with judicial propriety and were guilty of undue association with the broadcast industry.

"This memorandum," he said, "makes it appear that the members of the FCC are judges and only judges. It implies that most of their time is spent in deciding cases between litigants. . . . Probably ten per cent of our work involves litigated matters. In such cases, we sit as judges. When I *sit* as judge, I *act* as judge. When I have matters for decision between litigants, I do not discuss these matters with either side, or, for that matter, with anyone. But when I am a legislator looking for information to solve some of the great problems confronting communications in the country, I will talk to anyone . . . in my office . . . on the steps of the Capitol or at lunch with him at any public restaurant . . ."

With impassioned utterance (which brought applause from the crowded hearing room), he said that he "came to Washington a man of modest means. I am still a man of modest means. I followed my conscience in deciding every matter that came before me. I have done the best I know how and I am willing to subject my record to the sharpest scrutiny . . ."

With the conclusion of Mr. Doerfer's opening statement, the spotlight shifted to Dr. Schwartz. With dramatic ferocity, the probing professor grilled Chairman Doerfer for nearly three days. Among other things, he wanted to know if Doerfer had made trips at the expense of organizations regulated by the FCC. Doerfer readily admitted that he had made some, but was quick to point out that he was permitted to do so by Section 4(b) of the Communications Act which specifically provides that an FCC commissioner may accept a "reasonable honorarium or compensation" for the "presentation or delivery of publications or papers."*

But what about the trips he had made when he had received expense money from the group he addressed and at the same time had been reimbursed by the government for these expenses? With a kind of "mousetrap" finality in his

* Section 4(b) has since been repealed by Congress.

voice, the professor wanted to know if Chairman Doerfer thought Section 4(b) of the Act permitted him to make a profit at government expense.

Mr. Doerfer's face flashed fire at this innuendo. "That's a nasty way to put it," he indignantly replied. He explained that if a group offered him a reasonable honorarium or compensation for making a speech, which included a sum equal to what he could legitimately claim from the government, it was perfectly proper for him to accept it, and in no sense was there any violation of the law.

He further testified that in each case where he had received honorariums plus government reimbursement for expenses, his trips had had a double purpose. He explained that on all such trips he not only made speeches, but spent considerable time making studies and inspections of an official nature.

Never once during the three day ordeal did Doerfer wince under the whip-lash of cross-examination. With clear conscience and indomitable courage, he stoutly defended his actions and denied every charge made against him.

Shortly thereafter, Dr. Schwartz resigned as Chief Counsel under pressure from the Subcommittee which had become increasingly unhappy with his methods of operation. No punitive action of any kind was taken against Mr. Doerfer although there was a strong feeling on the part of some Congressman that he was unfit to continue in office. Despite all the furor on Capitol Hill, two other commissioners against whom the professor had made similar charges of misconduct, were subsequently re-appointed to the FCC for seven year terms and were confirmed by Congress with little difficulty.

While many people feel that Mr. Doerfer should have been more aloof in his relations with the broadcast industry, it is clear from the record that he violated no laws. There was no evidence that any of his decisions in official matters were affected by *ex parte* influences. While some may disagree with him as to how much a commissioner should associate informally with persons connected with industries regulated by the FCC (this writer certainly does), no thinking person, fully understanding the functions and responsibilities of the agency, would argue that a commissioner should be restricted to the same extent as a judge.

As Doerfer pointed out, an FCC official has important duties of a legislative and rule-making character. These require that he be free to move with intelligent discretion outside Commission walls and talk with those who are in a position to give him information about the problems of the communications industry. Except in adjudicatory cases, in important matters about which there is public interest and concern, he should be free to express his personal views and discharge his statutory duty to "encourage the larger and more effective use of radio in the public interest."

It has now been over a year since Mr. Doerfer appeared the first time before the Subcommittee on Legislative Oversight to answer questions regarding his official conduct. Until he resigned March 10, he and his colleagues at the FCC had been so busy with pressing regulatory matters that there was little time for him to brood over episodes of the past. The stack of agenda items which the FCC must consider at its regular meetings each week often measures a foot high. Some items, of course, are disposed of quickly. On the other hand, many involve highly technical questions and perplexing matters of public policy, requiring careful and prolonged study.

For example, during the past year or so, the problem of frequency allocation has demanded increasing time and attention. How can the limited radio spectrum be better divided and made to serve more effectively our growing civilian and military needs? How can this be done in the face of growing demands of other countries for larger slices of the spectrum to meet their needs?

Finding satisfactory answers to these questions is time-consuming and brain-racking. All FCC commissioners have been concerned with the problem at the domestic and international levels. Mr. Doerfer and two other commissioners found it necessary to travel abroad to negotiate with other countries and attempt to work out allocation agreements.

Related to the general allocation problem is the long standing, hotly contested issue whether to break up the clear channels and provide more frequencies for new stations in areas not now receiving adequate primary radio service. It has been hanging fire for fifteen years and a decision is long over-due.

Recently, the former Chairman and his fellow commissioners proposed to authorize new Class II stations on these clear channels in the western part of the country where local broadcast facilities are limited. While there is growing public sentiment in favor of such a proposal, clear channel stations and other broadcast interests will vigorously oppose it and the Commission, in all probability, will be pulled through the wringer before a final decision is made.

Just lately, the Commission concluded public hearings in Washington. These hearings were precipitated largely by public concern over the quiz scandals. During most of December, the FCC commissioners listened to witnesses complain about these deceptive programs, about payola practices, over-commercialization, crime thrillers and various other types of broadcasting.

As Chairman, Mr. Doerfer expressed the view that some of the grave charges of wide-spread corruption and deception in the broadcast industry are canards. He agreed, however, that there have been some reprehensible practices that must be uprooted. He favored reasonable measures by government to prevent their recurrence. In line with this belief, he went along with other commissioners in proposing, in February 1959, that rules be adopted to prohibit television stations from carrying rigged programs, unless an announcement is made by the station at the beginning and end of such programs that they are rigged, are in fact not spontaneous, and do not involve genuine contests of intellectual skill or knowledge.

Furthermore, the Commission under his leadership proposed a rule which would deny a license to any TV station having a contract with a network unless the station has received assurance that any network program of this type will be accompanied by announcements describing its true nature.

Mr. Doerfer hoped that these rules would be adopted. He was troubled, however, by the incessant demands of some segments of the public that the FCC prescribe specific program standards and attempt to define "program balance" for all radio and television stations.

Shortly before President Eisenhower made him FCC Chairman in 1957, in a speech to the Catholic Institute of the Press in New York City, he compared the American system of broadcasting to systems in several other countries where government plays a more dominant role. In making comparison, he said "the American way of broadcasting is, and promises to continue to be, a greater power for good because it is a free system. The people themselves are given the opportunity of developing their own programs, freedom to express their thoughts and ideas, and the power to discourage poor programming quickly and effectively by turning off the dials."

He further avowed that "the Federal Communications Commission has very limited power over programming." But he "sees no obstacle in such a limitation because it reasserts the tremendous faith of the American people in preserving the freedom of expressing themselves with a minimum of governmental interference."

Despite his belief that the FCC has limited authority with respect to programming, he was willing to take corrective action where the violation of specific statutes were involved. For example, in December 1958, he and his colleagues ordered a station in Denver to show cause why its license should not be revoked, on the basis of a complaint that the station had carried off-color and indecent language, in violation of the Criminal Code which specifically forbids such language.

He summed up his views regarding the FCC's powers over broadcasting in these words:

Congress did provide for Federal regulation of the radio spectrum in the public interest. This is mainly a problem of allocating the radio spectrum between broadcasting and other communication services. Assignment of radio frequencies is made to private persons or corporations so as to effect an efficient and equitable distribution among the several states and communities.

The licensees were to have a license for three-year periods subject to renewal if they can show that they have programmed in the public interest. Specifically, licensees are prohibited from broadcasting obscene, indecent or profane matter, or any information in the conduct of a lottery, or denying equal opportunities to political candidates.

Apart from this, the Federal Communications Commission has little power over programming—especially over a single program." (May 5, 1957, FCC Mimeo. No. 44910).

In a speech before the presidents of state broadcasting associations on February 25, 1959, he pointed out that the American system of broadcasting is not subsidized by the taxpayers' money. "It is financed by businessmen who are seeking a profit," he declared. "This needs no apology. It is the philosophy of the Communications Act and of our form of government. There are those who contend that the profit motive in broadcasting should be substituted by a government whip—not a big rawhide one—but just a *little one* for the time being."

He doesn't agree. As he told these state presidents, he believes the "solutions for higher levels of all programming are essentially grass roots problem. They must grow out of felt needs and not be imposed by the infusion of an insipid system from some government hierarchy."

Despite his feeling that government should play a limited role in broadcasting, as Chairman of the FCC he often expressed his views publicly as to what constitutes good programming. He said that it should not only serve "the cultural, spiritual, educational and entertainment needs of the public," but also "should preserve for the people uncensored news and discussion of public problems."

As a public official, he felt that it was his duty to encourage and lend endorsement to high quality programs. He was eager, as he said, to use his position in every legitimate way to help the industry and the general public to the end that their interests would be better served.

It has long been a practice of the FCC to hold informal conferences with representatives of the telephone industry. These discussions, he believes, have resulted in improved telephone service and reductions in rates. In fact, only recently, the Bell company, through informal negotiations with the FCC, agreed to substantial cuts in charges for some calls. Mr. Doerfer sees no good reason why the broadcast industry and the FCC might not carry on informal negotiations and, avoiding arbitrary standards set by governmental fiat, thereby achieve improved program service.

With the thought of being helpful along this line, he proposed in January

1959, that the three networks work out a cooperative arrangement by which each would make available a minimum of one hour per week, during good listening time, for informational, educational and cultural programming.

As a result, the networks did enter into such an agreement which will go into effect the second week of November following the political conventions and general election. It is understood that the networks will consult with each other, under the auspices of the FCC, so that the periods designated by each for these special programs will fall on the different nights and provide for a maximum spread during the week.

While there are many who would disagree as to the quality of his performance at the FCC, certainly John Doerfer came to his job with an outstanding professional background. He came to the Commission with a fine collegiate record and long years of successful professional experience as an accountant, lawyer and public servant.

He was born in West Allis, Wisconsin, a suburb of Milwaukee. His parents were of German extraction, his father having come to this country when he was four years of age. As a child, Doerfer attended parochial schools in West Allis. At an early age, he was selling newspapers and working as a caddy on the golf courses to make part of his expenses. His father was a skilled machinist and had a reasonably good income, but with seven children to support he was unable to provide his family with much more than the basic necessities. John Doerfer, therefore, was compelled to make his own way through high school and college.

He peddled ice in the summer time in Madison, Wisconsin to help defray his expenses as a student at the University of Wisconsin. After graduation there, he entered the Marquette Law School in 1931 and completed his J.D. degree in 1934 with *cum laude* honors.

He was quiet and studious and highly respected by the faculty and students for his fine personal qualities and scholastic ability. He was known for his friendly disposition and ability to get along well with his fellow students and instructors. His classmates elected him president of the Senior Class in the Law School.

Prior to his law school years, he married Ida M. Page, a charming and intelligent girl who was born in Vermont but had been reared in Wisconsin. In addition to carrying a full course of study in law, he worked long hours as an accountant to take care of his school and family expenses. (Mr. and Mrs. Doerfer have two grown sons, both of whom are now in college.)

Those who knew him in those early years, report that he was mild and modest, but that he never backed away from a fight where important principles were involved.

After graduation from law school, he practiced law in West Allis. He was elected Chairman of the Junior Bar Association in Milwaukee and later served as Chairman of the Public Utilities Section of the Wisconsin Municipal League.

He was elected City Attorney of West Allis. In his practice before the Wisconsin Public Service Commission, he specialized in public utility cases and, in 1949, was appointed Chairman of that commission.

It was his four year record of performance in this job that attracted the attention of the White House in 1953, and led to his appointment to the FCC the same year, replacing Paul A. Walker from Oklahoma who retired after nineteen years of service.

As previously pointed out, Mr. Doerfer was under almost constant surveillance by the House Committee on Legislative Oversight while he was Chairman of the Commission. In 1957 he was severely questioned by this committee regarding a visit in the home of George B. Storer, owner of a number of broadcast stations. More recently, he made another trip to Florida and was a guest on Mr. Storer's yacht for several nights.

This second trip was the subject of critical interrogation by several members of the House Committee when Mr. Doerfer appeared before the committee on March 4, 1960, to testify regarding what steps the FCC had taken to curb payola practices in the broadcast industry. For almost three hours, without one minute of recess, he was peppered with questions. Congressman Moss of California devoted a third of the time to cross-examination designed to show the impropriety of his accepting gratuities from Mr. Storer. It was a grueling experience for the Chairman, but he maintained a remarkable calm and restraint which were the object of comment by numerous observers at the hearing.

Mr. Doerfer responded to questions by saying that he had a right to choose his friends, that he had the right to make social contacts with any persons providing they were not involved in adjudicatory proceedings before the FCC, and that, while there might be differences of opinion, he did not feel that he had done anything wrong and that his conscience was perfectly clear.

When asked if he intended to resign as Chairman of the FCC following the three hour ordeal, he angrily replied that he had no such intention. But the rigors of Congressional scrutiny inevitably take their toll. No man can last for long as Chairman of the FCC. Mr. Doerfer, with all his courage, was no exception.

On the morning of March 4, this writer, on assignment, spent an hour and a half with the former Chairman in his office. He had graciously granted permission for an interview in connection with the preparation of this article. During that interview he gave no indication that he intended to resign. It was the wood-shed treatment that he received from the Harris committee on Capitol Hill that afternoon, because of his visit with Mr. Storer on the yacht, that aroused White House concern and precipitated his demise as Chairman of the most controversial and investigation-ridden agency in the federal government.

FCC CHAIRMAN, FREDERICK WAYNE FORD*

A lawyer's lawyer is the way one of his former colleagues described the man who was elevated to the chairmanship of the Federal Communications Commission on March 15, 1960 . . . Frederick Wayne Ford. The fifty-year old soft-spoken Ford has served the FCC as Commissioner since his appointment to that post by President Dwight D. Eisenhower thirty months ago. Held in high esteem by the FCC legal staff and by many communications lawyers in Washington who practice before the Commission, this "handsomest member" of the agency that regulates the broadcasting industry is considered "no patsy for the industry."

His philosophy for broadcast regulation is quite different from his predecessor, John C. Doerfer, whose resignation was asked for and received by President Eisenhower. In a speech which he made to the West Virginia Broadcasters Association entitled "The Role of the FCC in Programming," last August, he reviewed the legislative history of the Radio Act of 1927 and the Communications Act of 1934, as well as important judicial decisions and the consistent administrative practice of the old Radio Commission and the FCC. He expressed the view that the Commission's authority in this field is crystal-clear and has definite responsibility to evaluate the over-all program service of a station in

* The author collaborated with the Editor of *Telefilm* in the writing of this portrait of Mr. Ford and it is reprinted from the March 1960 issue with the Editor's permission.

terms of the public interest when that station comes up for renewal of its license. As pointed out by Walter B. Emery in his profile of John C. Doerfer elsewhere in this magazine, the former chairman seriously questioned the legal authority of the FCC to regulate programs, except where they violate specific statutes such as those forbidding lotteries and indecent presentations. Doerfer often got worked up emotionally about obscenity on-the-air, but made it clear that he doubted the FCC's power to establish general standards or "guidelines" for broadcast programming. The legal basis for his doubt was Section 326 of the Communications Act which forbids the Commission from censoring programs. Doerfer not only doubted the FCC's legal power, but he questioned the propriety of general surveillance in view of our traditional concern in this country for free speech as guaranteed by the First Amendment. From a social point of view, Doerfer objected to it. Furthermore, he did not think it was possible to set forth program criteria, applicable to all communities, because of the multiplicity and variety of cultural tastes in this country.

Contrary to Doerfer, Ford, West Virginia Republican, believes the Commission not only *can* set up some guidelines for the industry but *should* do so. "It has been my view for a long time," said he, in the speech at White Sulphur Springs, West Virginia, "that it is highly unfair for the Commission to lie in ambush, so to speak, while practices are developing which violates its concept of the public interest, convenience and necessity, and then make an example of an uninformed broadcaster. I believe, rather it is generally our duty to inform the public through appropriate orders or reports of the criteria we expect to apply in advance of action against an individual broadcaster," he continued.

On February 11, 1960 Ford, in a speech before the Television and Radio Advertising Club of Philadelphia on "Programming . . . The Commission and Its Broadcast Licensees" in regard to the development within the Commission of a reasonably well-defined policy of reviewing programs stated:

. . . the greatest freedom will be assured the broadcaster in programming his station and at the same time the Commission will perform its function of protecting the public interest, convenience and necessity with the minimum of interference to that freedom.

Following his graduation from the University of West Virginia Law School in 1934, with scholastic honors, he entered private law practice for several years before coming to Washington to serve in the general counsel's office of the Federal Security Administration in 1939. From there he went to the Office of Price Administration in 1942, later joining the U.S. Army Air Force. After several years of military service, he was discharged as a major and came back to Washington in 1946. After a short period of service with the OPA, he joined the FCC legal staff in 1947 in the Hearing and Review Sections.

Mr. Ford became Chief of the Hearing Division of the FCC in 1951 and, while serving in that capacity, he served as FCC co-counsel in two of the most important hearing cases ever conducted by the FCC. He had a major responsibility in the now-famous Paramount case, in which Paramount Television Productions and its subsidiary companies were seeking renewal of station licenses and were asking for authority to build new television stations. He also assumed important legal responsibilities in the celebrated Richards case, in which George (Dick) Richards was charged with news-slanting on three clear channel stations, KMPC, Hollywood, WJR, Detroit, and WGAR, Cleveland.

Regarding the Paramount case, the Paramount companies had been involved in an anti-trust litigation for more than 20 years. These companies were charged with monopolistic practices and restraints of trade, both at federal and state levels. On May 3rd, 1948, the U.S. Supreme Court handed down a decision finding Paramount substantially guilty of the charges, including price-fixing conspiracies and block-booking.

Paramount was required to split into two companies, one to be concerned with pictures and the other with theatres. The FCC was concerned that Paramount's monopolistic practices might carry over into the television field. The FCC received reports to the effect that Paramount and other motion picture companies had refused to make any of their films available for use by television stations.

Fred Ford was one of the principal attorneys for the FCC in the hearings on the broadcast applications of Paramount. The case went on for many days before an FCC examiner. Ford and his aides had prepared for the hearings with meticulous care. A former member of the Commission staff, Walter B. Emery has described Ford's voice, the clear and methodical mind, the courteous but firm manner of Ford in his cross-examination of witnesses. "He seldom antagonized the witnesses, but his skillful questioning usually brought forth the facts," relates Emery.

The Commission ultimately granted the Paramount applications and subsequently approved a merger of Paramount with the American Broadcasting Company, and the Commission held that the policies of the motion picture company (Paramount) with respect to their past use of film talent or stories on television did not constitute a bar to a grant of license and transfer applications.

No case in the history of the FCC has received more nation-wide publicity than the Richards' case. Benedict Cottone, then General Counsel of the FCC, was the principal attorney, with his capable right hand man, Fred Ford.

The hearing extended over a three-year period. Two hundred and ninety witnesses were heard in over a hundred days of testimony. More than 18,000 pages of testimony were taken. Mr. Richards spent a reported two million dollars in behalf of his own defense.

Mr. Richards died and the case came to an inconclusive end. The FCC Examiner in the case issued a brief opinion, holding that the death of Richards "had rendered the proceedings moot." The Commission, accordingly, renewed the licenses of the stations.

One can only speculate what the Examiner might have done, had Mr. Richards lived. But it should be pointed out that Mr. Ford and other FCC counsel in the case had in their proposed findings of fact and law (document ran more than 300 pages), recommended that the licenses of these stations be revoked. Some of the language in that document which bears the Ford name may be the key to what may be expected of the new FCC chairman in the field of program regulation:

For a broadcaster to treat the facilities licensed to him as a tool for the exploitations of his personal, private, political, social and economic beliefs in a manner which denies or suppresses expression or opportunity for expression of contrary points of view, or in a manner which creates difficult obstacles to the equal presentation of such contrary points of view over that broadcaster's facilities, would in fact constitute the exercise by the broadcaster of a power of 'thought control' through the utilization of a facility entrusted to his use by the public . . .

The language of this document also makes it clear that Mr. Ford did not hold the view then, at least in the context of the Richards case, that the statutory bar against censorship precluded the Commission from judging the program service of a station to determine whether it had served the public interest. In fact, some of his recent statements are quite similar to those which appeared in that 1951 document:

"It is provided in the Communications Act (Section 326)," reads that weighty treatise, "that there shall be no censorship by the government of the communications transmitted over a radio station. The language of this provision is plain. Simply put, it means that the Commission may not restrain any station in its intention to broadcast or not to broadcast any particular material subject to such exceptions as pertain to lotteries, obscene and profane language and broadcast by candidates for public offices. But the Act provides just as plainly that the Commission may not grant a license to any person unless that license will be used in the public interest (Section 309). The same requirement is applied to a broadcaster who seeks renewal of his license (Section 307 (d). In the latter case, the test of whether the broadcaster who seeks a renewal of his license may be expected in the future to serve the public interest, is his past conduct and the record of his past operations. This has been aptly put by the courts in the language of the scriptures: *"By their fruits ye shall know them."* (*Matt. VII*:20).

Ford has endorsed the plan to require licensees up for renewal not only to submit program logs for the required week but also state in narrative form what the community's needs are and how the licensee has met them. He has yet to take sides in the proposal by Representative Oren Harris of the House Oversight Subcommittee, that the FCC actually monitor licensees on a nation-wide basis (this issue divided Harris and Doerfer), but Ford according to sources close to him will probably oppose the proposal.*

Another issue involved is "option time" which the Department of Justice anti-trust division under acting Assistant Attorney General Robert A. Bicks considers a violation of the antitrust laws, while the FCC majority disagrees, calling it "reasonably necessary for network operations." Although there has been no record vote on the "option" issue, Mr. Ford's concurring statement on the reduction in option time from 3 to 2½ hours maintained:

I do not believe the foregoing proposed rule changes will entirely eliminate the legal questions involved in the option time practice. The proposed rule changes appear, however, to minimize those questions. I, therefore, concur in the Notice.

Since becoming chairman, Ford has stated to the press that he intends to make his thoughts on "option time" soon public.

The contrast in the regulatory philosophies of Doerfer and Ford is sharp and clear. It was James Lawrence Fly, former chairman of the FCC (1939-1944), who was said to rule the FCC and the industry with a "move of the eyebrow" technique and who inspired the adoption of the ill-famed Blue Book with its specific criteria for FCC control of programming. He made a kind of ignominious exit from the FCC because the famous Cox committee in Congress had lambasted him unmercifully for "dictation to the industry" and for a cold aloofness to the industry. Mr. Doerfer left in somewhat the same disrepute because the Legislative Oversight Committee thought he was too little concerned about program practices and fraternized too closely with those he had to regulate.

"My own idea," Chairman Ford said in his first interview as chairman, "dating back to when I was in the Commission's review section, is that I

* Since this article was written, under Ford's leadership a new unit in the Commission has been established to do some selective monitoring of problems where the public interest so requires.

wouldn't have lunch with those dealing with the Commission. I have gone to a few large parties, given by broadcasters where there were many guests. One rule, I guess, is safety in numbers." In regard to the long-proposed code of ethics for commissioners, Ford believes "it is something we must consider."

In his first appearance on Capitol Hill as FCC chairman, Ford told the House Commerce Committee that his agency considers proposed prohibitions against off-the-record contacts with FCC members to be too broad in both adjudicatory and rulemaking cases as the current proposal defines them. (HR 4800).

Ford has spent most of his adult years working for the government (20 years, including four in Air Force, which elevated him from second lieutenant to major), as an attorney at the FCC and the Justice Department (four years), he has been involved in investigatory and adversary proceedings that have required considerable aloofness from the parties involved. His performances over the years have exhibited a judicial temper and a clear understanding between judicial and administrative processes. His training and professional conditioning are such that he will have no difficulty in drawing the line, and he will draw the line if there is any reasonable question as to ethics or morality. He certainly will not be taking long trips in airplanes and cruises on the Florida seas with those he has to regulate unless it is unmistakably clear that the public interest and not private interest is to be served.

It must be said, however, that his expressed opinions on accepting small gratuities from the industry are not as far different from those of Mr. Doerfer as many people think. The proof for this is to be found in his statement to the House Committee on Legislative Oversight, dated January 20, 1958. In fact, a reading of his words shows Mr. Ford in somewhat a laughing and derisive mood, at that time, regarding concern on the part of Dr. Schwartz, then general counsel of the Committee, and others about commissioners accepting free lunches, Christmas gifts, etc., Ford remarked:

Since becoming a member of the Commission, I have received numerous items of a promotional nature, e.g., newspapers, books, ashtrays, magazines, some of which I ignored, others I acknowledged, still others I have read, and all of which had a nominal value. I have attended several luncheons and dinners given on behalf of various organizations in the broadcast industry, which may or may not come before the Commission for consideration, but nevertheless are an integral part of the business. They have accorded me an opportunity to learn many facets of these problems, of which I did not obtain an intimate knowledge as a member of the Commission's staff for a number of years, and to become acquainted with some of the people in the industry, whom I did not already know. I have also received from organizations in various sections of the country eatables, of a perishable nature (some of which had already perished when I received them), the value of which was small and I regarded as an exhibition of regional pride, common to us all for products of the sections from which we come.

In the same statement, he admitted that after a meeting in New York City, one of the broadcasting companies had brought him home in "order that I could attend an event incident to the assumption of control of a broadcast station."

With obvious sarcasm directed at those who were making picayunish jibes at the Commissioners when the House committee was hot on the war path, he said:

I have attended a number of social gatherings given by telephone users who have been long time friends and neighbors, but it is my understanding that you are not interested in matters of that kind, nor in stock which may be owned by the church which I attend.

I have obtained two loans since returning to the Commission, both from commercial banking institutions. I have given the details of them to your investigators. To my knowledge these commercial banks are not interested in matters pending before the Commission, but they very well could have some indirect interest. I am not in a position to require banks to disclose to me their holdings as a condition of making a loan to me, and consequently cannot say what their interests may be. In the past I have not received any honorariums or travel expenses, *but I expect to attend ceremonies opening broadcast stations, meetings of broadcasters, inspection of various types of radio and television operations at the expense of the industry, to that end that I may gain as complete an expertise in this field as possible, and my authority for that is the 1922 Attorney General's opinion which has the full force and effect of law.*

This is almost precisely the justification that Mr. Doerfer gave for his trips, except that he took such trips on his vacation and claimed that he had a right to select his friends, be they broadcasters or otherwise, and was free to play bridge with them, ride their airplanes, take yacht rides with them, so long as they had no adjudicatory matters pending before the Commission.

Twelve men have served as Chairman of the FCC since it was created in 1924. Not one of them has served without accepting some gratuities from the broadcast and telecommunications industry. It has never been proved that any of them were bribed or that small gratuities have influenced their decisions in adjudicatory matters. No one can be an effective chairman of the FCC and insulate himself in the same way as a judge. As an official in a legislative and rule-making role, he must have opportunity to mix and mingle with those he regulates. Mr. Doerfer did it, but he apparently went too far and with the political climate as it is, the Congressional cleaver brought about his sudden demise as Chairman. Mr. Ford is on record saying that he expects to do it.* He no doubt will. The question is: Will he be able to draw the delicate line? The experience of some of his predecessors should be helpful to him. The fact is . . . Ford is a career man in government. By the end of his present term at the FCC (June 30, 1964) he will have served in government for more than 25 years, will be only 54 years of age, and will have a retirement income of something like $8,000 per year. His chairmanship promotion resulted in collecting only a $500-per-year raise. With this kind of retirement security ahead, he can, if he has a mind to, call the shots as he sees them. Despite the wolves, which inevitably will howl and gang up on him, if he can avoid the political wood-shed and ultimate burning at the stake which have befallen most of his predecessors, he just might give that controversial and much-maligned commission new stature, and still justify the hopes expressed for it by Sam Rayburn when he breathed the breath of life into it in the Rooseveltian rah! rah! days of 1934.

OTHER MEMBERS OF THE FCC

A short distance from Mr. Ford's office in the New Post Office Building are the offices of the six other FCC commissioners. The Vice-Chairman, so designated by his fellow commissioners, is *Rosel Herschel Hyde,* a Republican from Idaho. His educational training includes study at Utah Agricultural College and B. A. and LL.B. degrees from George Washington University. He has been in government service since 1924. Prior to his appointment as an FCC commissioner in 1946, he served successively as attorney for the Federal Radio Commission, and

* Public utterances of Mr. Ford since he became Chairman of the FCC indicate that he will be more restrained in his contacts with the public than he had previously indicated, particularly with individual applicants and licensees—the author.

attorney, Examiner, Assistant General Counsel and General Counsel for the FCC. Following the retirement of Paul Atlee Walker on June 30, 1953, as previously indicated, he served as Chairman for one year. He recently was appointed for another seven year term which will expire June 30, 1966.[50]

He has always been a strong believer in the free enterprise system. In a speech at the convention of the National Association of Radio and Television Broadcasters on May 26, 1954, while he was still acting as FCC Chairman, he stated "that one of the things which has given broadcasting its vitality is its freedom from oppressive regulatory action." The Commission "wishes to be helpful and not place a single unnecessary burden upon a licensee . . . We have no interest in regulation just for the sake of regulation.[51]

Because he is a devotee of the free competitive enterprise system, he has given his full support to FCC regulations designed to prevent monopolistic control of broadcasting. He has strongly resisted attempts to break down the multiple ownership rules of the commission which limit the number of stations that may be owned by one group or organization. For example, in an address to a regional meeting of NARTB on September 24, 1956, he declared that he could think of no more serious blunder the Commission could make than "to permit large financial aggregates to acquire a dominant role in the television medium." He further said that "a competitive television system is a bulwark against governmental interference."[52]

While opposing censorship in any form, he has supported the concept that stations should provide a program service designed to serve community needs. Accordingly, he does not oppose reviewing the over-all operation of stations when they come up for renewal of their licenses to determine whether they have served the public interest.

Robert Taylor Bartley is a Democrat member from Texas. He was appointed March 6, 1952, coming directly from Capitol Hill where he had been serving as Administrative Assistant to the Speaker of the House Sam Rayburn.

Following his college work at Southern Methodist University, he served on the research and investigative staff of the House Committee on Interstate and Foreign Commerce, and later held staff appointments at the FCC and the Securities and Exchange Commission. Subsequently, he became Vice-President of the Yankee Network, Inc., and before going to Capitol Hill was with the National Association of Broadcasters for five years.[53] He is now serving his second term which will expire June 30, 1965.

He too has decried censorship and is repelled by the idea that the Commission should tell the broadcasters what particular programs they should or should not carry. But he has made clear his belief that the Communications Act not only gives the Commission the authority to review program performance but imposes a definite responsibility on it to exercise this authority when stations file their renewal applications. In such program review, he thinks the Commission should be concerned with such matters as whether the station has been fair in presenting both sides of public issues and in presenting news programs. Also, where there is over-commercialization (especially if the use of "artificial audience-stealing gimmicks" is involved) or if the broadcaster seems more concerned with making a "fast buck" than providing public service, the Commis-

[50] Biographical Sketch of Commissioner Rosel H. Hyde, FCC Public Notice 34398, July, 1956.
[51] *Broadcasting*, February 1, 1954, p. 50.
[52] *Ibid.*, October 1, 1956, p. 75.
[53] Biographical Sketch of Robert T. Bartley, FCC Public Notice 73828, March 6, 1952.

sioner has not hesitated to question whether the station is serving the public interest.[54]

The youngest member of the Commission is *Robert E. Lee,* a Republican whose residence is in the District of Columbia. Prior to his appointment, he did important administrative work with the FBI, and for a time was Director of Surveys and Investigations for the House Committee on Appropriations.

He was born in Chicago and studied Commerce and Law at De Paul University. He had considerable experience with business concerns in an auditing capacity prior to his government career.[55]

His appointment to the FCC was contested by a substantial number of Senators. It was alleged by some that he lacked broadcast experience. Others were fearful that he might attempt to impose strict controls on the broadcast media. There can be no doubt that some on Capitol Hill opposed him because of his friendship for and past associations with Senator McCarthy, whose behavior at the time had outraged many Congressmen and a substantial number of people throughout the Country.

After much debate the Senate confirmed his appointment by a vote of 58 to 25. Following confirmation, the February 1, 1954 issue of *Broadcasting* carried a report on an interview with him in which he was quoted as expressing confidence in the "free-enterprise radio-TV system." He expressed the view that the FCC must be "in the driving seat but light on the reins." He further said that "as long as broadcasters stay within the law they will have no trouble with me. I hope no station in any part of the U. S. feels even remotely that I would encourage it to carry a certain program as against another."[56]

Eight months later, he warned the broadcasters that they would need to find a way to clean their own house or the sins of the few would bring "the walls of the temple crumbling down on the heads of the vast majority of this great industry."[57]

He expressed concern about over-commercialization in broadcasting, the abuses of the "pitch" advertisers and the "growing cancer" in the form of advertising in bad taste.

He summed up his concept of the FCC's regulatory role as "one of protecting the spectrum in the public interest" with a "minimum of regulation."[58]

Tunis Augustus MacDonough Craven, a Democrat member residing in Virginia, graduated as an engineer from the U. S. Naval Academy in the class of 1913. During his long naval career he specialized in radio communication.

He has participated in many important conferences dealing with communications, and has had wide experience as a private engineering consultant. Like Rosel Hyde, he served on the staff of the old Federal Radio Commission. Later he was appointed Chief Engineer of the FCC, which post he held until his original appointment as Commissioner in 1937.

In 1944, he left the Commission to become a private radio engineering consultant in Washington, D. C. He accepted a second appointment as Commissioner on July 2, 1956, and his present term runs to June 30, 1963.[59]

As pointed out in Chapter 3, he opposed the adoption of the network regula-

---

[54] *Broadcasting,* August 6, 1956, p. 77.

[55] Biographical Sketch of Commissioner Robert E. Lee, FCC Public Notice 96382, October 6, 1953.

[56] *Broadcasting,* February 1, 1954, p. 50.

[57] *Ibid.* September 27, 1954, p. 40.

[58] *Ibid.*

[59] Biographical Sketch of Commissioner T. A. M. Craven, FCC Public Notice 33738, July 2, 1956.

tions more than seventeen years ago on the grounds that they involved control of programs and business practices of broadcast licensees. Also, as heretofore indicated, he has taken the position that the Commission exceeds its authority when it requires licensees to supply program information in terms of certain categories which are set forth in the renewal application form. He has stated:

From my point of view the Commission's position in this entire matter is patently both illegal and impractical. For, here the Commission prescribes what programs it considers to be in the best interest of the public and, by this prescription, creates either an artificial demand or an artificial need, or both—which does violence to principles of freedom of expression; to the clear statutory principle that choice of programs is the licensee's exclusive duty and responsibility; to every social aspect of programming as it applies to the varying tastes, customs, needs, and demands of the many communities of this nation; and to the economic well-being of the stations themselves.

The answer to this Commission-created problem is simple, legal, and practical. The Commission should discontinue using program proposals as one of the criteria on which it bases its approval or disapproval of an application for a broadcast permit or renewal of license. Only for the purpose of determining whether the law would be or is being violated by programming should an applicant or a respondent in a revocation proceeding be required to file program proposals or practices. Otherwise the Commission should leave the task of programming in the public interest exclusively to the licensee where it belongs as a matter of right and duty.[60]

On March 3, 1958, former Commissioner *Richard Alfred Mack* resigned his position, following disclosures of the Congressional Committee on Legislative Oversight which raised questions with respect to his qualifications. He had been appointed on July 7, 1955, taking the place of Commissioner Frieda B. Hennock, whose term expired on June 30 of the same year.

Almost immediately following Mr. Mack's resignation, President Eisenhower appointed *John Storrs Cross* to take his place. After confirmation by the Senate, Mr. Cross was sworn in as Commissioner on May 23, 1958. At the time of his appointment, he was Assistant Chief of the Tele-communications Division of the State Department. He received a degree in electrical engineering from Alabama Poly-technic Institute in 1923. He had a long career as a construction engineer, having held important positions with the South Carolina and Michigan State Highway Departments and the National Park Service.

It is noteworthy that Mr. Gross voted to approve the Commissions recent interim policy on programming, which says that broadcasters have a positive duty to ascertain the needs and interests of the listeners and provide programs accordingly.

A recent appointee to the Commission was Republican *Charles Henry King,* Dean of the Detroit College of Law. He was appointed by President Eisenhower in June 1960, to fill the unexpired term of former Chairman John C. Doerfer. Congress however adjourned without the Senate having confirmed his nomination. He was serving under a recess appointment when President Kennedy, in January 1961, appointed 34-year-old Newton Norman Minow, a lawyer from Chicago, to replace him and to succeed Fred Ford as Chairman.

[60] Notice of Proposed Rule Making, *In the Matter of Section IV (Statement of Broadcast Application Forms 301, 303, 314 and 315,* FCC Docket No. 12673 adopted November 19, 1958; 1 RR 98:26.

It was hot and humid in Washington, D. C. the afternoon of June 30, 1953. Despite the heat and humidity, a large number of government employees and representatives of the communications industry gathered in the New Post Office Building on historic Pennsylvania Avenue to pay tribute to a retiring public official.

The guest of honor was Paul Atlee Walker, whose nineteen years of service as an FCC commissioner officially came to an end at five o'clock that day.

As Walker sipped soft punch and mingled with his friends, there was a remarkable alertness and joviality in his manner that belied his seventy-one years. A rigorous half century of public life had left some physical marks, but there was no bitterness on his countenance, no rancor in his speech. His conversation was amiable and gracious. And when the FCC staff presented him with a scroll and gold watch as tokens of esteem, he was deeply touched and visibly overcome with gratitude.

One short hour of congratulations and good wishes and the party was over. As the big clock in the tower of the Old Post Office Building across Twelfth Street struck five, most of the guests were leaving, to be caught up in the mad rush of traffic which, at that hour, fans out in all directions from downtown Washington as government workers hurry to their suburban homes. But a few of the old-timers lingered to visit longer with the Commissioner. For they knew that when he left his office that day, not only would a great public career come to an end, but it would mark the close of an important and dramatic era in which government for two decades had played a positive and dynamic role in the field of communications.

The circumstances of Paul Walker's early life had prepared him for a role of leadership during this historic era. Born in a Pennsylvania log house in 1881, the son of a Quaker farmer who had been impoverished by the depression at that time, he had known much discomfort and hardship in his childhood. Farms were foreclosed, unemployment stalked the land, and there was hunger everywhere. These conditions made an indelible mark on Walker's mind.

By the time he was eighteen he was decrying the abuses of uncontrolled capitalism." In 1899, in a speech to his graduating class at Southwestern State Normal School in California, Pennsylvania, he declared that "a man backed by ambition and greed, holding in his grasp the happiness of millions, should not be permitted to increase his power by continued extortion, if the power of the state can prevent it."

The next twelve years were busy ones as he prepared himself for the big job ahead. During this time, he completed a Ph. B at the University of Chicago, taught and directed athletics in an Illinois High School, served as principal of an Oklahoma high school, and completed a law degree at the University of Oklahoma.

His formal education completed, he opened a law office in Shawnee, Oklahoma. It was here he made his first political race. He ran for Justice of the Peace and was elected by an overwhelming majority.

After a few months at this job, he ran for County Judge. "I had no cash,"

---

* The author has known Mr. Walker for many years; worked with him as his legal assistant when he was a member and Chairman of the FCC. This study is partially based upon a book the author wrote about him, *Paul A. Walker of the FCC: An Appreciation* (Lancaster Press, 1946).

he has related, "so I went to the bank and borrowed enough to buy a horse. I rode that animal all over the county; covered every district. I talked to farmers in their homes and in the fields. I helped them milk their cows. I spoke from cotton wagons, at picnics and pie suppers. My campaign slogan was honesty and justice for all with special favors to none.

"In the Democratic primary, I was nominated by a huge majority. Sometime later, two election officials came to me and said they could carry a certain district for me in the general election, but that in order to do it, they would have to have some money. My reply was: 'Gentlemen, in the first place, I have no money. In the second place, if I did, it wouldn't be right to give it to you. You are election officials in that district and responsible for counting the votes. I might be accused of bribery.' "

If he had dealt differently with these money-seeking election officials, he might have won the race. He was defeated by 102 votes. A change of only 52 votes would have made him winner. But he would not compromise his principles to achieve the victory.

When he refused to take part in or sanction what he thought might be interpreted as a misdeed, he set a pattern for his life from which he never deviated. In the years that followed, he had opportunities to join questionable financial enterprises, but he scrupulously avoided them. He turned down many social invitations, not necessarily because he suspected that those doing the entertaining had ulterior motives, but more because he feared the public, to whom he was responsible, might misunderstand.

Walker lost no time grieving over his political defeat. Oklahoma was a young and growing state. If he could not be county judge, he knew there would be other challenging opportunities for public service.

There was an industrial boom. In 1910, the state was producing over 250,-000 barrels of oil daily. A year later, 110 fields had been established and Oklahoma was producing one-third of the world's supply. With an abundance of coal, lead, clays, timber, building stone and other raw materials, manufacturing had gotten a good start. New railroads were being constructed. The telephone industry, electric light and power plants, and other public utilities were growing rapidly.

With the growth of business in the state there was a corresponding expansion in the powers of government. The Oklahoma Corporation Commission needed a competent lawyer to head up its campaign to cut the costs of public utilities and conserve the state's natural resources.

This was precisely the kind of challenge Walker was looking for. He was offered the job. He quickly accepted and began work at the State Capitol on January 1, 1915.

In the fifteen years that followed, he waged an almost continuous fight with the gas and light companies to secure lower rates and improved service for the people of Oklahoma. He assisted in getting the legislature to pass a law giving authority to the Commission to enforce oil and natural gas conservation measures. He also served as special counsel for the Commission in its war against freight rate discriminations.

As a result of these activities, he was urged to run for membership on the Commission. He made the race in 1930 and was an easy winner. "My campaign was pretty well made before I announced that I would run," he has related. "As special counsel for the Commission, I had handled the freight rate cases for farmers, oil producers, and for almost every major industry in the state. As a result, three-fourths of the newspapers supported me without my requesting it."

After his election, he was chosen by other members of the Commission to serve as Chairman. He immediately launched an investigation of gas rates in the state. He thought they were much too high. Oklahoma was in the worst throes of depression. Many people could not pay their utility bills and their service was being cut off.

Shortly after the probe began, a man came to see him about the gas rate matter. "He asked me to have lunch with him," Paul Walker remembers. "I said, 'yes, I'll have lunch with you, but each man will pay for his own meal, and we'll eat in the Capitol cafeteria."

"As we ate lunch, he said he couldn't understand my position on the rate matter and wanted to know what I expected to get out of it by carrying on the fight. 'Not a thing,' was my emphatic answer, 'except to see that the people of Oklahoma are treated right.' He did not seem to understand that a public official could be motivated by an unselfish desire to serve the people."

It is no overstatement to say that Paul Walker almost stood alone at times in these battles for rate reductions. Often opposed by other members of the Oklahoma Commission, and frequently denounced by the utilities, he, nevertheless, stood firm for what he considered to be the rights and interests of the people. He did not want to hurt the utilities, but he felt it was his duty to see that the consuming public got a square deal and he worked uncompromisingly toward this end.

In response to a joint resolution of the state legislature in 1933, he started an official inquiry of rates and practices of telephone companies operating in Oklahoma. He has recounted some of the difficulties involved. "In determining whether certain charges for telephone service were reasonable, we were handicapped because we could not get all the facts. It was discovered that the American Telephone and Telegraph Company with headquarters in New York, was charging its subsidiaries in Oklahoma large management fees, yet we had no jurisdiction over the New York company which would permit us to examine the books of that company to determine the basis for such a charge."

He, like many other state utility commissioners, became convinced that the only way to achieve effective regulation of the communications industries operating across state lines was to establish a new Federal agency with which state commissions could cooperate. When Congress was considering legislation to create the FCC, he appeared before the House Committee on Interstate and Foreign Commerce and declared that "the ramifications of the holding companies made it an impossibility for the state commissions to get anywhere in a telephone rate investigation," and that "if there is to be effective regulation at all of the telephone business, it must be brought about through the Federal Commission."

President Roosevelt had been fully briefed on Walker's philosophy, background and special talents when, in 1934, he telephoned from the White House and asked if he would accept appointment as a member of the newly created FCC. He knew that Walker had the exact qualifications for this rugged assignment. He expected an affirmative answer and he got it! In a few weeks Walker took the oath of office in the new, air-conditioned Post Office Building in Washington, expensively equipped by James Farley with handsome furniture and fancy, brass cuspidors.*

Walker promptly called on President Roosevelt and presented a proposal for a comprehensive investigation of the telephone industry. The President was agreeable. A resolution was submitted to Congress and $750,000 was appropriated for the investigation (later increased to $1,500,000).

* The cuspidors were found to be unnecessary and later were removed from the building. The writer often has wondered what happened to these expensive items.

Walker immediately was under pressure to make political appointments. How he resisted this pressure is typified by an incident that happened in his office shortly after the investigation got under way. A high government official called on him to *demand* that his cousin be employed for one of the key jobs. After a few minutes of fiery verbal exchange, the Commissioner, fearless and determined, got up from his seat. The high politico knew it was time to go. Mumbling threats, he moved toward the door. His eyes piercing, and biting his words, the Commissioner retorted with finality: "There will be no politics in this investigation. I will not recommend the appointment."

Walker was eager to choose competent persons and perfect an efficient organization. By October, 1935, nearly 200 accountants and engineers had been employed and were studying the books and operations of the Bell System. Public hearings were held intermittently from March, 1936 to June, 1937. Company officials were interrogated on profits, dividends, labor policies, lobby and propaganda methods and other matters coming within the scope of the inquiry.

On December 2, 1936, the Commission announced that as a result of informal discussions with the Company, rates had been reduced to the extent that telephone subscribers would save 12 million dollars a year.

The final report on the investigation was submitted to Congress on June 14, 1939. It disclosed that telephone rate reductions "in excess of thirty million dollars were effected in the interest and for the benefit of the American telephone-using public."

A week after the report was made, President Roosevelt reappointed Walker for a second term on the Commission. Without objection, the Senate confirmed the appointment on June 29, 1939. A few days before, Congressman Jed Johnson brought applause from the House when he referred to the "unusual mental attainments" of Paul Walker and said that the "nation needs more men of his caliber in public life."

Paul Walker's interest in communications was not limited to telephone service. While much of his time and energy were taken up with the telephone investigation during the early years of his FCC career, he kept a close eye on the expanding broadcasting industry.

Two years before the telephone investigation was completed, speeches were being made in the halls of Congress condemning "radio monopoly." The increasing fury of Congressional criticism prompted the Commission to order a probe of the billon-dollar radio industry.

Paul Walker had an important hand in determining the scope of the inquiry, which covered contractual relations between networks and their affiliates, monopolistic practices in the broadcasting industry, and network control of station programming. He was appointed a member of the Commission committee to carry on the investigation. More than seventy sessions of public hearings were held. Walker was present at all but three of them and took an active part in the questioning of witnesses.

The outcome was the adoption of network regulations (still in effect) designed to break the grip of network control over station affiliates and require these stations to exercise greater responsibility over programming.

The network regulations evoked a storm of protest from the broadcast industry. Their validity was contested in the courts. It was alleged that the Commission exceeded its statutory authority, and that the rights of free speech had been abridged in violation of the First Amendment. But the Supreme Court didn't agree and the regulations were confirmed in May of 1943.

Following the Supreme Court decision, the president of one of the networks stated that under the Court's interpretation of the law the Commission could now do whatever it wanted to do in regulating the business practices and programs of broadcasters. But Walker didn't see it this way. He never felt that the Frankfurter opinion went this far. He construed the opinion to mean that the Commission had to pass on the qualifications of applicants for broadcast facilities and, in connection with license renewals, review the overall operation of stations and determine whether they had operated in the public interest. In fact, in 1946, he voted to approve the famous Blue Book about which there has been so much discussion in Washington. This document, which has never been officially repudiated by the FCC, set forth some general criteria to be used in determining whether stations have kept their promises and discharged their public responsibilities. And, in the opinion of this writer, if Walker were on the Commission today he would take a firm position against the deception and over-commercialization which have characterized many radio and TV programs in recent years. There would be no question in his mind that the Commission has the authority and the responsibility to prohibit, through its licensing functions, such deplorable practices.

Despite the strong positions he had taken regarding some of the policies of the telephone and broadcasting industries, he came through the Congressional investigations of the forties unscathed. While charges and counter-charges were being made, with the Commission under scorching attack from Congress and special interests, Paul Walker fearlessly continued to "call the shots" as he saw them. Notwithstanding the inquisitorial atmosphere which pervaded Washington, not once was his integrity officially questioned.

He went through the long and exhaustive public hearings which lead to the adoption of the nation-wide television table with assignment of more than 2,000 TV channels throughout the country. He was greatly impressed with the showing made by educators in their appeal for reserved channels. While the proceeding was pending, however, he refrained from any extra-judicial, loud-mouthed advocacy. He waited until all the evidence was in before making up his mind on this and other phases of the hearing.

Paul Walker was passed up a half dozen times before he was finally made Chairman of the FCC. Because of his adamantine qualities and his unswerving devotion to the public interest, he was not always popular with some powerful political and economic interests. When matters of principle were involved, he was not one to pull his punches. For example, in 1943, he strongly rebuked a large utility concern for what he thought was gross mistreatment of a small, independent telephone company. "The wrongs committed," said he, ". . . will unless corrected, remain forever a reminder to the public of the arbitrary and hurtful actions which can be perpetrated by a powerful monopoly. The ultimate effect of such actions will be to destroy completely public trust and confidence in utility management . . ."

Such strong words tended to give segments of the communications industry an image of Walker as a "big corporation foe." This was a false image, of course, because those who were close to him knew that he was a real friend to the American free enterprise system. Nevertheless, the hostile attitude held by a few vested interests had its effect on the White House and militated against his appointment to the Chairmanship of the FCC.

Whatever may be said against Mr. Truman, it was to his credit that he recognized the true worth of Walker as a public administrator and, on February 28, 1952, elevated him to the top FCC position.

Walker had just passed his 71st birthday. He was cautioned by his associates to take it easy. Much younger men had succumbed to the strain of the office, he was reminded. Despite the warnings, he seemed to work harder the next fourteen months than ever before and he seemed to thrive on the responsibility.

Under his administration, the television freeze was lifted and the wild scramble for television channels began. For several months he and the FCC staff were working day and night setting up machinery to process more than 700 applications for new stations already on file with the Commission.

Just seven months after his appointment, the Commission announced that 200 TV stations had been authorized, and that the number of pending applications had increased to nearly 900. The legal battles for valuable channels in the big markets was feverish and intense. In one case involving competing applications, Walker was commanded to appear at the late Senator McCarthy's office and, in star chamber fashion, the Senator attempted coercive tactics. But Walker was fearless and unyielding. He respected Senators regardless of their character or party affiliation, but no power on earth could make him do what he thought was wrong.

With the election of the Republican administration, he stepped down as Chairman and was replaced by Rosel Hyde, a Republican from Idaho, who, as a member of the staff and the Commission, had worked with Walker since the agency was created in 1934.

Field Offices and Monitoring Stations of the FCC

FIELD ENGINEERING & MONITORING BUREAU

Headquarters: 718 Jackson Place, N. W., Washington 25, D. C.

George S. Turner, chief; Frank M. Kratokvil, assistant chief; Francis Keefe, administrative assistant; John H. McAllister, attorney advisor; Anne M. Ignatowich, secretary. Field Operating Div.: Frank M. Kratokvil, chief. Inspection & Examination Div.: Paul H. Herndon, Jr., chief. Monitoring Div.: Irving L. Weston, chief. Engineering Div.: Floyd W. Wickenkamp, chief.

DISTRICT OFFICES

District 1: 1600 Customhouse, Boston 9, Mass. Capitol 3-6608. Nathan A. Hallenstein, engineer in charge.

District 2: 641 Washington St., New York 14, N. Y. Watkins 4-1000, extension 245. W. D. Johnson, engineer in charge.

District 3: 1005 New U. S. Customhouse, Philadelphia 6, Pa. Market 7-6000, extension 277. Roger E. Phelps, engineer in charge.

District 4: 400 E. Lombard St., Baltimore 2, Md. Plaza 2-8460, extension 816. Hyman A. Cohen, engineer in charge.

District 5: Room 402, Federal Bldg., Norfolk 10, Va. Madison 2-4963. Edward Bennett, engineer in charge.

District 6: 50 Whitehall St., S.W., Atlanta 3, Ga. Jackson 2-4121, extension 6381. Arthur T. Cline, Jr., engineer in charge. Sub-Office: Room 214 Post Office Bldg., Savannah, Ga. Adams 2-7602. John W. Crews, engineer in charge.

District 7: 300 N.E. 1st Ave., Miami 1, Fla. Franklin 9-3900. Arthur G. Gilbert, engineer in charge. Marine Office: 221 N. Howard Ave., Tampa 6, Fla. 87-0661. Alfred L. Ritter, marine supervisor.

District 8: 600 South St., New Orleans 12, La. Express 2411, extension 594. William J. Simpson, acting engineer in charge. Sub-Office: 419 U. S. Courthouse & Customhouse, Mobile 10, Hemlock 2-3641, extension 209. George E. Franklin, radio engineer.

District 9: 7300 Wingate St., Houston 11, Tex. Walnut 6-3975. Everett H. Marshall, engineer in charge. Sub-Office: 300 Willow St., Beaumont, Tex. Terminal 2-8141. Eric D. Coburn, radio engineer.

District 10: 708 Jackson St., Dallas 2, Tex. Riverside 8-5611. Gerald M. Howard, engineer in charge.

District 11: 849 S. Broadway, Los Angeles 14, Calif. Richmond 9-4711, extension 1244. Bernard H. Linden, engineer in charge. Sub-Office: 1245 Seventh Ave., San Diego, Calif. Belmont 4-6211, extension 383. John W. Crews, radio engineer. Marine Office: 356 W. 5th St., San Pedro, Calif. Terminal 2-2389. William E. Clyne, marine supervisor.

District 12: 323-A Customhouse, San Francisco 26, Calif. Yukon 6-4141. Francis V. Sloan, engineer in charge.

District 13: 620 S. W. Main St., Portland 5, Ore. Capital 6-3361, extension 541. Joseph H. Hallock, engineer in charge.

District 14: 806 Federal Office Bldg., Seattle 4, Wash. Mutual 2-3000, extension 448. Herbert H. Arlowe, engineer in charge.

District 15: 521 New Customhouse, Denver 2, Colo. Keystone 4-4151, extension 227. Andrew Bahlay, engineer in charge.

District 16: 208 Federal Courts Bldg., St. Paul 2, Minn. Capitol 2-8011, extension 261. Donald A. Murray, engineer in charge.

District 17: 911 Walnut St., Kansas City 16, Mo. Baltimore 1-7000, extension 253. Harold W. Bourell, engineer in charge.

District 18: 219 S. Clark St., Chicago 4, Ill. Harrison 7-4700, extension 275. H. D. Hayes, engineer in charge.

District 19: 1029 New Federal Bldg., Detroit 26, Mich. Woodward 3-9330, extension 441. Edwin S. Heiser, engineer in charge.

District 20: 328 Post Office Bldg., Buffalo 3, N. Y. Washington 1744. Carolus L. Spencer, engineer in charge.

District 21: 502 Federal Bldg., Honolulu 13, Hawaii, 5-8831, extension 230. Paul R. Fenner, engineer in charge.

District 22: 323 Federal Bldg., San Juan 13, Puerto Rico, 2-4562. Eugene W. Klein, engineer in charge.

District 23: U. S. Post Office & Courthouse Bldg., Anchorage, Alaska. Broadway 2-5501. Harold D. DeVoe, engineer in charge. Sub-Office: 6 Shattuck Bldg., Juneau, Alaska, 6-1510. Hal S. Weidner, radio engineer.

District 24: 718 Jackson Pl., N.W. Washington, D. C. Executive 3-3620, extension 229. Alfred H. Kleist, engineer in charge.

For National Defense

(CONELRAD)

As pointed out in Chapter 5, Section 606(c) of the Communications Act provides that the President may proclaim a state of war or other national emergency. And thereupon, he may "suspend or amend for such time as he may see fit, the rules and regulations applicable to any or all radio stations or devices capable of emitting electromagnetic radiations within the jurisdiction of the United States as prescribed by the Commission."

The section further provides that he may close any such station or device operating on frequencies between 10 kc and 100,000 mc which is suitable for navigational aid beyond five miles. He may remove the equipment or authorize the use of any such station by any government department under such regulations as he may prescribe upon payment of just compensation to the owners. These emergency powers are applicable to both privately and governmentally owned stations.

On December 10, 1951, the President issued an order delegating authority vested in him by Section 606(c) of the Act to the Federal Communications Commission to prepare and put into effect plans with respect to radio stations under that agency's jurisdiction to minimize the use of electromagnetic radiations, which might give aid to the navigation of hostile aircraft, guided missiles, and other devices capable of direct attack upon the United States.

The delegation was made subject to the conditions that the FCC could not exercise any authority with respect to the content of station programs; could not take over and use any radio station or remove the apparatus and equipment of any station; and the plans of the Commission for exercising its authority under the order were not to become effective until approved by the Secretary of Defense and the appropriate civilian agencies concerned with national security.

Section 3 of the Order further provided that whenever, pursuant to the provisions of the Order, any radio station should be required to cease operations or should have its normal operations interfered with, "such station shall be allowed to resume operations or return to normal operations, as the case may be, at the earliest possible time consistent with the national security . . ."

Section 4 provided that the FCC, the Secretary of Defense and the head of each government department or agency could issue "appropriate rules, regulations, orders and instructions, and take such action as may be necessary, to assure the timely and effective operation of the plans and for carrying out their respective functions" and requiring compliance therewith.

Pursuant to this Order, on September 22, 1954, the Commission adopted initial plans for the operation of CONELRAD (Emergency Control of Electromagnetic Radiation). These plans have been extended and revised from time to time. Through the cooperative efforts of the FCC, the military establishment, civilian agencies concerned with national security, and all broadcast stations, an elaborate and effective system of communication has been worked out by which all stations may be swiftly notified of alerts and all clears in the event of enemy attack against the nation or the threat thereof.

The Commission has adopted specific regulations implementing the CONELRAD plans. Included in these regulations are definitions and detailed explanation as to supervision of CONELRAD activities, the required methods for sending and receiving radio alerts, restrictions on broadcast operations during alerts and the procedure for transmitting the all clear messages and for resuming normal broadcast operations.

After notification of an alert and until the period of the alert is ended, no Standard, FM or TV station is permitted to broadcast its identification unless expressly authorized by the FCC. Any operation permitted during this time must be on either one or both of two frequencies, 640 kc and 1240 kc, as determined by the Commission in the light of "pertinent engineering considerations."

Each broadcast station permitted to operate during a radio alert must observe operating procedures for the mode of operation to which it is assigned in accordance with instructions set forth in the CONELRAD manual for Broadcast Stations, copies of which may be secured from the FCC.

Tests of the alerting system are conducted from time to time. During these tests, all stations authorized to operate in the CONELRAD system must comply with the required procedures. Other stations will not be required to go off the air during these tests but will be subject to any interference which may result from the CONELRAD operation.

Stations authorized to participate in the CONELRAD system are required to maintain their equipment so that it is ready for instant use at all times. Appropriate entries of all tests must be made in the station logs.

The Commission has stated that "at some time it may be necessary to conduct an Air Defense Drill under conditions of simulated attack." Such drills will not be called unless agreed upon by the Department of Defense, Office of Defense Mobilization and the FCC. All stations will receive notice well in advance of the drills.

During a drill, all broadcast stations must take the same steps as such stations would be required to take in the event of an actual Radio Alert.

On August 17, 1960, the FCC announced augmentation of the CONELRAD program to include a continuity of service plan for the Emergency Broadcast System in the event of enemy attack. This plan will enable the President and other officials to communicate with the general public in the periods preceding, during and following such an attack. The complete text of the plan as approved and released by the Commission is as follows:

FEDERAL COMMUNICATIONS COMMISSION
WASHINGTON 25, D. C.

PLAN FOR THE CONTROL OF ELECTROMAGNETIC RADIATION (CONELRAD)
PURSUANT TO EXECUTIVE ORDER NO. 10312

Technical arrangements to insure nationwide continuity of the emergency broadcast system during CONELRAD *and the period following issuance of the* CONELRAD *radio all clear. Prepared by the National Industry Advisory Committee, appointed pursuant to Section 8, Executive Order No. 10312. Concurred in by Secretary of Defense July 28, 1960. Concurred in by Director, Office of Civil and Defense Mobilization July 22, 1960. Approved by F.C.C. July 29, 1960.*

I. PROBLEM

To develop a plan under which the President and other Federal Officials will be able to communicate with the general public in the period preceding, during and following an enemy attack. This plan must be capable of delivering to the general public a Presidential Message or national instructions, news and other information that will be available at the various Federal seats of Government. It must also provide for adequate arrangements for continuity of communications between State and Local Civil Defense Directors and the general public within their respective jurisdictions.

II. BACKGROUND

A. Under peacetime conditions, Presidential broadcasts to the population are handled entirely by existing non-government radio and television broadcast facilities. Under conditions that would call for the application of CONEL-RAD rules to all radio services, the normal flow of communications would probably be disrupted, destroyed or altered. This plan will insure, insofar as possible, that every available technical facility will be utilized to provide a continuity of service by the broadcasting industry and other FCC-licensed facilities of the communications industry of the nation consistent with the provisions of approved CONELRAD plans, mobilization orders and FCC Rules and Regulations.

B. The following assumptions form the basis for this plan:

1. Preceding, during and following an enemy attack, communications from the President to the people and the dissemination of news and information are essential to public morale, and for the survival and recovery of the nation.

2. In a post-attack period, communications to the surviving population will depend almost entirely upon the use of non-government broadcast facilities and personnel.

3. Sufficient numbers of the nation's non-government broadcast facilities will remain usable after a major attack to permit communication with a substantial portion of the surviving population.

4. Presidential communications, news and public information normally will originate from, or be transmitted for relay to, a site in the Federal relocation arc. Under pre-attack conditions, such programming will normally originate from the White House (See NIAC Order No. 1).

5. The White House Army Signal Agency (WHASA), acting as the Signal Office for the President, provides remote pick-up broadcast and communication facilities when the President is away from the normal seat of government. WHASA will deliver Presidential communications to the relocation sites to be selected as control points for the origination of Presidential Messages, and National Programming and News.

6. Although the program circuits normally employed by the nationwide commercial radio and TV broadcast networks will be seriously disrupted by a major attack, alternate routes will be available to continue nationwide distribution of Presidential Messages, and National Programming and News. Technical arrangements will be made to provide continuity of service by means of normal and alternate routes of radio and television network landline facilities, multiplexed FM broadcast and/or television aural facilities, remote pick-up broadcast facilities, studio-transmitter links, television intercity relays (privately owned), industrial microwave systems, and any other adaptable facilities now in existence

that can be made available at a future date as a result of research and development, and operated in accordance with approved CONELRAD plans, or as authorized by the Chairman, FCC, in accordance with Section 6(B), Executive Order 10312.

III. PROGRAMMING

A. Programming includes Presidential Messages, Local Programming, State (Regional) Programming and National Programming and News.
  1. Program priorities will be as follows:
    a. Under all conditions, top priority will go to a Presidential Message, which all stations must carry at time of transmission. Second priority will be given to Local Programming, third priority to State (Regional) Programming, and fourth priority to National Programming and News. Presidential Messages, National Programming and News will be made available to all stations by means of normal nationwide commercial radio and television network facilities with alternate backup facilities to replace missing links. If not broadcast at the time of original transmission, State (Regional) and National Programming and News must be recorded locally for broadcast at the earliest opportunity.
    b. Authentication procedures and specific channels for receipt of authentication information are outlined in Section IV-D, and Annex A.
  2. Following issuance of the CONELRAD Radio All-Clear (which means return to normal frequency), Presidential Messages and Civil Defense Programming relating to the protection of life and property continue to have the highest order of priority. Other National, State and Local Civil Defense information will be broadcast as bulletins or news programs.

IV. TECHNICAL PROGRAM CHANNELS AND AUTHENTICATION PROCEDURES

A. PRESIDENTIAL MESSAGES
  1. The following channels will be available for Presidential Messages:
    a. From the White House to the Nationwide major commercial radio and television broadcasting networks: American Broadcasting Company, Columbia Broadcasting System, Mutual Broadcasting System and National Broadcasting Company.
    b. From sites in the Federal Relocation Arc to the White House and then to the networks outlined in subparagraph a. of this paragraph.
    c. From sites in the Federal Relocation Arc to specified radio stations peripheral to the Washington metropolitan area that have been equipped to relay programs to the networks.
    d. From sites in the Federal Relocation Arc to Newspoint, thence to the major networks outlined in sub-paragraph a. of this paragraph.
  2. Technical Arrangements for the enumerated channels in paragraph 1 (See Annex B for diagram) will be provided as follows:
    a. Normal landline network interconnections are in existence and are maintained in a ready condition at all times and are used daily. Their use would be primarily in a pre-attack broadcast.
    b. Multiple communication links are installed between the White House and sites in the Federal Relocation Arc. These circuits are controlled by the White House Army Signal Agency.
    c. Circuits connecting the Federal Relocation Arc with the selected

peripheral stations will be provided by the Office of Civil and Defense Mobilization. These circuits are controlled by the White House Army Signal Agency. They will be two-way, record and voice communication systems and must be acceptable to the Presidential Press Secretary, the OCDM, the FCC and the White House Army Signal Agency from both a procedural and technical viewpoint.

B. NATIONAL PROGRAMMING AND NEWS

National Programming and News will utilize the same channels as a Presidential Message as designated in paragraph A-1, of this section. Presidential Emergency Broadcast circuits are available for National Programming and News when not in use for a Presidential Message. National Programming and News can normally originate at any one or all of the following points:

1. The White House
2. Sites in the Federal Relocation Arc
3. Newspoint

C. STATE AND LOCAL PROGRAMMING

State and Local Industry Advisory Committees in conjunction with state and local authorities will provide plans for their individual areas. Such plans shall be consistent with this plan and shall be approved by the cognizant Federal Government Agencies, following submission to the NIAC for its recommendations.

D. AUTHENTICATION

1. Presidential and National Programming. The NIAC will be responsible for establishing acceptable authentication procedures for use in the origination of Presidential Messages, National Programming and News. Such procedures must be concurred in by the White House Army Signal Agency. Authentication procedures will be set forth in Annex A.
2. State and Local Programming. State Industry Advisory Committees will be responsible for establishing authentication systems and procedures suitable for state and local broadcasting which are acceptable to State and Local Civil Defense officials of these areas, and the NIAC. The NIAC will insure that, as such systems and procedures are developed, they are submitted to the FCC for approval. All such procedures will be inserted in Annex A as they are developed.

V. OPERATIONAL AND TECHNICAL PROCEDURES

A. OPERATIONAL

1. Organization

   a. The NIAC will assist the cognizant Government agencies in the planning and coordination of the system for emergency broadcasting during and following the implementation of CONELRAD. (Annex C). The membership in this committee shall consist of a basic Technical Committee, appointed by the FCC, from representatives of the major nationwide commercial radio broadcasting networks and the National Association of Broadcasters. A member of this basic Technical Committee will act on a rotating basis as Chairman Pro-Tem. The permanent Vice Chairman will be appointed from The National Association of Broadcasters. The basic Technical Committee, with representatives of the programming departments and the Washington White House correspondents of the networks, shall, together with others as required from the broadcast industry, compose a Broadcast Services Committee. Other committees will be employed to maintain liaison with the entire non-government communications field to assist the Government in plans for operations under emergency conditions. These Committees shall consist of a Chairman and four members each, in the following areas: (See Annex C)

Aeronautical Communications Services Committee
Amateur Radio Services Committee
Broadcast Services Committee
Citizens Radio Services Committee
Consulting Engineers Committee
Disaster Radio Services Committee
Domestic Common Carrier Communications Services Committee
Electronics Industry Committee
Experimental Radio Services Committee
Industrial Communications Services Committee
International Communications Services Committee
Land Transportation Communications Committee
Legal Counsel Committee
Maritime Communications Services Committee
Public Safety Communications Services Committee

The purpose of NIAC will be to insure, insofar as possible, a workable national system of information dissemination by means of the Emergency Broadcast System, as outlined above, under all national emergency conditions and to provide technical advice and recommendations to the cognizant Federal Government agencies.

b. State Industry Advisory Committees composed of technical and programming people have been established. The individual State Broadcasting Associations have designated the members of these State Committees with FCC approval. The State Industry Advisory Committees shall function as liaison between the State Civil Defense officials and the broadcasters within their state. They will insure, insofar as possible, the formation of networks in their state enabling State Civil Defense messages to be carried by the broadcasting stations. They will cooperate with the FCC, the NIAC, the Local Industry Advisory Committees and appropriate Federal, National, State and Local officials and organizations within their state in all matters concerning their area.

c. A Local Industry Advisory Committee will be formed in each community as directed by the State Industry Advisory Committee, which Local Committee shall include broadcast station administrative, news, program and technical personnel and Local Civil Officials. Each Local Industry Advisory Committee will cooperate with the local head of government. Each Committee shall be responsible for the broadcasting of State and Local information including that supplied by appropriate State and Local Civil Defense, and for Presidential Messages and National Programming and News in their area. Outlets serving more than one state will arrange to receive and broadcast information as supplied by the appropriate authorities. Subject to the priorities established in Section III, the local programming and technical committees are responsible for continuous programming of their facilities, utilizing information received from all authentic sources in accordance with pre-established authentication procedures.

393

2. National Programming and News, for the most part, will originate from the following sources:
   a. The Vice President
   b. The Secretary of State
   c. The Secretary of Defense
   d. The Director, OCDM
   National Programming and News will be furnished intermittently, as available, on a 24-hour-a-day basis until resumption of normal broadcasting. This service will originate from a temporary seat of Government and/or its news center. These facilities will be manned by the programming personnel (news) of the broadcasting industry. Basic personnel will consist of the 16 member Emergency News Pool that currently exists in Washington. This Pool consists of members from the major networks, wire services, newspapers, magazines, photographic agencies, etc. National Programming and News will be handled by the radio and TV representatives. Those representing other services will be used as requirements may demand. National Programming and News shall consist of pronouncements by Federal Officials, such pronouncements to be made in person. Announcements released officially by the various departments will be read by qualified news correspondents on duty at the originating points.
3. Presidential Messages and National Programming and News will be preceded by a minimum of two minutes "talk up", stating:
   "A Presidential Message will be heard in_____minutes and_____ seconds from NOW."
   "A National Program will be heard in_____minutes and_____ seconds from NOW."
   If the length or subject matter can be made known, this information will be included in the "talk up." The above announcement will be made repeatedly during the two minutes, and the program will start at the announced time. The closing cue on all Presidential messages or National Programming and News will be:

   "THIS CONCLUDES THE PRESIDENTIAL MESSAGE"
   "THIS CONCLUDES THIS PORTION OF THE NATIONAL PROGRAM"

   At all other times, tone will be transmitted to indicate continuity of the circuits.
4. All broadcast stations will have a primary member of the local CONELRAD cluster, or a station close by, affiliated with one of the nationwide commercial radio broadcasting networks. The Presidential Message and National Program will be carried simultaneously by all nationwide commercial radio broadcasting networks, and in addition will be made available to all regional (state) broadcasting networks. The control station for each CONELRAD Cluster shall make its own necessary local arrangements to obtain the Presidential Message and National Program at the time of a CONELRAD Radio Alert in accordance with a pre-arranged plan of action. This feed is to be either through local tie lines already in existence in most cases to a network affiliated station, or by means of bridges of a network line at the nearest telephone company test room. All these arrangements shall be a local responsibility and a pre-arranged plan shall be filed with the U.S. Supervisor, CONELRAD. Radio back-up arrangements shall be made by utilizing the state and local intercity and intra-city Remote Pick-up Broadcast Emergency Inter

Communication Networks and other systems now under development and under proof-of-performance tests.

5. Presidential Messages and National Programming and News shall be transmitted by means of normal network facilities wherever possible. The operation of a broadcasting system requires the nationwide availability of trained personnel to engage in the setting up, testing and switching of facilities for the transmission of the Presidential Messages and National Programming and News to the CONELRAD stations. These skills are normally available only within the personnel of the telephone companies and the network control points. Alternate means of interconnection are under research, development and implementation.

6. Basic feeder circuits for the nationwide commercial radio broadcasting networks will be provided by utilizing one or more of the following means as a backup to normal network landline facilities.
   a. *Interstate*
      (1) Industrial radio microwave (grid networks)
      (2) Multiplexed FM off-the-air relay
      (3) AT&T express routes
      (4) Regional (State) inter-city Remote Pick-up Broadcast Intercommunication Networks.
      (5) Other means under development and proof-of-performance test.
   b. *Intrastate*
      (1) Remote Pick-up Broadcast Intercommunication Networks
      (2) Studio-transmitter links
      (3) Television (aural) intercity relay (privately owned)
      (4) Industrial radio microwave (grid networks)
      (5) Other means under development and proof-of-performance test.
   c. *Intracity*
      (1) Remote Pick-up Broadcast Intercommunication Networks
      (2) Normal Program lines between broadcast stations
      (3) Studio-transmitter links
      (4) Facilities of any other FCC-licensed services available that will be operated in accordance with FCC rules and regulations and approved CONELRAD plans and FCC approved interconnection arrangements.

These backup facilities must be consistent with the provisions of NORAD Regulations (55-7) and will be used only to replace, as required, facilities that have been disrupted or destroyed. Details will be provided to each State and Local Industry Advisory Committee by the FCC Field Supervisor, CONELRAD, Eastern, Central or Western United States.

7. Since Presidential Messages may conceivably originate from other than the normal network control points, (New York, Chicago, Los Angeles and Washington), procedures are being developed to provide the owned and operated radio and television stations of the nationwide networks with an alternate control-center capability. Standby traffic orders, when executed, will permit an authorized person to originate the Presidential Message from one of these points. Because of the complexity of the resulting network, which will be formed by combining all the affiliates of the four networks into one, it is impractical to switch "control" of the national network from point to point so long as the origination point in use remains available. Alternate control centers will be, as soon as practicable, added to allow for the Presidential Message and National Programming and News to originate from additional peripheral stations

throughout the nation. Initially, one broadcast station in each state will be designated by NIAC for program origination capability and interconnection to emergency communications facilities to bypass disrupted portions of normal nationwide commercial radio network facilities, and to provide re-entry thereto. Establishment of authentication procedures and an authentication teletype network between WHASA and the Emergency Broadcast System will be in accordance with Annexes A and D of this plan and with any special procedures desired by WHASA. All emergency services and authentication procedures discussed above and all subsequent NIAC Orders will be implemented automatically upon implementation of NIAC Order #1.

8. During pre-attack, Presidential Messages, National Programming and News shall normally be transmitted by WHASA to the White House, where it is available to the nationwide commercial radio broadcasting networks by means of already installed network facilities at this point. Selected peripheral stations will also be provided with program circuits (see Section IV, B, 1, b) concurrently with the establishment of a network program origination capability. Program circuits, acceptable to FCC, OCDM and DOD should also be provided from any other points from which government broadcasts or news broadcasts must originate; provided, however, that alternate circuits may be substituted in an emergency without prior approval. It is recognized that facilities routed through the White House would not be of value should a surprise attack destroy Washington. However, it is reasonable to assume that continuity of service to the specified stations on the outer periphery will be maintained, and provision is being made to interconnect these stations with the nationwide commercial radio broadcasting network facilities. It is felt that this provision would provide a readily available means for originating a Presidential Message, a National Programming or News.

9. So long as normal network control points are still operative, Presidential Messages, National Programming and News will be delivered to the normal network studios in Washington. If this means is unavailable, the program will be delivered to the Peripheral Stations.

10. The FCC has concurred in the issuance of NIAC Orders Number 1 and 2 and the procedures and details contained in letter dated October 20, 1959 (see Annex D). Further NIAC Orders will be issued that will provide for additional network interconnection points as the expanded capability becomes available.

B. TECHNICAL PROCEDURES

1. Requests for tests or drills of any portions of the Emergency Broadcast System will be forwarded to the FCC, U.S. Supervisor, CONELRAD, at least sixty days prior to any proposed test in accordance with FCC Rules and Regulations.

2. Close technical liaison will be maintained at all times between all Local Industry Advisory Committees and the appropriate State Industry Advisory Committees. The development of authentic channels of communication, as outlined in Section IV, D, 1 and 2, will be in close co-operation with the National Industry Advisory Committee and the FCC Field Supervisor, CONELRAD, Eastern Central or Western United States. The FCC Field Supervisors of CONELRAD will be the normal channel for communications with all stations in order that existing channels are not disrupted. All official instructions to the stations concerning the

plan will be furnished to them through the offices of the FCC, with copies to OCDM.
3. The FCC Field Supervisor, CONELRAD, will furnish detailed technical data, and instructions to the various State and Local Industry Advisory Technical Committees for use in implementing alternate facilities to replace primary broadcast and auxiliary intercommunication facilities that may be destroyed or disrupted by enemy action.

VI. PERSONNEL PROCEDURES

A. NATIONAL
1. The Technical Committee and the Broadcast Services Committee of the NIAC, and designated qualified newsmen, will proceed immediately upon receipt of the CONELRAD Radio Alert to report in person to the following specified government relocation sites at the earliest possible time consistent with prevailing conditions to assume their assigned responsibilities in connection with nationwide radio broadcasting operations. Two of the Technical Committee are assigned to the FCC Relocation Site and two to the OCDM Classified Location. The Broadcast Services Program group is assigned to the OCDM Classified Location; the Broadcast Services Washington Program group and designated qualified newsmen to Newspoint.
2. The sixteen-man Emergency News Pool will proceed with the Presidential Press Secretary to one of the sites in the Federal Relocation Arc. From this point, personnel from this group will be available as a backup to provide news service assistance.
3. Personnel of the National Capital Area Industry Advisory Committee will report to the selected Washington Metropolitan Area peripheral stations to perform operational control over all nationwide Presidential Messages National and News programming until the personnel in subparagraphs 1. and 2. of this paragraph report for duty.

B. STATE AND LOCAL
State and Local Industry Advisory Committees will arrange with appropriate State and Local Civil Defense Officials for inclusion of management, news and technical and program personnel as regular staff assistants at state and local relocation sites. These persons must ensure that adequate radio intercommunications, as approved by the FCC, exist among such sites and radio broadcast stations outside the metropolitan areas.

VII. DATA AND INFORMATION

A. Data, information, and detailed instructions will be required to fully implement the provisions of this plan. Annex C lists the various agencies that will participate in developing these details.
B. All proposals of a technical and policy nature will be forwarded to the FCC and the National Industry Advisory Committee prior to implementation.

Federal Trade Commission Guides and Form Letter Used by the Agency to Elicit Information Regarding Radio and TV Advertising

GUIDES AGAINST DECEPTIVE PRICING

The following guides have been adopted by the Federal Trade Commission *for the use of its staff* in the evaluation of pricing representations in advertising.[1] While the guides do not purport to be all inclusive, they are directed toward the elimination of existing major abuses and are being released to the public in the interest of obtaining voluntary, simultaneous and prompt cooperation by those whose practices are subject to the jurisdiction of the Federal Trade Commission.

In determining whether or not pricing practices are violative of the laws administered by the Commission, the facts in each matter are considered in view of the requirements of the Federal Trade Commission Act, as amended, and principles enunciated by the Courts in the adjudication of cases. The foremost of these principles are:

1. Advertisements must be considered in their entirety and as they would be read by those to whom they appeal.
2. Advertisements as a whole may be completely misleading although every sentence separately considered is literally true. This may be because things are omitted that should be said, or because advertisements are composed or purposely printed in such way as to mislead.
3. Advertisements are not intended to be carefully dissected with a dictionary at hand, but rather to produce an impression upon prospective purchasers.
4. Whether or not the advertiser knows the representations to be false, the deception of purchasers and the diversion of trade from competitors is the same.
5. A deliberate effort to deceive is not necessary to make out a case of using unfair methods of competition or unfair or deceptive acts or practices within the prohibition of the statute.
6. Laws are made to protect the trusting as well as the suspicious.
7. Pricing representations, however made, which are ambiguous will be read favorably to the accomplishment of the purpose of the Federal Trade Commission Act, as amended, which is to prevent the making of claims which have the tendency and capacity to mislead.

[1] For the purposes of these Guides "Advertising" includes any form of public notice which uses a claim for a product, however such representation is disseminated or utilized.

398

In considering particular types of pricing practices for the purpose of determining whether terminology and direct or implied representations, however made, i.e., in advertising or in labeling or otherwise, may be in violation of the Federal Trade Commission Act, the following general principles will be used:[2]

I. SAVING CLAIMS.

No statement, however expressed, whether in words, phrases, price figures, symbols, fractions, percentages or otherwise, which represents or implies a reduction or saving from an established retail price, or from the advertiser's former price, should be used in connection with the price at which an article is offered for sale unless,

(a) the saving or reduction statement applies to the specific article offered for sale as distinguished from similar or comparable merchandise,

(Note: Where a comparison is made between the price of the article offered for sale and the price of comparable merchandise Guide III applies.)

and, (b) or (c)

(b) the saving or reduction is from the usual and customary retail price of the article in the trade area, or areas, where the statement is made,

Examples of phrases used in connection with prices which have been held to be representations of an article's usual and customary retail price are:
"Maker's List Price"
"Manufacturer's List Price"
"Manufacturer's Suggested Retail Price"
"Sold Nationally At"
"Nationally Advertised At"
"Value"

(c) the saving or reduction is from the advertiser's usual and customary retail price of the article in the recent, regular course of business,

Examples of words and phrases used in connection with prices which have been held to be representations of the advertiser's usual and customary retail price are:
"regularly"
"usually"
"formerly"
"originally"
"reduced"
"was_____ now_____"
"made to sell for"
"woven to sell for"
"our list price"
"_____% off"
"save up to $_____"
"special"

[2] Pricing practices in connection with the sale and offering for sale of fur and fur products are governed primarily by the provisions of the "Rules and Regulations Under the Fur Products Labeling Act."

"you save $_____"
"$50 dress—$35"

and

(d) the statement clearly shows whether the saving or reduction is from the usual and customary retail price of the article in the trade area or from the advertiser's usual and customary retail price of the article in the recent, regular course of business.

II. LIMITATIONS.

No statement which represents or implies a reduction or saving from an established retail price or from the advertiser's usual and customary retail price should be used if,

(a) an artificial mark-up has been used to provide the basis for the claim, or

(b) the claim is based on infrequent or isolated sales, or

(c) the claim is based on a past price (i.e., one not immediately preceding the price used in the recent, regular course of business) unless this fact is clearly and adequately disclosed.

III. COMPARABLE AND SIMILAR MERCHANDISE.

Nothing in these guides is intended to preclude an advertiser from comparing his selling price for an article to the price at which similar and comparable merchandise is currently offered for sale, or sold, provided that,

(a) it is clearly and conspicuously disclosed in the statement, however made, that the comparison in price is being made between the article offered for sale and similar and comparable merchandise so that it is made clear that the comparative price is not the former or usual and customary price of the advertised article but is the price of such similar and comparable merchandise.

and

(b) the merchandise, to which the sales price of the advertised article is compared, is at least of like grade and quality in all material respects,

and

(c) said similar and comparable merchandise is generally available for purchase at the comparative price in the same trade area, or areas, where the claim is made, or, if not so available, that fact is clearly disclosed.

An example of a statement which would be proper within the provisions of Guide III if based on facts is:

"Dacron suit $20.00—
Comparable suits $25.00"

IV. "SPECIAL SALE, ETC."

No statement which represents or implies that because of some unusual event or manner of business, an article is offered for sale to the consuming public at a saving from the usual and customary retail price in the trade area, or areas, where the claim is made, or at a saving from the advertiser's usual and customary price for the article in the recent, regular course of his business should be made unless the claim is true.

400

Examples of words and phrases illustrative of representations to which Guide IV has reference are:
"Special Purchase"
"Clearance"
"Marked Down From Stock"
"Exceptional Purchase"
"Manufacturer's Close-Out"
"Advance Sale"
"Sale"

V. "TWO FOR ONE SALES."
No statement or representation of an offer to sell two articles for the price of one, or phrase of similar import, should be used unless the sales price for the two articles is the advertiser's usual and customary retail price for the single article in the recent, regular course of his business.

(Note: Where the one responsible for a "two for the price of one" claim has not previously sold the article and/or articles, the propriety of the advertised price for the two articles is determined by the usual and customary retail price of the single article in the trade area, or areas, where the claim is made.)

VI. "½ PRICE"—"1¢ SALE" CONDITIONED ON PURCHASE OF ADDITIONAL MERCHANDISE.
No statement or representation of an offer to sell an article at a saving through claims such as "½ price" or "50% off" or "1¢ sale," or expressions of similar import,[3] should be used when the offer is conditioned upon the purchase of additional merchandise, unless:

(a) the terms or conditions imposed are conspicuously disclosed in immediate conjunction with the offer,
and
(b) the represented saving in price is in fact true, and when the claim is "½ price," or an expression of similar nature, the saving is from the advertiser's usual and customary retail price for the article in the recent, regular course of business.
and
(c) the price charged for the additional merchandise required to be purchased is the usual and customary retail price for the merchandise in the recent, regular course of the advertiser's business.

(Note: Where the one responsible for the saving claim has not previously sold the article and/or the additional merchandise, the propriety of the claim will be governed by the usual and customary retail prices of the article and the additional merchandise at retail in the trade area, or areas, where the claim is made.)

VII. "FACTORY OR WHOLESALE PRICES."
No statement should be made in connection with the offering for sale of a product to the consuming public of a "factory" or "wholesale" price, or other such expression, which represents or implies that the consuming public can purchase the article at the same price that retailers regularly do, and provides a saving from the usual and customary retail price for the

[3] Similar claims, not conditioned upon the purchase of other merchandise, are governed by the provisions of Guide I (b) and (c).

article in the trade area, or areas, where the claim is made unless such statement is true.

VIII. "PRE-TICKETING."

No article should be "pre-ticketed" with any price figure, either alone or with descriptive terminology, which exceeds the price at which the article is usually and customarily sold in the trade area, or areas, where the "pre-ticketed" article is offered for sale.

(a) Those who disseminate "pre-ticketed" price figures for use in connection with the offering for sale of articles at retail by others (even though they themselves are not engaged in retail sales) are chargeable if the price figures do not meet the standard set forth in this Guide. As such, they are chargeable with knowledge of the ordinary business "facts of life" concerning what happens to articles for which they furnished "pre-ticketed" prices. One who puts into the hands of others a means or instrumentality by which they may mislead the public, is himself guilty of deception.

(b) For the purposes of this Guide "pre-ticketing" includes the use of price figures,
   (1) affixed to the article by tag, label or otherwise, or
   (2) in such a form as to be affixed to the product by others, or
   (3) in material, such as display placards, which are used, or designed to be used, with the article at point of sale to the consuming public.

IX. "IMPERFECT, IRREGULAR, SECONDS."

No comparative price should be quoted in connection with an article offered for sale which is imperfect, irregular, or a second, unless it is accompanied by a clear and conspicuous disclosure that such comparative price refers to the price of the article if perfect. Such comparative price should not be used unless (1) it is the price at which the advertiser usually and customarily sells the article without defects, or (2) it is the price at which the article without defects is usually and customarily sold at the comparative price in the trade area, or areas, where the statement is made, or if such article is not so available, that fact is clearly disclosed.

Nothing contained in these Guides relieves any party subject to a Commission cease and desist order or stipulation from complying with the provisions of such order or stipulation. The Guides do not constitute a finding in and will not affect the disposition of any formal or informal matter before the Commission.

Robert M. Parrish,
Secretary.

FEDERAL TRADE COMMISSION
WASHINGTON 25

BUREAU OF INVESTIGATION
OFFICE OF
CHIEF PROJECT ATTORNEY

Gentlemen: In re: *Commercial Broadcasts*

Pursuant to statutory authority the Federal Trade Commission is engaged in the review of current radio and television advertising, and requests that you forward to the Radio and Television, Advertising Unit, Federal Trade Commission, Washington 25, D. C., typed script representing the commercial text of all advertising originating in your studios and disseminated through your facilities on the following date(s):

Commercial continuities submitted should include those announcements, statements, and testimonials tending to or intended to create a demand for, or to induce the purchase of, any article of commerce, whether such commercial script opens, is interspersed with, or concludes a program. If commercial continuities are in a foreign language you are requested to submit an English translation of the continuities.

Date of dissemination and station call letters should be printed, stamped, or written, preferably at the bottom of each sheet of commercial continuity. Legible carbon copies of commercial continuities are acceptable. The advertiser's name and address should be indicated where not part of the script. Electrical transcriptions or films need not be transcribed. It will be sufficient to list the sponsor, the product advertised and the agency from which it is received.

Non-commercial script (i.e., without any commercial objective) covering lectures and similar programs, which are purely educational, religious, civic or political need not be submitted. Further, you may omit forwarding commercial advertising continuities of local banking institutions, building and loan associations, transportation companies, including local taxi services, local hotels, restaurants, theatres, night clubs, and mortuary establishments.

Please mail return promptly, in packages weighing not more than 4 lbs. each, and use the enclosed government franks for mailing. Please prepare the enclosed transmittal form FTC-R-6 covering individual station material, to distinguish your network material sent by originating key stations.

Very truly yours,
Charles A. Sweeney,
Legal Adviser in Charge,
Radio and Television
Advertising Unit.

Enclosures
FTC-R-7
L-3813 rev.

APPENDIX VI

Requirements for Construction, Marking and Lighting of Towers

Applications for broadcasting towers were formerly referred to the Airspace Subcommittee of the Air Coordinating Committee for special study. This Committee recently was abolished by Executive order. The Commission proposes to amend its rules (Section 17.4) to specify the Federal Aviation Agency. The referral is made under the following conditions:

(1) If the antenna structure is over 500 feet in height.

(2) Where antenna structures less than 500 feet would necessitate the raising of the minimum flight altitude within the Civil Airways and designated air traffic control areas in the country.

(3) If the structure is to be located in an established coastal area in which low level flight is required for Department of Defense and Coast Guard air stations located within 20 statute miles of the Atlantic, Pacific, and Gulf Coast.

(4) Where the structure would project above a landing area, or above the limited heights as set forth in Section 17.15 of the FCC Rules.

Section 17.21 provides that antenna structures shall be painted and lighted when they require special aeronautical study or exceed 170 feet in height above the ground. This requirement may be waived or modified if the applicant can show that the safety of air travel will not be impaired thereby.

Structures up to 150 feet in height must have installed at the top at least two 100 or 111-watt lamps enclosed in aviation red obstruction light globes. These lamps are required to burn simultaneously from sunset to sunrise and be in such position that unobstructed visibility of at least one of them at any angle of approach is assured. Automatic equipment may be used to control the lighting in lieu of manual control.

Higher towers reaching as high as 1500 feet must have at the top one 300 m/m electric code beacon with two 500 to 620 watt lamps which must burn simultaneously and be equipped with aviation red color filters. If an appendage of some kind not more than 20 feet in height and incapable of supporting the beacon is mounted on the tower, and view of this beacon by aircraft is not possible at every angle of approach, a second one must be installed in such position that unobstructed visibility is assured.

The Rules require that all beacons shall be so equipped to provide not more than forty nor fewer than twelve flashes per minute with the period of darkness equal to one-half of the luminous period.

For all towers higher than 150 feet, lower level illumination is also required. This consists of at least two 100 or 111-watt lamps enclosed in aviation red obstruction light globes, and mounted to insure unobstructed visibility of at least one light at any angle of aeronautical approach.

For antenna structures between 150 and 300 feet, the lower level for lighting

404

is specified as the midpoint of the overall height of the tower. In the 300 to 450 feet range, illumination is required at the one-third and two-thirds levels.

Towers within the 450 to 600 feet range must have the lower level lighting as just described at one-fourth and three-fourths of their overall heights. In addition, at about the midway point, a flashing beacon similar to those described above must be installed in such position that unobstructed visibility from approaching aircraft is possible. If one does not provide visibility from every angle of approach, a second one must be installed as is required at the top of the tower. The midpoint beacons must be mounted on the outside of diagonally opposite corners or opposite sides of the tower at the prescribed heights.

Requirements for the lower lighting of antenna structures ranging in height from 600 to 750 feet include the installation of lamps as described above at points approximately one, three and four-fifths of the tower heights plus the 300 m/m electric beacon installed at the two-fifths level.

Towers with heights from 750 to 900 feet require similar lamps at about their one-sixth, one-half, and five-sixths levels and the flashing beacons at their one-third and two-thirds levels.

Specifications for lighting towers higher than 900 feet are as follows:

From 900 to 1050 feet, similar lamps at one, three, five and six-sevenths levels with the beacons at points two and four-sevenths of the overall height;

From 1200 to 1350 feet, the specified lamps at one, three, five, seven and eight-ninths levels with beacons at two and four-ninths and two-thirds points;

Above 1350 and including 1500 feet, the specified lamps at points one-tenth, three-tenths, one-half, seven-tenths and nine-tenths distance up the tower with the flashing beacons at levels of one, two, three and four-fifths of the overall height; and

Antenna structures over 1500 feet in height must be lighted in accordance with specifications to be determined by the Commission after special aeronautical study.

The Rules specify that all lights regardless of height of tower or position thereon must burn continuously or shall be controlled by a "light sensitive device" adjusted so that they are turned on at a north sky light intensity level of about thirty-five foot candles and turned off at a north sky light intensity level of about fifty-eight foot candles.

During construction of an antenna structure, temporary lamps must be installed as provided in Section 17.36 of the Rules. These must be displayed nightly until the permanent obstruction lights have been provided.

Antenna structures must be painted throughout their height with alternate bands of aviation surface orange and white, terminating with aviation surface orange bands at both top and bottom. The width of the bands shall be approximately one-seventh the height of the structure, provided, however, that the bands shall not be more than 40 feet nor less than 1½ feet in width.

Uniform Definitions of Program Categories for Radio and TV Stations Prescribed by the FCC for Keeping Logs*

As to Commission policy in connection with program logs, the Commission's Report of March 7, 1946, *Public Service Responsibility of Broadcast Licensees,* should be consulted. Part V, C of that report, as amended July 2, 1946, states:

C. PROCEDURAL PROPOSALS

In carrying out the above objectives, the Commission proposes to continue substantially unchanged its present basic licensing procedures—namely, the requiring of a written application setting forth the proposed program service of the station, the consideration of that application on its merits, and subsequently the comparison of promise and performance when an application is received for a renewal of the station license. The ends sought can be best achieved, so far as presently appears, by appropriate modification of the particular forms and procedures currently in use and by a generally more careful consideration of renewal applications.

The particular procedural changes proposed are set forth below. They will not be introduced immediately or simultaneously, but rather from time to time as circumstances warrant. Meanwhile, the Commission invites comment from licensees and from the public.

1. UNIFORM DEFINITIONS AND PROGRAM LOGS

The Commission has always recognized certain basic categories of programs —e.g., commercial and sustaining, network, transcribed, recorded, local, live, etc. Such classifications must, under Regulation 3.404 [¶53:111], be shown upon the face of the program log required to be kept by each standard broad-

---

* The Commission is in the process of implementing its recent statement of policy with respect to broadcast programming (reported in Appendix VIII), and it is expected that some changes in program definitions and requirements will be made. The Commission, in cooperation with an industry committee, has been studying present requirements with the objective of modifying FCC application forms and providing clearer and more satisfactory program definitions and classifications to aid the broadcasters in keeping logs and reporting program information in connection with renewal and other types of applications.

Since the lengthy process of rulemaking is involved, it may be a considerable period of time before changes are made. In the meantime, the present program definitions and requirements must be observed.

cast station; and the Commission, like its predecessor, has always required data concerning such program classifications in its application forms.

Examination of logs shows, however, that there is no uniformity or agreement concerning what constitutes a "commercial" program, a "sustaining" program, a "network" program, etc. Accordingly, the Commission will adopt uniform definitions of basic program terms and classes, which are to be used in all presentations to the Commission. The proposed definitions are set forth below.

A commercial program (C) is any program the time for which is paid for by a sponsor or any program which is interrupted by a spot announcement (as defined below), at intervals of less than 14½ minutes. A network program shall be classified as "commercial" if it is commercially sponsored on the network, even though the particular station is not paid for carrying it—unless all commercial announcements have been deleted from the program by the station. Cooperative programs furnished to its affiliates by a network which are available for local sponsorship are network sustaining programs (NS) if no local sponsorship is involved and are network commercial programs (NC) where there is local sponsorship even though the commercial announcement is made by the station's local announcer.

(It will be noted that any program which is interrupted by a commercial announcement is classified as a commercial program, even though the purchaser of the interrupting announcement has not also purchased the time preceding and following. The result is to classify so-called "participating" programs as commercial. Without such a rule, a 15-minute program may contain 5 or even more minutes of advertising and still be classified as "sustaining." Under the proposed definition, a program may be classified as "sustaining" although preceded and followed by spot announcements, but if a spot announcement interrupts a program, the program must be classified as "commercial.")

A sustaining program (S) is any program which is neither paid for by a sponsor nor interrupted by a spot announcement (as defined below).

A network program (N) is any program furnished to the station by a network or another station. Transcribed delayed broadcasts of network programs are classified as "network," not "recorded." Cooperative programs furnished to its affiliates by a network which are available for local sponsorship are network sustaining programs (NS) if no local sponsorship is involved and are network commercial programs (NC) where there is local sponsorship even though the commercial announcement is made by the station's local announcer. Programs are classified as network whether furnished by a nationwide, regional, or special network or by another station.

A recorded program (R) is any program which uses phonograph records, electrical transcriptions, or other means of mechanical reproduction in whole or in part—except where the recording is wholly incidental to the program and is limited to background sounds, sound effects, identifying themes, musical "bridges," etc. A program part transcribed or recorded and part live is classified as "recorded" unless the recordings are wholly incidental, as above. A transcribed delayed broadcast of a network program, however, is not classified as "recorded" but as "network." A recorded program which is a local live program produced by the station and recorded for later broadcasting by the station shall be considered as a local live program.

A wire program (W) is any program the text of which is distributed to a number of stations by telegraph, teletype, or similar means, and read in whole or in part by a local announcer. Programs distributed by the wire news services are "wire" programs. A news program which is part wire and in part of non-syndicated origin is classified as "wire," if more than half of the program is usually devoted to the reading verbatim, or virtually verbatim, of the syndicated wire text, and otherwise is classified as "live."

A local live program (L) is any local program which uses live talent exclusively, whether originating in the station's studios or by remote control. Programs furnished to a station by a network or another station, however, are not classified as "live" but as "network." A program which uses recordings in whole or in part, except in a wholly incidental manner, should not be classified as "live" but as "recorded." Wire programs as defined above, should likewise not be classified as "live." A recorded program which is a local live program produced by the station and recorded for later broadcasting by the station shall be considered a local live program.

A non-commercial spot announcement (NCSA) is an announcement which is not paid for by a sponsor and which is devoted to a non-profit cause—e.g., war bonds, Red Cross, public health, civic announcements, etc. Promotional, participating announcements, etc. should not be classified as "non-commercial spot announcements" but as "spot announcements." War Bond, Red Cross, civic and similar announcements for which the station receives remuneration should not be classified as "non-commercial spot announcements" but as "spot announcements."

A spot announcement (SA) is any announcement which is neither a non-commercial spot announcement (as above defined) nor a station identification announcement (call letters and location). An announcement should be classified as a "spot announcement," whether or not the station receives remuneration, unless it is devoted to a nonprofit cause. Sponsored time signals, sponsored weather announcements, etc. are spot announcements. Unsponsored time signals, weather announcements, etc., are program matter and not classified as announcements. Station identification announcements should not be classified as either non-commercial spot announcements or spot announcements, if limited to call letters, location and identification of the licensee and network.

The Commission further proposes to amend Regulation 3.404 [¶53:111] to provide in part that the program log shall contain:

An entry classifying each program as "network commercial" (NC); "network sustaining" (NS); "recorded commercial" (RC); "Recorded sustaining" (RS); "wire commercial" (WC); "wire sustaining" (WS); "local live commercial" (LC); or "local live sustaining" (LS); and classifying each announcement as "spot announcement" (SA); or "sustaining public service announcement" (PSA).

The adoption of uniform definitions will make possible a fairer comparison of program representations and performance, and better statistical analyses.

2. SEGMENTS OF THE BROADCAST DAY

The Commission has always recognized, as has the industry, that different segments of the broadcast day have different characteristics and that different types of programming are therefore permissible. For example, the NAB Code, until recently, and many stations permit a greater proportion of advertising during the day than at night. The Commission's Chain Broadcasting Regulations recognize four segments: 8 a.m.—1 p.m., 1 p.m.—6 p.m., 6 p.m.—11 p.m., and all other hours. Most stations make distinctions of hours in their rate cards. In general, sustaining and live programs have tended to be crowded out of the best listening hours from 6 to 11 p.m., and also in a degree out of the period from 8 a.m. to 6 p.m. At least some stations have improved the ratios shown in reports to the Commission, but not the service rendered the public, by crowding sustaining programs into the hours after 11 p.m. and before dawn when listeners are few and sponsors fewer still. Clearly the responsibility for public service cannot be met by broadcasting public service programs only during such hours. A well-balanced program structure requires balance during the best listening hours.

	8 a.m. 6 p.m.	6 p.m. 11 p.m.	All other hours	Total
Network commercial (NC)				
Network sustaining (NS)				
Recorded commercial (RC)				
Recorded sustaining (RS)				
Wire commercial (WC)				
Wire sustaining (WS)				
Live commercial (LC)				
Live sustaining (LS)				
Total[1]				
No. of Spot announcements (SA)				
No. of Sustaining Public Service Announcements (PSA)				

[1] Totals should equal full operating time during each segment.

Statistical convenience requires that categories be kept to a minimum. In general, the segments of the broadcast day established in the Chain Broadcasting Regulations appear satisfactory, except that no good purpose appears to be served in connection with program analysis by calculating separately the segments from 8 a.m. to 1 p.m. and from 1 p.m. to 6 p.m. Accordingly, for present purposes it is proposed to merge these segments, so that the broadcast day will be composed of three segments only: 8 a.m.—6 p.m., 6 p.m.—11 p.m., and all other hours.

The categories set forth above, plus the segments herein defined, make possible a standard program log analysis as in the form shown above.

The above schedule will be uniformly utilized in Commission application forms and annual report forms in lieu of the various types of schedules now prevailing. In using it, stations may calculate the length of programs, to the nearest five minutes.

Report and Statement of Policy Re: Commission *en banc* Programming Inquiry*

The Commission en banc, by Commissioners Ford (Chairman), Bartley, Lee, Craven and Cross, with Commissioner Hyde dissenting and Commissioner King not participating, adopted the following statement on July 27, 1960:

On October 3, 1957 the Commission's Network Study Staff submitted its report on network broadcasting. While the scope and breadth of the network study as set forth in Order Number 1 issued November 21, 1955 encompassed a comprehensive study of programming, it soon became apparent that due to factors not within the control of the staff or the committee consideration of programming would be subject to substantial delay making it impracticable that the target dates for the over-all report could be met in the program area. The principal reasons were: (a) the refusal of certain program distributors and producers to provide the committee's staff with certain information which necessitated protracted negotiations and ultimately legal action (FCC v. Ralph Cohn, et al., 154 F. Supp, 899 [15 RR 2085]); and (b) the fact that a coincidental and collateral investigation into certain practices was instituted by the Department of Justice. Accordingly the network study staff report recommended that the study of programming be continued and completed. The Director of the Network Study in his memorandum of transmittal of the Network Study Report stated:

The staff regrets that it was unable to include in the report its findings and conclusions in its study of programming. It is estimated that more than one-fourth of the time of the staff was expended in this area. However, the extended negotiations and litigation with some non-network program producers relative to supplying financial data necessary to this aspect of the study made it impossible to obtain this information from a sufficient number of these program producers to draw definitive conclusions on all the programming issues. Now that the Commission's right to obtain this information has been sustained, it is the hope of the staff that this aspect of the study will be completed and the results included in a supplement to the report. Unless the study of programming is completed, the benefit of much labor on this subject will have been substantially lost.

As a result, on February 26, 1959, the Commission issued its "Order for Investigatory Proceeding," Docket No. 12782. That Order stated that during the course of the Network Study and otherwise, the Commission had obtained information and data regarding the acquisition, production, ownership, distribution, sale, licensing and exhibition of programs for television broadcasting. Also, that that information and data had been augmented from other sources including hearings before Committee of Congress and from the Department of Justice, and that the Commission had determined that an overall inquiry

* 25 F.R. 7291, August 3, 1960.

should be made to determine the facts with respect to the television network program selection process. On November 9, 1959, the proceeding instituted by the Commission's Order of February 26, 1959 was amended and enlarged to include a general inquiry with respect to programming to determine, among other things, whether the general standards heretofore laid down by the Commission for the guidance of broadcast licensees in the selection of programs and other material intended for broadcast are currently adequate; whether the Commission should, by the exercise of its rule-making power, set out more detailed and precise standards for such broadcasters; whether the Commission's present review and consideration in the field of programming and advertising are adequate, under present conditions in the broadcast industry; and whether the Commission's authority under the Communications Act of 1934, as amended, is adequate, or whether legislation should be recommended to Congress.

This inquiry was heard by the Commission en banc between December 7, 1959, and February 1, 1960, and consumed 19 days in actual hearings. Over 90 witnesses testified relative to the problems involved, made suggestions and otherwise contributed from their background and experience to the solution of these problems. Several additional statements were submitted. The record in the en banc portion of the inquiry consisted of 3,775 pages of transcript plus 1,000 pages of exhibits. The Interim Report of the staff of the Office of Network Study was submitted to the Commission for consideration on June 15, 1960.

The Commission will make every effort to expedite its consideration of the entire docket proceeding and will take such definitive action as the Commission determines to be warranted. However, the Commission feels that a general statement of policy responsive to the issues in the en banc inquiry is warranted at this time.

Prior to the en banc hearing, the Commission had made its position clear that, in fulfilling its obligation to operate in the public interest, a broadcast station is expected to exercise reasonable care and prudence with respect to its broadcast material in order to assure that no matter is broadcast which will deceive or mislead the public. In view of the extent of the problem existing with respect to a number of licensees involving such practices as deceptive quiz shows and payola which had become apparent, the Commission concluded that certain proposed amendments to our Rules as well as proposed legislation would provide a basis for substantial improvements. Accordingly, on February 5, 1960, we adopted a Notice of Proposed Rule Making to deal with fixed quiz and other non-bona fide contest programs involving intellectual skill. These rules would prohibit the broadcasting of such programming unless accompanied by an announcement which would in all cases describe the nature of the program in a manner to sufficiently apprise the audience that the events in question are not in fact spontaneous or actual measures of knowledge or intellectual skill. Announcements would be made at the beginning and end of each program. Moreover, the proposed rules would require a station, if it obtained such a program from networks, to be assured similarly that the network program has an accompanying announcement of this nature. This, we believe, would go a long way toward preventing any recurrence of problems such as those encountered in the recent quiz show programs.

We have also felt that this sort of conduct should be prohibited by statute. Accordingly, we suggested legislation designed to make it a crime for anyone to wilfully and knowingly participate or cause another to participate in or cause to be broadcast a program of intellectual skill or knowledge where the outcome thereof is prearranged or predetermined. Without the above-described amendment, the Commission's regulatory authority is limited to its licensing function. The Commission cannot reach networks directly or advertisers, producers, sponsors and others who, in one capacity or another, are associated with the presentation of radio and television programs which may deceive the listening or viewing public. It is our view that this proposed legislation will help to assure that every contest of intellectual skill or knowledge that is broadcast will be in fact a bona fide contest. Under this proposal, all those persons responsible in any way for the broadcast of a deceptive program of this type would be penalized. Because of the far reaching effects of radio and television, we believe such sanctions to be desirable.

The Commission proposed on February 5, 1960 that a new section be added to the Commission's rules which would require the licensee of radio broadcast stations to adopt appropriate procedures to prevent the practice of payola amongst his employees. Here again the standard of due diligence would have to be met by the licensee. We have also approved on February 11 the language of proposed legislation which would impose criminal penalties for failure to announce sponsored programs, such as payola and others, involving hidden payments or other considerations. This proposal looks toward amending the United States Code to provide fines up to $5,000 or imprisonment up to one year, or both, for violators. It would prohibit the payment to any person or the receipt of payment by any person for the purpose of having as a part of the broadcast program any material on either a radio or television show unless an announcement is made as a part of the program that such material has been paid for or furnished. The Commission now has no direct jurisdiction over the employees of a broadcast station with respect to this type of activity. The imposition of a criminal penalty appears to us to be an effective manner for dealing with this practice. In addition, the Commission has made related legislative proposals with respect to fines, temporary suspension of licenses and temporary restraining orders.

In view of our mutual interest with the Federal Trade Commission and in order to avoid duplication of effort, we have arrived at an arrangement whereby any information obtained by the FCC which might be of interest to FTC will be called to that Commission's attention by our staff. Similarly, FTC will advise our Commission of any information or data which it acquires in the course of its investigations which might be pertinent to matters under jurisdiction of the FCC. This is an understanding supplemental to earlier liaison arrangements between FCC and FTC.

Certain legislative proposals recently made by the Commission as related to the instant inquiry have been mentioned. It is appropriate now to consider whether the statutory authority of the Commission with respect to programming and program practices is, in other respects, adequate.

In considering the extent of the Commission's authority in the area of programming it is essential first to examine the limitations imposed upon it by the First Amendment to the Constitution and Section 326 of the Communications Act.

The First Amendment to the United States Constitution reads as follows:

Congress shall make no law respecting an establishment of religion or prohibiting the free exercise thereof; or abridging the freedom of speech, or of the press; or the right of the people peaceably to assemble, and to petition the Government for a redress of grievances.

Section 326 of the Communications Act of 1934, as amended, provides that:

Nothing in this chapter [Act] shall be understood or construed to give the Commission the power of censorship over the radio communications or signals transmitted by any radio station, and no regulation or condition shall be promulgated or fixed by the Commission which shall interfere with the right of free speech by means of radio communication.

The communication of ideas by means of radio and television is a form of expression entitled to protection against abridgement by the First Amendment to the Constitution. In United States v. Paramount Pictures, 334 U. S. 131, 166 (1948) the Supreme Court stated:

We have no doubt that moving pictures, like newspapers and radio are included in the press whose freedom is guaranteed by the First Amendment.

As recently as 1954 in Superior Films v. Department of Education, 346 U.S. 587, Justice Douglas in a concurring opinion stated:

Motion pictures are, of course, a different medium of expression than the radio, the stage, the novel or the magazine. But the First Amendment draws no distinction between the various methods of communicating ideas.

Moreover, the free speech protection of the First Amendment is not confined solely to the exposition of ideas nor is it required that the subject matter of the communication be possessed of some value to society. In Winters v. New York, 333 U.S. 507, 510 (1948) the Supreme Court reversed a conviction based upon a violation of an ordinance of the City of New York which made it punishable to distribute printed matter devoted to the publication of accounts of criminal deeds and pictures of bloodshed, lust or crime. In this connection the Court said:

We do not accede to appellee's suggestion that the constitutional protection for a free press applies only to the exposition of ideas. The line between the informing and the entertaining is too elusive for the protection of that basic right . . . Though we can see nothing of any possible value to society in these magazines, they are as much entitled to the protection of free speech as the best of literature.

Notwithstanding the foregoing authorities, the right to the use of the airwaves is conditioned upon the issuance of a license under a statutory scheme established by Congress in the Communications Act in the proper exercise of its power over commerce.[1] The question therefore arises as to whether because of the characteristics peculiar to broadcasting which justifies the government in regulating its operation through a licensing system, there exists the basis for a distinction as regards other media of mass communication with respect to application of the free speech provisions of the First Amendment? In other words, does it follow that because one may not engage in broadcasting without first obtaining a license, the terms thereof may be so framed as to unreasonably abridge the free speech protection of the First Amendment?

We recognize that the broadcasting medium presents problems peculiar to itself which are not necessarily subject to the same rules governing other media of communication. As we stated in our Petition in Grove Press, Inc. and Readers Subscription, Inc. v. Robert K. Christenberry (Case No. 25, 861) filed in the U.S. Court of Appeals for the Second Circuit, "radio and TV programs enter the home and are readily available not only to the average normal adult but also to children and to the emotionally immature . . . Thus, for example, while a nudist magazine may be within the protection of the First Amendment . . . the televising of nudes might well raise a serious question of programming contrary to 18 U.S.C. §1464 . . . Similarly, regardless of whether the 'four-letter words' and sexual description, set forth in 'Lady Chatterley's Lover,' (when considered in the context of the whole book) make the book obscene

[1] NBC v. United States, 319 U.S. 190 (1943)

for mailability purposes, the utterance of such words or the depiction of such sexual activity on radio or TV would raise similar public interest and Section 1464 questions." Nevertheless it is essential to keep in mind that "the basic principles of freedom of speech and the press like the First Amendment's command do not vary."[2]

Although the Commission must determine whether the total program service of broadcasters is reasonably responsive to the interests and needs of the public they serve, it may not condition the grant, denial or revocation of a broadcast license upon its own subjective determination of what is or is not a good program. To do so would "lay a forbidden burden upon the exercise of liberty protected by the Constitution."[3] The Chairman of the Commission during the course of his testimony recently given before the Senate Independent Offices Subcommittee of the Committee on Appropriations expressed the point as follows:

Mr. Ford. When it comes to questions of taste, unless it is downright profanity or obscenity, I do not think that the Commission has any part in it.

I don't see how we could possibly go out and say this program is good and that program is bad. That would be a direct violation of the law.[4]

In a similar vein Mr. Whitney North Seymour, President-elect of the American Bar Association, stated during the course of this proceeding that while the Commission may inquire of licensees what they have done to determine the needs of the community they propose to serve, the Commission may not impose upon them its private notions of what the public ought to hear.[5]

Nevertheless, several witnesses in this proceeding have advanced persuasive arguments urging us to require licensees to present specific types of programs on the theory that such action would enhance freedom of expression rather than tend to abridge it. With respect to this proposition we are constrained to point out that the First Amendment forbids governmental interference asserted in aid of free speech, as well as governmental action repressive of it. The protection against abridgement of freedom of speech and press flatly forbids governmental interference, benign or otherwise. The First Amendment "while regarding freedom in religion, in speech and printing and in assembling and petitioning the government for redress of grievances as fundamental and precious to all, seeks only to forbid that Congress should meddle therein." (Powe v. United States, 109 F. (2d) 147).

As recently as 1959 in Farmers Educational and Cooperative Union of America v. WDAY, Inc. 360 U. S. 525, the Supreme Court succinctly stated:

. . . expressly applying this country's tradition of free expression to the field of radio broadcasting, Congress has from the first emphatically forbidden the Commission to exercise any power of censorship over radio communication.

An examination of the foregoing authorities serves to explain why the day-to-day operation of a broadcast station is primarily the responsibility of the individual station licensee. Indeed, Congress provided in Section 3(h) of the Communications Act that a person engaged in radio broadcasting shall not be deemed a common carrier. Hence, the Commission in administering the Act and the courts in interpreting it have consistently maintained that responsibility

[2] Burstyn v. Wilson, 343 U.S. 495, 503, (1952).

[3] Cantwell v. Connecticut, 310 U.S. 926, 307.

[4] Hearings before the Subcommittee of the Committee on Appropriations, United States Senate, 86th Congress, 2nd Session on H.R. 11776 at page 775.

[5] Memorandum of Mr. Whitney North Seymour, Special Counsel to the National Association of Broadcasters at page 7.

for the selection and presentation of broadcast material ultimately devolves upon the individual station licensee, and that the fulfillment of the public interest requires the free exercise of his independent judgment. Accordingly, the Communications Act "does not essay to regulate the business of the licensee. The Commission is given no supervisory control of the programs, of business management or of policy . . . Congress intended to leave competition in the business of broadcasting where it found it . . ." [6] The regulatory responsibility of the Commission in the broadcast field essentially involves the maintenance of a balance between the preservation of a free competitive broadcast system, on the one hand, and the reasonable restriction of that freedom inherent in the public interest standard provided in the Communications Act, on the other.

In addition, there appears a second problem quite unrelated to the question of censorship that would enter into the Commission's assumption of supervision over program content. The Commission's role as a practical matter, let alone a legal matter, cannot be one of program dictation or program supervision. In this connection we think the words of Justice Douglas are particularly appropriate.

The music selected by one bureaucrat may be as offensive to some as it is soothing to others. The news commentator chosen to report on the events of the day may give overtones to the news that pleases the bureaucrat but which rile the . . . audience. The political philosophy which one radio sponsor exudes may be thought by the official who makes up the programs as the best for the welfare of the people. But the man who listens to it . . . may think it marks the destruction of the Republic . . . Today it is a business enterprise working out a radio program under the auspices of government. Tomorrow it may be a dominant, political or religious group. . . . Once a man is forced to submit to one type of program, he can be forced to submit to another. It may be but a short step from a cultural program to a political program . . . The strength of our system is in the dignity, resourcefulness and the intelligence of our people. Our confidence is in their ability to make the wisest choice. That system cannot flourish if regimentation takes hold.[7]

Having discussed the limitations upon the Commission in the consideration of programming, there remains for discussion the exceptions to those limitations and the area of affirmative responsibility which the Commission may appropriately exercise under its statutory obligation to find that the public interest, convenience and necessity will be served by the granting of a license to broadcast.

In view of the fact that a broadcaster is required to program his station in the public interest, convenience and necessity, it follows despite the limitations of the First Amendment and Section 326 of the Act, that his freedom to program is not absolute. The Commission does not conceive that it is barred by the Constitution or by statute from exercising any responsibility with respect to programming. It does conceive that the manner or extent of the exercise of such responsibility can introduce constitutional or statutory questions. It readily concedes that it is precluded from examining a program for taste or content, unless the recognized exceptions to censorship apply: for example, obscenity, profanity, indecency, programs inciting to riots, programs designed or inducing toward the commission of crime, lotteries, etc. These exceptions, in part, are written into the United States Code and, in part, are recognized in judicial decision. See Sections 1304, 1343 and 1464 of Title 18 of the United States Code (lotteries, fraud by radio, utterance of obscene, indecent or profane

[6] FCC v. Sanders Brothers, 309 U.S. 470, 475 (1940)
[7] Public Utilities Commission v. Pollak, 343 U.S. 451, 468, Dissenting Opinion.

language by radio). It must be added that such traditional or legislative exceptions to a strict application of the freedom of speech requirements of the United States Constitution may very well also convey wider scope in judicial interpretation as applied to licensed radio than they have had or would have as applied to other communications media. The Commission's petition in the Grove case, supra, urged the court not unnecessarily to refer to broadcasting, in its opinion, as had the District Court. Such reference subsequently was not made though it must be pointed out there is no evidence that the motion made by the FCC was a contributing factor. It must nonetheless be observed that this Commission conscientiously believes that it should make no policy or take any action which would violate the letter or the spirit of the censorship prohibitions of Section 326 of the Communications Act.

As stated by the Supreme Court of the United States in Joseph Burstyne, Inc. v. Wilson, supra:

. . . Nor does it follow that motion pictures are necessarily subject to the precise rule governing any other particular method of expression. Each method tends to present its own peculiar problem. But the basic principles of freedom of speech and the press, like the First Amendment's command, do not vary. Those principles, as they have frequently been enunciated by this Court, make freedom of expression the rule.

A review of the Communications Act as a whole clearly reveals that the foundation of the Commission's authority rests upon the public interest, convenience and necessity.[8] The Commission may not grant, modify or renew a broadcast station license without finding that the operation of such station is in the public interest. Thus, faithful discharge of its statutory responsibilities is absolutely necessary in connection with the implacable requirement that the Commission approve no such application for license unless it finds that "public interest, convenience and necessity would be served." While the public interest standard does not provide a blueprint of all the situations to which it may apply, it does contain a sufficiently precise definition of authority so as to enable the Commission to properly deal with the many and varied occasions which may give rise to its application. A significant element of the public interest is the broadcaster's service to the community. In the case of NBC v. United States, 319 U. S. 190, the Supreme Court described this aspect of the public interest as follows:

An important element of public interest and convenience affecting the issue of a license is the ability of the licensee to render the best practicable service to the community reached by broadcasts . . . The Commission's licensing function cannot be discharged, therefore, merely by finding that there are no technological objections to the granting of a license. If the criterion of 'public interest' were limited to such matters, how could the Commission choose between two applicants for the same facilities, each of whom is financially and technically qualified to operate a station? Since the very inception of federal regulation by radio, comparative considerations as to the services to be rendered have governed the application of the standard of 'public interest, convenience or necessity.'

Moreover, apart from this broad standard which we will further discuss in a moment, there are certain other statutory indications.

It is generally recognized that programming is of the essence of radio service. Section 307(b) of the Communications Act requires the Commission to "make such distribution of licenses . . . among the several States and communities as to provide a fair, efficient and equitable distribution of radio service to each

[8] Sections 307(d), 308, 309, inter alia.

of the same." Under this section the Commission has consistently licensed stations with the end objective of either providing new or additional programming service *to* a community, area or state, or of providing a new or additional "outlet" for broadcasting *from* a community, area or state. Implicit in the former alternative is increased radio reception; implicit in the latter alternative is increased radio transmission and, in this connection, appropriate attention to local live programming is required.

Formerly by reason of administrative policy, and since September 14, 1959, by necessary implication from the amended language of Section 315 of the Communications Act, the Commission has had the responsibility for determining whether licensees "afford reasonable opportunity for the discussion of conflicting views on issues of public importance." This responsibility usually is of the generic kind and thus, in the absence of unusual circumstances, is not exercised with regard to particular situations but rather in terms of operating policies of stations as viewed over a reasonable period of time. This, in the past, has meant a review, usually in terms of filed complaints, in connection with the applications made each three year period for renewal of station licenses. However, that has been a practice largely traceable to workload necessities, and therefore not so limited by law. Indeed the Commission recently has expressed its views to the Congress that it would be desirable to exercise a greater discretion with respect to the length of licensing periods within the maximum three year license period provided by Section 307(d). It has also initiated rulemaking to this end.

The foundation of the American system of broadcasting was laid in the Radio Act of 1927 when Congress placed the basic responsibility for all matter broadcast to the public at the grass roots level in the hands of the station licensee. That obligation was carried forward into the Communications Act of 1934, and remains unaltered and undivided. The licensee, is, in effect, a "trustee" in the sense that his license to operate his station imposes upon him a nondelegable duty to serve the public interest in the community he had chosen to represent as a broadcaster.

Great confidence and trust are placed in the citizens who have qualified as broadcasters. The primary duty and privilege to select the material to be broadcast to his audience and the operation of his component of this powerful medium of communication is left in his hands. As was stated by the Chairman in behalf of this Commission in recent testimony before a Congressional Committee:[9]

Thus far Congress has not imposed by law an affirmative programming requirement on broadcast licensees. Rather, it has heretofore given licensees a broad discretion in the selection of programs. In recognition of this principle, Congress provided in Section 3(h) of the Communications Act that a person engaged in radio broadcasting shall not be deemed a common carrier. To this end the Commission in administering the Act and the courts in interpreting it have consistently maintained that responsibility for the selection and presentation of broadcast material ultimately devolves upon the individual station licensee and that the fulfillment of such responsibility requires the free exercise of his independent judgment.

As indicated by former President Hoover, then Secretary of Commerce, in the Radio Conference of 1922-25:

The dominant element for consideration in the radio field is, and always will be, the great body of the listening public, millions in number, country wide in distribu-

[9] Testimony of Frederick W. Ford, May 16, 1960 before the Subcommittee on Communications of the Committee on Interstate & Foreign Commerce, United States Senate.

tion. There is no proper line of conflict between the broadcaster and listener, nor would I attempt to array one against the other. Their interests are mutual, for without the one the other could not exist.

There have been few developments in industrial history to equal the speed and efficiency with which genius and capital have joined to meet radio needs. The great majority of station owners today recognize the burden of service and gladly assume it. Whatever other motive may exist for broadcasting, the pleasing of the listener is always the primary purpose. . . .

The greatest public interest must be the deciding factor. I presume that few still dissent as to the correctness of this principle, for all will agree that public good must ever balance private desire; but its acceptance leads to important and far-reaching practical effects, as to which there may not be the same unanimity, but from which, nevertheless, there is no logical escape.

The confines of the licensee's duty are set by the general standard "the public interest, convenience or necessity."[10] The initial and principal execution of that standard, in terms of the area he is licensed to serve, is the obligation of the licensee. The principal ingredient of such obligation consists of a diligent, positive and continuing effort by the licensee to discover and fulfill the tastes, needs and desires of his service area. If he has accomplished this, he has met his public responsibility. It is the duty of the Commission, in the first instance, to select persons as licensees who meet the qualifications laid down in the Act, and on a continuing basis to review the operations of such licensees from time to time to provide reasonable assurance to the public that the broadcast service it receives is such as its direct and justifiable interest requires.

Historically it is interesting to note that in its review of station performance the Federal Radio Commission sought to extract the general principles of broadcast service which should (1) guide the licensee in his determination of the public interest and (2) be employed by the Commission as an "index" or general frame of reference in evaluating the licensee's discharge of his public duty. The Commission attempted no precise definition of the components of the public interest but left the discernment of its limit to the practical operation of broadcast regulation. It required existing stations to report the types of service which had been provided and called on the public to express its views and preferences as to programs and other broadcast services. It sought information from as many sources as were available in its quest of a fair and equitable basis for the selection of those who might wish to become licensees and the supervision of those who already engaged in broadcasting.

The spirit in which the Radio Commission approached its unprecedented task was to seek to chart a course between the need of arriving at a workable concept of the public interest in station operation, on the one hand, and the prohibition laid on it by the First Amendment to the Constitution of the United States and by Congress in Section 29 of the Federal Radio Act against censorship and interference with free speech, on the other. The Standards or guidelines which evolved from that process, in their essentials, were adopted by the Federal Communications Commission and have remained as the basis for evaluation of broadcast service. They have in the main, been incorporated into various codes and manuals of network and station operation.

It is emphasized, that these standards or guidelines should in no sense constitute a rigid mold for station performance, nor should they be considered as a Commission formula for broadcast service in the public interest. Rather, they should be considered as indicia of the types and areas of service which, on the basis of experience, have usually been accepted by the broadcasters as

[10] Cf. Communications Act of 1934, as amended, inter alia, Secs. 307, 309.

more or less included in the practical definition of community needs and interests.

Broadcasting licensees must assume responsibility for all material which is broadcast through their facilities. This includes all programs and advertising material which they present to the public. With respect to advertising material the licensee has the additional responsibility to take all reasonable measures to eliminate any false, misleading, or deceptive matter and to avoid abuses with respect to the total amount of time devoted to advertising continuity as well as the frequency with which regular programs are interrupted for advertising messages. This duty is personal to the licensee and may not be delegated. He is obligated to bring his positive responsibility affirmatively to bear upon all who have a hand in providing broadcast matter for transmission through his facilities so as to assure the discharge of his duty to provide an acceptable program schedule consonant with operating in the public interest in his community. The broadcaster is obligated to make a positive, diligent and continuing effort, in good faith, to determine the tastes, needs and desires of the public in his community and to provide programming to meet those needs and interests. This again, is a duty personal to the licensee and may not be avoided by delegation of the responsibility to others.

Although the individual station licensee continues to bear legal responsibility for all matter broadcast over his facilities, the structure of broadcasting, as developed in practical operation, is such—especially in television—that, in reality, the station licensee has little part in the creation, production, selection and control of network program offerings. Licensees place "practical reliance" on networks for the selection and supervision of network programs which, of course, are the principal broadcast fare of the vast majority of television stations throughout the country.[11]

In the fulfillment of his obligation the broadcaster should consider the tastes, needs and desires of the public he is licensed to serve in developing his programming and should exercise conscientious efforts not only to ascertain them but also to carry them out as well as he reasonably can. He should reasonably attempt to meet all such needs and interests on an equitable basis. Particular areas of interest and types of appropriate service may, of course, differ from community to community, and from time to time. However, the Commission does expect its broadcast licensees to take the necessary steps to inform themselves of the real needs and interests of the areas they serve, and to provide programming which in fact constitutes a diligent effort, in good faith, to provide for those needs and interests.

The major elements usually necessary to meet the public interest, needs and desires of the community in which the station is located as developed by the industry, and recognized by the Commission, have included: (1) Opportunity for Local Self-Expression, (2) The Development and Use of Local Talent, (3) Programs for Children, (4) Religious Programs, (5) Educational Programs, (6) Public Affairs Programs, (7) Editorialization by Licensees, (8) Political Broadcasts, (9) Agricultural Programs, (10) News Programs, (11) Weather and Market Reports, (12) Sports Programs, (13) Service to Minority Groups, (14) Entertainment Programming.

The elements set out above are neither all-embracing nor constant. We reemphasize that they do not serve and have never been intended as a rigid mold or fixed formula for station operation. The ascertainment of the needed

[11] The Commission, in recognition of this problem as it affects the licensees, has recently recommended to the Congress enactment of legislation providing for direct regulation of networks in certain respects.

elements of the broadcast matter to be provided by a particular licensee for the audience he is obligated to serve remains primarily the function of the licensee. His honest and prudent judgments will be accorded great weight by the Commission. Indeed, any other course would tend to substitute the judgment of the Commission for that of the licensee.

The programs provided first by "chains" of stations and then by networks have always been recognized by this Commission as of great value to the station licensee in providing a well-rounded community service. The importance of network programs need not be re-emphasized as they have constituted an integral part of the well-rounded program service provided by the broadcast business in most communities.

Our own observations and the testimony in this inquiry have persuaded us that there is no public interest basis for distinguishing between sustaining and commercially sponsored programs in evaluating station performance. However, this does not relieve the station from responsibility for retaining the flexibility to accommodate public needs.

Sponsorship of public affairs, and other similar programs may very well encourage broadcasters to greater efforts in these vital areas. This is borne out by statements made in this proceeding in which it was pointed out that under modern conditions sponsorship fosters rather than diminishes the availability of important public affairs and "cultural" broadcast programming. There is some convincing evidence, for instance, that at the network level there is a direct relation between commercial sponsorship and "clearance" of public affairs and other "cultural" programs. Agency executives have testified that there is unused advertising support for public affairs type programming. The networks and some stations have scheduled these types of programs during "prime time."

The Communications Act[12] provides that the Commission may grant construction permits and station licenses, or modifications or renewals thereof, "only upon written application" setting forth the information required by the Act and the Commission's Rules and Regulations. If, upon examination of any such application, the Commission shall find the public interest, convenience and necessity would be served by the granting thereof, it shall grant said application. If it does not so find, it shall so advise the applicant and other known parties in interest of all objections to the application and the applicant shall then be given an opportunity to supply additional information. If the Commission cannot then make the necessary finding, the application is designated for hearing and the applicant bears the burden of providing proof of the public interest.

During our hearings there seemed to be some misunderstanding as to the nature and use of the "statistical" data regarding programming and advertising required by our application forms. We wish to stress that no one may be summarily judged as to the service he has performed on the basis of the information contained in his application. As we said long ago:

It should be emphasized that the statistical data before the Commission constitute an index only of the manner of operation of the stations and are not considered by the Commission as conclusive of the over-all operation of the stations in question.

Licensees will have an opportunity to show the nature of their program service and to introduce other relevant evidence which would demonstrate that in actual operation the program service of the station is, in fact, a well rounded program service

[12] Section 308(a).

and is in conformity with the promises and representations previously made in prior applications to the Commission.[13]

As we have said above, the principal ingredient of the licensee's obligation to operate his station in the public interest is the diligent, positive and continuing effort by the licensee to discover and fulfill the tastes, needs and desires of his community or service area, for broadcast service.

To enable the Commission in its licensing functions to make the necessary public interest finding, we intend to revise Part IV of our application forms to require a statement by the applicant, whether for new facilities, renewal or modification, as to: (1) the measures he has taken and the effort he has made to determine the tastes, needs and desires of his community or service area, and (2) the manner in which he proposes to meet those needs and desires.

Thus we do not intend to guide the licensee along the path of programming; on the contrary the licensee must find his own path with the guidance of those whom his signal is to serve. We will thus steer clear of the bans of censorship without disregarding the public's vital interest. What we propose will not be served by pre-planned program format submissions accompanied by complimentary references from local citizens. What we propose is documented program submissions prepared as the result of assiduous planning and consultation covering two main areas; first, a canvass of the listening public who will receive the signal and who constitute a definite public interest figure; second, consultation with leaders in community life—public officials, educators, religious, the entertainment media, agriculture, business, labor—professional and eleemosynary organizations, and others who bespeak the interests which make up the community.

By the care spent in obtaining and reflecting the views thus obtained, which clearly cannot be accepted without attention to the business judgment of the licensee if his station is to be an operating success, will the standard of programming in the public interest be best fulfilled. This would not ordinarily be the case if program formats have been decided upon by the licensee before he undertakes his planning and consultation, for the result would show little stimulation on the part of the two local groups above referenced. And it is the composite of their contributive planning, led and sifted by the expert judgment of the licensee, which will assure to the station the appropriate attention to the public interest which will permit the Commission to find that a license may issue. By his narrative development, in his application, of the planning, consulting, shaping, revising, creating, discarding and evaluation of programming thus conceived or discussed, the licensee discharges the public interest facet of his business calling without Government dictation or supervision and permits the Commission to discharge its responsibility to the public without invasion of spheres of freedom properly denied to it. By the practicality and specificity of his narrative the licensee facilitates the application of expert judgment by the Commission. Thus, if a particular kind of educational program could not be feasibly assisted (by funds or service) by educators for more than a few time periods, it would be idle for program composition to place it in weekly focus. Private ingenuity and educational interest should look further, toward implemental suggestions of practical yet constructive value. The broadcaster's license is not intended to convert his business into "an

[13] Public Notice (98501), September 20, 1946, "Status of Standard Broadcast Applications."

instrumentality of the federal government";[14] neither, on the other hand, may he ignore the public interest which his application for a license should thus define and his operations thereafter reasonably observe.

Numbers of suggestions were made during the en banc hearings concerning possible uses by the Commission of codes of broadcast practices adopted by segments of the industry as part of a process of self-regulation. While the Commission has not endorsed any specific code of broadcast practices, we consider the efforts of the industry to maintain high standards of conduct to be highly commendable and urge that the industry persevere in these efforts.

The Commission recognizes that submissions, by applicants, concerning their past and future programming policies and performance provide one important basis for deciding whether—in so far as broadcast services are concerned—we may properly make the public interest finding requisite to the grant of an application for a standard, FM or television broadcast station. The particular manner in which applicants are required to depict their proposed or past broadcast policies and services (including the broadcasting of commercial announcements) may therefore, have significant bearing upon the Commission's ability to discharge its statutory duties in the matter. Conscious of the importance of reporting requirements, the Commission on November 24, 1958 initiated proceedings (Docket No. 12673) to consider revisions to the rules prescribing the form and content of reports on broadcast programming.

Aided by numerous helpful suggestions offered by witnesses in the recent en banc hearings on broadcast programming, the Commission is at present engaged in a thorough study of this subject. Upon completion of that study we will announce, for comment by all interested parties, such further revisions to the present reporting requirements as we think will best conduce to an awareness, by broadcasters, of their responsibilities to the public and to effective, efficient processing, by the Commission, of applications for broadcast licenses and renewals.

To this end, we will initiate further rule making on the subject at the earliest practicable date.

Adopted: July 27, 1960.

SEPARATE STATEMENT OF COMMISSIONER HYDE

I believe that the Commission's "Interim Report and Statement of Policy" in Docket No. 12782 misses the central point of the hearing conducted by the Commission en banc, December 7, 1959, to February 1, 1960.

It reiterates the legal position which was taken by the Federal Radio Commission in 1927, and which has been adhered to by the Federal Communications Commission since it was organized in 1934. This viewpoint was accepted by the executives of the leading networks and by most other units of the broadcasting industry as well as the National Association of Broadcasters. The main concern requiring a fresh approach is what to do in the light of the law and the matters presented by many witnesses in the hearings. This, I understand, is to be the subject of a rule-making proceeding still to be initiated. I urged the preparation of an appropriate rule-making notice prior to the preparation of the instant statement.

I also disagree with the decision of the Commission to release the document captioned "Interim Report by the Office of Network Study, Responsibility for Broadcast Matter, Docket No. 12782." Since it deals in part with a

[14] The defendant is not an instrumentality of the federal government but a privately owned corporation. McIntire v. Wm. Penn Broadcasting Co., 151 F. (2d) 597, 600.

hearing in which the Commission itself sat en banc, I feel that it does not have the character of a separate staff-study type of document, and that its release with the Commission policy statement will create confusion. Moreover, a substantial portion of the document is concerned with matter still under investigation process in Docket 12782. I think issuance of comment on these matters under the circumstances is premature and inappropriate.

Radio and Television Codes of the National Association of Broadcasters

The following are the recently revised radio and television codes of the National Association of Broadcasters, 1771 N. Street, N.W., Washington 6, D.C. These are reprinted by permission. For additional information regarding these codes, inquiries should be addressed to this organization.

A substantial number of radio and television stations in the country subscribe to these codes. More and more, these codes are having a helpful and constructive influence on the quality of broadcasting in this country.

I

RADIO CODE
OF GOOD
PRACTICES
OF THE
NATIONAL ASSOCIATION OF BROADCASTERS*

PREAMBLE

The radio broadcasters of the United States first adopted industry-wide standards of practice in 1937. The purpose of such standards, in this as in other professions, is to establish guideposts and to set forth minimum tenets for performance.

Standards for broadcasting can never be final or complete. Broadcasting is a creative art and it must always seek new ways to achieve greater advances. Therefore, any standards must be subject to change. In 1945, after two years devoted to reviewing and revising the 1937 document, new standards were promulgated. Further revisions were made in 1948, 1954, 1955, 1958, and 1960, and now there follows a new and revised Radio Code of Good Practices of the National Association of Broadcasters.

Through this process of self-examination broadcasters acknowledge their obligation to the American family.

The growth of broadcasting as a medium of entertainment, education, and information has been made possible by its force as an instrument of commerce.

* Promulgated 1937. Revised 1945, 1948, 1954, 1955, 1958, 1960.

This philosophy of commercial broadcasting as it is known in the United States has enabled the industry to develop as a free medium in the tradition of American enterprise.

The extent of this freedom is implicit in the fact that no one censors broadcasting in the United States.

Those who own the nation's radio broadcasting stations operate them—pursuant to this self-adopted Radio Code of Good Practices—in recognition of the interest of the American people.

THE RADIO BROADCASTERS CREED

We Believe:

That Radio Broadcasting in the United States of America is a living symbol of democracy; a significant and necessary instrument for maintaining freedom of expression, as established by the First Amendment to the Constitution of the United States;

That its influence in the arts, in science, in education, in commerce, and upon the public welfare is of such magnitude that the only proper measure of its responsibility is the common good of the whole people;

That it is our obligation to serve the people in such manner as to reflect credit upon our profession and to encourage aspiration toward a better estate for all mankind; by making available to every person in America such programs as will perpetuate the traditional leadership of the United States in all phases of the broadcasting art;

That we should make full and ingenious use of man's store of knowledge, his talents, and his skills and exercise critical and discerning judgment concerning all broadcasting operations to the end that we may, intelligently and sympathetically:

Observe the proprieties and customs of civilized society;

Respect the rights and sensitivities of all people;

Honor the sanctity of marriage and the home;

Protect and uphold the dignity and brotherhood of all mankind;

Enrich the daily life of the people through the factual reporting and analysis of news, and through programs of education, entertainment, and information;

Provide for the fair discussion of matters of general public concern; engage in works directed toward the common good; and volunteer our aid and comfort in times of stress and emergency;

Contribute to the economic welfare of all by expanding the channels of trade, by encouraging the development and conservation of natural resources, and by bringing together the buyer and seller through the broadcasting of information pertaining to goods and services.

Toward the achievement of these purposes we agree to observe the following:

I. PROGRAM STANDARDS

A. *News*

Radio is unique in its capacity to reach the largest number of people first with reports on current events. This competitive advantage bespeaks caution— being first is not as important as being right. The following Standards are predicated upon that viewpoint.

NEWS SOURCES. Those responsible for news on radio should exercise constant professional care in the selection of sources—for the integrity of the news and the consequent good reputation of radio as a dominant news medium depend largely upon the reliability of such sources.

NEWSCASTING. News reporting should be factual and objective. Good taste should prevail in the selection and handling of news. Morbid, sensational, or alarming details not essential to factual reporting should be avoided. News should be broadcast in such a manner as to avoid creation of panic and unnecessary alarm. Broadcasters should be diligent in their supervision of content, format, and presentation of news broadcasts. Equal diligence should be exercised in selection of editors and reporters who direct news gathering and dissemination, since the station's performance in this vital informational field depends largely upon them.

COMMENTARIES AND ANALYSES. Special obligations devolve upon those who analyze and/or comment upon news developments, and management should be satisfied completely that the task is to be performed in the best interest of the listening public. Programs of news analysis and commentary should be clearly identified as such, distinguishing them from straight news reporting.

EDITORIALIZING. Some stations exercise their rights to express opinions about matters of general public interest. Implicit in these efforts to provide leadership in matters of public consequence and to lend proper authority to the station's standing in the community it serves, is an equal obligation to provide opportunity for qualified divergent viewpoints.

The reputation of a station for honesty and accuracy in editorializing depends upon willingness to expose its convictions to fair rebuttal.

Station editorial comment should be clearly identified as such.

TREATMENT OF NEWS AND PUBLIC EVENTS. All news interview programs should be governed by accepted standards of ethical journalism, under which the interviewer selects the questions to be asked. Where there is advance agreement materially restricting an important or newsworthy area of questioning, the interviewer will state on the program that such limitations has been agreed upon. Such disclosure should be made if the person being interviewed requires that questions be submitted in advance or if he participates in editing a recording of the interview prior to its use on the air.

B. *Public Issues*

A broadcaster, in allotting time for the presentation of public issues, should exert every effort to insure equality of opportunity.

Time should be allotted with due regard to all elements of balanced program schedules, and to the degree of interest on the part of the public in the questions to be presented or discussed. (To discuss is "to sift or examine by presenting considerations pro and con".) The broadcaster should limit participation in the presentation of public issues to those qualified, recognized, and properly identified groups or individuals whose opinions will assist the general public in reaching conclusions.

Presentation of public issues should be clearly identified.

C. *Political Broadcasts*

Political broadcasts, or the dramatization of political issues designed to influence an election, should be properly identified as such.

D. *Advancement of Education and Culture*

Because radio is an integral part of American life, there is inherent in radio broadcasting a continuing opportunity to enrich the experience of living through the advancement of education and culture.

The radio broadcaster, in augmenting the educational and cultural influences of the home, the Church, schools, institutions of higher learning, and other entities devoted to education and culture:

Should be thoroughly conversant with the educational and cultural needs and aspirations of the community served;

Should cooperate with the responsible and accountable educational and cultural entities of the community to provide enlightenment of listeners;

Should engage in experimental efforts designed to advance the community's cultural and educational interests.

E. *Religion and Religious Programs*

Religious programs should be presented respectfully and without prejudice or ridicule.

Radio broadcasting, which reaches men of all creeds simultaneously, should avoid attacks upon religion.

Religious programs should be presented by responsible individuals, groups, or organizations.

Religious programs should place emphasis on broad religious truths, excluding the presentation of controversial or partisan views not directly or necessarily related to religion or morality.

F. *Dramatic Programs*

In determining the acceptability of any dramatic program containing any element of crime, mystery, or horror, proper consideration should be given to the possible effect on all members of the family.

Radio should reflect realistically the experience of living, in both its pleasant and tragic aspects, if it is to serve the listener honestly. Nevertheless, it holds a concurrent obligation to provide programs which will encourage better adjustments to life.

This obligation is apparent in the area of dramatic programs particularly. Without sacrificing integrity of presentation, dramatic programs on radio should avoid:

Techniques and methods of crime presented in such manner as to encourage imitation, or to make the commission of crime attractive, or to suggest that criminals can escape punishment.

Detailed presentation of brutal killings, torture, or physical agony, horror, the use of supernatural or climactic incidents likely to terrify or excite unduly;

Episodes involving the kidnapping of children;

Sound effects calculated to mislead, shock, or unduly alarm the listener;

Disrespectful portrayal of law enforcement;

The portrayal of suicide as a satisfactory solution to any problem.

G. *Children's Programs*

Programs specifically designed for listening by children should be based upon sound social concepts and should reflect respect for parents, law and order, clean living, high morals, fair play, and honorable behavior.

They should convey the commonly accepted moral, social, and ethical ideals characteristic of American life.

They should contribute to the healthy development of personality and character.

427

They should afford opportunities for cultural growth as well as for wholesome entertainment.

They should be consistent with integrity of realistic production, but they should avoid material of an extreme nature which might create undesirable emotional reaction in children.

They should avoid appeals urging children to purchase the product specifically for the purpose of keeping the program on the air or which, for any reason, encourage children to enter inappropriate places.

H. *General*

The intimacy and confidence placed in Radio demand of the broadcaster, the networks and other program sources that they be vigilant in protecting the audience from deceptive program practices.

Sound effects and expressions characteristically associated with news broadcasts (such as "bulletins", "flash", etc.) should be reserved for announcement of news, and the use of any deceptive techniques in connection with fictional events and non-news programs should not be employed.

The broadcaster shall be constantly alert to prevent activities that may lead to such practices as the choice and identification of prizes, the selection of music and other creative program elements and inclusion of any identification of commercial products or services, their trade names or advertising slogans, within a program dictated by factors other than the requirements of the program itself. This expressly forbids that acceptance by producer, talent, or any other personnel of cash payments or other considerations in return for including any of the above within the program.

When plot development requires the use of material which depends upon physical or mental handicaps, care should be taken to spare the sensibilities of sufferers from similar defects.

Stations should avoid broadcasting program material which would tend to encourage illegal gambling or other violations of Federal, State and local laws, ordinances, and regulations.

Simulation of court atmosphere or use of the term "Court" in a program title should be done only in such manner as to eliminate the possibility of creating the false impression that the proceedings broadcast are vested with judicial or official authority.

When dramatized advertising material involves statements by doctors, dentists, nurses, or other professional people, the material should be presented by members of such profession reciting actual experience, or it should be made apparent from the presentation itself that the portrayal is dramatized.

Quiz and similar programs that are presented as contests of knowledge, information, skill or luck must, in fact, be genuine contests and the results must not be controlled by collusion with or between contestants, or any other action which will favor one contestant against any other.

No program shall be presented in a manner which through artifice or simulation would mislead the audience as to any material fact. Each broadcaster must exercise reasonable judgment to determine whether a particular method of presentation would constitute a material deception, or would be accepted by the audience as normal theatrical illusion.

In cases of programs broadcast over multiple station facilities, the originating station or network should assume responsibility for conforming such programs to this Radio Code.

II. ADVERTISING STANDARDS

Advertising is the principal source of revenue of the free, competitive American system of radio broadcasting. It makes possible the presentation to all American people of the finest programs of entertainment, education, and information.

Since the great strength of American radio broadcasting derives from the public respect for and the public approval of its programs, it must be the purpose of each broadcaster to establish and maintain high standards of performance, not only in the selection and production of all programs, but also in the presentation of advertising.

A. *Time Standards for Advertising Copy*

As a guide to the determination of good broadcast advertising practice, the time standards for advertising copy are established as follows:

The maximum time to be used for advertising, allowable to any single sponsor, regardless of type of program, should be—

5 minute programs		1:30
10 " "		2:10
15 " "		3:00
25 " "		4:00
30 " "		4:15
45 " "		5:45
60 " "		7:00

The time standards allowable to a single advertiser do not affect the established practice of allowance for station breaks between programs.

Any reference in a sponsored program to another's products or services under any trade name, or language sufficiently descriptive to identify it, should, except for normal guest identifications, be considered as advertising copy.

While any number of products may be advertised by a single sponsor within the specified time standards, advertising copy for these products should be presented within the framework of the program structure. Accordingly, the use on such programs of simulated spot announcements which are divorced from the program by preceding the introduction of the program itself, or by following its *apparent* sign-off should be avoided. To this end, the program itself should be announced and clearly identified *before* the use of what have been known as "cow-catcher" announcements, and the programs should be signed off *after* the use of what have been known as "hitch-hike" announcements.

B. *Presentation of Advertising*

The advancing techniques of the broadcast art have shown that the *quality* and *proper integration* of advertising copy are just as important as measurement in time. The measure of a station's service to its audience is determined by its over-all performance, rather than by any individual segment of its broadcast day.

Programs of multiple sponsorship presenting commercial services, features, shopping guides, marketing news, and similar information, may include more material normally classified as "commercial" or "advertising", if it is of such nature as to serve the interests of the general public and, if properly produced and intelligently presented, within the established areas of good taste.

429

The final measurement of any commercial broadcast service is quality. To this, every broadcaster should dedicate his best efforts.

C. *Acceptability of Advertisers and Products*

1. A commercial radio broadcaster makes his facilities available for the advertising of products and services and accepts commercial presentations for such advertising. However, he should, in recognition of his responsibility to the public, refuse the facilities of his station to an advertiser where he has good reason to doubt the integrity of the advertiser, the truth of the advertising representations, or the compliance of the advertiser with the spirit and purpose of all applicable legal requirements. Moreover, in consideration of the laws and customs of the communities served, each radio broadcaster should refuse his facilities to the advertisement of products and services, or the use of advertising scripts, which the station has good reason to believe would be objectionable to a substantial and responsible segment of the community. The foregoing principles should be applied with judgment and flexibility, taking into consideration the characteristics of the medium and the form of the particular presentation. In general, because radio broadcasting is designed for the home and the entire family, the following principles should govern the business classifications listed below:
   a) The advertising of hard liquor should not be accepted.
   b) The advertising of beer and wines is acceptable only when presented in the best of good taste and discretion, and is acceptable subject to existing laws.
   c) The advertising of fortune-telling, occultism, spiritualism, astrology, phrenology, palm-reading, numerology, mind-reading, or character-reading is not acceptable.
   d) All advertising of products of a personal nature, when accepted, should be treated with special concern for the sensitivities of the listeners.
   e) The advertising of tip sheets, publications, or organizations seeking to advertise for the purpose of giving odds or promoting betting or lotteries is unacceptable.
2. An advertiser who markets more than one product should not be permitted to use advertising copy devoted to an acceptable product for purposes of publicizing the brand name or other identification of a product which is not acceptable.
3. Care should be taken to avoid presentation of "bait-switch" advertising whereby goods or services which the advertiser has no intention of selling are offered merely to lure the customer into purchasing higher-priced substitutes.

D. *Contests*

Contests should offer the opportunity to all contestants to win on the basis of ability and skill, rather than chance.

All contest details, including rules, eligibility requirements, opening and termination dates, should be clearly and completely announced or easily accessible to the listening public; and the winners' names should be released as soon as possible after the close of the contest.

When contestants are required to submit items of product identification or other evidence of purchase of product, reasonable facsimiles thereof should be made acceptable.

All copy pertaining to any contest (except that which is required by law) associated with the exploitation or sale of the sponsor's product or service, and all references to prizes or gifts offered in such connection should be considered a part of and included in the total time limitations heretofore provided.

All such broadcasts should comply with pertinent Federal, State, and Local laws and regulations.

E. *Premiums and Offers*

The broadcaster should require that full details of proposed offers be submitted for investigation and approval before the first announcement of the offer is made to the public.

A final date for the termination of an offer should be announced as far in advance as possible.

If a consideration is required, the advertiser should agree to honor complaints indicating dissatisfaction with the premium by returning the consideration.

There should be no misleading descriptions or comparisons of any premiums or gifts which will distort or enlarge their value in the minds of the listeners.

REGULATIONS
AND
PROCEDURES
OF THE
RADIO CODE
OF
GOOD PRACTICES
OF THE
NATIONAL ASSOCIATION OF BROADCASTERS
Issued July, 1960

The following Regulations and Procedures shall obtain as an integral part of the Radio Code of Good Practices of the National Association of Broadcasters:

I

Name

The name of this Code shall be the Radio Code of Good Practices of the National Association of Broadcasters, hereinafter referred to as the Radio Code.*

Definitions:

Wherever reference is made to programs it shall be construed to include all program material including commercials.

* "Radio Board. The Radio Board shall have power:—to enact, amend and promulgate Radio Standards of Practice or Codes, and to establish such methods to secure observance thereof as it may deem advisable;—". By-Laws of the National Association of Broadcasters, Article VI, section 8, B. Radio Board.

II

Purpose of the Code

The purpose of this Code is cooperatively to establish and maintain a level of radio programming which gives full consideration to the educational, informational, cultural, economic, moral and entertainment needs of the American public to the end that more and more people will be better served.

III

The Radio Code Board

SECTION 1. COMPOSITION

There shall be a continuing Committee entitled the Radio Code Board. The Code Board shall be composed of nine members. Members of the Radio Board of Directors shall not be eligible to serve on the above specified Board. The Chairman and members of the Code Board shall be appointed by the President of the NAB, subject to confirmation by the Radio Board of Directors. Due consideration shall be given, in making such appointments, to factors of diversification and the Board shall be fully representative of the radio industry. During the year 1960, five members shall be appointed to serve until immediately following the annual NAB convention of 1962; four members shall be appointed to serve until immediately following the annual NAB convention of 1961, provided that this term shall not count toward the limitation hereinafter provided. Starting in 1961, and every odd-numbered year thereafter, four members shall be appointed for two-year terms; and then in every even-numbered year thereafter, five two-year members shall be appointed.

A. *Limitation of Service:*

A person shall not serve consecutively as a member of the Board for more than two two-year terms or for more than four years consecutively.

A majority of the membership of the Radio Code Board shall constitute a quorum for all purposes unless herein otherwise provided.

Section 2. AUTHORITY AND RESPONSIBILITIES

The Radio Code Board is authorized and directed:

(1) To maintain a continuing review of all radio programming, especially that of subscribers to the Radio Code of the NAB; (2) to receive and clear complaints concerning radio programming; (3) to define and interpret words and phrases in the Radio Code; (4) to develop and maintain appropriate liaison with governmental agencies and with responsible and accountable organizations and institutions; (5) to inform, expeditiously and properly, a subscriber to the Radio Code of complaints or commendations, as well as to advise all subscribers concerning the attitude and desires program-wise of accountable organizations and institutions, and of the American public in general; (6) to review and monitor, if necessary, any certain series of programs, daily programming, or any other program presentations of a subscriber, as well as to request recordings, or script and copy, with regard to any certain program presented by a subscriber; (7) to make recommendations to advertisers concerning conformity of commercial copy with the standards set forth in the Radio Code of Good Practices; (8) to reach conclusions, and to make recom-

mendations or prefer charges to the Radio Board of Directors concerning violations and breaches of the Radio Code by a subscriber; (9) to maintain a continuing review of the Radio Code and to recommend to the Radio Board of Directors, amendments to the Radio Code.

A. *Delegation of Powers and Responsibilities:*

The Radio Code Board may delegate, from time to time, such of its above-specified responsibilities, as it may deem necessary and desirable, to a Staff Group of the NAB.

B. *Meetings:*

The Radio Code Board shall meet regularly semi-annually on a date to be determined by the Chairman. The Chairman of the Board may, at any time, on at least five days' written notice, call a special meeting of the Board.

IV

Subscribers

Section 1. ELIGIBILITY

Any individual, firm or corporation which is engaged in the operation of a radio broadcast station, or which holds a construction permit for a radio broadcast station within the United States or its dependencies, shall, subject to the approval of the Radio Board of Directors as hereinafter provided, be eligible to subscribe to the Radio Code of Good Practices of the NAB to the extent of one subscription for each station or each station which holds a construction permit; provided, that a non-radio member of NAB shall not become eligible via Code subscription to receive any of the member services or to exercise any of the voting privileges of a member.

Section 2. CERTIFICATION OF SUBSCRIPTION

Upon subscribing to the Code, subject to the approval of the Radio Board of Directors, there shall be granted forthwith to each such subscribing station authority to use the "NAB Radio Audio and Visual Symbols of Good Practice"; copyrighted and registered audio and visual symbols to be provided. The symbols and their significance shall be appropriately publicized by the NAB.

Section 3. DURATION OF SUBSCRIPTION

Subscription shall continue in full force and effect until thirty days after the first of the month following receipt of notice of written resignation. Subscription to the Code shall be effective from the date of application subject to the approval of the Radio Board of Directors; provided that the subscription of a radio station going on the air for the first time shall, for the first six months of such subscription, be probationary, during which time its subscription can be summarily revoked by an affirmative two-thirds vote of the Radio Board of Directors without the usual processes specified below.

Section 4. SUSPENSION OF SUBSCRIPTION

Any subscription, and/or the authority to utilize the above-noted symbols, may be voided, revoked or temporarily suspended for radio programming, including commercial copy, which, by theme, treatment or incident, in the judgment of the Radio Board constitutes a continuing, willful or gross violation of any of the provisions of the Radio Code, by an affirmative two-thirds vote of the Radio Board of Directors at a regular or special meeting; provided, however, that the following conditions and procedures shall govern:

A. *Preferring of Charges—Conditions Precedent:*

Prior to preferring charges to the Radio Board of Directors concerning violation of the Radio Code, the Code Board (1) Shall appropriately inform the subscriber of any and all complaints and information it possesses relating to the programming of said subscriber, (2) Shall have reported to, and advised, said subscriber by analysis, interpretation, recommendation or otherwise, of the possibility of a violation or breach of the Radio Code, and (3) Shall have served upon the subscriber by registered mail a Notice of Intent to prefer charges to the Radio Board of Directors; such Notice shall contain a statement of the grounds and reasons for the proposed charges, including appropriate references to the Radio Code and shall be transmitted at least twenty days prior to the filing of any charges with the Radio Board of Directors. During this interim period the Radio Code Board may, within its sole discretion, reconsider its proposed action based upon such written reply as the subscriber may care to make, or upon such action as the subscriber may care to take program-wise, in conformance with the analysis, interpretation or recommendation of the Radio Code Board.

B. *Time:*

In the event that the nature of the program in question is such that the Code Board deems time to be of the essence, the Code Board may prefer charges within less than the twenty days specified above, provided that a time certain in which subscriber may reply is included in the Notice of Intent, and provided further that the Code Board's reasons therefor are specified in its statement of charges preferred.

C. *Hearing:*

The subscriber shall have the right to a hearing before the Radio Board of Directors by requesting same and by filing an answer within 10 days of the date of receipt of the Notice of Intent. Said answer and request for hearing shall be directed to the Chairman of the Radio Board of Directors with a copy to the Radio Code Board.

D. *Waiver:*

Failure to request a hearing shall be deemed a waiver of the subscriber's right thereto.

E. *Designation:*

If hearing is requested by the subscriber, it shall be designated as promptly as possible and at such time and place as the Radio Board may specify.

F. *Confidential Status:*

Hearings shall be closed; and all correspondence between a subscriber and the Radio Code Board and/or the Radio Board of Directors concerning specific programming shall be confidential; provided, however, that the confidential status of these procedures may be waived by a subscriber.

G. *Presentation; Representation:*

A subscriber against whom charges have been preferred, and who has exercised his right to a hearing, shall be entitled to effect presentation of his case personally, by agent, by attorney, or by deposition and interrogatory.

H. *Intervention:*

Upon request by the subscriber-respondent or the Radio Code Board, the Radio Board of Directors, in its discretion, may permit the intervention of one or more other subscribers as parties-in-interest.

I. *Transcript:*

A stenographic transcript record may be taken if requested by respondent and shall be certified by the Chairman of the Radio Board of Directors to the Office of the Secretary of the National Association of Broadcasters, where it shall be maintained. The transcript shall not be open to inspection unless otherwise provided by the party respondent in the proceeding.

J. *Radio Code Board; Counsel:*

The Radio Code Board may, at its discretion, utilize the services of an attorney from the staff of the NAB for the purpose of effecting its presentation in a hearing matter.

K. *Order of Procedure:*

At hearings, the Radio Code Board shall open and close.

L. *Cross-Examination.*

The right of cross-examination shall specifically obtain. Where procedure has been by deposition or interrogatory, the use of cross-interrogatories shall satisfy this right.

M. *Presentation:*

Oral and written evidence may be introduced by the subscriber and by the Radio Code Board. Oral argument may be had at the hearing and written memoranda or briefs may be submitted by the subscriber and by the Radio Code Board. The Radio Board of Directors may admit such evidence as it deems relevant, material and competent, and may determine the nature and length of the oral argument and the written argument or briefs.

N. *Transcription, etc.:*

Records, transcriptions, or other mechanical reproductions or radio programs, properly identified, shall be accepted into evidence when relevant.

O. *Authority of Presiding Officer; of Radio Board of Directors:*

The Presiding Officer shall rule upon all interlocutory matters, such as, but not limited to, the admissibility of evidence, the qualifications of witnesses, etc. On all other matters, authority to act shall be vested in a majority of the Radio Board unless otherwise provided.

P. *Continuances and Extensions:*

Continuance and extension of any proceeding or for the time of filing or performing any act required or allowed to be done within a specific time may be granted upon request, for a good cause shown. The Board or the Presiding Officer may recess or adjourn a hearing for such time as may be deemed necessary, and may change the place thereof.

Q. *Findings and Conclusions:*

The Radio Board of Directors shall decide the case as expeditiously as possible and shall notify the subscriber and the Radio Code Board, in writing, of the decision. The decision of the Radio Board of Directors shall contain findings of fact with conclusions, as well as the reasons or bases therefor. Findings of fact shall set out in detail and with particularity all basic evidentiary facts developed on the record (with appropriate citations to the transcript of record or exhibit relied on for each evidentiary fact) supporting the conclusion reached.

R. *Reconsideration or Rehearing:*

A request for reconsideration or rehearing may be filed by parties to the hearing. Requests for reconsideration or rehearing shall state with particularity in what respect the decision or any matter determined therein is claimed to be unjust, unwarranted, or erroneous and with respect to any finding of fact shall specify the pages of record relied on. If the existence of any newly-discovered evidence is claimed, the request shall be accompanied by a verified statement of the facts together with the facts relied on to show that the party, with due diligence, could not have known or discovered such facts at the time of the hearing. The request for rehearing may seek:
   a. Reconsideration
   b. Additional oral argument
   c. Reopening of the proceedings
   d. Amendment of any findings, or
   e. Other relief.

S. *Time for Filing:*

Requests for reconsideration or rehearing shall be filed within ten (10) days after receipt by the respondent of the decision. Opposition thereto may be filed within five (5) days after the filing of the request.

T. *Penalty, Suspension of:*

At the discretion of the Radio Board, application of any penalty provided for in the decision may be suspended until the Board makes final disposition of the request for reconsideration or rehearing.

U. *Disqualification:*

Any member of the Radio Board may disqualify himself, or upon good cause shown by any interested party, may be disqualified by a majority vote of the Radio Board.

Section 5. ADDITIONAL PROCEDURES

When necessary to the proper administration of the Code, additional rules of procedure will be established from time to time as authorized by the By-Laws of the NAB; in keeping therewith, special consideration shall be given to the procedures for receipt and processing of complaints and to necessary rules to be adopted from time to time, taking into account the source and nature of such complaints; such rules to include precautionary measures such as the posting of bonds to cover costs and expenses of processing same; and further provided that special consideration will be given to procedures insuring the confidential status of proceedings relating to Code observance.

Section 6. AMENDMENT AND REVIEW

The Radio Code may be amended from time to time by the Radio Board of Directors which shall specify the effective date of each amendment; provided, that said Board is specifically charged with review and reconsideration of the entire Code, its appendices and procedures, at least once each year.

Section 7. TERMINATION OF CONTRACTS

All subscribers on the air shall be in compliance at the time of subscription to the Code.

V

Rates

Each subscriber shall pay fees in accordance with such schedule, at such time, and under such conditions as may be determined from time to time by the Radio Board (See Article VI, section 8, B. Radio Board By-Laws of the NAB); provided, that appropriate credit shall be afforded to a radio member of the NAB.

THE TELEVISION CODE
OF THE
NATIONAL ASSOCIATION OF BROADCASTERS

Sixth Edition. July, 1960

Preamble

Television is seen and heard in every type of American home. These homes include children and adults of all ages, embrace all races and all varieties of religious faith, and reach those of every educational background. It is the responsibility of television to bear constantly in mind that the audience is primarily a home audience, and consequently that television's relationship to the viewers is that between guest and host.

The revenues from advertising support the free, competitive American system of telecasting, and make available to the eyes and ears of the American people the finest programs of information, education, culture and entertainment. By law the television broadcaster is responsible for the programming of his station. He, however, is obligated to bring his positive responsibility for excellence and good taste in programming to bear upon all who have a hand in the production of programs, including networks, sponsors, producers of film and of live programs, advertising agencies, and talent agencies.

The American businesses which utilize television for conveying their advertising messages to the home by pictures with sound, seen free-of-charge on the home screen, are reminded that their responsibilities are not limited to the sale of goods and the creation of a favorable attitude toward the sponsor by the presentation of entertainment. They include, as well, responsibility for utilizing television to bring the best programs, regardless of kind, into American homes.

Television and all who participate in it are jointly accountable to the American public for respect for the special needs of children, for community responsibility, for the advancement of education and culture, for the acceptability of the program materials chosen, for decency and decorum in production, and for propriety in advertising. This responsibility cannot be discharged by any given group of programs, but can be discharged only through the highest standards of respect for the American home, applied to every moment of every program presented by television.

In order that television programming may best serve the public interest, viewers should be encouraged to make their criticisms and positive suggestions known to the television broadcasters. Parents in particular should be urged to see to it that out of the richness of television fare, the best programs are brought to the attention of their children.

I Advancement of Education and Culture

1. Commercial television provides a valuable means or augmenting the educational and cultural influences of schools, institutions of higher learning, the home, the church, museums, foundations, and other institutions devoted to education and culture.

2. It is the responsibility of a television broadcaster to call upon such institutions for counsel and cooperation and to work with them on the best methods of presenting educational and cultural materials by television. It is further the responsibility of stations, networks, advertising agencies and sponsors consciously to seek opportunities for introducing into telecasts factual materials which will aid in the enlightenment of the American public.

3. Education via television may be taken to mean that process by which the individual is brought toward informed adjustment to his society. Television is also responsible for the presentation of overtly instructional and cultural programs, scheduled so as to reach the viewers who are naturally drawn to such programs, and produced so as to attract the largest possible audience.

4. In furthering this realization, the television broadcaster:
   a) Should be thoroughly conversant with the educational and cultural needs and desires of the community served.
   b) Should affirmatively seek out responsible and accountable educational and cultural institutions of the community with a view toward providing opportunities for the instruction and enlightenment of the viewers.
   c) Should provide for reasonable experimentation in the development of programs specifically directed to the advancement of the community's culture and education.

438

Program materials should enlarge the horizons of the viewer, provide him with wholesome entertainment, afford helpful stimulation, and remind him of the responsibilities which the citizen has towards his society. The intimacy and confidence placed in Television demand of the broadcaster, the network and other program sources that they be vigilant in protecting the audience from deceptive program practices. Furthermore:

a) (i) Profanity, obscenity, smut and vulgarity are forbidden, even when likely to be understood only by part of the audience. From time to time, words which have been acceptable, acquire undesirable meanings, and telecasters should be alert to eliminate such words.

   (ii) Words (especially slang) derisive of any race, color, creed, nationality or national derivation, except wherein such usage would be for the specific purpose of effective dramatization such as combating prejudice, are forbidden, even when likely to be understood only by part of the audience. From time to time, words which have been acceptable, acquire undesirable meanings, and telecasters should be alert to eliminate such words.

b) (i) Attacks on religion and religious faiths are not allowed.

   (ii) Reverance is to mark any mention of the name of God, His attributes and powers.

   (iii) When religious rites are included in other than religious programs the rites are accurately presented and the ministers, priests and rabbis portrayed in their callings are vested with the dignity of their office and under no circumstances are to be held up to ridicule.

c) (i) Contests may not constitute a lottery.

   (ii) Any telecasting designed to "buy" the television audience by requiring it to listen and/or view in hope of reward, rather than for the quality of the program, should be avoided. (*See Contests, page 7*)

d) Respect is maintained for the sanctity of marriage and the value of the home. Divorce is not treated casually nor justified as a solution for marital problems.

e) Illicit sex relations are not treated as commendable.

f) Sex crimes and abnormalities are generally unacceptable as program material.

g) Drunkenness and narcotic addiction are never presented as desirable or prevalent.

h) The administration of illegal drugs will not be displayed.

i) The use of liquor in program content shall be de-emphasized. The consumption of liquor in American life, when not required by the plot or for proper characterization, shall not be shown.

j) The use of gambling devices or scenes necessary to the development of plot or as appropriate background is acceptable only when presented with discretion and in moderation, and in a manner which would not excite interest in, or foster, betting nor be instructional in nature. Telecasts of actual sport programs at which on-the-scene betting is permitted by law should be presented in a manner in keeping with Federal, state and local laws, and should concentrate on the subject as a public sporting event.

439

k) In reference to physical or mental afflictions and deformities, special precautions must be taken to avoid ridiculing sufferers from similar ailments and offending them or members of their families.

l) Exhibitions of fortune-telling, occultism, astrology, phrenology, palm-reading and numerology are acceptable only when required by a plot or the theme of a program, and then the presentation should be developed in a manner designed not to foster superstition or excite interest or belief in these subjects.

m) Televised drama shall not simulate news or special events in such a way as to mislead or alarm. (*See News, page 4*)

n) Legal, medical and other professional advice, diagnosis and treatment will be permitted only in conformity with law and recognized ethical and professional standards.

o) The presentation of cruelty, greed and selfishness as worthy motivations is to be avoided.

p) Excessive or unfair exploitation of others or of their physical or mental afflictions shall not be presented as praiseworthy.

q) Criminality shall be presented as undesirable and unsympathetic. The condoning of crime and the treatment of the commission of crime in a frivolous, cynical or callous manner is unacceptable.

r) The presentation of techniques of crime in such detail as to invite imitation shall be avoided.

s) The use of horror for its own sake will be eliminated; the use of visual or aural effects which would shock or alarm the viewer, and the detailed presentation of brutality or physical agony by sight or by sound are not permissable.

t) Law enforcement shall be upheld and, except where essential to to the program plot, officers of the law portrayed with respect and dignity.

u) The presentation of murder or revenge as a motive for murder shall not be presented as justifiable.

v) Suicide as an acceptable solution for human problems is prohibited.

w) The exposition of sex crimes will be avoided.

x) The appearances or dramatization of persons featured in actual crime news will be permitted only in such light as to aid law enforcement or to report the news event.

y) The use of animals, both in the production of television programs and as a part of television program content, shall at all times, be in conformity with accepted standards of humane treatment.

z) Quiz and similar programs that are presented as contests of knowledge, information, skill or luck must, in fact, be genuine contests and the results must not be controlled by collusion with or between contestants, or any other action which will favor one contestant against any other.

aa) No program shall be presented in a manner which through artifice or simulation would mislead the audience as to any material fact. Each broadcaster must exercise reasonable judgment to determine whether a particular method of presentation would constitute a material deception, or would be accepted by the audience as normal theatrical illusion.

III Responsibility Toward Children

1. The education of children involves giving them a sense of the world at large. However, such subjects as violence and sex shall be presented without undue emphasis and only as required by plot development or character delineation. Crime should not be presented as attractive or as a solution to human problems, and the inevitable retribution should be made clear.
2. It is not enough that only those programs which are intended for viewing by children shall be suitable to the young and immature. (*Attention is called to the general items listed under Acceptability of Program Materials, page 2.*) Television is responsible for insuring that programs of all sorts which occur during the times of day when children may normally be expected to have the opportunity of viewing television shall exercise care in the following regards:
   a) In affording opportunities for cultural growth as well as for wholesome entertainment.
   b) In developing programs to foster and promote the commonly accepted moral, social and ethical ideals characteristic of American life.
   c) In reflecting respect for parents, for honorable behavior, and for the constituted authorities of the American community.
   d) In eliminating reference to kidnapping of children or threats of kidnapping.
   e) In avoiding material which is excessively violent or would create morbid suspense, or other undesirable reactions in children.
   f) In exercising particular restraint and care in crime or mystery episodes involving children or minors.

IV Decency and Decorum in Production

1. The costuming of all performers shall be within the bounds of propriety and shall avoid such exposure or such emphasis on anatomical detail as would embarrass or offend home viewers.
2. The movements of dancers, actors, or other performers shall be kept within the bounds of decency, and lewdness and impropriety shall not be suggested in the positions assumed by performers.
3. Camera angles shall avoid such views of performers as to emphasize anatomical details indecently.
4. Racial or nationality types shall not be shown on television in such a manner as to ridicule the race or nationality.
5. The use of locations closely associated with sexual life or with sexual sin must be governed by good taste and delicacy.

V Community Responsibility

A television broadcaster and his staff occupy a position of responsibility in the community and should conscientiously endeavor to be acquainted fully with its needs and characteristics in order better to serve the welfare of its citizens.

VI Treatment of News and Public Events

News

1. A television station's news schedule should be adequate and well-balanced.

2. News reporting should be factual, fair and without bias.
3. Commentary and analysis should be clearly identified as such.
4. Good taste should prevail in the selection and handling of news:
   Morbid, sensational or alarming details not essential to the factual report, especially in connection with stories of crime or sex, should be avoided. News should be telecast in such a manner as to avoid panic and unnecessary alarm.
5. At all times, pictorial and verbal material for both news and comment should conform to other sections of these standards, wherever such sections are reasonably applicable.
6. Pictorial material should be chosen with care and not presented in a misleading manner.
7. A television broadcaster should exercise due care in his supervision of content, format, and presentation of newscasts originated by his station, and in his selection of newscasters, commentators, and analysts.
8. A television broadcaster should exercise particular discrimination in the acceptance, placement and presentation of advertising in news programs so that such advertising should be clearly distinguishable from the news content.
9. A television broadcaster should not present fictional events or other non-news material as authentic news telecasts or announcements, nor should he permit dramatizations in any program which would give the false impression that the dramatized material constitutes news. Expletives, (presented aurally or pictorially) such as "flash" or "bulletin" and statements such as "we interrupt this program to bring you . . ." should be reserved specifically for news room use. However, a television broadcaster may properly exercise discretion in the use in non-news programs of words or phrases which do not necessarily imply that the material following is a news release.
10. All news interview programs should be governed by accepted standards of ethical journalism, under which the interviewer selects the questions to be asked. Where there is advance agreement materially restricting an important or newsworthy area of questioning, the interviewer will state on the program that such limitation has been agreed upon. Such disclosure should be made if the person being interviewed requires that questions be submitted in advance or if he participates in editing a recording of the interview prior to its use on the air.

Public Events

1. A television broadcaster has an affirmative responsibility at all times to be informed of public events, and to provide coverage consonant with the ends of an informed and enlightened citizenry.
2. Because of the nature of events open to the public, the treatment of such events by a television broadcaster should be effected in a manner to provide for adequate and informed coverage as well as good taste in presentation.

VII Controversial Public Issues

1. Television provides a valuable forum for the expression of responsible views on public issues of a controversial nature. In keeping therewith the television broadcaster should seek out and develop with accountable individuals, groups and organizations, programs relating to controversial

public issues of import to his fellow citizens; and to give fair representation to opposing sides of issues which materially affect the life or welfare of a substantial segment of the public.

2. The provision of time for this purpose should be guided by the following principles:

   a) Requests by individuals, groups or organizations for time to discuss their views on controversial public issues, should be considered on the basis of their individual merits, and in the light of the contribution which the use requested would make to the public interest, and to a well-balanced program structure.

   b) Programs devoted to the discussion of controversial public issues should be identified as such, and should not be presented in a manner which would mislead listeners or viewers to believe that the program is purely of an entertainment, news, or other character.

VIII Political Telecasts

Political telecasts should be clearly identified as such, and should not be presented by a television broadcaster in a manner which would mislead listeners or viewers to believe that the program is of any other character.

IX Religious Programs

1. It is the responsibility of a television broadcaster to make available to the community as part of a well-balanced program schedule adequate opportunity for religious presentations.

2. The following principles should be followed in the treatment of such programs:

   a) Telecasting which reaches men of all creeds simultaneously should avoid attacks upon religion.

   b) Religious programs should be presented respectfully and accurately and without prejudice or ridicule.

   c) Religious programs should be presented by responsible individuals, groups and organizations.

   d) Religious programs should place emphasis on broad religious truths, excluding the presentation of controversial or partisan views not directly or necessarily related to religion or morality.

3. In the allocation of time for telecasts of religious programs it is recommended that the television station use its best efforts to apportion such time fairly among the representative faith groups of its community.

X Subliminal Perception

The use of the television medium to transmit information of any kind by the use of the process called "subliminal perception," or by the use of any similar technique whereby an attempt is made to convey information to the viewer by transmitting messages below the threshold of normal awareness, is not permitted.

XI Production Practices

The broadcaster shall be constantly alert to prevent activities that may lead to such practices as the use of scenic properties, the choice and identification of prizes, the selection of music and other creative program elements and inclusion of any identification of commercial products or services, their trade

443

names or advertising slogans, within a program dictated by factors other than the requirements of the program itself. This expressly forbids the acceptance by producer, talent or any other personnel of cash payments or other considerations in return for including any of the above within the program.

XII Presentation of Advertising

1. Ever mindful of the role of television as a guest in the home, a television broadcaster should exercise unceasing care to supervise the form in which advertising material is presented over his facilities. Since television is a developing medium, involving methods and techniques distinct from those of radio, it may be desirable from time to time to review and revise the presently suggested practices:

   a) Advertising messages should be presented with courtesy and good taste; disturbing or annoying material should be avoided; every effort should be made to keep the advertising message in harmony with the content and general tone of the program in which it appears.

   b) A sponsor's advertising messages should be confined within the framework of the sponsor's program structure. A television broadcaster should avoid the use of commercial announcements which are divorced from the program either by preceding the introduction of the program (as in the case of so-called "cow-catcher" announcements) or by following the apparent sign-off of the program (as in the case of so-called "trailer" announcements). To this end, the program itself should be announced and clearly identified, both audio and video, before the sponsor's advertising material is first used, and should be signed off, both audio and video, after the sponsor's advertising material is last used.

   c) Advertising copy should contain no claims intended to disparage competitors, competing products, or other industries, professions or institutions.

   d) Since advertising by television is a dynamic technique, a television broadcaster should keep under surveillance new advertising devices so that the spirit and purpose of these standards are fulfilled.

   e) Television broadcasters should exercise the utmost care and discrimination with regard to advertising material, including content, placement and presentation, near or adjacent to programs designed for children. No considerations of expediency should be permitted to impinge upon the vital responsibility towards children and adolescents, which is inherent in television, and which must be recognized and accepted by all advertisers employing television.

   f) Television advertisers should be encouraged to devote portions of their allotted advertising messages and program time to the support of worthy causes in the public interest in keeping with the highest ideals of the free competitive system.

   g) A charge for television time to churches and religious bodies is not recommended.

   h) The role and capability of television to market sponsors' products are well recognized. In turn, this fact dictates that great care be exercised by the broadcaster to prevent the presentation of false, misleading or deceptive advertising. While it is entirely appropriate to present a product in a favorable light and atmosphere, and techniques may be used to depict the characteristics of the product as they appear in actuality, the presentation must not, by copy or demonstration, involve a material deception as to the characteristics, performance or appearance of the product.

XIII Acceptability of Advertisers and Products—General

1. A commercial television broadcaster makes his facilities available for the advertising of products and services and accepts commercial presentations for such advertising. However, a television broadcaster should, in recognition of his responsibility to the public, refuse the facilities of his station to an advertiser where he has good reason to doubt the integrity of the advertiser, the truth of the advertising representations, or the compliance of the advertiser with the spirit and purpose of all applicable legal requirements. Moreover, in consideration of the laws and customs of the communities served, each television broadcaster should refuse his facilities to the advertisement of products and services, or the use of advertising scripts, which the station has good reason to believe would be objectionable to a substantial and responsible segment of the community. The foregoing principles should be applied with judgment and flexibility, taking into consideration the characteristics of the medium and the form and content of the particular presentation. In general, because television broadcasting is designed for the home and the family, including children, the following principles should govern the business classifications listed below:
    a) The advertising of hard liquor should not be accepted.
    b) The advertising of beer and wines is acceptable only when presented in the best of good taste and discretion, and is acceptable only subject to Federal and local laws.
    c) Advertising by institutions or enterprises which in their offers of instruction imply promises of employment or make exaggerated claims for the opportunities awaiting those who enroll for courses is generally unacceptable.
    d) The advertising of firearms and fireworks is acceptable only subject to Federal and local laws.
    e) The advertising of fortune-telling, occultism, astrology, phrenology, palm-reading, numerology, mind-reading, character reading or subjects of a like nature is not permitted.
    f) Because all products of a personal nature create special problems, such products, when accepted, should be treated with especial emphasis on ethics and the canons of good taste. Such advertising of personal products as is accepted must be presented in a restrained and obviously inoffensive manner.
    The advertising of intimately personal products which are generally regarded as unsuitable conversational topics in mixed social groups is not accepted. (*See Television Code Interpretation No. 4, Page 11*)
    g) The advertising of tip sheets, race track publications, or organizations seeking to advertise for the purpose of giving odds or promoting betting or lotteries is unacceptable.
2. Diligence should be exercised to the end that advertising copy accepted for telecasting complies with pertinent Federal, state and local laws.
3. An advertiser who markets more than one product should not be permitted to use advertising copy devoted to an acceptable product for purposes of publicizing the brand name or other identification of a product which is not acceptable.

445

4. "Bait-switch" advertising, whereby goods or services which the advertiser has no intention of selling are offered merely to lure the customer into purchasing higher-priced substitutes, is not acceptable.

XIV Advertising of Medical Products

1. The advertising of medical products presents considerations of intimate and far-reaching importance to the consumer, and the following principles and procedures should apply in the advertising thereof:
   a) A television broadcaster should not accept advertising material which in his opinion offensively describes or dramatizes distress or morbid situations involving ailments, by spoken word, sound or visual effects.
   b) Because of the personal nature of the advertising of medical products, claims that a product will effect a cure and the indiscriminate use of such words as "safe", "without risk", "harmless", or terms of similar meaning should not be accepted in the advertising of medical products on television stations.

XV Contests

1. In addition to complying with all pertinent Federal, state and local laws and regulations, all contests should offer the opportunity to all contestants to win on the basis of ability and skill rather than chance.
2. All contest details, including rules, eligibility requirements, opening and termination dates should be clearly and completely announced and/or shown, or easily accessible to the viewing public, and the winners' names should be released and prizes awarded as soon as possible after the close of the contest.
3. When advertising is accepted which requests contestants to submit items of product identification or other evidence of purchase of product, reasonable facsimiles thereof should be made acceptable.
4. All copy pertaining to any contest (except that which is required by law) associated with the exploitation or sale of the sponsor's product or service, and all references to prizes or gifts offered in such connection should be considered a part of and included in the total time allowances as herein provided. (*See Time Standards for Advertising Copy.*)

XVI Premiums and Offers

1. Full details of proposed offers should be required by the television broadcaster for investigation and approved before the first announcement of the offer is made to the public.
2. A final date for the termination of an offer should be announced as far in advance as possible.
3. Before accepting for telecast offers involving a monetary consideration, a television broadcaster should satisfy himself as to the integrity of the advertiser and the advertiser's willingness to honor complaints indicating dissatisfaction with the premium by returning the monetary consideration.
4. There should be no misleading descriptions or visual representations of any premiums or gifts which would distort or enlarge their value in the minds of viewers.
5. Assurances should be obtained from the advertiser that premiums offered are not harmful to person or property.
6. Premiums should not be approved which appeal to superstition on the basis of "luck-bearing" powers or otherwise.

XVII Time Standards for Advertising Copy

1. In accordance with good telecast advertising practices, the time standards for advertising copy are as follows:

Length of Pgm. (in Minutes)	5:00	10:00	15:00	20:00	25:00	30:00	35:00	40:00	45:00	50:00	55:00	60:00
"AA" and "A" Time	1:00	2:00	2:30	2:40	2:50	3:00	3:30	4:00	4:30	5:00	5:30	6:00
All Other Time	1:15	2:10	3:00	3:30	4:00	4:15	4:45	5:15	5:45	6:10	6:35	7:00

Length of Pgm. (in Minutes)	65:00	70:00	75:00	80:00	85:00	90:00	95:00	100:00	105:00	110:00	115:00	120:00
"AA" and "A" Time	6:30	7:00	7:30	8:00	8:30	9:00	9:30	10:00	10:30	11:00	11:30	12:00
All Other Time	7:35	8:10	8:45	9:20	9:55	10:30	11:05	11:40	12:15	12:50	13:25	14:00

Above time standards are for sponsored programs. "Participation" programs, carrying announcements for different individual advertisers, may not exceed one minute of advertising per five minutes of programming. (See paragraph 4.)

2. Reasonable and limited identification of prize and statement of the donor's name within formats wherein the presentation of contest awards or prizes is a necessary and integral part of program content shall not be included as commercial time within the meaning of paragraph 1, above; however, any oral or visual presentation concerning the product or its donor, over and beyond such identification and statement, shall be included as commercial time within the meaning of paragraph 1, above. (*See Television Code Interpretation No. 6, Page 12*)

3. Station breaks (spot announcements scheduled between programs) shall consist of not more than two announcements plus the conventional sponsored 10 second station ID. However, the aggregate total of the announcements shall not exceed 70 seconds within the station's highest rate period for announcements.

   Station break announcements shall not adversely affect a preceding or following program.

4. Announcement programs are designed to accommodate a number of announcements, which are carried within the body of the program and are available for sale to individual advertisers. Commercial announcements may not consume more than 6 minutes for any 30 minute program and no program shall have commercial content in excess of this ratio. Not more than 3 announcements shall be scheduled consecutively. Where the program exceeds 30 minutes in length, the required ID, not exceeding 10 seconds, may be in addition to these commercial time allowances.

5. Programs presenting women's services, features, shopping guides, market information, and similar material, provide a special service to the listening and viewing public in which advertising material is an informative and integral part of the program content. Because of these special characteristics the time standards set forth above may be waived to a reasonable extent.

6. Any casual reference by talent in a program to another's product or service under any trade name or language sufficiently descriptive to identify it should, except for normal guest identifications, be condemned and discouraged.

7. Stationary backdrops or properties in television presentations showing the sponsor's name or product, the name of his product, his trade-mark or slogan may be used only incidentally. They should not obtrude on program interest or entertainment. "On Camera" shots of such materials should be fleeting, not too frequent, and mindful of the need of maintaining a proper program balance.

8. The above commercial time standards do not include opening and closing "billboard" announcements which give program or announcement sponsor identification. Each opening and closing "billboard" regardless of the number of sponsors shall not exceed 20 seconds in programs longer than one half-hour or 10 seconds in programs of one half-hour or less.

XVIII Dramatized Appeals and Advertising

1. Appeals to help fictitious characters in television programs by purchasing the advertiser's product or service or sending for a premium should not be permitted, and such fictitious characters should not be introduced into the advertising message for such purposes.

448

2. Dramatized advertising involving statements or purported statements by physicians, dentists, or nurses must be presented by accredited members of such professions. (*See Television Code Interpretation No. 5, Page 11*)

XIX Sponsor Identification

Identification of sponsorship must be made in all sponsored programs in accordance with the requirements of the Communications Act of 1934, as amended, and the Rules and Regulations of the Federal Communications Commission.

XX INTERPRETATIONS OF THE TELEVISION CODE

TELEVISION CODE INTERPRETATION NO. 1

June 7, 1956
Revised March 3, 1960

Combination ("Piggy-Back") Announcements

The NAB Television Code Review Board has reviewed a number of spot announcements advertising more than one product. The Code Board observes that these may generally be separated into two classifications:

1. The *"integrated"* commercial advertising related (e.g., various frozen food products, or automobiles of one manufacturer) or compatible (e.g., pancakes and syrup, or furniture and carpeting) products within the framework of a single announcement. Such commercials may be treated as single announcements under the commercial Time Standards of the Television Code.

2. The *"piggy-back"* commercial advertising unrelated products and using a different and distinct production technique to present each product. The Code Board has concluded that the "piggy-back" commercial constitutes in effect two or more separate announcements and should therefore be treated as separate announcements under the commercial Time Standards of the Television Code.

TELEVISION CODE INTERPRETATION NO. 2

June 7, 1956
Revised June 9, 1958

"Pitch" Programs

The "pitchman" technique of advertising on television is inconsistent with good broadcast practice and generally damages the reputation of the industry and the advertising profession.

Sponsored program-length segments consisting substantially of continuous demonstration or sales presentation, violate not only the time standards estab-

449

lished in the Code, but the broad philosophy of improvement implicit in the voluntary Code operation and are not acceptable.

TELEVISION CODE INTERPRETATION NO. 3

June 7, 1956

Hollywood Film Promotion

The Television Code Review Board has formally concluded that the presentation of commentary or film excerpts from current theatrical releases in some instances may constitute "advertising copy" under section 1, "Time Standards for Advertising Copy." Specifically, for example, when such presentation, directly or by inference, urges viewers to attend, it shall be counted against the advertising copy time allowance for the program of which it is a part.

TELEVISION CODE INTERPRETATION NO. 4

June 7, 1956

Non-Acceptability of "Intimately Personal Products"

The Television Code Review Board has reviewed several advertisements in view of Paragraph 1f) "Acceptability of Advertisers and Products—General" and in particular of the specific language ". . . the advertising of intimately personal products which are generally regarded as unsuitable conversational topics in mixed social groups is not acceptable."

The Board has concluded that products for the treatment of hemorrhoids and for use in connection with feminine hygiene are not acceptable under the above stated language.

TELEVISION CODE INTERPRETATION NO. 5

July 17, 1958
October 2, 1958

Dramatized Appeals and Advertising (Paragraph 2)

1. The term "statement" shall include the portrayal in any manner, of a physician, dentist or nurse. Thus, the simulation of such professional people may not be undertaken even by visual means only.
2. There are instances presently on the air of advertising depicting persons obviously of some professional standing. By the nature of the props and setting, such portrayals *could* be that of medical, dental or nursing profession members, even though direct reference so indicating is not made. Such presentations, unless made by accredited members of these professions, are not acceptable.
3. This restriction does not preclude reference to comprehensive scientific research, studies or surveys, providing, however, that such claims can be fully supported.
4. The Board recognizes the need for time to change existing film commer-

cials affected by this amendment and advises that all such advertising produced prior to June 18th many be used until January 1, 1959. All "live" advertising and filmed announcements prepared subsequent to this date will be considered violations.

5. The term "accredited" defined. In this context the use of the word "accredited" is synonymous with "having legal sanction." Thus, an "accredited" member of the medical profession is one who has completed the required education in a recognized institution of learning, who has passed all necessary state examinations, and who has been granted leave by his resident state to practice a particular branch of medicine.

TELEVISION CODE INTERPRETATION NO. 6

Jan. 23, 1959

Prize Identification

The Television Code Review Board considers that oral and/or visual prize identification of up to ten seconds duration may be deemed "reasonable and limited" under the language of this Section. Where such identification is longer than ten seconds, the entire announcement or visual presentation will be charged against the total commercial time for the program period. The Board recognizes that some subscribers have current contractual obligations which will preclude immediate application, but advises that all prize agreements made after February 1, 1959 should comply with the interpretation.

TELEVISION CODE INTERPRETATION NO. 7

March 3, 1960

Paragraph 3, Page 7, "Contests"—does not mean that reasonable facsimiles must be acceptable in all instances where proof of purchase is a qualifying stipulation. This is necessary only when all elements of a lottery are present. They are prize, chance and *consideration.*

The official name of the Code is *The Television Code of the National Association of Broadcasters.* It was enacted effective March 1, 1952 by the Television Board of Directors of the NAB in accordance with the Association By-Laws, which read as follows: "Television Board. The Television Board is hereby authorized:—(4) to enact, amend and promulgate standards of practice or codes for its television members and to establish such methods to secure observance thereof as is may deem advisable;—". The administration of the Code is delegated to the Television Code Review Board, composed of seven members appointed from among telecast licensees to two-year terms by the president of the NAB, subject to confirmation by the Television Board of Directors. Its responsibilities include, among others, the defining and interpreting of words and phrases in the Code, the maintenance of appropriate liaison with responsible organizations, institutions and the public, as well as the screening and clearing of correspondence concerning television programming.

In addition to the substantive provisions of the Code contained in the present volume, the details of the regulatory and procedural functions of the Code and the Code Review Board may be found in the volume entitled *Regulations and Procedures of the Television Code*. For convenience—the headings specified therein are: I Name; II Purposes of the Code; III Subscribers; IV Affiliate Subscribers; V Rates; and VI The Television Code Review Board.

REGULATIONS AND
PROCEDURES OF THE TELEVISION CODE

Issued July, 1960

The following Regulations and Procedures shall obtain as an integral part of the Television Code of the National Association of Broadcasters:

I

Name

The name of this Code shall be *The Television Code of the National Association of Broadcasters.**

II

Purpose of the Code

The purpose of this Code is cooperatively to maintain a level of television programming which gives full consideration to the educational, informational, cultural, economic, moral and entertainment needs of the American public to the end that more and more people will be better served.

III

Subscribers

Section 1. ELIGIBILITY

Any individual, firm or corporation which is engaged in the operation of a television broadcast station or network, or which holds a construction permit for a television broadcast station within the United States or its dependencies, shall, subject to the approval of the Television Board of Directors as hereinafter provided, be eligible to subscribe to the Television Code of the NAB to the extent of one subscription for each such station and/or network which it operates or for which it holds a construction permit; provided, that a non-television member of NAB shall not become eligible via code subscription to receive any of the member services or to exercise any of the voting privileges of a member.

* "Television Board. The Television Board is hereby authorized:—(4) to enact, amend and promulgate standards of practice or codes for its Television members, and to establish such methods to secure observance thereof as it may deem advisable;—". By-Laws of the National Association of Broadcasters, Article VI, section 8, C. Television Board (4).

452

Section 2. CERTIFICATION OF SUBSCRIPTION

Upon subscribing to the Code, subject to the approval of the Television Board of Directors, there shall be granted forthwith to each such subscribing station authority to use the "NAB Television Seal of Good Practice", a copyrighted and registered seal to be provided in the form of a certificate, a slide and/or a film, signifying that the recipient thereof is a subscriber in good standing to the Television Code of the NAB. The seal and its significance shall be appropriately publicized by the NAB.

Section 3. DURATION OF SUBSCRIPTION

Subscription shall continue in full force and effect until thirty days after the first of the month following receipt of notice of written resignation. Subscription to the Code shall be effective from the date of application subject to the approval of the Television Board of Directors; provided, that the subscription of a television station going on the air for the first time shall, for the first six months of such subscription, be probationary, during which time its subscription can be summarily revoked by an affirmative two-thirds vote of the Television Board of Directors without the usual processes specified below.

Section 4. SUSPENSION OF SUBSCRIPTION

Any subscription, and/or the authority to utilize and show the above-noted seal, may be voided, revoked or temporarily suspended for television programming, including commercial copy, which, by theme, treatment or incident, in the judgment of the Television Board constitutes a continuing, willful or gross violation of any of the provisions of the Television Code, by an affirmative two-thirds vote of the Television Board of Directors at a regular or special meeting; provided, however, that the following conditions and procedures shall apply:

A. Preferring of Charges—Conditions Precedent:

Prior to the preferring of charges to the Television Board of Directors concerning violation of the Code by a subscriber, the Television Code Review Board (hereinafter provided for) (1) Shall have appropriately, and in good time, informed and advised such subscriber of any and all complaints and information coming to the attention of the Television Code Review Board and relating to the programming of said subscriber, (2) Shall have reported to, and advised, said subscriber by analysis, interpretation, recommendation or otherwise, of the possibility of a violation or breach of the Television Code by the subscriber, and (3) Shall have served upon the subscriber by Registered Mail a Notice of Intent to prefer charges, at least twenty days prior to the filing of any such charges with the Television Board of Directors. During this period the Television Code Review Board may, within its sole discretion, reconsider its proposed action based upon such written reply as the subscriber may care to make, or upon such action as the subscriber may care to take program-wise, in conformance with the analysis, interpretation, or recommendation of the Television Code Review Board.

(i) Notice of Intent

The Notice of Intent shall include a statement of the grounds and reasons for the proposed charges, including appropriate references to the Television Code.

453

(ii) Time

In the event that the nature of the program in question is such that time is of the essence, the Television Code Review Board may prefer charges within less than the twenty days above specified, provided that a time certain in which reply may be made is included in its Notice of Intent, and provided that its reasons therefor must be specified in its statement of charges preferred.

B. *The Charges:*

The subscriber shall be advised in writing by Registered Mail of the charges preferred. The charges preferred by the Television Code Review Board to the Television Board of Directors shall include the grounds and reasons therefor, together with specific references to the Television Code. The charges shall contain a statement that the conditions precedent, hereinbefore described, have been met.

C. *Hearing:*

The subscriber shall have the right to a hearing and may exercise same by filing an answer within 10 days of the date of such notification.

D. *Waiver:*

Failure to request a hearing shall be deemed a waiver of the subscriber's right thereto.

E. *Designation:*

If hearing is requested by the subscriber, it shall be designated as promptly as possible and at such time and place as the Television Board may specify.

F. *Confidential Status:*

Hearings shall be closed; and all correspondence between a subscriber and the Television Code Review Board and/or the Television Board of Directors concerning specific programming shall be confidential; provided, however, that the confidential status of these procedures may be waived by a subscriber.

G. *Presentation; Representation:*

A subscriber against whom charges have been preferred, and who has exercised his right to a hearing, shall be entitled to effect presentation of his case personally, by agent, by attorney, or by deposition and interrogatory.

H. *Intervention:*

Upon request by the subscriber-respondent or the Television Code Review Board, the Television Board of Directors, in its discretion, may permit the intervention of one or more other subscribers as parties-in-interest.

I. *Transcript:*

A stenographic transcript record shall be taken and shall be certified by the Chairman of the Television Board of Directors to the office of the Secretary of the National Association of Broadcasters, where it shall be maintained. The transcript shall not be open to inspection unless otherwise provided by the party respondent in the proceeding.

J. *Television Code Review Board; Counsel:*

The Television Code Review Board may, at its discretion, utilize the services of an attorney from the staff of the NAB for the purpose of effecting its presentation in a hearing matter.

K. *Order of Procedure:*

At hearings, the Television Code Review Board shall open and close.

L. *Cross-Examination:*

The right of cross-examination shall specifically obtain. Where procedure has been by deposition or interrogatory, the use of cross-interrogatories shall satisfy this right.

M. *Presentation:*

Oral and written evidence may be introduced by the subscriber and by the Television Code Review Board. Oral argument may be had at the hearing and written memoranda or briefs may be submitted by the subscriber and by the Television Code Review Board. The Television Board of Directors may admit such evidence as it deems relevant, material and competent, and may determine the nature and length of the oral argument and the written argument or briefs.

N. *Authority of Presiding Officer; of Television Board of Directors:*

The Presiding Officer shall rule upon all interlocutory matters, such as, but not limited to, the admissibility of evidence, the qualifications of witnesses, etc. On all other matters, authority to act shall be vested in a majority of the Television Board unless otherwise provided.

O. *Films, Transcriptions, etc.:*

Films, kinescopes, records, transcriptions, or other mechanical reproductions of television programs, properly identified, shall be accepted into evidence when relevant.

P. *Continuances and Extensions:*

Continuance and extension of any proceeding or for the time of filing or performing any act required or allowed to be done within a specific time may be granted upon request, for a good cause shown. The Board or the Presiding Officer may recess or adjourn a hearing for such time as may be deemed necessary, and may change the place thereof.

Q. *Findings and Conclusions:*

The Television Board of Directors shall decide the case as expeditiously as possible and shall notify the subscriber and the Television Code Review Board, in writing, of the decision. The decision of the Television Board of Directors shall contain findings of fact with conclusions, as well as the reasons or bases therefor. Findings of fact shall set out in detail and with particularity all basic evidentiary facts developed on the record (with appropriate citations to the transcript of record or exhibit relied on for each evidentiary fact) supporting the conclusion reached.

R. *Reconsideration or Rehearing:*

A request for reconsideration or rehearing may be filed by parties to the hearing. Requests for reconsideration or rehearing shall state with particularity in what respect the decision or any matter determined therein is claimed to be unjust, unwarranted, or erroneous, and with respect to any finding of fact shall specify the pages of record relied on. If the existence of any newly-discovered evidence is claimed, the request shall be accompanied by a verified statement of the facts together with the facts relied on to show that the party, with due diligence, could not have known or discovered such facts at the time of the hearing. The request for rehearing may seek:

    a. Reconsideration
    b. Additional oral argument
    c. Reopening of the proceedings
    d. Amendment of any findings, or
    e. Other relief.

S. *Time for Filing:*

Requests for reconsideration or rehearing shall be filed within ten (10) days after receipt by the respondent of the decision. Opposition thereto may be filed within five (5) days after the filing of the request.

T. *Penalty, Suspension of:*

At the discretion of the Television Board, application of any penalty provided for in the decision may be suspended until the Board makes final disposition of the request for reconsideration of rehearing.

U. *Disqualification:*

Any member of the Television Board may disqualify himself, or upon good cause shown by any interested party, may be disqualified by a majority vote of the Television Board.

Section 5. ADDITIONAL PROCEDURES

When necessary to the proper administration of the Code, additional rules of procedure will be established from time to time as authorized by the By-Laws of the NAB; in keeping therewith, special consideration shall be given to the procedures for receipt and processing of complaints and to necessary rules to be adopted from time to time, taking into account the source and nature of such complaints; such rules to include precautionary measures such as the posting of bonds to cover costs and expenses of processing same; and further provided that special consideration will be given to procedures insuring the confidential status of proceedings relating to Code observance.

Section 6. AMENDMENT AND REVIEW

Because of the new and dynamic aspects inherent in television broadcasting, the Television Code, as a living, flexible and continuing document, may be amended from time to time by the Television Board of Directors; provided that said Board is specifically charged with review and reconsideration of the entire Code, its appendices and procedures, at least once each year.

Section 7. Termination of Contracts

All subscribers on the air at the time of subscription to the Code shall be permitted that period prior to and including the earliest legal cancellation date to terminate any contracts, then outstanding, calling for program presentations which would not be in conformity with the Television Code, provided, however, that in no event shall such period be longer than fifty-two weeks.

IV

Affiliate Subscribers

Section 1. Eligibility

Any individual, firm or corporation, which is engaged in the production or distribution, lease, or sale of recorded programs for television presentation, subject to the approval of the Television Code Review Board as hereinafter provided, shall be eligible to become an affiliate subscriber to the Television Code of the NAB.

Section 2. Certification of Subscription

Upon becoming an affiliate subscriber to the Code, subject to the approval of the Television Code Review Board, there shall be granted forthwith to each such affiliate subscriber authority to use a copyrighted and registered seal and declaration, in a manner approved by the Television Code Review Board, identifying the individual firm or corporation as an affiliate subscriber to the Television Code of the NAB. Such authority shall not constitute formal clearance or approval by the Television Code Review Board of specific film programs or other recorded material.

Section 3. Duration of Affiliate Subscription

The affiliate subscription shall continue in full force and effect until thirty days after the first of the month following receipt of a written notice of resignation. The affiliate subscription to the Code shall be effective from the date of application subject to the approval of the Television Code Review Board.

Section 4. Suspension of Affiliate Subscription

Any affiliate subscription and the authority to utilize and show the above-noted seal may be voided, revoked, or temporarily suspended for the sale or distribution for television presentation of any film or other recorded material which by theme, treatment, or incident, in the judgment of the Television Code Review Board, constitutes a continuing, willful or gross violation of any of the provisions of the Television Code, by a vote of three members of the Television Code Review Board at any regular or special meeting. The conditions and procedures applicable to subscribers shall not apply to affiliate subscribers.

Section 5. Representation of Affiliate Subscribers

Any affiliate subscriber or group of affiliate subscribers may authorize an individual or association to act for them in connection with their relations with the Television Code Review Board by filing a written notice of such representation with the Board. Such representation, however, in no way will limit the right of the Television Code Review Board to suspend individual affiliate subscribers in accordance with the provisions of Section 4.

Rates

Each subscriber and affiliate subscriber shall pay 'administrative' rates in accordance with such schedule, at such time, and under such conditions as may be determined from time to time by the Television Board (see Article VI, section 8, C. Television Board (3) and (4), By-Laws of the NAB); provided, that appropriate credit shall be afforded to a television member of the NAB against the regular dues which he or it pays to NAB.

VI

The Television Code Review Board

Section 1. COMPOSITION*

There shall be a continuing committee entitled the Television Code Review Board. The Review Board shall be composed of seven members, all of whom shall be from the Television membership of NAB. Members of the Television Board of Directors shall not be eligible to serve on the above specified Review Board. Members of the Review Board shall be appointed by the President of the NAB, subject to confirmation by the Television Board of Directors. Due consideration shall be given, in making such appointments, to factors of diversification of geographical location, company representation and network affiliation.

During the year 1960, four members shall be appointed to serve until immediately following the annual NAB convention of 1962.

Starting in 1961, and every odd-numbered year thereafter, three members shall be appointed for two-year terms; and then in every even-numbered year thereafter, four two-year members shall be appointed.

A. *Limitation of Service:*

A person shall not serve consecutively as a member of the Review Board for more than two two-year terms or for more than four years consecutively after April 30, 1953.

A majority of the membership of the Television Code Review Board shall constitute a quorum for all purposes unless herein otherwise provided.

Section 3. AUTHORITY AND RESPONSIBILITIES

The Television Code Review Board is authorized and directed:

(1) To maintain a continuing review of all television programming, especially that of subscribers to the Television Code of the NAB; (2) to receive, screen and clear complaints concerning television programming; (3) to define and interpret words and phrases in the Television Code; (4) to develop and maintain appropriate liaison with governmental agencies and with responsible and accountable organizations and institutions; (5) to inform, expeditiously and properly, a subscriber to the Television Code of complaints or commendations, as well as to advise all subscribers concerning the attitude and desires program-wise of accountable organizations and institutions, and of the American public in general; (6) to review and monitor, if necessary, any certain series of programs, daily programming, or any other program presentations of a subscriber, as well as to request recordings, aural or kinescope, or script and

* As amended by the NAB Television Board of Directors June 18, 1959.

copy, with regard to any certain program presented by a subscriber; (7) to reach conclusions, and to make recommendations or prefer charges to the Television Board of Directors concerning violations and breaches of the Television Code by a subscriber; (8) to recommend to the Television Board of Directors, amendments to the Television Code.

A. *Delegation of Powers and Responsibilities:*

The Television Code Review Board may delegate, from time to time, such of its above-specified responsibilities, as it may deem necessary and desirable, to a Staff Group of the NAB.

B. *Meetings:*

The Television Code Review Board shall meet regularly once each quarter of the calendar year on a date to be determined by the Chairman. The Chairman of the Review Board may, at any time, on at least five days' written notice, call a special meeting of the Board.

STATION CODES

Some stations, in addition to subscribing to the NAB Code, establish their own rules of conduct. A sample is the following statement of *General Policies and Rules Governing the Acceptance of Program Material and Advertising Copy of Station WJR* in Detroit.

FOREWORD

WJR has always subscribed to the industry code of the National Association of Broadcasters and it subscribes to the N.A.B. Code as revised from time to time, and republished in January, 1960. However, WJR believes higher standards of service and advertising can be adopted on a regional rather than a national basis where conflicting thoughts and interests and varying community conditions require an appreciable degree of compromise in the formulation of nationwide standards.

The practices and policies for WJR, now revised and brought up to date, represent to a considerable extent a restatement of those practices and policies which have been developed and carried out over a period of years by this Station.

Amplification and clarification in certain areas is based on the continuing development and advance in broadcasting, which is a creative art, and upon the experience of the station in its daily operations and contacts with the public for a period of thirty-eight years.

These rules will serve as a guide to all employees and any others concerned in the preparation and broadcasting of news, educational and public affairs programs for WJR.

WJR POLICY

The unchanging policy of WJR, The Goodwill Station, Inc., Detroit, remains an unwavering devotion to the United States of America, with special emphasis on the public needs and wants of the people residing in the area covered by the ground-wave signal of this station.

In brief, it is our purpose—

To exercise our stewardship in broadcast communications to keep unsullied the stream of news and information that is directed to our listening audience . . .

To provide the finest entertainment, including a wide variety, live and recorded, of musical, dramatic and documentary material, designed to appeal to all tastes.

To maintain on the air the freedom of opinion which is the bulwark of American liberties by reflecting all important phases of thought and policy on issues before the American people . . .

To serve the community, the state and the nation by focusing public attention on the vital problems of the day, by championing the good cause and by exposing without fear or favor forces that would undermine our democratic institutions . . .

To provide a continuing forum of religious service and education, Protestant, Catholic and Jewish alike; to serve the cause of political education by presenting the various schools and varieties of political thought and opinion, and to cooperate in the public interest with the social and welfare organizations representative of the communities which our station serves . . .

To provide a medium for American business to advertise its goods and services to the public and to maintain high standards of product acceptability and copy presentation.

This is our policy and our credo.

WJR STANDARDS OF PRACTICE
Section I
PUBLIC AFFAIRS AND COMMUNITY SERVICE

At WJR the licensing requirement of "serving public interest, convenience and necessity" is regarded as a privilege rather than a mandate.

Every effort should be made to foster and further strengthen a longstanding heritage of distinguished public service to civic, educational, cultural and welfare organizations. WJR will present information from these groups on sustaining time.

Organizations in this field, not operating for profit, should be encouraged to report their activities and problems to the station, and will be offered counsel and assistance, if desired, in preparing and presenting their story to the public effectively.

Sustaining time should be made available, to the extent consistent with existing commitments and good balance, for broadcasting programs or announcements on behalf of welfare or charitable groups engaged in raising funds from the public.

In time of disaster or public emergency, the facilities of the station will be made available without charge for the broadcasting of programs or messages authorized by public officials or agencies responsible for public safety, health and emergency relief measures. The station will exercise due care to insure that any statements or appeals broadcast at such times are properly presented and have been authorized or approved by a responsible official or organization.

Specifically, the facilities of the station should be available to—

1. Promote worthy and bonafide philanthropic charitable causes such as the United Foundation, hospitals, children's organizations, etc.
2. Aid in programs for the prevention and reduction of delinquency and crime in the community.
3. Disseminate knowledge of mental and physical health.
4. Assist in safety drives.
5. Promote city, state and national improvement projects.

6. Help reduce and prevent infectious diseases in the community.
7. Promote parents and teachers activities in public schools.
8. Promote racial and religious intergroups understanding and good citizenship.
9. Assist in the improvement of public educational and civic facilities.
10. Assist worthy men's and women's service clubs in their efforts to promote the social welfare of the community.

A policy of widespread personal participation in civic, educational, welfare and service organizations is encouraged so that WJR personnel cover the many varied facets of public service activity. WJR personnel, under management coordination, are encouraged to serve on committees and to play an active role in worthwhile public service campaigns.

Section II
CONTROVERSIAL PUBLIC ISSUES, INCLUDING POLITICS

WJR, The Goodwill Station, Inc., is impartial in its handling of controversial public issues and questions. As a general policy, time for discussion of such matters is made available without charge. However, during the campaign period preceding primary and general elections, time is sold at regular published rates to or on behalf of legally qualified political parties and candidates. Also under unusual circumstances (each case to be judged on its merits) time may be sold for the discussion of controversial public issues.

Strict adherence to Section 315 of the Communications Act of 1934 as amended will be observed in making time available to legally qualified candidates. This law as well as FCC regulations and court decisions pertaining thereto are reviewed regularly by management and appropriate staff members.

Time for discussion of all other controversial subjects, and for political discussion at times other than the campaign periods mentioned, is made available without charge by the station. The station policy is to maintain a fair balance of opposing viewpoints. As far as practicable, such discussion, debate, or presentation of controversial subjects is normally scheduled in time periods or program series regularly maintained for that purpose. Special broadcasts may be arranged from time to time. In all cases the station will exercise its best judgment to insure overall fairness and maintenance of free speech.

Every effort will be made to assure the presentation of such material by responsible and competent individuals or groups, and they will be clearly identified to the listener.

The station accepts, and reserves to itself, the responsibility for allotting time for presentation and discussion of current controversial subjects, bearing in mind on the one hand the natural desire of persons and organizations to make their views known, and on the other hand, the obligation to the listener to maintain a balanced program of entertainment and information.

The station exercises impartial judgment in maintaining free expression on programs of controversial nature, but reserves the right to require advance submission of script and to refuse to accept programs, announcements or statements which in its opinion are contrary to laws, including those of sedition and defamation, and to refuse any program, announcement or statement which it believes might violate the rights of others.

Our station does not accept fictional treatment of strictly political issues relating to candidates or their candidacies.

461

Section III
STATION EDITORIALS

In order to promote better public understanding of timely issues, WJR will broadcast station-sponsored editorials whenever appropriate and compelling subjects warrant editorial treatment.

Station management alone is responsible for the editorial. Editorials must reflect the position of the station and not an individual employee. Editorials will be voiced by various staff members and as a general rule will not be personalized.

Subjects will be selected by a WJR editorial board after careful analysis of all known facts about an issue. After the subject has been selected, an individual will be assigned to conduct further research and to prepare a well-documented editorial for final approval.

Editorials are completely separate and distinct from WJR newscasts. WJR rigidly maintains its policy of objective, factual news reporting.

The station provides equal and comparable time to responsible spokesmen to express opposing or divergent views from those expressed on the WJR editorials. If subject is deemed controversial, effort will be made to seek out authoritative spokesmen for opposing viewpoints to assure fairness of overall presentation.

Editorials may take a stand on any local issue and on national issues with local implications.

WJR's editorial board is appointed by the General Manager and is directly responsible to him.

Section IV
NEWS

The basic policy of WJR news is to present facts, not opinions.

News programs will present facts accurately and honestly with the greatest possible fairness and completeness. Those responsible for broadcasting the news should exercise constant professional care in the selection of sources and in the editing.

Competent and experienced News Editors will be responsible for the preparation and broadcasting of news programs.

Commentary programs, when scheduled, shall be clearly identified as such, so as to be readily distinguished from straight news reporting.

Good taste will be observed by WJR newsmen in the handling of all news, particularly news of a sensational or tragic nature. Morbid or alarming details not essential to the factual report should be avoided. Special care must be taken in connection with stories that might cause panic or unnecessary alarm.

The commercial content of a news broadcast may be cancelled when the news at hand is such that an advertising message might be in poor taste.

Commercial messages shall be, as a general rule, handled by a voice other than the newscaster. The commercial message must be set apart from the news, so that the listener may easily distinguish between them. No attempt shall be made to make the commercial message sound like a news item.

Newscasts may not contain dramatized news items or any sound material that is not authentic.

All news interview programs should be governed by accepted standards of ethical journalism, under which the interviewer selects the questions to be asked. Where there is advance agreement materially restricting an important or newsworthy area of questioning, the interviewer will state on the program that such limitation has been agreed upon. Such disclosure should be made if the person being interviewed requires that questions be submitted in advance or if he participates in editing a recording of the interview prior to its use on the air.

Section V
RELIGIOUS PROGRAMS

Time will be contributed by the station for religious broadcasts on a balanced program basis. As a general rule, time will not be sold for religious broadcasts. The station will maintain regular weekly periods for religious broadcasts, and will allot additional time at such periods as the religious holidays or special observances for the various faiths, Protestant, Catholic and Jewish.

The station will invite representatives of all major faiths and denominations to participate in the broadcasting schedule of religious programs, and will make every effort to extend invitations also to responsible persons and groups representing religious faiths and beliefs of less widespread membership.

Religious broadcasts will not include attacks on any faith nor on its clergy or lay members as representatives of such faith. No religious belief, ritual or custom will be held up to ridicule or prejudice.

Religious programs should place emphasis on broad religious truths, excluding the presentation of controversial or partisan views not directly or necessarily related to religion or morality.

Section VI
ENTERTAINMENT AND MUSIC PROGRAMS

WJR's concept of quality broadcasting is built around a skillful blend of entertainment, information and public service, with the accent on complete range programming to serve the many varied interests of listeners.

WJR entertainment programs should reflect the general policy of serving every taste and every age with "something for everyone." Entertainment programs should be wholesome and designed to enrich the experience and to afford helpful stimulation to the listener.

WJR presents both live music, by the station musical staff, and recorded music by program personalities. Musical programs are scheduled for every taste and include popular, folk, classical, symphonic, choral and religious music. Music to be broadcast should be selected for its enduring appeal, its melody, quality of composition and, in use of recorded music, its excellence of performance. Other factors to be considered by WJR staff personnel are popular appeal and the effect on program balance. Identification of records will be limited to the title of the selection and the performer's name.

Management determines policy for the type of recorded music to be played. Music personalities, and, in some cases, the music transcription librarian, select records within the framework of that policy under supervision of the program manager.

Quiz and similar programs that are presented as contests of knowledge, information, skill or luck must, in fact, be genuine contests and results must not be controlled by collusion with or between contestants, or any other action which will favor one contestant against any other.

The acceptance of money, services or other valuable consideration by staff personalities or program personnel from sources other than this company for performance of any music or mention of any product or service is specifically prohibited.

463

Section VII
CHILDREN'S PROGRAMS

Programs broadcast particularly for children should be both wholesome and, whenever possible, educational. They should inspire respect for the family, the community, and the fundamentals of the American way of life.

Children's programs should aim to project educational values through the medium of entertainment. These programs will discourage a child's tendency to admire or emulate anti-social persons or customs. Every effort will be made to instill respect for the law and law enforcement agencies, and generally accepted moral codes. Producers of children's programs should cooperate with agencies combatting juvenile delinquency.

Programs broadcast during hours when children may normally be expected to listen should foster the accepted moral, social and ethical ideals characteristic of American life.

Section VIII
ADVERTISING STANDARDS

Advertising is the principal source of revenue of the free, competitive American system of broadcasting . . . it makes possible the presentation of the finest programs for all WJR listeners. WJR requires its staff and advertisers to maintain high ethical standards and good taste in the selection and production of all programs and presentation of advertising.

The following regulations have been voluntarily promulgated by WJR in order to benefit the listener and to assure him of information which is accurate, authentic, reliable, and in conformance with the highest standards of good taste and professional ethics:

. . . Prior to broadcast of any advertising copy, WJR will verify any product or service benefit, claim or statement made in advertising copy.

. . . All advertising of products of a personal nature, when accepted, should be treated with special concern for the sensitivities of listeners.

. . . Advertising of hard liquors will not be accepted.

. . . Advertising of beer or light wines is acceptable when presented in the best of good taste and discretion and is acceptable subject to existing laws.

. . . No advertising of products or services claiming to cure will be accepted.

. . . No financial advertising of a speculative nature is acceptable, nor any investment advertising which does not comply fully with all laws.

. . . The station will not act as a receiving agent for money submitted in payment for advertised products or services.

. . . The advertising of tip sheets, publications, or organizations seeking to advertise for purposes of giving odds or promoting betting or lotteries, is unacceptable.

. . . Advertising of schools or training courses will not be acceptable if they offer any questionable or untrue promises of employment as inducements for enrollment.

. . . Fortune telling, character reading, palm reading, numerology, and astrology programs or announcements are not acceptable.

. . . No advertising copy may contain claims or statements disparaging competitors, or other industries, professions, or institutions.

When dramatized advertising material involves statements by doctors, dentists, nurses, or other professional people, the material should be presented by members of such profession reciting actual experience, or it should be made apparent from the presentation itself that the portrayal is dramatized.

. . . All contest details, including rules, eligibility requirements, opening and termination dates, should be clearly and completely announced or easily accessible to the listening public; and the winners' names should be released as soon as possible after the close of the contest.

When contestants are required to submit items of product identification or other evidence of purchase of product, reasonable facsimiles thereof should be made acceptable.

All copy pertaining to any contest (except that which is required by law) associated with the exploitation or sale of the sponsor's product or service, and all references to prizes or gifts offered in such connection should be considered a part of and included in the total time limitations heretofore provided.

All contests broadcast by the station should comply with pertinent Federal, State, and Local laws and regulations.

. . . Commerical copy shall not exceed the time limitations in the N.A.B. Code, and any time devoted to sponsor advertising shall be included in calculating the commercial time on a program or in length of announcement.

. . . All advertising copy shall conform to stipulations of the Federal Trade Commission and fair trade laws. The station further reserves the right to require any advertiser to meet any business or industry codes currently prevailing and to meet the standards of the Better Business Bureau.

. . . No advertising matter will be accepted which, in the opinion of the station, would be injurious to the interests of the public, WJR, The Goodwill Station, Inc., or to the fundamental principles of honest advertising and reputable business.

. . . Each program or announcement shall be broadcast in a manner acceptable to the station, and the right is reserved to refuse to broadcast any program or announcement which, in the station's opinion, would not reflect credit upon the station and the advertiser.

Time Standards for Advertising Copy

As a guide to the determination of good broadcast advertising practice, the time standards for advertising copy are established as follows:

The maximum time to be used for commercial copy allowable to any single sponsor, regardless of type or time of program, should be:

5 minute programs	1:15
10 minute programs	2:10
15 minute programs	3:00
25 minute programs	4:00
30 minute programs	4:15
45 minute programs	5:45
60 minute programs	7:00

The time standards allowable to a single advertiser do not affect the established practice of allowance for station breaks between programs.

Programs of multiple sponsorship presenting commercial services, features, shopping guides, marketing news, and similar information may include more material normally classified as "commercial" or "advertising," if it is of such nature as to serve the interests of the general public and, if properly produced and intelligently presented, within the established areas of good taste.

The final measurement of any commercial broadcast service is quality. To this, every staff member should dedicate his best efforts.

THE RADIO
BROADCASTER'S CREED

(From the Code of the Broadcasting Industry, as revised January 25, 1960)

We believe:

That Radio Broadcasting in the United States of America is a living symbol of Democracy; a significant and necessary instrument for maintaining freedom of expression, as established by the First Amendment to the Constitution of the United States;

That its influence in the arts, in science, in education, in commerce, and upon the public welfare is of such magnitude that the only proper measure of its responsibility is the common good of the whole people;

That it is our obligation to serve the people in such manner as to reflect credit upon our profession and to encourage aspiration toward a better estate for all mankind; by making available to every person in America such programs as will perpetuate the traditional leadership of the United States in all phases of the broadcasting art;

That we should make full and ingenious use of man's store of knowledge, his talents, and his skills and exercise critical and discerning judgment concerning all broadcasting operations to the end that we may, intelligently and sympathetically:

Observe the proprieties and customs of civilized society;

Respect the rights and sensitivities of all people;

Honor the sanctity of marriage and the home;

Protect and uphold the dignity and brotherhood of all mankind.

Enrich the daily life of the people through the factual reporting and analysis of news, and through programs of education, entertainment, and information;

Provide for the fair discussion of matters of general public concern; engage in works directed toward the common good; and volunteer our aid and comfort in times of stress and emergency;

Contribute to the economic welfare of all by expanding the channels of trade, by encouraging the development and conservation of natural resources, and by bringing together the buyer and seller through the broadcasting of information pertaining to goods and services.

Information Regarding Sales of Stations in 1958

With funds made available through an All-University Research Grant provided by Michigan State University, the author spent several weeks in Washington, D. C. reviewing the official files of the FCC and collecting data with respect to stations that were sold during the calendar year 1958. With the help of Dr. Paul Deutschmann, Director of the Communications Research Center, and his staff at Michigan State University, the following tabulations were compiled. These tabulations do not reflect station transfers of control in which there was little or no substantial consideration involved.

Table 1

KINDS OF SALES AND NUMBER OF STATIONS INVOLVED

Class of Sale	Number of Stations		Number by Class of Stations
Single AM	347		
Multiple AM	9		
AM-FM Combination	38	AM	386
AM-TV Combination	13		
AM-FM-TV Combination	18	FM	43
Single FM	17	TV	32
Single TV	19		
Total	461		461

Table 2

STATIONS SOLD BY REGIONS OF COUNTRY

Region	Number of Stations
Far West	118
Southwest and Plains	60
South	163
Midwest	67
East	40
Puerto Rico and other Islands	4
Total	461

467

Table 3

TOTAL AND AVERAGE SALE PRICES OF STATIONS
SOLD BY CLASSES*

Class	No. in Single Station Sales	No. in Package Sales	Total Sales Price	Average Sale Price**
AM	364	22	$ 43,549,000	$ 112,821
FM	16	27	198,000	12,375
TV	30	2	60,869,000	1,902,156
Total	410	51	$104,616,000	$ 226,932

* The figures represent sale prices reported to the FCC. Only 79 per cent of sales involved full ownership; accordingly these figures represent what was paid—on the average—for about 80 per cent of the "value" of 461 stations.

** A total of 51 stations were sold in package deals involving some combination of kinds of stations or a number of stations of the same class. No information is available to pro-rate the sale price of the units in such "package" transactions. Accordingly, the sale price was assigned to the most expensive unit. This tends to inflate sale price figures slightly for TV and AM stations. To obtain averages, and correct for this partially, the number of FM stations sold as single units was used as a base for that average, while total number of AM and TV stations sold was used as base for these averages.

Table 4

TOTAL AND AVERAGE VALUES OF STATIONS
SOLD BY CLASSES*

Class	No. in Single Station Sales	No. in Package Sales	Total Value	Average Value**
AM	364	22	$ 45,117,000	$ 116,883
FM	16	27	308,000	19,250
TV	30	2	68,636,000	2,144,870
Total	410	51	$114,061,000	$ 246,880

* The figures given in this table are TOTAL VALUES of stations involved in transactions. They were computed by taking FCC information on percentage of value involved in the transaction and computing the 100 per cent value figure for every sale involving a partial interest. About 21 per cent of the sales involved less than 100 per cent of ownership.

** A total of 51 stations were sold in package deals involving some combination of kinds of stations or a number of stations of the same class. No information is available to pro-rate the value of the units of such "package" transactions. Accordingly, the value was assigned to the most expensive unit. This tends to inflate the value figures slightly for TV and AM stations. To obtain averages, and correct for this partially, the number of FM stations sold as single units was used as a base for that average, while total number of AM and TV stations sold was used as base for these averages.

Selective Bibliography

BOOKS:

Barnouw, Erik. *Mass Communication: Television, Radio, Film, Press.* New York: Rinehart, 1956.
Barrett, Edward W. *Truth Is Our Weapon.* New York: Funk and Wagnalls Company, 1953.
Bogart, Leo. *The Age of Television.* New York: Frederick Ungar Publishing Company, 1956.
Bryson, Lyman. *The Communication of Ideas.* New York: Harper and Brothers, 1948.
Bureau of the Census. *Telephones and Telegraphs.* Washington, D. C.: U. S. Government Printing Office, 1902.
Casson, Herbert N. *The History of the Telephone.* Chicago: A. C. McClung, 1910.
Chafee, Zechariah, Jr. *Government and Mass Communication.* Chicago: University of Chicago Press, 1947.
Chase, Francis, Jr. *Sound and Fury.* New York: Harper and Brothers, 1942.
Chester, Giraud, and Garrison, Garnet. *Radio and Television.* New York: Appleton-Century-Crofts, Inc., 1950.
Commission on Freedom of the Press. *A Free and Responsible Press.* Chicago: University of Chicago Press, 1947.
——. *Peoples Speaking to Peoples.* Chicago: University of Chicago Press, 1946.
Cushman, Robert E. *The Independent Regulatory Commissions.* New York: Oxford University Press, 1941.
Daugherty, William, and Janawitz, Morris. *A Psychological Warfare Case Book.* Baltimore: Johns Hopkins Press, 1958.
Dunlap, Orrin Elmer, Jr. *Dunlap's Radio and Television Almanac.* New York: Harper and Brothers, 1951.
——. *The Story of Radio.* New York: The Dial Press, Inc., 1935.
Ernst, Morris Leopold. *The First Freedom.* New York: The Macmillan Company, 1946.
——, and Seagle, William. *To the Pure: A Study of Obscenity and the Censor.* New York: The Viking Press, Inc., 1929.
Federal Communications Commission. *Network Broadcasting, Report of the Study Staff to the Network Study Committee.* Washington, D. C.: 1957.
——. *Public Service Responsibility of Broadcast Licensees.* Washington, D. C.: 1946.
——. *Report on Special Telephone Investigation.* Washington, D. C.: 1937.
Filgate, John Thomas. *Theory of Radio Communication.* Brooklyn: Radio Design Publishing Company, 1929.

Frankfurter, Felix. *The Public and Its Government*. New York: Oxford University Press, 1930.

Head, Sydney. *Broadcasting in America*. Boston: Houghton Mifflin, 1956.

Holt, Robert T. *Radio Free Europe*. Minneapolis: University of Minnesota Press, 1958.

Husing, Ted. *Ten Years Before the Mike*. New York: Holt, Rinehart, Winston, Inc., 1935.

Hyneman, Charles S. *Bureaucracy in a Democracy*. New York: Harper and Brothers, 1950.

Joint Council on Educational Television. *Four Years of Progress in Educational Television*. Washington, D. C.: 1956.

Kerwin, Jerome Gregory. *The Control of Radio*. Chicago: University of Chicago Press, 1934.

Kingsbury, John E. *The Telephone and Telephone Exchanges*. New York: Longmans, Green, and Company, Inc., 1915.

Kirkpatrick, Evron M. *Target: The World; Communist Propaganda Activities in 1955*. New York: The Macmillan Company, 1956.

Landis, James M. *Report on Regulatory Agencies to the President-Elect*. Washington, D. C.: December, 1960.

Landry, Robert J. *This Fascinating Radio Business*. Indianapolis: The Bobbs, Merrill Company, Inc., 1946.

Levin, Harvey J. *Broadcast Regulation and Joint Ownership of Media*. New York: New York University Press, 1960.

MacNeal, Harry B. *The Story of Independent Telephony*. Washington, D. C.: The Independent Pioneer Telephone Association, n.d.

Morecroft, John H. *Elements of Radio Communication*. New York: John Wiley and Sons, Inc., 1934.

Morse, Edward Lind. *Samuel F. B. Morse, Letters and Journals*. Boston: Houghton Mifflin Company, Inc., 1914.

Moser, Julius G., and Lannie, Richard A. *Radio and the Law*. Los Angeles: Parker, 1947.

Murray, Edelman. *The Licensing of Radio Services in the United States*. Urbana: University of Illinois Press, 1950.

National Association of Broadcasters. *Broadcasting and the Bill of Rights*. Washington, D. C.: National Association of Broadcasters, 1947.

Oleck, Howard L. *Non-Profit Corporations and Associations*. Englewood Cliffs, New Jersey: Prentice-Hall, Inc., 1956.

Paulu, Burton. *British Broadcasting*. Minneapolis: University of Minnesota Press, 1960.

Pike and Fischer. *Radio Regulation*. Washington, D. C.: 1945–.

Pilpel, Harriet, and Zavin, Theodora. *Rights and Writers, A Handbook of Literary and Entertainment Law*. New York: E. P. Dutton and Company, Inc., 1960.

Rhyne, Charles S. *Municipal Regulations, Taxation and Use of Radio*. Washington, D. C.: National Institute of Municipal Law Officers, 1955.

Robinson, Thomas Porter. *Radio Networks and the Federal Government*. New York: Columbia University Press, 1943.

Salomon, Leon I. *The Independent Federal Regulatory Commissions*. New York: H. W. Wilson Company, 1959.

Schramm, Wilbur. *Communications in Modern Society*. Urbana: University of Illinois Press, 1948.

———. *Mass Communications*. Urbana: University of Illinois Press, 1949.

————. *Responsibility in Mass Communication.* New York: Harper and Brothers, 1957.

Schwartz, Bernard. *The Professor and the Commissions.* New York: Alfred A. Knopf, Inc., 1959.

Shaffner, Tal. P. *The Telegraph Manual.* Pudney and Russell, 1859.

Shurick, E. P. J. *The First Quarter Century of American Broadcasting.* Kansas City: Midland Publishing Company, 1946.

Siebert, Frederick S. *Clearance, Rights and Legal Problems of Educational Radio and Television Stations.* Washington, D. C.: National Association of Educational Broadcasters, 1955.

————. *Four Theories of the Press.* Urbana: University of Illinois Press, 1956.

Siepmann, C. A. *Radio's Second Chance.* Boston: Little, Brown and Company, 1946.

————. *Radio, Television and Society.* New York: Oxford University Press, 1950.

Smead, Elmer A. *Freedom of Speech by Radio and Television.* Washington, D. C.: Public Affairs Press, 1959.

Thompson, Robert L. *Wiring a Continent.* Princeton, New Jersey: Princeton University Press, 1947.

University of Chicago. *Print, Radio, and Film in a Democracy.* Chicago: University of Chicago Press, 1942.

University of Michigan Law School. *Lectures on Communication Media, Legal and Policy Problems.* Ann Arbor: University of Michigan, 1955.

Warner, Harry P. *Radio and Television Law.* Albany, New York: Matthew Bender and Company, Inc., 1948.

————. *Radio and Television Rights.* Albany, New York: Matthew Bender and Company, Inc., 1953.

White, Leonard Dupee. *Introduction to the Study of Public Administration.* New York: The Macmillan Company, 1955.

PERIODICALS:

Agee, W. K. "Cross-Channel Ownership," *Journalism Quarterly,* XXVI (December 1949), 410–416.

Armstrong, Edwin H. "A Method of Reducing Disturbances in Radio Signaling by a System of Frequency Modulation," *Proceedings of the Institute of Radio Engineers,* May 1936, 689.

Baker, Warren E. "Policy by Rule or *Ad Hoc* Approach—Which Should It Be?" *Law and Contemporary Problems,* XXII (Autumn 1957), 658–671.

Barrow, Roscoe L. "Network Broadcasting—The Report of the FCC Network Study Staff," *Law and Contemporary Problems,* XXII (Autumn 1957), 611–625.

Bendiner, Robert. "The FCC—Who Will Regulate the Regulators?" *The Reporter,* XVII (September 19, 1957), 26–30.

Brown, Ralph S., Jr. "Character and Candor Requirements for FCC Licensees," *Law and Contemporary Problems,* XXII (Autumn 1957), 644–657.

Butler, James J. "Radio Can Be Denied on Monopoly Ground," *Editor and Publisher,* LXXXIII (January 28, 1950), 9.

Carson, Saul. "The Richards' Licenses," *New Republic,* CXXI (August 8, 1949), 22–23.

Carter, Roy E., Jr. "Radio Editorializing Aboard the New Mayflower," *Journalism Quarterly,* XXVIII (Fall 1951), 49–53.

471

Courtney, Jeremiah, and Blooston, Arthur. "Development of Mobile Radio Communications—The Workhorse Radio Services," *Law and Contemporary Problems*, XXII (Autumn 1957), 626–643.

"Diversification and the Public Interest: Administrative Responsibility of the FCC," *Yale Law Journal*, LXVI (January 1957), 365–396.

"FCC Attacks Radio Give-Away Program," *Stanford Law Review*, I (April 1949), 475–485.

"FCC Disclaims Power to Limit Competition in Broadcasting," *Columbia Law Review*, LVII (1957), 1036–1038.

"FCC May Properly Consider Past Competitive Practices of Newspaper Applicant as Basis for Denial of Radio License," *Harvard Law Review*, LXIII (May 1950), 1274–1275.

Fisher, Ben C. "Communications Act Amendments, 1952—An Attempt to Legislate Administrative Fairness," *Law and Contemporary Problems*, XXII (Autumn 1957), 672–696.

Fisher, John. "TV and Its Critics," *Harper's*, CCIX (July 1958), 10–14.

Griffith, Emlyn I. "Mayflower Rule—Gone But Not Forgotten," *Cornell Law Quarterly*, XXXV (Spring 1950), 574–591.

"Gross Receipt Tax on Radio Stations," *Stanford Law Review*, I (June 1949), 741–756.

Hansen, Victor R. "Broadcasting and the Antitrust Laws," *Law and Contemporary Problems*, XXII (Autumn 1957), 572–583.

Hoover, Herbert. "Radio Gets a Policeman," *American Heritage*, VI (August 1955), 73–76.

Houn, Franklin W. "Radio Broadcasting and Propaganda in Communist China," *Journalism Quarterly*, XXXIV (Summer 1957), 366–377.

Irion, H. Gifford. "FCC Criteria for Evaluating Competing Applicants," *Minnesota Law Review*, XLIII (January 1959), 479–498.

Kalodner, Howard I., and Vance, Verne W., Jr. "The Relation Between Federal and State Protection of Literary and Artistic Property," *Harvard Law Review*, LXXII (April 1959), 1079–1128.

Kennedy, Roger. "Programming Content and Quality," *Law and Contemporary Problems*, XXII (Autumn 1957), 541–548.

Knickerbocker, Daniel C., Jr. "Licensee's Right to Hearing on Modification of License," *Cornell Law Quarterly*, XXXIV (1949), 608–615.

Koop, Theodore F. "Equality of Access for Radio in Covering Washington News," *Journalism Quarterly*, XXXIV (Summer 1957), 338–340.

Lawrence, Edmund. "Radio and the Richards' Case," *Harper's*, CCV (July 1959), 82–87.

McMahon, Robert S. "Harris Subcommittee Report: Fifty Years of Broadcasting Regulation," *Journal of Broadcasting*, III (Winter 1958–1959), 56–87.

Pike and Fischer. *Radio Regulation*. Washington, D. C.: 1945–.

Remmers, Donald H. "Recent Legislative Trends in Defamation by Radio," *Harvard Law Review*, LXIV (March 1951), 727–758.

Rosenburg, Herbert H. "Program Content," *Western Political Quarterly*, II (September 1949), 375–401.

Salant, Richard S. "The Functions and Practices of a Television Network," *Law and Contemporary Problems*, XXII (Autumn 1957), 584–610.

Schwartz, Bernard. "Contemporary Television and the Chancellor's Foot," *Georgetown Law Journal*, XLVII (Summer 1959), 655–699.

Siebert, Frederick S. "The Right to Report by Television," *Journalism Quarterly*, XXXIV (Summer 1957), 333–337.

Siepmann, C. A. "Scramble for Air Time," *The Nation,* CLXXVIII (May 15, 1944), 422–424.

Smythe, Dallas W. "Facing Facts About the Broadcast Business," *University of Chicago Law Review,* XX (1952), 96–106.

Tannenbaum, Samuel W. "Titles in the Entertainment Field," *American Bar Association Journal,* XLV (May 1959), 459–462.

Terry, Hugh B. "Electronic Journalism in the Colorado Courts," *Journalism Quarterly,* XXXIV (Summer 1957), 341–348.

"Transit Broadcasting: The Problem of the Captive Audience," *Columbia Law Review,* LI (January 1951), 108–118.

Walker, Paul A., and Emery, Walter B. "Post War Communications and Speech Education," *Quarterly Journal of Speech,* XXX (December 1944), 399–402.

Warner, Harry P. "Legal Protection of the Content of Radio and TV Program Content," *Iowa Law Review,* (Fall 1950), 14–28.

Yoder, R. M. "They Track Down Outlaw Broadcasters," *Saturday Evening Post,* CCXXIV (December 1, 1951), 17–19; (December 8, 1951), 34.

Index

Block-booking, 167.
"Blue Book": adoption of, 237-238; controversy over, 298; problems of enforcement, 298-300.
Board of War Communications, 257, 358.
Booster stations: See Repeater stations.
Bori, Lucretia, 11.
Brinkley, John R., 12.
Broadcast Bureau (FCC): functions of, 51, 185-186.
Broadcast channels: ownership of, 32-33.
Broadcasting industry: size of, 291.
Broadcast Music Inc. (BMI), 282.
Broadcast regulation: bills introduced in Congress relating to, 303; proposals to improve, 303-312.
Broadcast services: extent of and use, 80-81.
Brown, Thaddeus Harold, 355.
Buchanon, James, 5.
Burden of proof: assumed by FTC counsel in false advertising cases, 61.
Bureau of Consultation (FTC), 59.
Bureau of Economics (FTC), 59.
Bureau of Investigation (FTC), 58-59.
Bureau of Litigation (FTC), 59.
By-laws: importance of, 70.

Cantor, Eddie, 20.
Carrier frequency, 78.
Caruso, Enrico, 10.
Case, Norman Stanley, 355.
CBS: See Columbia Broadcasting Company.
Cease and Desist orders: against unlawful advertising, 61; failure to comply with, 61; grounds for issue, 263-264; procedure for issuance, 264; when may be issued, 35.
Celler, Emanuel, 217.
Censorship: early complaints against, 15; federal, prohibition of, 38; local, 72-73; of political speeches, 276-278.
Chief Accountant (FCC), 48.
Chief Engineer (FCC), 53-54.
Chief Hearing Examiner, 53.
Civil Aeronautics Administration: reports on tower lighting failures, 209.
Civil Service Commission: removal of hearing examiner, 52.
Class I Station (AM): defined, 89.
Class II Station (AM): defined, 89-90.
Class III Station (AM): defined, 90.
Class IV Stations: defined, 90; number of, 91; power increases authorized, 90-91; power increases prohibited, 91.
Classification Act of 1949, 46.

Clearances, 283-284.
Clear Channel Case, 91-93.
Clear channels: defined, 88; number of, 89; proposal to break up, 368.
Cobb, Irvin S., 11.
Columbia Broadcasting System: Church of the Air, 21; interpretation of Section 315, 221-222, 234; organization of, 14; School of the Air, 21.
Commerce Clause: prohibits burden on interstate commerce, 70.
Commissioners (FCC): appointment of, 44; factors against good appointments, 293-294; limitations on activities, 44-45; qualifications, 44-45, 292-293; responsibilities, 33-37; salaries, 44; terms of office, 44.
Communications Act of 1934: as amended, 315-353; basic purposes of, 30.
Communications media: early history of, 3-8; government ownership advocated, 29-30.
Communications Subcommittee of the House Interstate and Foreign Commerce Committee: concern with frequency allocations, 83.
Community antenna TV: description of, 136; FCC jurisdiction, 143; pending court actions, 136-137.
Competition: broadcasting, 32; restraints against, prohibited, 32.
Complaints and Compliance Division (FCC): purposes of, 240-242.
Complaints: unlawful advertising, 62.
CONELRAD, 388-397.
Congress: appropriation for experimental telegraph line, 3; concern for FCC workload, 49-50; influence on broadcast regulation, 67-68; investigation committees, 67-68.
Congressional Subcommittee on Legislative Oversight, 294, 300.
Congressmen: influence on FCC, 68.
Construction permit: when granted, 192.
Control of stations: unlawful assignment of, 267-270.
Copyright restrictions, 279-288.
Corporations: organizational procedure, 70.
Cosmetic: defined in FTC Act, 60.
Coughlin, Charles E., 12.
Council of Chief State School Officers, 118, 122.
Court review: See Appeals.
Courts: review actions of FCC, FTC and FDA, 68.
Cox, James R., 12.
Cox Investigation, 296-298.

Coy, Wayne, 129, 291, 362-364.
Craven, T.A.M., 313, 378-379.
Crosley Corporation, 258-259.
Cross, John Storrs, 379.

Daley, Richard J., 221.
Daly, Lar, 221.
Damrosch, Walter, 21.
Danaher, John A., 104-105.
Davis Amendment, 181.
Daytime Broadcasters' Association, 93.
Daytime stations, 206.
Deceptive contests, 232-233.
Defamation, 243-249, 274-276.
Defense Commissioner (FCC), 55.
Defense Department: concern with frequency allocations, 83.
Deforest, Lee, 8, 10.
Denny, Charles R., 123, 360-361.
Department of Justice: functions of antitrust division, 69-70.
Device: defined by FTC Act, 60.
Diathermy machines: interference from, 72.
Direct waves: nature of, 79; utility for broadcasting, 80.
District Courts: enforce orders of FCC, FTC, FDA, 68.
Division of Defense Coordination: functions of, 55.
Doctrine of fair use, 284.
Doerfer, Charles John, 365-371.
Don Lee Broadcasting Company case, 272-274.
Dramatic materials: restrictions on use, 279-281.
Dramatico-musical materials: restrictions on use, 279-280.
Drew, John, 11.
Drugs: as defined in FTC Act, 60.
Durr, Clifford Judkins, 236, 357, 359-360.

Editorialization: FCC policy, 245-246; prohibited under Mayflower decision, 244; reactions against FCC policy, 246-247.
Educational stations, frequency modulation: extent of, xx; identification of, 213; number of, xx; operators, 208; requirements for frequency measurement, 195.
Educational stations, television: dimensions of, xx; eligibility for, 119-120; growth of, 118-119; how financed, 118.
Eisenhower, Milton S., 118.
Electromagnetic waves: early uses for communication, 8; nature of, 77-78.
Emergency powers: exercised by the President, 66.

Emergency Relocation Board, 55.
Engineering Department (FCC), 47.
Equipment: proofs of performance, 197; repair and replacement, 204; requirements for broadcast stations, 193-197; requirements for type acceptance, 196-197; tests of, 197, 204.
Examiners: appraisal of positions, 306-307; authorized by Administrative Procedure Act, 52-53; duties of, 187; initial decisions, 61; restrictions on, 52-53.
Executive Director (FTC), 59.
Ex Parte representations, 307.
Expenditures (FCC): legislative authority for, 46.
Experimental broadcast stations: application and licensing procedure, 145; assignment of frequencies, 149-150; developmental, 148-149; dimensions of, 151; limitations on ownership, 150; operational requirements, 149-150; requirements for renewal of licenses, 150; studies of, 151-152; television, 148.
Experimental radio stations: application and licensing procedure, 144-145; classified, 144; operational requirements, 145-146; reports to FCC, 146; statutory authority for, 144; student authorizations, 147; studies by, 147-148.

False advertising: defined, 59; FTC guides on, 63; unlawful, 59.
Federal Aviation Agency: concern with allocations, 83.
Federal Communications Commission: administrative procedure, 306; annual reports to Congress, 45-46; chronology of, 355-375; cooperation with state utility commissions, 31; creation of, 23-24; Democratic leadership, 355-364; divisions abolished, 47-49; early problems and accomplishments, 355-356; inquiry on Daytime Broadcasters' petition, 93; investigations of, 295-298; leadership of, 355-379; number of authorizations issued by, xx; organization of, 46-55; powers of, 30-40, 45-46, 54, 311; proceedings open to public, 45; program policies, 411-423; quorum, 45; regulatory problems, 291-302; workload, 291-292. *See also* Commissioners (FCC).
Federal Radio Commission: abolished, 24; allocations by, 181; established, 20-21; license revocation by, 12; powers of, 20.
Federal Spectrum Authority, 83.
Federal Trade Commission: administra-

477

tive procedures, 61-62; basic functions, 58; bi-partisan character, 58; commissioners, 58; condemnation of radio monopoly, 15; cooperative arrangements with the FCC, 249; creation of, 58; duties of, 58; form letter on broadcast advertising, 403; grounds for attacking objectionable advertising, 62; guides against false advertising, 398-402; monitoring services, 63-64; Radio and Television Advertising Unit, 63-64; working agreement with Food and Drug Administration, 65-66.

Fictitious pricing, 63.

Field, Cyrus, 5.

Field Engineering and Monitoring Bureau: functions of, 52; inspections by, 204; offices of, 204, 386-387.

Field intensity requirements: 93-94; factors determining, 78; measurement of, 78.

Fly, James Lawrence, 356-358.

Folsom, Marion B., 118.

Food: defined in FTC Act, 60.

Food and Drug Administration: powers of, 65-66; staff offices, 65.

Food, Drug and Cosmetic Act, 65.

Ford Foundation: contributions to educational TV, 118.

Ford, Frederick R.: address of, 313; statement on Complaints and Compliance Division, 240-242.

Forfeitures, 271-272.

Frequency allocation: problems of, 83-85.

Frequency Allocation Board: proposed, 87; proposed functions, 84

Frequency hours for international broadcast stations, 128.

Frequency Modulations Stations (FM): advantages over AM operation, 99-100; area requirements, 102-103; channel assignments, 101-103; classes of stations, 101-103; construction permits, xix; early allocation by FCC, 100; early development of, 100; field inten sity requirements, 102-103; identification of, 213; pattern of decline and growth, 100-101; problems since the War, 100; requirements for operators, 206-208; schedule requirements, 206; service areas, 102.

Frequency Modulation Stations (FM), noncommercial educational: early history, 107-108; eligibility requirements, 109-110; frequencies assigned, 109; program requirements, 109-110; progress since 1944, 108-109.

Functional music: See Subsidiary Communications Authorizations.

Fund for Adult Education: contributions to educational TV, 118.

Gary, Eugene, 296-297, 302.

Gary, Hampson, 354.

General Counsel (FCC), 53.

General Counsel (FTC), 59.

General Electric Company: early broadcasting interests, 14.

Gershwin, George, 11.

Give-away shows: FCC rules regarding, 226.

Government ownership: early advocates, 29-30.

Grand rights: in copyrighted material, 281-282.

Grange, Harold "Red," 11.

Gross receipts tax, 70-71.

Ground wave service: attenuation, 80; nature of, 79, 87; transmission, 80; utility for broadcasting, 80.

Harding, Warren G., 11.

Harris, Oren: introduces bill to establish the Frequency Allocation Board, 84; regarding activities of committee to investigate FCC, 365-366.

Hartford Television Company, 141.

Holmes, Oliver W., 30, 279.

Hoover, Herbert: attempts to regulate radio, 16-19; calls radio conferences, 17-18; regulatory philosophy, 18-19.

Hoover Commission, 49.

Horse racing information: broadcasts of, 243, 249.

Hough, Howard O., 12.

House Interstate and Foreign Commerce Committee: concern with operations of FCC and FTC, 67.

Husing, Ted, 21.

Hyde, Rosel: 364, 376; dissent to FCC interpretation of Section 317 of Act, 219.

Hyneman, Charles, 48-49.

Indecent programming; prosecutions for, 70.

Independent telephone companies, 7.

Injunctions: against injurious advertising, 61.

Interference: causes, 78; objectionable, 181-182; objections to, 16-17; permissible, 181; prohibited by municipal regulations, 72.

Intermittent service area, 88, 94-95.

International Broadcast Stations: application form and showing required, 123; assignment of frequencies for, 124;

contract operations, 128; defined, 123; frequency hours of, 128; identification of, 213; operating requirements, 124-125, 208; private operation, 128; program requirements, 125; target areas, 127; Voice of America, 125-127.

Interstate commerce: discrimination against, prohibited, 31; radio transmissions so classified, 31.

Interstate Commerce Commission: authority regarding communications transferred to FCC, 30.

Intrastate communication: regulated by states only, 30-31.

Ionosphere, 79-80.

Irion, Gifford, 178-179.

Jessel, George, 20.

Jett, Ewell K., 358.

Joint Committee on Toll TV, 138.

Joint Council on Educational TV: xx; comments regarding toll TV, 137-138; evaluation of TV growth, 119.

Kaltenborn, H. V., 11.

King, Charles Henry, 379.

Koop, Theodore F., 288.

Kreisler, Fritz, 11.

La Follette, Robert, 15.

La Fount, Harold, 21.

Landry, Robert J., 13.

Lea, Congressman, 297.

Lee, Robert E.: 378; dissent of, 219.

Legislation: Act of 1910, 16; Act of 1912, 16-17; Radio Act of 1927, 19-20; recommendations for, 303-311.

Legislative Oversight Committee: recommendations of, 303-308, 312.

Libel: See Defamation.

Licenses: length of, 198; limitations imposed, 198; operators', 35; operators', suspension and revocation of, 35-36; posting of, 208; requirements for, 197-198; revocation of, 35; taxes on, 71.

Lincoln, Abraham, 4.

Liquor advertising, 243, 249.

Literary works: restrictions on broadcast use, 282-283.

Local channel, 89.

Logs: entries required, 208-209; keeping, 210; retention of, 210.

Long, Huey P., 295.

Lopez, Vincent, 11.

Lotteries: cases involving, 243, 249; FCC rules against, 225-226; laws against, 224-225; prosecution of offenders, 70.

Mack, Richard Alfred, 379.

Magnusen, Warren, 297.

Marconi, Guglielmo, 8.

Marlowe, Julia, 11.

Mayflower decision, 244.

McConnaughey, George D., 364.

McCormack, John, 11.

McNamee, Graham, 11.

McNinch, Frank Ramsey, 355-356.

Mechanical reproductions: broadcasting of, 213-214.

Medical treatments: broadcast of, 243.

Michigan Broadcasters Association: petition of, in reference to "Payola," 218-219.

Michigan State University: report of Committee on Future, 301.

Misleading advertising: pertaining to oleomargarine, 59.

Misrepresentation of facts to FCC: cases involving, 264-267; grounds for license revocation, 264; Supreme Court attitude toward, 266-267.

Monitoring stations, 386-387.

Monitors, 195, 204.

Monopolistic practices: FCC concern for, 167; penalties for, 159; prohibited in broadcast field, 31-32; telephone and telegraph, 31-32.

Morrill Act, 118.

Morse, Samuel: 3-4; advocated government ownership of telegraph, 29; completes telegraph line, 3-4; predicts worldwide telegraphy, 5.

Motions Commissioner, 55.

Multiple ownership rule, 176-178.

Multiplex stations: See Subsidiary Communications Authorizations.

Municipal regulations, 72-73.

Music materials: restrictions on broadcast use, 280-281.

National Association of Land Grant Colleges and Universities, 118, 122.

National Association of Radio and Television Broadcasters: codes of, 247, 424-459; opposes toll TV, 138.

National Association of Railroad and Utilities Commissioners, 51.

National Broadcasting Company: interpretation in Lar Daly case, 222; organized, 14.

National Citizens' Committee on Educational Television, 118.

National Education Association, 118.

National Television and Radio Center, 118.

NBC: See National Broadcasting Company.

Network regulations: 229-232, 272-274; history of, 228-229; opposed by Commissioner Craven, 39; revisions recommended, 232; Supreme Court decision, 39-40.

Networks: growth of, 14.

Non-profit organizations: proposal to allocate broadcast facilities to, 37-38.

North American Regional Broadcast Agreement: 25; regarding interference, 182.

Office of Administration (FCC): functions of, 53.

Office of Civil and Defense Mobilization: concern with frequency allocations, 83; duties of director, 66-67.

Office of Hearing Examiners: functions of, 52-53.

Office of Network Study: functions of, 51.

Office of Reports and Information: functions of, 54.

Oleomargarine Act, 59.

Operator requirements: AM stations, 206-208; educational FM stations, 208; FM stations, 206-208; international stations, 208; television stations, 208.

Option time: *See* Network regulations.

Organization (FCC): 51-55; limitations on, 176; originally constituted, 46-49.

Paramount Television Productions, Inc.: 372-373; involved in antitrust litigation, 165-169.

Payne, George Henry, 355.

Payne Fund, 118.

Payola practices: Congressional concern, 217-219; FCC concern, 215-219; penalties for, 219.

Pearl, Jack, 20.

Peddlers of the air, 12-13.

Penner, Joe, 20.

Personnel (FCC): statutory authority to select, 46.

Petitions: requesting denial of applications, 248.

Pirating programs, 285.

Political broadcasting: 276-277; statutory provisions regarding, 219-220.

Political candidates: involved in newscasts, 223-224; presidential, 224.

Porter, Paul A.: 358-360; leadership of, 298.

Postal Telegraph: merger with Western Union, 358.

Post Master General, 29-30.

President, U.S.: appointive powers, 67; influence on commissioners, 67; statutory powers in regard to broadcasting, 66.

President's Special Advisory Committee on Communications, 83.

Prettyman, E. Barrett, 171.

Price-fixing: motion picture industry, 166.

Primary service area: factors determining, 87-88; signal requirements, 94.

Profane language, 227-228.

Programming: deceptive, 368; deceptive contests, 232-233; early FCC concern for standards, 236-237; FCC cases raising public interest questions, 238-240; FCC concern for over-all operation, 240; FCC policy statement, 242, 410-422; FCC surveillance of, 240-242; identification of sponsors, 214-215, 217-218; obscene and indecent, 226-227, 243, 249; political, 219-224; representations required in applications, 183-184; types disfavored by FCC, 243-244; types favored by FCC, 243-244; uniform definitions by FCC, 406-409.

Program service: FCC authority over, 36-38; Commissioner Craven's views, 36.

Proofs of performance, 197.

Protection of program ideas, 284.

Public interest broadcasting: elements of, 37-39.

Public Responsibility of Broadcast Licensees: analyzed, 237-238; enforcement problems, 298-300.

Quiz shows, 232-233.

Quorum: FCC, 45.

Quota system of frequency allocations, 181.

Racial and religious attacks: broadcasts of, 243, 249.

Radiating systems: specifications for, 195.

Radio and TV codes, 247, 424-466.

Radio City, 20.

Radio communication: how accomplished, 77-78.

Radio Corporation of America: early network broadcasting, 14.

Radio frequencies: classification of, 80-83; propagation characteristics, 79-80.

RCA: *See* Radio Corporation of America.

Receiving sets, xx.

Recordings: restrictions on broadcast use, 280-282.

Regional channels: 88-89; number of, 91.

Regulation: early problems, 17-19; inadequacy of, 21-22; need recognized by industry, 37; theories on, xx-xxi.

Religious programs: proposal to require, 37-38.